BEMUS POINT, N.
SAT., AUG
DANCING starts at 8:30 E.S.T.
EMUS POINT, N. Y.
JUNE 25TH
DANCING 8 to 1, E.S.T.
DUKE
LLINGTON
ND HIS FAMOUS ORCHESTRA
ELMWOOD
USIC HALL
BUFFALO
$1.10 Person Tax Inc.
21
"The Ace Drummer Man"
GENE KRUP
GLEN PARK
CASINO
83c
WILLIAMSVILLE
N. Y.
Dancing 9 to 2
DOOR Sale
99c
Including TAX
IN PERSON
Presents
RED NORVO
AND THEIR Orchestra
Bob
ROSBY
MILDRED
Rockwell O'Keefe, Inc.

THE BIG BANDS

WITH A FOREWORD BY

George T. Simon

☆

THE BIG BANDS

FRANK SINATRA

Fourth Edition

SCHIRMER BOOKS
A Division of Macmillan Publishing Co., Inc.
NEW YORK

Collier Macmillan Publishers
LONDON

Schirmer Books
A Division of Macmillan Publishing Co., Inc.
866 Third Avenue, New York, N. Y. 10022
Collier Macmillan Canada, Inc.

Library of Congress Catalog Card Number: 81-51633

Printed in the United States of America

printing number
4 5 6 7 8 9 10

Library of Congress Cataloging in Publication Data

Simon, George Thomas.
    The big bands.

    Discography: p.
    Includes index.
    1. Big bands—United States. 2. Jazz musicians—United States—Biography. I. Title.
ML3518.S55 1981   785'.06'66   81-51633
ISBN 0-02-872420-8   AACR2
ISBN 0-02-872430-5 (pbk.)

To
Bev,
Julie,
and
Tom

Also by George T. Simon:

The Big Bands Songbook
The Best of the Music Makers
Glenn Miller and His Orchestra
Simon Says: The Sights and Sounds of the Swing Era
The Feeling of Jazz
The Bandleader
Don Watson Starts His Band

CONTENTS

PART THREE:

INSIDE MORE OF THE BIG BANDS

The Arranging Leaders 459

Van Alexander, Archie Bleyer, Sonny Burke, Ted Fio Rito,
Ralph Flanagan, Jerry Gray, Joe Haymes, Lennie Hayton, Carl Hoff,
Quincy Jones, Billy May, Sy Oliver, Don Redman, Johnny Richards,
Sauter-Finegan, Bobby Sherwood

The Horn-playing Leaders 465

Louis Armstrong, Ray Anthony, Randy Brooks, Henry Busse,
Billy Butterfield, Lee Castle, Les Elgart, Maynard Ferguson,
Erskine Hawkins, Jack Jenney, Henry Jerome, Clyde McCoy,
Johnny McGhee, Buddy Morrow, Phil Napoleon, Louis Prima,
Shorty Sherock, Muggsy Spanier, Cootie Williams, Si Zentner

Art Hickman, Tiny Hill, Richard Himber, Dean Hudson, Jack Hylton,
Spike Jones, Louis Jordan, Jimmy Joy, Roger Wolfe Kahn,
Gene Kardos, Al Katz, Al Kavelin, Herbie Kaye, John Kirby,
Eddie Lane, Lester Lanin, Bert Lown, Clyde Lucas, Richard Maltby,
Matty Malneck, Ralph Marterie, Billy Maxted, Lani McIntyre,
Benny Meroff, Lucky Millinder, Art Mooney, Spud Murphy,
Ruby Newman, Harry Owens, Louis Panico, Ray Pearl,
Paul Pendarvis, Perez Prado, Barney Rapp, Joe Ricardel,
Riley and Farley, Rita Rio, Buddy Rogers, Dick Rogers,
Luigi Romanelli, Sal Salvador, Terry Shand, Milt Shaw,
Beasley Smith, Paul Specht, Phil Spitalny, Harold Stern,
Eddie Stone, Justin Stone, Lew Stone, Bob Strong,
The Sunset Royal Serenaders, Paul Tremaine, Frankie Trumbauer,
Fats Waller, Alvy West, Ran Wilde, Gene Williams, Griff Williams,
Bob Wills, Gerald Wilson, Barry Wood, Austin Wylie

. . . plus a listing of two hundred *more* big bands

PART FOUR:

BIG BANDLEADERS REVISITED

PART FIVE:

THE BIG BANDS—NOW

PART SIX:

A SELECTIVE BIG BANDS DISCOGRAPHY

PART SEVEN:

THE BIG BANDS' THEME SONGS

FOREWORD

MR. JOSEPH D. OAKES
1234 OAK STREET
MIDDLETOWN, U.S.A.

Dear Joe:

Thanks for your letter. I can understand how you feel.
I'm sure a few zillion others who weren't around during
the big band era ask themselves the same questions you
asked me: what made them so great, how things were in
those days, and why the bands were (and still are) an
important part of the scene.

When you were born, the band era was just beginning
to wilt. By the time you were in grade school, the old and
new eras were overlapping; you could see it symbolized
when Elvis Presley got a couple of his first big breaks on
the Dorsey Brothers' television show (yes, Joe, there was
a Dorsey Brothers TV series). Within a year or two after
that, the Dorseys were gone. In a sense, an era died with
them, because Tommy and Jimmy had been symbols of
so much that happened during the band years, through
their impeccable musicianship, their contribution to the
betterment of musical values and standards, their friend-
ships and quarrels, their discoveries of new talent (instrumental and vocal) and their part in molding America's
musical tastes.

It's hard to say exactly when the bands moved away
from center stage to the sidelines, and it's even tougher to
fix the precise point in history when they were born. It
seems there were some ragtime groups that played for
dancing just before World War I, but many of them were
of small combo dimensions. Certainly, though, while my
generation was growing up, in the 1920's and '30's we
were thoroughly indoctrinated into the sounds of the big
bands via radio remotes.

"Big Band" in those days meant ten men or more. As long as there was that feeling of teamwork, of a group of saxophones blending, a tightly knit brass section, it qualified. This didn't mean you were typecasting it, because, you see, Joe, those bands ranged all the way from the Guy Lombardos and Wayne Kings on through the Goodmans, Ellingtons and Dorseys.

The big bands differed as much in personality as any random bunch of individuals you might pass on the street. Some tried for a strictly commercial style and a mass audience; sometimes the corn was as high as a piccolo's A. Others, and this was especially true when the swing era began, had objectives that reached beyond entertainment and dancing; they played for fans who wanted to listen, think, and even analyze.

Regardless of which segment of the public they aimed at, the big bands became vitally important, at home and abroad. In the years between the two world wars, some of our greatest bands toured all over the world; and wherever they went, they told a little bit about America.

The bands molded everyone's musical tastes. Their listeners (including teen-agers like yourself) were emotionally and physically involved. For the fans, these orchestras were a healthy and meaningful pastime; for young musicians, they were illustrations of how to work as part of a team.

Fortunately, my own career got under way just in time for me to take advantage of the opportunities the big bands offered. Working with a good band in those days was the end of the rainbow for any singer who wanted to make it in this profession.

My association with the bands started just after a panic period when I was running around doing every sustaining radio show I could reach. Sustaining—that meant no sponsor, Joe, and you better believe it, that routine sustained everyone but me. I was on four local stations, and sometimes I had it planned so I'd be on the air someplace or another every three hours all through the day. Don't think I was doing all this work for nothing—I got seventy cents carfare from Jersey to the Mutual studios.

On top of the eighteen sustainers a week, I landed a

real paying job at a dance hall called the Rustic Cabin in Englewood, New Jersey. I still went into New York every morning to rehearse with Bob Chester's band; then in the afternoon I'd rehearse with another band. Get the picture, Joe? I simply dug that big band sound around me.

At the Rustic Cabin I was emceeing the show and doing a little singing too. One night, when I sang a number on the air with Harold Arden's band, Harry James heard me. He had left Benny Goodman four months earlier and started his own band. A couple of days later he asked me to meet him at the Paramount Theater, and we set the deal. I was on the road with Harry's band for the second half of 1939; then when Tommy Dorsey made me an offer, Harry agreed to let me out of the balance of my contract.

I made my first records with Tommy on February 1, 1940, and stayed with the band until September 10, 1942. By that time, Dorsey had a vast band complete with string section, which gassed me. I was always crazy about strings for a vocal background; if James had had strings at the time I was with the band, maybe I'd never have left him, because in 1940 Tommy didn't have strings.

Whether you were an instrumentalist or a vocalist, working in a band was an important part of growing up, musically and as a human being. It was a career builder, a seat of learning, a sort of cross-country college that taught you about collaboration, brotherhood and sharing rough times. When it comes to professional experience, there's nothing to beat those one-nighter tours, when you rotate between five places around the clock—the bus, your hotel room, the greasy-spoon restaurant, the dressing room (if any) and the bandstand. Then back on the bus to the next night's gig, maybe four hundred miles away or more.

I've said this many times, but it can never be said too often: a singer can learn, should learn, by listening to musicians. My greatest teacher was not a vocal coach, not the work of other singers, but the way Tommy Dorsey breathed and phrased on the trombone.

It was while I was with the James band that I got my first important write-up. The September, 1939, *Metronome* carried a review of the band mentioning the "very pleasing vocals of Frank Sinatra, whose easy phrasing is especially commendable." The review was signed by a young fellow named George T. Simon, who spent his time listening to bands of every kind and doing his best, through the great magazine that *Metronome* was in those days, to inform and enlarge the public for bands and singers.

Ever since the great band days, Joe, there has been a need for one really definitive book to answer questions like yours, to document the fabulous stories that fellows like you should know. Maybe you didn't even know there was a Paramount Theater or a Rustic Cabin; perhaps even the names of the Dorseys are dim memories to you. But in *The Big Bands,* George T. Simon tells it all like it was. It's a fascinating book. Don't let your father swipe it; tell him to go buy his own copy. I know he'll find it as hard to put down as you will; for him, though, it will be a well of nostalgia. For you and others like you, it will be an education.

Have fun reading this book, Joe, and don't forget—if it hadn't been for the big bands, there are a lot of lucky guys who might not have been so lucky, including

Yours truly,

Frank Sinatra

PREFACE

"It's great to look back, but don't stare!"

What a great attitude to take, especially from someone who truly enjoyed the past, like the legendary black baseball pitcher, Leroy "Satchel" Paige, who reportedly made that remark!

It's an attitude made-to-order for those of us who lived through the big band era and who still love to listen to its music. With us, it's great to listen again, though, if we listen too hard and won't open our ears to anything else, life can become frustrating, distorted and even just plain monotonous.

This isn't a book meant for staring. Instead, it's meant to be more of a vehicle that will help you *listen* back easily and lovingly to some of the musical joys and romance that filled the airwaves and record grooves and those ballrooms and night clubs and college gyms and theaters in which the bands played. The text, which has been revised and updated for this edition, will, I hope, help those of you who were there to remember even a little more clearly, and those of you who weren't to get a real feeling of the era and its music.

One new feature that I feel pretty certain will evoke many fond memories is the list of theme songs we have put together. So will, I hope, the dozens of new pictures we have inserted into this new edition. And then, too, there's a much larger discography than ever appeared in any of our earlier editions—close to 200 currently available long-playing albums—that will help you listen once more to the true sounds of that era.

Like many of you, I welcome the availability of the big band sounds on these albums. I like to listen to them, as well as to some of the 78s that have not been reissued. But those are by no means *all* the records I like to play. Why? Because I feel strongly that there's nothing that will age a guy more quickly than a morbid desire to live only in the past. I'm sure that's what "Satchel" Paige had in mind when he said, "Don't stare!"

Let me share with you what I can look back on. I guess you could say that I headed the list of all those "lucky" guys Frank Sinatra refers to in his foreword. For early in 1935, when I joined *Metronome,* the oldest and most respected popular music magazine, the big band movement was just beginning. And there I would be for the next twenty years (except for time-out in the army), living day and night in the midst of all those great sounds and people, listening not only to their music but also to what they had to say about it and how they felt about it and about one another and about everything related to the big bands. It was like having a twenty-season pass on the fifty yard line. Nobody who loved the big bands ever had it so good!

It began about eight months after graduation from college, where I had led a band called "The Confederates," because we didn't belong to the union. An old family friend, Herb Marks, introduced me to the publisher of *Metronome,* who couldn't understand what I meant when I said I'd like to review bands, but, since Herb was a valued advertiser, said he'd take me on at twenty-five bucks a month. Fortunately, the magazine had a much more knowing editor, a wonderful gent named Doron K. Antrim, who gave me my editorial head and let me write just about anything I wanted to. Actually, he let me assume a lot of heads, because it didn't make much sense to list the same byline under each of the many articles I contributed each month. So I also became Gordon Wright and Henry S. Cummings, who wrote record reviews, radio columnist Arthur J. Gibson, reporters Peter Embry and Joe Hanscom, and author of a lengthy, rambling column, filled with inside "scoops," gossip, and opinions, called "The Diary of Our Own Jimmy Bracken." I was having myself one magnificent schizophrenic ball!

As the magazine attracted more readers and advertisers, we were able to enlarge our editorial staff. During the following years, many good and dedicated writers joined us: Amy Lee, Dick Gilbert, Ed Dunkum, John Stolzfuss and Barry Ulanov, who, during my three-year hitch in the service during which I played in Glenn Miller's band and then produced V Discs of most of the top bands, assumed the editorship that Antrim had turned over to me in 1939. Later during the big band era, Leonard Feather, Peter Dean, Barbara Hodgkins, Bob Bach, Dave Dexter, Jr. and others added their critical pens and opinions.

At times, we wrote some pretty strong stuff, and I wonder when I look back at it now whether sometimes we weren't unnecessarily cruel, just as I find some of today's rock critics tend to be. But Ned Bitner, who had become publisher soon after I was made editor, never interfered. Instead, he encouraged our dedication to high musical standards. Those bands that entered the business purely for what they could get out of it monetarily distressed us with their often unconscionable gimmickry and blatant commercialism, and we kept on saying so. (I wonder how we would have reacted to all the hype that's going on in the business today!) On the other hand, those bands that kept trying to create something musically worthwhile, even something that might not have appealed to us, that did their best to maintain a high level of musicianship, that continued to respect artistic creativity and, in the final analysis, to put music above money, drew both our moral and our critical support.

This attitude or preference or bias or whatever you might want to call it pervades this book as well. I've tried to make the approach primarily repertorial, though, I must admit, not consistently objective. That's because I can never completely bridle my enthusiasm and respect for true musical creativity, talent and, above all, integrity. On the other hand, even though it's now thirty-five years since the end of the big band era (and presumably I have mellowed since then and begun to develop a greater understanding of why some bands were forced to be so crassly commercial in order to exist), my enthusiasm and respect for those less musicianly bands, no matter how successful they became, have grown not at all.

So, as you can see, this is in a sense a report with a definite point of view —a report of the big bands that focusses mostly on their greatest years— from 1935 through 1946. For it I have drawn not only upon the music itself, but also upon the often very personal words that were expressed to me by the leaders, the musicians, the singers, the arrangers and so many others whose thoughts and ideas and feelings, as well as their music, made the world of the big bands such a wonderfully rewarding one in which to live.

For making this book possible, my deepest thanks go to Neil McCaffrey and Donald Myrus, who first approached me about writing it; to Bob Markel, my first editor, and Bruce Carrick, his successor, and to my most recent editor, Ken Stuart, Jr., who agreed that it was about time to publish this new edition, and who worked so hard with me to give it a new life and a new look. I'd also like to extend similar thanks to Bob Asen, the last owner of *Metronome,* which ceased publication in the early 1960s, and who has carried on its name ever since, and to his partner, Milton Lichtenstein, who have permitted me to quote so copiously from the magazine and to utilize its magnificent collection of photographs; to one of the big bands' most illustrious alumni, Frank Sinatra, for his charming foreward; to all those quoted in these pages who have shared with me and you their thoughts and remembrances, and, finally, to all the many magnificent, creative people for whose outstanding musical contributions all of us who ever loved the big bands will remain forever grateful.

GEORGE T. SIMON
New York, April 1981

Part One:
The Big Bands—Then

What it was like: Benny Goodman and fans

The Scene

DO YOU remember what it was like? Maybe you do. Maybe you were there. Maybe you were there in New York two-thirds of the way through the 1930's, when there were so many great bands playing—so many of them at the same time. You could choose your spots—so many spots.

You could go to the Madhattan Room of the Hotel Pennsylvania, where Benny Goodman, the man who started it all, was playing with his great band, complete with Gene Krupa.

You could go a block or so farther to the Terrace Room of the Hotel New Yorker, and there you'd find Jimmy Dorsey and his Orchestra with Bob Eberly and Helen O'Connell . . . or to the Blue Room of the Hotel Lincoln to catch Artie Shaw and his band with Helen Forrest . . . or to the Green Room of the Hotel Edison for Les Brown's brand new band.

Maybe you'd rather go to some other hotel room—like the Palm Room of the Commodore for Red Norvo and Mildred Bailey and their soft, subtle swing . . . or to the Grill Room of the Lexington for Bob Crosby and his dixieland Bob Cats . . . or to the Moonlit Terrace of the Biltmore for Horace Heidt and his huge singing entourage . . . or down to the Roosevelt Grill for Guy Lombardo and his Royal Canadians and their extrasweet sounds.

And then there were the ballrooms—the Roseland with Woody Herman and the Savoy with Chick Webb. Not to mention the nightclubs—the Cotton Club with Duke Ellington, or the Paradise Restaurant, where a band nobody knew too much about was making sounds that the entire nation would soon recognize as those of Glenn Miller and his Orchestra.

Maybe you didn't feel so much like dancing but more like sitting and listening and maybe taking in a movie too. You could go to the Paramount, where Tommy Dorsey and his band, along with Jack Leonard and Edythe Wright, were appearing . . . or to the Strand to catch Xavier Cugat and his Latin music . . . or to Loew's State, where Jimmie Lunceford was swinging forth.

And if you had a car, you could go a few miles out of town . . . to the Glen Island Casino in New Rochelle to dance to Larry Clinton's music with vocals by Bea Wain . . . or to Frank Dailey's Meadowbrook across the bridge in New Jersey to catch Glen Gray and the Casa Loma Orchestra with Peewee Hunt and Kenny Sargent.

Of course, if you didn't feel like going out at all, you still were in luck—and you didn't have to be in New York either. For all you had to do was to turn on your radio and you could hear all sorts of great bands coming from all sorts of places—from the Aragon and Trianon ballrooms in Chicago, the Palomar Ballroom in Hollywood, the Raymor Ballroom in Boston, the Blue Room of the Hotel Roosevelt in New Orleans, the Mark Hopkins Hotel in San Francisco, the Steel Pier in Atlantic City and hundreds of other hotels, ballrooms and nightclubs throughout the country, wherever an announcer would begin a program with words like "And here is the music of ————!"

The music varied tremendously from style to style and, within each style, from band to band. Thus you could hear all types of swing bands: the hard-driving swing of Benny Goodman, the relaxed swing of Jimmie Lunceford, the forceful dixieland of Bob Crosby, the simple, riff-filled swing of Count Basie, the highly developed swing of Duke Ellington, and the very commercial swing of Glenn Miller.

Many of the big swing bands were built around the leaders and their instruments—around the clarinets of Goodman and Artie Shaw, the trumpets of Harry James and Bunny Berigan, the trombones of Jack Teagarden and Tommy Dorsey, the tenor sax of Charlie Barnet, the pianos of Ellington and Count Basie and the drums of Gene Krupa.

And then there were the sweet bands. They varied in style and in quality too. Some projected rich, full, musical ensemble sounds, like those of Glen Gray and the Casa Loma Orchestra, Isham Jones, Ray Noble and Glenn Miller. Others depended more on intimacy, like the bands of Hal Kemp and Guy Lombardo and of Tommy Dorsey when he featured his pretty trombone. Others played more in the society manner—Eddy Duchin with his flowery piano and Freddy Martin with his soft, moaning sax sounds. And then there were the extrasweet bandleaders. Lombardo, of course, was one. So was his chief imitator, Jan Garber. So was the Waltz King, Wayne King.

And there were the novelty bands, generally lumped in with the sweet bands—Kay Kyser, with all his smart gimmicks, including his College of Musical Knowledge and his singing song titles; Sammy Kaye, who also used singing song titles and introduced his "So You Wanna Lead a Band" gimmick; and Blue Barron, who aped Kaye . . . and so many others who aped Barron, who aped Kaye, who aped Kyser, who aped Lombardo.

There were so many bands playing so many different kinds of music—some well, some adequately, some horribly—all with their fans and followers. The *Metronome* poll, in which readers were invited to vote for their favorite bands in three divisions (Swing, Sweet and Favorite of All), listed almost three hundred entries in each of the four years from 1937 through 1940. And those were merely the bands that the readers liked most of all! There were hundreds more all over the country that didn't even place.

Why were some so much more successful than others? Discounting the obvious commercial considerations, such as financial support, personal managers, booking offices, recordings, radio exposure and press agents, four other factors were of paramount importance.

There was, of course, the band's musical style. This varied radically from band to band. A Tommy Dorsey was as far removed from a Tommy Tucker as an Artie Shaw was from an Art Kassel or a Sammy Kaye was from a Sam Donahue. Each band depended upon its own particular style, its own identifiable sound, for general, partial or just meager acceptance. In many ways, the whole business was like a style show—if the public latched on to what you were displaying, you had a good chance of success. If it rejected you, you'd better forget it.

Generally it was the band's musical director, either its arranger or its leader or perhaps both, who established a style. He or they decided what sort of sound the band should have, how it should be achieved and how it should be presented, and from there on proceeded to try to do everything possible to establish and project that sound, or style.

Secondly, the musicians within a band, its sidemen, played important roles. Their ability to play the arrangements was, naturally, vitally important. In some bands the musicians themselves contributed a good deal, especially in the swing bands, which depended upon them for so many solos; and in the more musical bands, whose leaders were willing to listen to and often accept musical suggestions from their sidemen.

But the musicians were important in other ways too. Their attitude and cooperation could make or break a band. If they liked or respected a leader, they would work hard to help him achieve his goals. If they had little use for him, they'd slough off both him and his music. The more musical the band and the style, the greater, generally speaking, the cooperation of its musicians in all matters—personal as well as musical.

Salaries? They were important, yes, in the bands that weren't so much fun to play in. But if the band was good musically and if the musicians were aware that their leader was struggling and couldn't pay much, money very often became secondary. Pride and potential and, most importantly, respect usually prevailed.

Thirdly, the singers—or the band vocalists, as they were generally called—often played important roles in establishing a band's popularity, in some cases even surpassing that of the band itself. A good deal depended upon how much a leader needed to or was willing to feature a vocalist. Most of the smarter ones realized that any extra added attraction within their own organization could only redound to their credit. Even after many of those singers had graduated to stardom on their own, their past relationships with the bands added a touch of glamour to those bands and their reputations.

Thus such current stars as Frank Sinatra and Jo Stafford still bring back memories of Tommy Dorsey, Doris Day of Les Brown, Ella Fitzgerald of Chick Webb, Peggy Lee of Benny Goodman and Perry Como of Ted Weems.

Tommy Dorsey's Frank Sinatra

Les Brown's Doris Day

And there were many others who meant very much to their leaders—Bob Eberly and Helen O'Connell to Jimmy Dorsey, Ray Eberle and Marion Hutton to Glenn Miller, Dick Haymes and Helen Forrest to Harry James, Kenny Sargent and Peewee Hunt to Glen Gray, Bea Wain to Larry Clinton, Ivy Anderson to Duke Ellington, Mildred Bailey to Red Norvo, Anita O'Day to Gene Krupa, June Christy to Stan Kenton, Ginny Sims to Kay Kyser, Dolly Dawn to George Hall, Wee Bonnie Baker to Orrin Tucker, Amy Arnell to Tommy Tucker, Jimmy Rushing to Count Basie, Al Bowlly to Ray Noble, Eddy Howard to Dick Jurgens, Bon Bon to Jan Savitt, Skinnay Ennis to Hal Kemp and, of course, Carmen Lombardo to brother Guy.

But of all the factors involved in the success of a dance band—the business affairs, the musical style, the arrangers, the sidemen and the vocalists— nothing equaled in importance the part played by the leaders themselves. For in each band it was the leader who assumed the most vital and most responsible role. Around him revolved the music, the musicians, the vocalists, the arrangers and all the commercial factors involved in running a band, and it was up to him to take these component parts and with them achieve success, mediocrity or failure.

Jimmy Dorsey's Helen O'Connell and Bob Eberly

The Leaders

SOME were completely devoted to music, others entirely to the money it could bring.

Some possessed great musical talent; others possessed none.

Some really loved people; others merely used them.

Some were extremely daring; others were stodgily conservative.

Some were motivated more by their emotions, others by a carefully calculated course of action.

And for some, leading a band was primarily an art; for others, it was basically a science.

That's how much bandleaders varied—in their ambitions, their ideals, their motivations, their talents and their personalities, as well as in their musical and ethical standards and values. They were as different personally as their bands were musically. Yet, with varying degrees of intensity, each sought success in one form or another—from the most purely artistic to the most crassly commercial.

Their approaches varied with their personalities and their talents. Highly dedicated and equally ambitious musicians like Glenn Miller, Benny Goodman, Artie Shaw and Tommy Dorsey approached their jobs with a rare combination of idealism and realism. Well trained and well disciplined, they knew what they wanted, and they knew how to get it. Keenly aware of the commercial competition, they drove themselves and their men relentlessly, for only through achieving perfection, or the closest possible state to it, could they see themselves realizing their musical and commercial goals.

Others, equally dedicated to high musical standards but less blatantly devoted to ruling the roost, worked in a more relaxed manner. Leaders like Woody Herman, Les Brown, Duke Ellington, Gene Krupa, Count Basie, Harry James, Claude Thornhill and Jimmy Dorsey pressured their men less. "You guys are pros," was their attitude, "so as long as you produce, you've got nothing to worry about." Their bands may have had a little less machine-like proficiency, but they swung easily and created good musical and commercial sounds.

Other leaders, often less musically endowed and less idealistically inclined, approached their jobs more from a businessman's point of view. For them

Two perfectionists and rivals:
Benny Goodman and Tommy Dorsey at the 1939 Metronome *All-Star record date*

music seemed to be less an art and more a product to be colorfully packaged and cleverly promoted. The most successful of such leaders, bright men like Guy Lombardo, Kay Kyser, Sammy Kaye, Horace Heidt, Shep Fields, Wayne King and Lawrence Welk, were masters at creating distinctive though hardly distinguished musical styles; men respected more for commercial cunning than for artistic creativity. They might have been faulted by *Metronome* and *Down Beat* but never by *Fortune* or *The Wall Street Journal.*

At the other end of the bandleading scale were those not nearly wise or calculating enough to realize that they never should have become bandleaders in the first place. Among these were some of the most talented and colorful musicians on the scene, to whom the music business meant all music and no business. Their lives were undisciplined and so were their bands. They swung just for the present, for a present filled with loads of laughs and little acceptance of their responsibilities as leaders. Unfortunately, almost all of this last group wound up as bandleading failures. For no matter what they would have liked to believe, leading a band was definitely a business, a very competitive, complex business consisting of almost continuous contacts— and often difficult and crucial compromises—with a wide variety of people on whom not merely the success but the very life of a dance band depended.

The leaders were called on to deal daily and directly—and not only on a musical but also on a personal basis—with their musicians, their vocalists and their arrangers, directing and supervising·and bearing the responsibilities of each of these groups. But that wasn't all. For their survival also depended a great deal on how well they dealt with all kinds of people outside their

Leaders greet Will Bradley and Ray McKinley at their Famous Door opening.
Left to right: *Teddy Powell, Art Kassel, Bradley, Charlie Barnet, Ella Fitzgerald
(who took over Chick Webb's band), Bob Crosby,
McKinley, Les Brown, Gene Krupa*

bands—with personal managers, with booking agents, with ballroom, night-club and hotel-room operators, with headwaiters and waiters and busboys, with bus drivers, with band boys, with the press, with publicity men, with music publishers, with all the various people from the radio stations and from the record companies and, of course, at all times and in all places—and no matter how tired or in what mood a leader might be—with the ever-present, ever-pressuring public.

No wonder Artie Shaw ran away to Mexico!

The Public

THE ever-present public knew. It was hip. The kids followed the bands closely, and they recognized not just the leaders themselves but also the songs they played, their arrangements, and who played what when with whom.

The big bands were like big league ball teams, and the kids knew all the players—even without a scorecard. Ask them to name Casa Loma's clarinet player and they'd tell you Clarence Hutchenrider. Ask them what trombonist played jazz for Bunny Berigan and they'd tell you Sonny Lee. Ask them what trombonist in Benny Goodman's band never played jazz at all and they'd tell you Red Ballard. Ask them who sang and played lead alto for Count Basie and they'd tell you Earle Warren. Ask them who played drums for Tommy Dorsey and—after *they'd asked you* on what records and you'd told them "Song of India" and on "Opus No. 1"—they'd tell you Davey Tough and Buddy Rich.

About records, which so many fans collected, they could answer most readily and specifically. They could tell you that it was Jerry Gray who arranged "Begin the Beguine" and Jack Jenney who played that great trombone solo of "Stardust" for Artie Shaw; that it was Tex Beneke followed by Al Klink on the series of tenor-sax passages on Glenn Miller's "In the Mood"; that it was Bon Bon who sang "720 in the Books" on the Jan Savitt recording; Bea Wain who sang "Deep Purple" for Larry Clinton; Bill Harris who was featured on trombone on Woody Herman's "Bijou"; Herschel Evans, not Lester Young, who played the sax solo on Count Basie's "Blue and Sentimental"; and Irene Daye, not Anita O'Day, who sang on Gene Krupa's "Drum Boogie."

But phonograph records offered merely one link between the bands and their public. It was an important one, even though only three companies, Columbia (including its Brunswick label), Decca and RCA Victor (including its Bluebird label), were issuing almost all the big band sides, and even though there weren't nearly so many disc jockeys to plug the music over the radio as there are today.

Radio stations did help to enlarge the big band audience, however, by broadcasting many live performances—a few on regular commercial series, but most on sustaining shows, many of them complete with crowd excitement, directly from where the bands were playing. Every night the airwaves would

PERSONNELS OF 1938's LEADING BANDS

SAX SECTIONS

Bands	1st Sax	2nd Sax	3rd Sax	4th Sax
1—Count Basie	Earl Warren (ha)	Lester Young (h)	Ronald Washington	Hershal Evans (h t & c)
2—Bunny Berigan	Milton Schatz	George Auld (b)	Gus Bivona (c)	Clyde Rounds
3—Larry Clinton	Mike Doty	Tony Zimmers (h)	Leo White (c)	Hugo Winterhalter
4—Bob Crosby	Joey Kearns	Eddie Miller (h)	Fazola (c)	Gil Rodin
5—Jimmy Dorsey	Milt Yaner	Herbie Hamyer (h)	Leonard Whitney	Charles Frazier (h)
6—Tommy Dorsey	Hymie Schertzer	Babe Russin (h)	Johnny Mince (c)	Dean Kincaide (h)
7—Duke Ellington	Otto Hardwick	Barney Bigard (hc)	Johnny Hodges (h)	Harry Carney (hb)
8—Benny Goodman	Milton Yaner	Bud Freeman (h)	Dave Matthews (ha)	Arthur Rollini (h)
9—Glen Gray	Art Ralston	Pat Davis (h)	C. Hutchenrider (c)	Kenny Sargent
10—Horace Heidt	Frank DeVol	Bob Riedel	Bill Tieber	
11—Hal Kemp	Henry Dankers	Saxey Dowell	Ben Williams	Bruce Milligan
12—Gene Krupa	Bob Snyder	Sam Donahue (h)	Mascagni Ruffo	Sam Musiker (h)
13—Kay Kyser	Armand Buissaret	Morton Gregory	Herman Gunkler	Sully Mason
14—Guy Lombardo	Carmen Lombardo	Fred Higman	Lawrence Owen	Victor Lombardo
15—Jimmie Lunceford	Willy Smith (ha & c)	Joe Thomas (h)	Ted Buckner (ha)	Earl Carruthers
16—Glenn Miller	Hal McIntyre (c)	Gordon Beneke (h)	Wilbur Schwartz (c)	Stan Aaronson
17—Red Norvo	Frank Simeone	George Berg (h)	Hank D'Amico (h)	Maurice Kogan (h)
18—Artie Shaw	Les Robinson	Tony Pastor (h)	Hank Freeman	Ronny Perry
19—Chick Webb	Chauncey Haughton (c)	Ted McCrea (h)	Hylton Jefferson	Waymond Carver
20—Paul Whiteman	Al Gallodoro	Art Dollinger (h)	Sal Franzella (c)	Frank Gallodoro

BRASS SECTIONS

	1st Trumpet	2nd Trumpet	3rd Trumpet	1st Trombone	2nd Trombone
1—	Ed Lewis	Buck Clayton (h)	Harry Edison (h)	Dan Minor	Benny Morton (h)
2—	John Naptan	Harry Goodman	Berigan (1st & h)	Nat LeBrousky	Ray Conniff
3—	Snapper Lloyd	Jimmy Sexton	Walter Smith (h)	Joe Ortolano	Ford Leary (h)
4—	Zeke Zarchi	Sterling Bose (h)	Bill Butterfield (1st & h)	Ward Silloway	Warren Smith (h)
5—	Ralph Muzzillo	Shorty Sherock (h)	Don Mattison (3 trmb)	Bobby Byrns (h)	Sonny Lee (h)
6—	Charles Spivak	Yank Lausen (h)	Lee Castaldo (h)	Moe Zudecoff	Les Jenkins (h)
7—	Wallace Jones	Cootie Williams (h)	Rex Stewart (h)	Lawrence Brown (h)	Juan Tizol (h)
8—	Harry James (h)	Ziggy Elman (h)	Chris Griffen (h)	Vernon Brown (h)	Red Ballard
9—	Frank Zullo	Grady Watts (h)	Sonny Dunham (h)	Billy Rausch	Peewee Hunt (h)
10—	Warren Lewis	Frank Strasek		Jimmy Skyles	
11—	Clayton Cash	Mickey Bloom (h)	Harry Wiliford (h)	Ed Kusborski (h)	Leo Moran
12—	Nick Prospero	C. Frankhauser (h)	Tom Goslin (h)	Toby Tyler	Bruce Squires (h)
13—	Robert Guy	Merwyn Bogue	H. Carriere	Harry Thomas	Max Williams
14—	Lebert Lombardo	Dudley Fodsick (mellophone)		Jim Dillon	
15—	Eddie Tompkins (h)	Paul Webster (h)	Sy Oliver (h)	James Young (h)	Russell Boles
16—	Bob Price	Bob Barker	Johnny Austin (h)	Al Mastren	Lightnin
17—	Johnny Owens	Jack Palmer (h)	Barney Zudecoff	Danny Russo	Al George
18—	John Best (h)	Claude Bowen	Chuck Peterson (h)	Rusell Brown	George Arus (h)
19—	Dick Vance	Bobby Stark (h)	Taft Jordan (h)	Nat Storee	Sandy Williams (h)
20—	Don Moore	Charley Teagarden (h)	Harry Goldfield	Jose Gotierrez	Jack Teagarden (h)

RHYTHM SECTIONS AND VOCALISTS

	Piano	Guitar	Bass	Drums	Vocalists
1—	Count Basie	Freddy Green	Walter Page	Joe Jones	Helen Humes and James Rushing
2—	Joe Bushkin	Dick Morgan	Hank Wayland	Buddy Rich	Jayne Dover and Morgan
3—	Sam Mineo	Jack Chesleigh	Walter Hardman	Charlie Blake	Bea Wain & Chesleigh
4—	Bob Zurke	Nappy Lamare	Bob Haggart	Ray Bauduc	Marion Mann, Crosby, Lamare & Miller
5—	Freddy Slack	Roc Hilman	Jack Ryan	Ray McKinley	Bob Eberle & Mattison
6—	Howard Smith	Carmen Mastren	Gene Traxler	Maurice Purtill	Edythe Wright and Jack Leonard
7—	Duke Ellington	Fred Guy	Bill Taylor	Sonny Greer	Ivy Anderson
8—	Jess Stacey	Ben Heller	Harry Goodman	Dave Tough	Martha Tilton
9—	Howard Hall	Jacques Blanchette	Stan Dennis	Tony Briglia	Sargent and Hunt
10—	Lou Bush	Alvino Rey	Edward McKimey	Bernie Matthewson	Lysbeth Hughes, Larry Cotton, etc.
11—	Van Nordstrand		Jack Shirra	Emery Kenyon	Judy Starr, Bob Allen, Dowell & Wiliford
12—	Milton Raskin	Ray Biondi	Horace Rollins	Gene Krupa	Irene Daye & Leo Watson
13—	Lyman Gandee		Lloyd Snow	Eddie Shea	Ginny Sims, Harry Babbitt, Mason & Bogue
14—	Frank Vigneau	Francis Henry	Bernie Davis	George Gowans	Carmen & Lebert Lombardo
15—	Edwin Wilcox	Albert Norris	Mose Allen	Jimmy Crawford	Grissom, Oliver, Webster, Thomas & Young
16—	Chummy MacGreggor		Rolly Bundoc	Bob Spangler	Marion Hutton, Ray Eberle, Beneke & Miller
17—	Bill Miller	Allen Hanlon	Pete Peterson	George Wettling	Mildred Bailey & Terry Allen
18—	Les Burness	Al Avola	Sid Weiss	Cliff Leeman	Billie Holiday
19—	Tommy Fulford	Bobby Johnson	Beverly Peer	Chick Webb	Ella Fitzgerald
20—	Roy Bargy	Art Ryerson	Artie Miller	Rollo Layland	Joan Edwards & Teagarden

OTHER MEN IN ABOVE BANDS 1. Dick Wells, 3rd & hot trmb. 5. Jimmy Dorsey, hot alto & cl. 6. Fred Stulce, 5th sax; Dorsey, hot & lead trmb; Elmer Smithers, 3rd trmb. 7. Joe Nanton, 3rd (plunger) trmb. 8. Goodman, hot cl.; Matthews also 1st sax. 9. Dan D'Andrea, 1st & 5th sax; Gray, 6th sax; Murray MacEachern, 1st & hot trmb. 12. Dalton Rizzotto, 3rd trmb. 15. Lunceford, Dan Grissom, saxes; Elmer Crumbley, 3rd & most hot trmb. 16. Bill Stagmire, 5th & hot alto. Miller all hot & sweet trmb. 18. Shaw, hot cl.; Harry Rodgers, 3rd trmb. 19. Jefferson also 1st sax; George Matthews, 3rd trmb. 20. Bob Cusumano also 1st trpt; Hal Matthews, 3rd trmb.; Frank Signorelli, 2nd piano.

SYMBOLS: a, alto; b, baritone; c & cl, clarinet; h, hot; t, tenor; trpt, trumpet; trmb, trombone.

be filled with the music of the big bands. In addition, whenever the networks had open time, either in the early evenings or at mid-day, or even sometimes at nine o'clock in the morning, they would schedule similar broadcasts.

With all those records and radio shows inundating homes, anyone at all interested in the big bands could learn a great deal about them and their music. To educate the fans even more, magazines like *Metronome* and *Down Beat* devoted their monthly issues almost entirely to news and reviews of the bands. Occasionally some of the country's major magazines wrote pieces about some of the biggest names, but seldom did much of the daily press devote significant space to any of them, except, of course, when some self-appointed watchdog of the country's morals might spout off about how decadent swing music was or when some reporter might become impressed with the sociological implications of a batch of kids getting excited listening to a band in a theater. But the lack of interest, understanding and often ability to get facts straight on the part of the newspapers was positively appalling and proved pretty conclusively that, when it came to big bands, one good arrangement or one outstanding trumpet chorus could be worth more than a thousand words!

Of course, records and radio and the press couldn't even approach the potent impact of hearing a band in person. This was it! To stand in front of one of your favorite swing bands *watching* its musicians make the sounds you'd been *hearing* over the air and on records, and, most of all, hearing it in all its roaring purity—with the trumpets and trombones blasting away right at you and the saxes supporting them and the rhythm section letting loose with those clear, crisp, swinging beats—it all added up to one of the real thrills in life.

Nothing has ever matched it. The whining electrified guitars and the flabby-sounding electronic basses of the sixties and seventies had power, all right —they could virtually steamroller you. But hearing big bands in person was completely different. They didn't knock you down and flatten you out and leave you lying there, a helpless victim of sodden, sullen, mechanized musical mayhem. Instead they swung freely and joyously. And as they swung, they lifted you high in the air with them, filling you with an exhilarated sense of friendly well-being; you joined them, emotionally and musically, as partners in one of the happiest, most thrilling rapports ever established between the givers and takers of music.

The free, spontaneous communication between the big bands and their fans was a natural culmination of the music itself. The approach of most outfits was so honest and direct that their fans could recognize instinctively whether the bands were really trying or merely coasting. When a musician played an especially exciting solo, they'd cheer him for it, and when the band as a whole reached especially high musical and emotional heights, it would be rewarded with enthusiastic, honest, heartfelt yelling and cheering—not the kind of hysterics evoked by a rock and roller's shaking his long tresses, but real approval for a musical job well done.

It was easy to tell when a band was communicating with its audience, for

The public inside—listening to Harry James

when it did, many couples would crowd as close to the bandstand as they could in order to catch every visual and aural nuance. Behind them, other couples would be dancing happily to the swinging sounds. Then later, when the band would lapse into a romantic mood, the listeners would usually join the others, dancing gracefully to the mellower music.

The public's appreciation and awareness of the music and the musicians kept the big bands honest. When a jazz soloist recorded what the fans thought was a great solo, like Bunny Berigan's on "Marie" or Charlie Barnet's on "Cherokee," they'd remember it, and they'd expect to hear it when the band came to their town.

Jimmy Dorsey once recalled how this dedication could extend beyond reasonableness. After his band had completed an engagement in a midwestern town, he was invited to go to an after-hours spot to hear a local group that featured a clarinetist who apparently idolized Jimmy. He could play the Dorsey clarinet choruses note for note, just the way Jimmy had recorded them. But the big shock came when the band went into a number on which Dorsey had played a chorus of which he had been particularly ashamed. Out came that same chorus note for note, including all the bad ones that Jimmy had never meant to blow and had never blown since. Obviously here was one king who could do no wrong.

The kids could also spot personnel changes within bands. Naturally they would expect to see such established stars as Flip Phillips with Woody Herman or Johnny Hodges with Duke Ellington or Roy Eldridge with Gene Krupa. But such astuteness wasn't limited just to the top bands and top soloists. If Nappy Lamare wasn't playing guitar for Bob Crosby, if Alec Fila wasn't playing lead trumpet with Bob Chester, or if Harry Terrill wasn't

. . . and ogling Stan Kenton's June Christy.

playing lead alto for Mitchell Ayres, there'd usually be one or more followers who'd want to know why.

Ayres himself reportedly once became the victim of the keen ears of his audience. He had been hired several months in advance for a school prom. Meanwhile he had been booked into a steady engagement, and when the Saturday for the prom rolled around, the spot's manager wouldn't release him. So Mitch cut out, picked up a local band near the school and probably figured he was doing all right with the substitutes, despite some doubting looks from the dancers, until a couple of kids, either because they became disenchanted with the music or for more personal reasons, decided to sit in their car. There they tuned in their radio. Out came a familiar sound, followed by a shocking revelation as the announcer intoned, "From Murray's Restaurant in Tuckahoe, New York, we are bringing you the music of Mitchell Ayres and his Orchestra!"

If distinctive sounds, special arrangements, individual musicians and singers and over-all styles hadn't become so important to the public, a misadventure such as the one that befell Ayres (and he wasn't the only leader who had been caught with his baton down) would probably never have occurred. But the big bands, by their very emphasis on individuals and individuality, had brought to dance bands a highly personal touch that they had never had before. And the more successful they became, the more new outfits, each emphasizing its own hopefully distinctive style, began to appear on the scene. By 1940 there must have been close to two hundred dance orchestras, any one of which a knowing fan could identify after hearing only a few of its stylized musical measures.

Nothing like it had ever happened before.

The Musicians

ONE night in 1937 while we were driving—I can still remember it was under the old Third Avenue El in New York—Glenn Miller turned to me and said, "You know, you'd better make up your mind right now what you want to be —a musician or a writer."

The cause of his ultimatum was clear. I'd been moonlighting from my job as assistant editor of *Metronome* to play drums with his band, at rehearsals and even on its first recordings. But my course was just as clear as his cause. "Thanks just the same," I said, "but I'd better stick to writing."

Pass up a chance to play drums with Glenn Miller? Of course I did. I'd been working for *Metronome* for only a couple of years, but I'd already learned one important fact: a big band could be a wonderful place to work for an outstanding musician, which I knew I wasn't. As a writer—well, I figured I still had a chance.

The big band days were exciting and rewarding for the top musicians. For them there was glory, there was glamour and there was good money. For them it could be a thrilling ball, a daydream come true. But for others it could develop into a chilling bore, a nightmare come much too true.

The big rewards—the recognition and often the top money—came readily to those who, in addition to playing their instruments exceptionally well, could also communicate easily with the public. Among them were most of the top soloists, the individualists in each band who provided their own special brand of musical excitement. Eventually several of them, like Harry James, Lionel Hampton, Gene Krupa, Bunny Berigan, Charlie Spivak and Tony Pastor, became successful leaders. Others, such as Benny Goodman's Ziggy Elman, Duke Ellington's Johnny Hodges, Tommy Dorsey's Bud Freeman, Glenn Miller's Tex Beneke, remained sidemen during the big band era, rewarded handsomely by their leaders and by the adulation of their fans.

It was a good life for the star soloists. So it was, too, for many of the lead men, the most important members of the brass and reed sections, mainly responsible for the band's ensemble sounds. These were the musicians often accorded the greatest respect by their fellow sidemen. What's more, a potent, dependable, yet flexible lead trumpeter could always find work, and the best of them, such as Ralph Muzzillo and Zeke Zarchy and Andy Ferretti and

Jimmy Campbell, could and would choose their spots with any of the most successful, best-paying bands. The same sorts of reward came to the outstanding lead saxists like Hymie Shertzer, Toots Mondello, Milt Yaner and Sam Marowitz and to lead trombonists like Buddy Morrow and Murray MacEachern. These were the unsung heroes of the big bands.

Tommy Dorsey once compared a dance band to a football team. In the backfield he put the soloists, the obvious stars. And in the line he put his lead men—first trumpet, first sax and first trombone—along with the four men in his rhythm section—the pianist, guitarist, bassist and drummer.

But there were a great many lesser-known men in the bands, those who played in the sections but didn't lead them and who didn't get a chance to play solos. These were strictly supportive players, their lives filled with little glamour and seldom any overt appreciation. Whether life as big band musicians was any fun at all for them depended a great deal on the specific band they happened to be in.

The morale of the musicians was generally highest in the bands that played the best music and were headed by leaders who knew how to treat not only their music but also the men who played it. Les Brown was an outstanding example of such a leader. Woody Herman was another. So were Duke Ellington, Harry James, Count Basie, Jimmy Dorsey, Jimmie Lunceford, Gene Krupa, Claude Thornhill, Stan Kenton and sometimes Tommy Dorsey. Life in bands like these, as well as in some less successful ones in which respect for good music and musicianship prevailed, could be and often was one continuous ball.

In the bands led by the most exacting perfectionists, like Glenn Miller, Benny Goodman and Artie Shaw, the living may have been a little less easy, the atmosphere more tense and the good times less intense. But for any musician who had pride in his music, working with such exacting but experienced leaders usually offered superior artistic rewards. Not so, however, in many other, less musical bands, in which routine and discipline and protocol too often assumed greater importance than the quality of the music itself.

This preoccupation with effect for effect's sake appeared most often in bands that emphasized musical tricks, gimmicks that required precise musicianship but provided few opportunities for musical expression. Playing in such purely commercial outfits could become both depressing and frustrating for musicians with much of a creative urge of their own. I often wondered how much pride, how much self-respect and how much *joie de vivre* men could retain playing in bands like Sammy Kaye's or Horace Heidt's or Kay Kyser's of the thirties or in some of the many other mickey-mouse bands. Too often members of strictly commercial bands were treated more like employees than artists, more like Boy Scouts than grown-ups, and in extreme cases more like robots than musicians.

Life in general, though, was rewarding to most of the big band musicians. It was, after all, a life they had selected for themselves, and the fact that they

They traveled by car:
Dick Stabile and wife-vocalist Grace Barrie on the outside; musicians Frank Gibson,
Charley Arlington, Hank Reinecke and Pinky Savitt on the inside.

could earn a living doing what many of them would have done without pay was certainly a big plus.

But there were also numerous minuses. The actual living conditions for most musicians would have been pretty difficult to take if they hadn't had their love of music to sustain them. The numerous one-nighter routines could be especially discouraging. Planes and trains were too expensive and impractical, so that traveling was confined almost entirely to chartered buses or private cars, none of which offered the riding ease or the luxuries of today's vehicles. Many times bands would arrive by bus at a ballroom or dance pavilion, wash up and change clothes in dingy dressing rooms or even in a men's washroom, play the job, hang around for something to eat, climb back on the bus and grab some sleep while riding to the next spot. This time they'd probably check into some hotel, usually a second-rater, wash up, eat, play the job, eventually get to bed, then rise, much too early, to clamber back on the bus and ride on to the next job. (By sleeping in hotels only every other night they could save substantial sums, for leaders did not pay for lodging or food.)

Some of the one-nighter jumps were pretty horrendous, especially during winters and in mountainous areas. Near-misses seemed almost routine. And some accidents really hit home, like the head-on crash that took Hal Kemp's life, and the accident that killed Chu Berry, the brilliant tenor saxist then with Cab Calloway's band. In another crash, Charlie Barnet lost two musicians, while other road accidents seriously maimed several more musicians,

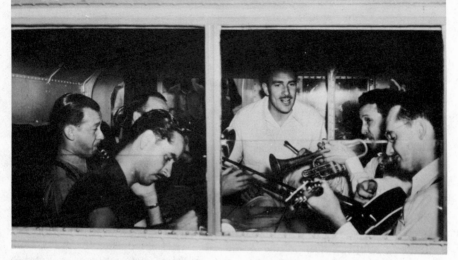

They traveled by bus:
clarinetist Clarence Hutchenrider, saxist Dan D'Andrea, unidentifiable trombonist,
leader Glen Gray, trumpeter Grady Watts, guitarist Jacques Blanchette.

They sometimes traveled by plane:
Guy Lombardo and His Royal Canadians beside a specially chartered
United airliner; the Lombardos, Guy, Liebert and Carmen at left in front row.

like Enoch Light, whose career was almost ended, and Barclay Allen, Freddy Martin's brilliant pianist, who was paralyzed for life.

One chief cause of the accidents was the length of the daily jumps—some as long as five hundred miles—that the booking offices imposed on the bands. The ridiculousness of it all was once beautifully expressed by members of the Bob Crosby band. At a party, one musician stated that "We will now play a game called 'Rockwell-O'Keefe' [the band's booking office]." Whereupon they produced a globe and a blindfold. "Here's how we book the Crosby band," announced one of the musicians as he spun the globe. Then another musician, securely blindfolded, stuck out his finger and stopped the globe. "There's where you play tomorrow night," he announced, and the process was repeated until a whole week's tour had been arranged: Canada; New Zealand; Terre Haute, Indiana; New Delhi; Fairbanks, Alaska; and so on.

Eventually the musicians' union provided its men some sort of protection by limiting jumps to four hundred miles a day, then during the war years, when worn tires and worn-out buses made traveling even more hazardous, to three hundred miles.

The union also succeeded in securing better working conditions for musicians. Wage scales set by each local differed vastly from town to town, and often within a city there were different scales for different types of spots. (Colored bands, whicn often belonged to separate locals, almost always played at lower scales.) As the economy improved, so did musicians' pay. This also held true for working hours. In New York, for example, musicans for years had been working seven days a week; finally, late in 1938, their union won a six-day week.

With so much time spent in traveling and work, musicians' extracurricular activities were necessarily limited. During bus rides, however, in addition to sleeping, they talked, played cards, read and drank. Often cliques developed within bands—again, the card players, the readers, the drinkers and the sports fans.

Baseball was the favorite sport among musicians. Not only did they follow the big league scores, but quite a few bands fielded teams. There wasn't a more enthusiastic player than Harry James, who captained, pitched and led the Goodman band in hitting during his first year in the big band league, a season that saw Benny's team win fourteen games while losing none.

"Our most recent victory," Harry wrote in July, 1938, "was an eighteen-inning affair against Count Basie's Bulldogs, and we finally won out only after Benny Heller (guitarist) tallied after some hard running from second on Red Ballard's (trombone) prodigious triple to deep left center. We've had three road games. We walloped Glenn Miller's Millers 15 to 5, Gene Krupa's Kangaroos 19 to 7 (which really steamed Gene, too), and in a very tight pitchers' battle just nosed out Woody Herman's Herd by 26 to 15."

On the subject of pitchers, Tommy Dorsey, a highly competitive gent, once hired an old-time idol of his, Grover Cleveland Alexander, to coach his team,

*Avid ball player
Harry James*

while Muggsy Spanier took on another hurler, Pat Malone of the Cubs, to teach his men.

Gene Krupa, an avid Chicago White Sox fan, whose team once beat Jan Garber's by 18 to 8 ("due to the fact," Krupa stated, "that I didn't play"), has pointed out the striking similarity between the lives led by ballplayers and musicians: ". . . the road, the living out of suitcases, the constant time pressures to get to another place so that you can perform on schedule, the working with the same people every day, being watched all the time by the public, trying to live up to a reputation, and, of course, all the mental and emotional intangibles that must affect ballplayers just the way they affect musicians."

GOODMAN'S GARGANTUANS

	AB	R	H
Bernardi 3b	4	1	2
H. Goodman ss	5	3	3
Elman lf.	5	2	2
James p.	5	2	3
Brown 1b.	5	1	3
Freeman rf	5	0	1
Rollini cf.	5	0	1
Griffin 2b.	4	0	2
Heller sf.	4	0	1
Godfrey c.	4	2	2
	51	11	20

BASIE'S BAD BOYS

	AB	R	H
Washington 2b	5	0	3
Warren ss	4	1	2
Morton 3b.	5	0	2
Evans 1b.	5	0	2
Lewis c.	5	0	2
Clayton rf.	5	0	1
Green lf.	4	1	2
Young p.	4	1	2
Edison cf.	3	0	0
Roberts sf.	4	0	4
	44	3	20

This Goodman-Basie box score appeared in a 1938 edition of Metronome.
Lester Young pitched for Basie, Harry James for Goodman.

GOODMAN.. 2 0 4 1 0 0 3 0 1—11 20 0
BASIE....... 1 2 0 0 0 0 0 0 0— 3 20 0

Home run: James. Three base hits: Elman, James. Two base hits: Bernardi (2). H. Goodman (2), Godfrey. Struck out by James: 6. Base on Balls off James: 2; of Young: 1.

Those intangibles often affected not only the playing but also the behavior of musicians. Seemingly inconsequential actions and reactions within a band could make a musician loose or tight, happy or depressed, ebullient or tired. So could even more strictly personal matters.

There were, of course, many musicians who lived primarily for their art. But there were others who wanted to lead fuller lives. Some were married men, and if they happened to be worried about things at home, about finances, about their wives or about their kids, their playing and their general behavior could be affected. It wasn't uncommon for a musician to play exceptionally well one night and very uninspiringly the next. Also it wasn't unusual for the same musician to mingle graciously with his fans in one town and then to fluff them off completely the next night in another town. Any number of extenuating circumstances could have affected his mood, his outlook and his creativity—a run-in with his leader, a bad reed, an out-of-tune piano, a hangover, a new musican sitting next to him who played terribly, a toothache, lack of sleep, lousy food, a cold, a date who failed to show up and so on.

Musicians had numerous consuming interests outside of music. Harry James and others had their baseball. Jack Teagarden loved to tinker with cars. Bobby Byrne and Larry Clinton were involved in flying. Tex Beneke and Kenny Sargent were fascinated by shortwave radio. Bud Freeman always harbored a yen to become an actor. Artie Shaw was an avid reader, Davey Tough an avid writer.

Of all the people who have written about jazz, Tough remains my favorite. A wiry little man who weighed less than a hundred pounds but who could swing big bands like Goodman's and Shaw's and Herman's with a fantastic drive, he was a midget dynamo. He was also a warm, witty, wonderful person, and it all showed in the column on drum playing that he wrote in 1937 for *Metronome*.

One of my favorite passages, quite indicative of Davey's wry way of treating the many frustrating conditions that faced musicians, appeared in answer to a letter writer who had complained about his music school, about having to buy a lot of books and about his drum teacher, who wasn't a drummer. Wrote Davey: "The realization that one has no natural aptitude, no technique and no knowledge of the instrument, along with the fancy that he would have been a rather neat plumber, is too often followed as a sort of defense mechanism by the morbid desire to teach. These abortionate percussionists head for the facilities of music schools like homing pigeons, and for this reason alone the schools should be avoided like the plague. . . .

"Being an old meany-andrew at heart, I should like to recommend to those drummers who can neither teach, play nor plumb, the job of control man at a recording studio. The only requirement for such a position demands that you must know something about anything generally and you must not have the foggiest wisp of an idea about music specifically. When the trumpet is playing too loudly just say 'too much brushes.' Say everything is awful, and when you think you should break down and say 'yes,' say 'no,' twice loudly."

Frustrations and aggravations, such as those created by control men in recording studios; ballroom and hotel-room managers who seemed to be constantly complaining about bands playing too loud; bookers, many of whom never seemed to indicate that they cared at all about musicians as human beings; fans who kept wanting to squeeze more and still more from musicians so tired they could barely sit up in their chairs; out-of-tune pianos; bandstands too small for anything resembling comfort; acoustics that made it impossible to hear the musician in the next chair; public-address systems that didn't work —all these and many more frustrations and irritations haunted the big band musicians almost continually throughout their careers. I doubt whether any other group of artists has ever managed to develop and produce so consistently well under such trying conditions as did the musicans in the big bands.

Obviously they were all part of something more inspiring than mere materialism. They shared what too few other working groups share: a love of what they were doing, a love coupled with a healthy conviction that they were both playing and fighting for a cause to which they were deeply dedicated. In addition, most musicians, jazz musicians especially, were then, as some still are today, blessed with their own brand of humor, the kind that let them laugh not only at humorous events that concerned others but also at themselves. Unlike many other artists, most jazz musicians have possessed the happy faculty of not taking themselves too utterly seriously. Their work, yes. But themselves, no. It was this ability to look at themselves and their circumstances with some degree of objectivity that frequently helped them to rise above the frustrations that might have discouraged other artists from further productivity.

Many big band graduates often reminisce with varying degrees of enthusiasm, but always with deep appreciation, about their experiences—experiences that they freely admit taught them so much, not merely about music, but also about people and places and things *outside* their world of the big bands. Theirs was a tremendous education—unique, perhaps; unorthodox, certainly. It was, as Frank Sinatra pointed out to Joe D. Oakes in the introduction to this book, like attending "a cross-country college." With, he might have added, a major in music and a minor in human relations.

The Rise, the Glory
and the Decline

IT BEGAN with Benny Goodman. His was the band that sparked the whole big band scene; he was the first truly important horn blower to bridge the gap between the leaders and their bands and the general public.

Benny and his clarinet became a symbol, a direct line of emotional and musical communication betwen those on the stand and those who gathered around to watch, to worship, to dance and to listen—in person, on records and over the radio.

The Benny Goodman band in early 1936:
pianist Jess Stacy; bassist Harry Goodman; guitarist Allan Reuss;
vocalist Helen Ward; drummer Gene Krupa; Goodman; trumpeters Harry Geller,
Ralph Muzzillo, Nate Kazebier; trombonists Joe Harris, Red Ballard;
saxists Dick Clark, Bill Depew, Hymie Shertzer, Arthur Rollini

Several things set Goodman's apart from all the bands that had preceded it. One, of course, was the type of music it played—a crisp, clean, driving, always swinging and exciting, always easily understood kind of music. Another was its consistently superior musicianship. And then, of course, there was Goodman himself, with the personalized excitement that he projected through his horn. He and his clarinet created a kind of identity that hadn't existed before, providing an aura of glamour and personality and excitingly superb musicianship that set the mood and the pace for a dozen glorious years.

Before Benny there had been many big bands—some very good, some very successful. The most important of the early ones, Paul Whiteman's, forsook the accepted but dull routine of merely repeating chorus after chorus after chorus of a song. Instead, like another band that started on the West Coast, Art Hickman's, it featured its own special arrangements. Other leaders soon followed suit—Ben Selvin, Vincent Lopez, Fred Waring, Coon-Sanders, Don Bestor and the Benson Orchestra, Abe Lyman, Eddie Elkins, Art Landry, Bert Lown, George Olsen, Don Voorhees, Leo Reisman, Jan Garber, Paul Ash, Paul Specht, Paul Tremaine and many more. A few were interesting, some were merely adequate, many were unbearably dull.

Most musically creative and exciting during the twenties were some of the black bands, which played more than just gentle dance music. With almost all the best hotel rooms and vaudeville houses reserved for white bands, these spirited, pre-swing-era outfits blew their wares mostly in ballrooms and, in the case of at least one of them, the brilliant Duke Ellington Orchestra, in nightclubs that featured black talent for a white clientele.

In addition to Ellington's, there were several other top bands, including two white ones, that played what by the then current standards must have been considered progressive music. Many of their arrangements projected a pure jazz feeling, not only in the ensembles but also in the freedom that they gave their soloists: Fletcher Henderson's, on whose style Goodman's and many other later bands built their arrangements; McKinney's Cotton Pickers, who

Before the big band boom began:
Henry Busse and Paul Whiteman
in Coral Gables, Florida, 1926

The early Duke of Ellington

rivaled the Henderson band in musical proficiency and excitement; Bennie Moten's riff-filled Kansas City band, which later spawned Count Basie's; Jean Goldkette's, which featured jazz stars like Bix Beiderbecke, Joe Venuti, Eddie Lang and the Dorsey Brothers (before they joined Whiteman); and Ben Pollack's, which in the late twenties sported arrangements by a young trombonist, Glenn Miller, and the clarinet of a young Chicagoan, Benny Goodman.

Then in 1929 came the stock-market crash and the Depression. The high-living and the tempos slowed down. The mood and the music of the country changed. The search for security, for sweetness and light was reflected in the country's musical tastes—in its acceptance of crooners like Rudy Vallee and Will Osborne, and then Bing Crosby and Russ Columbo, in its preference for dance music that encouraged romance and sentiment and escape.

This was the era that nurtured several outstanding sweet bands—Guy Lombardo and his Royal Canadians and their saccharine sounds, Hal Kemp and his light, tricky, don't-take-me-too-seriously romantic approach, Isham Jones and his broad, reassuring, melodic ensembles, Eddy Duchin and his personalized pianistics, Ozzie Nelson and Harriet Hilliard and their sweet simperings, and Wayne King and his whimpering waltzes.

Whiteman and Waring and Reisman and Lyman and some of the other commercial bands kept going too. So did the great Ellington and Henderson outfits. And another great colored band, Jimmie Lunceford's, started to challenge them.

Unnoticed at first by the general public, though impressing the musicians and jazz fans as early as 1930, were the brisk, brittle, semi-swinging big band sounds produced by the midwestern Casa Loma Orchestra. Perhaps they never would have reached more ears if someone connected with the band hadn't hit upon the idea of interspersing its blaring, brassy bombasts with some of the most mood-provoking ballads ever wafted by a dance orchestra. By 1933 this group of smartly dressed sophisticated-looking musicians had added to its repertoire of up-tempo killer-dillers ("Blue Jazz," "Wild Goose Chase" and "Casa Loma Stomp") a flock of beautifully arranged ballads such as "For You," "Under a Blanket of Blue" and "It's the Talk of the Town."

Soon not only musicians were listening to Glen Gray and the Casa Loma Orchestra. Kids, especially those in the colleges, flocked to hear the handsome-looking band that produced such mellow, musical moods, then stood around in awe as it let loose with an excitingly different-sounding big band barrage. More than any other group, the Casa Loma Orchestra set the stage for the emergence of the swing bands and eventually the blossoming of the entire big band era.

By 1934 other musical outfits were also making attractive sounds. The Dorsey brothers were noodling in the background; Ray Noble was threatening from across the sea. In New York, Benny Goodman organized a band that played at a nightclub, Billy Rose's Music Hall, and attracted nobody except musicians.

But early in 1935 came Goodman's big chance, a weekly Saturday-night appearance on a coast-to-coast radio show. For the first time, all of America could now hear a truly outstanding swing band.

The times were changing. FDR had instilled hope into the hearts and spirits of Americans. Sentimental music, emphasizing self-pity, had satisfied a need during the days of the Depression. But now it wasn't enough. The country, especially the kids, could envision happy, glistening daylight. Joy and excitement, the sort that can be expressed so ideally through swinging

The band that led the way: Glen Gray and the Casa Loma Orchestra
Left to right: *Pat Davis, Clarence Hutchenrider, Peewee Hunt, Bobby Jones,*
Gray, Grady Watts, Billy Rausch, Sonny Dunham, Art Ralston, Fritz Hummell,
Tony Briglia, Jacques Blanchette, Stan Dennis, Kenny Sargent, Joe Hall, Mel Jenssen

music and dancing, lay ahead. And Benny Goodman, the Pied Piper of Swing, had arrived to lead the way!

Lead it he did—joyously, exultantly, and spiritedly—with a brand of swinging dance music that captivated both the kids and many of their elders. A whole new era of dance bands—the kind you not only listened to but watched and worshiped—began to take over the American musical scene.

Goodman's success paved the way for others. The Dorsey brothers suddenly found acceptance, first in tandem, then individually. The Casa Loma Orchestra's popularity perked up perceptibly. Ellington gained many new converts. And several outstanding instrumentalists, who'd been hiding their horn-trimmed splendor in the radio and recording studios, emerged blowing in front of their own bands—Artie Shaw, Bunny Berigan, Glenn Miller, Will Bradley, Charlie Spivak, Jack Jenney and more.

From the field of pure jazz came more leaders—Jack Teagarden, Count Basie, Charlie Barnet, Red Norvo and others. And eventually, from the ranks of the new swing bands, came still more like the three famous Goodman graduates, Gene Krupa, Lionel Hampton and Harry James, and Artie Shaw alumni Tony Pastor and Georgie Auld.

Not all were strictly jazz players. With the emphasis now switched to the leader of the band and the instrument he played, other instrumentalists who communicated in a more romantic yet highly personal way gained their followers—Charlie Spivak and his trumpet, Claude Thornhill and his piano, Hal McIntyre and his alto sax, Freddy Martin and his tenor sax, and all those Eddy Duchin piano imitators.

As more and more bands vied for popularity, the element of style grew increasingly important. The easier it was to identify, the better chance a band had for success. Thus arrangers began to front their own bands, figuring their individual writing styles to be as distinctive and as rewardable as the sounds created by mere instrumentalists. Topflight arrangers like Larry Clinton, Les Brown, Will Hudson (of Hudson-DeLange), Raymond Scott and, eventually Glenn Miller, and finally Stan Kenton all doubled successfully on pen and podium.

During the first couple of years following the start of Goodman's triumph in August, 1935, the greatest emphasis among the big bands was on swinging sounds—bristling brass, pungent saxes, rollicking rhythm sections—and, of course, on numerous jazz soloists. But not all of America understood or even liked this exciting and rhythmic approach. This was especially true in certain conservative sections in the Midwest. Cleveland, for example, proved to be an especially tough place for many swing bands. Chicago, despite its acceptance of them in hotel rooms such as in the Congress and the Sherman, featured sweet bands almost exclusively in its large ballrooms, like the Aragon and the Trianon. And many other dance emporiums throughout the middle part of the country found they could attract crowds more consistently by featuring a blander, more conservative type of dance music.

Fortunately, the appeal of the big bands had grown to such proportions that both sweetness and swing prevailed. There was room at or near the top for all kinds of bands, including Guy Lombardo's and Kay Kyser's and Sammy Kaye's and Jan Garber's and Blue Barron's and Lawrence Welk's and Art Kassel's and all the others that featured syrupy-sounding saxes, emasculated brasses and reticent rhythm sections ("What does Guy Lombardo's drummer tell people he does for a living?" quipped one swing fan), plus such musical minutiae as singing song titles, funny faces and silly hats.

But even though there was room for all—in theaters, ballrooms, night-clubs, hotel rooms and on radio and records—the element of competition remained. Artie Shaw strongly challenged Benny Goodman for his King of Swing crown. The two Dorseys kept trying to outdo each other. Bands raided one another for their top stars. Sammy Kaye tried to wrest away sweet-band honors from Kay Kyser, who in turn was trying to top Guy Lombardo's popularity. Count Basie began giving Duke Ellington and Jimmie Lunceford a stiff battle. Glenn Miller finally emerged with more fans than any other band, only to find Harry James challenging him strongly and then in 1942 overtaking him in station WNEW's highly rated popularity poll, which listed James, Miller, Tommy Dorsey, Jimmy Dorsey, Vaughn Monroe, Benny Goodman, Woody Herman, Kay Kyser, Charlie Spivak, Sammy Kaye, Alvino Rey, Claude Thornhill, Gene Krupa, Count Basie, Artie Shaw, Charlie Barnet, Johnny Long, Freddy Martin, Guy Lombardo and Hal McIntyre as its top twenty.

1942 was also the year in which many leaders and musicians entered the armed services. The first leader to go was Dean Hudson. Artie Shaw enlisted in the Navy in April. Shortly thereafter, Orrin Tucker and Eddy Duchin received Navy commissions. In October, Glenn Miller became an Air Force captain, Claude Thornhill became an apprentice seaman in the Navy, and Clyde McCoy's band enlisted as a unit. Two months later, Ted Weems and six of his musicians joined the Coast Guard en masse. And more maestros, Bob Crosby, Larry Clinton, Ray McKinley, Alvino Rey, Bobby Byrne, Sam Donahue and others, began donning uniforms quite different from those that they had been wearing on the bandstand.

The contributions of the leaders and the musicians to the war effort was massive. Miller's, of course, has become legendary. Shaw's, Thornhill's and those of numerous others have often been cited. Perhaps the most dramatic of all, however, were the exploits of Saxie Dowell, once Hal Kemp's portly saxist and singer of novelty tunes, who along with his Navy musicians, according to a 1945 *Metronome* report, "played through the fire and water and muck of a crippled airplane carrier, the U.S.S. *Franklin,* as she lay on her side in Pacific waters and crawled away from the scene of her disastrous encounter with the Japanese in March.

"Dowell was at his battle station in a third deck machine shop when the *Franklin* was hit. He stayed there for two hours before he was forced to leave. Then he and his musicians put on an improvised musical show, with

*The AAF goes overseas:
Glenn Miller conducts
as guest vocalist Dinah Shore
sings in London.*

*The Navy goes overseas:
Claude Thornhill leads his sailors on a remote Pacific island.*

whatever instruments they could rescue, deep in water on the charred flight deck. They played, fought fires and stayed with the battle through to its triumphant end, losing five of their number."

Other leaders and musicians still in civvies also pitched in by playing in service camps, and some bands, such as those of Hal McIntyre, Shep Fields and Spike Jones, toured with USO units to play in person for the servicemen overseas.

Back at home, band business was booming. Tommy Dorsey once remarked, "We all had it pretty good wherever we went. It was a cinch to break records. And if we didn't want to travel, it was excusable, because it was tough to get transportation then. Even Army camps were hard to get to. There weren't enough musicians to go around, and the few good ones went from band to band, trying to get the most money."

Though some of the top bands, like Tommy's and Harry James's and Les Brown's, continued to do well playing camps for the USO and for Coca Cola Spotlight shows, certain problems did arise, some of which were eventually to contribute to the decline of the big bands. Gas shortages made traveling not only difficult for bands but also almost impossible for dancers who wanted to go to places outside city limits. Top spots like Glen Island Casino and Meadowbrook were forced to close. The government levied a 20 per cent amusement tax, which discouraged people from going out to dance, then imposed a midnight curfew, known as the brownout, as an added deterrent.

But the bands might have survived these developments had it not been for some others that hurt them even more intimately. One was the attitude of the musicians themselves. Those who escaped the draft had themselves a field day. Many acted like spoiled brats. The economic law of supply and demand was completely in their favor, and some exploited leaders by demanding exorbitant salaries and playing one against the other. The attitudes of many sidemen too often reflected contempt for the public and for the war effort. I can remember one group of musicians in a top band cursing servicemen because they had to get up as early as noon to go out and play at a nearby camp.

Many of the bands, especially those who couldn't bid for the best sidemen, offered inferior music. The leaders became disgusted. But worse, so did the public. It was not uncommon for kids to leave a dance thoroughly disappointed by the sloppy, uninspired sounds of a band they had once admired.

And then in 1942 came the monstrous recording strike, one that neither the recording bands nor the record companies nor the public wanted. The strike couldn't have been more ill-timed. The girls at home and the boys overseas or in camps were equally lonely, equally sentimental, and for the most part preferred to listen to Frank Sinatra crooning instead of Harry James blaring or to Peggy Lee whispering instead of Gene Krupa banging his drums. The time was ripe for the singers, with their more personalized messages, and the strike helped them blossom by leaving the entire popular recording field wide open to them. It was theirs to take over, and take it over they did.

By the war's end, the world of popular music had become primarily a singer's world. Not only on records, but also on radio shows that once featured the top bands, Sinatra, Perry Como, Dick Haymes, Nat Cole, Andy Russell, Dinah Shore, Jo Stafford, Peggy Lee and more had replaced Miller, James, Tommy Dorsey, Goodman and other bands as top musical attractions.

The vocalists start to take over: Perry (Ted Weems's) Como and Frank (Tommy Dorsey's) Sinatra, sponsored by Chesterfield and Lucky Strike respectively.

The excitement and general feeling of celebration that followed the armistice, plus the return of most of the top musicians and leaders, brought some brighter days and nights to the big bands. But they didn't last. The public's new tastes had been pretty well firmed. The musicians, either tired of traveling or spoiled by the unusually high wartime wage level, became more apathetic about hitting the road again. A number of them were attracted to bop and to the progressive sounds emanating from bands like Kenton's, Raeburn's, Gillespie's and Herman's.

But many of the new, more complicated big band sounds were difficult to dance to. The beat became too vague. Kenton himself has admitted that his band's involved music contributed directly to the decline of the dance bands. The idea of going out to hear a big band had been made even less attractive by the higher prices the night spots were charging so that they could afford bands with higher salaries and transportation costs and, of course, by the continuing 20 per cent amusement tax. What's more, Americans became more appreciative of and attuned to home life, and soon came the greatest of all home entertainment—television.

Finally in December, 1946, almost a dozen years after Benny Goodman had blown the first signs of life into the big band bubble, that bubble burst with a concerted bang. Inside of just a few weeks, eight of the nation's top bandleaders called it quits—some temporarily, some permanently: Benny Goodman, Woody Herman, Harry James, Tommy Dorsey, Les Brown, Jack Teagarden, Benny Carter and Ina Ray Hutton.

For a few year the bands hung on, but slowly more and more began to hang up their horns for good, and the world that was once theirs now became the property of a group of their most illustrious graduates—the singers!

The Vocalists

HOW important were the vocalists to the big bands? Very! Some hipper jazz-oriented fans and musicians may have resented them and their intrusions. But in the over-all picture, it was the singers who provided the most personal, the most literal and often the most communicative link between the bandstands and the dance floors, between stages and seats, and between recording and radio studios and the perennial "unseen audiences."

The era was filled with band vocalists. Some were terrible, some were mediocre, some were great. But so long as they could communicate, whether on ballads, novelties or swinging numbers, they earned their keep.

Not that the keep was usually very much. Unestablished vocalists were generally paid less than the musicians in the band. One reason: they had no union to protect them. Another: the supply was so great that as a group they possessed little financial muscle. It wasn't at all uncommon, therefore, for boy singers, in order to protect their jobs, to double in various ways—watching over the music library, helping with the instruments, aiding with travel arrangements, and so on. As for the girl singers—well, they didn't double as much as they sometimes were given discredit for.

Doris Day, one of the most respected of all girl singers, recently told me, "Being on the road is not easy, especially for one girl among a lot of guys. There's no crying at night and missing mama and running home. So it makes you become a stronger person. You have to discipline yourself, musically and in every way. Being a band singer teaches you not only how to work in front of people but also how to deal with them."

Another highly successful big band alumna, Peggy Lee, elaborates even further on the musical-discipline aspect. "Band singing taught us," she notes, "the importance of interplay with musicians. We had to work close to the arrangement. Even if the interpretation of a particular song wasn't exactly what we wanted, we had to make the best of it. I can remember some songs I sang with Benny when I felt they should have been treated just the opposite way he'd had them arranged. So, like all band singers, I learned to do the best with what they gave me.

"I will say this: I learned more about music from the men I worked with in bands than I've learned anywhere else. They taught me discipline and the value of rehearsing and how to train."

*Les Brown's Doris Day, Stan Kenton's June Christy
and Woody Herman's Frances Wayne*

Frank Sinatra has often commented on how much he learned merely by sitting on the same bandstand with Tommy Dorsey and watching him breathe as he blew his trombone. Because of that breath control, Sinatra pointed out, "Tommy could make it all sound so musical that you never lost the thread of the message." So impressed was Frank with Tommy's physical prowess that he began taking extra breathing and physical-fitness exercises, including a series of underwater sessions in the hope that he would be able to breathe as effortlessly as his leader.

Sinatra has noted many times how important he feels it is for singers to get their training with bands. Several years ago I ran into him in New York when his son was appearing there with the Tommy Dorsey band directed by Sam Donahue. Frank was absolutely delighted that Frank, Jr., was getting this sort of experience. "I hope he'll stay with the band for quite a while," he stated then.

The comment jibed with one he'd made a generation earlier to his teacher, John Quinlan. "If I were starting all over again," he told Quinlan, "I'd get a job with a band. I would sing and sing and sing. If a leader gave me forty songs a night, I would tell him to give me sixty.There's no teacher like experience."

Not all singers were either as appreciative or as dedicated as Sinatra. It showed, too. Spoiled too often by too much attention, especially from teen-age girls more impressed by gender than talent, some of the big band vocalists, including some with the top bands, paid far too little attention to musical development and far too much to the fuss that was being made over them.

Bob Eberly, one of the greatest of all band singers, as well as one of the best liked by all who knew him, recently admitted to me that "lots of times I didn't concentrate on what I was doing. I was preoccupied with other things —like romance. I'm still surprised though," he added, referring to the adulation he and other boy singers received, "that something could have been that important to somebody."

The hysteria that greeted boy singers during the forties almost matched that spewed on the vocal groups of the sixties. Mobs would wait for them outside stage doors. In the theaters they'd howl and scream—perhaps not as blatantly as the kids in the sixties did in the presence of their idols, but certainly with a good deal more musical justification.

The relationships between boy vocalists and their leaders varied, depending upon how much talent the boy had and how much the leader wanted his singer to be starred. If the boy could really sing and if the leader appreciated his talents and his value to the band, he could go far, as singers like Sinatra and Eberly and Dick Haymes and Perry Como and Jimmy Rushing and Jack Leonard and Billy Eckstine and Eddy Howard and Skinnay Ennis did. But no matter how good a singer might be, if his leader didn't set him up properly, either through poor planning or because of jealousy, his chances for success were negligible.

Numerous circumstances, over none of which vocalists exercised much control, often determined how well a singer sounded and thus ultimately how successful he could become. Some singers were forced to stray and strain outside their vocal range because an arranger happened to goof or because they were saddled with arrangements inherited from differently pitched predecessors.

Tempos, too, could help or hinder vocalists. Too often leaders sacrificed singability for danceability, and singers, both male and female, would be forced to rush through their choruses at ridiculous paces, unable to phrase properly and sometimes not even able to make the words intelligible. I have always felt that one reason Bob Eberly (who liked the looks of his last name better spelled with a final "y") was able to sound so much more convincing than his brother, Ray Eberle, was that Jimmy Dorsey gave him slower, more romanticized tempos than Glenn Miller ever gave Ray.

On recordings, singers often appeared to disadvantage because tunes were tossed at them at the last minute and they didn't have time to familiarize themselves with them. After they had sung them several times during regular engagements, they would do them more justice, making the lyrics more meaningful and phrasing the tunes in a more relaxed manner. But they still couldn't erase the indelible impression of the inferior recording.

And there were other factors that singers often had to overcome—out-of-tune pianos, not to mention out-of-tune bands and bands that played too loud, and PA systems that were so inadequate that the singers couldn't hear themselves at all. Then, too, there were purely physical problems, such as keeping one's throat in condition at all times (colds and lack of sleep were murder), looking well dressed and well groomed at all times despite the lack of money, getting sufficient sleep and finding adequate laundry and tailoring facilities.

With girl singers some of these physical factors were even more important. Good looks, a good figure, good grooming, attractive dresses (girls sometimes had to make up on bouncing buses and iron dresses in ladies' rooms) and, of course, poise were almost as vital to success as talent itself. And so was, as Doris Day pointed out, an ability to deal with all kinds of people.

A single girl among a pack of men certainly had her problems. If her leader was especially wolf-bent, as some of them were, the difficulties increased in proportion to his demands and/or his ardor. In addition, of course, there were the musicians themselves. The female vocalist had to be tactful in dealing not only with the men interested in extracurricular activities but also with the group as a whole in the usual day-to-day relationships. Some girls tried very hard to be one of the boys, an attitude that was often resented. Others protected themselves with a pronounced air of independence, which might have been a good defensive maneuver but also produced much loneliness. Still others tried the extra-feminine approach, which sometimes resulted in the capture of one man for good.

Extra-feminine in their approach or not, many of the singers with the top bands wound up with musicians from the same bands as husbands. Doris Day married Les Brown saxist George Weidler; Peggy Lee married Benny Goodman guitarist Dave Barbour; Jo Stafford married Tommy Dorsey arranger Paul Weston; Frances Wayne married Woody Herman arranger-trumpeter Neal Hefti; Mary Ann McCall married Herman tenor saxist Al Cohn; June Christy married Stan Kenton tenor saxist Bob Cooper; Kitty Kallen married Jack Teagarden clarinetist Clint Garvin. Other girl singers married their bosses: Harriet Hilliard to Ozzie Nelson, Georgia Carroll to Kay Kyser, Irene Daye to Charlie Spivak, Dorothy Collins to Raymond Scott, Ginnie Powell to Boyd Raeburn, Ann Richards to Stan Kenton. Obviously a girl's career as a band singer was not necessarily a dead-end street.

Sometimes a girl singer would do so well with a band that she would carry it to greater heights. Certainly Ella Fitzgerald, especially after she introduced "A-Tisket, A-Tasket," helped Chick Webb tremendously. Wee Bonnie Baker's "Oh, Johnny" brought brand-new fame to Orrin Tucker. And George Hall made such a star out of Dolly Dawn that he finally turned over his entire band to her.

Many of the singers became as important and familiar to the public as the bands themselves. And when the musicians' union called a lengthy and self-defeating record strike in the early forties, a number of the vocalists whose debut and development had occurred in those bands began to take the play away from them.

When the big bands started to fade in the mid-forties, it was their former vocalists—especially those with the most talent and the most brains—who emerged as big stars. Among the men were Sinatra and Como and Haymes and

Jimmy Dorsey's Helen O'Connell   Goodman's Peggy Lee

Clinton's Bea Wain   Tommy Dorsey's Edythe Wright   Goodman's Martha Tilton

Barnet's and Venuti's
Kay Starr   Shaw's, Goodman's and James's
Helen Forrest   Whiteman's and Norvo's
Mildred Bailey

Miller's Marion Hutton   *Tommy Dorsey's Jo Stafford*   *Pastor's Rosemary Clooney*

Weeks's Dale Evans   *Tommy Tucker's Amy Arnell*   *Goodman's Helen Ward*

Raeburn's Ginny Powell   *Goodman's and Bradley's*   *Kemp's Nan Wynn*
Louise Tobin

Eckstine and Vaughn Monroe and Count Basie's Joe Williams and Freddy Martin's Merv Griffin and Kay Kyser's Mike Douglas and Dick Jurgens' Eddy Howard and Sammy Kaye's Don Cornell and Gene Krupa's and Glenn Miller's Johnny Desmond.

And then among the girls there were Peggy and Doris and Ella and Jo and Charlie Barnet's Kay Starr and Earl Hines's Sarah Vaughan and Vincent Lopez' Betty Hutton and Shaw's, Goodman's and James's Helen Forrest and Krupa's Anita O'Day and Kenton's June Christy and Tommy Dorsey's Connie Haines and Lionel Hampton's Dinah Washington and Noble Sissle's and Barnet's Lena Horne and, of course, Billie Holiday, who had been a band singer with Basie and Shaw for two much-too-short periods, and Red Norvo's Mildred Bailey, who had started her own career even before most of the big bands, including Red's, had started theirs.

That's quite an impressive list of graduates. What's more, in the years immediately following the big band era and preceding that of the rock and rollers (roughly from 1947 to 1953), just about every top pop singer, with the exception of Nat Cole, Dinah Shore and Kate Smith, had come out of the big bands. Even Bing Crosby, firmly established as the world's foremost singer by the time the big bands had begun to take over in 1935, had already received his musical experience and education and had paid his dues in the bands of Paul Whiteman and Gus Arnheim.

The vocalists may have done a lot for the big bands, but it was nothing compared with what the big bands did for them!

Webb's Ella Fitzgerald   *Orrin Tucker's Bonnie Baker*

The Arrangers

THE two men most directly responsible for the style of a band, and thus often for its success or failure, were its leader and its arranger. The importance of the first is obvious, that of the second somewhat less so. And yet without the specific talents and contributions of the arrangers, none of the bands would have had any individuality; all would have sounded very much alike, and dance bands would never have become colorful, distinctive and entertaining enough to attract such a large segment of the populace.

As more and more bands appeared on the scene and as radio and recordings began giving each of them greater exposure, the importance of the arrangers continued to increase. For as competition became keener, so did the public's ears, and attractive and distinctive sounds—musical styles—became a more and more crucial factor in the potential success of each band.

Arranging music well is a difficult task. It requires a knowledge not only of the basic elements of music but also of form and of exactly what notes each instrument can play and of how they can be most effectively voiced to produce the desired musical effects. Many arrangers knew all this. But it was those with imagination as well as knowledge and training who created the most successful, original, colorful, ear-catching sounds.

The list of those who did so well for themselves that they eventually rose above the bands for whom they wrote is an impressive one. For just as the big bands provided exceptional training grounds for musicians and vocalists, so did they offer both the experience and often the exposure necessary for the arrangers' development and in many cases their own success as well-known arranger-conductors.

Let's take a look at some of the famous arranger-conductors who graduated from the big bands. Paul Weston, Sy Oliver, and the late Axel Stordahl all worked for Tommy Dorsey; Tutti Camarata and Sonny Burke for Jimmy Dorsey. Nelson Riddle wrote for Charlie Spivak; Ray Conniff and Johnny Mandel for Artie Shaw; Henry Mancini for Tex Beneke; Billy May for Glenn Miller; Gordon Jenkins for Isham Jones; John Scott Trotter for Hal Kemp; Gil Evans for Claude Thornhill; Pete Rugolo for Stan Kenton; Frank DeVol for Horace Heidt; Neal Hefti and Ralph Burns for Woody Herman; Gerry Mulligan for Gene Krupa and Elliot Lawrence; Eddie Sauter for Red Norvo, Benny Goodman and Ray McKinley.

Benny Goodman and style-setter Fletcher Henderson

The role of the arrangers extended beyond merely writing down the notes. Many leaders depended upon them for musical direction. Some worked closely with their writers in the planning of arrangements; others gave them completely free rein. Usually, after an arranger had completed a work, he would be the one who would run it through with the musicians, coaching them in precisely how he wanted the notes to sound. Meanwhile the leader would listen, and depending upon his knowledge of music, his patience and tolerance, not to mention his ego, he'd approve, try to improve or else disapprove of the arrangement.

Some leaders were also their own chief arrangers. Before the big band era had begun, Fletcher Henderson and Don Redman, who had led his own band and McKinny's Cotton Pickers, had already formed their own styles. And, of course, all through the pre-big band, the big band, and the post-big band eras, Duke Ellington was creating his great music for his band. In addition, during the big band days he took on an assistant, Billy Strayhorn, who soon developed into one of the outstanding arrangers of all time.

Glenn Miller's success was predicated principally on his own arrangements, though after commercial interests began taking so much of his time, he turned over most of the writing chores to Bill Finegan, Jerry Gray and Billy May. Claude Thornhill created his own particularly tasty music, later to be helped by Gil Evans, Bill Borden and Gerry Mulligan. And the hard-hitting excitement of Stan Kenton's music was created by Stan himself, with Pete Rugolo, Bill Holman and others eventually supplying most of the arrangements.

And there were other important arranger-leaders—Les Brown, Benny Carter, Larry Clinton, Will Hudson, Elliot Lawrence, Russ Morgan, Ray Noble, Boyd Raeburn and Raymond Scott, for example.

Musicians within the bands often developed into important arrangers. Sy Oliver played trumpet for Jimmie Lunceford, John Scott Trotter piano for Hal Kemp, Ray Conniff and Johnny Mandel trombones for Artie Shaw; Tutti Camarata played trumpet, Joe Lipman piano for Jimmy Dorsey; Neal Hefti played trumpet, Ralph Burns piano for Woody Herman; Henry Mancini was a pianist in the postwar Miller band; Nelson Riddle played trombone for Charlie Spivak, Gerry Mulligan sax for Gene Krupa. And three excellent musicians, bassist Bob Haggart and saxists Matty Matlock and Deane Kincaide, wrote almost all the important arrangements for the Bob Crosby band.

Numerous musicians figured in the bands' arrangements in a more informal way too, for in many bands there were men who provided all sorts of musical ideas, even though most of them never made any attempt to write them down. This cooperative approach was especially prevalent within the swing bands. There the musical *esprit de corps* was generally excellent. The musicians, proud of what they were playing and often creative themselves, would offer suggestions for improving or embellishing or perhaps even cutting certain segments within an arrangement. Often this occurred not when an arranger had first brought in his work, but later on, after the band had been playing it for a while and the musicians had become familiar enough with all its components to be able to offer valuable ideas.

Some of the most exciting of all the swing band arrangements were essentially composite works out of the heads of several musicians. Called head arrangements, these often began with some simple musical figure, or riff, that one of the men had been noodling around with. Others would pick up on the idea and start helping to develop it. Perhaps some of the developments would be discarded and others offered instead. Then, after one section—say, the saxes —had established the musical figure, the brass might come along and offer a counterfigure, and the whole piece would begin to jell.

Other times, swinging riff pieces evolved from spontaneous backgrounds that one or more musicians had been blowing behind a soloist playing a well-known piece. The background itself might provide such a catchy phrase that it would become the central theme of an entirely new work. The technique lent an element of spontaneity to the music. Lionel Hampton's thrived on this procedure. And the great Count Basie band, strapped as it was financially through its early period, produced one catchy riff tune after another—many of them based on the twelve-bar-blues theme—all head arrangements from the collective craniums of its enthusiastic and creative sidemen.

Pay for arrangements varied considerably, depending a great deal on the financial condition of each band. Sy Oliver revealed in an article published in the February, 1946, *Metronome*, that he had been so enthusiastic about arranging for the Jimmie Lunceford band when he first joined it that he had been perfectly content to supply it with some of its greatest scores for the grand total of two and a half dollars per arrangement—and fully copied, at that! On the other hand, when Sy joined the more affluent Tommy Dorsey band, Tommy told Oliver that he'd guarantee him five thousand dollars a year more than Lunceford had been paying him, no questions asked.

Established arrangers like Dorsey's Oliver and Weston and Stordahl, Goodman's Fletcher Henderson and Jimmy Mundy, and others generally made out better financially than most of the sidemen. Usually they were guaranteed a certain sum over a specified period, during which they would supply an agreed-upon minimum number of arrangements. So long as they met their quotas, they could continue living rather rewarding lives.

In addition to those arrangers who worked exclusively for a specific leader, there were numerous writers who peddled their wares from band to band. Some of them did very well, though naturally they enjoyed less financial security.

Many leaders welcomed these free-lancers. Often at rehearsals, which many bands held after work, they would audition new works by new writers, and though much of the stuff turned out to be unusable, once in a while a gem would be unearthed.

Jimmie Lunceford's arranger, Sy Oliver,
and Duke Ellington with his arranger, Billy Strayhorn

Some free-lancers made a good living working not for bands directly but instead for music publishers. To get their tunes plugged on the air, some publishers would supply bands with free orchestrations, written especially for them. Generally these arrangements were pretty second rate, however, because the arrangers didn't know the bands very well and because they had little inspiration other than cold cash. Yet these arrangements served a purpose for the leader, permitting him to vary his fare on radio broadcasts and, of course, to save money. It's worth noting that few really musical bands bothered with this sort of subsidization, fully aware that too many lapses in the quality of their music might not only reduce their popularity but also impair the valuable spirit of their musicians.

The field of arranging for dance bands offered a wide variety of opportunities, from the most prosaic to the most inspirational. Writing for publishers was generally dull and tedious. So was arranging for mickey-mouse bands, whose heavily stylized, highly restrictive formulas permitted nothing more exciting than the sound of a wet washrag crashing on a damp bath mat.

Chances for creativity naturally increased within the more musical bands. And yet life could get pretty dull there too, especially when a writer was called upon to rush through an arrangement of some stupid pop tune that the band had been assigned to record the next day. Such assignments became purely commercial ventures, requiring mere craftsmanship as opposed to artistic creativity.

Some of the best bands did permit the arrangers greater freedom, encouraging them not merely in their interpretations of pop tunes, but also in the composition of their own material. Often this resulted in wonderfully fresh-sounding originals that redounded to the credit of the band as well as the arrangers. A classic example was the series of inspiring instrumentals performed by the Woody Herman band in the mid-forties—Ralph Burns's "Bijou" and "Early Autumn" (part of his "Summer Sequence" suite), Neal Hefti's "The Good Earth" and "Wild Root," and Jimmy Giuffre's "Four Brothers." So pleased was Woody with the results of such originals that he even commissioned a classical composer, no less a personage than Igor Stravinsky, to write an original for the band. The result: Stravinsky's "Ebony Concerto."

Stan Kenton went Herman even one better: he encouraged his writers to create not merely the usual swinging originals that followed in general the over-all pattern of such numbers, but even more adventurous pieces, admittedly unsuitable for dancing, that utilized classical forms. The results frequently astounded and confounded Kenton's most devoted fans and his severest critics.

Few other leaders gave writers so much leeway. The great majority of arrangers were limited by specific restrictions. Since they were writing for bands that made their money playing for dancing, their scores had to be danceable. This meant sticking to a basic four-four rhythm. Disonances were too risky—they might scare listeners away. Complicated voicings tended to confuse many musicians and required additional rehearsal time, which many leaders were loathe to supply.

And yet, just as singing with a band had trained vocalists to work within specific restrictions, so did writing for one train arrangers. Certainly they learned a great deal from their work with the big bands, and the proof of the value of this training is attested to by the impressive list of graduates who today have become the country's recognized arranger-conductors.

Eddie Sauter, who wrote for Red Norvo, Benny Goodman and Artie Shaw, and Bill Finegan, who wrote for Tommy Dorsey and Glenn Miller

Of all those who received training in the big bands, the arranger who kept on impressing many of us, no matter which band he was writing for, was Eddie Sauter, cited by his fellow-arranger Glenn Miller as being "ten years ahead of his time." Like other talented and creative writers, Eddie was faced with many frustrations. Others, though, found it easier to compromise. But for Sauter, a man of high ideals and equally high principles, writing within the dance-band milieu remained a constant chore. In an interview a few years ago, he stated categorically what other dance band arrangers may also have felt but seldom admitted publicly. "Writing commercially," he said, "is not an art. But who knows," he added hopefully, "maybe I'll be able to earn enough money in the commercial field so that I'll be able to retire for a while and *really* write!"

The Businessmen

FOR most successful bandleaders, the music business consisted of two equally important words, "music" and "business." To arrange their music, they engaged creative and communicative arrangers; to arrange their business, they depended upon topnotch managers and bookers.

The terms "manager" and "booker" were often considered synonomous by the public. But they weren't. Most band managers worked with one specific band; bookers worked with many. Conversely, bookers performed primarily one function: they found jobs for their bands. But managers handled a number of business affairs for their particular bands, and how well they handled them often had just as much to do with the success of a band as how well its musicians played, its vocalists sang or its arrangers wrote.

Band managers functioned in various capacities—as travel agents, as accountants, sometimes even as valets and often as fathers. They arranged all travel arrangements and hotel accommodations. They handled all financial transactions. Some concerned themselves with the appearance of the band, making sure that each man was properly dressed and showed up on time for each engagement. Many band managers spent many hours listening to and trying to solve their musicians' personal problems, often acting as buffers or peacemakers between sidemen and leaders.

Equally important were the band managers' activities outside the band—with booking offices, with radio stations and recording companies and with dance promoters and hotel and ballroom managers. They became the direct financial links with those upon whom the bands' very existence depended, and it wasn't uncommon for a band manager, after having spent the evening checking attendance at the entrance of a ballroom, to collect the band's fee and carry the wad of bills around with him until it came time to pay off the musicians.

Some of the bands, after they'd become especially successful and had expanded their field of activity, operated with more than one manager. They would employ both a regular band manager, who stayed with the band, supervising its regular day-to-day operations, and a personal manager, an executive back in the band's headquarters office who concentrated on bookings, contracts, finances and many of the leader's personal business matters.

The most effective personal manager I ever knew was a large, quiet, stolid Bostonian named Si Shribman, who, along with his brother, Charlie, owned and/or operated a string of New England ballrooms. Si evinced a great love of bands in general and a great faith in a few new leaders in particular— young unknowns like Artie Shaw, Glenn Miller, Tommy Dorsey, Woody Herman, Claude Thornhill and Tony Pastor. To them, Si gave more than mere advice. He lent them money to get started, then kept them working in his ballrooms and on college dates, which he booked, until they'd had a chance to develop musically and to establish themselves financially. Leaders loved Si Shribman, not only for what he did for them but also because of the quiet, gentlemanly way in which he treated them. He was both a rare manager and a rare man.

In New York another manager-booker, Moe Gale, helped his new, struggling bands by booking them into his own Savoy Ballroom. Chick Webb developed there, as did Teddy Hill and Willie Bryant, and Erskine Hawkins made it his home away from home while his Alabama Collegians tried to achieve national recognition.

One of the most famous of all manager-bookers was Joe Glaser, who single-handedly guided the career of Louis Armstrong. Joe's hard-sell dedication established not only Armstrong but also other important leaders, such as Les Brown and Lionel Hampton; and after the big band era, his office, Associated Booking Corporation, became one of the most important of all band-booking outfits.

About the softest-sell booker-manager I ever knew was a kindly looking, nonpushing gentleman named Francis (Cork) O'Keefe. By the early thirties, he had developed the Casa Loma Orchestra into one of the hottest properties on the scene, and soon he joined forces with Tom Rockwell to form the Rockwell-O'Keefe organization, which later became General Artists Corporation (GAC).

Unlike O'Keefe, Rockwell was an extrovert. He was a great salesman, especially when he believed in his product, and fortunately for the good of many musical bands, he appreciated talent. As a recording executive, he had guided the careers of Bing Crosby, Louis Armstrong, the Mills Brothers and the

Tom Rockwell and Cork O'Keefe (second from left and far right) with Glenn Miller (far left) and friend

Boswell Sisters as well as the Casa Loma band. As a booking-office executive, he surrounded himself not only with artists but also with businessmen who appreciated some of the finer points of music.

Rockwell-O'Keefe was only the second largest of the band-booking offices, but it always seemed to be trying harder, possibly because many of its personnel really enjoyed music. Its enthusiasm and dedication attracted many of the new bands headed by musicians who needed understanding and encouragement. Jimmy Dorsey, Artie Shaw, Bob Crosby, Woody Herman, Glenn Miller and Claude Thornhill all migrated toward GAC when they launched their bands.

They might have gone to Music Corporation of America (MCA), the biggest of all booking offices, once tabbed the "Star Spangled Octopus." But MCA could never match GAC's understanding of the specialized problems of musicians-turned-leaders. Working out of plush, handsomely furnished, distressingly formal offices, MCA's approach was strictly business—cold, dry, hard but tremendously effective business. For bandleaders like Guy Lombardo, Eddy Duchin, Horace Heidt, Xavier Cugat, Sammy Kaye, Wayne King and those less interested in musical notes than in bank notes, MCA performed magnificently well—especially its charming and tremendously convincing salesman Sonny Werblin, who years later created such a furor with his brilliant behind-the-scenes exploits in professional sports.

Not that MCA represented no outstanding swing bands. Thanks to the foresight and insight of one of its young bookers, Willard Alexander, the company did sign Benny Goodman and Count Basie when they first started out. Harry James, a Goodman alumnus, also joined up. So did Tommy Dorsey, conceivably because his brother, Jimmy, had already gone with GAC and there was no other major office with whom he could sign. Tommy never seemed to be happy at MCA. He fought constantly with the office, for years refusing to set foot in it, and when his contract finally expired, he took out a huge ad in a trade paper which read in part: "Whew . . . I am finally out of the clutches of you-know-who!"

MCA's more conservative musical tastes reflected those of its two most

Jules C. Stein,
founder and president
of Music Corporation of America

important executives, Jules Stein and Billy Goodheart, two very bright businessmen who during the twenties had worked as musicians with midwestern hotel-type bands. But so firmly established had their office become by the time the big band era began that they could afford to coast along with the less controversial new bands. Thus the field was left open for GAC to ferret out and develop the more progressive new bands, and this it did with great success.

In 1939 MCA lost Alexander when he opened a band department for William Morris, an agency which for years had booked many theatrical, vaudeville and nightclub stars but which had done little along big band lines. Willard, aided by Billy Shaw, a former trumpeter and bandleader, soon developed a highly creative and efficient organization, servicing such veterans as Duke Ellington, Paul Whiteman and Count Basie, plus numerous new and musical bands like those of Dizzy Gillespie, Hal McIntyre, Charlie Spivak, Boyd Raeburn and Billy Eckstine.

GAC, MCA and William Morris—these were the biggest band-booking agencies. The ever-driving, highly experienced Joe Glaser continued to do well with Armstrong, Brown, Hampton, Andy Kirk, Jan Savitt, Teddy Powell, Russ Morgan and a host of top black jazz stars. Moe Gale kept his office operating under full steam and added new bands and singers.

And there were others: Consolidated Radio Artists, which started strong but faded after a few years; Stan Zucker, who had a few good bands; and a couple of midwestern-based offices, Fredericks Brothers and McConkey Music Corporation, both of which concentrated on their portion of the country and the mickey-mouse bands that appealed to most of their clients' tastes.

How much did all these booking offices contribute to the success of the big bands? Obviously some contributed more than others. But what many of the executives in their high-backed swivel chairs too often forgot was that the bands contributed to their success in return. In their frantic, competitive efforts, they frequently overlooked the long-term aspects of their clients' careers as they made shortsighted decisions to solve an immediate booking problem that might never have arisen had the office planned more carefully and knowingly in the first place.

Stan Kenton, whose music remained outside the ken of most businessmen, once expressed his feelings and those of others like him when he stated, "Bookers know less about music than anybody in the music business, but they're always shooting off their mouths to all young bandleaders, giving 'em the stuff about how they've been in the business for so many years and they know what the public wants and just listen to them and you can't help being a success.

"If we [his band] become a really big success—and I sure hope we do, because I feel I owe music something, and the best way I can repay it is to help raise its standards—I feel that we'll have become a success despite all the things the guys in the offices tried to straighten us out on."

Recordings

RECORDS were important to the big bands—but not so greatly important as they are to today's musical groups, who without echo chambers and other electronic trappings would be completely uncommunicative. The big bands had more than records going for them. They had one-nighters, ballrooms, theaters and live broadcasts. And most importantly, they had musicianship, so that no matter where they went, they could duplicate in person what they had played on records.

The musicians in the big bands differed from many of those of the most popular recording groups a generation later. Far less concerned with show business, they focussed strictly on their music. Many spent years studying music theory and mastering their instruments, starting in school bands and working through territory outfits into the big league of dance bands.

Good musicianship and an ability to read quickly were necessities. Not only were the musicians expected to complete their four (and sometimes six) sides in three hours, but many times the music they played was music they were seeing for the first time right on the recording date. Speed and accuracy were essential, because bands often vied with one another to be the first on the market with new songs.

Star vocalist Frank Sinatra, producer George T. Simon, recording supervisor Mitch Ayres, drummer Buddy Rich and interested spectator Alec Wilder on a Metronome *All-Star session*

There were few of the stop-and-go routines that later became accepted procedure at recording sessions. There was no tape to splice. Bands recorded directly on either wax or acetate discs, and so it was not possible to utilize the technique of combining part of one take and part of another and more of a third to make up a complete performance. It all had to be recorded as one unit.

In addition, what went into a record came out exactly the same way, with no souped-up electronic gimmicks. Until an astute recording supervisor, Morty Palitz, hit upon the idea of placing a speaker and a mike in the men's room next to Brunswick's studio to produce the first echo chamber—a move that was great for a band's music but rough on its musicians' kidneys—most of the recordings had a dry, dead sound that made recorded performances seem dull compared with live ones. Eventually, as the companies began utilizing larger studios, such as Columbia's famed Liederkranz Hall, the records took on a more brilliant, exciting sound. And as microphones and other equipment were improved, records took on ever-greater fidelity. However, most of this took place after the end of the big band era.

Of course, the pressure of recording four sides in three hours could have its disadvantages. Often a band's first reading of a song would turn out to be quite different from the way it played it later in person. Familiarity with an arrangement breeded new attempts at different phrasings, voicings and tempos, as musicians continued trying to improve upon their too often hurried and harried recorded performances.

A few years ago, after listening to Gene Krupa's original recording of "Let Me Off Uptown," I mentioned to Gene that I was very surprised to hear how slow the tempo was, that I'd remembered the band playing it much faster. "I guess we did," Krupa said. "But you know, it's a funny thing about tempos. After you've played a number many times, it seems you almost automatically increase the tempo. Maybe it's because subconsciously you feel that you need to give it some added excitement and you can't think of another way to do

Stan Kenton, standing, assists recording supervisor Carl Kress (one of the era's top guitarists), as Nat Cole peers into control to see how he's been doing.

it. But you can work it another way too—you can slow down a tune purposely, just to get it into a different groove."

Tommy Dorsey, when he recorded "I'll Never Smile Again," used that slowing-down-the-tempo routine to produce a big hit. Glenn Miller had recorded the same tune three months earlier at a much faster, less intimate tempo, but nothing had happened with his version. Tommy's found the right groove, and that was it. And Tommy Tucker used the same slow-down routine with his big hit record "I Don't Want to Set the World on Fire," which had already been recorded by Harlan Leonard's band, but at such a fast tempo that his version had gone completely unnoticed.

A band's name power, as well as its interpretation of a song, helped create big hits. For example, Erskine Hawkins had already gained a bit of fame with his Bluebird version of "Tuxedo Junction," when Glenn Miller came along and parlayed the tune into an even bigger hit—and on the same record label at that! And Count Basie recorded his "One O'Clock Jump" in July, 1937, but the big hit version was Benny Goodman's, recorded seven months later.

New interpretations gave new life to old standards. Artie Shaw resurrected "Begin the Beguine" and "Indian Love Call," Bunny Berigan "I Can't Get Started," Tommy Dorsey "Song of India," Larry Clinton "Martha," Charlie Barnet "Cherokee," Les Brown "I've Got My Love to Keep Me Warm," Harry James "You Made Me Love You" and Freddy Martin "Tchaikovsky's Piano Concerto." And there were many more. Usually the bandleaders came up with the idea of resurrecting such old standards. Sometimes they met with strenuous objections from the record company artists and repertoire (A&R) men, who were under constant pressure from their superiors to record "sure hits," and from music publishers, who constantly kept assuring them that their particular tunes were those "sure hits." It's gratifying to those of us who were constantly fighting for higher musical standards that the big band record hits that have survived have almost always been those which the bands, not the businessmen, dug up and fought to get on wax—standards like those listed above plus instrumentals like Miller's "Moonlight Serenade" and "In the Mood," Woody Herman's "Woodchoppers' Ball" and "Apple Honey," Jimmie Lunceford's "For Dancers Only," Frankie Carle's "Sunrise Serenade," Lionel Hampton's "Flyin Home" and, of course, the many brilliant pieces written and recorded by Duke Ellington.

Of the three major companies that recorded most of the big band sounds, Decca and Victor seemed more conservative, Columbia more daring. For years, jazz and other creative musicians recording in Decca's small, stuffy studio were intimidated by a sign that read: "Where's the Melody?"—which reflected the basic philosophy of the company's bright though often very stubborn president, Jack Kapp. Victor's recording supervisor, Eli Oberstein, was an equally astute and equally self-confident executive who also liked to run things his way. Both Kapp and Oberstein made lots of money for their companies, but few converts among musicians.

Columbia, on the other hand, especially on sessions run by Morty Palitz and John Hammond, seemed to sympathize more with the leaders and musicians. They were more willing to listen to other ideas, to experiment and to approach recording sessions from the long-range rather than from the quick-buck point of view.

Most bands were impressed with the promotional value of recordings, but a couple of top leaders had little use for them. Both Paul Whiteman and Fred Waring felt that recordings played over the air were self-defeating because they were competing with live radio performances. Waring wouldn't record for ten years; it wasn't until late in 1941 that he broke down and signed up with Decca.

But the man who seemed to recognize even less the importance of recordings to the big bands was the most influential man on the entire big band scene, James Caesar Petrillo. Elected national president of the American Federation of Musicians in June, 1940, and perturbed by the possible adverse effects of recording on his membership, he hired Ben Selvin, a highly respected recording executive and orchestra leader, to conduct a thorough study of the entire recording field as it affected musicians.

James Caesar Petrillo:
the most influential man

Selvin's report was exhaustive. Presented at the annual convention of the musicians' union, it received a standing ovation from the delegates. Estimating that by the end of 1941 the recording industry would have paid out more than three million dollars to working musicians, Selvin recommended that "it would be unwise, if at all possible, to curtail industries where such large amounts are spent for musicians. There are remedies for the unemployment caused by this mechanization of music, but a knockout blow, which could not be delivered, is not the answer."

So what did Petrillo do? On August 1, 1942, he tried for a knockout—he ordered his musicians to stop all recording. His argument was simple but specious. If the record companies couldn't devise some system whereby musicians were paid for the use of their recordings on radio programs and in jukeboxes, then he wouldn't let them record at all. The big band leaders almost to a man disagreed violently with Petrillo's actions. They recognized far better than he the importance of records to their future. But James Caesar stuck dictatorially to his battle plan.

For more than a year no major company made any records with instrumentalists. They did record singers, however, usually with choral backgrounds. Finally in September, 1943, Decca signed a new contract with the union. A month later, Capitol followed suit. But the companies with most of the big name bands, Columbia and Victor, fought for more than a year longer.

It was a big mess. Late in 1943 the War Labor Board (WLB) was asked to help. Four months later, finding in favor of the record companies, it recommended that the strike be ended and "conditions prevailing on July 31, 1942, be restored." But Petrillo refused to accept the recommendation. Even President Roosevelt got into the act, requesting an end to the strike. Again Petrillo said no. Finally in November, 1944, Columbia and Victor capitulated and agreed to pay the union a royalty for all records released.

Petrillo was jubilant. He claimed "the greatest victory for labor . . . in the history of the labor movement." In a way he may have been right. The rank-and-file membership, two-thirds of whom, according to the WLB report, did not depend upon music for a livelihood, had won a victory. As for the knockout blow that the Selvin report had predicted couldn't be delivered—well, it may not have been a knockout, but it certainly was a knockdown. Unfortunately, though, it didn't hit the recording companies nearly so hard as it did the big bands. And then, when the bands finally did get up from the floor, after a long count of two years and two months, they found that they were no longer champions of the recording field. While they had been down, the singers had taken over, and the recording field would never again be the same for the big bands.

Radio

THE big bands depended just as much on radio for exposure during the thirties and forties as did the singers and the vocal groups in the fifties and sixties. But there was one huge difference: much of the music of the big bands went over the air live instead of on records.

Of course, there were disc jockey shows. But these were almost exclusively on a local, unsponsored basis. To be sure, some attracted such large audiences that they became important to a band's success. Martin Block on WNEW in New York and Al Jarvis on KFWB in Los Angeles, with their "Make Believe Ballrooms," a program idea each claimed to have originated, drew large and faithful audiences. And so did other disc jockeys throughout the country who concentrated on big bands and who often succeeded, through records, in re-creating the sound of broadcasts from ballrooms.

A rare photo of WNEW's Martin Block surrounded by an all-star musicians' cast of Coleman Hawkins, Jack Jenney, Tommy Dorsey, Gene Krupa, Harry James, Bunny Berigan, and Count Basie

Almost every bandleader sought and welcomed such exposure. Some romanced disc jockeys with intense and sometimes nauseating ardor. Some jockeys reacted in kind. But many, genuinely interested in the music and its makers, willingly lent valuable support. Not stymied, as many of their successors in the sixties were to be, by strict adherence to a "top-forty" type of programming, many disc jockeys actually sought out records by new, upcoming bands and promoting such discoveries remained a labor of love for many a big band disc jockey.

Naturally they also played the records of the top bands, and this sometimes led to difficulties between those outfits and the sponsors of their live commercial series. For why, reasoned some of the clients, should we pay good money to these bands for live programs when some local stations can imitate our show, almost selection by selection, through records? They had a valid point.

Some of the top leaders took steps to protect their sponsors. For years, for example, Hal Kemp refused to record his theme song, thereby preventing disc jockeys from re-creating his live broadcasts. And Paul Whiteman and Fred Waring, both heavily sponsored, stayed out of the recording studios during much of the big band era, thus avoiding all competition with their live shows.

Big bands headlined numerous top radio series. Many were starred for several years on the Fitch Bandwagon, which, during the late thirties, presented most of the leading orchestras on programs that featured an MC named Tobe Reed, who talked with the leaders and generally tried to humanize the bands and musicians. Later, Coca-Cola with its Spotlight series also broadcast music of many name bands direct from numerous locations, including, during the war years, service camps.

As a group, the cigarette manufacturers really got behind the big bands. Camels sponsored the Benny Goodman and Bob Crosby bands in series highlighted by a weekly commentary on the news, called "Newsy Bluesies," composed and sung by Johnny Mercer, with Dan Seymour, now head of J. Walter Thompson, a major advertising agency, as announcer. Later the same cigarette company sponsored Vaughn Monroe's band. Chesterfield allied itself with several top bands—Hal Kemp's, Glenn Miller's and Harry James's, with future movie star Paul Douglas as announcer. Raleigh-Kool sponsored the Tommy Dorsey band for a number of years, with future television star Bud Collyer as announcer. Philip Morris went along with Horace Heidt, while Old Gold used numerous groups—Paul Whiteman, Artie Shaw, Larry Clinton, Frankie Carle and Woody Herman.

But the longest-lived cigarette-sponsored series was that of the American Tobacco Company, which in addition to its Kay Kyser's College of Musical Knowledge, sponsored what was first called "The Lucky Strike Hit Parade" and later simply "Your Hit Parade." Here the songs rather than the bands became the big attraction as listeners were kept in suspense right to the end of each program waiting to hear what tune had gained the number-one spot on

"The Lucky Strike Survey," a poll whose results sometimes baffled publishers and bandleaders who felt that it should have been conducted more thoroughly and analytically.

Lucky Strike, after going along for years with the almost martial music of B. A. Rolfe and his Orchestra, eventually switched to the more danceable and slightly more subtle sounds of Mark Warnow and his Orchestra. A large, well-disciplined studio outfit, it employed some of the top musicians in town, who, unfortunately, because of the sponsor's and agency's preconceived notions of tempos and volume, seldom got a chance to project much of the warmth or color that typified the music of the big name bands.

Studio bands continued to flourish during the big band era. Some had taken on and continued to use the names of their sponsors, like Harry Horlick and the A&P Gypsies, Sam Lanin and the Ipana Troubadors, and Harry Reser and the Cliquot Club Eskimos. Reser, by the way, eventually emerged from his carbonated commercial and formed an excellent band composed of some fine young swing musicians.

Although some of the leading studio musicians, such as the Dorseys and Benny Goodman and Artie Shaw and Glenn Miller and Claude Thornhill and Will Bradley and Charlie Spivak, left to form their own bands, often taking some friends with them, enough good musicians remained to stock very commercial orchestras led by Paul Baron, Lud Gluskin, Al Goodman, Gus Haenschen, Gordon Jenkins, Jack Miller, who was Kate Smith's steady conductor, Raymond Paige, Jacques Renard, Willard Robison, who led an especially musical group called the Deep River Boys, Rubinoff, who featured his magic violin, whatever that was, and Ben Selvin.

An All-Star radio session:
violinist Jack Benny, trumpeter Dick Powell, clarinetist Ken Murray,
drummer Bing Crosby, trombonist Tommy Dorsey, pianist-singer Shirley Ross

And there were more successful studio conductors—the Shilkret brothers, Nat and Jack, Harry Sosnick, Leith Stevens, Axel Stordahl, who appeared later on the scene as Frank Sinatra's maestro, John Scott Trotter, who conducted for Bing Crosby, Peter Van Steeden, Paul Weston, Meredith Willson, later to gain fame as composer of *The Music Man,* and Victor Young, who, when he wasn't conducting for the top singers, was busy writing a flock of wonderful songs.

Most of their music was different from that of the big dance bands. Much of it was strictly background for singers. A good deal consisted of uninspired readings of mundane arrangements. And almost all of it was constricted by the penny-pinching of network executives who allowed their studio bands a minimum of rehearsal time and personnel, by the old-fashioned attitudes of some leaders who were coasting on their reputations, and by insecure, hard-shelled advertising agency executives, who constantly kept quashing creativity lest anything outside the norm offend their clients. Much of the radio network programming of the thirties and forties rivaled in the vastness of its wasteland the kind of adolescent drivel that television was soon to spew forth.

Once in a while a studio band with a distinctive, musical sound would emerge. Raymond Scott fronted an outstanding outfit in New York. And Philadelphia produced three topflight bands: Jan Savitt's, Joey Kearns's and Elliot Lawrence's.

But by far the most exciting sounds came from the established dance bands, some during their commercial programs but many more during their broadcasts direct from where the bands were playing—Frank Dailey's Meadowbrook, the Palomar, the Hotel Sherman, Glen Island Casino, the Aragon, Elitch's Gardens, the Palladium and many, many more spots throughout the country that featured name and semi-name bands.

These network broadcasts were exceedingly important to the bands. They gave the groups exposure and publicity that they couldn't possibly afford to buy. Consequently, competition for these jobs became keen. This meant that bands would accept low wages for engagements in spots with radio outlets, often staying on for weeks and losing money while hopefully gaining enough national recognition through air time so that when they finally did go out on one-nighters and theaters tours they could demand and get more money.

The vast majority of remote broadcasts took place at night—from eleven to one on CBS and both NBC networks and from eleven to two on the Mutual network. There were also early evening airings, and during the late thirties and very early forties, when the competition for air time became especially keen, bands would show up at all sorts of weird hours just to get network exposure. Alvino Rey, for example, broadcast at noon on Sundays from the Rustic Cabin in New Jersey, while both Jack Teagarden and Tommy Tucker put on 11 A.M. shows from their locations.

Just as the bands fought for top spots, so did the networks fight for top bands. The big battles in the mid-sixties between NBC and CBS over the rights to telecast games of top football teams were an extension of other fights, twenty-five years earlier, in which they vied for tie-ins with the top name bands.

In 1939 NBC proudly announced summer broadcasts over its two networks, the Red and the Blue, of a total of forty-nine name bands, including those of Charlie Barnet, Blue Barron, Count Basie, Larry Clinton, Jimmy and Tommy Dorsey, Horace Heidt, Woody Herman, Gene Krupa, Glenn Miller, Jan Savitt and Artie Shaw. CBS at the same time trumpeted a list of twenty-one signatories that included Cab Calloway, Jan Garber, Benny Goodman, Sammy Kaye, Hal Kemp, Kay Kyser, Ozzie Nelson, Jack Teagarden and Paul Whiteman.

But those seventy bands by no means represented the total that were playing over the air. Both networks featured others. And there was also the vast Mutual network, which brought its microphones into clubs that the others didn't have time for, spots that featured some of the younger and often equally exciting bands.

The quality of the broadcasts varied tremendously. A great deal depended on a room's acoustics. Big dance halls generally projected more exciting sounds; smaller, more intimate hotel and nightclub rooms produced smaller, deader tones. Engineers were all-important too. Some had good ears for music. They could recognize which instruments should predominate and adjusted their dials accordingly. Others had tin ears, and some of their broadcasts were horrendous.

NBC and CBS sent an announcer and an engineer to each broadcast, but Mutual, a less wealthy network, had one man perform both functions. This required both a good ear and a good voice. Unfortunately very few men had both.

The right announcer was important to the big bands. If he projected enthusiasm for the music, the entire tenor of the broadcast could be uplifted. Consequently, many bandleaders wined and dined these men, hoping that they would respond with the sort of inspirational gab that would let the nation know just how great the band was. Sometimes, though, the results were pretty ridiculous, as overzealous, underinformed announcers spieled inane jive talk and clichés in hysterical attempts to match the band's musical excitement.

The attention that leaders heaped on announcers was nothing compared with that which one group of men, the music publishers, piled on the leaders. Called song pluggers or, more respectfully, contact men, the publishers' representatives wooed bandleaders with such varied gifts as liquor, theater and baseball tickets, clothes, women, jewelry, resort vacations, musical arrangements for their bands and just plain money.

Some leaders were constantly taking; others just as constantly refusing. Some publishers treated the leaders with courtesy, respect and consideration; others merely plowed bullishly ahead, intent only on getting one particular plug for the tune, caring little for the bandleader's feelings or for establishing a more lasting relationship.

*Music publishers descend on Tommy Dorsey at his June 1, 1939, opening at
the Roof Garden of New York's Pennsylvania Hotel.*
Seated: *Johnny Green, Jonie Taps, Eddie Wolpin, organist Jessie Crawford,
TD, Jack Mills*
Standing: *Dick Coester, Murray Baker, Nicky Campbell,
George (not George T.) Simon, Charlie Ross, Stan Stanley, Sidney Kornheiser,
Al Porgie, Lester Stanley (behind Porgie), Joe Santley, Norman Foley,
Charlie Warren (rear), Larry Spier, Willie Horowitz (front), Mac Goldman,
Billy Chandler (rear), Elmore White (front)*

The pressure on the publishers' representatives was intense. They had to
produce or they lost their jobs. Publishers often designated a certain week as
"plug week" for a special tune, and their men had specific instructions to get
that song played during that week. The so-called logic behind all this was to
try to get the song high up on the charts that were based on the number of
times a tune was played during a seven-day period, a chart that had a big
bearing on where the tune would rank on the "Hit Parade" survey. It was a
pretty synthetic setup, especially since only NBC and CBS broadcasts counted.
Mutual, which broadcast more hours per week and often over more stations
than the other networks, was for some reason not considered important enough
to count in the plug tally. As a result, bandleaders would often be thanked
profusely for an NBC or a CBS plug but be greeted with grumbles for having
played a song over Mutual.

Some bandleaders resented what they openly called the hypocrisy of the
song pluggers. Tommy Dorsey once expressed what many leaders felt: "They
come in and instead of a direct 'Here's a tune that I think will be good for
the band; please look it over,' they try hard as hell to be subtle, put their arms
around me, shake my one hand with two of theirs—all in an attempt to have
me believe that they love me and that I'm really one helluva wonderful guy.

"But through it all I know exactly what they're driving at and that any minute they're going to drive in for the kill with the usual stuff about the most 'terrific tune' of the year."

Not all publishers acted either so obviously or so hypocritically. Many became close and often very valuable friends of the leaders and didn't, as some others did, forget entirely about a leader whenever his orchestra wasn't playing in a spot with a radio wire.

The bandleaders weren't blameless either—not by a long shot. Some relished the warped attention they received. At times their demands for favors exceeded the ridiculous. And many publishers resented bitterly the "publishers nights" and "official openings" at which they were expected to appear, generally with large entourages, all for the benefit of the band.

There was, of course, no denying the value of air plugs to exploit songs. No other medium, not even phonograph records, provided as much impact, and both the publishers and the leaders knew it. As a result, many "plug" tunes, which had little musical merit, received frequent airings, while other, often better songs, with none of the financial support that the publishers shelled out so willingly, were heard once or twice and then forgotten.

During 1941, so far as radio broadcasts were concerned, some of the great tunes of all time were completely overlooked. That was the year in which the radio networks and ASCAP (the American Society of Authors, Composers and Publishers), which collected for almost all the top composers, waged their big war. The cause was simple: ASCAP wanted more money for licensing its music; the networks refused to raise the ante.

It turned out to be a battle between two powerful and rich groups. For a full year, until they finally reached an agreement with the Society, the networks banned all ASCAP tunes from their networks. To fill the void they set up their own collection agency, BMI (Broadcast Music, Inc.), offering attractive terms to new writers and any ASCAP composers who would defect. At first their music suffered badly when compared with that of top ASCAP writers like the Gershwins, Rodgers and Hart, Cole Porter, Harold Arlen, Johnny Mercer, Jerome Kern, Irving Berlin and others of their stature, though in later years it improved perceptibly. Meanwhile, bandleaders, faced with having to play music they didn't especially like, often turned to very old standards whose copyrights had expired and were no longer controlled by ASCAP. Thus appeared a sudden overdose of swing versions of "I Dream of Jeanie with the Light Brown Hair," "London Bridge Is Falling Down," "My Old Kentucky Home," "Comin' Through the Rye," "My Bonnie Lies over the Ocean," plus many other nineteenth century tunes that might never had been embalmed had it not been for the ASCAP-BMI war.

The quality of dance band remotes deteriorated rather drastically. The less-inspiring songs were one factor. But equally important was the "no ad-libbing" ban that the networks imposed on musicians. This meant that all solos were required to be written out and submitted to the networks before each broadcast so that no strains of any ASCAP tunes might possibly seep

TUNES PLAYED MOST ON AIR

Title	Publisher	Broadcasts
1—Please Be Kind	Harms, Inc.	28
2—One Song	Irving Berlin, Inc.	27
3—Ti-Pi-Tin	Leo Feist, Inc.	25
4—You Couldn't Be Cuter	Chappell & Co.	25
5—Cry, Baby, Cry	Shapiro, Bernstein, Inc.	24
6—I Fall In Love Every Day	Famous Music Corp.	24
7—You're An Education	Remick Music Corp.	22
8—Bewildered	Miller Music, Inc.	21
9—Don't Be That Way	Robbins Music Corp.	20
10—How'd Ja Like to Love Me?	Famous Music Corp.	20
11—On the Sentimental Side	Select Music Co.	20
12—Heigh Ho	Irving Berlin, Inc.	19
13—I Love to Whistle	Robbins Music Corp.	19
14—Sunday in the Park	Mills Music, Inc.	18
15—In My Little Red Book	E. B. Marks Music Co.	18
16—Who Are We to Say?	Leo Feist, Inc.	17
17—Good Night, Angel	Irving Berlin, Inc.	17
18—Let's Sail to Dreamland	Larry Spier, Inc.	17
19—Something Tells Me	Witmark & Son	17
20—Garden in Granada	Schuster-Miller, Inc.	16
21—Always and Always	Leo Feist Inc.	16
22—Joseph Joseph	Harms, Inc.	15
23—Two Bouquets	Shapiro, Bernstein, Inc.	15
24—At a Perfume Counter	Donaldson-Douglas-Gumble	14
25—So Little Time	Shapiro, Bernstein, Inc.	14
26—It's Wonderful	Robbins Music Corp.	14
27—Thanks for the Memory	Paramount Music Corp.	13
28—Whistle While You Work	Irving Berlin, Inc.	13
29—Dipsy Doodle	Lincoln Music Corp.	12
30—I Simply Adore You	Ager-Yellen-Bornstein	12
31—Lovelight in the Starlight	Paramount Music Corp.	12
32—Toy Trumpet	Circle Music Co.	12
33—I Can Dream Can't I?	Marlo Music Co.	11
34—Love Walked In	Chappell & Co.	11
35—More Than Ever	Miller Music, Inc.	11
36—Where Have We Met Before?	Robbins Music Corp.	11
37—Just Let Me Look at You	Chappell & Co.	11
38—Girl in the Bonnet of Blue	Crawford Music Corp.	10
39—Let Me Whisper	Chappell & Co.	10
40—Loch Lomond	Robbins Music Corp.	10
41—In Shade of New Apple Tree	Chappell & Co.	10
42—I See Your Face Before Me	Crawford Music Corp.	10
43—How Can You Forget	Harms, Inc.	9

BEST SHEET MUSIC SELLERS

No.	Title	Publisher
1	Ti-Pi-Tin	Leo Feist, Inc.
2	Love Walked In	Chappell & Co.
3	Please Be Kind	Harms, Inc.
4	Heigh Ho	Irving Berlin, Inc.
5	Whistle While You Work	Irving Berlin, Inc.
6	Good Night, Angel	Irving Berlin, Inc.
7	Moon of Manakoora	Kalmar-Ruby Music Corp.
8	I Love to Whistle	Robbins Music Corp.
9	New Apple Tree	Witmark & Son
10	Some Day My Prince Will Come	Irving Berlin, Inc.

BEST RECORD SELLERS FOR MARCH

Bluebird

Ti-Pi-Tin .... Jerry Blaine
Perfume Counter ...... Blue Barron
Cry, Baby, Cry .... Calif. Ramblers
Please Be Kind ... Dixieland Band
New Apple Tree ...... Ozzie Nelson

Brunswick

I Let a Song .... Duke Ellington
Please Be Kind—Weekend of Secretary .... Red Norvo
If You Were in My Place
— Scrounch .... Ellington
Oh Dear .... Ella Logan
Moon of Manakoora ...... Ray Noble

Decca

Cry, Baby, Cry .... Dick Robertson
Perfume Counter—Love Walked In
Jimmy Dorsey
Shortnin Bread—Oooh Boom
Andrews Sisters

Pop Corn Man—Campbells Swinging
Milt Hearth
Ti-Pi-Tin .... Andrews Sisters

Victor

Don't Be That Way .. Benny Goodman
Martha .... Larry Clinton
Ti-Pi-Tin .... Guy Lombardo
Yearning .... Tommy Dorsey
Snow White Album

Vocalion

Love Walked In ...... Sammy Kaye
Ti-Pi-Tin .... George Hall
Don't Be That Way—I Can't Face
Music .... Mildred Bailey
Thanks for the Memory—I See Your
Face .... M. Bailey
Chinatown .... Slim and Slam

These were the songs most played on the radio, on pianos and on phonographs according to the April, 1938, issue of Metronome.

through. Consequently, much of the spontaneity that sparked the broadcasts of the swing band was lost during all of 1941.

Obviously, bands could no longer play their well-known hit arrangements on the air. Nor could they play their theme songs, for which they substituted a rash of melodies, almost all of which have long since been forgotten. Not so, however, their regular themes, which returned in 1942, and the memories of which still release waves of nostalgia for big band fans everywhere.

These theme songs varied in mood, in quality and in nostalgic power. There were literally hundreds of them, and many of them, and the way they were performed, bring back wonderful memories: Louis Armstrong and his trumpet on "When It's Sleepy Time Down South"—Mitchell Ayres and the sweeping lead sax on "You Go to My Head"—Charlie Barnet's jumping, pumping tenor sax on "Cherokee" and "Red Skin Rumba"—Blue Barron's syrupy version of "Sometimes I'm Happy"—Count Basie's light, swinging "One O'Clock Jump"—Bunny Berigan's emotional, broad-toned trumpet on "I Can't Get Started"—Ben Bernie's lovely opening theme, "It's a Lonesome Old Town" and his cozy closer, in which he talked the lyrics of "Au Revoir, Pleasant Dreams."

Les Brown also had two themes, his jumping "Leap Frog" and his doleful "Sentimental Journey"; the lesser-known Willie Bryant band had a great old ballad, "It's Over Because We're Through"; Henry Busse featured his corny, commercial "Hot Lips"; Billy Butterfield blew his brilliant trumpet on "What's New?"—the song he had introduced with Bob Crosby's band; and Bobby Byrne blew his pure, soothing trombone through "Danny Boy."

And there were many more: Cab Calloway's showmanly "Minnie the Moocher"—Frankie Carle's brittle piano on his "Sunrise Serenade"—Benny Carter's alto sax on his "Melancholy Lullaby"—Larry Clinton's light, swinging ensembles on his "Dipsy Doodle"—the Bob Crosby band's slow, languid, nondixieland version of George Gershwin's "Summertime"—and Xavier Cugat's Latinized version of "My Shawl."

Jimmy Dorsey blew his alto sax on his theme, "Contrasts" with its tempo changes, and Tommy his trombone on one of the most beautiful of all theme sounds, "I'm Gettin' Sentimental over You." Eddy Duchin sounded almost classical when he played "My Twilight Dream" on the piano; Sonny Dunham sounded almost frantic when he blew "Memories of You" on his trumpet.

Duke Ellington used "East St. Louis Toodle-oo" as his theme for years; then when Billy Strayhorn's "Take the 'A' Train" became popular, he switched to that swinging opus. Benny Goodman also used two themes—"Let's Dance" was his opener; for a closer, the Goodman clarinet gently caressed Gordon Jenkins' mournful ballad "Goodbye." Glen Gray and the Casa Loma orchestra were also associated with two themes: "Was I to Blame for Falling in Love With You?"—an unusually beautiful song—and then later the better-known "Smoke Rings," which featured Billy Rausch's trombone.

Mal Hallett had a jumping original called "Boston Tea Party," Lionel

Hampton an even jumpier one with his "Flyin' Home," Horace Heidt a sleepy ballad, "I'll Love You in My Dreams," and Fletcher Henderson his loping, swinging "Christopher Columbus."

Woody Herman featured the dramatic "Blue Flame" for years, then added "Woodchoppers' Ball." Richard Himber used a fine old standard, "It Isn't Fair," Earl Hines a semi-eerie "Deep Forest," Claude Hopkins a delicately swinging "I Would Do Anything for You," and the Hudson-DeLange band a similar sort of rhythm tune, "Eight Bars in Search of a Melody."

Each Harry James broadcast opened and closed with his biting trumpet blowing "Ciribiribin"; each Jack Jenney program opened and closed with his wonderfully mellow trombone playing a lovely theme called "City Lights." The broad, rich tones of the Isham Jones ensemble played their leader's "You're Just a Dream Come True," while Dick Jurgens featured a sweeping theme song called "Day Dreams Come True at Night." Sammy Kaye's brass and saxes smeared through "Kaye's Melody," while Hal Kemp's staccato trumpets and unison reeds closed every show with "How I Miss You When Summer Is Gone."

Stan Kenton had one of the most stentorian theme songs, "Artistry in Rhythm," Henry King one of the loveliest—Frank Signorelli's "A Blues Serenade," Wayne King one of the laziest, "The Waltz You Saved for Me." Gene Krupa used "Apurksody" for a while, then switched to the more dramatic "Star Burst." Kay Kyser set a pretty mood with a lovely ballad, "Thinking of You," Elliot Lawrence an intimate one with "Heart to Heart."

Several bands used really old tunes for themes: Ted Lewis "When My Baby Smiles at Me"—Guy Lombardo "Auld Lang Syne"—Johnny Long an old fraternity song, "The White Star of Sigma Nu"—Vincent Lopez "Nola."

Jimmie Lunceford began with a screaming "Jazznocracy"; later he switched to the moodier "Uptown Blues." Freddy Martin used "Bye Lo Bye Lullaby"; then after it became a hit he also used "Tchaikowsky's Piano Concerto," later called "Tonight We Love." Frankie Masters featured a ricky-ticky pop tune called "Scatterbrain," while Clyde McCoy went even cornier with his personalized trumpet treatment of "Sugar Blues." Ray McKinley's theme was personal too—a swinging "Howdy, Friends," during which Ray welcomed his listeners vocally.

To many the most nostalgic, mood-provoking of all theme songs was Glenn Miller's original melody "Moonlight Serenade," complete with the clarinet lead and the ooh-wah brass. The strained strains of Vaughn Monroe's singing of "Racing with the Moon" began each of his broadcasts; the wah-wah trombone trick on "Does Your Heart Beat for Me?" identified the band of the song's composer, Russ Morgan. The eerie, growling trumpet of Red Nichols on "Wailing to the Four Winds," one of the catchiest of all themes, opened and closed each of his band's broadcasts; the simple piano and pretty orchestral sounds of "The Very Thought of You" always brought on the band of its composer, Ray Noble.

Red Norvo had an infectious, light-swinging riff theme, seldom identified, called "Mr. and Mrs. Swing," which featured his xylophone; Tony Pastor, a more dramatic one, "Blossoms," which focused on his warm tenor sax. Ben Pollack's band came on with an old standard, "Song of the Islands," Carl Ravazza's with a tune its leader invariably sang, "Vieni Su," Don Redman's with a haunting instrumental, "Chant of the Weed," written by its leader.

Alvino Rey had two themes, both electronically treated: an opening instrumental called "Blue Rey" and a closing vocal by Yvonne King called "Nighty Night." Jan Savitt came on strong with a pulsating instrumental called "Quaker City Jazz," Raymond Scott more delicately with one of his many originals, "Pretty Little Petticoat," and Artie Shaw, dramatically with his provocative, seering composition "Nightmare," which spotted tom-toms and growling brass under his exciting clarinet lead.

Bobby Sherwood had a swinging dixieland original, "The Elks' Parade," Freddy Slack a moodier piece, "Strange Cargo," which had been the Bradley band's theme when Freddy was its piano player. Charlie Spivak featured his trumpet on a pretty piece called "Star Dreams." One of the most haunting themes of all was Harold Stern's "Now That It's All Over," a lovely melody sung with great feeling by Bill Smith, the band's drummer.

Jack Teagarden's bluesy trombone set the mood for each of his band's broadcasts as it played "I've Got a Right to Sing the Blues," while Claude Thornhill's light piano, backed by his beautifully voiced ensemble, played a delicate "Snowfall" at the start and completion of each of his band's airings. The Tuckers, Orrin and Tommy, both had sentimental themes—Orrin, the well-worn standard "Drifting and Dreaming"; Tommy, a pretty ballad, "I Love You, Oh, How I Love You," sung romantically by a vocal trio.

For years Fred Waring's orchestra and glee club were identified by the pretty strains of "Sleep." Chick Webb used an infectious, swinging version of "I May Be Wrong," Ted Weems a haunting rendition of "Out of the Night," Lawrence Welk an effervescing, clippety-cloppety spraying of "Bubbles in the Wine," and Paul Whiteman a rich, sumptuous version of the major strain of George Gershwin's "Rhapsody in Blue."

And there were many more melodies that set each band apart from the others—at least at the opening and close of each broadcast. After that it wasn't always possible to make out just who was imitating whom. Nothing, though, was more personal to a band than its theme.

Many of the big band memories revolve around those musical identifications. In the summer of 1966 I happened to pick up a late-evening broadcast from station WHAM in Rochester. All I heard was theme songs. I contacted Bill Givens, the announcer, who said that the show had been such a success that the station was planning another one. Sure enough, several weeks later there it was—a six-and-a-half hour program that featured 102 theme songs! Again, the response was immense.

The big bands may have died, but their themes—never!

Movies

THE big bands were well established by the time Hollywood decided to cash in on their popularity. During the thirties the movie moguls gave them short shrift. Oh, sure, after Benny Goodman became a phenomenon, they latched on to him and put him in a mediocre film called *Hollywood Hotel*. And a couple of years later, when Artie Shaw captured so much news space via his bands and his verbal outbursts, they featured him in a thing called *Dancing Co-Ed,* in which he was assigned lines like, "Greetings, swing cats and alligators," and "Hi ya, jive hounds, I'll dig ya and I'll plant ya," which he steadfastly refused to utter.

Hollywood treated dance bands with consistent inaccuracy. Instead of presenting them as they really were, it tried adapting them to its own preconceived ideas of how musicians acted and played. Producers and writers created all sorts of ridiculous, unbelievable plots and situations into which it thrust one band after another. Good taste and honesty were too often sacrificed for what a bunch of studio executives, most of whom had little feeling for the music, hoped would sell.

Take what they did to Gene Krupa in *Ball of Fire*—they had him drumming not on his drums but on a match box, not with his sticks but with matches. When this feat of phony phosphorescence finally reached its climax, what happened? The matches burst into flame! And what did Hollywood do to poor Woody Herman's band so that it would fit into the plot of *Winter Wonderland?* It was stranded where it wouldn't possibly have been in the first place—way out in the woods of Canada! Even the booking offices must have cringed at that one.

Unbelievability popped up everywhere. In Tommy Dorsey's first picture, *Las Vegas Night,* the band was photographed on the bandstand with seven brass, five saxes and a rhythm section. And what came out of the sound track? A full string section, of course.

Another Dorsey film, *The Fabulous Dorseys,* provided a typical, nonsensical cliché. The hero is constantly plagued by his inability to create a musical theme he has been assigned to write. And how does it finally come to him? Easy. He's sitting with his girl friend at a table and happens to hit a few water glasses—and, sure enough, out comes the theme he'd been searching for!

The Tommy Dorsey band in Paramount's Las Vegas Nights
Front row: *saxists Heine Beau, Johnny Mince, Freddy Stulce,*
Don Lodice, leader Dorsey, pianist Joe Bushkin
Second row: *trombonists Lowell Martin, Les Jenkins, George Arus.*
Third row: *trumpeters Jimmy Blake, Ray Linn, Chuck Peterson,*
Ziggy Elman, drummer Buddy Rich, bassist Sid Weiss
Back row: *The Pied Pipers with Jo Stafford, Connie Haines, Frank Sinatra*

Tommy provided one of the few "inside" laughs in a picture called *Swing Fever,* which featured Kay Kyser's band. In one short sequence Dorsey and Harry James are spotted as sidemen in Kyser's band. Suddenly, after playing only a few bars, they get up and walk out as Tommy mutters disdainfully, "That square'll never get anywhere. He looks too much like Kay Kyser."

Tommy could do lines better than most leaders, including his arch rival, Benny Goodman, who in a film called *The Gang's All Here* uttered little more than a few "Uh-huh's," "Yeah's" and "Right's." He also sang two mediocre tunes with untelling effect. Remember "Minnie's in the Money" and "Paducah"? Few do.

During the summer of 1941, many popular bands were busying themselves before the cameras—Charlie Barnet, Tommy Dorsey, Woody Herman, Harry James, Sammy Kaye, Gene Krupa, Jimmie Lunceford, Freddy Martin, Glenn Miller, Alvino Rey and Jack Teagarden. In fact, so intent was Hollywood with featuring name bands that several companies decided to bunch batches of them together. *Stage Door Canteen* presented six—the bands of

Count Basie, Xavier Cugat, Benny Goodman, Kay Kyser, Guy Lombardo and Freddy Martin—and presented them well by just letting them play instead of trying to weave them into plots. And *Jam Session* followed a similar, more natural procedure with the bands of Louis Armstrong, Charlie Barnet, Jan Garber, Glen Gray and the Casa Loma Orchestra, Teddy Powell and Alvino Rey, plus Jo Stafford and the Pied Pipers.

The movies gradually realized that band presentations didn't have to be all gimmicked up in order to be effective. Soon some companies took a more realistic approach via some intelligently prepared and produced shorts (a whole series of two-reelers by Universal Pictures and a batch of shorties called "soundies" often showed off bands quite effectively) as well as a few full-length films. Glenn Miller, a man who could not be easily pushed around, managed to make both his pictures, *Sun Valley Serenade* and *Orchestra Wives* (Jackie Gleason acted in the latter), fairly believable. *The Fleet's In* featured Jimmy Dorsey's band and did very well by its two attractive vocalists, Bob Eberly and Helen O'Connell, who sang as they would on any real bandstand. And Harry James, who turned out to be quite a ham, made a good impression with his band in *Best Foot Forward*. What's more, all four films turned out to be box-office successes.

The James band and many others began headquartering in Hollywood during the latter part of 1942. Their motivation wasn't entirely love of the movies; there was also the matter of general unemployment and the need for promotion. Petrillo had called his recording strike, so that medium was closed to them. On top of that, war restrictions, especially the gas shortage, had crippled the one-nighter business. So why not stick around Hollywood, where prospects were bright? In addition to James, Charlie Barnet, Benny Carter, Jimmy and Tommy Dorsey, Benny Goodman, Horace Heidt, Woody Herman, Stan Kenton, Kay Kyser, Hal McIntyre, Vaughn Monroe, Artie Shaw, Freddy Slack and Charlie Spivak began concentrating their activities in the film capital.

The intensive activity lasted a couple of years. Few really good pictures resulted, which may have been why the movie companies began to show less interest in the bands. By the end of 1944 they had little use for them.

For several years thereafter, movies and the big bands drifted farther apart. But after the big band era had ended and segments of the public began thinking nostalgically of what they were missing, some of the picture companies decided to film some biographical movies. Again Hollywood's penchant for showing things as they weren't took over. *The Fabulous Dorseys* turned out to be a fabulously unreal film. Tyrone Power fingered the piano to synchronize with Carmen Cavallaro's playing on the sound track in *The Eddy Duchin Story*. Steve Allen played clarinet, after coaching from Sol Yaged, in the movie of Benny Goodman's life. Sal Mineo gave *The Gene Krupa Story* a method-acting approach. *The Five Pennies* was an oversentimentalized biography of Red Nichols, played in simpering fashion by Danny Kaye.

In many ways the most effective of all the biographical films was *The Glenn Miller Story,* chiefly because the Miller-style music was played so well by a group of musicians, some of whom had actually worked for Miller, and because of June Allyson's moving portrayal of Glenn's wife. But there were also some glaring inconsistencies. Vital periods of the band's career were omitted, some characters became caricatures, and incidents that never happened were created as Hollywood followed its accepted procedure of stretching the truth in order to stretch its box-office lines.

The definitive big band movie has yet to be produced.

The Glenn Miller Band during Sun Valley Serenade
Front row: *trombonists Paul Tanner, Jimmy Priddy, Frank D'Anolfo, pianist Chummy MacGregor, Miller, vocalist Paula Kelly, saxists Ernie Caceres, Hal McIntyre, Willie Schwartz*
Second row: *Ralph Brewster (of the Modernaires) doubling on trumpet, trumpeters Ray Anthony, Mickey McMickle, vocalist Ray Eberle, Modernaires Hal (Spooky) Dickenson, Chuck Goldstein, Bill Conway, saxists Tex Beneke, Al Klink*
Back row: *trumpeters Johnny Best, Billy May, guitarist Jack Lathrop, drummer Maurice Purtill, bassist Trigger Alpert*

The Press

THE big bands received surprisingly little sympathetic treatment from the national press. Instead of commenting on their music, many of the papers preferred concentrating on the foibles of the leaders and their musicians. What mattered—apparently because it made for more colorful copy—was not how well Gene Krupa played drums but how avidly he chewed gum, not how well Artie Shaw played clarinet but how balefully he glared at the jitterbugs, not how much the dancers enjoyed the music but how far it presumably sent them into the upper stratosphere.

Typical of the sort of copy that big bands had to overcome was an article written for the usually reliable *New York Times* by someone called Gama Gilbert on August 14, 1938. After suggesting that swing might be responsible for emotional unbalance, sexual excess and even rape, the article quoted a psychologist about the "dangerously hypnotic influence of swing," which purportedly had been "cunningly devised to a faster tempo than seventy-two bars to the minute—faster than the human pulse." By being exposed to it, the psychologist explained, "young people, presumably unfamiliar with the ways of the world, . . . can reasonably be expected to break down conventions," and this would "lead to moral weakness."

Then the article went on with the usual clichés about musicians: "Many swingsters require some artificial stimulus of immediate effect. They find it in the cup and the weed. Marijuana is cheaper than alcohol. . . . The swingster will smoke his reefer so long as the demands of his job and his material rewards remain incompatible with human physical resources." What nonsensical sensationalism!

Another article, this one in the Tulsa *Tribune,* quoted an unnamed "profound psychologist" and expert on swing, which for the writer of the article included the music of Sammy Kaye and Guy Lombardo. It was, the psychologist noted, "a manifestation of the restless hysteria which is sweeping the world in advance of the coming war. In Germany it is the shovel brigade. In Italy it is the Fascist Youth Marchers. In France it is the war-babies."

Not all the comments by the daily press were derogatory. Some were just stupid. In 1940 a nationally syndicated article noted that Glenn Miller was one of several who lead "what musicians call 'Mickey Mouse bands'; that is, they don't swing with confusing arrangements but emphasize rippling rhythms with a tic-toc tone."

As late as 1945 Elsa Maxwell came up with a beaut in one of her columns: "The drums are forerunners of all music and still hold great power over a vast majority of the younger set—as witness the popularity of one Artie Shaw and other skin beaters."

More than anything else it was the uninformed comments by writers that irked the big band leaders and musicians. Few dailies had any men on their staffs who had either a feeling for or a knowledge of popular music, swing in particular. Time and again, reviewers versed only in classical music were sent to cover performances of swing bands. Time and again, they came up with nonsensical pieces.

Few major magazines covered the field regularly. Occasionally some printed articles by fairly knowledgeable writers, and several of them, *Colliers, Look* and *Esquire* especially, gave fairly frequent coverage to the bands in general and to jazz in particular.

Surprisingly, there were no major big band fan magazines. Once in a while one would spring up with a name like *Bqton, Preview* or *Band Leaders* (the latter did a complete fan-style job), but none could attract enough steady readers or advertisers to survive.

With the trades it was different. Both *Billboard* and *Variety* covered the big band business thoroughly, and for those concerned with bookings and other commercials aspects, those two weeklies became required reading. There were also three trade monthlies, *Orchestra World,* which was more of a puff sheet, *Down Beat* and *Metronome.*

Down Beat, published in Chicago, started off strictly as a sensation sheet. Edited by Carl Cons and published by Glenn Burrs, both former working musicians, it ran numerous lurid and often misleading headlines. But after Ned Williams, a former press agent who loved music, took over, it turned into a much more respectable magazine, mixing a sharp news approach with numerous feature articles by such respected writers as John Hammond, Marshall Stearns, Charles Edward Smith, George Hoefer and its various New York staff members, Dave Dexter, Dixon Gayer, Mike Levin and John S. Wilson. It is still published today.

Metronome was less sensational. It covered the news, using contributors from cities throughout the country, and devoted much space to instrument-instruction columns. But the staff—which at various times during the big band era included Barry Ulanov, Leonard Feather, Amy Lee, Barbara Hodgkins, Peter Dean, Bob Bach, Johnny Stulzfuss, Dick Gilbert and Doron K. Antrim, who was editor in 1935, when a guy named Simon also joined—was devoted mostly to intelligent and constructive criticism. It covered the big bands regularly, employing a rating system that went from A to D, with pluses and minuses included. Founded in the 1880's, it lasted into the 1960's.

For years, at the end of each of my reviews I would rate each band with a "Simon Says B plus" or "Simon Says C minus" or whatever I felt the band deserved. This monthly ritual amused Davey Tough, the great little drummer who wrote a column for *Metronome,* and in December, 1937, he tried to describe precisely how the rating system worked. In an article titled "The Crazy Professor," he opined:

> Dr. Simon is one of the most lovable characters on the *Metronome* campus. He potters absentmindedly about the ivy arbors muttering some cabalistic formula concerning B plus, C minus, B plus. That's all one hears; just that: B plus, C minus, B plus. To the uninitiated it's a little eerie.
>
> In his briefcase he carries a slide rule, a caliper, and micrometer and McKinley's record of "Milk Bottle Caps." He is working out a formula of musical criticism. But at the moment he is confronted by a real B plus obstacle. Postulating that:
>
> $$\frac{(6 \text{ saxophones}^2 \times \text{Ray Bauduc}^3)}{(\text{Pi plus Ray McKinley}^6)} = \frac{(2 \text{ tom-toms} \times \text{Chick Webb}^3)}{(\text{Big Sidney plus Zutty})}$$
>
> he has a tentative, three-dimension equation that will set the musical cognoscenti back on its heels. Still the answer refuses to come out B plus.
>
> I think the error here is one of simple arithmetic: 6 take away one times Bauduc squared, carry three. (Note: I multiply Bauduc squared; not, as Dr. Simon does, subtract Bauduc squared.) The answer is obvious. It fairly leaps at you B plus, C minus, B plus.
>
> Good God, he's got me doing it, too!

For the pages that follow, I have decided to dispense with the formula that Tough described. Instead, I will write—sometimes analytically, sometimes critically, sometimes sentimentally, but always, I hope, accurately—about the big bands as I knew them then and as I remember them now.

Drummer and writer Davey Tough

Part Two:
Inside the Big Bands

Charles Daly Barnet

Charlie Barnet

"THE band business was a romping, stomping thing, and everybody was swinging, and I can't help but think back to the group of boys in the band—it was a happy band, and even with the one-nighters it was a ball."

For Charlie Barnet and the many fine musicians who played in his ever-swinging outfit, the big band days must indeed have been a ball. For Charlie was the kind of a guy who believed in a good time—not only for himself, but also for all those around him. He and his cohorts projected a happy, carefree, swinging feeling both in their music and very often in their attitude toward life. They were disciplined in their playing, for Charlie always respected music, and they took their task seriously. But take themselves seriously—no! This was a band that reflected the wonderful ad-lib spontaneity that characterizes jazz. Its music always had a beat. And, like its leader and many of his sidemen, it was always, but always colorful.

Barnet was a handsome, Hollywood-hero sort of man—in fact, at one time he tried making it as a movie actor, appearing in two films, *Irene and Mary* and *Love and Hisses*. But his heart wasn't in acting, for it always remained so very much in jazz.

As a kid he revolted toward jazz. His family wanted him to study piano. He wanted to play drums, so he began banging on his mother's hatboxes and sundry pots and pans, probably expensive paraphernalia too, because his was a wealthy family. His mother's father, Charles Daly, had been the first vice-president of the New York Central Railroad, and Charlie's parents had all sorts of "respectable plans" for their son. They sent him to Rumsey Hall and Blair Academy, two very respectable boarding schools, and he was enrolled at Yale. But this wasn't for Charlie. By the time he should have been preparing for his freshman midterms at Yale, he was in the South, blowing his wild tenor sax in various local outfits.

Admittedly Barnet's style was influenced greatly by that of Coleman Hawkins. When Charlie was twelve his family gave him a C-melody sax, which is a cross between an alto and tenor. "I learned to play hot by fooling around with the Victrola," he recently told writer George Hoefer. "I was nuts about the Fletcher Henderson band, and when I heard Hawkins play, I just naturally switched to the tenor." Later, when he heard Duke Ellington's

Johnny Hodges play alto and soprano sax, he just naturally switched to those horns too.

Ellington's band had a profound effect on Barnet, and when, after having fronted a fairly commercial outfit for several years, Charlie decided to cash in on the big swing-band craze, he patterned his arrangements after those of the Duke. As I noted in an August, 1939, review of his band (headed "Barnet's—Blackest White Band of All!"), he and his musicans made no attempt to hide the fact "that they're aping Duke Ellington, copying many of his arrangements, adapting standards and some pops to his style, using his sax-section setup of two altos, tenor, and baritone and his growling trumpets and trombones." So dedicated was Barnet to the Duke that, it has been noted, when he built a fallout shelter after the war, he stocked it with a superb collection of Ellington recordings.

Charlie's first important band, formed as early as 1933, featured some unusually good and even advanced arrangements written by two of his trumpeters, Eddie Sauter and Tutti Camarata. The third trumpeter was Chris Griffin, who a couple of years later became a mainstay of the Goodman section that also included Harry James and Ziggy Elman. For a singer, Barnet used, believe it or not, Harry Von Zell, later to become a famous radio announcer.

Barnet also sang, and sang well too. His voice was rather nasal, but he had a good beat and a good sense of phrasing, and in later years I often wondered why he didn't sing more. Of course he featured his tenor sax a great deal— an exciting, booting, extremely rhythmic horn. He could also play very soul-fully too, as he proved on several Columbia sides he made in 1934 with an all-star group led by Red Norvo. Two of these, "I Surrender, Dear" and "The Night Is Blue," are highly recommended, not only for Norvo and Barnet, but also for three then-obscure recording musicians, clarinetist Artie Shaw (this was his first featured solo), pianist Teddy Wilson and trombonist Jack Jenney.

Barnet liked to surround himself with inspiring musicians. Many of them were black, and it could well have been because of his liberal attitude on the racial question (especially liberal for those days) that his band was not picked for any of the commercial radio series that featured the big name bands. He even had some troubles securing engagements in certain hotels because he clung so strongly to his principles.

Not that Barnet was entirely a do-gooder. He could get into trouble, some attributable to his zest for having a ball and presumably not worrying too much about the consequences, and some over which he had no control. For example, in 1939, just after his band had opened an extremely important engagement at the famed Palomar in Los Angeles, the ballroom burned to the ground. The band lost everything—its instruments, its music, even most of its uniforms. Barnet, though, took it in stride. "Hell, it's better than being in Poland with bombs dropping on your head!" he exclaimed. He also showed a kooky sense of humor by featuring on the band's first engagement after the fire two new swing originals titled "We're All Burnt Up" and "Are We Hurt." It's significant to note that Ellington as well as Benny Carter, then, as now, one of the world's most respected arrangers, upon hearing of Barnet's plight, shipped him batches of new scores.

Two years later, also out on the West Coast, the Barnet band was again hit when Bus Etri, its brilliant guitarist, and trumpeter Lloyd Hundling were killed in a car crash.

Although Charlie was doing fairly well in the mid-thirties, playing the 1936 summer season at the Glen Island Casino, where he introduced a new vocal group out of Buffalo, the Modernaires, and spotting such black jazz stars as John Kirby and Frankie Newton in 1937, it wasn't until 1939 that his band really caught fire—figuratively this time. This was the year in which it recorded the wild, romping version of Ray Noble's tune "Cherokee," which soon became the band's theme song. (Before then the group had used a lovely ballad, which probably everyone has since forgotten, called "I Lost Another Sweetheart.") It was also the year in which Billy May joined the band as trumpeter and, perhaps more importantly, as arranger. The cherubic, humorous, wildly imaginative May and a more staid but equally effective writer named Skip Martin began to build a book for the Barnet band that gave it a recognizable style that it theretofore had never been able to achieve.

The band was really cooking. It made a slew of great sides for Bluebird, including "The Count's Idea," "The Duke's Idea," "The Right Idea," and "The Wrong Idea." The last, a takeoff on the day's mickey-mouse bands, was subtitled "Swing and Sweat with Charlie Barnet." Then there were "Pompton Turnpike," "Wings over Manhattan," "Southern Fried" and "Redskin Rumba," which was a follow-up to "Cherokee" and bore an expedient resemblance to it, since the latter was an ASCAP tune, and ASCAP tunes, because of the Society's war with the radio networks, were not permitted to be played on the air.

Many of the sides featured vocals by Mary Ann McCall, a good, jazz-tinged singer. Then early in 1941 Barnet took on a new vocalist, one who had made some sides with Noble Sissle's band. Her name: Lena Horne. She recorded four tunes with the band, the most notable of which was "Good for Nothin' Joe." Bob Carroll, the robust baritone who sang with Barnet at the time, recalls the day Lena joined the band. "We were working at the Windsor Theater in the Bronx, and something had happened to the girl we were using. Somebody remembered this pretty girl who was working in a movie house, and they sent for her. It was Lena. I remember she had long, straggly hair, and her dress wasn't especially attractive. She ran down a few tunes in the basement of the theater, and then, without any arrangements, she did the next show—not only did it but stopped it cold. She was just great!"

Charlie had a knack for finding fresh talent. By the following year he had assembled a slew of outstanding young musicians: trumpeters Neal Hefti,

Peanuts Holland and Al Killian, clarinetist Buddy DeFranco and pianist Dodo Marmarosa, plus a new singer, Frances Wayne, who, like Hefti, was to become an important part of Woody Herman's most famous Herd several years later.

Other stars followed: singers Kay Starr, Fran Warren, Dave Lambert and Buddy Stewart, pianist-arranger Ralph Burns, trombonist Trummy Young, guitarist Barney Kessel, bassist Oscar Pettiford, and some years later trumpeters Clark Terry, Jimmy Nottingham and Doc Severinsen.

If you talk to almost any of these people, you'll find that they have pretty much the same remembrances about their Charlie Barnet days. "It was a ball," they'll say. "Charlie was a terrific leader to work for. He had great musical and personal integrity, and even though things got kind of wild sometimes and maybe even out of hand, it was a rewarding experience. Most of all you could say that things never got dull—never."

Eventually, Barnet gave up his big band. He settled down on the West Coast, headquartering in Palm Springs, and for years he led a sextet or septet, always finding enough work to keep him occupied. In the mid-sixties he headed a romping big band, organized especially for an exciting two-week stint at New York's Basin Street East. Financially he has never had any real worries. He has been able to do pretty much what he has wanted to do. He has owned his own homes and flown his own planes. And he has had at least ten wives and, one suspects, many attendant alimony payments.

Charlie Barnet, now in his sixties, has mellowed. But that great charm and vitality are still there. And so is his undying love of pulsating big band sounds that communicate with large audiences. "I still like to hear the beat," he said recently. "I don't like it when it's too abstract. To me, jazz should be exciting. Remember, there's a difference between 'exciting' and 'startling,' which is what some of the younger kids don't realize."

Charlie Barnet was one of the "younger kids" for a long time.

Count Basie

HE HAS that faraway look, yet he always knows where he's at, what's going on and what to do about it. For Count Basie, leader of one of the most consistently swinging bands in history, very definitely has both feet firmly planted on the ground—except when one of them happens to be tapping lightly in time, which is whenever his ever-swinging band is playing.

For almost half a century and without radically changing its style, Basie's has remained one of the greatest, most admired of all big bands. The style? Large, robust and always swinging ensemble sounds, interspersed with numerous fine solos and, of course, the light, infectious piano tinkling of its leader.

The Count

Basie's band has also managed to sound surprisingly fresh through the years. Perhaps that's because it has maintained an exceptionally good *esprit de corps.* One reason: the musicians have always been given the opportunity to play the kind of music they enjoy playing. For the Basie style, because of its simplicity and directness, has been able to reach a large segment of the public and, unlike other bands that have tried more complicated routines, has seldom been called upon to play down in order to communicate with its listeners.

Basie has been a good leader. He has chosen his musicians carefully, for their emotional maturity as well as for their musical ability, and he has treated them with respect and dignity. He is a warm, gentle man, full of humor. On the surface he appears to be exceptionally easygoing, and he is just that when there is no crisis. But when called upon to face up to a difficult situation, of which there have been several in his band's history, the Count has come through with great firmness and determination in following the path that he feels is musically and morally right.

His musicians have been given a great deal of leeway. But should any of them step too far out of bounds, Basie yanks them back firmly, making it obvious to one and all who's boss. Sometimes, if a musician strays too far out, the Count will just let him go entirely. This happened in 1940 to Lester Young, Basie's most famous tenor saxist, whom the Count fired on the spot for missing an important recording date, the last of several infractions. Some years later he dismissed another top sideman who constantly kept challenging his leader's authority.

The first time I heard the Basie band, it didn't sound particularly well disciplined. It was in December of 1936 during a broadcast from Chicago to which the band had migrated from Kansas City, where it had been playing in a spot called the Reno Club and where it had been discovered by John Hammond, the wealthy jazz enthusiast, who had already done so much to further the career of Benny Goodman. "I heard the band one night when I was in Chicago with Benny," John recalls. "I happened to tune in to an experimental radio station at the very top of the dial, just beyond the last station on the regular AM wavelength." The band—it was just a nine-piece band then—thrilled Hammond, and he immediately told his friend, Goodman, about it.

MCA's Willard Alexander, who was then booking Goodman, reports that shortly thereafter he received a phone call from Benny. "He told me about the band, only he kept calling it Count *Bassie,* and he kept urging me to get to Kansas City to hear it. John, of course, had been the instigator, and so he and I flew out there.

"We arrived late in the evening and went directly to the Reno Club. The band was just great—rough in spots, but terribly exciting. John introduced me to Basie, and I signed him up that night. Bands used to play all night long in those clubs out there, so after a while John suggested we go to hear Andy Kirk at another club. He was great too, and I wanted to sign him as

The Basie band of 1940 at Harlem's Apollo Theater
Front: *The Count, saxists Buddy Tate, Tab Smith, Jack Washington, Lester Young*
Back: *bassist Walter Page, drummer Jo Jones, guitarist Freddie Green,*
trumpeter Buck Clayton, trombonists Vic Dickenson (hiding Ed Lewis),
Dickie Wells, trumpeters Al Killian, Harry Edison, trombonist Dan Minor

well, but Andy said he was sorry, we were a little late; he had just signed with Joe Glaser.

"The next day at the airport, we ran into Glaser. I didn't know him, and he didn't know me, but he knew John, and after telling John that he had signed Kirk, he added that he had missed out on Basie because some ———— named Alexander had signed him first. And so John said, 'Joe, meet Willard Alexander.' "

Both the Kirk and the Basie band were subjects of a column I wrote in the January, 1937, *Metronome*. About Andy's band I said several complimentary things. But Basie's, which I'd heard on several broadcasts, impressed me less. "Basie, who'll be in a New York ballroom by the time this gets into print," I noted, "hasn't been nearly as impressive. True, the band does swing, but that sax section is so invariably out of tune. And if you think that sax section is out of tune, catch the brass! And if you think the brass by itself is out of tune, catch the intonation of the band as a whole!! Swing is swing, but music is music. Here's hoping the outfit sounds better in person."

Many years later both Basie himself and Buck Clayton, who played trumpet in that edition of the Basie band, threw that quote about the intonation back at me—word for word. "And you know what?" they added. "You were absolutely right. We did play terribly out of tune."

Poor intonation was somewhat prevalent among black bands in those days, however, and the reasons for it were more obvious than most people realized. As numerous members of those bands have since pointed out to me, many black musicians, unable to afford topflight instruments, were forced to blow substantially inferior horns. Many of these, no matter how good the player might be and how hard he might try, could not be blown consistently in tune simply because the notes themselves just weren't in tune with one another.

There was another reason, also basically economical, for poor intonation: few black musicians could afford the luxury of prolonged instruction. What's more, because of social limitations, few were able to study with any of the highly trained and experienced teachers—graduates of top music schools or top studio musicians. Instead, they learned from those who may have been quite competent in what they did teach but who hadn't had the breadth of experience or the concentrated tutelage that had been made available to white instructors and musicians.

When the Basie band did appear at Roseland Ballroom in New York the following month for its big eastern debut, it wasn't much more impressive. Basie had rehearsed his men carefully for the opening, and my review in the following issue noted "a vast improvement in the band." However, it still played ballads out of tune. But it did jump wonderfully on "some smartly written faster numbers . . . brilliantly conceived stuff . . . figures that not only swing in their own right, but which also fit into some cleverly worked out swing patterns."

It should be noted that this was by no means the all-star outfit that many people think played that first Roseland date. Clayton and Young and tenor saxist Hershal Evans and drummer Jo Jones and Walter Page were there, but there were also several soon-to-be-forgotten musicians, sidemen like Joe Keyes, Claude Williams, Cauche Roberts and George Hunt and no sign yet of some of the stars that were soon to strengthen the band.

One of those stars was one of the brightest ever to work with Basie. This was the legendary Billie Holiday, who joined the band shortly after the Roseland engagement but who, according to Basie, "never worked any important location with us except the Savoy Ballroom. She was our first girl vocalist and she was beautiful to work with. I used to be just as thrilled to hear her as the audience was."

Billie never had a chance to record with the band (she can be heard on two sides taken from a radio broadcast from the Savoy and included in a Columbia album) because she was under contract to Brunswick while Basie was tied to Decca. "I'd given Count some of Billie's records to listen to," recalls John Hammond, who was both Basie's and Billie's most ardent and effective supporter, "but it wasn't until I almost twisted his arm and took him to Munro's up in Harlem to hear her in person that he decided to hire her." Billie fitted in wonderfully with the band, whose members appreciated her impeccable musicianship and with several of whom, notably Freddie Green and the late Lester Young, she struck up especially rewarding relationships.

Following the Roseland engagement, Basie played the Paramount. "The band wasn't ready yet," reports Alexander, who kept trying valiantly, despite

Billie Holiday

opposition from top MCA executives, to keep the band going. "It wasn't until it opened sometime later at the Famous Door that New Yorkers began to hear how great the band really was."

Until the Basie booking, the Famous Door, a small club—approximately twenty to twenty-five feet wide and maybe fifty to sixty feet deep—had played only small jazz combos. But Alexander figured that such an intimate setting might be just the right spot for Basie. His argument about how great the band was didn't carry much weight with the owners. But when Willard pointed out that the place could do much better business if it had an air-conditioning unit and offered to lend the club twenty-five hundred dollars to install one, the deal was made. "Basie got only about thirteen hundred dollars a week —maybe even less. But we had a bunch of radio network shots. And that's when the whole fire started."

The personnel of the band had changed appreciably by then. Some of the deadwood had been replaced by such Basie stalwarts as guitarist Freddie Green, who was to stay with the band for at least forty years more and was to become one of its bulwarks; trumpeters Harry Edison and Ed Lewis;

Mr. Five By Five: Jimmy Rushing

trombonists Benny Morton and Eddie Durham, soon to be replaced by Dickie Wells; lead saxist Earle Warren; and Jimmy Rushing, Basie's great blues shouter. Billie Holiday had left to join Artie Shaw, who had offered her more money, and Helen Humes, whom John Hammond had arranged to "audition" for Basie by getting her into an amateur contest at the Apollo, where the Count was playing, took over. Helen was really no amateur; she had been working with Vernon Andrade's band, along with her husband, tenor saxist Al Sears, but John wanted Basie to "discover" her. "It almost didn't work," he relates, "because some girl who was imitating Ella Fitzgerald won the contest. But Helen still impressed Basie enough to get the job."

The band sounded ever so much better. Musicians flocked to the Door to hear it. And the band began to record a batch of great sides for Decca— "Sent for You Yesterday," "Jumpin' at the Woodside," "Every Tub," "John's Idea" (dedicated to Hammond) and "One O'Clock Jump," the band's famous theme song.

Helen supplied some wonderful vocals, not as stylized as Billie's, but full of good jazz feeling just the same. In a later vocal change, Jimmy Rushing, the original "Mr. Five By Five," was replaced by a warm-hearted, big-voiced blues singer, Joe Williams. Basie also had a famous basso as his vocalist for a few hours with whom, in October, 1941, he recorded a two-sided opus, though hardly an epic, called "Big Joe." The vocalist: Paul Robeson.

The caliber of musicians kept improving. Brilliant, exciting trumpeters like

Emmet Berry, Al Killian, Joe Newman, Snooky Young, Clark Terry and Thad Jones, eventually filled that famous top row in the Basie band. But even more impressive was the succession of stars who sat down front in the tenor-sax chairs.

In its early days the band invariably highlighted the brilliant but completely divergent tenor saxes of Lester Young and Hershal Evans. Young proved to be one of the most important style setters of modern jazz. Harmonically he was far ahead of his time, and his tone, too, was equally startling—light, airy, liquid, more like that of an alto than a tenor sax. On the other hand, Evans blew a much mellower, more emotional horn (his recording of "Blue and Sentimental" remains a classic), one of the "moodiest" saxes of all time. Herschel, for me one of the truly great tenor saxists of all time, died after a heart attack early in 1939, before he'd had an opportunity to garner all the acclaim due him. Young, after having been fired, returned for a short time several years later and then became a star of the traveling Jazz at the Philharmonic group. His influence on other tenor saxists became tremendous; many later stars, like Stan Getz and Zoots Sims, patterned their playing directly on that of the hard-living Young, who died in 1959 of various causes.

Other famous tenor men followed—Buddy Tate, Don Byas, Illinois Jacquet, Lucky Thompson, Frank Wess, Frank Foster, Eric Dixon and Eddie (Lockjaw) Davis. Basie once told me, "The band has always been built from the rhythm section to the tenors and then to the rest of the band." Interestingly, that's the way its most famous of all numbers, "One O'Clock Jump," is routined. It starts with just the rhythm section, then goes into a tenor-sax chorus or two, and eventually leads into the entire band.

Of course, as the Count pointed out, his rhythm section has always been extremely important. His light yet invariably swinging piano has set its style, and what is generally refered to as "the Original Basie Rhythm Section" still serves as a model for many quartets today. It consisted of Basie at the piano, the wonderously light yet propulsive guitar of Freddie Green, the pungent bass of the late Walter Page, and the highly sensitive, ever-swinging drums of Jo Jones. Actually, after Jones left the band, the rhythm section never sounded quite the same. In later years it may have grown more assertive, but Jones gave it a subtlety that it has never known since.

The importance of the drummer has been stressed by Basie. "You may think you're the boss," he once said, "but that drummer is *really* the head man. When he's not feeling right, nothing is going to sound good."

Drummers certainly can inspire bands to do things they never did before. This actually happened with the Basie band one time when it was playing at the Palladium in Hollywood. Jones had been taken ill, so Basie asked Buddy Rich to fill in for the evening. Buddy, when he feels like playing, is undoubtedly the most inspiring drummer in the world, and as any musician would, he was thrilled at the opportunity of working with the Basie band. According to those who were there that night, the men performed brilliantly.

As the Count reported some time later, "We asked Buddy to play again the next night. And you know what happened? The entire band showed up *early* for work. Now, you know that was just about unheard of in that band!"

Even though Basie credits the drummer with being "head man," don't let him fool you. Basie is strictly in charge at all times. This may not be obvious to those on the outside, though if they watch the band long enough, they'll realize that all the directions come from little, subtle motions from the Count at the piano. He may shrug his shoulders in a certain way to give a specific warning to the drummer. He may cock his head at a special angle to

Three-fourths of a great rhythm section: drummer Jones, bassist Page, pianist Basie

tell the entire band to come way down in volume. Or he may hit just one key note to cue the ensemble into a rousing, roaring finale.

Blasting ensembles taking over from a light piano solo; big brass explosions behind a moving, murmuring sax solo; a bit of light piano tinkling after a brilliant brass barrage—these dynamic devices have always been part of the excitement that the Basie band has brewed. As the Count once told me, "I want those solid ensembles, and I want that brick wall behind the solos. There's nothing like those shout licks. But they gotta be able to play those shout things softly too!"

Just that ability—to play softly and still swing—perhaps figured prominently in one of the band's most important successes. In 1943 it was signed to play at the famous Blue Room of the Hotel Lincoln—the first black band to perform there—and did so well that it was re-signed a few months later with an increase in salary.

And yet an ability to swing softly was only part of the reason. What attracted customers—and continued to attract them throughout the band's career—was its ability to play big band jazz that almost anybody could understand. For the Basie band's appeal remained basically emotional and surprisingly simple. The beat was always there, sometimes subtley submerged, yet forever insinuating itself into everything the band was playing, both charming and stimulating audiences throughout the world.

For throughout the years, Basie's band, unlike other big bands that helped to develop jazz as a whole, seldom played above the heads of the average listener. Its rhythmic and melodic approaches always projected a certain contagious quality. And the Count remained a master of working to an audience, knowing just how far to go in tempo, in volume and in harmonic complexity. Few leaders in history ever walked the tight-rope between commercial appeal and musical integrity as daintily and yet as assuredly as Count Basie.

Except for a short time in the early 1960s when economic pressures made Basie reduce his band to a sextet, the instrumentation remained the same and with a lower turnover of personnel than that of any other band. During the late 1970s and early 1980s, a series of illnesses deprived the band of its leader, though it still carried on with arranger Nat Pierce at the piano. Early in 1981, Basie was hospitalized again, but his spirit never ebbed. Unable to walk well after rejoining his band, he bought himself an automated wheel chair, much like a golf cart, in which he would gleefully drive right onto a stage, even in such an imposing edifice as Carnegie Hall, sliding gracefully from cart to piano stool, from which he continued to steer his band on its ever-swinging course.

Bunny Berigan

"I CAN'T GET STARTED" was Bunny Berigan's theme song. It was also a pretty apt description of his career as a bandleader.

Bunny could have and should have succeeded handsomely in front of his own band. He was a dynamic trumpeter who had already established himself publicly with Benny Goodman and Tommy Dorsey via brilliant trumpet choruses that many of the swing fans must have known by heart—like those for Benny on "King Porter Stomp," "Jingle Bells" and "Blue Skies" and for Tommy on "Marie" and "Song of India." So great were Berigan's fame and popularity that he won the 1936 *Metronome* poll for jazz trumpeters with five times as many votes as his nearest competitor!

It wasn't just the fans who appreciated him, either. His fellow musicians did too. One of them—I think it was either Glenn Miller or Tommy Dorsey—once told me that few people realized how great a trumpeter Bunny was, because when he played his high notes he made them sound so full that hardly anyone realized how high he actually was blowing! Red McKenzie, referring to the notes that Bunny did and didn't make, once said, "If that man wasn't such a gambler, *everybody* would say he was the greatest that ever blew. But the man's got such nerve and likes his horn so much that he'll go ahead and try stuff that nobody else'd ever think of trying."

All of these men, Miller, Dorsey, McKenzie, plus many others, including Hal Kemp, featured Bunny on their recordings. How come Kemp? Because his was the first big name band Bunny ever played with. Hal had heard him when he was traveling through Wisconsin in 1928, was attracted by his style, but, according to his arranger-pianist, John Scott Trotter, "didn't hire him because Bunny had the tinniest, most awful, ear-splitting tone you ever heard." Berigan broadened his sound considerably (it eventually became one of the "fattest" of all jazz trumpet tones), came to New York, joined Frank Cornwall's band, was rediscovered by Kemp ("Bunny had discovered Louis Armstrong by then," Trotter points out), joined the band, then went off into the radio and recording studios (he cut some great sides with the Dorsey Brothers Orchestra) and was at CBS doing numerous shows, including one of his own, which featured Bunny's Blue Boys, when Goodman talked him into joining his band. He stayed six months, returned to the studios and then joined Dorsey for a few weeks—long enough to make several brilliant records.

Even while he was with Tommy's band, Bunny began organizing his own, with a great deal of help from Dorsey and his associates. First he assembled an eleven-piece outfit, which recorded several sides for Brunswick and which really wasn't very good, and then in the spring of 1937 he debuted with a larger group at the Pennsylvania Roof in New York.

The band showed a great deal of promise, and it continued to show a great deal of promise for the close to three years of its existence. It never fulfilled that promise, and the reason was pretty obvious: Bunny Berigan was just not cut out to be a bandleader.

As a sideman, as a featured trumpeter, as a friend, as a drinking companion, he was terrific. The guys in his band loved him, and for good reason. He was kind and considerate. Unlike Goodman, Dorsey and Miller, he was not a disciplinarian—neither toward his men nor, unfortunately, toward himself. Playing for Bunny Berigan was fun. And it was exciting too—like the night a hurricane blew the roof off Boston's Ritz-Carlton Hotel, where the band had just begun to establish itself, or the time it showed up for a Sunday-night date in Bristol, Connecticut, only to find Gene Krupa's band already

Bunny

on the stand (Berigan had gotten his towns slightly mixed—he was supposed to have been in Bridgeport, Connecticut, that night.)

The band projected its share of musical kicks too. On that opening Pennsylvania Roof engagement, it unveiled a new tenor sax find from Toronto, Georgie Auld, who perhaps didn't blend too well with the other saxes but who delivered an exciting, booting solo style. It had a good arranger and pianist in Joe Lipman and several other impressive soloists, including a girl singer, Ruth Bradley, who was also a clarinet player.

Berigan was good at discovering musicians. Ray Conniff started with him, and so did two brilliant New York lads, a swinging pianist named Joe Bushkin and a rehabilitated tap-dancer-turned-drummer named Buddy Rich.

The band recorded a batch of sides for Victor; some were good, some were pretty awful. Naturally his "I Can't Get Started" was his most important. (He had recorded the number earlier with a pickup band for Vocalion, and to many musicians this was a more inspired version.) Also impressive were "Mahogony Hall Stomp," "Frankie and Johnny," "The Prisoner's Song," "Russian Lullaby," several Bix Beiderbecke numbers and a few pop tunes, especially if Kitty Lane happened to be the singer. He featured other girl singers, such as Ruth Gaylor, Gail Reese and Jayne Dover, and sang occasionally himself, but not very well.

As Berigan's self-discipline grew even more lax, his band became less successful. By late 1939 it was obvious that as a leader, Bunny was not going anywhere. Early in 1940 he gave up.

Almost immediately his friend Tommy Dorsey offered him a job. Bunny accepted and sparked the Dorsey band to brilliant heights, blowing great solos and infusing new life into a band that had begun to falter. (For a sample of how Bunny was playing then, try Tommy's record of "I'm Nobody's Baby.")

Bunny's stay lasted only six months, however. There was marked disagreement about why he suddenly left the band on August 20, 1940, after a radio broadcast at the NBC studios. Dorsey said, "I just couldn't bring him around, so I had to let him go. I hated to do it." Berigan, on the other hand, complained about not "enough chance to play. Most of the time I was just sitting there waiting for choruses, or else I was just a stooge, leading the band, while Tommy sat at somebody else's table."

So he reorganized and for a while the new band, composed entirely of unknown musicians, showed promise, according to writer Amy Lee, who reviewed a May, 1941, air shot from Palisades Park in New Jersey: "That fifteen minutes was enough to tell the listener that Bunny is playing more magnificently than ever, that he has a band with a beat which fairly lifts dancers or listeners right off their seat or feet . . . his range, his conception, his lip, and his soul are without compare, and to hear him again is the kick of all listening kicks."

But again Bunny couldn't get started quite enough to last. The combination of too many one-nighters and unhealthy living began to catch up with him again. The last time I heard the band was in a Connecticut ballroom during the summer of 1941, and for one who admired Bunny's playing so tremendously and who liked him so much personally, it was quite a shattering experience. I reported in *Metronome*:

> The band was nothing. And compared with Berigan standards, Bunny's blowing was just pitiful. He sounded like a man trying to imitate himself, a man with none of the inspiration and none of the technique of the real Berigan.
>
> He looked awful, too. He must have lost at least thirty pounds. His clothes were loose-fitting; even his collar looked as if it were a couple of sizes too large for him.
>
> Apparently, though, he was in good spirits. He joked with friends and talked about the great future he thought his band had. But you had a feeling it would never be. And when, after intermission, Bunny left the bandstand, not to return for a long time, and some trumpeter you'd never heard of before came down to front the band, play Bunny's parts, and spark the outfit more than its leader had, you realized this was enough, and you left the place at once, feeling simply awful.

Shortly thereafter he gave up the band, and Peewee Erwin, who had replaced him in both Goodman's and Dorsey's outfit, took it over. Berigan declared bankruptcy. He was obviously quite ill, but he carried on doggedly, fronting yet another band. He broke down several times. He was hospitalized in Pennsylvania with a severe case of pneumonia. More than anything and almost anyone else, Bunny needed a rest and help. But probably out of sheer loyalty to his men, and faced with the responsibilities of supporting a wife and two young children, he refused to give up.

On June 1, 1942, he was scheduled to play a job at Manhattan Center in New York. The band showed up. Bunny didn't. He was seriously ill in Polyclinic Hospital with cirrhosis of the liver. Benny Goodman, playing at the Paramount Theater, brought over his sextet and filled in as a gesture of friendship toward his first star trumpeter.

On June 2, 1942, Bunny Berigan died, a financially and physically broken man. Like another wonderful trumpeter with the same initials, Bix Beiderbecke, whose horn had also been stilled a decade earlier by too much booze, Bunny lived much too short a life. He was only thirty-three when he died. And yet during that brief span, he grew to be a giant on the jazz scene—perhaps not as a big bandleader but certainly as one of the best-liked musician-leaders of his day and one of the most inspiring jazz soloists of all time.

Will Bradley

THE Will Bradley Band was a great band while it lasted, but it didn't last long because (1) it could never quite decide what it really wanted to be, and (2) by the time it did decide, it was too late.

Even though it never admitted it in lights, the Will Bradley Band had in effect two leaders, Will Bradley and Ray McKinley. They were good friends, they respected one another, each was a top musician in his own right. Each was also stolid and stubborn, with very definite ideas of what was best in music and what was best for him and for this particular band. Unfortunately, their ideas were too often too divergent.

Bradley, a very successful studio trombonist, had been working on some

Will

plans with intellectual, classical overtones when Williard Alexander, who had already launched the swing bands of Benny Goodman and Count Basie, approached him with the idea of starting his own outfit that would feature a down-to-earth, high-swinging drummer, Ray McKinley. Ray was no stranger to Will, for they had played together several years before in a group called Milt Shaw's Detroiters. And he liked his playing. The only trouble was that McKinley was firmly ensconced in Jimmy Dorsey's band. But Alexander, who had his pulse on the day's music and its musicians, had a pretty good idea McKinley was ready to spring.

"Ray was playing with Jimmy in New Jersey at the Meadowbrook," Will recalls, "so Willard and I met him in a cocktail lounge in Newark. All three of us were sitting there and everything was going along fine, when I'll be damned if Jimmy didn't just happen to walk into the same place. Things were a little tense, because I'm sure he knew what was going on, but Jimmy just smiled and said, 'Go ahead. I don't mind. I know what you're talking about.'"

However, McKinley states today that even though Dorsey may not have admitted it, he did care. "After I'd handed in my notice, Jimmy kept asking me to stay on. He kept saying he couldn't find anyone to replace me. After a while I got impatient, and so I figured I might as well look for a drummer myself. So I went for the best available one, Davey Tough, and asked him if he'd come out to Meadowbrook and take over for me. Davey said, 'Sure,' and he came right out, and that's how I finally got to leave."

The band got started late in 1939, ostensibly a partnership but with Will leading. Both men offered explanations for the setup. Will noted the need for someone in front of the band to direct, to lead effectively because of the increasing emphasis on dynamics, citing Glenn Miller as an example, and because of the "size and rapid turnover of the band's music libraries."

McKinley said, "A drummer isn't a natural leader for a band. For instance, as a leader, I'd have to do three things—lead the band, play and sing. It's too much. Another thing—drummer-leaders are apt to be poison to hotel managers. Say 'drummer' and they hear tom-toms."

So Bradley, handsome and urbane, with an almost continual expression of a guy who thought he'd said something bright but wasn't quite certain he'd got his point across, fronted the band. I reviewed it during one of its first steady engagements, at New York's Famous Door, and acclaimed it "one of the most musically thrilling units in all dancebandom . . . certainly the most polished and most exciting band yet produced in 1940." McKinley, then my favorite drummer because of his imagination, taste, humor and propulsive beat, came in for his share of raves. So did pianist Freddie Slack, who had followed Ray from Dorsey's band, a young tenor saxist from Syracuse named Mike (Peanuts) Hucko (today a great jazz clarinetist, he was reportedly fired from Bradley's band because he was so weak on that horn), singer Carlotta Dale and, of course, Will's trombone.

The band swung, all right, but its ballads, built around its leader's horn, were less impressive. Bradley played exquisitely, as always, but the band's "major defect," the review noted, "is its inability to create a really mellow mood when playing popular ballads. Musically, like most large radio orchestras, it plays them just about flawlessly. But radio groups are liable to be a bit frigid, and so is Bradley's." What's more, the tempos, like those of the radio's studio bands, were too often too fast to establish any sort of romantic rapport.

Radio tempos could well have become ingrained with Bradley, because, except for a short stay with Ray Noble's band, he had spent many of his previous years in the studios—with leaders such as Jacques Renard, Victor Young, Nat Shilkret, Raymond Paige and Andre Kostelanetz and singers such as Kate Smith, Eddie Cantor and Al Jolson.

The reason Bradley had worked with many stars was simple: he was very good. Yet those of us outside the studios hadn't heard much about him. I recall that in 1935, during one of my first talks with Glenn Miller, the subject of trombone players came up and I told Glenn that my favorite was Jack Jenney, whose playing I had recently discovered. Glenn agreed he was good. "But the best of them all," he stated emphatically, "is Wilbur." He meant, of course, Wilbur Schwichtenberg, his fellow trombonist in Ray Noble's band. Several years later, realizing full well that there probably weren't enough marquees that could hold a name as long as Wilbur Schwichtenberg, let alone enough people who could remember how to spell it, Wilbur changed his name to Will Bradley. But Miller never changed in his admiration for Bradley. One night in the early forties, after he and Will and Tommy Dorsey had performed as a trio at a benefit, playing Don Redman's famous trombone chorus of "I Got Rhythm," Glenn confided to me that "we'd never have gotten through that thing if it hadn't been for Will. He really held us together."

For the first eight or nine months of its existence, the band had no set style. It played many musical arrangements by Leonard Whitney, who wrote most of its early book, Slack, Hugo Winterhalter and Al Datz. It recorded numerous pretty ballads for Columbia, such as "This Changing World," "Watching the Clock" and "I Don't Stand a Ghost of a Chance," which featured Miss Dale. There were also some rompers, such as "You're Lucky to Me," "As Long As I Live," "What Can I Say After I Say I'm Sorry?" plus other swingers with vocals by McKinley: "Old Doc Yak," "I Get a Kick Outa Corn" and, with Carlotta, the humorous "It's a Wonderful World."

Other good singers eventually joined the band—Louise Tobin, then Harry James's pretty wife, who had sung with Goodman and Bobby Hackett and who cut a version of "Deed I Do" that's still talked about; a bright, vivacious blonde named Phyllis Miles (her real first name was Dyllis, but nobody would have believed that any more than they would Schwichtenberg!); and a sultry brunette named Lynn Gardner. There were also some boy singers—Larry Southern; Terry Allen, an impressive baritone who sang with several bands and made several outstanding sides such as "Don't Let Julia Fool Ya" and

"Get Thee Behind Me, Satan"; and a discovery out of Texas, Jimmy Valentine, whom McKinley had first heard when the Dorsey band played a date down there and who had made a tremendous impression on everyone, including Dorsey's own famed vocalist Bob Eberly. "I'll never forget it," Eberly said later. "We were playing in Austin and I thought I was doing pretty well for myself. Then, along about the middle of the dance, some of 'em started calling for Jimmy Valentine. So this quiet fellow comes up to the bandstand and sings 'Stardust.' Well, I was just a has-been after that—the girls wouldn't even look at me—it was all Jimmy Valentine!"

Bradley recalls Valentine, whose tenor style never really captured the general public, as "a very bashful, very shy guy. I remember when we were playing the Paramount. It was his first time on a New York stage, and when he had finished his chorus, he just bolted into the wings. Unfortunately, somebody had left a baton lying at the head of the staircase going off the stage, and poor Jimmy fell right down all the steps."

Valentine might have been featured more with the band if it hadn't uncovered a gimmick that changed its style drastically and shifted the emphasis far away from ballads and directly into an old-fashioned jazz style—boogie-woogie.

McKinley, around whom the stylistic change revolved, says it all began when he and Slack, who played that style so well, and arranger Whitney began wondering out loud among themselves how a big band would sound playing the boogie-woogie jazz that Meade Lux Lewis and the team of Albert Ammons and Pete Johnson were then making so popular. So they experimented with a couple of instrumentals based on the blues with an eight-to-the-bar boogie beat. "We were playing one of them one night at the Famous Door, and two songwriters, Don Raye and Hughie Prince, were there. There was one part where I had a drum break, and for some reason or other that night, instead of playing the break, I sang out, 'Oh, Beat Me, Daddy, Eight to the Bar!' After the set, Hughie called me over to the table and asked if they could write a song using that break. I told him to go ahead, and they offered to cut me in on the tune. That was fine with me—only, they were signed with Leeds Music and I was with Robbins. So I had them put the name of my wife, Elinor Sheehy [Ray's first wife], on the song instead of mine.

"There's something I'd like to set straight about that song," McKinley went on, "and that's the line I wrote about 'In a little honky-tonky village in Texas, there's a guy who plays the best piano by fa '[*] A lot of people seemed to think I was referring to Peck Kelley [the legendary pianist], and some years later Peck even thanked me for it. But, you know, I didn't have anybody— Peck or anybody else—in mind, just an imaginary pianist in an imaginary town."

"Beat Me, Daddy, Eight to the Bar" turned out to be the band's biggest

* "Beat Me, Daddy, Eight to the Bar," by Don Raye, Elinor Sheehy and Hughie Prince. © 1940 by MCA Music, a division of MCA Inc., New York, N. Y. Used by permission. All rights reserved.

hit. "A month after the record came out, we got a wire from Ted Wallerstein, the president of Columbia Records, congratulating us for having sold over one hundred thousand copies. That's like a million seller today."

From then on came a batch of boogie-woogie sides, each trying to top "B.M.D.8.T.T.B." There were "Rock-a-Bye Boogie," "Down the Road a Piece" (done by just a trio of piano, bass and drums), "Scrub Me, Mama, with a Boogie Beat," "Bounce Me, Brother, with a Solid Four," "Fry Me, Cookie, with a Can of Lard" and many more. Early in 1941, Slack left to start his own band, and a young Worcester, Massachusetts, pianist named Bob Holt moved in for a while, to be replaced by Billy Maxted, another eight-to-the-bar expert.

Double-threat McKinley

Other new and often better musicians arrived. Trumpeter Joe Weidman and clarinetist Jo-Jo Huffman, whom McKinley had discovered out west when he took a honeymoon trip after leaving Dorsey, departed, and Lee Castle (then Castaldo) and Mahlon Clark replaced them. Clark was the only member of the reed section who stayed on when Bradley, dissatisfied with the way the quintet sounded, fired all five of them, only to rehire Mahlon. The band had become a swinging success, but, according to Will, "hadn't planned to play that much jazz. Besides, I don't think some of those sax players knew what a sharp key was. I'd want to lift some of our arrangements up a halftone to get more brilliance, but then we'd be in keys they couldn't play in."

The wholesale changes improved the band musically. But what it didn't do was break the increasing tension between Bradley and McKinley. Ray wanted to continue to emphasize boogie-woogie, while Will yearned to play the sort of music that satisfied him more.

According to Ray, "Will was bitching a lot. He complained that his feet hurt him from standing up there in front of the band so much. The boogie-woogie style didn't suit him, and I can understand that. But I felt we should continue to feature it, especially after a guy as knowing as Glenn Miller remarked one night, 'You guys sure have got that market cornered!'

"But Will always had high musical standards. I remember one night, shortly before we split up, we heard Benny Goodman at the Palace Theater in Cleveland with a really great band, and he sounded awfully good compared with us."

According to Will, the break had similar causes. "Ray couldn't stand to play several ballads in a row, and I remember one night, at the Hotel Sherman in Chicago, it must have gotten to him, because right in the middle of a pretty trombone solo he went into one of those heavy press rolls on the snares. I jumped him for it afterwards, right in front of the whole band, and yelled, 'Don't you dare ever do that to me again.'"

That one occurrence didn't, of itself, bring about the split, but it was symptomatic of what had been going on. So, early in 1942, McKinley left, taking Clark and a young trumpeter named Pete Candoli with him. However, little personal animosity existed between the two ex-partners, as evidenced two months later when Will and his wife, celebrating their fifth wedding anniversary, attended the debut of Ray's band.

Bradley revamped the band completely, retaining only guitarist Steve Jordan and singers Terry Allen and Lynn Gardner. Among the young musicians he assembled were a New York drummer, Shelly Manne, and an unknown kid trumpeter from Massachusetts, Shorty Rogers.

But Bradley's new band didn't last long. Because of the expanding draft, musicians were becoming increasingly scarce. "We were playing in Detroit when they took six men from us all at one time—most of them trumpets. From there we had to go directly to Denver. Now, where could you find six men in Denver to replace the guys we'd lost? I had no idea, so I didn't even try. I just gave up the band."

For all intents and purposes, that was the end of the Will Bradley band. During the war, it recorded several good sides for Signature Records, but, as Will points out, "we used all studio men. It was never an organized band." It wasn't long before Bradley reestablished himself as a major trombonist in the studios, where he has remained ever since, appearing occasionally on camera on the "Tonight" show and living a very comfortable life. Essentially an artistic soul (he studied serious music for years and was the first person to make me aware of a then very far-out composer Alban Berg), he has broadened his activities and now, in addition to music, has become most adept at gem cutting and silversmithing.

More than many others, Will Bradley's band evokes gushes of nostalgic comments from big band fans. One of them, Tom Connell, sent a passionate plea to *Metronome* that was printed in the June, 1946, issue. Noting that Bradley was forced to heed the call of the kids for boogie-woogie, Connell wrote:

> So he played it for them, and played himself right out of the business. It is therefore my purpose to ask Will to give it one more try in the interests of modern American music. . . . The type of hot trombone he played in many of his Columbia waxings is as bright and as fresh today as it was the day he blew it. Listen to his passages on "Strange Cargo" [the band's theme], "In the Hall of the Mountain King," "When You and I Were Young, Maggie," "Celery Stalks at Midnight," "Basin Street Boogie," "Jimtown Blues" and many others, and you'll find a style of hot that is completely his own. He is as fluent as the early Teagarden, as graceful as Dorsey, even in the fastest of passages, and as imaginative as McGarity at his Goodman best. And without any clinkers! . . .
>
> So I say, give it one more try, Will. You won't find life as secure as you do now in your studio work. But there are a lot of fans who suffered with you and for you through your boogie-woogie days. . . . Pick up your golden sliphorn and we won't let you down again.

But Will never heeded the call.

Les Brown

LES BROWN refers to his band as "The Malted Milk Band." If you equate malted milks with leading a relaxed, youthful life, with liking and trusting people, with enjoying what you're doing, with retaining a certain amount of unabashed naiveté, then Les's description is quite accurate.

This band had fun. The guys always seemed to take pride in their music, and for good reason: it was always good music. Maybe it wasn't as startlingly creative as Ellington's or Goodman's or that of some other bands, but it was never music that the men would have any cause to be ashamed of. The arrangements (many of the early ones were written by Les himself) were topnotch, and throughout most of the band's history the playing of them was equally good.

Les's spirit and musicianship pervaded his band. Few leaders have ever been accorded such complete respect by their sidemen. Back in 1940 I wrote in *Metronome* what now, more than a generation later, still holds true:

> It's difficult to find a better liked and more respected leader in the entire dance band business than Les Brown. Of course, a healthy personality and an honest character don't make a great leader by themselves. But they help an awful lot when the guy can do other things such as make fine arrangements, rehearse and routine a band intelligently, treat men as they want to be treated, and then impress himself on the public by playing a good clarinet. . . . Talk to some of the fellows in his band. A number of them have had better offers, for there have been some lean Brown band days, but they've refused them. "This band's too fine and a guy can't be happier than when he's working for Les. He knows just what he wants, how to get it, and he treats you right." So explain men as they ruthlessly turn down a Miller or a Goodman or a Dorsey in rapid succession.

Though there always existed a warm, close relationship among the members of the band, a preoccupation with musical precision prevented an equally close rapport with their audiences. Thus, during its first three or four years, the band made a stronger impact on other musicians than it did on the public.

Organized at Duke University, the band, known as the Duke Blue Devils, left the college in the spring of 1936 as a complete unit. The men, almost all still undergraduates, spent the summer at Budd Lake, New Jersey, and then, with the exception of two men who returned to school in the fall, took to the road for a year. During the summer of 1937, they played at Playland Casino in Rye, New York. Les recalls that "the guys made twenty-five bucks a week, and I made all of thirty-five. I was pretty green in those days. I remember that the song pluggers used to come up to see me to talk business, but most of the time I'd go off between sets with the guys and play shuffleboard."

The band broke up right after Labor Day—the parents of most of the boys had decided that their sons should go back to college and get their degrees. So Les moved in with another arranger named Abe Osser, later better known as Glenn Osser, and supported himself by writing for Larry Clinton, Isham Jones, Ruby Newman and Don Bestor.

For the summer season of 1938, Les returned to Budd Lake, fronting a local band which had also served as a road band for Joe Haymes. There he finally noticed a very pretty girl who had hung around the bandstand during

Les and . . .

the band's engagement two years earlier—noticed her enough to marry her. Today Les and Claire (Cluny) Brown are one of the most popular and respected couples in West Coast musical circles, parents of two grown children, a daughter, Denny, mother of two boys, and Les, Jr., a businessman, who married Missi Murphy, daughter of actor and former Senator George Murphy.

Meanwhile back at Budd Lake. The romance had been good; the band had been only fair. Les wanted out before the end of the season so he could go with Larry Clinton as chief arranger. But the customers liked Les and his band, so the management wouldn't let him quit.

At that time, RCA Victor had a very shrewd A&R chief named Eli Oberstein, who saw great promise in Brown. (Les had switched from Decca to Victor's subsidiary Bluebird label.) Oberstein convinced Les he should organize a better band and arranged a booking in the Green Room of New York's Edison Hotel, for which Les received a hundred dollars a week—quite a salary for him in those days. The twelve-piece outfit wasn't an astounding success, but it satisfied the management and soon attracted booker Joe Glaser, who threw his support, financial as well as otherwise, behind the outfit. Thus

. . . *Doris*

began a warm relationship that was to last more than a quarter of a century.

Glaser was intensely devoted to the band. One summer, while *Metronome* was running its annual dance-band popularity poll, I received a telephone call from him. He wanted to buy 250 copies of the magazine. When I asked him why, he said he needed them for his friends, so they could use the ballot to vote for Les. When I told him we couldn't sell them to him because we wanted the contest to reflect a true picture of our regular readers' tastes (with our circulation, 250 votes could have made a strong impact), he said nothing and hung up. Our attitude must have made quite an impression, however, because for a long time thereafter, Les subsequently told me, Glaser kept referring to me as "What's his name—the guy at *Metronome* who couldn't be bought."

When it was formed in late 1938, the band had twelve men. As its engagements grew (it played the Arcadia Ballroom in New York and also spent a good part of the summer of 1940 at the New York World's Fair Dancing Campus), its personnel also grew, in quality as well as in numbers. It featured a couple of excellent tenor saxists in Wolffe Tannenbaum and Stewie McKay; a brilliant lead saxist, Steve Madrick, who later became the chief audio engineer for NBC-TV's "Today" show; and, starting in the summer of 1940, a very attractive seventeen-year-old ex-dancer from Cincinnati named Doris Day.

Doris had been discovered by the Bob Crosby band, but something went wrong. One report had it that a member of the band had made some pretty serious passes at the very young lady, which frightened her so that she gave her notice. In any event, Les heard her at the Strand Theater, was immediately impressed, and, having heard the grapevine stories about her unhappiness, offered her a job in what was probably his most boyishly charming manner. She accepted and joined the band in New England in August of 1940, eventually to become one of its most important assets.

Twenty-five years later, Doris told me, "I was awfully lucky working with Les. The boys were so great. They softened things up for me when everything could have disillusioned and soured me."

Doris's stay with the band lasted less than a year. She recorded a few sides. Says Les, "I remember the first one was a thing called 'Beau Night in Hotchkiss Corners.' What was she like? Very easy to work with—never a problem."

How was she as a performer? I reviewed the band both at the Arcadia and at Glen Island Casino during the fall of 1940 and came away with this impression: "And there's Doris Day, who for combined looks and voice has no apparent equal: she's pretty and fresh-looking, handles herself with unusual grace, and what's most important of all, sings with much natural feeling and in tune."

However, the band's chief failing still remained evident: it lacked intimacy. "Only at times does it ever get really close to the dancers," continued the same review. More novelties and more spotlighting of soloists were suggested.

That winter the band went to Chicago for a two-week engagement at Mike Todd's Theater Café. It stayed for six months. But before it returned East, Doris had left. She'd fallen in love with a trombonist in Jimmy Dorsey's band, become Mrs. Al Jorden and retired—temporarily.

During the following summer, the band really found itself. It spent the entire season at Log Cabin Farms in Armonk, New York, where the guys had a ball. Most of the men lived in houses in the area, and during the day they played softball and tennis and went through quite a health-kick routine. The band took on a new, even younger girl singer (some reports stated she was only fourteen, though she didn't look it) named Betty Bonney and with her made its first hit record, a timely opus called "Joltin' Joe DiMaggio." Inasmuch as the band was made up preponderantly of avid Yankee fans (Joe Glaser had a season's box at Yankee Stadium that Les and his friends frequently occupied), the effort proved to be quite a labor of love.

The band's approach, which up till then had been good but always quite serious, began to reflect the personalities of its members, and the rapport between musicians and audiences that had been missing for all the previous years was finally established. They had a very personable, romantic singer named Ralph Young, and a brilliant clarinetist named Abe Most, each of whom had a wild sense of humor. One of their favorite gags involved Most's pretending to sing a pretty ballad. Abe happened to have a horrible voice, but Ralph would sneak a mike off behind the bandstand and supply the sounds while Abe would lip-sync. Then, of course, as Abe would reach the climax of his chorus, Ralph would sing ridiculous lyrics or stop singing altogether, while Abe continued mouthing to no avail.

But the band's big novelty hits were performed by a cherubic baritone saxist named Butch Stone. "I caught him first when he was with Larry Clinton's band at Loew's State Theater in New York," reports Les. "I remembered he did a thing called 'My Feet's Too Big,' and he broke me up. Right after that, Larry was commissioned an Air Force captain, and so I offered Butch a job, and he's been with me ever since."

Stone was just one of many replacements Les started to make—not all of his own volition—when the draft started gobbling up some of the best musicians around. "It got so you wouldn't hire a guy," Les reports, "unless you were sure he was 4-F."

But the band continued to sound better and better all the time. And it found the formula for reaching the dancers and holding them—not merely through novelties but via some lovely ballads, like "'Tis Autumn," which Les arranged, and a series of swinging versions of the classics, most of them scored by Ben Homer, including such items as "Bizet Has His Day," "March Slav" and "Mexican Hat Dance."

Obviously the band had found its commercial groove. In October of 1941, it started a one-month engagement at Chicago's Blackhawk Restaurant and stayed for almost five. It followed that with a series of lengthy dates at top

Les and fans

hotel rooms like the Café Rouge of the Hotel Pennsylvania, New York's prestige room, and the College Inn of Chicago's Hotel Sherman, the most coveted spot in that city. In 1942 it scored a big hit at the Palladium in Hollywood, made its first movie, *Seven Days Leave,* with Lucille Ball, Victor Mature and Carmen Miranda, then began a whole series of appearances on the Coca Cola-sponsored radio show that emanated from service camps throughout the country. "We'd just travel and blow, and blow and travel, and travel and blow some more," Les relates. "Tommy Dorsey was supposed to have done the most of those Coke shows, but I'm sure we were a close second —it must have been something like eighty-two for him to seventy-six for us."

For several years, Les had been calling Doris, who by then had become a mother. For him she had remained the ideal girl singer—the ice-cream-soda girl for the ice-cream-soda band—and he wanted her back. It was during the band's Coke travels that he called her one more time. "We were in Dayton, Ohio, and I told her that's as close as we'd be coming to Cincinnati, where she was living. 'So how about it?' I asked her. And when she couldn't quite seem to make up her mind because of her kid, I told her the band would send her son *and* her mother ahead to the Pennsylvania Hotel, where we were going to open in a few days, and fix them up there and everything if she'd join us right away in Ohio. That's when she agreed to come back."

With Doris in the band again, Les started turning out a series of successful records, such as "My Dreams Are Getting Better All the Time," "You Won't Be Satisfied," and Doris' biggest hit with the band, "Sentimental Journey."

The first time the band played the tune, the reaction was negligible. "It was at one of those late-night rehearsals we used to have at the Hotel Pennsylvania," Doris recalls. "Nobody was especially impressed. But after we played it on a couple of broadcasts, the mail started pouring in. Before that I don't think we'd even planned to record it. But of course we did—right away—and you know the rest."

This was the same period in which Les recorded his other big hit, "I've Got My Love to Keep Me Warm." To show you how imperceptive recording companies can be, it wasn't released until almost five years later. "We did it between recording bans," Les reports. "We'd taken it along as one of those extra numbers you sometimes get a chance to do on a date, and we did the whole thing in fifteen minutes. For years after that it stayed in the barrel at Columbia.

"Then one night in 1948, when we were running out of tunes, we played it as a band number on one of our Hope shows. The reaction was terrific. Right away we got a wire from Columbia telling us to get into the studio the next day and record it. I wired back, 'Look in your files.' They did, and of course they found it and released it, and it became a big hit. I've often wondered if Columbia had released it when we first did it whether it would have been as big for us. I have a feeling it might not have made it then. And you know what? Columbia still has a lot of things of ours that they've never released."

Actually, by the time the record came out, Les had given up his band, supposedly for good. It happened late in 1946, and the move wasn't entirely surprising to some of us. In the February issue of *Metronome*, after praising the band, especially saxists Steve Madrick, Ted Nash and Eddie Scherr, trumpeters Don Jacoby and Jimmy Zito, trombonist Warren Covington, pianist Geoff Clarkson, and Doris Day, "now THE band singer in the field, who is singing better than ever and displaying great poise," I concluded with: "As for Les himself, he is becoming sort of an enigma these days, apparently more interested in songs and the publishing field, less eager and enthusiastic about his band. . . . Such a change is discouraging and causes some uneasy wondering about the Brown future."

A few months later he verified his retirement plans, first verbally, then actively. He quit in December, 1946. "I wanted to settle in L.A., where the weather would be nice and I could relax. It rained steadily for the first twelve days."

Les's plan was to take twelve months off. But he had a contract for a March date at the Palladium. "I'd forgotten all about it. The guys had taken other jobs. But the management wouldn't let me out of it, even though I had no band." So he reorganized. "I think we rehearsed about three times before we opened. We had some great men. But the band was uneven."

They broadcast twice a night from the Palladium. "Stan Kenton heard one of our early shows one night and, according to the guy he was with, said he thought the band sounded terrible. He was right. But then later on that same night, he tuned in our second broadcast, without knowing who it was, and asked the same guy he was with, 'Whose band is that? It sounds great!' He was right again. That's just how unpredictable we were with that new group."

Two years later, Les still had a band. But, he noted then, "I've given up the idea of being the number-one band in the country. It's not worth it. I'd much rather stay here in California, maybe doing radio work like I'm doing. . . . I've got a home here and I can be with Cluny and the kids and I can make a pretty good living."

Thirty-five years after he had emigrated to there, Les was still in California. For most of those years he earned an excellent living from radio and television shows—Bob Hope's, Dean Martin's, the Grammy Awards salutes, etc. He and his band also traveled extensively with Hope to service camps all over, a regimen that Les gladly surrendered in the latter 1970s in favor of one that allowed him to remain at home in his warm, delightful, early-American style abode in Pacific Palisades, where he and Clare spend evenings listening to classical music and entertaining their many friends. Several nights a week, Les still leaves home to play west coast gigs with his band, but in the winter of 1981 he concluded what he insisted would be his final one-nighter tour. And this time, even more so than in 1946, when he issued a similar statement, he really meant it. Or at least, that's what he was saying!

The Les Brown band today

Bobby Byrne

BOBBY BYRNE could never be faulted for not trying. He could, however, be faulted for trying too hard. When the brilliant young trombonist left Jimmy Dorsey's band late in 1939, he had everything going for him—ability, good looks, experience, a big booking office that believed in him, and a Decca recording contract. His band was a good one too, tabbed in my February, 1940, review of its initial New York appearance (actually it was in Brooklyn's Roseland Ballroom) as "one of the finest young outfits to pop over the dance band horizon in a long time." The write-up went on to rave about Byrne's fantastic prowess as a sweet trombonist, then also complimented him for his newfound ability to play quite good jazz.

The following month, Bobby got a big break. Michael DeZutter, who had known young Byrne when he had played with Jimmy Dorsey in 1935, hired Bobby's band for the full 1941 summer season at Glen Island Casino, the country's top booking plum. In addition, just as he had the year before, when he found out that Glen Island had booked Glenn Miller, Frank Dailey hired Byrne's band for an April stint at his famed Meadowbrook.

Byrne was an intense young man, deadly serious about his music and equally serious about becoming a successful leader. Younger than many of his musicians, but a musical perfectionist, Bobby drove his men exceptionally hard. Mistakes seemed to bother him more than they did other leaders. His band impressed me as being unusually tense, which was reflected in Bobby's own straining for ambitious and too often missed notes. If only he wouldn't try so hard, I used to think about the eager young man, who reportedly rehearsed his band seven afternoons a week, how much more relaxed his music could sound!

In addition to Bobby's glorious trombone tone, the band featured some good ensemble sounds, an exquisite bassist named Abe Siegel (a mature person, he gave the band some extra emotional stability), a cute, vivacious and very effective singer, Dorothy Claire, an exciting clarinetist, Jerry Yelverton and, for a while, a pretty good kid drummer with not too definite a beat. His name: Shelly Manne.

But though Byrne kept trying to eliminate the fluffs, he couldn't do anything about a chronically troublesome appendix. In October, while his band was playing the Paramount Theater, he was rushed to Leroy Sanitarium for an emergency operation. While he was gone, various top name leaders filled in for him, and it is interesting to note that the favorite of them all so far as Byrne's musicians were concerned was not Benny Goodman or Charlie Barnet or Jan Savitt, but the veteran Abe Lyman. As for Guy Lombardo, the guys had an amusing reaction: they liked him personally but were completely confused by the way he waved his long baton strictly out of tempo!

When Marion Hutton left Glenn Miller quite suddenly at the start of the following year, Glenn lured Dorothy Claire away from Bobby. This was a big blow, for Dorothy had become an important fixture in the band. Byrne appeared hurt and angry, and for a while it looked as if a big feud would erupt. But Dorothy did not seem to fit too well into the Miller picture, and in March she returned to Byrne. Along about the same time, Bobby discovered the best boy singer he ever had, Stuart Wade, a handsome baritone with a great sense of phrasing and exceptional control, who later achieved even greater success with Freddy Martin's band.

Though he had captured the Raleigh-sponsored radio show, Bobby still kept trying harder. To improve his book, he hired the veteran Don Redman, an exceptionally talented arranger. Don wrote some great though difficult charts for the band, and Byrne worked exceptionally hard to do them justice. But he just never could seem to establish the kind of relaxed groove that Redman's swinging scores required. Too much tension? Perhaps. In August, I noted: "You probably never did see a bandleader who tried to bring out the mechanics of music more earnestly than Bobby Byrne does. It's gotten to be almost a phobia with him now." In regard to the importance he placed on not fluffing notes, I added: "Not only has it become a dread mania where he, himself, is concerned, but Byrne makes it plenty obvious, via his glowerings, that he won't tolerate bad notes from the musicians beneath him." Then, after commenting that creative musicians tighten up under such pressure, I reasoned: "That tension is the only apparent reason for the Bobby Byrne band not being one of the country's leading crews."

Bobby Byrne (far right) with Dorothy Claire and band

Not that everything was all young Byrne's fault. Certainly he couldn't help the appendicitis attack. And it was not because of him that one of his earliest and most important engagements, at the Hotel New Yorker, was canceled at the very last minute because of an electricians' strike.

And who could have predicted his great humiliation when he decided to regale his New York Strand Theater audience with a solo on the harp? He could play the instrument quite well, identifying the notes via various colored strings. In his opening show, he was just about to begin a very pretty solo, when, it has been reported, the light man had a sudden brainstorm: why not enhance the mood by bathing Bobby and his harp in a lovely purple spotlight? It was a noble thought, but the purple light completely washed out the colors of the strings, and poor Bobby had no way of telling a B flat from an F sharp! According to the guys in the band, Byrne suffered even more than his audience.

By 1942, Bobby had changed arrangers and modified the style of his band. Redman had gone, and in his place had come a former trombonist, Sid Brantley, who wrote simpler yet equally effective arrangements. And, being a trombonist, he knew exactly how to write for Bobby.

In the summer of 1942, Barry Ulanov, reviewing the band, found it to be well disciplined but less tense than before, the best band Bobby had ever had. The very fact that the arrangements were easier to play helped the musicians relax more, causing Ulanov to remark that the band was filled with "good cheer, good humor and good taste." It may be, Barry summed up, "the sensation Bobby has promised himself and his large public."

But Bobby had little time to find out. Long interested in and adept at flying, he disbanded when, early in 1943, he was offered a commission in the Air Corps, where he served for several years.

Following his stint in the service, Byrne organized another band, fairly good musically but still not completely relaxed. Bobby was blowing as beautifully as ever, but the fluffs were still there. "He is an absolutely amazing trombonist," I wrote in July, 1946. "There's just about nothing he can't do, and the little he can't do, he tries anyway. . . . Grandstanding of that sort is entirely unnecessary," I concluded.

His band improved, though, thanks in part to Larry Elgart's sax and arrangements by Charlie Albertine, who later developed the Elgart band style. But Byrne, like other leaders who had returned from the service, found fewer audiences and places to play. However, since he was an exceptionally good trombonist, he was most welcome in the recording studios, where he did very well for himself.

Eventually, he began concentrating less on playing and more on producing, and in the late fifties he took over as a top executive at Command Records, a post in which he performed excellently for many years and where he never again had to worry about fluffing notes on his trombone.

Cab Calloway

WHEN people mention Cab Calloway, they invariably bring up things like "Heigh-de-ho" and "Minnie the Moocher" and all the screaming novelties and unhip "hip" phrases he used to utter when he was trying to make an impression at the Cotton Club in the early thirties.

Better they should think of him in the early forties, when he led one of the truly great outfits of the big band era, one that too few people seem to remember, one that was brutalized by the AFM recording strike, and one that is seldom even mentioned nowadays by anyone except musicians. Yet that band, with its rich, clean ensemble sounds, its brilliant soloists, and its persuasive swing and great spirit, must go down as Calloway's greatest contribution to American music.

Cab (composed of song titles)

As critic Barry Ulanov wrote in the January, 1943, issue of *Metronome:* "How many people realize what a great band Cabell is leading right now, a band extraordinary in every aspect, in its clean musicianship, its jazz kicks and its brilliant showmanship. Here's one of the magnificent bands of our time!"

Another writer, Harry Lim, fourteen months later attributed the band's impressive brilliance to the musicians themselves. Lim was not the only one to make this observation. Calloway himself once told me, "I'm up front there doing my act, but it's the guys themselves who are making this band what it is."

He once admitted, as many of us who had been listening to his music through the years had often noted, that "there was something missing in the band for a long time, but nobody could ever put his finger on it. About four months ago, when we were in New York, I sent for Buster [Buster Harding, who took over musical directorship of the band and wrote its arrangements]. . . . He's turning out stuff that's inspirational. That's why they're playing so fine. . . . Now, for the first time in my life, I've got a band I can be really proud of. Harding and all the rest of them have built themselves a real band for me to stand in front of."

But the band that "they" built was really built by Calloway himself. For despite the fact that he gave his men great freedom and encouragement, he was the one who assembled, shaped and routined this outstanding group, which during the few years of its greatness included such stars as tenor saxists Chu

Cab Calloway:
ballad singer

Berry and Ben Webster, alto saxist Hilton Jefferson, trumpeters Dizzy Gillespie and Jonah Jones, bassist Milt Hinton and drummer Cozy Cole.

What set Calloway apart from most other leaders, though, especially among black bands, was that he could afford to and did pay his musicians high salaries. Thus he gave them both musical and financial encouragement and security. Little wonder, then, that the *esprit de corps* of the Calloway band was tremendous, and the great pride that the musicians possessed as individuals and as a group paid off handsomely in the music they created.

Calloway, whose singing of ballads always impressed me more than his vocal clowning (try his record of "You Are the One in My Heart" as a sample), was an extremely alert, appreciative and articulate man, full of wit and good humor, some of which is revealed in his biography, *Of Minnie the Moocher and Me*. I remember once during a radio interview I asked him what he thought of a popular arranger who liked to attract his listeners with stentorian introductions. "The trouble with him," he explained, "is that he comes on like 'Gangbusters' but goes off like 'The Good Will Hour.'"

When the big bands died down, Cab kept right on going, working for a while with a smaller unit and often as a single act, spreading his good cheer and talents through the movies and even into the operatic field, touring Europe and the United States as Sportin' Life in George Gershwin's *Porgy and Bess*. To most he will be best remembered as the "Prince of Heigh-de-ho." But at least some of us will always admire and thank him most for that great band he led in the early forties.

Frankie Carle

FRANKIE CARLE became an important big band leader late in his career. In show business since 1918, according to his own admission, he'd gained fame as a pianist with Horace Heidt's band, with whom he was starred for many years, even becoming Heidt's co-leader in 1943. Then in 1944, the quiet, self-effacing New Englander (his first important job had been with Mal Hallett's band), whose relaxed attitude contrasted sharply with his more intense, brittle piano style, went out on his own.

He'd had a big opportunity several years earlier. "I received a wire from my late friend, Eddy Duchin," Frankie recently wrote me. "He was playing the Palmer House in Chicago, and I was appearing in Omaha with Heidt. Eddy was entering the service, and he wanted me to take over his band and library for 25 per cent of the gross. Jokingly I showed Heidt the wire and told him I was leaving to head Eddy's band. Right then and there he offered me a thousand dollars weekly and 5 per cent of the gross to stay with him."

It turned out to be a good deal for Carle. But several years later, and with Heidt's blessings, he finally formed his own band, a good one, which debuted in February, 1944, at the Café Rouge of New York's Hotel Pennsylvania. Its arrangements by Al Avola, who once had written many scores for Artie Shaw, were musical, the band played them well, and the total effect was like an extension of Frankie's piano playing. "They possess," my *Metronome* review stated, "that Rotary-Club-After-Luncheon-Speaker's directness—never too subtle for anyone to understand, always pleasant, enjoyable and almost boy-scoutish in their down-to-earthness."

Naturally, Frankie used "Sunrise Serenade," his big hit of several seasons earlier, as his theme and featured himself at the piano, playing simply and straightforwardly. On rare occasions, some other musician might solo. As a starter, Carle hired Betty Bonney, Les Brown's former vocalist, to sing with the band, and the pretty girl, who later became known as Judy Johnson, turned in a good job.

After Betty Bonney came Phyllis Lynne and then later another girl, whose discovery Frankie describes with pardonable pride. He had been auditioning singers in person and via demo records. All in all he listened to about one hundred of them—fifty in person and fifty on discs.

Frankie Carle and Marjorie

"Among the records," Carle noted in his letter, "unknowingly to me, my Mrs. slipped in a demo that was taken off a radio program, and it happened to be my daughter, who was singing with a local band [Paul Martin], getting her first start. I liked the record, and when my Mrs. said it was my daughter, I was asked to give her a chance with my band. I did not want the public to know she was any relation of mine until I found out whether she could make the grade or not. I gave her three months and had her change her name to Marjorie Hughes."

Marjorie Hughes (Carle) did very well with the band. When she recorded a hit side, "Oh, What It Seemed to Be," Walter Winchell broke the news that she was actually Frankie's daughter.

Carle's band continued on its successful and always pleasantly musical way, gaining cross-country acclaim via two radio series—one for Old Gold and the other for Chesterfield cigarettes. Meanwhile, Frankie kept on writing songs and, according to his musicians, tuning pianos. "All I did really," he explains about his unusual habit, "was tune certain strings that were out of tune. I just couldn't stand a piano out of tune, and I feel the same way today."

During the mid-1970s, Frankie toured successfully with a big band package that played concerts throughout the country. He recorded sporadically and led a band on occasional dance dates. Looking hale and hearty, with little loss of enthusiasm, he eventually settled down in Mesa, Arizona, a welcome neighbor to many who years earlier had admired him from afar.

Benny Carter

WHEN the big band era began, Benny Carter was in Europe. Already accepted by leading jazz musicians as one of the most talented musicians and arrangers around, he had written scores for Fletcher Henderson, McKinney's Cotton Pickers and Chick Webb. He had also recorded with his own musically but not commercially successful band, which included such then-obscure musicians as pianist Teddy Wilson, drummer Cozy Cole, tenor saxist Chu Berry and trombonist Dickie Wells. But Europe, then as now, more discerning about and more receptive to American jazz than America, offered more opportunities for a talent like Carter's. There he arranged in the London studios of the British Broadcasting Company, became the first American jazz musician to play in Spain and organized an outstanding international orchestra that included one Scotsman, one Welshman, one Cuban, one Frenchman, one West Indian, one Dutchman, one Panamanian, two Englishmen and, as Carter tells it, "one Yank: me."

In 1938, Carter, an extremely intelligent and affable man, returned to the States to find the big band boom well under way. He soon organized the first of several fine outfits, hoping to place high in the big band sweepstakes. But none ever did, for Carter always communicated better with musicians than with the public.

His first outfit, which opened in Harlem's Savoy Ballroom early in 1939, included two fine trombonists, Tyree Glenn and Vic Dickenson, as well as a budding pianist, Eddie Heywood. The band didn't last long. A year and a half later, he was fronting another edition, again in New York, this time at the Famous Door on Fifty-second Street. This one I found to be well rehearsed and disciplined, playing excellent arrangements, displaying fine musicianship, but lacking warmth.

But Carter was accorded his usual rave: "His playing is the rare combination of a ripened intellect and a complete, musical soul, produced via complete mastery of his instrument." The instrument in question was the alto sax. Benny was also an excellent trumpeter. Other musicians invariably admired him, for he had a keen harmonic sense and an inventive mind. Not always, though, did he project emotionally the way Goodman or James or Dorsey did, and this could have been one reason for his lack of greater public popularity.

Carter's Famous Door outfit didn't make it either, but Benny was neither discouraged nor unemployed. Mark Warnow, who was conducting the "Hit Parade" radio series, hired Carter to write arrangements. It wasn't much of a job from a musical-satisfaction viewpoint, but it kept Benny clothed and fed and enabled him early in 1942 to start another band (Jonah Jones played in this one), which worked as a team in theaters with the late Billie Holiday. But it, too, fizzled out.

So Benny decided to leave New York and try his luck on the West Coast. There he organized again, taking two top trumpeters, Gerald Wilson (later a successful leader) and Snooky Young from Les Hite's band, and uncovering a young trombonist destined for jazz stardom, J.J. Johnson. The outfit worked with a singer, Savannah Churchill, who sang the vocal on the most popular record Carter ever made, an emotional blues titled "Hurry, Hurry."

The West Coast was where Benny was to remain. He engaged in various recording activities, most of them with Capitol Records. The band he led there at the Swing Club in Hollywood during 1944 was probably the best he ever led, "soothing and exciting musically," wrote critic Barry Ulanov. "And something new has been added. This band jumps!"

That last comment is significant, for not too many of Carter's various editions, beamed more at musicians' heads than at dancers' feet, jumped very much. This one, though, featured drummer Max Roach and pianist Jerry Wiggins, and with them a band had to jump. Yet even this crew didn't last too long. "Band after band of Benny Carter's," *Metronome* finally concluded, "has died, some painfully, some so slowly that rigor mortis never set in."

Still, Benny Carter's musical productiveness has never died. Eventually he settled in the studios, making an occasional record under his own name, composing for television and the movies, and continuing to arrange for singers. In the latter 1970s, he re-emerged as a soloist, lending his lovely horns to concerts and night club appearances, reminding everyone what an especially talented and gentlemanly human being he had always been—and still was.

The multi-talented Benny Carter

Casa Loma

MORE than any other single musical organization, the Casa Loma Orchestra set the stage for the big band era. For during the early thirties, this very elegant-looking group of fairly good musicians succeeded in bringing to the public at large and to the college kids in particular an exciting and refreshing mixture of arranged big band jazz and slow, sentimental ballads matched by no other bands of its day.

Alternating such "killer-dillers" as "Casa Loma Stomp" and "White Jazz," "Blue Jazz" and "Black Jazz" with sentimental ballads like "For You" and "Under a Blanket of Blue" and "It's the Talk of the Town," complete with Kenny Sargent's romantic vocals, the band succeeded in doing what no other outfit had yet been able to do: it reached the kids on two completely different and contrasting yet equally emotional levels.

In the very early thirties, some of us college musicians had latched on to the band before many of our nonplaying friends had. During my freshman year, I had been appointed leader of the official freshman dance band (actually, I had wanted to be the drummer, but when somebody else proved to be better, the guys decided that since I knew something about tempos, they might as well put me up front). Tremendously impressed by a very early Casa Loma record on the Okeh label of "Alexander's Ragtime Band" and "Put on Your Old Grey Bonnet," I had convinced our pianist to copy the arrangements off the record. They turned out to be our two most impressive numbers—so much so that when I arrived back at college the next September, one of my friends, who, like many others, had been unaware of Casa Loma, announced that during the summer he had heard a band called "Casa Nova or something like that, and they copied two of your arrangements, note for note!"

Perhaps I should have been prepared for such unfamiliarity with the Casa Loma Orchestra, because just before I returned to college I met one of those "ideal girls," who told me she "just loved jazz." But when I asked her how she liked Casa Loma, she replied, "I don't know. How does it go?"

When it first started, the Casa Loma Orchestra was known only around Detroit. A mid-twenties offshoot of one of Jean Goldkette's numerous outfits in the area, it was called the Orange Blossoms. Henry Biagini led it, with Glen Gray (Knoblaugh) on sax. Trombonists Walter (Peewee) Hunt and Billy

Rausch, along with pianist Howard (Joe the Horse) Hall, joined in 1927, and in 1929 two other future Casa Lomans, guitarist-arranger Gene Gifford and tenor saxist Pat Davis, came along. With several forgettable musicians, the band was scheduled to open a new Canadian nightclub, the Casa Loma, erected especially for the visit of the Prince of Wales. The club never opened, but in a sort of memorial move, the men decided to call their band the Casa Loma Orchestra.

Eventually the men dismissed Biagini, and several of the regulars formed a corporation—the first cooperative band of its kind—with Gray as president, Francis (Cork) O'Keefe, who was to become co-partner of the famous Rockwell-O'Keefe booking office, as manager, and Davis as secretary-treasurer. Hunt, Rausch, Hall and Gifford, along with three recent additions, drummer Tony Briglia, bassist Stan Dennis and lead trumpeter Bobby Jones, also received stock.

"After the crash of 1929," O'Keefe reports, "Spike [Glen Gray] phoned me from Detroit to say they had no work and they wanted to come to New York. So I got them a job at the Roseland Ballroom, and while they were there, Bob Stevens of Okeh Records heard them and immediately offered them a deal." Thus began the band's recording career. Significantly, all six of the sides (they completed only two on their first date) were up-tempo jump tunes, the sort that first attracted the collegians. Judged by later swing standards, or even compared with what bands like Ellington's, Henderson's McKinney's Cotton Pickers and Goldkette's were recording in those days, the Casa Loma sides sounded stiff and corny, but they were tremendously flashy, and this is what attracted the kids.

Though he was nominally the head of the band, Gray, a magnificently handsome man, then sat in the sax section. The front man was Mel Jenssen, a dancer-turned-fiddler, never a member of the corporation, who served adequately as buffer between musicians and dancers.

The personnel of the band remained very steady during its first years. In the spring of 1931, the co-leaders hired a handsome saxist who also sang, Kenny Sargent. A few months later, they brought in the band's outstanding jazz soloist, clarinetist Clarence Hutchenrider, who had insisted that they also hire his buddy, Grady Watts, a pleasant, dixielandish trumpeter. Shortly thereafter an entirely different kind of trumpeter, a real screamer, Sonny Dunham, joined.

Dunham was my first connection with the band. He was a bright, intense, affable man whom many of us admired, and one evening at the Glen Island Casino I, still a college kid, got up enough nerve to talk with him. At that time one of the big jazz favorites among musicians was "China Boy," so I asked Sonny whether the band ever played it. "We have an arrangement of it," he told me, "but we've only had it for three weeks, and I don't think the boys know it well enough yet."

His answer was disillusioning. Three weeks to learn an arrangement? I

Peewee Hunt, Glen Gray and Kenny Sargent surround guest vocalist Connee Boswell (the hands are Connee's, not Gray's).

couldn't imagine musicians needing *that* much time. Later I discovered two things: (1) that the band had some very weak readers who required long rehearsals and (2) that it placed great emphasis on accuracy.

In discussing what he terms "five years of phenomenal success" (1930–1935), O'Keefe credits two members especially, "Gene Gifford, the arranger, whose tremendous musical imagination set the entire musical flavor of the band, and Billy Rausch, who had an obsession for meticulous perfection and who insisted that the band perform with machinelike precision. Billy was so insistent upon everything being just right that he'd practice his trombone steadily for an hour before every broadcast to make sure that he wouldn't fluff those high notes on the band's 'Smoke Rings' theme."

Not merely the college kids were attracted to Casa Loma during those first five years. Some of the top recording stars of the times were too. That's why singers like Mildred Bailey, Connee Boswell and Lee Wiley and, in later years, Louis Armstrong and Hoagy Carmichael recorded with it.

After its first Okeh sides, the band switched to Brunswick Records, for which it turned out its most memorable ballad sides. On that label it was known as simply the Casa Loma Orchestra. But so great had its popularity grown that Victor Records also bid for its services, and for a while the band recorded for both labels, appearing on Victor under Glen Gray's name without the Casa Loma appendage. Eventually it recorded exclusively for Brunswick, using the title Glen Gray and the Casa Loma Orchestra, one it continued to use when it switched in 1934 to Decca Records.

In 1933 and 1934 the band appeared on the first radio commercial series to feature a swing band, the "Camel Caravan." During those years it spent its summers at Glen Island Casino, where its national popularity soared, thanks to frequent air shots, and part of its winters in the Colonnades of New York's Essex House.

By 1935, when the big band era was beginning, Casa Loma was widely known and, like many highly acceptable, highly exposed products, was getting the familiar American obsolescence treatment. Thus my May, 1935, review began with: "It's a characteristic of band boys in general to praise a new, good individual band to the skies; then, when it's made the grade and the boys have heard it for a while, they turn right around, pick on every minor flaw, and say that the band is lousy, that it's pulling the same stuff all the time. . . . They want something else in place of what they used to think good, and, if they hadn't heard it a lot, would still think good. . . . That's the kind of a deal the Casa Loma boys have been getting."

After complimenting the band for its cleanliness, accuracy and danceability, I noted one failing that plagued it throughout much of its career—its over-emphasis on arrangements. "You've got to give the boys, especially Gene Gifford, credit for starting a subtler ballroom style of music, but they should realize that by over-emphasizing that aspect [the arrangement] they're harming themselves. Paying so much attention to arrangements, playing everything just as writ, tends to make the boys stale. They have to spend so much time and energy concentrating on the finer points of the intricate arrangements that they're unable to do themselves justice on the less mechanical and more imaginative aspects, such as phrasing and hot choruses."

Actually, there was very little good jazz being blown in the band. Except for Hutchenrider and occasionally Dunham and Watts, the solos were pallid. Hunt could blow a fairly good trombone chorus now and then, but Davis played tenor sax with great fervor and little else, while pianist Hall was just plain dull. On top of that, the band was hampered by a miserable rhythm section, which I described in a later article as being "as solid and as supple as a marble pillar."

Where the band really did shine, though, was in its ability to "raise duck bumps on the kids" (another later quote). This it did by contrasting its fast if unswinging numbers with some absolutely lovely ballads, played at much slower tempos than other dance bands were then using. As O'Keefe has noted, "The band really never came into its own until it interspersed ballads with up-tempos." And Larry Clinton, who took over as chief arranger when Gifford left, recently described Casa Loma as "primarily an effect band, not a jazz band. It was Glen's great ability to play for an audience that made it what it was."

Clinton joined the band after Gifford, who'd become quite unreliable, departed. That was in the spring of 1935. In the fall of that year, the Casa Lomans inaugurated one of the most colorful and important projects in the history of the big bands. They appeared on the stage of New York's Paramount Theater, to launch the emporium's famous stage-band policy. Shortly thereafter they succeeded Ray Noble's band in the swank Rainbow Room atop Radio City.

The band seemed to reek class—at least on the stand. The men all wore tails and their decorum was superb. Off the stand, the impression wasn't as consistent, for though the majority of the men were gentlemen, some of them were hard-drinking gentlemen—or boozers—and many a night 'neath the elegant aura, rigor mortis was setting in on some deeply defiant hangovers.

Perhaps because he realized the necessity for greater control of the men, Gray, who had been sitting among the saxes, decided in 1937 to front the band himself. This meant the dismissal of Mel Jenssen. With characteristic modesty, Glen told O'Keefe, "We can get a better sax player in my place."

Actually the band had already improved its reed section with the addition in 1934 of Art Ralston, who added considerable color by doubling on numerous horns. It had also improved its rhythm section by taking on Jacques

Trombonist Billy Rausch plays "Smoke Rings," the Casa Loma theme, in the Hotel New Yorker's Terrace Room as Glen Gray conducts.

Blanchette for Gifford (Blanchette, Jenssen and new trombonist Fritz Hummel formed a fiddle trio).

When Gray took over the baton—and there probably was never a more glamorous-looking big band leader than this huge, handsome, dimpled, mustachioed charmer—the band added another saxist, Danny D'Andrea. So successful was the group by this time that it was able to entice two outstanding men from other top bands. From Benny Goodman's number-one band, it snatched his number-one trombonist, a young Canadian with a terrific lip. This was Murray McEachern, who also doubled on sax, so that at times, with Murray and Glen blowing too, the band was able to field a sax septet.

This was ideal for the other new arrival, arranger Dick Jones, who had left Tommy Dorsey's new band to join Gray's. Jones, an extremely sensitive and skilled writer, especially adept at writing pretty scores, also succeeded in adding more color to the band. In 1938, Larry Wagner joined to write some swing originals that helped to show once more that this was a much better sweet band than a swing outfit.

Though it blazed few trails and excited few musicians, the Casa Loma band continued to survive quite comfortably during the ensuing years. In February of 1939, two months before Glenn Miller recorded "Sunrise Serenade," the band waxed the same number, with composer Frankie Carle on piano. That was the year that it lost its fine lead Frankie Zullo, who died suddenly and was replaced by Frank Ryerson. And in the next year, it lost another trumpeter, Sonny Dunham, who set out to start his own band. His chair was taken by Sy Baker.

By 1940 the Casa Loma band had passed the ten-year mark in its history. Though it continued to impress immensely as a sweet band (it wound up second in *Metronome's* sweet poll and sixth in the swing category, quite a change from the second in swing and seventh in sweet of three years before), much of the excitement it had generated had begun to wane. Several of the stalwarts started to leave, and by 1942 Casa Loma rookies such as trombonist Don Boyd, with a biting jazz style, tenor saxist Lon Doty, who blew a big-toned, emotion-laden horn, and Corky Cornelius, a swinging, often screeching trumpeter, along with a vocal trio, the LeBrun Sisters, had infused a new flavor into the band. So did the new arrangers, Tutti Camarata and Harry Rodgers, who had come over from Jimmy Dorsey and Artie Shaw, respectively.

In 1943 two of the most important members departed. Billy Rausch, the most impressive musician in the band, decided to take his trombone into the New York studios so that he could spend more time with his family, while Kenny Sargent returned to his home in Memphis, there to begin a career as a disc jockey. To replace Sargent, Gray hired Eugenie Baird, the band's first girl vocalist, whom I described in a June, 1944, review as "the prettiest girl I've ever seen in front of a band, and, in addition, the possessor of one of the prettiest voices I've ever heard in back of a microphone. (Later she became a top jingle singer and wife of the chairman of the board of the SCM Corp.)

That same review, though also complimenting a brilliant young guitar find, Herbie Ellis (today one of the greats on his instrument), and veteran trumpeter Red Nichols, who stayed with the band for a short time (Bobby Hackett also served for a few months), noted that "Gray's band sounds very uninspired as it goes through an evening of some of the dullest, least modern-sounding arrangements played by any top band today, lacks color and imagination, and, in general, exhibits too few moments of musical brilliance."

Nothing reflected more accurately the over-all decline of the Casa Loma Orchestra than what happened to it at the Paramount Theater in December of 1944. Appearing on the same bill with singer Andy Russell, it was allowed only three numbers to itself. In years gone by, it would have played at least a dozen. It was, I stated, in my final burst of loyalty to a band that I had admired and revered for so many years and that had attracted me as well as other fans and musicians to big bands in the first place, "an insult to the band that had started its [the Paramount's] name policy."

But though the Casa Loma Orchestra was never again the same, Glen Gray did score an impressive comeback in the fifties when, at the suggestion of Dave Cavanaugh of Capitol Records, he led a handpicked studio orchestra in a series of re-creations of the music of many of the best of the big bands. The project proved to be a huge success, and, though Gray was offered substantial sums to appear publicly with his own outfit, he preferred to spend the rest of his days in his adopted home of Plymouth, Massachusetts, where, in August, 1963, he died of cancer.

The Casa Lomans in 1935. Back row: trumpeters Sonny Dunham,
Grady Watts and Bobby Jones; drummer Tony Briglia; pianist Joe Hall.
Second row: trombonists Peewee Hunt and Billy Rauch;
arranger and guitarist Gene Gifford; bassist Stan Dennis.
Front row: saxists Pat Davis, Clarence Hutchenrider,
Glen Gray and Kenny Sargent. Conducting: violinist Mel Jensen.

Bob Chester

TO SOME, Bob Chester's band was just a carbon copy of Glenn Miller's. But that was only to those who didn't listen beyond his Miller-like reed sound. There was a good deal more to Bob's band.

The idea of latching on to the Miller reed style may have been Bob's, or it may have been that of Tommy Dorsey, then a big Miller rival, who took a liking to the wealthy Detroiter (his mother's second husband was the head of the Fisher Body Company). For after Bob's band failed at the Detroit Athletic

Chester

Club, Tommy invited him to come East and live with him and his family. Chester, a big, easygoing, bearish guy accepted. With the help of Dorsey and his manager, Arthur Michaud, Chester's new career was launched.

Coincidentally the band, when it finally got working, played at some of the same spots that Miller's had during its formative period—the Adolphus Hotel in Dallas, the Nicolette in Minneapolis and the Raymor Ballroom in Boston. As for its Miller reed style, I noted in my September, 1940, review that "the blend isn't as polished, the breathing isn't as effortless and therefore the phrasing isn't as legato, and the tonal quality is decidedly inferior."

But the band had a couple of assets the Miller band didn't have. One was an absolutely sensational singer named Dolores (Dodie) O'Neill, whom I raved about month after month and Bluebird record after Bluebird record. Hers was a highly individualistic and musical style—breathy and ethereal-sounding, warm and terribly intimate in phrasing, and yet with a free feeling common only among jazz singers and therefore utterly amazing from a band vocalist. *Metronome*'s readers may have become a bit bored after reading one rave record review after another for her singing of songs such as "Don't Make Me Laugh," "Don't Let It Get You Down," "When I Leave This World Behind" and "Pushin' the Conversation Along," a duet with Al Stewart, and yet, heard today, her singing still stands up splendidly.

The band's other asset was an eighteen-year-old trumpeter whom it plucked out of Juilliard School of Music. He was Alec Fila, and the way he led the Chester brass was truly thrilling. His powerful, pulsating horn seemed to inspire and carry the entire band, providing the push that was often lacking in the mediocre rhythm section.

For a while, Dodie and Alec (who were soon married) and Bob and Edna Chester (who were already married) carried on a wonderful personal relationship. But Fila was too good a trumpeter not to go on to better things, and he left to join Benny Goodman's band (Fletcher Henderson, who was back arranging for Benny then, described him to me as the best lead trumpeter he

Chester's Dolores (Dodie) O'Neill

knew and hired him for his own recording dates.) Dodie also left the band to replace Dinah Shore on NBC's "Chamber Music Society of Lower Basin Street" radio series and eventually to bear Alec five children, two of whom turned out to be excellent singers. But their marriage finally broke up. (So did Bob's and Edna's, with Chester returning to a business career in the automotive industry in Detroit, where he died in 1977.)

As for the band, it did improve despite the losses of its lead trumpeter and singer. Chester gave up the Miller sound at the beginning of 1941, when Dave (not David) Rose provided different and more imaginative arrangements. The over-all musicianship of the band perked up considerably, and Bob was able to engage good singers like Betty Bradley, Bob Haymes and Gene Howard, so that Dodie wasn't missed too much. Later, he also hired an excellent lead trumpeter in Louis Mucci, and he began to feature Garnett Clark, who played a pleasant two-beat trumpet style.

As a writer on the scene, I was immensely impressed as well as refreshed by the way the Chesters, as well as Dodie and Alec, refused to take themselves too seriously, unlike some other leaders, musicians and singers, not to mention leaders' wives. Typical of their light, humorous attitude was their reaction to a story I'd run in the magazine. Its headline read: "Bob Chester Lays Eggs in Wilkes-Barre." Right after the issue appeared on the stand, I received a telegram that read: DEAR GEORGE, WE DID NOT LAY AN EGG IN WILKES-BARRE. IT WAS IN SCRANTON. SINCERELY BOB AND EDNA CHESTER.

It's too bad there weren't more people like the Chesters—the big band days might have been even happier times!

Larry Clinton

LARRY CLINTON was best known for his renditions of "My Reverie" and "Deep Purple," both with vocal choruses by Bea Wain, and for his original theme song, "The Dipsy Doodle." The first two were big hit records for him. But not "The Dipsy Doodle." Why? Simply because he did not—in fact, he could not—record it. For Tommy Dorsey had already cut the song for RCA Victor, for whom Clinton also recorded, and neither Victor nor Dorsey wanted a competitive version.

Tommy had come by the song naturally, for in 1937 Larry, then on Dorsey's staff, had written and arranged it and other instrumentals, such as "Satan Takes a Holiday," for the band. This had been during the mild-mannered, mustachioed Clinton's second stint with Tommy. Several years before, he'd enjoyed a two-week association with TD, as an arranger for the Dorsey Brothers Orchestra. "But almost as soon as I came in, Tommy went out," Clinton says. He did write two well-known jazz pieces that the band recorded, "Tap Dancers' Nightmare" and "Dusk in Upper Sandusky," the last portion of which, Clinton, himself, points out, sounds like "The Dipsy Doodle." Both were issued under Jimmy Dorsey's name, but, according to Larry, they were actually recorded by the Dorsey Brothers with Tommy before he left the band.

From Jimmy's band, Larry went to Glen Gray and the Casa Loma Orchestra to write swing pieces, the most famous of which was "A Study in Brown," and to build a reputation as one of the country's top composer-arrangers. After a couple of years, he joined Tommy, who, late in 1937, backed Larry as a bandleader. Actually, both were part of an organization that included not only Dorsey, who put up whatever money was needed (Clinton always lived frugally and had saved some himself), but also RCA Victor's recording chief, Eli Oberstein. "They had sort of a stable of bands in which Eli and sometimes Tommy participated. There was Bunny [Berigan] and Van Alexander and Les Brown. To save money, Les and I used to swap some of our arrangements."

At first Larry recorded with studio men, whom he also used on an RCA Victor dance band radio program on which he alternated with Dorsey and Berigan. The next year he organized a permanent band.

In 1938 it played the summer season at Glen Island Casino, and like other leaders who spent their summers there in those years, Clinton wound up with a hit band on his hands. In my review of the band at the Casino, I termed it "unexciting." I complimented the brass, especially Walter Smith for his work on a then-obscure instrument, the mellophone, but faulted the damp-sounding saxes, which, however, did boast of a tenor man, Tony Zimmers, who had a lovely tone and ideas to match. Clinton also featured the clarinet a great deal, often several in unison. "I was looking for a semi-symphonic sound," he says.

The review also complimented his singer, Bea Wain, who turned out to be one of the most outstanding stylists of her day. "Chuck Rinker, the music publisher, originally told me about her," Larry recalls. "I needed a girl at the time, and he suggested I listen to Bea, who was a member of the Kay Thompson Choir. She sang eight solo bars on a radio show, but I knew immediately that she was what I wanted." Bea was featured on some very impressive sides, notably "True Confession" and "Old Folks," before her "Deep Purple" and "My Reverie" hits. Later, she married announcer André Baruch, shared a disc jockey show with him in Florida, then settled down with him in the late 1970s in Beverly Hills, California.

Ace New York Giants' pitcher Carl Hubbell showing Larry Clinton how he threw his Dipsy Doodle screwball

At that time, Clinton concentrated more on sweet rather than on swinging sounds. He recalls one negative reason for this emphasis. "We were playing a battle of music at the Green Key Ball at Dartmouth College. Jimmie Lunceford's was the other band. We were there bright and early, but Jimmie, who was supposed to go on first, didn't arrive until just a few minutes before he was to play. They'd been riding all night long, all the way from some town in the middle of Pennsylvania. So Jimmie asked me if I'd mind opening the dance while he and his guys got dressed and washed up.

"Well, we played about an hour, and I trotted out all our flag-wavers with the trumpets playing high C's. Then Jimmie came on, and after he'd played just a minute or so of 'For Dancers Only,' with that great beat his band had and the trumpets tossing their horns in the air and everything, I made up my mind right then and there that I could play nothing but sweet things if I were going to survive that night. Maybe that's why I continued to concentrate on pretty things from then on."

Several years later, however, with swing so firmly established, Clinton again began featuring faster tempos. He brought in more jazz-oriented musicians, especially when he found he could get "a package deal from Van Alexander. He had given up his band and joined us, and he brought along Butch Stone and Irv Cottler, whose drumming made all the difference in the world." For a while Hugo Winterhalter played sax and Joe Mooney arranged.

Larry proceeded to concentrate on writing originals. "It was more lucrative," he explains simply. Many of those originals were adaptations of well-known classics and sometimes even of well-known popular songs, which caused one wag to comment about Larry that "it goes in one ear and comes out his pen."

Clinton, an easygoing, well-liked man, didn't seem to be bothered by such criticism. He was a realist and a businessman. "I learned from the best of them, Tommy Dorsey and Glen Gray. The business then was a real rat race. We were all trying to do the best we could." Even as a front man, Clinton went all out, doubling on trumpet (his original instrument), trombone and clarinet. His explanation today is amusing: "It was a little easier than waving a baton, that's all. The only guy I can ever remember who looked good waving a stick was Paul Whiteman."

After Bea Wain left, a girl named Mary Dugan joined, to be followed by Helen Southern and then by Peggy Mann, who, like Bea, was an exceptionally musical singer. Throughout a good part of its career, the band featured two boy singers, trombonist Ford Leary on rhythm tunes and novelties, such as "Shadrack," and a handsome baritone with a rich voice, Terry Allen, who recorded many good sides with the band, including a slow, romantic version of future jazz musicians' biggest favorite, "How High the Moon."

Clinton had always been fascinated by flying and had developed into such a good pilot that in 1942 the U.S. Air Force was delighted to accept him and give him a lieutenant's commission. He became a flight instructor, serving first in the States, then moving to China, and eventually gaining his captaincy and being placed in charge of entertainment in the Calcutta, India, area. One of his top aides was Sergeant Tony Martin.

After being separated from the service in 1946, Larry recorded several albums for Herb Hendler on the Cosmo label, including such items as "The Dipsy Doodle Dance Contest" and an original Hendler opus called "Romeo Loves Juliet." But in restrospect, those sides loom very small in the Clinton recording career—a survey of his output for RCA Victor and the related Bluebird label reveals that the Larry Clinton Orchestra, during a period of less than four years, recorded a grand total of 214 sides! As an indicator of Clinton's well-disciplined, businesslike approach, as well as his musical efficiency and proficiency, it is worth noting that whereas almost all bands were fortunate to record four sides during their three-hour dates, Clinton very often succeeded in completing six in the same time.

Clinton's conservative businesslike approach to bandleading paid off well. He saved his money, and when he decided he'd had enough, he just quit. First, he and his wife, Wanda, moved to Florida, where Larry played a lot of golf. Later, approaching their golden wedding anniversary, they migrated to Green Valley, Arizona, where Larry busied himself by writing, not musical arrangements, but humorous and science fiction articles, which, in addition to his ASCAP earnings, have left him, he has admitted, quite at ease and with no kicks coming.

Larry Clinton (right) reviews
young Metronome editor George T. Simon.

Bob Crosby

BOB CROSBY led one of the swingingest and most colorful bands of all time. It was also one of the most controversial.

What set it apart from all the rest was its dixieland style, a brand of jazz considered old-fashioned by some of the hipper younger set, for whom jazz began with Benny Goodman's band. But for those with tastes catholic enough to appreciate all kinds of music, just so long as it was good, the Crosby band supplied some of the great thrills of the big band era.

It was a band with tremendous spirit, one filled with men who believed thoroughly in the kind of music they were playing and, what's more, who respected and admired one another as musicians and as people. For several years before it began to be known as the Bob Crosby band, its musicians had been working together as members of Ben Pollack's band. But Ben, who gave starts to such future stars as Benny Goodman, Glenn Miller, Jack Teagarden and Charlie Spivak, seemed to be more interested in the career of his wife, singer Doris Robbins, than in that of his band. So the men quit, first going their separate ways to various parts of the country, then, late in 1934, reassembling in New York under Gil Rodin, Pollack's right-hand man.

Gil, a serious-looking, amazingly patient and extremely dedicated man, secured work for the men. They played a radio series, the "Kellogg College Prom," under Red Nichols' baton. They recorded a few sides, using the name of Clark Randall and his Orchestra, a pseudonym for a wealthy Alabamian, Frank Tennill, who was the featured singer.

With Goodman's sudden success in 1935, Rodin and the men realized this was the right time to start out on their own. Gil, for all his fine qualities, was not the leader type. So the men decided to form a corporation and were preparing to make Jack Teagarden their leader, when Jack suddenly recalled he was still contractually bound to Paul Whiteman. Soon thereafter, Gil had a meeting with Cork O'Keefe, partner in the Rockwell-O'Keefe organization, which was building an impressive stable of bands. Cork liked the idea of a corporation, whose stockholders, he proposed, should be the musicians, his office and a leader. That was great with Rodin. But what leader?

"I know three guys you can have," said O'Keefe, "Johnny Davis, Goldie and Bing's kid brother." But Davis, a scat singer with Fred Waring's Pennsyl-

The early Bob Crosby Orchestra:
pianist Gil Bowers, Crosby, violinist Eddie Bergman, guitarist Nappy Lamare,
saxists Gil Rodin, Eddie Miller, Noni Bernardi, Matty Matlock,
bassist Bob Haggart, drummer Ray Bauduc, trumpeters Yank Lawson,
Andy Ferretti, trombonists Ward Sillaway, Mark Bennett

vanians, duplicated what the band already had in its guitarist, Nappy Lamare, while Goldie, the tricky trumpeter with Paul Whiteman, was considered too corny. On the other hand, Gil had met "Bing's kid brother" at the Palais Royale, where he had been working with the Dorsey Brothers band. He hadn't been knocked out by his singing, but he'd liked his attitude and youthfulness—and quite possibly his family ties. Bob got the job.

It was a relationship that could have been a mess. But it wasn't, for Gil, as recognized headman, remained discreetly in the background, running the band in his own quiet, efficient way, while Bob fronted for the public. A strong mutual understanding and respect resulted—one that lasted many years. What's more, Bob admired all the musicians tremendously and he let them know it. And perhaps best of all, he was wise and honest enough to recognize and admit to his own limitations. "I'm the only guy in the business," he once said, "who made it without any talent." (Not true.—GTS)

It was quite a band that young Crosby fronted, stocked with such brilliant musicians as tenor saxist Eddie Miller, clarinetist and arranger Matty Matlock, saxist and arranger Deane Kincaide, trumpeter Yank Lawson, pianist Gil Bowers, guitarist Nappy Lamare and drummer Ray Bauduc. In addition, the men had uncovered a sensational bass player, who also wrote exceptional arrangements. This was Bob Haggart, recently described by Crosby as "the undiscovered George Gershwin of our day." Adds Eddie Miller today, "Haggart still doesn't know how much talent he has."

I first heard the band during its initial New York engagement early in 1936 at the Hotel New Yorker. Seldom in all the years that I reviewed for *Metronome* did any band hit me as hard. It was one of the most exciting evenings of my life, and I, of course, gave it a rave review, one with which not all readers agreed. To some, two-beat jazz was and always would be old-fashioned and corny, so that in essence most of their arguments were beamed not so much at the band in particular as against the style of music in general.

There are many things I remember about the Crosby Crew, as I called it.

(I was a real alliterative hack in those days. I came up with such inimitable names as the Goodman Gang, the Herman Herd, the Dorsey Dervishers, etc.—I used to read the sports pages—and at times became so startlingly creative that I produced bits of sheer though condensed genius, such as calling Tommy Dorsey "TD" and Benny Goodman "BG.") There was Miller's tenor sax, warm, swinging, equally impressive on slow ballads and up-tempo numbers. There was the way Miller and Matlock functioned as a sax-clarinet team. There was Bauduc's loose, imaginative two-beat drumming, and there was Lawson's rollicking, rocking trumpet, the most propulsive I'd ever heard. I don't think many people realized how much Yank meant to the band, for it was his great rhythmic feeling, more than anything else, that inspired Bauduc to play his best drums.

The arrangements by Matlock, Kincaide and, above all, Haggart also impressed me. Though he came from Long Island, the lean, lanky bassist with the infectious smile and subtle sense of humor did an amazing job of creating for a big band those jazz sounds which had for so many years been indigenous to New Orleans, where Miller, Lamare and Bauduc had been born and raised. And his bass playing was also magnificent.

And then, of course, the Crosby band also had, as I once noted, "a unanimity of purpose, of thought, both musical and otherwise, plus a sense of freedom and play—all combined with an air of maturity—that you won't find in any other orchestra."

Its personnel changes were far fewer than those of other bands. From 1935, when it was first organized, until the draft started taking away some of its men, it included Rodin, Haggart, Miller, Bauduc, Lamare, and, except for a few time-outs, Matlock, Lawson and Kincaide. Trombonist Ward Silloway stayed for three years, trumpeter Billy Butterfield for almost three and pianist Jess Stacy for two. It was a happy and satisfying band.

Following its initial New York City engagement, the band traveled across town for a stay in the Hotel Lexington's Silver Grill (now the Hawaiian Room), where non-Hawaiian name bands once held forth. There it took on its first girl singer (the men still had a bad taste from the Ben Pollack–Doris Robbins setup). She was Kay Weber, with whom Bob had sung in the Dorsey Brothers band and who later married Ward Silloway, Kay, a lovely lady with a warm, soft style, was followed by Teddy Grace, Marion Mann and others.

Also at the Lexington, the band hired a top jazz pianist, Joe Sullivan, whom all the men admired tremendously. He was a big, hulking man whom nobody suspected was soon to be hospitalized for a long time, a victim of tuberculosis. Several months later, while the band was playing at the Congress Hotel in Chicago, it ran a mammoth benefit that defrayed many of Joe's expenses. Sullivan's place was taken by a hard-driving, hard-drinking Detroiter named Bob Zurke, one of whose most famous recorded solos with the band was a tune called "Little Rock Getaway." It was written by Joe Sullivan.

Right from the start, the band produced a series of exceptionally good sides for Decca, from "Dixieland Shuffle" and "Muskrat Ramble" on its first date through "Come Back, Sweet Papa," "Pagan Love Song," "Sugar Foot Strut" and Zurke's initial recording with the band, "Gin Mill Blues." But the two recordings for which it has been best remembered are two Haggart creations, the brilliantly exciting portrayal of a New Orleans marching band on "South Rampart Street Parade" and the delightfully zany yet thoroughly musical Haggart-Bauduc duet on "The Big Noise from Winnetka," complete with Bob's toothsome whistling and Ray's use of drumsticks on Bob's bass strings.

Haggart recently told me how "Big Noise" was born. "One afternoon at one of those concerts at the Blackhawk, the crowd just wouldn't stop yelling after we'd finished a number called 'The Big Crash from China.' So as an encore, I, for some reason or other, started whistling that little phrase. I'd always liked to whistle, ever since I'd heard that whistling waiter who used to spin his tray at the same time at the Hotel President in New York. So after I started whistling that silly little thing, Ray and I fell into our routine, and it went over so big that we recorded it the following week."

"South Rampart Street Parade" was also a Haggart-Bauduc collabora-

"The Big Noise
from Winnetka":
Haggart and Bauduc

tion. Recalls Bob: "One night in 1936, when we were playing at the New Yorker Hotel, Ray and I were sitting at a table, and he said he had an idea for a parade jazz march. He sang some of it to me, and I wrote it down on the tablecloth." Fortunately, Haggart remembered to swipe the tablecloth that night. He took it home with him and in a few days returned with the complete arrangement of the number that was to become a jazz classic.

During the band's stay at Chicago's Congress Hotel, it met up with one of the most charming and colorful characters ever to invade the dance-band scene. This was Mrs. Celeste LeBrosi, a large and attractive widow who developed such an intense attachment to the band that she followed it wherever it went. And just to make her behavior seem completely logical to her many blue-blooded society friends, she arranged to have her strapping teenage son serve as assistant-assistant band manager.

No group of musicians ever lived so well. She gave the band a huge party in her swank Long Island home when it stopped off in New York for a record date. When it played on the roof of Boston's Ritz-Carlton Hotel, she reserved a huge table every night right next to the bandstand, where drinks were waiting for all band members, and after the boys were through work, she served them luscious buffets in her suite. Reportedly her hotel tab ran over eleven hundred dollars for the first week alone.

In September of 1937, the band traveled across country before its engagement in Los Angeles' Palomar Ballroom. Mrs. LeBrosi went too, renting a huge Beverly Hills mansion, where she continued to entertain sumptuously. So loyal was she to the band that she never forgave John Hammond for reading a newspaper at a ringside table while the band was playing in the Congress Hotel.

It was at another Windy City spot, the Blackhawk Restaurant, that the Crosby band played some of its greatest music. Before then, it had had some tough sledding. Following a disappointing showing at the Palomar (which had probably the most unromantic-sounding name of all time for a line of chorines: the Hudson-Metzger Girls), Bob Zurke broke his leg while fooling around with Haggart in a midwestern town, and the band broke its contract with Rockwell-O'Keefe because of deep disagreements about service charges. It signed with MCA, which immediately booked it into its top New York spot, the Hotel Pennsylvania. Unfortunately, Benny Goodman had just completed a sensational run, and anything that followed him had to suffer by comparison. The Crosby band most certainly did.

But then came the Blackhawk and "South Rampart Street Parade" and "The Big Noise from Winnetka." The band was flying high again, until a guy named Tommy Dorsey stuck in his heavy hand.

Tommy was playing a Chicago theater engagement and must have been as impressed as everyone else was by the Crosby trumpet section, which by this time had, in addition to Lausen, Charlie Spivak, the brilliant lead man, who had returned to his alma mater, and a young man named Billy Butterfield.

The Bob Cats serenade their namesake:
Crosby, Ray Bauduc, Nappy Lamare, Eddie Miller, Bob Haggart, pianist Jess Stacy,
Billy Butterfield, Warren Smith, Irving Fazola.

The roly-poly, pink-cheeked Ohioan blew not only fine jazz, but also a potent lead as well as some of the most beautiful ballads this side of Bix and Berigan. (In a burst of enthusiasm in the August, 1939, issue of *Metronome,* I tabbed Butterfield as "the greatest all-around trumpeter in jazz today," a rave for which I received several rounds of ribbing from fellow writers but which, as I now look back, I realize was pretty well justified.) Dorsey didn't touch Billy, but he did offer both Spivak and Lawson, as well as arranger Deane Kincaide, substantial sums to join his band. They did, and the Crosby music and morale immediately took a nose dive.

Lawson's loss was especially hard on the Crosby band. His drive had inspired it in general and Bauduc in particular, and without big Yank to boot him along, Ray's drumming fell off, and the band lost much of its rhythmic sparkle.

And yet much good music remained. The band recorded a gorgeous tune of Haggart's called "I'm Free," which featured Butterfield's horn to telling effect. In case you're wondering whatever happened to the song, it was retitled some months later as "What's New?" And then, too, there were the lovely, relaxed, opulent clarinet sounds of a huge clarinetist from New Orleans, Irving Prestopnick, better known by his nickname, Fazola.

In 1939 the band, growing more and more commercial and concentrating less and less on dixieland sounds, captured the Camel Caravan radio series, which featured the band's current vocalist, Dorothy Claire, and Benny Goodman's original singer, Helen Ward, plus Johnny Mercer in the triple-threat role of singer, MC and composer.

The lineup, which had remained relatively stable, began to undergo numerous changes. Zurke left to start his own group, and Sullivan returned for a short but disappointing stay, to be followed by former Goodman pianist Jess Stacy, a sensitive musician and a witty man (of sorts) who liked to tell people he'd just left "Benny Badman" and had chosen the Crosby band despite offers from "Tommy Doorstep" and "Jan Savage." The trumpeters kept changing regularly, with men like Zeke Zarchy, Shorty Sherock, Billy Graham, Sterling Bose, Bob Peck, Eddie Wade and Muggsy Spanier coming in and out.

The trombonists also had their turnover. Warren Smith, who blew most of the hot and blew it well, was replaced by Floyd O'Brien, who fitted in excellently. Two future bandleaders, Moe Zudekoff, better known in later years as Buddy Morrow, and Ray Conniff, sat in the section for a while, and when Fazola left, Hank D'Amico took over the clarinet chair until Matlock came back once again.

During 1940 the band developed into a big bringdown for its dixieland fans. It veered from the two-beat style, hiring Jimmy Mundy, who had written many of Goodman's scores, and Paul Weston, Tommy Dorsey's ex-arranger. It also took on a nondescript vocal group known as the Bob-o-Links, with which it made many recordings, none of any distinction whatsoever. Vocalists, including a young Johnny Desmond who had yet to find himself, kept popping up all over the place, just as they did with the highly successful Tommy Dorsey band. But there was one big difference: Tommy had Sinatra, Jo Stafford, Connie Haines and the Pied Pipers; Crosby only had the Bob-o-Links, some undistinguished boy singers and himself. For very short periods the band's female vocal slot had been filled by Doris Day, Gloria DeHaven and Kay Starr. "But we never held on to them," Bob recently admitted. "Come to think of it, we fired some pretty great arrangers too, like Ray Conniff, Henry Mancini, Nelson Riddle and Paul Weston!"

Bob turned out to be a fine front man. He had a delightful sense of humor, he handled crowds with great grace and ease, and he got along very well with his musicians. But though he tried hard, he was never a truly first-rate singer and for some not even a truly second-rate singer. Thus, all the emphasis on his vocals did nobody any good.

Everybody connected with the band was pretty unhappy. Then, in the middle of 1941, Lawson returned. Immediately the important trumpet section, which also included the powerful and exuberant Lyman Vunk and a strong leader, Maxie Herman, perked up perceptibly. So did the entire band's music and morale. And the Bob-o-Links left.

I spent a full week with the band at Catalina Island during the summer of 1941. It was one happy ball, both on and off the stand. The band was really swinging. "It's the best dixieland band in the land again!" I wrote in the October issue. "In fact, it's the best all-around band the dixieland band has ever had," I added, singling out not merely the jazz, but also Liz Tilton's singing, the band's over-all showmanship, and, of course, the Bob Cats, the eight-piece dixieland band that had been an integral part of the larger unit ever since 1937, when it had made the first of many outstanding sides for Decca.

It was a happy season for the Crosby band. It had learned its lesson. Ballads, more modern four-four swing, vocal groups, and so on—these were not its groove. For deep down, this always had been and always would be an enlarged dixieland jazz band, a magnificent extension of the free-feeling, free-wheeling two-beat jazz that Les Brown once called "the happiest music in the world."

Unfortunately, it couldn't last. Not that the men didn't want it to. But in the following months, Bauduc and Rodin were drafted. Soon some of the others went into the service. Bob could see the end coming, so when he was offered a movie career, he called in the men, told them just what was what, and suggested that they make Eddie Miller their leader. They agreed. But soon Miller was drafted, and shortly thereafter the greatest dixieland band in the land was no more.

Crosby soon received a commission in the Marines, but his movie career blossomed briefly after the war in a weedy sort of way when he made a picture called *The Singing Sheriff*. We made it in exactly ten days," he told me in 1946, "and do you know it set back Western pictures exactly three years! Why, Randolph Scott—he and I used to be pretty good friends—but after he saw that picture, he wouldn't talk to me for six months. Claimed I was trying to ruin his racket!"

Bob made these remarks one night backstage at the New York Strand, where his new band was playing. This one was quite different in style. It emphasized ballads. The shift was necessary, Bob explained, because the kids no longer were flocking up to the bandstand to hear bands play up-tempo numbers. "When we do, they just walk away. It seems they're more interested in romancing than dancing."

The band never achieved nearly the recognition that the original Crosby band had. Still, it survived for a while, thanks to an Old Gold and a Ford radio series. But as soon as television came along, Bob Crosby concentrated more and more on working as a single. For several years he made out well, not only on TV but also in nightclubs, spreading his sphere of activity to Honolulu and during the mid-sixties to Australia. He occasionally reunited some of the Bob Cats, who sounded especially good (Miller was still magnificent!) during a 1966 engagement in New York's Rainbow Grill. Then in the early seventies, Bob toured the country with a big band package that used a set group of musicians fronted by Bob and by various leaders like Freddy Martin, Frankie Carle, Buddy Morrow and Art Mooney.

And what happened to the various Bob Cats? Thanks in part to his wife's happy inheritance, Bauduc was able to retire comfortably in Texas. Lamare and Matlock worked the lounges in Las Vegas, where the latter passed away in 1978. Miller, a proud grandfather and father of a successful physician, returned to New Orleans to work with Pete Fountain's dixieland group, and then came back to California where he was featured in several jazz concerts. As for Lausen and Haggart, they more than any of the others continued the music and spirit of the Bob Cats. For years, both had settled for the security of New York's radio, TV and recording studios, with Haggart also enjoying a successful jingle writer's career. But they also recorded as the Lawson-Haggart Jazz Band and then, in the late 1960s, with financial help from friends, launched The World's Greatest Jazz Band. A success for awhile, it featured some great arrangements by Haggart, and included in its personnel their old pal, Bud Freeman, and on numerous occasions, their Crosby band compatriot, Billy Butterfield. But as the 1970s waned, so did their bookings, so by the end of the decade Haggart was spending most of his time in his new home in Mexico and Lausen in his old home in Maine.

As for the Crosby band's president, Gil Rodin embarked on an entirely different career. Bright, shrewdly farsighted, and an indefatigable worker, he used his GI privileges to learn the art and science of television. Eventually, he became the producer of TV shows that starred Jack Benny, Fred Astaire and Crosby, and of two very successful hour-long spectaculars, "The Swinging Years" and "The Singing Swinging Years," that re-created the sounds of the big band era interspersed with some "Gee-whiz-wasn't-it-really-great-fellas-and-gals!" type of exclamations, emoted with cozy frenzy by none other than later-to-be President Ronald Reagan.

Rodin later parlayed his recording experience into yet another successful career in which he produced some top-selling albums by W. C. Fields, the Marx Brothers and other comedians. Later he also produced hit singles and albums for the motion pictures "The Sting" and "American Graffiti," and was instrumental in launching the career of a young composer/arranger, Marvin Hamlisch. Eventually, Rodin became a corporate vice-president and built himself a home in Palm Springs where he hoped to enjoy the rest of a life that was cut much too short in June of 1974 by a sudden heart attack.

Xavier Cugat

XAVIER CUGAT'S name has always been synonomous with Latin-American dance music. The reason is simple. The crafty Spaniard, who spent part of his youth in Brooklyn, has always been a superb showman and has succeeded in presenting to the American public in a most captivating manner the music of South America. To be sure, other bandleaders have tried through the years to do the same thing. Some have had a modicum of success. But none has managed to package the music with as much color and glamour as did Cugat, who once employed Rita Hayworth in his band. As a result, whenever tangos or rumbas or congas are mentioned, the average American immediately thinks of Cugie.

It was as a violinist in Phil Harris's band that Cugat began his name band career. Thereafter he was hired to lead the relief band at the Waldorf Astoria, a spot in which he was to be starred many times in subsequent years. The band was nothing sensational, but the way it dressed was most attracting. Larry Barnett, one of the best-known and most influential talent-agency executives (he headed MCA's West Coast operation for years and later became president of GAC), recalls that Lucius Boomer, the Waldorf's director, almost fired Cugat one night, not because the music wasn't satisfactory, but because the bandsmen had neglected to wear the flaming red jackets that had become their trademark.

During the early forties, the Cugat orchestra achieved its greatest musical distinction, partly because of Miguelito Valdes, its magnificent Cuban singer. The band also featured a beautiful Latin female vocalist, Lena Romay, and during one period blended her vocals with those of a chorus of five men and four women that Cugat used as a regular section in the band—just like reeds or brasses—with telling effect.

In front of the excitingly garbed orchestra and the sensuous singers, all of whom produced unexpectedly good music, stood Cugat, a master showman, a man of great charm and wit. Some of us sometimes felt that he was overdoing the personality bit—and chances are we were often right. But this was Cugie's way of reaching an audience, one of his life's prime aims.

He is a man of numerous other talents. Exhibit A: his hundreds of distinctive and at times almost distinguished caricatures of famous people, distributed to hundreds of newspapers via Kings Syndicate. Exhibit B: his glib tongue,

Cugie

used to great advantage in radio and TV interviews. Exhibit C: his attraction for several very lovely females, including his first two wives, Carmen and Lorraine (both exceedingly pretty), and his subsequent, more famous spouses, Abbe Lane and Charo.

It may be argued that Cugat's was not the greatest of the Latin-American bands, that those of Machito and Tito Puente and a few more have played the music more authentically and with more conviction than Cugat's ever did. Possibly this is true. But certainly no other Latin bandleader ever captured the fancy of the American public more than did Cugat, for none could come close to him when it came to his superb sense of showmanship, his ability to sell his music, his girls and himself so successfully.

The Dorsey Brothers

ON A spring evening in 1934, several of us fellow college musicians stood transfixed in front of the bandstand at Nuttings-on-the-Charles, in Waltham, Massachusetts, listening to a band we'd never heard of before and the likes of which we hadn't known until then even existed.

This was the brand-new Dorsey Brothers Orchestra, organized just a few weeks earlier but, so far as we were concerned, one of the slickest, most exciting musical aggregations ever to enter our musical lives. A few of us had heard of Jimmy and Tommy Dorsey, but only through records and, at that, mainly as leaders of a group that accompanied singers like Bing Crosby, Mildred Bailey and the Boswell Sisters. And one or two of us may have heard their studio-band recordings featuring Bunny Berigan and some other top musicians. But none of us expected anything like this.

It was a stupendously, solidly swinging band that impressed us that night— much more solid and much more swinging than Glen Gray and the Casa Loma Orchestra, which had become *the* outfit among collegians. As a drummer, I was immediately impressed by the tremendous drive of Ray McKinley, the way his style fit right in with that of the horns, the sound he got from his instrument and the light, subtle wit that permeated his playing. (That night, I recall, he even sang rather than played a couple of drum breaks, just the way he did several years later, when, as part of Will Bradley's band, he gave birth to "Beat Me Daddy, Eight to the Bar.")

What amazed all of us, however, was the huge sound coming from just eleven men. Instead of three trumpets and two trombones, the orthodox brass setup, the band had just one trumpet but three trombones, giving the ensemble a round-bellied resonance we'd never heard before. Of course, when one realizes in restrospect that two of the trombones were those of Tommy Dorsey and Glenn Miller and that Miller had written many of the arrangements, it's pretty easy to understand why we were so impressed.

The things Miller wrote for the band were replete with repeated riffs, notably in such numbers as "St. Louis Blues," "Dinah," the long-running "Honeysuckle Rose" and the fans' favorite, "Stop, Look and Listen." They all came complete with rhythmic interludes and fade-outs, the same devices

142

Glenn was to use years later for his own band on such tunes as "In the Mood" and "Tuxedo Junction."

Glenn was responsible not only for the band's style but also for half its personnel. He and McKinley had been working in Smith Ballew's band (Glenn was trombonist, arranger and manager) when it played in Denver and was looking for replacements. There, in Vic Shilling's band, Glenn discovered a vocal trio of good instrumentalists—saxist Skeets Herfurt, trombonist Don Matteson and guitarist Roc Hilman. In the Donnelly-James band he heard a fine girl singer named Kay Weber. He invited all four to join the Ballew band for its next engagement in Miami. They accepted. But the plans were changed and instead the band was booked into the Roosevelt Hotel in New York. The group arrived in town, only to find this date had been canceled too.

Kay Weber, who recalls Ballew as "a man with a beautiful voice and great personal charm—he used to remind me of Gary Cooper," still feels indebted to Glenn for his hard work in "keeping us in eating money until he got us with the Dorseys. They had been planning a band, but it took Glenn to really crystallize everything for them and set the style of their band."

According to McKinley, "the emphasis on the trombones was to give the band a Bing Crosby quality. The Dorseys had often played for Bing, and they felt that they could achieve some relationship if they pitched their sound like his."

A great deal of planning went into the venture. Kay Weber recalls rehearsing arrangements in the offices of Rockwell-O'Keefe, the band's bookers, several nights from seven in the evening till eight in the morning. Both the Dorseys and Miller were then, as they continued to be, sticklers for musical perfection, and few bands began their careers in as good musical shape as did the Dorsey group.

The saxes included Jimmy, Skeets and Jack Stacey; the rhythm section, in addition to McKinley and Hilman, had pianist Bobby Van Epps and bassist Delmar Kaplan (a magnificent musician); the trombonists were Tommy, Glenn and Matteson; and, to start with, Bunny Berigan played trumpet. Berigan lasted too short a time. Charlie Spivak followed him for a brief period, and then Jerry Neary, who was with the band when I heard it at Nuttings-on-the-Charles, took over. A few weeks later, when the band began its first steady engagement, at Sands Point Casino on Long Island, George Thow, a Harvard graduate, replaced Neary. To give the band greater color, Jimmy and Stacey would occasionally double on trumpets.

Kay Weber, the only girl vocalist the band ever had, sang ballads beautifully. "There was a tenor for a short time," McKinley recalls, "but his voice didn't fit at all. So Rockwell-O'Keefe, which was also handling Bing, sent over his kid brother, Bob."

According to Kay, "Tommy resented the booking office telling him whom to hire, and he took it out on Bob, who was a pretty scared kid at the time. The office had told the band to let Bob sing on the next broadcast, and so as soon as Bob joined the band, Tommy started needling him. He kept calling off names of tunes and saying, 'Can you sing this one and that one,' and Bob kept saying 'No,' until finally George Thow called out from the back of the band. 'Can you *sing*?' It was cruel, but it broke the tension, and even Tommy laughed."

After the summer at Sands Point, during which the band recorded some very fine sides for Decca, came engagements at Ben Marden's Riviera in New Jersey and the Palais Royale nightclub on Broadway, where McKinley created a minor furor by shooting pins off rubber bands and bursting the girl dancers' bubbles, and where Miller left to organize the Ray Noble Orchestra (Joe Yukl replaced him).

Following some more one-nighters, the Dorseys landed the coveted Glen Island Casino gig for the 1935 summer season, opening there on May 15. The spot had already built up a great clientele via its two-summer booking of Glen Gray and the Casa Loma Orchestra, and the future of the Dorsey Brothers Orchestra looked very bright. But some drastic changes were soon to take place.

During the spring of 1935, the band played a one-nighter in Troy, New York. As Ray McKinley remembers it, "The police hired a young kid to sing too. I remember he came up playing a four-string guitar, and he sang very well." The "young kid" recalls the night very well. "I'd won the Allen's Amateur Hour on the Fred Allen radio show," says Bob Eberly, "but I hadn't done much else except sing around the Troy area—that's where my hometown, Hoosick Falls, is. Tommy seemed to like me, and so when Bob Crosby left, he sent for me. I remember one of the first things I did was record a couple of sides, 'Chasing Rainbows' and 'You're All I Need,' and, believe me, they were two of the worst things I've ever heard in my life! I also remember one of the first things Tommy did was to borrow ten bucks from me. And all I had to my name was eleven! You know, I don't ever remember him paying me back, either."

Eberly was deeply impressed by Tommy's tremendous drive and energy. "He was doing everything—leading the band, making up the radio programs and all the things a leader does. He resented Jimmy for several reasons. For one thing, Jimmy was drinking quite a lot, and Tommy, even though he may have wanted to, didn't. That alone made him mad. But, then, Jimmy used to like to needle Tommy too. He'd just sit there in the saxes, and when Tommy was leading, he'd make cracks like, 'Smile, Mac,' and, 'You're the big star!' and that sort of thing.

"Tommy just kept on working harder. I remember how he used to drive himself. He never had more than five hours sleep a night, and every evening, when we were finished work, he'd drive all the way home to Bernardsville, New Jersey, going ninety miles an hour on back roads. I know, because I lived with him."

Tommy, who had difficulty getting along with Jimmy and at times with the rest of the band, sometimes drove his car instead of traveling in the bus with the others. Kay Weber recalls one time when Tommy passed the bus in his car, got out, signaled for it to stop, then climbed on board and, obviously very emotionally upset, blurted out, "Why don't you guys like me?" There was an embarrassing silence, then McKinley broke in with, "Tommy, you always say this was a band of handpicked musicians. Then why don't you treat us with respect? That's all we want."

In the months that followed, the tension continued to mount. Tommy kept resenting Jimmy more and more. And when Michael De Zutter, who ran Glen Island Casino, seemed to take a stronger liking to the older Dorsey (Tommy was the younger brother), making him his drinking companion, Tommy, according to McKinley, became even more upset.

Something had to happen. Early in June it did. One night on the bandstand, Tommy beat off the tempo to a tune called "I'll Never Say 'Never Again' Again." Jimmy looked up. "Isn't that a little too fast, Mac?" he asked. Tommy didn't say a word. He just picked up his horn and walked off the stand and out of the band—forever.

Both Tommy Rockwell and Cork O'Keefe tried to talk Tommy into returning. He wouldn't budge. So Jimmy became the leader.

"Jimmy didn't want it that way," Eberly remembers. "He was too shy. He never thought he could be a leader." But a leader he became just the same.

According to Ray McKinley, Tommy gave Rockwell an interesting explanation. "He didn't say anything wrong," he complained, referring to Jimmy. "He just bawled me out with his eyes!"

Jimmy Dorsey

JIMMY DORSEY never had the drive or the ambition or the boundless energy that his brother Tommy had. Quite possibly he would have been content to sit there in the sax section of the Dorsey Brothers Orchestra, letting Tommy take over, for the rest of his life. There are those who saw him in the fifties, when he and Tommy had been reunited and Tommy was again calling the shots, who submit that they hadn't seen Jimmy as happy and as relaxed in a long, long time.

Jimmy

Happy and relaxed is basically what Jimmy was by nature. He was not a competitor, so that the idea of having to lead a band against all the hard-nosed leaders who had been around and who were coming around as the big band boom got under way was probably not too much to his liking. But he had a job to do—and he did one hell of a great job!

Of course he had the basic ammunition, for Jimmy was an excellent musician—in some ways better rounded than Tommy. He also knew instinctively how to get along with people, and though his band may never have reached the dynamic heights that Tommy's did, it managed to exist on an evener keel, with fewer flare-ups and crises and with a more consistent *esprit de corps*. Jimmy was extremely well-liked by all his men—not just by those, as was more prevalent in Tommy's case, whom *he* happened to like. And like Tommy, he too had a keen sense of humor. There were many laughs in the Jimmy Dorsey band, and Jimmy supplied lots of them.

There was a softness, too, about Jimmy that was very lovable. He cared about people and their problems. He had little pet philosophies, such as one that arranger Harold Mooney (later an executive with Mercury Records) recalls: "If you don't feel well, stop thinking about yourself and rise above it." It was a bit of philosophy that, Mooney says, "he tried to force on the men in the band. But it never really worked."

Indicative of Jimmy's thoughtfulness—and his sly sense of humor perhaps—was his reaction to Mooney's joining the band along with nine pieces of luggage plus a phonograph. "The guys made fun of it," Mooney remembers. "But when next Christmas came around, Jimmy gave my wife and me two wardrobe trunks."

The big problem Jimmy had to face when Tommy walked out was finding a trombone replacement. For several weeks, various friends sat in, including two excellent musicians, Jack Jenney and a CBS staff trombonist named Jerry Colonna. But the substitutes either didn't want the job or weren't good enough. Then Jimmy remembered a kid trombonist he and Tommy had heard in Cass High School in Detroit. This was sixteen-year-old Bobby Byrne, possessor of a fantastic tone and range.

Larry Clinton, who was arranging for the band then, recalls that Byrne arrived with three trombones and a harp. "They took up so much room in the dressing room at Glen Island that the guys could hardly get in. But I will say this for Bobby: he was the only trombone player out of all those who came up who wasn't scared by Tommy's book. And, believe me, that was one tough book too!"

Ray McKinley remembers Byrne with a certain amount of admiration and also a bit of credulity. "He really wasn't what you'd call a true jazz musician. His idea of the greatest hot trombone player in the world was Peewee Hunt."

Byrne's debut with the band was like that of a rookie pitcher tossing a no-hitter his first time out in the majors. He was absolutely fantastic. According to those present, he knew just how good he was too. Under a leader less sympathetic than Jimmy, Bobby Byrne's debut could have been disastrous.

Following its summer at Glen Island, the band went into hibernation insofar as most dance band followers, other than those around Los Angeles, were concerned. It had captured the assignment on Bing Crosby's "Kraft Music Hall" radio series, which emanated from Hollywood, and it stayed out there for eighteen months. McKinley notes that an old Dorsey and Crosby compatriot, Fud Livingston, was hired to do most of the arrangements for the show. They were written, of course, for Bing, which was just great for Eberly, because Crosby was his idol, and "it was a tremendous kick for me to be able to sing those arrangements whenever the band played a one-nighter."

The band underwent few changes, and the style of its instrumental numbers didn't vary much. It played basically a two-beat sort of jazz, especially when it featured McKinley on numbers like "The Parade of the Milk Bottle Caps." Ray, along with Don Matteson, sang the up-tempo novelties. Eberly and Kay Weber shared the ballads, as well as a minor romance. "She used to call me the Country Bumpkin," Bob reports. "I guess she was right in a way. I remember one time we went to the movies—the picture was *The Great Ziegfeld*—and after a while she held my hand. I almost died!"

There was little left for Kay to do in the band. A warm, gentle person with a small-town midwestern background, she loved to sing and to act. But Dorsey concentrated almost entirely on the radio series, on which she didn't appear, and Kay says she felt "as if I were stagnating. I really wanted to be an actress more than a singer in those days, and so I decided to go back to New York to see what I could do there." Soon thereafter she continued her singing career in the new band led by her old Dorsey singing partner, Bob Crosby. Her immediate replacement was Vicki Joyce, who remained only a short time. And then came a young, pretty and effervescent lass, Martha Tilton, who stayed for quite a while, though she never recorded until she joined Benny Goodman later in 1937.

Eberly stayed on. Being near his idol was enough of an inducement. But more than that, he and Jimmy had become very close friends, a relationship that was to exist for the rest of Jimmy's life. They lived together, and Bob attended all rehearsals and broadcasts. He was then, as he still is today, an immensely witty person, and, according to McKinley, "he used to break us up at rehearsals with his ad-lib cracks." What people don't know, though, is that many of those quips showed up as "ad libs" by Bob Burns, the bazooka player on the Kraft broadcasts.

During that period, the band made several unusual sides, including a hilarious takeoff on "What's the Reason I'm Not Pleasing You," with Jimmy clucking away in chicken fashion on his clarinet and the rest of the band corning it up as well, and an ambitious version of "Listen to the Mocking Bird," which featured an operatic soprano, Josephine Tumminia, and which could have been considered funny, depending on how you happened to listen to it.

The band's vocal department got quite a lift early in 1938 when June Richmond joined. She was an extremely effervescent and very large black woman, and such a racial breakthrough was considered a pretty daring move in those days. But Jimmy and his sensitive personal manager, Billy Burton, stuck to their convictions, and June became a vital and welcome member of the organization. She may not have been the world's greatest singer, but she was a top-flight entertainer who broke up many a stage show.

Somewhere near the beginning of 1939, Jimmy heard a singer at a Houston jam session who impressed him so greatly that he hired her on the spot. June had already left, and Vi Mele had been singing temporarily with the band. But young Ella Mae Morse, who had to borrow carfare to get to the jam session, seemed like the ideal girl for the band.

For once Jimmy was wrong. Ella Mae came to New York and lasted about a month. She had a great beat and a remarkable sense of phrasing, but she was totally inexperienced and musically undisciplined. Eberly recalls that on one broadcast she sang some very risqué and network-banned lyrics instead of the network-approved set, and on another air shot she forgot the words of a song completely. And so, seemingly oblivious of the fact that she was on the air, she simply smiled sweetly at the mike and then, turning to Jimmy and, for all the listening nation to hear, murmured something like, "I forgot the words. Now isn't that just awful? I don't know what to do. I can't catch up to the band now, can I?"

Ella Mae must have made quite an impression on the band's pianist, Freddy Slack, though, for three years later she was starred on his first hit record, "Cow Cow Boogie," and soon thereafter became an established star.

One reason Jimmy could easily let Ella Mae go was that Burton had in the meantime discovered a very pretty blonde singer working with Larry Funk and his Band of a Thousand Melodies at the (Greenwich) Village Barn in New York. Helen O'Connell was a very sweet person—she usually wore a religious cross when she sang—whose singing I never happened to like especially, for she had a tendency to overphrase and not always to sing in tune. But obviously the public adored her, and she turned out to be not only the most popular girl singer Jimmy ever had, but also such a favorite among fans of all bands that she won the *Metronome* poll of 1940.

Many people remember Helen primarily for the duets she sang with Bob. Yet for the first two years of her stay with Jimmy, she sang only solos of songs ranging from novelties like "Six Lessons from Madame La Zonga" and "The Bad Humor Man" to dainty bits like "Little Curly Hair in a High Chair" and out-and-out torch songs like "When the Sun Comes Out." According to Bob, she was never too happy about singing swing tunes, believing she sounded best on torchers. Eberly still feels today that she was most effective on songs "that fit her personality, like 'Embraceable You' and 'All of Me,'" numbers during which she exploded certain notes so forcefully that I always pictured some little man standing behind her and pinching her at crucial times in crucial spots.

Bob and Helen

The series of famous Eberly-O'Connell duets was born out of necessity. On its radio series for Twenty Grand cigarettes, one of several dime-a-package brands that had become popular, the band was allotted a three-minute spot near the close in which it was supposed to feature all its stars. And so arranger Tutti Camarata devised a special routine during which Bob sang the first chorus as a ballad, the tempo would pick up and Jimmy would play part of a jazz chorus of the tune, and then the tempo would slow down again for Helen to come on for a semi-wailing finale.

The gimmick proved to be a sensation. Eberly notes that an important Decca Records executive was dead set against recording the routine because "people would break a leg trying to dance to all those tempo changes." But he was out-argued, obviously happily for his sake, because, according to Bob, "Green Eyes" sold ninety thousand copies in the first few days, at a time when twenty-five thousand copies was considered a great seller.

"Green Eyes" actually was the third song recorded in the tempo-changing manner. "Amapola" and "Yours" had been cut a month earlier, in February, 1941. Another duo-vocal hit, "Tangerine," was recorded in the following December. But "Green Eyes" was the biggest hit, and Bob credits much of its success with "the way Helen took those pickup notes, 'those cool and limpid green eyes!'[*] It really killed them." What amuses Eberly is that because of her limited vocal range, Helen couldn't sing the notes the way they were written, the way Bob sang them on the first chorus, that is, starting low and going up. Instead she sang alternate and easier notes, and the effect on the public was devastating.

The Eberly-O'Connell relationship, according to Bob, "could have made the perfect setting for one of those happy family TV situation series, the way Helen and I would kid and tease each other while Jimmy guided and watched over us." On radio interviews, each with mock seriousness would jokingly claim complete credit for the success of the record, though both were acutely aware of the other's contribution. They were completely aware of each other's more romantic attributes too—something many of us never realized at the time. But some of the men in the band felt sure they would be married. The feeling, according to them, was stronger on Helen's part, and after Bob married Florine Callahan in the early forties, Helen became romantically interested in both Jimmy Blumenstock, a Fordham College football star, and a handsome Ivy League type named Cliff Smith. The band was rooting for Jimmy, but eventually Helen married Cliff, and, as some suspected it might be, the marriage turned out to be disastrous. Helen has since made frequent public appearances, singing more surely and more musically than she ever did with Jimmy and also for a time making an excellent impression as the hostess of NBC-TV's "Today" show and of a beauty contest series.

Certainly his two singers played vital roles in the success of Jimmy Dorsey's Orchestra. But, of course, his musicians, though not as well known as Bob and Helen, were every bit as important and impressive, for Jimmy always insisted upon a high level of competence in all who worked for him.

Following its year and a half on the Coast, the band traveled east, eventually winding up in New York in the latter part of 1937. The saxes had been augmented from three to four, the brass from four to five. Tutti Camarata, who was to become the band's chief arranger, played lead trumpet for a while, and two other arrangers, Dave Matthews and Leonard Whitney, played tenor sax.

During those days, *Metronome* often printed thumbnail sketches of various band personnel. To give you an idea of what Jimmy was like, here's my 1937 item on him:

> Jimmy Dorsey (leader and alto sax)—an inveterate golfer . . . plays in the eighties and a light blue gaucho shirt and a light blue half sweater . . . and mostly with Bette Davis and Oliver (Laurel &) Hardy . . . a great reed worrier . . . sports two new Packards but would gladly trade them for some spare ribs in Houston, Texas, sans any vegetables . . . fiery temper but never bears a grudge . . . favorite pastime is amusing audiences at rehearsals and never getting anything done.

In 1938 the band couldn't quite make up its mind what it wanted to be. It played two different kinds of jazz—dixieland two-beat and a more modern, swinging four-beat. However, it featured some great musicians notably tenor saxist Herbie Haymer, first trumpeter Ralph Muzzillo, jazz trumpeter Shorty Sherock, lead trombonist Bobby Byrne and drummer Ray McKinley. And, of course, there was Jimmy himself, starred on both alto sax and on clarinet, the instrument on which he had originally achieved fame with the Scranton Sirens, with Red Nichols and his Five Pennies and with Paul Whiteman's huge orchestra.

With Don Redman added to an arranging staff that included Tutti Camarata, Hal Mooney and Joe Lipman, the band settled into a more distinctive and distinguished groove. In July of 1939, the rhythm section was shaken by the departure of Ray McKinley, a musical and spiritual stalwart. Davey Tough took over for a brief period, Buddy Schutz for a much longer one.

In 1939 Jimmy experienced a happy reunion with Tommy when his band closed an engagement at the New Yorker Hotel and Tommy's opened one—both on the same night. Everyone knew they weren't getting along, and it was quite an emotional scene when they finally appeared in public. My report was pretty emotional too:

> When Tommy handed over the bandstand to his brother, their arms entwined, the two of them talking back and forth to each other, ad-libbing joking perhaps to hide the embarrassment occasioned by so many people staring at them, there arose a feeling of sincerity and reality that'll seldom be equalled in the history of dancebandom. You felt it and you felt that the brothers felt it and that their parents, sitting nearby, felt it too. You couldn't describe it, but it did make you feel that even in hard-boiled dancebandom a human element arises that sometimes obliterates all questions of vibratos, split commissions, intonation, song pluggers, press agents and so forth.

Though the Dorseys were getting along (for a night, anyway), other controversies were raging. One was the question of the relative importance and popularity of swing and sweet music. In a letter to the Chicago *Daily News*, Jimmy noted that Americans, habitually trying to digest everything too

The Jimmy Dorsey Orchestra of 1940
Seated: *Tutti Camarata, Don Matteson, Bobby Byrne, Bruce Squires.*
Standing: *Jimmy, Bob Eberly, Roc Hilman, Shorty Sherock, Jack Ryan,*
Ray McKinley, Dave Matthews, Leonard Whitney, Charlie Frasier, Freddy Slack

quickly, had not fully digested swing, "so that it has become distasteful because of overindulgence." Still he felt that swing was here to stay, that sweet music had never been "out," and that "we are now arriving at the stage of the middle-of-the-path popular music, where slow, torrid tunes will vary with hot jam sessions." Then, pointing out that bands that emphasize only swing or sweet are "beginning to slide and slide fast," he concluded, "the issue is not that swing is losing out to sweet; it is more that a happy medium is being approached that will give equal ranking to both."

On this subject, *Metronome* in October, 1939, polled fifty kids picked at random at Frank Dailey's Meadowbrook, asked them about Jimmy's band, and found out that twenty-eight preferred its sweet, eleven its swing, while eleven more were undecided. In another poll late in 1939, the magazine discovered that Eberly, responsible for many of the band's pretty sounds, had become an immensely popular singer, his total of 527 votes being just 110 less than that of perennial victor, Bing Crosby. (Interesting side observation: Frank Sinatra received twenty-one votes.)

Bob credits Jimmy's concern for his singers for much of his success. "He got away from the usual form of an arrangement—you know, when the band always plays a first chorus and then the singer gets his chance. Instead, he'd let the singer start off—in fact, he'd build entire arrangements around us." Thus on such big Dorsey hit records as "I Understand," "I'm Glad There Is You," "I Get Along Without You Very Well," "Marie Elena" and many others, almost the complete side was given over to Eberly's vocal.

Bob was a great singer who might have been even greater had he not succumbed to a tendency to overphrase, to sing too ponderously, instead of just allowing his magnificent voice box and innate good taste to carry him along. There were times when he could absolutely chill you, and more than one critic hailed him as the best of all band singers, even at a time when Sinatra's popularity with Dorsey was at its highest.

Eberly was immensely popular with everyone who knew him. Whereas musicians generally were rather critical of band vocalists, those in Jimmy's band swore by Bob. It is doubtful whether the entire big band era ever turned out a more beloved person than Bob Eberly, and even today those associated with him during his Dorsey stay recall with great reverence and enthusiasm the man's honesty, humility, wonderful values and terrific sense of humor.

What was great about the band era in general and the Dorsey band in particular, so far as Eberly was concerned, was the fact that "we all spoke the same language. The band days offered you a big education, as a musician and as a human being. A selfish person would soon learn that his was the wrong attitude to take simply by seeing so many examples of selflessness right in front of him."

As noted earlier, Eberly and Dorsey remained the closest of friends. But sometimes Jimmy felt compelled to set Bob straight. Eberly recently recalled one such occasion. "We were on a movie lot, and a man stopped me and said he'd heard me sing and liked what I did. Then he asked me if I'd mind putting a few notes on mike for him. So he sat down at the piano and backed me on a chorus of 'They Can't Take That Away from Me.' When it was over, I turned to him and told him, maybe even a little too condescendingly, that I thought he played real good piano and he thanked me and then I rejoined Jimmy. 'How'd you like George?' Jimmy asked me. 'George who?' I asked him. 'Why, George Gershwin,' he said. I could have fallen right through the floor. Can you imagine what a dope I must have felt like—*me* telling George Gershwin *he* played good piano!"

Eberly had numerous offers to go out on his own. "Paramount Pictures at one time wanted me to replace Dick Powell, but they weren't definite about it." According to Hal Mooney, song publisher and personal manager Lou Levy once offered Bob a hundred-thousand-dollar guarantee to go out as a single. Someone else wanted to build a band around him and put him in Glen Island Casino. And right after Sinatra had scored such a tremendous hit at the Riobamba Club in New York, Eberly was invited to go into a competing club at a fabulous guarantee.

At this point, manager Burton wanted Bob to sign a contract to assure his staying with the band. "But I didn't want to leave, and I told Jimmy so. I was very happy making my four hundred dollars a week and twelve hundred and fifty dollars extra when we made movies. I didn't feel a contract was necessary, and Jimmy told Billy that my word was good enough for him. So I never did sign a contract."

Eberly, who once tried to help Sinatra by asking Jimmy to record a song Frank had written, "This Love of Mine" (Jimmy turned it down cold), insists to this day that he has never envied Frank ("He was a great singer then, and he's even greater today"), not even during those days when Bob was still with Jimmy and when Sinatra, who had cut out from Tommy's band, had become so successful. "I was very content where I was, maybe in a lazy sort of way. But I never felt adequate, and perhaps it was that feeling, more than loyalty, that made me stay where I was."

The question of staying or leaving the band became academic in December, 1943, when Bob entered the Army, spending many of his days working for Wayne King. One of his fondest remembrances is receiving a letter from Crosby that said, in essence, "Wish you could get out and make a lot of money and wear tweed suits the way so many of us are doing."

The two years that Eberly spent in the service diminished his popularity. Before he entered, he was idolized by a young singer named Dick Haymes (Dick has frequently admitted this). But Haymes, like Sinatra a civilian, gained greatly in popularity during those two years, and it must have been quite a shock to Bob to have someone compliment him after he got out of the Army with, "You sing just like Dick Haymes!"

After his discharge, Bob auditioned for the "Chesterfield Supper Club" radio series with, of all things, a slight brain concussion. Maybe that's why Perry Como wound up with the plum. But Eberly kept on singing, often in small clubs, his wit and good humor never diminished, though the removal of one lung in 1980 did curtail his activities.

With both Eberly and O'Connell gone, the Dorsey band altered its style to fill the void. Kitty Kallen proved to be an excellent replacement for Helen, though stylistically she was quite different. And though boy singers like Buddy Hughes and Bob Carroll did quite well at various times, nobody could ever replace Eberly.

The band had reached its zenith in 1943, surpassing even Tommy's in popularity and in musicianship. At that time, Jimmy sported a nine-piece brass section (five trumpets instead of the original one) and some exceptional soloists, such as tenor saxist Babe Russin, trumpeter Nate Kazebier and pianist Johnny Guarnieri. During the following years, the band kept up its high standards, and by the end of the war, Jimmy had the swingingest band he had ever led. In early 1946, I reviewed it at the 400 Club in New York and was enthralled with its bite and vigor, the guitar playing of Herb Ellis, the piano of Lou Carter and the drumming of young Earl Kiffe.

But the band never had the same personality. The warmth and the humor and the distinctiveness were gone. Jimmy tried gimmicks, such as featuring a small dixieland jazz band that included trumpeter Charlie Teagarden. It was all good musically, but nothing, not even Jimmy's alto (which, by the way, I always thought was better than his clarinet), could rekindle the flame, though late in his career the band created a bright though brief spark via Jimmy's hit recording of "So Rare."

Jimmy struggled along for a number of years and finally, like so many other leaders, gave up. Then in the middle of 1953, eighteen years after Tommy had walked off the Glen Island Casino bandstand, the brothers were reunited. The band was basically Tommy's, but both of them led it. According to the report in *Metronome*: "Tommy leads the band, playing his library, for the first hour and a half or so of the date. Then he introduces Jimmy, who performs as featured soloist for several numbers. After that they play a number or two together. Then comes intermission. After the siesta, Jimmy takes over with his library, going through all the things that made him famous. Toward the close he brings on Tommy, who is featured in a few numbers as Jimmy conducts. The finale has them both out front for a short enough time so they can't fight."

The partnership lasted for two years, until Tommy's sudden death. Jimmy, who had already been quite ill and had undergone a major operation, quickly went downhill. It was obvious to all who knew how deep-seated his cancer had grown that he had only a short time to live. "It was so hopeless," Bob Eberly reports, "that the doctors even allowed him to drink as much as he wanted to. There was no way of saving him."

On June 12, 1957, just a little more than six months after Tommy died, Jimmy Dorsey passed away, and all the wonderful contributions that these two brothers had made to American music came to an end.

Eberly, surveying a current music scene that has changed so drastically since the days of the well-trained, perfection-minded Dorseys, recently noted with mixed solemnity and sentimentality, "If Jimmy and Tommy were alive today, they'd be so unhappy with music. Boy, how things have changed!"

Tommy

Tommy Dorsey

WHEN Tommy Dorsey walked off the Glen Island Casino bandstand and out of the Dorsey Brothers band that spring evening in 1935, he had no idea just where he was going. He could have done the easy thing: he could have returned to the radio and recording studios where he had been making a mint of money and forgotten all about ever having a band of his own. But those who knew Tommy Dorsey best knew he wouldn't, in fact, couldn't, do that.

For Tommy, who was soon to achieve fame as "The Sentimental Gentleman of Swing," was a fighter—often a very belligerent one—with a sharp mind, an acid tongue and intense pride. He had complete confidence in himself. He felt he could do so many things better than so many other people could. And so many times he was absolutely right.

This time he set out to prove one specific thing—that he could have an even more successful band than his brother Jimmy had. And prove it he most certainly did.

In restrospect—and in big band history—Tommy Dorsey's must be recognized as the greatest all-round dance band of them all. Others may have sounded more creative. Others may have swung harder and more consistently. Others may have developed more distinctive styles. But of all the hundreds of well-known bands, Tommy Dorsey's could do more things better than any other could.

It could swing with the best of them, first when it featured stars like trumpeters Bunny Berigan and Peewee Erwin, tenor saxist Bud Freeman, clarinetist Johnny Mince, drummer Davey Tough and Deane Kincaide's arrangements; later when it spotlighted Ziggy Elman's and for a while once again Berigan's trumpet, Don Lodice's tenor, Buddy DeFranco's clarinet, Buddy Rich's drums and Sy Oliver's arrangements.

Sure, the bands of Ellington, Goodman, Basie, Lunceford and possibly one or two others could outswing Dorsey's. But they couldn't begin to match it in other ways. For example, none could come close to Tommy's when it came to playing ballads. Tommy Dorsey, "The Sentimental Gentleman of Swing," was a master at creating moods—warm, sentimental and forever musical moods—at superb dancing and listening tempos. And, what's more, Tommy selected arrangers who could sustain those moods—Paul Weston, Axel Stordahl and Dick Jones. And he showcased singers who could project those moods wonderfully—Jack Leonard, Frank Sinatra, Jo Stafford and the Pied Pipers and others. With the possible exception of Claude Thornhill's, no other band ever played ballads so prettily, so effectively and always so musically.

And, of course, to top it all there was Tommy's trombone. It has often been suggested that his band was built around his singers and his sidemen and its arrangements. And yet throughout the twenty years of its almost continuous existence, its most pervading and distinguishing sound remained the warm, silken, sometimes sensuous, more times sentimental horn of its leader.

Tommy didn't start his band exactly from scratch. An old friend of his, Joe Haymes, was leading a band at New York's McAlpin Hotel. Joe wasn't getting anywhere, and it's not at all inconceivable that he wasn't completely averse to letting Tommy take over his band. At any rate, the entire Haymes sax and trumpet sections, his trombonist, his pianist, his guitarist, his bassist and his arranger, a young Dartmouth graduate, Paul Weston—twelve men in all—joined Dorsey en masse.

One of the first things Tommy did after changing the style of the Haymes band to suit his personal likes and needs—it had been playing essentially "hotel swing" with little distinction—was to record some sides for RCA Victor in September of 1935. In the first set of record reviews I ever wrote for *Metronome*, I commented on three of the Dorsey band's initial efforts, "On Treasure Island," "Back to My Boots and Saddles" and "Santa Claus Is Coming to Town," giving the nod to Edythe Wright's vocal over Cliff Weston's and summing up with: "The three sides show a band with lots of promise, a great trombone and trumpet [Sterling Bose's], a good clarinet [Sid Stoneburn's] and drums [Sam Rosen's], some nice ideas in arrangements and a lack of polish. But the polish should come in time."

Several months later the band made its New York debut—in the Blue Room of the Hotel Lincoln. Tommy instituted numerous personnel changes, bringing in drummer Davey Tough and tenor saxist Bud Freeman. He also snatched three formidable talents from Bert Block's local band—trumpeter Joe Bauer, vocalist Jack Leonard and a young, flaxen-haired arranger who'd been known as Odd Stordahl but who, as Axel Stordahl, was to develop into one of the most sensitive and musical arrangers of all time, a man who was to contribute immensely to the success of Dorsey and, in later years, to the rise of Frank Sinatra. These three Block graduates, Leonard, Stordahl and Bauer, also functioned as a vocal trio, known as The Three Esquires.

Other important musicians soon joined. Tommy had played often with Bunny Berigan in the studios, and he persuaded the great Wisconsin trumpeter to join him. A young clarinetist named Johnny Mince, fresh out of Chicago Heights, had been making some attractive sounds around town (he played for Ray Noble for a while). Tommy got him, too, as well as Joe Marsala's guitarist, Carmen Mastren.

The Tommy Dorsey Orchestra of 1936
Front row: *arranger-vocalist Axel Stordahl, Tommy,*
Edythe Wright, Jack Leonard, pianist-arranger Dick Jones
Second row: *trombonists Les Jenkins, Walter Mercurio,*
saxists Joe Dixon, Freddy Stulce, Bud Freeman, Clyde Rounds
Back row: *trumpeters Joe Bauer, Steve Lipkins, Maxie Kaminsky,*
drummer Davey Tough, guitarist Carmen Mastren, bassist Gene Traxler

Actually, the band went through numerous personnel changes in its formative years—a procedure that continued to plague it through a good part of its early history. Tommy was a perfectionist, and if his men didn't measure up to what he expected from them, he'd let them know so in no uncertain terms. It didn't matter who else was listening, either, so muscans with thin skins or tin ears weren't likely to last long in the band. Later, as he mellowed a bit, his musicians stayed with him longer.

There's no doubt about it—Tommy knew what he wanted. He'd had years of experience, first during his early days in Pennsylvania, later with Paul Whiteman and other bands and most consistently in the radio and recording studios, where his ability had made him the most "in-demand" of all trombonists. His big trouble, one which earned him a number of impassioned enemies, was his lack of tolerance of others' mistakes and his lack of tact when they were made.

But he was able to transmit his musical knowledge to those who were willing to listen—and who were able to put up with his temper tantrums. Paul Weston, later a top conductor in television, recently credited Dorsey for "teaching me just about everything I know. I have such great respect for his musicianship and his musical integrity." And the influence that Dorsey had on Frank Sinatra has been reported often. As Frank put it in the mid-forties in a *Metronome* interview: "There's a guy who was a real education to me in every possible way. I learned about dynamics and phrasing and style from the way he played his horn, and I enjoyed my work because he sees to it that a singer is always given a perfect setting."

This regard and respect for singers made singing with Dorsey's band the top spot for all vocalists of the big band era. Tommy began with a big, bearish man named Buddy Gately, who recorded one impressive side called "Love Will Live On," and then featured the lighter-voiced Cliff Weston, a Haymes holdover, before he snatched Jack Leonard from Block's band.

Jack turned out to be a real find and for several years rivaled Bing Crosby as the kids' favorite singer. He was a warm, decent, straightforward person, very handsome and rather shy. I have a feeling he never really knew how important he was. I remember once when he and I were going to the World's Fair together and we talked about taking some girls along with us I suggested he ought to be able to dig up a couple of really great ones and he said very simply, "You know, I hardly know any at all." That amazed me until he followed up with, "I meet a lot of them, but I don't really know what they look like. You see, I'm very near-sighted, and I can't wear glasses because that would ruin my romantic image!"

Jack stayed with the band for almost four years, recording such fine sides as "For Sentimental Reasons," "Dedicated to You," "If It's the Last Thing I Do," "Little White Lies," "You Taught Me to Love Again," "Once in a While" and probably the most famous of all Dorsey sides, "Marie."

The "Marie" side, with the band singing vocal riffs as Jack emoted a straight lyric, was so successful that Dorsey recorded several more standard tunes with the same formula—"Who," "Yearning" and "East of the Sun." "Marie" was recorded in January, 1937, after Tommy and his band had played a battle of music in Philadelphia with Doc Wheeler's Sunset Royal Serenaders. From Norman Pierre Gentieu's report in the November, 1937, issue of *Metronome* comes this excerpt about the battle between the two bands at Nixon's Grand Theater:

> Although the Dorsey band was as good as reports had promised, I think that the Sunset Royal lads were a trifle more in the groove. . . . The Sunset Royal Orchestra (who arrived here in a pitiful second-hand bus) was in the pit. The leader wielded a baton which might have served for a Zulu spear. . . . The band played but three numbers (other than for the vaudeville acts): "Limehouse Blues," which indicated again the smoothness of the boys in their more frenzied moments; "Marie" in which the Don Redman influence became apparent when the band sang hot vocal licks back of the vocalist, and "Blue."

Tommy, himself, writing in *Metronome* in June, 1938, verified the report in this way:

We were playing a theatre in Philly once upon a time, and there was a colored band playing the same show called the Royal Sunset Serenaders. They had the arrangement of "Marie" and all of us in the band liked it; in fact, after a couple of days we all knew it by heart. I figured that we could do more with it than they could, and so I traded them about eight of our arrangements for one of theirs.

The funny part of it is that I tried to get Eli Oberstein [Victor's recording chief] to let us record it. Eli couldn't see it, and so I tried it out on our studio audience after one of our commercials. It went over so big that I tried it out on the program. We got so many requests that we had to repeat it the next week. It was then that Oberstein let us record it.

In the following issue, Dorsey wrote about how "fed up" he and his band had become with having to play "Marie" so often. Realizing that it wasn't so much the tune as the arrangement that people were clamoring for, he decided "to get out some similar arrangements of different songs and see what happens. That started our cycle. We finally hit upon 'Who.' The arrangers got busy and wrote something that sounded pretty much like 'Marie' only different. Edythe [Wright], aided by a couple of the fellows, wrote some band lyrics for the background behind Jack's vocal. After a while 'Who' started to wear us down, so we dug up 'Yearning.' "

The other side of "Marie" was also a huge Dorsey hit. It was "Song of India," which, Tommy admitted, was suggested to him by the same Eli Oberstein who had turned down "Marie." "The funny part of it," Tommy reported, "was that for months, driving home at night, I had been singing to myself that lick we use on the introduction—you know: DUH—duh dee da dee duh duh duh duh duh—DA DA—but I could never get a tune to follow that figure. As soon as Eli suggested 'Song of India' I saw the connection. The next night (we were at Meadowbrook then) a whole bunch of us in the band got together and started working out the arrangement. By the following night we had everything arranged through Bunny Berigan's chorus. He was playing with us at the time. So we tried it out on the folks at Meadowbrook, and when Bunny got through his chorus we just stopped and explained that we hadn't finished the arrangement. Well, finally, to make a long story short —or to make a longer arrangement short—we just decided to go back to the original intro—and there we were." [The arrangement has always been credited to Red Bone, a Dorsey trombonist, who whipped it into shape.]

Berigan, of course, was a Dorsey favorite. And so was Bud Freeman. Tommy loved to listen to Bud's tenor-sax passages, and many was the time when he would let him blow chorus after chorus (especially on "Marie"), each time holding up a finger indicating "one more" as the panting but forever-swinging saxist grew wearier and wearier and wearier. It was Tommy's way

Jack Leonard (far right) sings "Marie" aided by glee club
of (front row) saxists Fredy Stulce, Skeets Herfurt, Johnny Mince,
and (back row) trumpeters Peewee Erwin, Andy Ferretti, Joe Bauer,
leader Dorsey and trombonist Walter Mercurio.

of showing his appreciation of Bud's talents while at the same time engaging in a typical Dorsey practical joke.

One thing about Tommy, he never failed to show his admiration if a musician did something well, not only the many men he featured in his band —Berigan, Freeman, Johnny Mince, Davey Tough, Peewee Erwin, Yank Lawson, Babe Russin, Joe Bushkin, Buddy Rich, Ziggy Elman, Chuck Peterson, Buddy DeFranco, Don Lodice, Boomie Richman, Charlie Shavers and others—but also his arrangers, Weston, Stordahl, Kincaide, Oliver and two young trombonists Tommy encouraged, Nelson Riddle and Earle Hagen, currently among the most successful arranger-conductors in the world..

But the man who inspired the most awe in Tommy was a fellow trombonist —Jack Teagarden. I saw it plainly one night—the only time I ever saw Tommy ill at ease and even a bit flustered. The occasion was the first *Metronome* All Star date, during which we recorded two sides by the winners of the magazine's poll. The first had featured a Teagarden solo, and since Tommy had also been picked as a trombonist, I suggested that he solo on the next tune. Tommy appeared embarrassed as he refused. "Nothing doing," he said. "Not when Jack's in the same room." (As a matter of fact, we finally did get Tommy to solo; he played a pretty chorus of blues, absolutely straight, while Jack improvised around it. The result was really quite emotional.)

Tommy's relationship with the men he liked in his band—and he seemed to like most of them—was social as well as musical and extended well beyond the bandstand. Often many of them weekended at his sumptuous home in Bernardsville, New Jersey—complete with tennis court, swimming pool, pinball machines and a fabulous hi-fi set, one of the first of its kind. Invited too would be other friends, like Johnny Mercer, Lennie Hayton and Clay Boland, to share the food, the drinks and the many laughs.

Tommy was a fine host, and his first wife, whom everyone called "Toots," was a wonderfully warm and gracious hostess. Unfortunately, their marriage broke up. In October, 1939, Tommy's bright and attractive singer, Edythe Wright, of whom Toots had been more than critical, also departed from the Dorsey scene. She was replaced by Anita Boyer, a very good singer, in what was the first of several changes in the vocal department which were to reshape rather drastically not only the music but also the career of the Dorsey band as a whole.

The next change was an important one: Jack Leonard left the band and an interim singer named Allan DeWitt was hired.

Jack was extremely popular not only with the public but also with the musicians in the band. There had been talk about his going out on his own as a single, but so far as anyone could determine, Jack himself had never been part of that talk, nor had he evidenced much interest in departing. However, it was entirely possible that Tommy heard some of these murmurings. It soon became apparent to many connected with the band that his attitude toward Leonard was cooling. Tommy was like that—impetuous and inclined to be suspicious. One day Leonard was late for rehearsal. It had been reported that he and Jimmy Blake, a trumpeter in the band, had been balling it up the night before. Those who knew Jack best doubted the story, but it seemed to be the final straw. In November of 1939 he left the band.

"I'll be back the first or second week in December," he said at the time. "That talk about Tommy and me having a fight is just talk. After five years of steady work, I was run down and just needed a rest—that's all. But I'm on one of those plenty-of-milk-to-bed-at-nine kicks now. I'll be back soon."

Jack never made it. And Allan DeWitt wasn't what Tommy was looking for. What he was looking for, however, happened to be working at the Sherman Hotel in Chicago at the same time Tommy's band was at the Palmer House, a few blocks away. He was referred to as "that skinny kid with James." Tommy sent an emissary over to see if he was interested. Sinatra talked it over with James, with whom he was very close. Harry agreed to let him out of his contract. One reason: Nancy Sinatra was pregnant at the time and Frank could use the extra pay. So Sinatra told Dorsey "O.K." A few weeks later in Milwaukee he joined the band.

Jack Egan, the veteran press agent who handled Dorsey in those days, recalls that Sinatra never got a chance to sing with the band in Milwaukee, where it was playing a theater engagement: "He had to wait until Allan DeWitt had worked out his two weeks' notice.

"Tommy had planned for Frank meanwhile to work on some new arrangements with Sy Oliver, who'd recently joined the band. But Jimmy Blake had taken sick, and Sy, who also played trumpet, had to sub for him. [According to Oliver, it was Lee Castle whom he replaced when an energetic dentist broke Lee's jaw.] That left no time for him to write for Frank. So when Frank made his first appearance with the band—it was at the Lyric Theater in Indianapolis —he had only two songs to sing. First he did a ballad—I forget what it was —it may have been 'My Prayer'—and then, of course, he did 'Marie,' which was still our big number.

"Well, he broke it up completely. And that was tough to do because a lot of the kids were big Jack Leonard fans. They kept yelling for more, but Frank had no encore prepared. So there right onstage he and Tommy went into a huddle and Frank suggested they fake 'South of the Border.' Well, that broke it up even more, especially when Frank started slurring down on those notes. You know, right then and there, when he went into the slurring bit, the kids started screaming, just the way they did later at the Paramount. And there was nothing rigged about it either. I know, because I was the band's press agent. And I was also Jack Leonard's close friend, and I wasn't inclined to go all out for any other singer. No, those screams were real!"

Dorsey must have been delighted at the response to his new singer. He had, as it turned out, already predicted Frank's success even before he had sung a note with the band. During a disc jockey interview while the band had played that week in Milwaukee, Tommy had stated that he thought Sinatra would become as big as Crosby. Maybe he really believed it. Maybe he was just showing his pique at Leonard for having quit the band. In any case, he was clairvoyant.

Sinatra blossomed with Dorsey, and with Sinatra the Dorsey band became more successful than ever. Frank has often admitted how listening to Tommy helped him develop his phrasing, his breathing, his musical taste and his musical knowledge. Dick Jones, once a Dorsey arranger and later a close friend of Sinatra, says simply, "Frank's musical taste was developed at Tommy's elbow."

It wasn't purely osmosis, however. Frank was never content to sit back and let things happen. He always wanted to improve himself and he was always working at singing. Jo Stafford recalls that after Frank joined the band he made a special effort to get a good blend with the Pied Pipers. "Most solo singers," she points out, "usually don't fit too well into a group, but Frank never stopped working at it and, of course, as you know, he blended beautifully with us. He was meticulous about his phrasing and dynamics. He worked very hard so that his vibrato would match ours. And he was always conscientious about learning his parts."

Frank blended wonderfully well with Tommy on a personal basis. He was young and eager and effervescent, and he needed approbation. Tommy, wise and outgoing, found it easy to encourage his young singer, for he liked him as a person and tremendously admired his singing. The happy relationship continued while Frank remained with the band. Unfortunately it came to an end thereafter, for, just as Tommy could not forgive Jack Leonard for leaving him, he resented Frank's departure. What's more, Sinatra could be just as stubborn as Dorsey, so that in the years that followed, neither seemed to be willing to be the first to give. Apparently the antagonism became even more intense than many of us realized, because years later, when Frank was asked to join all the other Dorsey alumni in a special memorial broadcast for Tommy, he refused because, as he reportedly told an associate, "it would be hypocritical of me."

Sinatra had joined the band when it had been undergoing numerous changes. Some of these were caused by Dorsey's loss of his radio commercial, which forced him to cut salaries. Some of the high-priced stars in the band didn't like the idea, especially since he had just added four extra singers to his payroll in the persons of the Pied Pipers. (They were originally an octet, but Dorsey couldn't afford that many new singers!)

Tommy spoke out fiercely, as he so often did. He blasted those who refused to take cuts, claiming they were getting too big for the band. Anyway, he said, he'd rather lead a bunch of young kids than the stars he had built.

Sinatra was young. So was Jo Stafford, the distaff member of the Pipers, a remarkably cool, self-possessed person with musical control to match and a sly sense of humor that endeared her to all. After Anita Boyer left, Jo began to sing many solos, concentrating on ballads. There were also two more young newcomers—cute Connie Haines, who came in to sing the rhythm songs, and Buddy Rich, the brash, exciting drummer who'd been with Artie Shaw.

And then there was Sy Oliver, a bit older than the rest but also new with Dorsey. His scintillating arrangements created a fresh style for the band. Tommy had grabbed Sy when the latter had left Jimmie Lunceford's band, where he had been a mainstay for many years. "It happened one night out at Brighton Beach in Brooklyn." Sy recalls, "I'd given my notice to Jimmie, and Bobby Burns, Tommy's manager, was out there and said 'Come on in and talk with Tommy.' So he drove me in to the hotel and we went up to Tommy's room. I remember he was shaving, and he turned to me and said, 'Sy, whatever you are making playing and writing for Jimmie, I'll pay you $5,000 a year more.' I said, 'Sold!' and that was it."

The Bobby Burns that Sy refers to was often the go-between in matters concerning Tommy and his men. He managed the band, not only handling all the usual details but also taking the pressure off the rest of the men. Many times when Tommy would lose his temper he'd yell out, "Burns! Burns! Come here!" And Burns, who somehow always seemed to be within hearing distance if not always in sight, would amble over to Tommy, wearing a sort of whipped-dog look, bear the brunt of Tommy's wrath, and do, or make believe he was doing, what was supposed to be done, and soon Tommy would be all smiles again. I always had a feeling this was all part of a game on Bobby's part, a game he partially enjoyed, for behind that vague look of his, intensified by thick glasses, was the mind of a sharp young man fresh out of Dartmouth College. There's no doubt about it—Tommy needed Burns very much and Bobby knew it. And if Bobby would do something that Tommy felt he couldn't do personally, like contacting Sy Oliver before it was known that he had resigned from Jimmie Lunceford's band, that was great with Dorsey.

Oliver infused the band with a new musical spirit. It was sort of a gentler version of the rocking, rhythmic sounds that he had created for Lunceford, now toned down somewhat and played with more precision and slightly less excitement by the Dorsey band. But swing they did, including some great original pieces Sy wrote for the band—things like "Easy Does It," "Quiet Please," "Swing High," "Yes, Indeed," "Swingin' on Nothin'," "Well, Get It!" and "Opus No. 1."

Oliver also had a unique way of approaching a straight pop tune, injecting a soft, two-beatian feeling into it. This he did with resounding success in such arrangements as "What Can I Say After I Say I'm Sorry," "For You," "Swanee River," "Mandy, Make Up Your Mind," "Chicago" and "On the Sunny Side of the Street."

As for the singers, they worked individually and they worked together, and they turned out a slew of hit sides, all of them of superior quality. Thus there were Sinatra's "Everything Happens to Me," "Violets for Your Furs" and "This Love of Mine"; Jo Stafford's "For You" and "Embraceable You"; and the Pied Pipers and Sinatra's "There Are Such Things," "Just As Though You Were Here," "Street of Dreams," "Oh, Look at Me Now" and, of course, their biggest hit of all, the one that established vocal groups forever, "I'll Never Smile Again," a song that Glenn Miller had recorded at a faster tempo three months earlier. But Sinatra and the Pipers wanted to create a more intimate version (they met the song's writer, Ruth Lowe, who had recently lost her husband), and though they tried several times for just the right take, they could not seem to project a personal enough mood. Dorsey, noting how hard they were trying, finally suggested that they sing it as though they'd just gathered around the piano at somebody's house. They followed his advice, and a wonderfully personalized performance was the result.

The revamped Dorsey band got better and better throughout 1940. Bunny Berigan was back, but his erratic behavior finally forced Tommy to let him go. It was at this point that he raided Benny Goodman's band (Tommy always seemed to be raiding somebody's outfit) and pulled in Ziggy Elman. It was also in this period that Tommy, who had taken on a number of Joe Marsala's alumni, like guitarist Carmen Mastren, pianist Joe Bushkin and drummer Buddy Rich, received a wire that read: "Dear Tommy, how about giving me a job in your band so I can play with mine. Joe Marsala."

On Halloween Eve of 1940 a huge new ballroom opened in Hollywood. The Palladium was probably the most lavish of all dance palaces, and for the opening night the management chose the Dorsey band as its star attraction. Prices, incidentally, were upped from the usual one dollar to five dollars per person, but this included "a deluxe dinner." The regular price scale ranged from thirty-five cents for women to fifty cents for men on Saturday matinees; fifty cents for the ladies and seventy-five cents for the gents on weekday nights, with Saturday nights pulling the top admissions: seventy-five cents for ladies and a dollar for men.

Just as there has never been a band singer like Sinatra, so there has never been a drummer like Buddy Rich. Each respected the other's talents immensely, and yet they both had such fantastic egos that neither seemingly could stand seeing the other get too much attention.

One of the greatest bits of deflation that Rich ever devised was the night up at the Astor Roof when he talked a pretty girl he knew into asking Sinatra for his autograph. She waited in line with some other girls and then, after she had got Frank's signature, murmured very sweetly—per Buddy's instructions—"Gee, thank you so much, Frankie. Now if I can get just three more of these, I can trade them in for one of Bob Eberly's!"

Rich loved to tease Sinatra in other ways, chiefly by playing too loud during Frank's ballads. It wouldn't be an over-all high volume—just an occasional thud or rim shot, deftly placed, that would completely destroy Frank's mood.

One night, also on the Astor Roof, Sinatra finally erupted. He cornered Rich backstage and tossed a water pitcher filled with ice directly at him. Fortunately he missed. However, he did take a huge chunk of plaster out of the

Jo Stafford and Frank Sinatra, surrounded by Pied Pipers Lowrey, Yocum and Huddleston, receive Dorsey's down beat to start smiling again.

Buddy Rich and TD

wall, and for quite some time thereafter the spot was encircled. Next to it was scrawled the simple but searching epitaph: "Who said it can't happen here?"

Of course, both Sinatra's and Rich's egos in those days paled in comparison with Tommy's. His was colossal. And yet Tommy had one tremendous attribute that his younger employees, more intense and less worldly, apparently lacked—he had a great sense of humor about himself. He could and would get terribly mad—he had a trigger temper—but he would also calm down very quickly. Many times, after a blast was all over, he'd sit around and kid about himself.

During several rides back with him when we were returning from those Bernardsville weekends, I had begun to gain a better understanding of that volatile, complex man. I learned, for example, that he respected more than anything else a man with a good education. He confessed to me one time that he would give just about anything he had—and he had just about anything that money could buy—if only he could have gone to college.

Another time he confided that he was sick and tired of the daily grind. He felt he had made enough money and that he had proved himself as a bandleader. "One year from now," he predicted, "I definitely will not have a band. That's all I give myself."

This, of course, was a big scoop for an editor of a music magazine. I printed the prediction, but, in order not to injure Tommy's bookings, I merely identified him as one of the top bandleaders in the world. Well, one year later Tommy was still very much in the business, with no sign of quitting, and my prediction would have looked like a completely phony story except that during that very month Artie Shaw decided he'd had enough, gave up his band and ran away to Mexico. So I turned out to be a great scoop artist after all.

Tommy continued griping vociferously: "My life's not my own." "I want to get out to the ball park, but instead I'm stuck here in my dressing room all day." "I never made more than $750 a week when I was a musician in the studios, but when that week was over I could go home and forget about it. Nowadays I can't forget about anything. I make more money but what happens? The government takes about half of it. I have the other half left, but what can I do with it? You can't have fun with your money when you can't take time off to spend it." These were typical protests, and yet he grew more and more active.

For one thing, since he couldn't get out to all the ball games he wanted, he concentrated on having his own games. He outfitted his band with uniforms, and at one time he hired one of his early baseball pitching idols, Grover Cleveland Alexander, to coach his team.

Other interests kept taking his time, too. With all the hit records coming his way, he figured, why give away so much money in performance royalties to other music publishers? The solution was simple: he began two of his own publishing companies, Sun and Embassy Music, and both they and he did very well.

Farther afield, but still within publishing, was a far less successful Dorsey venture. This was in the field of magazines. Tommy noted that musical publications seemed to be doing rather well. Certainly they were noticed within the business. So why not publish his own magazine, which could also help to publicize his own business ventures, and which would be beamed not just at the trade but at the public at large, especially his fans?

Tommy revealed his plans to me on one of these rides back from Bernardsville. He wanted to know if I'd be interested in leaving *Metronome* and editing his paper. My polite "no thank you" turned out to be one of my more intelligent decisions, for after six issues of the tabloid-sized *Bandstand*, Tommy's career as a magazine publisher ended.

Jack Egan, who doubled as press agent and editor, notes that "the issues got larger and larger. It was a give-away, and at one time it had a circulation of a hundred and eighty thousand. The guys in the band contributed columns, and Tommy even had Zeke Bonura writing on baseball. I will say this for the man: when he ran a college poll and found that his wasn't the most popular band, he printed the results just the same."

But *Bandstand* proved to be such an expensive proposition, costing Dorsey about sixty-five thousand dollars, that his personal manager, Johnny Gluskin, was rather easily able to convince him that the price was too high to pay for publicity and the satisfaction of a personal whim.

Dorsey dabbled in all sorts of other ventures, some rather immature, like toy trains (he stocked his home with more paraphernalia than he had time to unpack!) and some quite grown-up, like financial investments. The story of how several of his men lost money on one of his oil-well tips was well known in band circles, although it took a statement from Tommy many years later to set it in proper perspective. "Morton Downey gave me a tip," he said, "and so I invested four thousand dollars. I mentioned it to the guys in the band, and they got excited and wanted to invest too. Well, it wound up with them putting in four thousand dollars and I put in twelve thousand dollars and when the whole thing collapsed I gave all the boys their money back. See, I'm not as bad a character as some people might think."

In the spring of 1941 Dorsey took his biggest business plunge. Long fed up with the activities and inactivities of booking offices, he finally decided to book himself. This meant putting together a complete organization, which he called Tommy Dorsey, Inc. He rented the penthouse atop the famous Brill Building in New York, which housed many of music's top publishing firms, and opened his thirteen-thousand-square-foot offices with a gigantic party that eventually turned into a gigantic brawl. But his new venture was launched, nevertheless, and from then on Tommy Dorsey became as much of a business-man as he had been an orchestra leader.

This was the era in which the band was at its best. In the summer of 1941 it outranked even Glenn Miller's to finish first in one of the most indicative of all popularity polls—Martin Block's "Make Believe Ballroom" contest. Actually, this may have pleased Tommy less than most people suspected, because for years he had subscribed to the theory that it's best not to be Number One because, once you get there, you have no place to go except down. Jack Egan reports that at one time, on Tommy's instructions, he went out on the road and extolled the virtues, not of Tommy's band, but of Artie Shaw's because Tommy was scared that he himself might be getting too popular!

Tommy's involvement with business extended in other directions. For example, when Sinatra—wanting to start his career as a single before Bob Eberly, whom he admired greatly and who was rumored to be leaving Jimmy Dorsey, could start his—decided in 1942 to go out on his own, Dorsey made sure that he owned a big piece of him.

Dorsey's cut and that of his manager, Leonard Vannerson, amounted to almost fifty per cent. But eventually, Sinatra, with help from outsiders, in-cluding his booking agency, bought his release. According to Harry James, the irony of it all was that in all probability Sinatra's contract with the Dorsey band had been invalid in the first place. "When Frank left the band," Harry recently told me, "he was still legally under contract to me, so that any con-tract he would have signed with Tommy when he joined his band would have been null and void."

Before Frank and others started to leave, Tommy had put together what was literally the biggest band he ever had. To his regular complement of eight brass, five saxes, four rhythms and six singers he added a full string section of seven violins, two violas, a cello, plus a harp! Most of the strings had come from Artie Shaw's band, which had disbanded when their leader had enlisted in the Navy. Reviewing the huge Dorsey ensemble, I began with: "It's wonderful, this enlarged Tommy Dorsey band. It's really wonderful! It does all sorts of things, and it does all sorts of things well, too! It can rock the joint with the mightiest sort of blasting jazz, and then it can turn right around and play the soothingest sort of cradle music that'll rock any little babe fast asleep."

This was written in the summer of 1942. Shortly thereafter Sinatra departed of his own will, and the drafting of some of the top stars began. Elman went into the Army, Rich into the Marines, and Jo Stafford went home to spend some time with her husband, who also was about to go into the service. It was the beginning of the end of one of the greatest aggregations of all time. But it was by no means the beginning of the end of Tommy Dorsey as a bandleader.

For a while the band floundered. The replacements didn't measure up. Sinatra and Stafford and Rich and the Pied Pipers were sorely missed. Frank was replaced by another great singer, Dick Haymes, who stayed for just a few months, but long enough to realize that "Tommy was the greatest leader in the world to work for. He actually knew all the words of every song I sang!" Then came Teddy Walters, Betty Brewer, and the Sentimentalists. But Tommy was never the sort of a guy who'd settle for anything less than the best. Slowly he improved his band once again. Gene Krupa came in. Bill Finegan, no longer tied to Glenn Miller, who had gone into the service, returned to write more arrangements. And Buddy Rich, discharged from the Marines in the early summer of 1944, came back to spark the band with his drumming.

But it was especially in the world of business that Dorsey began to flourish. In that same summer (1944) he pulled a typical TD move. He had been feuding over money with the management of the Hollywood Palladium. They had offered him eighty-five hundred dollars a week. Tommy felt he was worth much more—and in this estimate he was supported by many other leaders who'd been feeling that the Palladium had been underpaying them while reportedly making a mint of money itself. So one night Tommy walked up to the mike at the Palladium and calmly announced to the thousands of customers that he had just bought his own ballroom, the Casino Gardens, in nearby Ocean Park, and wouldn't they like to come down next weekend and dance to his music?

Tommy had partners. One was Harry James. Another was his brother, Jimmy, whose band wracked up a house record at the Palladium that summer and then, a few short weeks later, moved into the Gardens, where it did just as well.

This was an era when the two feuding brothers seemed to be getting together again. In fact for a while Jimmy seemed to have gained the upper hand in popularity, so that Tommy, shrewd as he was, must have realized that he could gain by collaborating with his brother. Suffice it to say, during that summer they staged a gigantic battle of music that highlighted the Casino Gardens' season. Then at Liederkranz Hall in New York they combined their bands to record a memorable V-Disc that featured two rhythm sections (including a couple of the world's loudest drummers, Buddy Rich and Buddy Schutz) plus ten saxes and fifteen brass.

Other exciting things happened. In his personal life, Tommy, now married to movie actress Pat Dane, got into a headlined brawl in his own home with movie actor Jon Hall. So much bad publicity ensued that Tommy lost his radio commercial, and the future of his band seemed to be in jeopardy. His friend, Charlie Barnet, sent him a telegram which read, "I am now in a position to offer you the first trombone chair in my orchestra. You will receive feature billing. Can also use Pat as featured singer. Please advise at once." Tommy immediately replied to the ribbing with "Accept offer. How much dough?" and then went right ahead and began reorganizing his own band.

Eventually the Hall affair was settled, and the fears that the Dorsey career was in trouble were soon dispelled. As a matter of fact, several months later, when the 400 Club opened in New York, a spot that was to feature many of the country's top bands, Dorsey was chosen as its first attraction.

Soon thereafter, Tommy made another important move: he hired his first black musician, Charlie Shavers, who had been a star of the John Kirby Sextet and then had played at CBS with Raymond Scott's band. Shavers immediately added a flair to the band's music that had been sadly lacking since the exits of Berigan and Elman.

And yet for several years, despite the presence of Shavers and Rich and the subsequent additions of good jazz musicians like clarinetist Buddy DeFranco and tenor saxist Boomie Richman, plus a superb singer named Stuart Foster, Tommy's band tried but could never quite reach the brilliant heights of before. By now some of the enthusiasm that had always fired Dorsey had waned. He was concentrating more and more on outside interests. In the winter of 1945–1946 he was signed by the Mutual radio network as Director of Popular Music. Shortly thereafter he began a series of weekly radio shows during which he read what was generally a pretty tired-sounding script about bands, vocalists and arrangers.

And there were other, even more obvious reasons for this loss of enthusiasm. One was the inability all bandleaders were experiencing in trying to get musicians to go out on the road. The other was the increasing difficulty of finding places in which bands could play.

By late 1946 it was becoming apparent that the band business was getting worse and worse. The reason was obvious: the supply of bands far exceeded the demand. All at once this simple economic fact seemed to dawn on eight top bandleaders at one time, for in the single month of December, 1946, eight of them announced they were calling it quits—Woody Herman, Benny Goodman, Harry James, Les Brown, Jack Teagarden, Benny Carter, Ina Ray Hutton and Tommy Dorsey!

For all intents and purposes, this was the official end of the big band era. Herman, Goodman, James, Brown, Teagarden, Carter, Hutton and Dorsey, all gone at once. What was left?

Not much. And yet it was Tommy Dorsey, more than any of the other big names, who in the years immediately following was to fight the cause of the big bands—with words and with action. Less than two years later he was fronting a formidable new group that featured Shavers and Chuck Peterson on trumpets, Richman on tenor sax, Paul Smith on piano, Louie Bellson on drums and vocals by Lucy Ann Polk, her brother Gordon and England's Denny Dennis.

"It's about time somebody started things going again," Tommy said at the time. "You can't expect to have any real interest in dance bands if the bands don't go around the country and play for the kids." And so Dorsey went right ahead where others, like James, Goodman and Brown, feared to tread.

Actually, Tommy never gave up trying until the very end. Much help came from his old pal, Jackie Gleason, who featured the Dorsey band on its own TV series, which spotted, in addition to the usual band numbers, various guests, including two comparatively unknown singers uncovered by Gleason and producer Jack Philbin—Elvis Presley and Connie Francis. But Tommy still felt he needed first-rate exposure on records, and so when he couldn't get the right sort of a deal from any record companies—for big bands were hard to sell—he recorded his band himself and then found outlets for his masters later on.

The band, into which he had brought his brother Jimmy and which was once more known as the Dorsey Brothers Orchestra, continued to work, though the pickings were getting leaner and leaner. Tommy himself was becoming increasingly more interested in forming a mammoth record company in which he would be joined by other top recording stars. His plan: each of the artists would have a financial interest in the company, each would own his own masters, each could make more money than by recording on the usual royalty basis for another company because his profits could be realized in capital gains and thus fall into a lower tax bracket and because other financial returns could conceivably come from profits of the company itself. It is interesting to note that Tommy's plan was not unlike the one which Sinatra instituted when he started his Reprise label several years later.

I saw quite a bit of Tommy during those final days. He was by no means a contented man, but then he always seemed to be fighting for something that he didn't have. But the general demise of the band business, as well as the change in musical styles and values, depressed him. Then too, despite all his efforts and keen desires, his last marriage, complete with two adorable children and a wonderful house in Greenwich, Connecticut, was working out badly.

Who knows what went through his mind on the night of November 26, 1956, exactly one week after his fifty-first birthday. Certainly he must have been filled with all sorts of conflicts. He dreaded his impending divorce. The thought of the disintegration of his home life was upsetting him terribly, for, just as Tommy had been a man of intense hatreds, he had also been a man full of love, which he gave and shared willingly.

Impulsive he most certainly was too. Impulsive and impatient, as well, and the two traits of character formed a lethal and fateful combination that night when, possibly to get relief from the terrific tension that had been building up at home, he took several sleeping pills in hopes of getting a good night's rest.

That was the night he reportedly also had eaten a huge dinner. It was a dinner that apparently did not sit well. In his sleep, it has since been surmised, he became nauseous, then violently sick to his stomach. He began to vomit, and then to gag . . . and then to choke . . . and all the while the sleeping pills kept him in such a state that he was unable to rouse himself.

The next morning he was found dead in his bed. Apparently he had choked to death.

A few days later a whole bunch of us, headed by Jackie Gleason, put on a one-hour television show called "A Tribute to Tommy Dorsey." It was a fantastic affair, in which a host of musicians and singers who had been associated with Tommy took part.

Jimmy was there. So were other old friends like Joe Venuti, Eddie Condon and Russ Morgan. And there were some of his former sidemen, like Max Kaminsky and Peewee Erwin and Joe Dixon and Howard Smith and Sandy Block and Carmen Mastren and Bud Freeman and Boomie Richman and Bobby Byrne, who had taken his place in the Dorsey band more than a generation before. Connie Haines sang "Will You Still Be Mine?" while Axel Stordahl conducted and composer Matt Dennis played piano. Dick Haymes sang "Daybreak," and Jo Stafford, with Paul Weston conducting, sang the first song she had ever recorded with the band, "Little Man with a Candy Cigar." Bob Crosby sang "Dinah" as he had done with the Dorsey Brothers

Tommy and Jimmy introduce a rising new star, Elvis Presley, on their "Stage Show" telecast.

band, and finally there was a long and emotional medley that began with "Well, Git It," featuring Charlies Shavers, followed by a short trombone passage of "Once in a While," then Stuart Foster singing "This Love of Mine," the full band playing "Opus #1," Tommy Mercer (Tommy's last boy singer) doing "There Are Such Things," Sy Oliver singing his special version of "On the Sunny Side of the Street" and dueting with Lynn Roberts (who also had been singing with the last band) on "Yes, Indeed." Then the band went into a chorus of "Song of India," followed by a sax chorus of "I'll Never Smile Again," then into "Boogie Woogie" and finally into "Marie," with Jack Leonard returning to sing a final farewell vocal.

Gleason opened the show with a moving speech in which he stressed that "I don't think Tommy would want us getting sentimental over him, so in the next hour you'll be hearing a tribute that represents *all* the sentiments, happy and sad, that made up his music."

Just before the close of the show, Paul Whiteman came on and said a few very simple, yet very meaningful words about Tommy: "I've been watching and I've been listening this evening to all the wonderful tributes to Tommy and I know there's not a thing I could possibly say that would match their sincerity and eloquence. . . . It's the sort of tribute that fits Tommy perfectly . . . simple, straightforward and beautiful . . . and right from the heart.

"Just as I'm sure there'll never be another trombone player like Tommy, so I know there'll never be another man like him. . . . There was always a certain graciousness and greatness about everything he did. I first sensed this when he joined our band close to twenty-five years ago, and I felt it, perhaps even a little bit more, just a few weeks ago when he graciously rejoined the band and blew his last recorded notes in our fiftieth anniversary album.

"Looking back at his music is now—and I'm sure always will be—one of the real big pleasures in the lives of all of us."

The script's closing lines, assigned to Gleason, reflected the mood of the program: "I wish I could say, the way the announcers used to do, 'Join us again tomorrow night for more music by Tommy Dorsey and his Orchestra.' But I can't, because there are no tomorrows left for us with Tommy. . . . Good night, everybody."

Eddy Duchin

"I CLOSE my eyes, hum to myself, and then play what I happen to feel inside of me."

That's how Eddy Duchin described his style of piano playing to me back in 1935 when he had become firmly established as the country's top piano-playing maestro. "I think it's the first time that any dance orchestra pianist has adopted that formula—playing what he feels rather than what he sees," he continued. "It's inspirational rather than mechanical."

There's no doubt about it, Duchin did have a way of communicating to his public his emotional approach to music. He did so not only through his flowery phrasing but also by the great visual show he put on—weaving back and forth at the piano, crossing his hands as with one finger of his right hand he coaxed forth the melody from the piano's bass, tilting his head this way and that way, smiling graciously and often insinuatingly, projecting Duchin, the personality, every bit as much as Duchin, the musician.

"Many people didn't really listen to him as much as they looked at him," one of his veteran sidemen recently pointed out. "I'll say this for the man, he was the only musician I've ever known who could play a thirty-two bar solo with thirty-two mistakes and get an ovation for it afterwards."

Duchin, an extraordinarily handsome, well-mannered man with a captivating personality that mesmerized most of the women who watched him (he was, in a way, a virile Liberace), communicated easily with his audiences. With his band, though, it was somewhat different, for he was not a well-rounded musician who knew exactly where his music was going and why. He left most of the details of the running of his orchestra to Lew Sherwood, his trumpeter, vocalist and close confidant throughout his entire bandleading career. For example, after hearing his men run through a new arrangement that didn't especially strike his fancy, Eddy, instead of working closely with the arranger and trying to explain just what he wanted to have changed, would be more inclined to state merely that he didn't like it, he didn't know why, but, no, he just didn't like it and would let it go at that. Then it would be up to the more musically trained members of his organization to revise the arrangement, trying to guess what it was that Eddy hadn't liked and what might please him.

He could talk well in generalities about his music. For example, one thing of which he was proud, he told me, was the way his orchestra would "swell." He was referring, of course, to its dynamics, which, so far as most musicians were concerned, were overdramatized, but which, so far as Eddy was concerned, produced in his audience precisely the emotional effect he had intended. Impressing and pleasing dancers seemed to be his pervading concerns. "You must remember all the time," he emphasized, "that your dance music is for dancing primarily. If the crowd finds your music easy to dance to, then you're a success."

Such a simple, direct and, to some, musically naive approach was rather typical of Duchin. Communication was his forte. It had certainly helped when, after just two years of professional experience, he auditioned with many other pianists for a chair in Leo Reisman's orchestra. Eddy won the job and for three years thereafter was featured with the Reisman band at the Central Park Casino, then New York's most popular and poshest spot for dancing. So popular did young Duchin become with the regular patrons that in 1931 he took over Reisman's place as leader at the Central Park Casino.

Andy Wiswell, for years a top producer at RCA Victor Records, played trombone for Duchin during those early days. "It was just a ten-piece orchestra and we had no second trumpet, so I played those parts on trombone," he recalls. The band played its music straight with Duchin taking all the fill-ins at the end of phrases with his piano flourishes. "Eddy was a wonderful performer," Wiswell says. "He had very strong hands and he would really take over. And, of course, when he introduced that one finger playing the melody in the lower register he had something big going for him."

The reaction to Duchin was tremendous. According to Wiswell, the band played at the Casino seven nights a week and "the rope was up every night. And that was all the more remarkable when you realize that people had to be dressed formally to be allowed in the place."

In addition to the seven nightly sessions, the band also played for tea dances on Saturdays and Sundays. The Saturday *dansants* were broadcast coast to coast and more than anything else were responsible for Duchin's great national popularity. The band played a few other class spots, such as the Persian Room of the Plaza in New York and the Cocoanut Grove of the Ambassador in Los Angeles, and eventually wound up with several radio series, one for Texaco with Ed Wynn and Graham McNamee, the most golden-voiced announcer of his day, another called "Going Places," a national talent show in which tenor Kenny Baker emerged as the eventual winner, and a third series with George Burns and Gracie Allen.

Duchin's music varied little for years. It was built around his flashy piano (the guys in the band used to rib him because the kid pianist in the relief band at the Casino, Carmen Cavallaro, could play even flashier piano), embellished by three saxes (two tenors and an alto with a tenor playing lead)

Eddy Duchin

moaning away, plus the two brass often blowing into harsh-sounding mutes.

But as the big bands, with their more interesting sounds, began to grow more popular, and as so many other bands began imitating his, Duchin, a sharp businessman, must have realized that he could go no further. So he organized a more orthodox group with the usual saxes and brass comple- ment, and it played some pretty good music. But the concentration was on the Duchin piano style, one that often seemed to be totally removed from that of the rest of the band. Eddy's apparent obsession with playing what he felt, regardless of what else was taking place, still prevailed. This was especially evident in his attempts to retain the rushing feeling of society tempos in arrangements meant to be played in a more relaxed fashion. It was what I described in a 1940 review as his "I'll - run - ahead - for - a - cou- ple - of - measures - and - see - what - it's - like - up - there - and - then - wait - for - the - rest - of - the - rhythm - section - to - catch - up - to - me" style.

The modernized band was well received, not only in the swankiest hotel rooms in North America but also, in the early forties, on a very successful South American tour, during which Eddy spread around his personal charm as part of a good-will gesture. Within a few years he was again out of the country, this time wearing a Navy lieutenant's uniform. Duchin's service career had very little to do with music; he was, according to his son, Peter, intensely and completely dedicated to his military ventures.

After the war Eddy continued with his band where he had left off. For a while he led his most musical outfit; then, as illness started affecting him, he cut down on his activities. In 1951 he died of leukemia. Several years later *The Eddy Duchin Story* was produced in Hollywood, with Tyrone Power playing the part of Duchin and Carmen Cavallaro playing the piano.

The sixties saw the rise of another Duchin as Peter Duchin emerged as one of the most popular of society bandleaders. A more accomplished musician than his father, he had absorbed the elder Duchin's pleasant, personal approach, while adding to it a more developed brand of musicianship—a pianist as much worth listening to as his father had been worth looking at.

Duchin talks to the accompaniment
of two members of the King Cole Trio.

Sonny Dunham

THE guys in the Bob Crosby band used to refer to him as "The Man from Mars" because he blew so high on his trumpet. Swing band fans probably remember him most readily for his featured role on "Memories of You," his tour de force when he played with Glen Gray and the Casa Loma Orchestra, and which he later used for a theme song. To those who knew him best, Sonny Dunham brings back fond recollections of a sensitive, somewhat emotional gentlemen who fronted a band that showed occasional signs of brilliance but which never actually dug deeply enough into any sort of musical or even commercial groove to rank as one of the country's top outfits.

Sonny, whose real name was Elmer, was one of the most sophisticated musicians of his time. He had a highly developed sense of humor and interests in numerous intellectual pursuits. He began his career as a trombonist, singer and arranger for Paul Tremaine's orchestra, left to start his own group called Sonny Lee and his New York Yankees, then joined Casa Loma in 1932. He took a short sabbatical in March, 1937, to start his own band of fourteen men, ten of whom doubled on trumpet. "If they can't book us, we can always join Ringling Brothers," Sonny quipped. "They" couldn't book the band frequently enough, so in November of the same year Dunham rejoined Casa Loma, with which he stayed until early 1940, when he formed a band that did last.

For a while he toured the country, under the auspices of a trumpet mouthpiece manufacturer, looking for young talent. He discovered some, too, as witness the outfit that played Frank Dailey's Meadowbrook in the summer of 1941. There was very young Corky Corcoran on tenor sax and a completely unknown trumpeter, Pete Candoli, who was to develop into one of the most wanted of all lead men. There was also an excellent singer, Ray Kellogg, later a successful Hollywood actor.

But the band as a whole was only fairly impressive, principally because it always seemed to be playing under wraps. I noted in an August, 1941, review that its future would have been much more assured if it could adopt "a hell-bent-for-leather attitude instead of that of a posing, young, pipe-smoking adolescent."

What also seemed to be missing, both then and in the years that followed, was proper emphasis on Dunham's horn or horns. His was a very sensational-sounding trumpet style, yet too few of the very good arrangements written by George (The Fox) Williams spotted Sonny sufficiently. He could also play excellent trombone, yet this horn was pretty much subjugated to playing with the section.

Perhaps it was all part of Dunham's apparent inability to let himself and his band go. Off the stand he was a bright, articulate, enthusiastic, witty man. On the stand he came across as almost affectedly cool, and this unfortunate posture seemed to be reflected in almost everything the band did. Perhaps he was much more self-conscious and ill at ease than any of us suspected. Whatever the cause, neither Dunham, still playing trombone in Florida, nor his band ever realized their commercial or musical potential.

Sonny Dunham with vocalist Harriet Clark

Billy Eckstine

BILLY ECKSTINE, whose name was Eckstein until some nightclub owner decided it looked too Jewish, had a modern, swinging band during the mid-forties. He had been singing with Earl Hines for a number of years when one of his fellow bandsmen, Dizzy Gillespie, suggested to Billy that he ought to go out with his own crew.

It was a sensible suggestion, because Billy, an outstandingly handsome man with a great deal of charm, had built up quite a following not merely among musicians, who admired him as a person and as a singer, but also among a segment of the public that followed the jazz-oriented bands.

In the spring of 1944 Billy left the Earl. He took with him the band's chief arranger and tenor saxist, Budd Johnson, who, along with Gillespie, became one of the two musical directors of the new group. So great was the emphasis upon instrumental music and what was then considered to be progressive jazz that Billy's strong, masculine but highly stylized vocals were often subjugated to the playing of some young, budding jazz stars like Charlie and Leo Parker, Miles Davis, Art Blakey, Fats Navarro, Howard McGhee, Kenny Dorham, Lucky Thompson, Gene Ammons and Dexter Gordon. And for a while Eckstine also featured a timid young girl vocalist with a marvelously clear, vibrant voice. To this day Sarah Vaughan still looks back fondly on her association with the band and credits it for much of her musical development.

Singing bandleader Billy Eckstine serenades then-rising singing-dancing star Sammy Davis, Jr.

The Eckstine band was an exciting one, especially for musicians and fans who appreciated its boppish sounds. Unfortunately its recordings were horrendous. It was signed to a couple of minor labels, one of which seemed to be trying for a new sound by pressing its discs off-center, while the other recorded Billy in such a small, dead studio that the band sounded as though it were trying to blow its way out from under a pile of blankets. Consequently much of the exposure that the outfit needed was not forthcoming, and even when radio stations did play its records, they sounded so bad that they made few Eckstine converts.

On recordings, Billy sang numerous ballads, many of them too pompously and backed by pedantic, overly precious-sounding arrangements. To satisfy his fans he also recorded some blues, but none approached the popularity of his earlier "Jelly, Jelly," which he had waxed with Hines.

Billy was in a dilemma. Ballads interested him commercially. Bop intrigued him musically. But the blues bored him. "I hate blues," he told Barbara Hodgkins in a September, 1947, *Metronome* interview. "You can't do anything with them." And, explaining why he seldom sounded as good with his own band as he had with Hines's, or, for that matter, when he was performing as a single, Eckstine said, "My band was on a bebop kick, and you can't sing with that so well."

The love of bop undoubtedly swayed Billy too much for his band ever to achieve a style that would set him off as a singer. He did play an occasional valve trombone. "I liked the sound of it, maybe because it's a low instrument," explained Billy, whose own vocal lower register was often a sound of rare beauty. He seemed constantly to be trying to convince everyone, including himself, that he could succeed with a large, modern band, rather than one that would be more easily understood by the general public. Accordingly he featured his bop stars a great deal and himself too little. Had he spent as much effort setting himself up as well as he did his sidemen, Billy Eckstine might easily have emerged as a much more successful bandleader. As it was, the musicians were his biggest fans, and there just weren't enough of them.

Several years later, by then a successful single attraction, Eckstine expressed a sense of relief about the demise of his band. "You feel so much freer singing by yourself," he said. "You're not constantly singing in tempo; you get a chance to express yourself more fully. I like it better than singing with my own band. 'They' wanted me to get a commercial band, to be a background for my singing. So what happens when I'm not singing? They'd be playing some old-time stuff, and *I* wouldn't be on the stand. I decided the best thing was to do a single and go hear Dizzy for kicks."

During the post-big band period, the Gillespie band scored more of a success with its modern sounds than Eckstine's, playing basically the same sort of big band jazz, ever had. "We were trying to play music," Billy concluded sadly, after the demise of his big band, "and I guess it was a little too early for that."

How right he was!

Duke Ellington

WHEN the country started latching onto the big band sounds in the mid-thirties, it was merely discovering the music that Duke Ellington and his band had already been playing for close to ten years—but to none of the rewarding hoopla or fanfare that greeted appearances by Benny Goodman, Artie Shaw, Tommy Dorsey and the rest of the white swing bands.

Such idolatry heaped upon those "Benny- and Artie- and Tommy-Come-Latelys" must have been discouraging for Ellington, whose orchestra, even then, was regarded by most musicians and jazz followers as the best of all the big bands. I once asked him how the sudden popularity of the new bands affected him. "Competition," he said, "only makes you play better. Besides," he added, "a guy may go to a lot of fancy restaurants, but he always comes home to that soul food!"

Duke's analogy contained a touch of irony. For, though most of the swing bands could play in fancy restaurants and hotel rooms, Duke's, like numerous other black bands of the thirties, was not accepted in most of such spots. How did he feel about that? "I took the energy it takes to pout," he said, "and wrote some blues."

The biggest influence on the popular swing bands was Fletcher Henderson, who had temporarily left his band to create Goodman's new style. "You know what," Duke once confided, "my big ambition was to sound like Fletcher. He had such a wonderful band. But his was basically an ensemble group, and in our band the solos—you know all the various stars we have had—always dominated everything."

Ellington very often credited his sidemen with the success of his band. But those who knew Duke and his music best—and they included those very sidemen—would invariably tell you what always set Ellington's apart from, and almost always above other bands, was just one thing—the brilliant conductor-composer-arranger-pianist-bon vivant and leader of men, Duke Ellington himself.

A wonderfully warm and witty and urbane gentleman, the Duke was creating his own particular jazz sounds as far back as 1924, when he had organized his first small jazz band. Two years later it had developed into a twelve-piece outfit, playing music composed and arranged by its leader. And this was the role it was to play ever after, that of an interpretive instrument for the unique material that came from Ellington's fertile mind, material sometimes geared to the general public but often too advanced to be understood by those more readily attracted by Paul Whiteman and Rudy Vallee and the simpler swing bands that followed them.

The general public may have preferred the Duke's more commercial competition. Not so, though, the jazz musicians and the leaders of other big bands. This intense admiration and respect was impressed very forcibly on me some years ago at a benefit in New York's Jazz Gallery, attended by a large number of music's leading figures. Many of them were introduced. Some performed. Some merely took bows. And the applause ranged from polite to enthusiastic. But when Duke Ellington was introduced, it was something else again. The club, which was jammed with a cross section of musicians and fans, ranging from the coolest hippies to the most mellow old-timers, broke out into more than polite or even enthusiastic applause. It rose to its feet and gave the Duke a standing ovation that made the message quite clear: "Duke, you are the Greatest!"

Outside America, Duke invariably found even broader acclaim. There no other band in the history of American music has ever been revered so warmly and so consistently. One reason for this, of course, is that jazz, as an art form, has generally found much readier acceptance abroad than at home. Certainly it is significant that long before Duke Ellington had ever been received at the White House, he had been accorded magnificent receptions by the leaders of numerous foreign nations, including the King and Queen of England!

If Ellington was all that great, why then were other bands more popular back home in America? How come he won England's *Melody Maker* poll in 1937, while in the United States, Benny Goodman and Artie Shaw and others continued to top him?

Not being permitted to play in spots open only to white bands certainly was a big reason. White bands not only could play in person for more people in more places—hotels and theaters especially—but they also were given greater exposure on radio, both from the spots in which they played as well as on commercially sponsored series.

And there was another important factor—the Ellington band's comparatively slight concern for the current commercial pop tunes, which meant so much to the average American. The image and the music of Ellington's band had been built around his own compositions and the band just wasn't especially interested in the era's musical trivia. Thus, for the many who insisted upon hearing most of the latest songs, Duke's band was not entirely acceptable.

Not that Ellington refused to play pop tunes. He performed a select quota, including those—many of them exceptionally good—which he, himself, had written. For he felt then, as he still feels today, that in order to develop

The Duke surrounded by Junior Raglin, Lawrence Brown,
Johnny Hodges, Ray Nance, Sonny Greer and Freddy Guy.

it is important not to close oneself in an ivory tower but, instead, to try earnestly to communicate with people. "That's why," he told me in an interview some years ago, "it still means so much to me to go out and play for people in person. It's a give-and-take-proposition. You make them feel good, and then you feel good when out somewhere in the provinces a doctor, or a car washer, or a farmer may travel two hundred miles just to hear you. And then they start talking to you, and usually one of them says, 'I liked that last record of yours, but you know the one that really knocked me out. . . .' And he mentions something you haven't even thought about in a long time but you've always liked, and you realize here is a real listener."

Ellington himself was also a real listener. In another interview he told me, "The biggest thing I do in music is listen." He was referring only in part to what other musicians were playing. "While I'm playing," he added, "I also listen ahead to what I will be playing. It may be thirty-two or just one or merely an eighth of a bar ahead, but if you're going to try to play good jazz, you've got to have a plan of what's going to happen."

The chief planner of the Ellington band was always its leader. Without his men, though, he would have been lost. Keeping them often incurred a tremendous financial burden on a man who, in his sixties, could easily have afforded to retire and to live off the royalties of his recordings and many hit songs. "But," he asked, "without the men what could I do? I could keep on composing, something I always intended to do, but then I'd have nobody to play the things I write so that I can hear what they sound like." Without his band Duke Ellington would have been a lost man. Fortunately, for him and his musicians, it was a luxury he could afford to keep.

Many of his musicians had been with him for many years. Harry Carney, the handsome, quiet, eternally youthful-looking baritone saxist, joined in 1926. Two years later dour-faced, whimsical Johnny Hodges brought his alto sax into the band. The following year Cootie Williams, he of the famous growl trumpet, joined, and in 1932 Lawrence Brown with his sensuous-sounding trombone became a member. All four willingly remained with the band for many, many years.

Playing with Ellington's band entailed more than just following Duke's directions, His manuscripts were invariably tailored for particular musicians in his organization. Many times his works did not arrive for a first rehearsal in finished form. Duke would then experiment as he was running them down, making what he deemed to be appropriate changes. Sometimes this would turn into a team effort, especially for those who had been associated with the band for any length of time and thus familiar with Duke's ideas and routines. These veterans would offer their own suggestions. Duke would listen to all, accept some, reject others.

Freedom of expression, Duke's and that of his men, always permeated much of Ellington's music. Any arrangement was subject to change, sometimes even without notice. This fluid approach could be very mystifying to the less-initiated Ellington sidemen. Al Sears, who played tenor sax in the band in the early forties, once described what faces an Ellington newcomer: "It's not like any other band where you just sit down and read the parts. Here you can sit down and read the parts and suddenly you find you're playing something entirely different from what the rest of the band is playing. It's not logical. You start at the beginning of the arrangement at letter 'A' and go to letter 'B' and then suddenly, for no reason at all, when you go to letter 'C,' the rest of the band's playing something else which you find out later on isn't what's written at 'C' but what's written at 'J' instead. And then on the next number, instead of starting at the top of the arrangement at letter 'A' the entire band starts at 'R'—that is, everybody except me. See, I'm the newest man in the band and I haven't caught on to the system yet."

The reason for many of the changes in routine, Sears explained, was Duke's willingness to accept suggestions after the arrangements had already been written. "The band plays it through a few times and then one or two men come up with ideas for changes and soon the whole routine may be altered and the brass is playing a different figure behind the sax chorus, and the part that the trombone is playing is out entirely because it has been given to the baritone sax, which had been playing a part that had gone to one of the trumpets in the first place. After a while you feel you're not reading just a musical arrangement but a road map as well."

Louie Bellson, who has played drums for Benny Goodman, Tommy Dorsey, Harry James, Count Basie, Johnny Carson and Ellington, has also stressed the great impromptu feeling that consistently permeated the Duke's band. "There was something different every night," he once told me. "Duke always gave us a great deal of freedom. I learned a lot about tempos and blending from Benny and Harry and Basie, and about endurance from Tommy. But from Duke I learned the importance of sound. Playing with his band was the highlight of my career."

The Ellington career, itself, has had so many highlights that it's just about impossible to list them all. One of them occurred in 1933, just before the big band era began, when his band toured Europe. As Barry Ulanov wrote in *A History of American Jazz* (Viking, 1952), "Everywhere he went Duke was received with such adulation and ceremony that it was inevitable he should rub noses (figuratively) and indeed play some jazz (literally) with two future Kings of England, the Prince of Wales and the Duke of York." (For a complete biography of Ellington through 1946, Ulanov's book, *Duke Ellington,* published by Creative Press, is highly recommended.)

At the time the general public was becoming completely conscious of big band sounds, Duke was recording his for Brunswick. During that 1935–1936 period he had a wonderful, tightly knit group whose personnel varied very little and which produced such works as Duke's "Reminiscing in Tempo," a two-sided recording that traced Ellington's interpretation of his musical history; "Clarinet Lament" and "Echoes of Harlem," two pieces that featured clarinetist Barney Bigard and trumpeter Cootie Williams respectively; and several more sides containing outstanding performances by Ivy Anderson, the bright, pert, metallic-sounding singer who suited the band so wonderfully. Ivy was a slim, bright-looking young lady whose appearance contrasted sharply with her strong, almost strident and uncompromising "take-charge" way of phrasing. When Ivy sang such songs as "Oh Babe, Maybe Someday," "It Was a Sad Night in Harlem," "I'm Checkin' Out, Goombye" and "Rocks in My Bed," she sang them the way nobody else did—or could. Her voice became as much of an integral part of the Ellington band as did the saxes of Hodges and Carney, the trombones of Brown and Juan Tizol or the trumpets of Williams and Rex Stewart.

For a while during 1937 the band recorded on the Master label, which was run by Irving Mills, who had long been associated with Ellington in a business capacity and who, for reasons best known to Ellington, shares composer credits on a great many of Duke's hit tunes published by Mills Music. Some years ago I was invited by a friend to come with him to a party at Mills's Hollywood mansion. "I want you to notice one thing," he said, "and that's that huge expanse of red carpeting that covers the ground floor. That's Duke's blood."

By the end of 1937 the band had returned to the Brunswick label and immediately recorded another important two-sided Ellington work, "Diminuendo in Blue" and "Crescendo in Blue," which Duke frequently uses even today when he feels like stirring up a crowd to some sort of frenzy. This was also the period during which the band recorded what remains for me the most subtley swinging of all Ellington sides, a comparatively simple, little-known work called "Steppin' into Swing Society."

Through 1938 the band continued to make many records for Brunswick. It also continued to play, as it had been doing for so many years, places that were actually far below the stature of its music. True, musicians the

The Duke's Ivy Anderson and Jimmy Blanton

world over considered Ellington's the greatest of all bands—it again won the poll of England's widely distributed music paper, *The Melody Maker,* while Goodman, Shaw and others continued to sweep American contests— but enough of the public never had a chance to hear the Ellington band in person. It did play theaters—many of them—but in New York, for example, where the big stage-show houses were the Paramount and the Strand, the Ellington band did well to make it at Loew's State.

In 1939 many changes occurred. One of these concerned bookings. For years these had been handled by the Mills office, to whom Duke felt he owed a debt of gratitude, especially to Irving Mills for his faith in the band during its early days. But the office had limited contacts. With big bands doing so well all over, Duke must have felt that his, too, should play some of the top spots. He turned over his business affairs to Willard Alexander at the William Morris Agency, which soon booked him into such prestige spots as the Ritz Carlton Roof in Boston and the Hotel Sherman in Chicago.

Musically the band underwent several changes, too. Duke discovered a magnificent young bassist, Jimmy Blanton, whose playing inspired all the members of the orchestra and with whom Ellington recorded several duet sides. Ben Webster, who had recorded occasionally with the band, was made a permanent member of the sax section, and his inspiring, highly emotional solos also helped bring new fire and inspiration to the organization.

But the most important addition of all was a young pianist and arranger out of Pittsburgh. This was Billy Strayhorn, who was to become Duke's musical confidant and often his collaborator, his protégé and also the creator of some of the finest music the band ever performed. Strayhorn proceeded to write many arrangements for Duke, especially for Ivy Anderson and a handsome baritone who joined shortly thereafter, Herb Jeffries. He also composed a number of extremely musical songs—including two that featured Johnny Hodges, "Day Dream" and "Passion Flower," a lovely opus called "Something to Live For," which Jean Eldridge sang so well with the band, and "Lush Life," which Billy himself used to sing and which became a hit when Nat Cole recorded it.

In 1940 and during the next two years the band recorded many of its greatest sides, including Ellington compositions like "Jack the Bear," "Cotton Tail," "All Too Soon," "Warm Valley," "Just a-Settin' and a-Rockin'," "Perdido," "C Jam Blues," plus two Billy Strayhorn originals, "Chelsea Bridge" and "Take the A Train," which soon became Duke's theme. During this era the band waxed two other Ellington melodies, "Concerto for Cootie," which, with Bob Russell's lyrics added, became more famous as "Do Nothing Till You Hear From Me," and "Never No Lament," which turned into "Don't Get Around Much Anymore."

Duke's output as a composer of hit songs was immensely impressive. In addition to hundreds of strictly instrumental compositions such as his early "Black and Tan Fantasy" and "Creole Love Call" and "The Mooche," all of which the band played for years, he wrote "Mood Indigo," "It Don't Mean a Thing If It Ain't Got That Swing," "Sophisticated Lady," "In My Solitude," "In a Sentimental Mood," "I Let a Song Go Out of My Heart," "I'm Beginning to See the Light," "Satin Doll," "I Got It Bad and That Ain't Good" and "Jump for Joy." What about "Things Ain't What They Used To Be"? No, Duke didn't write it. But his son, Mercer, a quiet, handsome, talented man who lived in the shadow of his father's brilliancy, did.

Probably the most important work that Duke wrote in the early forties, and to some his most important of all, was a three-part suite called "Black, Brown and Beige." Subtitled "A Tone Parallel," it was debuted in a glamorous concert in New York's Carnegie Hall on January 23, 1943.

The band had made practically no New York appearances for a couple of years before the concert, and so anticipation and interest ran high. Produced for the benefit of Russian War Relief, the affair attracted a capacity crowd, to which the band responded magnificently. "Black, Brown and Beige" lasted almost forty-five minutes. It featured just about everyone in the band: Ellington on piano, singer Betty Roche, saxists Hodges, Carney, Webster and Toby Hardwick, trombonists Brown, Tizol and Joe (Tricky Sam) Nanton and trumpeters Rex Stewart, Harold Baker and Ray Nance. The great bassist Jimmy Blanton unfortunately was not there; he had died a few months before at the tender age of twenty-four.

Barney Bigard, the fluent clarinetist, had also left before the concert, and during the months that followed, Webster, Hardwick, Stewart and Brown also departed. And yet, the band, spurred by Duke's leadership and the unceasing flow of his inspiring music, continued to produce great sounds, so great, that in the August, 1943, issue of *Metronome,* Barry Ulanov awarded it the only A plus rating in the magazine's history. And New York audiences, so long deprived of an Ellington appearance, were treated to six consecutive months of his music at a club called The Hurricane.

The years that followed were generally good ones for Duke and his men. For a while he featured two impressive singers, Betty Roche, who could sing the blues so magnificently but whose undisciplined attitude kept her from achieving the success due her tremendous talents, and Al Hibbler, he of the deep scoops, who, though never as musicianly or polished a singer as Herb Jeffries, the man he replaced, still attracted a host of fans. And late in 1944, after Betty Roche had left, Duke bedecked his bandstand with three girl singers, each especially attractive-looking and each a good song stylist in her own right. They were Kay Davis, who sang in an almost pure soprano voice but who still imparted a feeling for jazz, Joya Sherrill, an especially vivacious and pretty girl who sang with fine rhythmic sense, and a charming lady, Maria Ellington (no relation of Duke's), who contributed some deeper-pitched, more emotional solos and who later became even better known to the general public as the wife of Nat (King) Cole and later as the mother of Natalie Cole.

The Duke's feminine court: Kay Davis, Joya Sherrill, Maria Ellington

The band continued to play many of the better spots. And it continued to make more frequent appearances in concert halls, often enchanting its audiences with its spirited, fresh performances of new compositions and arrangements by Ellington and Strayhorn. But sometimes the band just coasted, disappointing its devoted fans by dwelling on too-frequent reprises of Ellington hits delivered in an "and-then-I-wrote" lackluster style.

That is how it had always been with the Ellington band. On those fortunately frequent occasions when it had been really "on," it reached musical heights that no other bands had ever scaled. But there would also be those inexpliciable times when the band would play so poorly, so lacking in inspiration, that it would be difficult for those who had heard the Ellingtonians at their best to realize that this was the same group of musicians.

Of course, it always wasn't the same group. Through the years the band underwent a great many changes in personnel, and some of the new men required time to become accustomed not merely to the music itself but also to the attitude of the band, an attitude that at times seemed to be almost fatalistic, as though the men realized and accepted the fact that there would be those nights when they would be unable to feel and play as one, when the great music their leader had written and arranged just for them would somehow sound like something someone else, less talented, had written for a group of mediocre musicians who didn't care very much in the first place.

What happened then? Did they panic? No. Did they worry? Never! It didn't pay. Duke always impressed this philosophy on his men, just as he impressed it on me at the close of an interview some years ago. "What keeps a man like you going at such a terrific pace?" I had asked him. And Duke had smiled at me in his most disarming way and said simply, "Because I can't and I don't want to stop creating." "But what about that back-breaking schedule of yours?" I continued. "Doesn't that worry you?" And that's when he started philosophizing. "Worry," he said, "is the shortcut to the end of the line. Nothing's worth worrying about because worrying destroys you." But, he explained patiently, though he didn't worry, he could become concerned, as every man should. And he went on to explain the difference. "A man who's concerned," he pointed out, "is concerned about something he can do something about. He can solve a problem. But a man who worries can do nothing because worrying is purely negative. It eats, and it eats only you. It's completely destructive."

Perhaps it was this refusal to worry, coupled with a willingness to be concerned—the realization that the only action worthwhile was positive action—that enabled Ellington to sustain through all those years. Certainly the problems he had to face during more than half a century of leading a band remained immense, especially on a band that depended so much on his ability to create and control and inspire night after night. No other bandleader ever did this nearly so long so well as Duke Ellington. No other bandleader created as much and contributed as much to American music. Until he died late in May of 1974 of lung cancer, he was still writing magnificent works, some devoted to the culture of other countries, others to religious music with which he was becoming increasingly involved. As jazz writer Ralph Gleason noted back in 1953 in the San Francisco *Chronicle*, "His is the greatest single talent to be produced in the history of jazz. I would like to predict that a quarter of a century hence, Duke's music will be studied in the schools and critics will grant him his true place beside the great composers of this century."

Thanks to Duke's son Mercer, the music continued to be performed, sometimes in its original form, sometimes with surprising and perhaps even devastating deviations. "The Duke Ellington Orchestra Under the Direction of Mercer Ellington" apparently decided not to compete with the original, but instead to change some of the music to fit the so-called "contemporary" mode. To many die-hard Ellingtonians, this amounted to blasphemy, especially when the music was fitted into the constricted disco style. But to Mercer, an intelligent, sensitive, but, according to his book about his father, also a resentful man, this seemed to be a better way in which to express himself while still keeping the band working, even though hardly any members of the group that Duke had been leading were present.

Then in March of 1981 came *Sophisticated Ladies,* a musical made up entirely of Duke's works. With Mercer as its musical director, the big, lavish, hit show became a fitting tribute to a great man, a dramatic reminder of his father's prodigious and prolific talents.

Shep Fields

WHENEVER people talk about Shep Fields they always mention his Rippling Rhythm. That's not surprising, because this tricky, ricky-tick style made a lasting impression on the big band scene. But there was much more to this man and his music than just a simple expression of mickey-mousism, and eventually he showed his love of good music via one of the most remarkable, least remembered of all the big bands.

Shep, a very relaxed person, who came across like the uncle in whom you like most to confide, started his career in 1934, when, as a sax-playing leader, he replaced Jack Denny in New York's Hotel Pierre. He'd been there for some time when Veloz and Yolande, the top dance team of the era, dropped in with Jules Stein, head man at MCA. They were looking for a band that would go on the road with them, and as Shep once pointed out, "it turned out to be between us and Freddy Martin who was playing at the Hotel Bossert in Brooklyn. I could say that they chose our band over Freddy's, but I wouldn't be honest, because to this day I'm not sure that Freddy wanted the job. Anyway, they took us.'"

The first engagement of the "Veloz and Yolande Orchestra under the direction of Shep Fields" was at the swank Palmer House in Chicago. Says Fields, "Till then we had been playing nothing but stock arrangements, just like the other society bands. But three of us, Sal Gioa, our pianist and arranger, Lou Halmy, who played trumpet and arranged, and I, started experimenting. We had a lot of air time; we were bucking all those bands with their own styles, and we realized we had to come up with something distinctive of our own."

Such perception wasn't outstandingly shrewd. However, the way Shep developed his unique style, without ever creating anything really original, turned out to be a masterful bit of adapting. He once confessed all in his sumptuous office in Beverly Hills, where he had become an important cog in Creative Management Associates, one of the country's top talent outfits.

He and his arrangers began listening to the more successful sweet bands. They heard the solo trombone glissing in Wayne King's orchestra; they took that sound and transferred it to the solo viola in their band. They heard Eddy

Duchin's flowery right-hand embellishments on the piano; these they assigned to their very talented accordionist, Jerry Shelton, who, Shep noted, "played well with his right hand only anyway." They liked the sound of Hal Kemp's trumpet triplets and the distinctiveness of Ted Fio Rito's temple blocks, so they featured the triplet style in a new combination of flutes, clarinets and temple blocks. And one thing Shep had always liked was the effective use Ferdy Grofe had made of the trombone (along with temple blocks too) in his *Grand Canyon Suite*. This stylistic device they assigned to muted trumpets.

"We had very little money for our own arrangements," Shep reported, "and so we took the published arrangements, and I'd sing the parts we'd worked out to the men, and then they'd write them down."

The results sounded completely original. Radio listeners responded so enthusiastically that the Mutual network gave the band many extra air shots. "We needed a name for our style and so we started a contest among our listeners. The first prize was a free weekend for two at the Palmer House. We had about five thousand responses and of those more than three thousand had the word 'rippling' in the title. And over four hundred of them suggested 'rippling rhythm.' Naturally we couldn't give each of them a prize, so we gave only one. I imagine there must be close to four hundred couples around who still must hate us."

From Chicago, Veloz and Yolande went to the Cocoanut Grove in Los Angeles. By then Shep felt he had built a big enough name to go out on his own. Despite objections from Veloz and Yolande and MCA, Shep quit, and on his own called Mr. Pierre, head of the New York hotel bearing his name, and got his old job back.

"On the way East," Shep recalled, "we did a one-nighter in Rockford, Illinois. One thing we'd been looking for was a distinctive sound effect that would introduce our music, one that would let everyone know right away that they were listening to rippling rhythm. Out in L.A. we had gone into several studios trying to come up with just the right device, but we had no luck. And then it happened in Rockford.

"Now this may sound corny and hard to believe and like one of those ridiculous movie scenes, but it's the truth. My wife, Evy, and I were sitting in a little confectionary shop between shows, drinking sodas. Well, you guessed it. She's sitting there, thinking, blowing through her straw into her soda glass, and she makes that noise. Right away I knew that was the exact sound we needed to introduce our rippling rhythm."

It's doubtful if any bandleader has ever received more ribbing for anything than Shep Fields has for blowing through a straw. But that's exactly what he did, before every one of hundreds of broadcasts, and the ridiculous sound became the harbinger of his rippling rhythm for many years.

The band scored a big hit in New York. "There was lots of talk and interest, but no hit record—in fact, no record at all. Then I remembered when I'd been in Chicago that Benny Goodman (sic!) had heard the band and appar-

Shep ripples some rhythm

ently liked it enough to call Eli Oberstein, head of RCA Victor, and told him about us. Eli told Benny to tell me to call him if I ever got back into town. So I did and we got a recording date, and incidentally, Eli became my best friend."

The first record was a coupling of "Us on a Bus" and "On the Beach at Bali Bali." Shep was driving up to Grossinger's in the Catskills ("I started there and I'd go back to see Jennie Grossinger whenever I could") when he heard Martin Block play the record for the first time on his "Make Believe Ballroom" program, complete with raves about the new band and all sorts of predictions about its success. Block was right, too, because shortly thereafter Fields came in No. 1 not only in Block's poll but also in that of the Paramount Theater.

Surprisingly, despite his instant success, Fields wasn't entirely happy with his band. Other successful mickey-mouse leaders remained intensely devoted to their ticks and tricks throughout their careers. But Fields, to the amazement of many of us who thought he'd ripple the rest of his life, grew restless. He was, he intimated, interested in forming a more musical band. Of course the success of the era's big, swinging sounds undoubtedly influenced his decision, for Shep was not only an imaginative musician, but also an astute businessman.

Shep's brother, Freddy, had been deeply impressed by some records Paul Whiteman had made with just a sax section. This was the same Freddy who for years headed Creative Management, was married to Polly Bergen and who manages many top TV performers. Then, though, he was still a trombone player. Recalls Shep: "Freddy thought it would be a great idea to embellish what Whiteman had recorded. So we went all the way."

I caught the band when it first began rehearsing early in 1941. Shep certainly had gone all the way. Whereas Whiteman had featured a few saxes, Fields paraded a total of thirty-five instruments, including one bass sax, one baritone, six tenors, four altos, three bass clarinets, ten regular clarinets, nine flutes, including one alto flute and one piccolo.

At first Shep considered filling one of the sax chairs. "But, I reasoned, why should I play if for a hundred and a quarter a week I can get a guy who can *really* play!"

It turned out to be one of the most musical dance bands of all time. The varied reeds produced wonderful tone colors, via some fine arrangements, first by Glenn Osser and Lew Harris, and later by Freddy Noble, who became Shep's musical director, a post he held for twenty-three years. In a February, 1942, review I commended the band for its great blend and its lack of obtrusiveness, while still projecting all the excitement of a band with brass sections. The more one listened to the music, I noted, the more one could appreciate it. I added that its over-all approach wasn't too startlingly different from that of the more orthodox bands, for Shep, in dividing his reeds into two distinct sections—generally altos vs. tenors—used them the way the other bands used saxes vs. brass. The big difference, though, was the amazingly rich ensemble sounds the all-reed band achieved when all nine horns played similar lines. Even critic Leonard Feather, in those days impressed only by jazz sounds, lauded the band for its sheer beauty.

To play the difficult book, Fields hired some top-notch musicians. He also hired some future TV stars, saxophonist Sid Caesar and singers Ken "Fustis" Curtis and Ralph Young. But during the war there just weren't enough good musicians available who would go out on the road. Furthermore, Fields found during his USO tours that most servicemen didn't appreciate his new sound; they kept yammering for his old rippling rhythm.

Shep, the musical idealist, had to give in to Shep, the commercial realist. And so in 1947, back to the soda straws and the rickey-tick sounds he went. For many years thereafter he continued to ripple successfully in hotels throughout the land, continuing his career long after leaders of more musical bands had been forced to give up theirs.

For Fields, who died in February, 1981, of a heart attack, his fondest memories centered about that multi-reed band. With great pride he noted that famed musical arranger and educator Joseph Schillinger once described it as "one of the most colorful bands ever assembled. And for a guy who had sold corn almost all of his life, that certainly was my biggest thrill!"

Dizzy Gillespie

DIZZY GILLESPIE often acted like his nickname during the big band era—wild, unpredictable and brash, sporting a bop beret, dark glasses and a goatee. Yet John Birks Gillespie, tremendously creative and as uninhibited in his music as in his behavior, knew all along what he was doing. He was, as one of his fellow musicians noted, "about as crazy as a fox." He was, most of all, a tremendously inventive and inspiring musician, whose influence extended far beyond the many big bands in which he played trumpet.

Dizzy's nonconformity may have been part of a huge act—none of us was ever too sure. Neither, apparently, were some of the leaders for whom he worked, several of whom refused to countenance being hit by a barrage of spitballs deftly blown from the brass section, or a young trumpeter's suddenly stalking off the bandstand in disapproval of some musical turn. And yet Dizzy

Dizzy—then

Dizzy—later

was seldom out of work, so attractive were his musical contributions. During the big band era he blew his horn in the bands of Cab Calloway, Duke Ellington, Billy Eckstine and Boyd Raeburn, as well as that of any one of eight "H's" —Claude Hopkins, Les Hite, Edgar Hayes, Fletcher and Horace Henderson, Earl Hines, Teddy Hill and Woody Herman, for whom he wrote a dedicatory instrumental, "Woodyn You," which became one of the jazz classics of the forties.

Gillespie's influence on the big bands was stronger as a musical pacemaker and sideman than as a leader. After forming a combo in 1945, he organized a big band. It lasted only a few months because, as one writer pointed out, "the band as a whole couldn't keep pace with Dizzy's frantic fingering." So he went back to leading another combo, and then, when the big band era was just about over, assembled an outstandingly good, modern big jazz outfit that featured his brilliant, boppish trumpet, Sonny Stitt on sax, Milt Jackson on vibes, Ray Brown on bass, Kenny Clarke on drums, the legendary Chano Pozo on congo drums and either Thelonious Monk or John Lewis, leader of the Modern Jazz Quartet, on piano. Lewis, Tad Dameron and Walter Fuller wrote a batch of exciting scores for the young, exuberant group, which made some sides for Victor (none was especially well recorded and thus all failed to project the true excitement of the music) and which worked fairly regularly during the late forties, primarily in jazz clubs and in concert.

Dizzy has always been one of the most communicative of jazz musicians, verbally as well as instrumentally. He has recognized that his has been a big influence on jazz, though he has always been quick to point out that the late Charlie Parker and Thelonious Monk had at least as much to do with the development of bop as he did. Despite his outward behavior, he is deadly serious about his music and those who play it, and he is deeply concerned about the importance of the fundamentals of music. In the mid-forties, during the height of the bop craze, when so many young musicians were trying to emulate him, Gillespie displayed a refreshing perspective for an idol when he warned that "some of the kids try to pick up in a single day everything that's taken years to develop. They get the superficial things but not the fundamentals. They could get something new themselves if they could find out what it is they're doing."

A few years ago Dizzy again emphasized the importance of fundamentals, while at the same time crediting the big bands for his development. He spoke fondly of his first important big band job, the one with Teddy Hill's band at the Savoy Ballroom, with which he made his first recordings back in 1937. "Just by sitting next to Bill Dillard [Hill's first trumpeter] and listening to him and having him show me things," Gillespie related, "I began to develop. He told me how to hold the notes the right way, and how to attack and how to use my vibrato and all that. I learned not only what to do but also what *not* to do. Without the big bands, kids today don't get a chance to learn like that."

Actually how much has Dizzy Gillespie learned? Enough to bring forth from one of today's most thoroughly schooled and accomplished musicians, André Previn, an opinion that is shared by many top jazz musicians. "Dizzy Gillespie is the perfect jazz musician," said Previn. "He is a great trumpet player. He's inventive. He swings and he has a sense of humor that jazz should have. He has," Previn concluded, "developed the proper perspective that comes with maturity and confidence."

(Those who would like to know even more about Dizzy Gillespie should read his delightful biography, "To Bop Or Not to Bop," published in 1978 by Doubleday and Company.)

Benny Goodman

"BENNY GOODMAN and his 'Let's Dance' band are a truly great out-fit—fine arrangements and musicians who are together all the time—they phrase together, they bite together, they swing together. And there are plenty of individual stand-outs—Papa Benny's clarinet, Helen Ward's vocals, Gene Krupa's drums, Frank Froeba's piano, Jack Lacey's trombone, Peewee Erwin's trumpet, Arthur Rollini's tenor sax, ad infinitum . . . wonderful."

This rave appeared as part of the first column I ever wrote for *Metronome*. It was in the March, 1935, issue, and, after it came out, Gus Greiff, the assistant advertising manager, took me aside and said rather solicitously, "You know, you made a mistake in your column. His name isn't *Benny* Goodman, it's *Al* Goodman." That's about how well Benny Goodman was known at the time—certainly not as well as Al Goodman, who as conductor on several regular radio shows was far more familiar to most Americans—including Gus Greiff.

Benny's band, of course, hadn't been making much noise or an impression—except on the few jazz initiated who had bought some of its few Columbia records and who might have caught it at Billy Rose's Music Hall. There a radio producer named Joe Bonime had also heard it. Fortunately he happened to be among the minority: he liked it. He liked it so much, in fact, that when his agency, which represented the National Biscuit Company, decided to put on a three-hour marathon dance band program every Saturday night, he selected Goodman's as one of the three orchestras. The other two were those of Xavier Cugat, who provided the Latin music, and Kel Murray (a fiddle player named Murray Kellner), who led one of those big but undistinguished outfits that played purely vanilla music. By contrast Goodman's had to sound at least colorful. Actually it sounded downright thrilling.

The program lasted twenty-six weeks. The band was beginning to make a good reputation. Willard Alexander, the MCA agent in charge of Goodman, decided he was ripe for a New York hotel engagement. He picked the Grill Room of the Roosevelt Hotel, where Guy Lombardo normally held forth. Guy had been on tour, and the spot had been occupied by the less popular Bernie Cummins' Orchestra, which wasn't as difficult an attraction to follow.

The Goodman band opened in May of 1935. It was, I stated in my

Metronome review, "the closest to perfection this reviewer has heard in many moons. Benny and the rest of the boys have adapted themselves [to the room] beautifully; they produce a subdued type of swing that is a credit to the profession and which clicked immediately with all the varied ages the grill down there draws."

As a sample of criticism, the piece wasn't bad. Reportorially it was something else. I faintly recall now that there weren't many people in the place the night I reviewed the band, so it's possible that the band might have satisfied "all the varied ages" who were there—all twelve customers. But so far as the manager of the hotel was concerned, the "new-fangled swing" band was monstrous. "Opening night," Alexander recalls, "they got their two weeks' notice."

It was a tough blow for Benny. It was tough for Alexander, too, because the young agent, who had recently given up his own orchestra to go to work for MCA, had been fighting for the band even though Jules Stein, the president, and Billy Goodheart, in charge of the New York office, had much less use for Goodman. "Like Benny, they were both from Chicago," Willard relates. "Only they used to play society music rather than jazz—in fact Billy was one of the 'Nola'-type pianists. When Casa Loma started making it, MCA decided it ought to have a band like that too. I'd heard Benny on records and so I sent for him and we signed him, even though I never felt that Jules or Billy really wanted him."

But Alexander kept plugging. He drew strong support from John Hammond, the most enthusiastic and influential jazz buff around, who had encouraged Benny to organize a band in the first place. After the Roosevelt fiasco, Willard booked Goodman on some one-nighters, and these, plus some record dates, kept the band working.

Between the middle of April and the beginning of July, Goodman cut some of his best sides, including the now-famous Fletcher Henderson arrangements of "Blue Skies," "Sometimes I'm Happy" and "King Porter Stomp." These simple yet insistently and incessantly swinging scores typified the band's style—simple, swinging arrangements in which complete sections played with the feeling of a single jazz soloist. In addition, Henderson would set off one section against another, rolling saxes vs. crisp brass, an approach quite different from the less rhythmic, more lethargic-sounding ensembles of most dance bands.

Of course Henderson, and other Goodman arrangers such as Fletcher's brother Horace, and Edgar Sampson and Jimmy Mundy, also allowed plenty of room for the soloists, especially Benny, to get off on their own. However, the arrangements still continued to emphasize the rhythmic power of ensemble sounds by inspiring the soloists with swinging group backgrounds.

The band was soon set for a cross-country tour. Before it left New York, though, two of its members, Benny and Gene Krupa, participated in a historic recording session.

At a party at the home of the Red Norvos (Mrs. Norvo was Mildred Bailey) Goodman had played in a trio format with Teddy Wilson, the young, black pianist and Hammond protege, who was with Willie Bryant's band at the Savoy Ballroom. His clean, well-articulated swinging style had thrilled Benny so much that he had invited Teddy to make some recordings with him. Thus in mid-July, Benny and Gene and Teddy cut the first four Benny Goodman Trio sides. The tunes were "After You've Gone," "Body and Soul," "Who" and "Someday Sweetheart."

Wilson didn't join the band then. But Bunny Berigan did. And so did a fine pianist out of Chicago, Jess Stacy.

Nothing eventful happened until the band reached Denver. There, at Elitch's Garden, where most of the top bands had been playing, Goodman underwent what he later described to writer Richard Gehman as "just about the most humiliating experience of my life." On opening night people started asking for their money back and the manager wouldn't be mollified until the band started playing waltzes. It proved to be a horrendous engagement, so that what happened shortly thereafter on the band's first West Coast engagement, a one-night stand in Oakland, California, became all the more gratifying.

For the first time the band scored a resounding triumph. People had lined up outside waiting to get in to hear the new group and responded with cheers to each swinging number. From Oakland, Goodman went to the most famous of all West Coast ballrooms, Hollywood's Palomar, for an August 21 opening. Apparently Benny still wasn't too sure how the band would be received, because on the first night, Gene Krupa recalls, "we played the first couple of sets under wraps. We weren't getting much reaction, so Benny, I guess, decided to hell with playing it safe and we started playing numbers like 'King Porter Stomp.' Well, from then on we were in!"

The engagement was a smash. Kids gathered around the bandstand and screamed for more. Their cheers and the band's swinging sounds were swept coast to coast via a series of broadcasts from the Palomar. Swing was really in!

Following the Palomar, the band played several one-nighters, then began what was supposed to be a three weeks' engagement in the Urban Room of Chicago's Congress Hotel. Three weeks? Maybe that's what the original contract called for. But Benny Goodman, now tabbed "The King of Swing," and his Orchestra stayed there for eight months! When they finally left, there was only one thing the management could do for a follow-up: it closed the room and redecorated it.

While in Chicago the band continued to record, waxing one of its big hits, "Stompin' at the Savoy." This was written and arranged by Edgar Sampson, a modest, talented arranger-saxist who worked in Chick Webb's band and who also composed "Don't Be That Way" and "Blue Lou," two more big instrumental hits of the day.

During this period Helen Ward recorded the vocals on several of Benny's greatest pop sides—"Goody, Goody," "It's Been So Long" and "No Other

One." For me, and, I presume, for many others who gathered around the Goodman bandstand, Helen was an especially stimulating singer, visually as well as vocally. Her style embodied a warm, sensuous jazz beat, and her body moved in a very sexy manner. She had, in addition to her physical attributes, a fine ear, and she could also play a pretty good piano.

In Chicago the band started a new radio series for Elgin watches. It also instituted a series of Sunday afternoon concerts at the Congress, and it was at one of these that Benny contributed an important breakthrough in race relations: without any fanfare he presented Teddy Wilson. Any fears he might have had were immediately dispelled by the crowd's enthusiastic reception and acceptance. From then on Teddy appeared as a featured member of the trio on all Goodman engagements.

On April 27, 1936, the Goodman Trio recorded several more memorable sides. On the following night the band closed its engagement at the Congress Hotel. Helen Oakley (now the wife of noted respected jazz critic Stanley Dance) commented in her *Metronome* column that "the evil day has fallen. Benny Goodman left the Congress Hotel on April 28th."

It was becoming obvious that Goodman's popularity was no longer confined just to the Congress or to the Palomar. The results of *Metronome*'s national swing band poll showed Goodman topping the popular Casa Loma band by nearly 2 to 1.

Following its Congress triumph, the band returned to New York, added a brilliant, young trombonist, Murray McEachern, made some more records and continued its radio commercial. Then in early summer, it returned to Hollywood to begin work on its first movie, *The Big Broadcast of 1937*. While there it took on two extremely exciting musicians.

One of these was a big, burly tenor saxist with tone and attack to match. He was Vido Musso, one of the few members of the Goodman band who was not a thoroughly schooled musician but who blew exciting jazz and who was such a delightfully disarming character that Benny never seemed to have the heart to let him go. Besides, who else could regale the bandsmen with stories about "boats that drowned" and visits to doctors who "glanced" his boils?

The other new entry was the drummer with Les Hite's band, who happened to be a pretty fair vibraphone player too. At John Hammond's suggestion, Benny went out to hear Lionel Hampton play. He immediately offered him a job, thus enlarging his trio to a quartet. In August of 1936 the new group recorded its first sides, "Dinah," "Moonglow" and "Vibraphone Blues," the latter a head arrangement that also featured Lionel on some original blues lyrics.

When Goodman opened in October, 1936, in the Madhattan Room of the Pennsylvania Hotel, Benny's New York fans finally got their first chance to listen to the band in person. Night after night they crowded into the Madhattan Room, down in the hotel's basement. It wasn't as sumptuous or as

The original Goodman Quartet: Lionel, Benny, Teddy, Gene

glamorous as the Café Rouge, which opened a year later, but it had fine acoustics and its small size and low ceiling lent an aura of immediacy conducive to jazz listening.

Those were thrilling nights down there, made all the more so after several weeks when young, gaunt Harry James, fresh out of Ben Pollack's band, was added to the trumpet section. Chris Griffin had already joined in April, and shortly before the Pennsylvania opening Benny had heard and hired a big-toned, blasting trumpeter, who blew out of the side of his mouth and yet managed to spark the entire Alex Bartha band, which had been playing opposite Goodman on Atlantic City's Steel Pier. This was Ziggy Elman, a colorful, enthusiastic, cigar-smoking extrovert.

When James and his driving horn joined in December, not merely the brass section but the entire band started jumping as it never had before. Besides being an inspiring lead trumpeter and an exciting soloist, James was also an excellent reader. Goodman must have been tipped off by his old boss, Pollack, because, according to Harry, when he arrived in New York and called Benny to ask "When's rehearsal?" Benny replied, "There won't be any. Just come on down and play tonight." Harry did, and that night one of the great trumpet sections of all time was born!

Gene swings, Harry blasts, Ziggy dreams.

People used to argue about who was playing the potent lead trumpet in that section—Harry, Ziggy or Chris—for each could blow with convincing brilliance. Some fans persisted in crediting James for everything. But they were wrong about two-thirds of the time. James explained in his *Metronome* column of June, 1938:

> I'm just one of the lead trumpeters in the band. There's no definite rule about dividing the first book, either—nothing like Chris taking all the pretty tunes and Ziggy and I dividing the ride numbers. We just get the first parts in rotation. If an arrangement comes in and it's Ziggy's turn to get the lead, he takes it; if it's Chris's turn, he takes it, and if it's my turn, it's handed over to me. . . .
>
> The funny part is, though, that most people can't tell just by listening which one of us is playing lead. And it seems funny that we should have such similar tones and style when we play so differently. Chris has a one-third top, two-thirds bottom embouchure, Ziggy's is two-thirds top and one-third bottom and dangerously close to his ear, while mine's a slightly off-center, half and half, puffed-out-cheek affair.

The band was a smash hit in the Madhattan Room. And when it went into the Paramount Theater shortly thereafter, the fans started lining up outside at seven o'clock in the morning, yearning to get inside to hear their idol. Some fairly hysterical scenes followed, with kids dancing in the aisles while up on the stage the Goodman gang blew its killer-diller arrangements.

One reason the band sounded especially good was that the personnel had at last been firmly set. For months there had been no changes. Only in the vocal department was there a murmur—when Helen Ward became engaged to a wealthy jazz enthusiast named Albert Marx. Realizing that she would soon leave, Benny began looking around for another singer. By the time a November record date came up, he still hadn't found one he liked enough to hire as a regular, so he reached into Chick Webb's band and borrowed his exciting young singer, Ella Fitzgerald. She recorded three sides with the band, "Good Night, My Love," "Take Another Guess" and "Did You Mean It?" But when

Decca Records, for whom Ella recorded with Chick, found out what had happened, they threatened to sue. So the three sides were promptly recalled and for years remained collectors' items. Not so, though, the fourth side, "T'ain't No Use," on which the band used another vocalist, Benny Goodman. How well did he sing? The song title gave the answer.

The vocal chair found no steady sitter for several months. Benny was considering Beatrice Wayne, who sang with the Kay Thompson group and who later shortened her name to Bea Wain and joined Larry Clinton's band. Helen's first replacement was Margaret McCrae, who was soon followed by Frances Hunt, a good singer who'd been working with Lou Bring's orchestra. However, again romance interfered, for Frances loved Lou and Lou loved Frances, and so she returned to his band and married him.

Next came Peg LaCentra, who had been singing impressively with Artie Shaw's band. Apparently she and Benny didn't hear ear to ear, and in a few weeks she was back with Artie. Then came a very voluptuous girl, Betty Van, who could sing fairly well. Finally, in the summer of 1937, Benny found Martha Tilton and his vocal problems were solved.

The cute little blonde, a warm, friendly person, fitted in beautifully, though she ran into a bit of embarrassment on one of her first nights with the band. That was at the Sunnybrook Ballroom in Pennsylvania, where Benny, intending to give her a big buildup, introduced her as "a singer from Hollywood who's going places." But Martha forgot her cue, and when she didn't appear, Goodman quipped, "Boy, she isn't going places; she's already gone!"

Of course, Benny could be pretty forgetful, too, and the stories of his absent-mindedness have become legendary among jazz musicians—like the time he hailed a taxi, opened the door, got in, sat back in his seat and asked the driver, "How much do I owe you?" Or the time he and a friend took a couple of girls to a nightclub and when the girls, apparently wanting to go to the ladies room, said, "Will you excuse us, please?" Benny replied, "Why certainly," and got up and walked away.

Contrary to what one might expect, Benny is quite aware of his tendency to fog up. At lunch some years ago he told two of his favorite stories about himself. One concerned his earlier days in New York when, walking along Fifty-third Street after a snowstorm, he noticed an open Ford convertible parked at the curb and filled with snow. "The poor jerk," he murmured to himself, "leaving a car out like that all night." And then it suddenly hit him. It was his own car!

The other story concerned his being jolted out of a sound sleep one night in his Pennsylvania Hotel room. "We'd been doubling at the hotel and at the Paramount Theater. It was quite a schedule, and each night I'd go to bed right after we finished working at two so that I could get some sleep. But on this particular night I was awakened by a pounding on the door. I got up and asked who was there. 'It's the waiter from Tony Pastor's,' a voice said. 'You didn't pay your check and we followed you here.' We talked back and forth a while and then I decided to open the door to let him see I'd been in bed. Well, when I opened it, I found nobody there. But standing in front of the door to the next room was this guy in a waiter's outfit. He'd been talking through one transom and I'd been talking through the other!"

Benny's fogginess or absentmindedness has often been taken for rudeness. Now, Benny has never been known as the most tactful man in the world, and at times he has been quite thoughtless. But often his vagueness and seemingly rude behavior have been caused by nothing more evil than simple preoccupation. For Benny can and does easily get lost in whatever he happens to be concerned with at any particular moment, so that his lack of communication with someone who might be thinking about something other than what Benny happens to be totally immersed in, shouldn't necessarily be classified as premeditated hostility.

During the band's stay at the Pennsylvania, Goodman came in for some caustic criticism, with one musician's trade paper running an editorial titled "Is Benny Goodman's Head Swollen?" and discussing "the universal expressions of dislike for Benny among musicians, bookers, publishers and other band leaders in New York."

At *Metronome* we interviewed several of those "other band leaders" and came up with the following quotes:

Artie Shaw: "That statement is stupid; it's out of the question; it's just not so. Benny has a lot more on his mind than he used to have, but he still doesn't come close to having a big head. Anyway, anybody who makes a crack like that is likely to make the same sort about any orchestra leader, and I'm going to protect myself, too!"

Tommy Dorsey: "Hey, that guy's so busy right now he doesn't know if he's coming or going most of the time. I just saw him the other day and he had nothing even remotely resembling a big head."

Glenn Miller: "Benny and I came to New York together. We roomed together when we were with Ben Pollack. He was a swell gent then and he still is one today. You've got to really know Benny to appreciate his many wonderful qualities."

Not only among bandleaders, but among sidemen and just about anyone else who has worked with him, Benny Goodman has emerged as one of the most controversial of all the personalities who made up the big band scene. And the fact that he played an important role emphasized anything he did just that much more.

Appraisals of Goodman by his former musicians vary from "he's a penny-pinching s.o.b." to "he's absolutely the greatest." One thing almost everyone agrees with concerning Benny is that he does watch a buck very carefully. Even when he was at his richest, he was constantly trying to bargain with musicians about salaries. Today some of them still harbor resentment; others, especially some of the veterans, laugh it off with a shrug and a "that's Benny for you, so what are you going to do?"

Some probe a little deeper and comprehend that a self-made man, someone brought up in a very poor family, as Benny was, is never likely to lose the instinct or the impulse to bargain and fight for the best deal he can get, no matter with whom and for what—even if he has it made and commutes between a beautiful home in Connecticut and a sumptuous East Side apartment in New York.

The turnover among musicians in the various Goodman bands was quite high, but the cause wasn't usually money. Most often it was more Benny's penchant for perfection, coupled with a low tolerance level. If musicians delivered consistently for Benny, they seldom had trouble with him. But those who didn't, especially those who goofed because of lack of effort, received what has become well known among musicians as "the Goodman ray."

The "ray" is best described as "a fish stare," with which Benny seems to be not so much as looking at a person as looking through him. For anyone feeling the least bit unsure or the least bit guilty, such a look can be quite unnerving, especially when it comes from the boss.

Harry James and I were discussing this look recently. "He used it only on some guys," Harry explained. "And then there were some guys who thought he was giving them the ray when he really wasn't. Instead, he'd be looking in their direction, but at the same time he'd be completely occupied about something else, usually something about music, and he'd actually be looking off into space."

Goodman himself has often admitted that he is a perfectionist and that musicians' mistakes, especially the careless ones, bug him. "I'll never be satisfied with any band," he told me in 1946. "I guess I just expect too much from my musicians, and when they do things wrong I get brought down."

Unlike Tommy Dorsey and Glenn Miller, Goodman seldom blew his top at his musicians. His method was more subtle. When a musician displeased him, Benny would usually just ignore him, a sort of negative method of informing the musican that he was in trouble. Frequently the situation would become so uncomfortable that the musician would quit. Thus Goodman did not actually fire many of his men; usually what happened was more like a passive fadeout.

"Very few bands I've ever had," Benny admitted just a few years ago, "didn't squawk about something."

One of the biggest squawks ever let out from the Goodman bandstand came from Benny's famous drummer, Gene Krupa, on the stage of the Earle Theater in Philadelphia, and it marked the beginning of the gradual breakup of what many refer to as "The Original Benny Goodman Band."

Just before then, though, Benny and his men had participated in one of the greatest triumphs ever registered by a swing band. This was its famous Carnegie Hall concert.

The band's fame had been spreading and spreading, thanks to its recordings, its numerous air shots from the Pennsylvania and its new half-hour, prime-time radio commercial, "The Camel Caravan," on which it was allowed to play all its best numbers with practically no sponsor interference. It was a well-produced show, with commentary by such respected literary figures as Clifton Fadiman and Robert Benchley, plus some brilliant special material by Johnny Mercer, to give it additional class.

What next? "How about Carnegie Hall?" suggested publicist Win Nathanson. Benny hesitated. Willard Alexander was enthusiastic. Sol Hurok agreed to promote the bash, and *Metronome* announced that on January 16, 1938, the Goodman band would be "replacing Jack Barbirolli and his Philharmonic Cats, the regular band in that spot."

Before the concert Benny made a couple of personnel changes. Murray McEachern had gone over to the Casa Loma band, so Goodman brought in Vernon Brown. At the same time he replaced Vido Musso with Babe Russin.

After tabbing the concert "a howling success," my *Metronome* review noted that "it started off a bit gingerly. Benny, quite nervous, beat off 'Don't Be That Way' a bit too slow, and for one chorus it was quite obvious that his men were neither relaxed nor in any sort of a groove. Suddenly, though, Gene Krupa emitted a tremendous break on drums. The crowd cheered, yelled, howled. Gene's hair fell into his eyes. The band fell into a groove, and, when

Backstage at the "Camel Caravan":
unidentified paunch, Allan Reuss, Ziggy Elman, Johnny Mercer,
BG, Gene Krupa, Murray MacEachern

it had finished this fine Edgar Sampson opus, received tumultuous applause. Now the concert was in a groove, too."

It was a lengthy, enthusiastic review that described the great ovation the band received for its "One O'Clock Jump," the ending of which was "drowned out by applause and cat-calls"; the amusing history of jazz, during which Benny imitated Ted Lewis; the appearance of three members of Duke Ellington's band (Cootie Williams, Johnny Hodges and Harry Carney) in a short salute to Duke's music; the Goodman band's "return to the stage, from which it almost blasted itself off with Harry James's 'Life Goes to a Party,'" the ineffectual jam session with Count Basie, Lester Young, Buck Clayton and several others; the relaxed numbers played by the trio and the big hand accorded Teddy Wilson; the show-stopping ovation that followed Martha Tilton's singing of "Loch Lomond"; Jimmy Mundy's "Swingtime in the Rockies" in which "all of a sudden, blasting like hell, riding on high out of the ancient alcoves came Ziggy Elman with a trumpet passage that absolutely broke everything up. . . . The crowd began to yell; the band began to dig and blast at a pace it had never approached before Ziggy's outburst."

There was little letup thereafter as the band approached "the real finale of the evening. Gene, hanging on for dear life by now, began the tom-tom-toming that started 'Sing, Sing, Sing.' It was the occasion for a wild outburst. After many choruses the band began to build to a climax. As it did so, one kid after another commenced to create a new dance: trucking and shagging while sitting down. Older, penguin-looking men in traditional boxes on the sides went them one better and proceeded to shag standing up. Finally Benny

Part of the Carnegie Hall program

and Gene alone—just clarinet and drums—hit the musical highlight of the concert with both of them playing stupendous stuff. Came the full band, and then suddenly soft, church-music from Jess Stacy at the piano. It was wonderful contrast. Benny started to laugh. Everybody started to laugh. And then everybody started to applaud, stamp, cheer, yell, as the band went into the number's final outburst. And long after it was completed, they kept on yelling."

Several days after the concert, Krupa was doing some yelling too—only of a different sort and in a different place. He and Benny had been having some pretty sharp disagreements about how their music should be played. In addition, Gene had been gaining a great deal of national publicity, and possibly Benny wasn't overjoyed at being upstaged by one of his men. Tremendously popular, Gene felt he could make it on his own, and so a few weeks after the Carnegie Hall triumph and a few hours after an outburst in Philadelphia, Gene announced he was leaving.

Goodman wasn't unprepared. He immediately hired another former Chicago drummer, Davey Tough, who instilled a new looseness into the band with his driving yet tremendously simple playing. Benny began featuring the free, unfettered arrangements of Edgar Sampson instead of the more intense, complex scores of Jimmy Mundy. He hired Dave Matthews as a lead saxist, and though Dave wasn't nearly as polished a musician as Hymie Shertzer had been, he too contributed a more relaxed feel. And on tenor sax in place of Babe Russin, who turned out to be only a temporary replacement, Goodman hired his and Tough's old Chicago pal, Bud Freeman, whose humorous and ever-jumping solos added some delightful levity.

The band's lighter approach suited two precedent-shattering engagements during the summer and fall of 1938. The first was on the Roof of the Ritz-Carlton Hotel in Boston, the second was in the Empire Room of the Waldorf-Astoria. Neither spot had ever booked a swing band before, but so tastefully did Benny swing in both those rooms that he opened the way for many other swing bands.

But for the two years that followed, life was far less pleasant for Benny Goodman. His orchestra underwent an unhealthy number of personnel changes and finally, through no fault of Benny's, was forced to disband.

Davey Tough, the tremendously talented, sensitive, swinging drummer, didn't last long, victim of one of a series of collapses that hounded him throughout his career. Davey was an extraordinary human being with many fine qualities—exceptional intelligence, a keen intellect, a great wit and an amazing compassion for other people. But he also was filled with haunting frustrations, and when these became too great to bear he would take a couple of drinks and go to pieces. After a few absences, during which Lionel Hampton filled in for Davey, Benny finally had to let Tough go. Buddy Schutz was his replacement, but Buddy and Benny didn't hit it off musically and soon thereafter Nick Fatool joined the band.

But the biggest blow of all was the departure of Harry James early in 1939. The reason was simple: Harry wanted to have his own band. Benny understood and even helped out financially. Brother Irving, whom Harry had replaced, came back for a few weeks, to be followed by Corky Cornelius. And brother Harry Goodman, who had been playing with the band since the very beginning, gave way to one of the finest bassists of all time, Artie Bernstein.

There were more changes. Lead saxist Toots Mondello returned, so Hymie Shertzer immediately quit. George Rose replaced the ebullient Benny Heller on guitar. Jerry Jerome replaced Bud Freeman. Several men, including Arthur Rollini, quit. And Benny, in a masterful display of tactlessness, suggested to Martha Tilton that as long as so many were leaving, perhaps she'd like to go too. Martha probably didn't want to go, and certainly the men in the band, who had become so attached to her, didn't want her to. But with Benny acting as he did there was little else she could do. She was immediately replaced by a very vivacious and pretty Texan, Mrs. Harry James, better known as Louise Tobin.

The summer of 1939 wasn't an easy one for Goodman, but it was nothing compared with the first half of 1940.

Benny's relationship with MCA had never been the greatest, but thanks to Willard Alexander, the man who had believed in Goodman from the start and who knew how to handle him ("Benny gave me less trouble than any three musicians I ever knew," Alexander recently told me), no serious trouble ever erupted. But when Willard left to form a band department for the William Morris Agency, and Bob Crosby's band was assigned Benny's old "Camel Caravan" show, Goodman wouldn't even set foot in the MCA offices or talk to any of its representatives.

Benny's recording relations also underwent a metamorphosis, and in July, after almost five years with Victor, he signed with Columbia. The fact that his friend, admirer and confidant John Hammond had been appointed an executive there undoubtedly influenced Goodman.

Hammond had also been responsible for drawing Benny's attention to one of the greatest of all jazz musicians, a driving, probing guitarist from Oklahoma, Charlie Christian. Benny hired him in August, and began featuring him extensively on his small group recordings. Unfortunately this brilliant musician, one of the most influential jazz creators, remained with the band for only two years; he died of tuberculosis early in 1942. Fortunately his genius has been preserved on such great Goodman sextet recordings as "Soft Winds," "Seven Come Eleven," "Shivers," "As Long As I Live," "A Sm-o-o-oth One" and "Air Mail Special."

The band underwent more personnel changes, and several of the departees blasted Benny. Toots Mondello, the highly respected lead saxist, who himself had once quit the band, defended Goodman, stating that "some of the guys haven't been able to take criticism. When guys started taking it easy—well, then he just started to bear down." And the veteran Chris Griffin noted just before leaving the band after a four-year stay: "The guy is easier to work for now than at any time during the last four years. . . . I have nothing but respect for Benny, both as a musician and as a person."

Some of Mondello's and Griffin's opinions were challenged by at least one Goodman veteran, his mild-mannered pianist Jess Stacy, who left the band in 1939, stating, "I never want to play with Benny Goodman's band again. . . . There were no hard feelings between Benny and me. He's a fine guy. But it was too much of a strain. You never knew just where you were with Benny, and I feel terribly relieved that it's all over." Stacy was replaced by Fletcher Henderson, who remained in the band for several months until Johnny Guarnieri came in for the first of his two stays.

Two of the best things that ever happened to the Goodman band took place during the latter half of 1939. One of these was the addition of Eddie Sauter to the arranging staff; the other was Helen Forrest's transferring from Artie Shaw's band to Benny's.

Eddie had been writing wonderfully imaginative, subtle yet ever-swinging arrangements for Red Norvo's band, and when the group broke up, Eddie, a mild-mannered, shy man, acceded to Benny's frequent offers to write for his band. He was not a writer in the Goodman band tradition. His was neither a simple nor a direct style. But it was so musical, so full of refreshing harmonic and contrapuntal innovations, that it infused a new spirit into a band that at that particular moment was in danger of going stale.

Helen, of course, was a wonderfully warm and musical singer who had become a national favorite with Shaw's band, which was rumored at that time to be breaking up. She joined Benny after Louise Tobin had left to have a baby and her replacement, Kay Foster, had not satisfied Goodman. Mildred Bailey, by the way, cut a few sides with the band just before Helen joined.

Neither Eddie nor Helen made their greatest contributions to the Goodman band until after the hiatus of 1940. Starting late in 1939, Benny had begun to experience increasing pain in one of his legs. It was diagnosed as sciatica, and, though Goodman underwent treatments and tried desperately to continue with his band (he even played a benefit at Chicago's Hull House, his alma mater, with a brace on his leg), the pain grew increasingly unbearable. He took a short leave of absence, during which Ziggy Elman led the band, but then in July, 1940, he gave up the fight and entered Mayo Clinic for a corrective operation.

The band's popularity was still great among musicians, who in the 1940 *Metronome* poll gave it a greater than 2 to 1 majority over the fast-rising Glenn Miller band in the swing division, and a 3 to 2 edge over Miller in the favorite-band-of-all category.

During his Mayo Clinic stay, Benny was reported to have planned several innovations, including the addition of a double string quartet to his band. The idea never materialized, but several others did.

One was the hiring of Duke Ellington's brilliant trumpeter, Cootie Williams, an event of such significance that Raymond Scott wrote a special composition for his band called "When Cootie Left the Duke." Williams gave the band a trumpet spark it hadn't known since James's days. His magnificent, rich tone and his spirited drive highlighted several records by the new Goodman sextet, which sported Count Basie on piano. Cootie also starred with the full band and made one especially great side, a sparkling Sauter original written especially for and dedicated to Cootie. Its title: "Superman."

The band began reaching new musical heights. Benny gave Sauter greater leeway, and Eddie responded with some superb scores, one of which, "Benny Rides Again," still stands as one of the truly great big band sides of all time. I must admit that when I heard it the first couple of times at rehearsal, I didn't have much of an idea of what Eddie was trying to do, and, in a way, I almost felt sorry for him, figuring he had composed something so complicated that it just couldn't swing. However, Eddie and Benny and the band worked hard and long on the piece, and as soon as I heard the record, I knew I was wrong. And when Eddie followed this with another exciting original, "Clarinet a la King," I realized, as many others did, that a new and wondrous dimension had been added to Goodman's music, one that can still be heard today in such Sauter-arranged recordings as "It Never Entered My Mind," "More Than You Know," "The Man I Love" and "Cornsilk."

Of those who had been with the band when Benny had gone into the hospital, only Charlie Christian, Artie Bernstein, trumpeters Jimmy Maxwell and Irving Goodman, and Helen Forrest were back with the reorganized band when it debuted on October 25 at Lehigh University. Two weeks later, Goodman again recorded for Columbia, with a band that included Lou McGarity, the wonderful, Teagarden-like trombonist who had been playing for Ben Bernie, Georgie Auld as featured tenor saxist (Sam Donahue had been in for a couple of weeks), Alec Fila, Bob Chester's young star, as one of the trumpets, sometimes Bernie Leighton and sometimes Fletcher Henderson on piano, and Harry Jaeger on drums.

But soon there were changes. One of these saw Davey Tough returning to the band, which immediately began to swing mightily again. It was during this period that it recorded a Buster Harding original called "Scarecrow," which continues to stand up for me as the swingingest Goodman side of all time, an appraisal that's bound to go challenged!

Shortly thereafter, when Artie Shaw disbanded, Benny grabbed several of his stars, including pianist Johnny Guarnieri, trumpeter Billy Butterfield and lead saxist Les Robinson, and the band sounded better than ever.

At Mayo Clinic Benny had also been doing some serious thinking about serious music. For several years he had indicated that he would like to broaden his scope as a performer. After he came out of the hospital, he did just that.

On December 12, 1940, he appeared in Carnegie Hall as guest soloist with the New York Philharmonic in a performance of the Mozart Clarinet Concerto and Debussy's First Rhapsody. It was so successful that Columbia issued a Masterworks version. On April 29, 1941, again in Carnegie Hall, he was featured clarinetist on Prokofiev's Overture on Yiddish Themes in a concert also starring Paul Robeson and staged for the American Russian Institute.

In October, Goodman was due to conduct the Philadelphia Orchestra at Robin Dell. The selection was a tango by Igor Stravinsky. But José Iturbi, scheduled to perform at the same concert, refused to do so, claiming Goodman had no right to conduct. The management, in effect, told Iturbi to get lost, a wise commercial gesture since Benny attracted nine thousand paying customers, plus an estimated five thousand crashers, conducted quite adequately and also performed as soloist in the Mozart Clarinet Concerto with which he had now become so familiar that when the wind blew his music off his stand he was able to continue purely from memory. Oh yes, the full Goodman band also performed.

Four nights later he appeared with the New York Philharmonic at Lewisohn Stadium. Since I felt unqualified to review the concert, I asked my long-haired brother, Henry W. Simon, then music critic for *PM,* to cover the event. Said he of Benny: "His playing couldn't be distinguished from any other longhair's excepting that the tone was better than most and he didn't seem entirely at home on the classical stuff."

In the months to come, Goodman appeared with other important orchestras —the Cleveland, the Pittsburgh and the National symphonies.

During the 1941 summer season the Goodman band participated in one of the biggest flops in danceband history. Producer Monte Proser decided he'd play big bands in, of all places, New York's Madison Square Garden. As an opening attraction he hired "The King of Swing." The band itself was good, though few people realized it because the Garden had probably the worst acoustics for a danceband either east or west of the Mississippi. Within a few weeks the gigantic venture folded.

It was while he was playing at the Garden that Benny hired one of the most talented and exciting musicians of the early forties, a man who has since made quite a reputation for himself in the field of classical and electronic music. This was Mel Powell.

The hiring of Powell serves as a classic example of how unintentionally exasperating Goodman can be. Knowing that Benny was looking for a new pianist, I told him about Powell, who was playing with a dixieland group at Nick's. Benny suggested I bring him over to the MCA rehearsal room the next afternoon. At the audition, Benny seemed quite impressed, but after Mel had left he kept asking me, "Is there anybody better around?" and I kept answering "No, no, no!" So that night Mel sat in at the Garden and reportedly did very well. But sure enough, the next day, Benny, after telling me how well Mel had performed, popped the same question, "Is there any-body better around?" When I emphasized my flat "no" with a couple of "for Chris' sakes!" Benny said, "O.K. I guess I'll take him."

Powell became one of the bright stars of the band, recording some great sides, beginning with his own composition "The Earl," whose swinging feeling is astounding when you realize the band didn't have a drummer. Tough had collapsed again, so Benny hired the talented Jo Jones especially for the session. But somehow Jo didn't work out, so Benny sent him home and recorded "The Earl" without any drums—killing once and for all the theory that a big band couldn't swing without a drummer. Powell recorded several more brilliant sides, including his own composition "Mission to Moscow," which turned out to be the last side the Goodman band was to wax for several years, thanks to James C. Petrillo's destructive recording ban of 1942.

Right after "The Earl" session, the drummer-less Goodman pulled a *coup.*

He hired "Big Sid" Catlett, who had just left Louis Armstrong's group, and Sid proceeded to impart to the band a sharply defined, swinging solidarity it hadn't known since the days of Krupa and James. His time was so sure, his taste was so pure, and the way he took rhythmic charge was an inspiration to all the musicians. Big Sid was quite a giant!

Still another star of the most musical band Benny ever had was soon to join. This was Peggy Lee, whom Goodman first heard singing with a small combo in a Chicago cocktail lounge and whom he hired in August of 1941 when Helen Forrest suddenly decided to quit. Peggy had become an integral part of the band when a few months later it played one of its most impressive of all engagements, the one in the Terrace Room of the Hotel New Yorker.

In a rave review I gave the band at that time, I noted that "Peggy Lee, who wasn't too impressive till she got over the shock of finding herself with Benny's band, is slowly turning into one of the great singers in the field. The lass has a great flair for phrasing—listen to her on those last sets at night, when the band's just noodling behind her. . . . That she gets a fine beat, that she sings in tune, and that she's awfully good-looking are self-evident."

I remember many things about that engagement, including composer Alec Wilder's regular visits with batches of new songs for Peggy, whom he admired greatly, a romance starting between Peggy and guitarist Dave Barbour which culminated in marriage, and a very striking lady always sitting at the same table at the side of the band.

The latter was Mrs. Alice Duckworth, an attractive divorcée, who was also John Hammond's sister. Whereas John would aggravate musicians by sitting up close to them and seemingly concentrating more on his newspaper than on their music, his sister would create the same reaction by sitting right by the bandstand and either knitting or playing gin rummy. (She was a master at the game, as I found out after having been handed something like a dozen consecutive schneids.)

But Alice's interest was never so much in the band as it was in its leader, and on March 21, 1942, Benny Goodman, whom just about all of us had figured would be a lifelong bachelor (after all, who could compete with that consuming interest in music?), married John Hammond's sister.

Meanwhile, outside the busy Terrace Room of the New Yorker and inside Columbia's large recording studio, the band produced more fine sides, many of which featured excellent vocals by Peggy—things like "My Old Flame," "Let's Do It," "I Got It Bad and That Ain't Good," "Somebody Else Is Taking My Place," "How Long Has This Been Going On?" "Blues in the Night," "All I Need Is You" and one of Peggy's own tunes, "Why Don't You Do Right?"

Peggy was a talented and prolific songwriter. I recall one Christmas Eve when she came down to my house after work and I put on an instrumental recording by Teddy Wilson, Red Norvo and Harry James of "Just the Blues," and Peggy sat there and ad-libbed some of the most tender verses, all about

The Goodman Band at the New Yorker (late 1941):
pianist Mel Powell; vocalists Art (Lund) London and Peggy Lee; bassist Sid Weiss;
Goodman; saxists Vido Musso, Clint Neagley, Julie Schwartz, George Berg,
Chuck Gentry; trombonists Lou McGarity and Cutty Cutshall;
drummer Ralph Collier; trumpeters Jimmy Maxwell, Billy Butterfield, Al Davis.
Guitarist Tommy Morgan is hidden behind Goodman.

how she'd like to be "a little girl who plays with dolls and such, a little girl
who wished she'd never had that touch," etc., etc. Peggy may have looked
sophisticated and sensuous, but in reality she was rather insecure, extremely
sensitive and terribly sentimental.

She and Benny got along very well most of the time, though there was a
period when he didn't seem to approve of her phrasing. This bothered her
considerably, especially because she couldn't quite seem to understand what
Benny, who wasn't always the most articulate man in the world, was trying
to tell her. One night Harry James came into the room and Peggy told him
about her problem. Harry, recognizing one of the phases that Benny was
inclined to go through, suggested placation. He advised her to tell Benny
before her next vocal that she understood what he meant and that she'd
follow his suggestion. "Just sing the way you've always been doing and see
what happens," Harry said. Peggy did, and when she was finished, Benny
turned to her and smiled graciously, and never again did he try to tell her
what she hadn't been able to comprehend in the first place. How come?
Probably only Benny knows. Certainly Peggy never knew!

In retrospect, the original Goodman band, with the James-Elman-Griffin
trumpet section and Gene Krupa on drums, and the 1941 band with Mel
Powell and Big Sid (and for a time Davey Tough) and Lou McGarity and
Cootie Williams and Billy Butterfield and Peggy Lee—with those superb
Eddie Sauter arrangements—rate for me as the greatest bands of Benny's
illustrious career.

There were still more editions to come, however. The 1941 band remained relatively intact through a good part of 1942. Benny seemed to be playing better than ever. Marriage seemed to agree with him. His solos seemed to show renewed vitality, and if the band faltered occasionally, Benny was always there to pick it up with electrifying performances.

In the spring of 1942 Benny took on his third boy vocalist, Dick Haymes, who made one good record of "Idaho" before the recording ban. Dick replaced Art Lund (first known as Art London), who then was not the polished performer he turned out to be several years later on the Broadway stage, but who did record an impressive "Winter Weather" duet with Peggy. The first Goodman male vocalist (first since the very early thirties when Ray Hendricks had sung briefly with the band) had been Tommy Taylor.

By the end of 1942 Benny's band, like so many others, was beginning to feel the effects of the draft. As more of the regulars departed, the precision and spirit which had permeated the group for so many months went with them. Barry Ulanov, reviewing a November broadcast, stated: "Never before, in this reviewer's experience, has Benny's band sounded so bad. In four numbers not one shred of distinction was uncovered, while every kind of limitation and mistake and lapse was displayed. . . . Benny's musicianship is so profound that he needn't countenance this sort of drag. This reviewer hopes he never again has to go through the humiliating experience of hearing such a performance from the great man."

Apparently Benny's sentiments weren't greatly dissimilar, because early in 1943 he began replacing some of the ineffectual youngsters in the group with seasoned veterans. Besides, the latter were less likely to be drafted, and Benny, who had been classified 4-F because of the effects of his sciatica, knew he'd be around to lead a band for a while longer.

So in came the old pros—Hymie Shertzer on lead sax, Miff Mole on trombone (Jack Teagarden and Jack Jenney played for a couple of evenings too), and others—and soon the band settled into a surer groove. For a while it played it simple and safe. The brass section was cut from seven to five men, the saxes from five to four, and it featured more of the older and easier arrangements.

Gene Krupa soon returned, getting along better than ever with Benny. Allan Reuss, one of the great rhythm guitarists of all time, who had played next to Krupa in the Goodman band of the thirties, returned, too, as did the brilliant lead trumpeter Ralph Muzzillo. Lee Castaldo, now Castle, was the jazz trumpet player. And Benny had uncovered a sensational trombonist who played wild choruses that thrilled all the guys in the band. This was Bill Harris, who later was to achieve fame with Woody Herman's band.

But by the end of 1943, many of the key men had departed. Gene joined Tommy Dorsey's band, Shertzer, Castaldo and Muzzillo, tired of traveling, quit to take jobs in New York. On March 9, after another battle with MCA, Benny put the entire band on two-weeks' notice and for the remainder of the year took it easy, gathering together groups of studio men to fulfill such engagements as recording for a Walt Disney film called *Swing Street* and making some V-Discs.

As producer of the V-Disc dates, I was able to see Benny in quite a different light. One of the sessions was also a radio broadcast, and especially for this Benny put together an astoundingly good group, whipping it into shape with a minimum amount of rehearsal, and turning in an excellent performance for us. More than ever I began to appreciate his passion for perfection.

What delighted me in addition to Benny's musical talents, of which I had of course been aware, was his attitude toward the V-Disc program. Nobody was paid for making these records, and it wasn't always easy to get a leader to agree to make even one session. But Benny offered to make several of them, and on each he worked extremely hard and came up, I think, with some magnificent sides, which featured sidemen like Teddy Wilson, Red Norvo and Slam Stewart.

These were the men who became part of the band he led in 1945, and they stood out as the most important members, next to Benny, of course, who himself continued to play elegantly and began to come across as a more relaxed, fun-loving character as he sang songs like "It's Gotta Be This or That" in a half-kidding, half-swinging fashion. By the end of the year, though, he was beginning to find it increasingly difficult to staff his band with the sort of musician who could play up to him. For a while he featured Kai Winding on trombone and Stan Getz on tenor sax, an indication of the kind of more modern music he tried to produce with minimal success in later years.

But for all intents and purposes, the great Goodman band had pretty much passed out of the picture during 1946. But Benny himself? No, not by any means. Tom Connell, writing in the August issue of *Metronome* that year, traced the band's career briefly, then concluded: "The truth begins to dawn. Goodman himself is as far out front as he ever was. But the band he leads is inferior by modern standards. In fact it is uncomfortably inferior. The King has abdicated! And long live the King!"

Benny Goodman let his hair down to me late in 1946. Now Benny, when he's in the mood, can be the charmer of charmers. When he's relaxed with people, when he tells them just how he feels and why he feels the way he does, he makes a great deal of common sense. I've often wished that Benny, during his brightest days, could have felt and acted more relaxed; that he could have given as much of himself as a human being as he did as a musician. For Benny, I discovered slowly through the years, has a great deal to give—a great deal of warmth, intelligence and understanding. What's more, he is basically a very honest man and, when he allows himself to be, extremely honest with himself. All this adds up to a greater person than Goodman himself ever permitted many people to know. It's too bad he kept his personal self under such wraps.

"I'm sick and tired of rehearsing," Benny admitted. "I've had enough of that stuff. I guess I've just passed the stage where I want to knock myself out. For what? To get everything just the way I want it, I'd have to rehearse all the time, and even then I'm not sure I'd get it."

"Goodman no longer wants to do it the hard way," I commented. "He likes to spend as much time as possible on his big estate in Bedford Village with his charming wife, Alice, his two daughters and his three stepdaughters, whom he sometimes calls simply 'Pops' because he's absent-minded and doesn't remember their names too well. He plays tennis, golf and bridge and keeps company with other wealthy folks. He has had his kicks, and now he wants his contentment too."

Perhaps it was just as well. Certainly by 1946, when the music world was being invaded by boppers with whom Goodman and his music had little in common, it was time for us to evaluate the man in the context of what he had given to, and, I guess, had taken from his world during the past dozen years—the world which he had helped so much to create—his world of the big bands. I wrote then and would still write today:

> Swing can thank Benny Goodman, and Benny Goodman can thank Swing. Swing can thank Benny Goodman for making possible its acceptance in a world which, before the advent of the King's reign, thought that the best swing hung between two trees in a backyard and that a beat was reserved exclusively for cops and reporters. Benny Goodman can thank Swing for making possible his attaining a huge house, a swimming pool, a tennis court, a wife, two daughters, a slew of managers and the security that allies itself with a million cabbage leaves, all autographed either by Vinson or Morgenthau.

In the generation that followed the end of the big band era, Goodman continued to blow his clarinet—sometimes in front of a big band of young, modern musicians to whom he seldom related very well; sometimes in front of a group of veterans with whom he played his old arrangements, many of which sounded distressingly dated; sometimes in front of a smaller group with which he appeared to excellent advantage in some of the country's smarter supper clubs; and sometimes in the role of a classical musician as he played with various chamber music groups and symphonies throughout the country.

But it was outside America that Benny made his most dramatic contributions. In the winter of 1956–57 he toured the Far East on a trip that was highlighted by a jam session in the Royal Palace in Bangkok, during which the King of Thailand played alongside the King of Swing. In 1958 he took a band to the Brussels Fair in Belgium, and in 1962 he made a most memorable trip. With a band of hand-picked jazz stars, he toured Russia, the first American band to do so. The journey was highly successful, even though some of the musicians balked at Benny's insistence upon playing the simpler sort of swing which he felt would best reach the natives, and even though our

State Department exhibited an amazing lack of understanding of American jazz and its players.

After his return from Russia, I asked Benny if this U.S. indifference had bothered him. His reply was direct, succinct and, I believe, very typically Benny Goodman. "Of course it didn't bother me," he said. "I don't look for help. I'm not used to being helped in America. We know our business and what we have to do. And we do it, that's all."

And Benny kept on doing things his way during the years that followed. He continued to take groups abroad, and he continued to disagree with some of his musicians, and some of them continued to come home, teed off at the boss. But most important of all, he continued to blow great clarinet and produce some of the swingingest excitement in the world of music—here at home, as well as overseas. I recall especially an early seventies television show, "The Timex All Star Swing Session," from Carnegie Hall, for which Benny reunited his original quartet and tore up the joint with a stupendous version of "I'm a Ding Dong Daddy from Dumas."

And I recall another reunion of the same group during the summer of 1973 for the Newport Jazz Festival. Carnegie Hall was again the scene. But this time trying to recapture all the excitement of previous appearances there was much harder. Gene Krupa, his health rapidly deteriorating, had dragged his weary body to make the gig. I was sitting on stage, right behind the quartet, and after every few numbers, I could see Benny come over to Gene, put his arm gently around him, and ask him how he was doing. He was deeply concerned, as were those of us who knew how sick Gene really was, and as I look back upon it all now, I have the feeling that the reason Benny didn't play especially well that evening was because for one of the few times in his life he was concerned with something that mattered even more than his music.

The classical BG and the classical LB (Leonard Bernstein)

George Hall

GEORGE HALL is probably best remembered for Dolly Dawn. That's natural. The popular vocalist was the focal point of his band, which broadcast so consistently and often insistently for years from the Grill Room of the Hotel Taft.

In the beginning it wasn't a good band and its arrangements were usually pretty dull. What's more, Hall, an affable man who looked more like the chief buyer in a men's clothing store than a bandleader, persisted in playing an overlapping fiddle along with the band, giving the outfit the ensemble sound of a vaudeville house pit orchestra.

But along about 1940, after he had left the Taft, Hall began developing a better band, composed principally of younger and more enthusiastic musicians. He played his fiddle less and left the music pretty much in the hands and horns of his youngsters. The results were more modern and more interesting.

Of course Dolly Dawn, a chubby, ebullient miss, remained the band's most potent asset. She may not have always sung in tune, and purists might well have cringed at the sneaky way she attacked notes, but the gal certainly knew how to sell a song. Like all belters, she was even more impressive in person than she was on the air.

Eventually, Hall grew tired of leading. He saw a bigger potential in Dolly, whom, reportedly, he had adopted, and so on July 4, 1941, in a fancy ceremony at New York's Roseland Ballroom, where he had become a favorite, George officially turned over the band to his protégé. From then on it was officially Dolly Dawn and Her Dawn Patrol.

Dolly did fairly well as a leader of the band, which continued to feature young New York musicians. But the wear and tear, physical as well as financial, of keeping the unit at work soon became an unnecessary handicap. Dolly's records on Bluebird had been selling well. Booking her as a single performer into nightclubs was easier and more rewarding than trying to sell her as a "maestress." And so in March, 1942, she gave up her band, and the Hall-Dawn dance band dynasty came to an end.

George Hall (left) and Dolly Dawn help Mal Hallett celebrate his twenty-year association at Roseland. Ballroom manager Joe Belford is at right.
Plaque reads: "To Mal Hallett, a Grand Person and a Great Maestro —1940—in Appreciation of 20 Years of Happy Association, Roseland Ballroom, New York [Signed] Louis Brecker."

Mal Hallett

MAL HALLETT led a very musicianly band for a long time. For years his base of operation was New England, where he had settled down as a bandleader after having toured France during World War I as a member of Al Moore's band, which had been sent over to entertain the troops.

The best band Hallett ever had swung through New England and other parts of the country in the early thirties. Included in its ranks were drummer Gene Krupa, trombonists Jack Teagarden and Jack Jenney, pianist Frankie Carle and saxophonist Toots Mondello.

Hallett's hard-hitting, driving style kept his band out of the better hotel supper rooms. On the other hand, ballrooms, better able to absorb his musical barrage, welcomed Hallett. Backed by the Shribman brothers, two of the most astute bookers of all time, the band worked consistently in every major New England ballroom and in many others throughout the country. No wonder it became known as the "one-nightingest" band of them all.

Mal was an impressive-looking man. He was almost six and a half feet tall. He had long, wavy hair, which he used to push back nervously, and he always seemed proud of his long, neatly waxed mustache. To me he looked more like a circus ringmaster than the leader of one of the better swing bands.

His musicians liked and respected him. He gave them opportunities to play good music, even before Goodman made it fashionable. True, he worked his men hard and made them engage in novelties—he insisted that bands should entertain as well as play music—but his enthusiasm, much like that of an early-day Stan Kenton, was persuasive. Besides, he was a good musician who had studied at the Boston Conservatory.

Although he worked regularly during the big band era, Hallett achieved only a modicum of success. His hard-selling appeal captivated certain audiences, but to the youngsters, indoctrinated to seeing younger leaders playing an instrument rather than an older uncle waving a baton, his approach must have seemed old-fashioned.

Hallett always evinced great pride in his work, and he surrounded himself with good and often colorful sidemen, like his almost lifelong bassist, Joe Carbonero, a huge man who doubled as comedian, and an almost equally rotund vocalist-saxist, Buddy Welcome. Clark Yocum, who became one of the mainstays of the Pied Pipers singing group, also sang and played guitar. Mickey McMickle, who was to emerge as one of the trumpet stalwarts of Glenn Miller's band, developed under Hallett.

Throughout the later thirties and earlier forties, the Hallett band underwent numerous changes. As it continued to tour the country, it continued as well to uncover good, young musicans, and it is somewhat ironic that two of the best Mal took into his band, saxist Buddy Wise and trombonist Dick Taylor, were snatched by Gene Krupa, who so many years before had, himself, been a sideman in the Hallett organization.

Though the general public may have forgotten Mal Hallett, who died in Boston in 1952, many musicians remember him well and remain grateful to him for pioneering a swing band long before it was fashionable to do so, and for always treating them and their music with the respect both he and they felt they deserved.

The early 1930s version of the Mal Hallett band on the boardwalk in Atlantic City. Included are (back row) bassist Joe Carbonero (far left), trumpeter Dale McMickle (second from left), Hallett (center), trombonist Jack Jenney (second from right), and drummer Gene Krupa (far right). At bottom are trumpeter Frank Ryerson (far left), pianist Franke Carle (second from left), and saxophonist Toots Mondello (center).

Lionel Hampton

THE exuberance and excitement and feeling of exultation that Lionel Hampton contributes to any musical occasion with which he is associated are absolutely amazing. No other single performer in American jazz—and in American big bands, too—has so consistently and joyously incited and inspired his fellow musicians and his listening audiences. For Hamp invariably projects a wonderful, uninhibited aura of spontaneity that brightens every place in which he performs and that assures everyone within earshot that music, fast or slow, screaming or sentimental, can be a joy forever—or at least as long as Lionel happens to be playing it.

Hampton left Benny Goodman in the latter half of 1940 to start his own big band. He had already been an unofficial leader since early in 1937 when he organized for RCA Victor some superb recording groups that included jazz stars like Gene Krupa, Harry James, Jonah Jones, Charlie Christian, Dizzy Gillespie, Nat (King) Cole and, on one spectacular session, a sax team of Benny Carter, Coleman Hawkins, Chu Berry and Ben Webster.

When Lionel decided to take the plunge with a big band, he couldn't quite make up his mind where and how he wanted to jump. Such indecision wasn't entirely unpredictable, for Hamp was then and is still noted for acting on the spur of the moment. According to someone close to him at that time, Hamp would change his mind daily. "Tuesday, he told me he was going to have a band built around the King Cole Trio. Wednesday, he said that he thought he'd take over most of Earl Hines's old band. Thursday, he was looking for some saxes who doubled on fiddle so that he could have a band that could play sweet."

The band that Hamp eventually led, and continued to lead for many years thereafter, was primarily a swinging one, a high-flying swinging one, complete with brilliant showmanship and musicianship from Hampton and a whole series of talented musicians whom he discovered and inserted into his lineups.

Throughout its career it reflected its leader's personality. Lionel played for the fun of it, and his remained a gleeful-sounding group. Often Hamp would appear like a man possessed of something or other (nobody ever

knew exactly what), and his band would reflect the same sort of inspirational feeling. As he told me during the early sixties, "Sometimes when I play jazz, it's like a spiritual impulse comes over me." And so he will grunt and groan and grind and moan as he becomes completely immersed in his music. Jazz, he has always admitted, is first and foremost an emotional experience for him, one that can carry him and his men away. This almost happened—literally—one night when his band was playing its famed version of "Flyin' Home" on a barge in the Potomac River and everyone was getting highly charged as the number was reaching its climax. According to Lionel, "Just as we were gettin' down to the part in the last chorus when everyone goes 'rum-ba-da, dum-ba-da, rum—pow!' I yelled to the bass player to 'hit the water.' And he got so excited that he jumped right in!"

"Flyin' Home" had always been associated with Hampton, even in his Goodman days, and when he recorded it for Decca in May of 1942 it turned out to be a smash hit for him. But no record could possibly do justice to a performance of Hamp's. This can be a shattering experience, visually as well as aurally, as he flays away first on vibes, then on piano, using just two fingers like vibraphone mallets, then switches to a frantic, stick-tossing session on drums, and eventually climaxes the whole affair by jumping up onto a tom-tom and dancing wildly on top of it! There's no doubt about it, Lionel Hampton must go down in history as one of the most inspiring and surely the most perspiring jazz musician of all time.

I've been associated with Lionel several times as a producer on both recording dates and on TV shows. The way the man never stops going is utterly fantastic. I recall especially one of the Timex All-Star Jazz television shows we did together during which Hamp kept driving his men at rehearsal, making sure everything was going just right, and then refusing to quit when his allotted rehearsal time was over. We finally did get the next act on stage, but for the rest of the afternoon Hamp kept following me around the studio, begging for more rehearsal time, as though nothing else on the show mattered. To him, probably nothing did.

Yet this was nothing compared with what happened on the show later on. We had his numbers routined perfectly—we thought. Every camera shot was worked out to fit his arrangements, so that as each man started his solo we'd cut directly on camera to him. Well, Hamp got so carried away with how great his men were doing, that when we got on air he forgot all about the set routines. Thus, after a tenor man had finished his sixteen bars and we

were ready to cut to a trumpet for the next sixteen, we suddenly found a trumpeter, not beginning his passage, but still sitting in his section with nothing but a blank look on his face. Hamp, it seems, had signaled the tenor to go on blowing but never let us know about it. The rest of the number turned out to be quite a video shambles, because none of us in the control room was sharing those same "spiritual impulses" that were re-routing the entire number for Hamp.

There was one particular musician, in addition to Hampton, who injected great spirit into the band. This was a little, round pianist named Milt Buckner, who, besides playing some excellent boogie-woogie–styled piano, also wrote many of the band's arrangements.

Hamp always surrounded himself with outstanding musicians, and though there were times when the band couldn't afford to pay top salaries, the music was so much fun to play and the spirit of the band was so moving, that whenever one musician would decide to cut out, there'd always be plenty waiting to replace him.

Hamp had a good ear and a good eye for new talent, and the list of musicians he has discovered is truly an amazing one. "We've been the breeding place of some fine jazz musicians," he told me one day, as he reeled off, with obvious pride, such names as Charles Mingus, Quincy Jones, Illinois Jacquet, Lucky Thompson, Joe Newman, Ernie Royal, Cat Anderson, Kenny Dorham, Art Farmer and many more, as well as singers Dinah Washington and Joe Williams. Joe, to be sure, never became a fixture with Hampton; he left in the middle of 1943, the month after Barry Ulanov, in an otherwise highly favorable review of the band, commented that "Joe has a fine voice but a godawful tremolo which shakes the whole house when he sings. Somebody ought to tell him." Apparently Hampton did. This was also the year in which *Metronome,* for whom Ulanov was writing, selected Hampton's as The Band of the Year.

As the band became more successful, its music became somewhat more pretentious. This was especially obvious in April of 1945 when it performed at Carnegie Hall and Hampton trotted out, in addition to his seventeen usual swinging musicians, something like three dozen nonswinging strings. To some the experiment was interesting, to say the most. To most Hampton fans it was a bring-down, to say the least.

This sort of striving to do more, to create something new, to broaden his outlook, became more and more a part of Lionel Hampton's life. In later years he spent a great deal of time working on behalf of and visiting Israel, where Lionel, always an intensely religious man, has become as much of a celebrity as in his own country.

Typical of Hamp's sense of dedication is an incident he related after one of his visits to Israel. He wanted to learn the sheheheyanu, a Hebrew prayer, so that he could recite it to an audience that had come to hear him play. Before the concert started, someone wrote it out for him phonetically, "and I studied it and then I took my Bible and read in it and asked God to help me. Then I laid the prayer down on the corner of my vibes and while I was playing the wind came and blew it away. But I had faith, and I was determined to recite the prayer, so I just closed my eyes and something like electricity took my soul and body and I recited exactly like I was supposed to, and when I got through there was great quietness and then the audience started applauding, and, you know, they applauded and yelled so loud that they blew out the radio transmitter that was broadcasting our concert. All night long I stayed in a trance."

Faith has become a large part of Lionel Hampton's life. What's more, he never hesitates to let anyone know he is grateful for any favor or kindness or other token of friendship. There is, so far as I have been able to determine, not an ounce of phoniness in this amazing man, who sometimes impresses you as a kid who has never quite grown up and then suddenly comes through as a remarkably mature human being—mature and, in his generous contribution of his talents to one benefit after another, compassionate. One of these days this big world of ours may stop turning. I doubt, though, that even then Lionel Hampton will stop swinging!

Horace Heidt

HORACE HEIDT was always an enigma to me. For years he had one of the most showmanly, most corny, most successful bands in the world. And then, when those of us who liked better music had become convinced that there was no musical hope for Heidt, he suddenly began hiring some of the best swing musicians, gave them their heads, and their hearts, and wound up with a thoroughly impressive outfit.

He was a difficult man for many of us to know, and the "us" included many of the musicians who worked for him. He had what I once described as "a self-conscious, yet winning personality." He moved stiffly, almost clumsily, somewhat in the manner of Richard Nixon. He smiled a great deal, but it was seldom a complete smile, so that one wondered whether he was really happy or whether the smile was just part of an astonishingly effective coverup for an ill-at-ease leader of one of the most formidable of all show bands.

Heidt's band beginnings had been in vaudeville. During the twenties and the earlier thirties he directed one of the most entertaining, well-rehearsed, well-paced outfits ever to grace a stage. It's significant that today few, if any, people can recall the name of a single musician in that early Heidt band. And yet everyone who ever watched it will remember one performer: Lobo. Who was Lobo? A trained dog!

The first time I ever heard Heidt on a dance job was in 1937 at the Biltmore Hotel in New York during an engagement that helped establish the group as a dance rather than a stage band. The music wasn't very exciting, though it was danceable, despite a plethora of singers, such as Lysbeth Hughes, the harpist; Alyce, Donna, Louise and Yvonne, the King Sisters; Jerry Bowne, trumpeter; Art Thorsen, bassist; Larry Cotton and the Glee Club consisting of Bob McCoy and Charlie Goodman, soloists, plus Jack Millard, Myron Ernhardt, Rollin Butts, L. L. Smith, Ray Berrington and Lee Throm. That made sixteen singers all told with a band of fourteen musicians.

Some of the musicians were pretty good, too—men like Frank DeVol, who played lead sax and wrote arrangements and who since has become better known as a conductor-arranger and character actor; Ernie Passoja, who could and did play way high up on his trombone, though not always in tune; and a guitarist who'd had to put aside his jazz ambitions when he joined the band. He was Alvino Rey.

Heidt's musicians were full of musical tricks. The trumpets triple-tongued all over creation; the saxes slid and slurped like Lombardo's; the three violas glissed in and out of passages; and Rey created all sorts of novelty effects with his electric guitar. While hardly ecstatic about its musical qualities, I did tab "Horace Heidt's Brigadiers the greatest spectacle in dancebandom today. You can't get away from that. In fact, if you happen to be in the Moonlit Terrace of the Biltmore, you'll find that you can't get away from them. They're all over the place. When they're not playing dance music, they're singing and playing harps and cocktail shakers. Any minute you expect one of them to come swooping down at you from the ceiling on a flying trapeze."

In looking back at the band, Alvino Rey recently admitted to me that "it may have sounded awful, but it was a great band. It did so many things. Heidt had a good feeling for playing for dancers. He was kind of clumsy-looking all right." Horace seemed to try to emulate Fred Waring when he conducted. He obviously also idolized Lombardo.

Rey also credits Heidt for starting and nurturing "a family feeling." Little did Horace realize, however, how this prescribed socializing would ultimately disrupt his band. "Several of us were going around with several of the girls," reports Rey, who was soon to marry Louise King. "I remember one night when Alyce accidentally knocked over a mike and it hit a girl who was dancing by. Heidt got so mad that he fired Alyce right on the spot. But we had grown so close in that 'family,' that one by one the King Sisters and all their boy friends quit too!"

Larry Barnett, the former MCA executive who worked closely with Heidt and became one of his best friends, confirms that "Heidt could be a tyrant. He demanded perfection. If you didn't do something right, he'd get rid of you tomorrow. He had no sense of personal loyalty that way.

"He was a very smart businessman. One thing he was sharp enough to realize was that he himself had no real talent as a performer. That's why he was always looking for something new and different to present."

In essence, Heidt was more of a producer than a bandleader. In that role it was important for him constantly to dig up attractive talent and to present it in a way that would redound as much to his credit as to that of the individual performer. And so he worked hard, and successfully, to build the careers of such members of his group as singers Gordon MacRae, Ronnie Kemper, Larry Cotton, an especially good tenor, Donna and the Don Juans (Art Carney sang in that group), Fred Lowrey, the blind whistler, and pianist Frankie Carle.

Heidt also managed to sell his orchestra, which later became known as "Horace Heidt and His Musical Knights," on numerous radio series. Some of these sometimes featured music but often concentrated mostly on gimmicks. One series called "The Pot o' Gold," in which Horace would thumb through

Horace

telephone directories of cities throughout the United States, handing out impressive prizes to those who answered his ring and his questions, was one of the first big-time give-away successes.

When swing bands started to prove themselves more than just a fad, Heidt, much to the amazement of those of us who looked upon him as strictly a cornball leader, began giving good-paying jobs to outstanding musicians. The first important one he hired was Bobby Hackett, the trumpeter, who played with the band for about a year, 1939–1940.

Of course Heidt continued also to feature Frankie Carle, whose gimmicks included playing piano with his hands behind his back. And Horace, though he seemed to try hard to loosen up, still kept on presiding over his clan, looking, to at least one viewer, like a high school principal who expected the student body to erupt at any moment.

When Glenn Miller's band broke up late in 1942, Heidt reportedly made offers to several of his men and succeeded in landing Glenn's top arranger, Bill Finegan, who wrote some pieces for the band that immediately sent its musical stock skyward. During this period, Carle, who had been given a partnership in the band for staying with it when he could have taken over Eddy Duchin's orchestra, served as Heidt's musical director. The music continued to improve with the addition of Fazola (Irving Prestopnik), the great New Orleans clarinetist, and a brilliant lead trombonist named Warren Covington.

After Carle left in 1944 to start his own band—with Heidt's blessings—more top jazz musicians joined—men like Jess Stacy, Benny Goodman's old pianist; Shorty Sherock, who had starred on trumpet with Jimmy Dorsey and who was soon to lead his own band; Frankie Carlson, who had played drums for years with Woody Herman; and Joe Rushton, considered by many to be the country's top jazz bass saxophonist.

Heidt also showed his appreciation of jazz—artistic or financial—who knows?—in booking such artists as Louis Armstrong and Jack Teagarden into the West Coast Trianon Ballroom, which he had purchased. As a matter of fact, so involved and diverse had his financial affairs become by 1945 that he finally decided to give up his band and to concentrate entirely on his various real estate holdings as well as "The Horace Heidt School for Stammering." It is significant to note that Heidt, who had suffered from that very speech affliction, had succeeded by sheer tenacity in correcting the condition. He could, it was apparent, discipline himself just as firmly as he did others.

After he broke up his band, Heidt appeared on several more radio and TV shows but with no overwhelming success. Yet, because of shrewd investments, he grew more and more prosperous, until today, according to his friend Larry Barnett, "he is probably the wealthiest businessman of all the former bandleaders."

Fletcher Henderson

FLETCHER HENDERSON'S contribution to the big bands was tremendous. It consisted not so much of leading a band during the thirties and forties as it did in establishing during the late twenties and early thirties a style that was used by Benny Goodman and that by its infectious directness served to start the entire swing band cycle.

During that earlier period, Henderson had fronted one of the truly great bands of its day. Playing a whole batch of simple but ever-swinging instrumentals, many composed and arranged by Henderson, it unleashed pulsating ensemble sounds interspersed by a series of brilliant solos blown by such jazz greats as Louis Armstrong, Coleman Hawkins, Benny Carter, Buster Bailey, Fats Waller (on recordings), Lester Young (briefly), Benny Morton, Don Redman, Rex Stewart, Cootie Williams, J. C. Higginbotham and Edgar Sampson. There was also a banjo player named Clarence Holiday. He was Billie Holiday's father.

Henderson, a genteel and gentle man, might have become even more successful had he not been so genteel and so gentle. John Hammond, a close friend of Fletcher's who helped him so much during his career, noted in the booklet that accompanies Columbia's imposing Henderson record collection, "A Study in Frustration," that Fletcher's "early success as a bandleader, un-

Fletcher Henderson surrounded by admiring alumni at a 1941 reunion
Front row: pianist-arranger Henri Woode, trumpeter Russell Smith,
bassist John Kirby, Henderson, trumpeter Henry (Red) Allen, Jr., clarinetist Buster
Bailey, drummer Kaiser Marshall, trombonist Fernando Arbello,
saxist-trumpeter-arranger Benny Carter
Back row: Trombonists J. C. Higginbotham and Sandy Williams, drummers
"Big Sid" Catlett and Walter Johnson,
guitarist Lawrence Lucie, saxist Russell Procope

rivaled social acceptance as a college-trained son of teaching parents, and an unparalleled skill in assembling great musicians should have made him a fortune and given him stability." But, as Hammond pointed out, Henderson as a businessman was his own worst enemy, though "his easy-going nature made for a loose and happily swinging group of top-flight instrumentalists who would not have tolerated the kind of discipline either Ellington or Lunceford would have imposed."

Henderson's style was deceptively simple. It consisted primarily of pungent, pushing brass and rolling saxes with the former stating the theme in ensemble fashion on opening and closing passages, while the latter filled in with trim, rhythmic riffs. Then he'd reverse the procedure, giving the lead to the saxes, with the brass cutting in with clipped punctuations. Typical of what Henderson had been doing for many years are some of the arrangements he later wrote to help launch the Goodman band. "Sometimes I'm Happy," "King Porter Stomp," "Blue Skies," "Down South Camp Meeting" and many more were typical not only of Goodman band sounds but of those of the many other successful swing bands of the future which based their styles on Fletcher's.

Goodman, at Hammond's urging, had hired Henderson soon after Fletcher had disbanded in the winter of 1934. But after a half-year stay with Benny, "Smack" as Henderson was called by his friends, decided he'd like to have a band again. So he reorganized and settled back into the Grand Terrace Café in Chicago, where he featured some more jazz greats: Roy Eldridge on trumpet, Ben Webster on tenor sax, Hilton Jefferson on alto sax, bassist John Kirby, drummer Sid Catlett and Fletcher's brother Horace, also a good arranger, on piano. The band made a batch of fine sides, including the big instrumental hit of the times, "Christopher Columbus." Henderson recorded this before any other leader did, but because of lack of promotion it never achieved the popularity of Benny Goodman's or several other bands' versions of the tune.

Such seemed to be a way of life for Fletcher Henderson. Even when he led great units, his band never seemed to achieve the recognition that his fine arrangements brought to other organizations. In 1939 he returned to Goodman, serving as an arranger and, for several months, also as pianist. Eventually he left, not because of any disagreement or any real desire to lead his own band again but because his failing eyesight made writing too difficult for him. In 1941 he did organize one more band. It played at the New York Roseland, the scene of his great triumphs in the late twenties and early thirties, but even though it included several excellent musicians, it never approached the brilliance of any of Henderson's previous units.

In the ten years preceding his death in 1952 (he suffered a crippling stroke in 1950), Henderson continued to arrange a bit (he wrote for Goodman in 1946 and 1947), to appear occasionally as head of a small group, and even to serve as an accompanist for Ethel Waters. But his chief contributions had already been made, many years before, contributions for which so many, many swing bands must remain eternally grateful.

Woody Herman

"HE'S a clean-cut-looking lad with a nice smile that should attract the dancers; he sings very nicely and plays good clarinet, both attributes that command musical respect, and he's very much of a gentleman and real all-around nice guy whom you'd like to know even better off the stand."

That's what I wrote about Woody Herman in January, 1937. It was a part of the very favorable review I'd accorded his brand new band at New York's Roseland Ballroom. As the years went by, I realized my wish. I got to know Woody "even better off the stand," very much better, in fact, and discovered, as so many others have during the past thirty years, that this is one of the real pros, both as a performer and as a mature human being. His warmth, his enthusiasm, his intelligence and his integrity—in addition, of course, to his musical taste, talent and perception—have made him one of the most thoroughly successful and popular leaders of all time.

He's always had good bands, and one major reason has been that musicians invariably like to work for him. Nat Pierce, who served as his pianist, arranger and general aide for many years, recently put it this way: "We never

"He's a clean-cut-looking lad with a nice smile that should attract the dancers."

feel we're actually working *for* the man. It's more like working *with* him. He appreciates what we're doing and he lets us know it. And the guys appreciate him and respect him. So they work all the harder."

Jake Hanna, the superb drummer who, after having played for other leaders, finally blossomed in Woody's band, has this explanation: "Woody's flexible. He goes along with the way the band feels instead of sticking strictly to the book. That makes it always interesting and exciting for us. If a man's really blowing, Woody doesn't stop him after eight bars because the arrangement says so. He lets him keep on wailing."

"Flexible" is the key word here. Woody has managed through the years to adjust himself to the wants, talents and even the personalities of his musicians; yet he has retained their respect so completely that he has rarely had to assert himself as their leader. He has succeeded, too, in adjusting his music to the times, so that during its thirty-year history his band has never sounded old-fashioned even while staying within the bounds of general public acceptance. "I think," he once told writer Gene Lees in *Down Beat*, "I'm a good organizer and a good editor."

Leonard Feather once wrote: "No name bandleader has ever been better liked by the men who worked for him as well as those for whom he works." That comment reminds me of what happened during the band's initial Rose-land date. Woody had both a loud band and high musical ideals. The ballroom manager, a man named Joe Belford, who looked like a Green Bay lineman, used to bellow to the band to play waltzes, rumbas, tangos and sambas, none of which it had in its books and none of which it would have played on principle anyway. Woody handled Joe beautifully. He'd just bust out in a grin, bellow back kiddingly at Belford, tell him to get lost and quit bothering him. And he'd continue playing what he wanted to. So good-natured was Woody's approach, and yet so firm and so positive, that Belford not only took it but became one of the band's biggest fans.

Woody was already familiar with most phases of show business. He'd been playing sax professionally since he was nine years old, first in vaudeville, later in numerous name bands. The first was Tommy Gerun's, in which Woody shared vocal honors with a pretty miss named Virginia Simms, who later was better known as Ginny Sims of Kay Kyser fame, and a handsome baritone named Al Morris, who later changed his name to Tony Martin. Woody, like Morris-Martin, played tenor sax then. How good was Woody? "I sounded like Bud Freeman with his hands chopped off," he says.

After stints with Harry Sosnick and Gus Arnheim, Woody landed with the Isham Jones band. When that good musical group broke up, Herman and several of its other alumni decided to form their own cooperative band. Gordon Jenkins and Joe Bishop, who had been members of the Jones band, contributed some free arrangements, guitarist Chick Reeves wrote many more, and after six weeks of rehearsals the band debuted late in 1936—first at the Brooklyn Roseland and then at the New York Roseland.

Bishop, who had played tuba with Jones, stayed on, switching to flugelhorn. Other corporation members were saxist Saxey Mansfield, trumpeters Clarence Willard and Kermit Simmons, trombonist Neal Reid, violinist Nick Hupfer, bassist Walter Yoder and drummer Frankie Carlson. They called themselves "The Band That Plays the Blues" and they took their name literally. For example, when the new outfit first played Frank Dailey's Meadowbrook, for which it received six hundred dollars a week for its fifteen members, it filled its radio shows almost entirely with blues. "That was a little too strong," Woody admitted later.

For the first couple of years the band really struggled. It tried hard to please, but there weren't many Joe Belfords scattered around the country, and at the Rice Hotel in Houston the manager responded to the band's full-bodied blues and Woody's vocals with a curt note that read: "You will kindly stop singing and playing those nigger blues." And at Cincinnati's Netherlands-Plaza, at Detroit's Eastwood Gardens and even at the Hotel Schroeder in Woody's hometown of Milwaukee, the reaction, though perhaps not quite so vulgar, was still not very much more encouraging.

The band persisted in living up to its name. Accordingly it recorded a slew of blues sides for Decca, including "Dupree Blues," "Laughing Boy Blues," "Blues Upstairs" and "Blues Downstairs," "Indian Boogie Woogie," "Casbah Blues" and "Blues on Parade." It also recorded its two theme songs, "Blue Prelude," which it used for the first few years, and then a new theme, "Blue Flame."

Finally, in mid-1939, the blues formula paid off. The band recorded Joe Bishop's rollicking blues original called "Woodchoppers' Ball." Based on a simple, repetitive blues riff, the record became a smash hit and ever since has remained the band's most requested number.

Soon, big engagements began pouring in. The band went back into Meadowbrook—this time at a decent salary—and then in the fall of 1939, after Glenn Miller's band had completed the first of its smashingly successful summer seasons at Glen Island Casino, Woody's took over there. It also landed the Panther Room at Chicago's Hotel Sherman, followed Larry Clinton into the New Yorker Hotel, and played twice at the Famous Door on New York's swinging Fifty-second Street.

In those early days Woody was looking hard for a new girl singer. I had heard one who was then working with Peter Dean's swinging band at Nick's in Greenwich Village. I thought she'd be great. But Woody, after hearing her, felt differently. We still kid about it. Why? Because he missed hiring Dinah Shore.

During its career his band did have some very good girl singers, some that weren't much more than fair, plus a few who knew how to get their man. First there was Sharri Kaye, wife of arranger Deane Kincaide, to be followed at one time or another by Dillagene, who married drummer Carlson; Carol Kaye, Carolyn Grey, Muriel Lane, Kathleen Lane, Jean Bowes, Sue Mitchell,

Lynne Stevens, Mary Ann McCall, who married saxist Al Cohn; Anita O'Day (briefly), Billie Rogers, who married band manager Jack Archer and who doubled in the trumpet section; and Frances Wayne, who married trumpeter-arranger Neal Hefti.

But the best singer Woody ever had, for my dough, was Woody himself. He sang a lot of blues, and a good many uptempoed swingers and novelties, but it was as a ballad singer that he impressed me and many musicians the most. His phrasing was immensely warm and musical; he used his vibrato well, and his voice had both a sensuous and sensitive timbre. (He retains all these qualities today, by the way.) He made a batch of fine recordings in those days, like "It's a Blue World," "If I Knew Then," "Don't You Know or Don't You Care?" "It's My Turn Now," "I'll Remember April," " 'Tis Autumn" and "This Time the Dream's on Me."

The last, complete with good glee club effects, was the other side of the band's second big record hit, "Blues in the Night," recorded late in 1941. This brought even greater public recognition for the band, which also began to appear in such movies as *What's Cookin'?* with the Andrews Sisters and *Quota Girl* and *Summer Holiday*, two of several films it made with skating star Sonja Henie. (One wag suggested Woody adopt "The Skaters' Waltz" as a theme and book the band as "Woody Herman and His Gay Blades.")

Like many other bands, Woody's experienced personnel difficulties as the draft started calling up musicians. But Woody, because the word had got around that he was a good man to work for, and because he kept his eyes and ears open for men, suffered less than most leaders did. And sometimes, when he couldn't find just the men he wanted for a particular occasion, he'd borrow them from other bands. Thus he corralled several of Duke Ellington's star sidemen—Johnny Hodges, Ben Webster, Ray Nance and Juan Tizol—to make some records with his band.

The Duke's band had always impressed Woody. That this was so became more apparent than ever during the early forties when he hired Dave Matthews, who could write in the Ellington style, to arrange for the band. "We were getting one-slotted anyway," Woody explained. "I was beginning to realize there was more to music than what we were playing. We even went pretty far out for a while. I remember I got Dizzy Gillespie to write a couple of things for us. He played with us for a short time too—I think it was for a week at the Apollo Theater—and after I'd heard him I advised him strongly to stick to writing and to give up the trumpet. That was what you might call 'one of my strongest decisions!' "

Because of Petrillo's recording ban, much of the music that Woody was playing during 1943 and early 1944 had a limited audience. Thus, after not having heard the band for quite a while, I experienced a considerable shock the first time I heard what has been since referred to as The First Herd. (Actually, we'd been calling it the Herman Herd for years at *Metronome*, but somehow this brilliant bit of name-calling didn't catch on until 1944.)

It was a summer's night in 1944. I had driven out to Pleasure Beach in Bridgeport, Connecticut, to listen to Woody, not knowing quite what to expect. What I heard gave me one of the big thrills of my life, and I said as much in a rave review that appeared in the September *Metronome*. It began " 'Before you can have a really great band,' Woody Herman once told me, 'you've got to be able to play really fine music all night long. You can't just coast on a few arrangements and then just play average stuff for the rest of the evening.'

"Today Woody Herman's band qualifies in terms of Woody Herman's own exacting requirements, with no reservations whatsoever, as 'a really great band.' It can and does do everything!"

Thanks to a brilliant rhythm section, led by Davey Tough, the band laid down a massive, swinging beat, aided by bassist Chubby Jackson, guitarist Billy Bauer and pianist Ralph Burns. Ralph and another young arranger, Neal Hefti, were writing most of the new, modern-sounding manuscripts. And there were a batch of brilliant soloists, including Flip Phillips on tenor, Bill Harris on trombone, and the Candoli Brothers, Pete and Conte (Conte was only sixteen then and had to return to school a few weeks later), Hefti and Sonny Berman on trumpets. And, of course, there was Woody.

Throughout his band's career, Herman's clarinet playing has too often been taken for granted. He may not always match the brilliance or the modernity of some of his band's other stars, and yet he has invariably managed to adapt his style to whatever style his band might be playing. He has also contributed —perhaps not often enough—some lovely ballad solos on his alto sax.

The Herman Herd in Republic's Earl Carroll's Vanities *(early 1945)*
Front row: *pianist Ralph Burns, vibist Marjorie Hyams, guitarist Billy Bauer,*
saxists Flip Phillips, John LaPorta, Sam Marowitz, Pete Mondello, Skippy DeSair
Second row: *bassist Chubby Jackson, drummer Davey Tough, trombonists*
Ralph Pfiffner, Bill Harris, Ed Kiefer
Back row: *trumpeters Neal Hefti, Charlie Frankhauser, Ray Wetzel,*
Pete Condoli, Carl (Bama) Warwick

*"Caldonia . . . Caldonia
. . . what makes your
big head so hard?!"* *

Woody was ecstatic about his new band. Not only did it please him musically, but its spirit and excitement captivated all its listeners. It was soon rewarded with its own radio series, first replacing Frankie Carle's band on the Old Gold program, then starring on one of the swingingest of all radio adventures, the Wildroot series.

There was one drawback, though. Because the Petrillo ban was still in effect, the band couldn't record. Woody got around this by waxing several spirited, high-swinging V-Disc sides, all of which it was my pleasure to supervise. Thus at least the members of the armed forces were able to hear such romping Herman selections as "Apple Honey," "Caldonia," "Goosey Gander," "Northwest Passage" and "Your Father's Mustache."

The records were great, not just because of the musicianship, but because the *esprit de corps* was so immense and the exuberance so thoroughly contagious. The men loved to play, and they especially loved to play the charts by Ralph Burns and Neal Hefti, both of whom have since become notably successful, Ralph in the Broadway theater and Neal on television (the "Batman" theme for example), on records and as composer of several catchy instrumental themes popularized by the Count Basie band.

Both Burns and Hefti, as well as Neal's wife, singer Frances Wayne, had joined The Herd on Chubby Jackson's recommendation. "What an immense influence Chubby had on us," Woody recently told me. "And what enthusiasm! He used to get around to hear everything. He was always screaming about this musician and that musician, and his taste was so good."

Jackson's forte was finding and recommending new young blood. So it was not surprising that when Woody wanted to hire Davey Tough, the Chicago veteran who had played so brilliantly for Goodman, Shaw and Tommy Dorsey, Chubby objected. "He doesn't play modern enough," he said. But after Davey had been with the band only a couple of days, Jackson was converted.

Tough's contribution to the band was tremendous. Unlike many other drummers, especially those considered modern in the forties, he played very simple, basic drums. But so definite and so swinging was his beat, and so subtle were the little additions he made to color the arrangements, that in poll after poll musicians of all kinds kept voting him their favorite drummer. The honor had been a long time coming.

Tough turned out to be only one of several poll winners. Flip Phillips, whom Woody had taken out of Russ Morgan's band, captured the tenor sax post. And Bill Harris, who had failed to last with Benny Goodman and Bob Chester because of his poor reading, but who had since learned to read, was the top trombone choice. And there was Sonny Berman, the young New Haven trumpeter, "one of the happiest characters I've ever known," according to Woody. "What fire and feeling and warmth he had!" The fire and feeling and warmth were to pass away all too soon: Berman would be found dead of a heart attack at the age of twenty-two.

Even though it was just a little over a year old, The First Herd was really riding high by the end of 1945. Its Wildroot commercial was a big success. Columbia was recording again, and the Herman discs were selling well. The band was breaking records in theaters and ballrooms. It won both the *Metronome* and the *Down Beat* musicians' polls; and Phillips, Harris and Tough again copped top instrumentalists' crowns.

But even before Tough's victory appeared in print, the little drummer—he weighed scarcely ninety-five pounds—departed from the band, the victim of the same troubles that had hounded him during his Dorsey and Goodman days. He was replaced by Don Lamond.

Shortly thereafter, Hefti and Frances Wayne—the latter had scored a big hit with the band with her rendition of "Happiness Is Just a Thing Called Joe"—left too. But soon Shorty Rogers, also an arranger-trumpeter, filled Hefti's spot, and Lynne Stevens, soon to be followed by Mary Ann McCall, took Frances' place. As others departed, Herman made more good replacements. Early in 1946 he took on the wonderful vibraphonist Red Norvo, with whom Woody and eight of the sidemen, known as the Woodchoppers, recorded eight superb sides.

But so great was the success of the Herman recordings that it began to boomerang. Wherever the band played, the same selections were requested over and over again and the young, eager but bored musicians began to find fewer and fewer opportunities to play any new numbers.

One new piece they did get a chance to play, though, was written especially for them by one of the world's most distinguished composers, Igor Stravinsky. He was a fan of the band and when Woody, very much aware of the prestige potential, suggested that he write a piece for his orchestra, Stravinsky said "da."

The result was "Ebony Concerto." Performed at Carnegie Hall in March, 1946, the work drew mixed reactions. Barry Ulanov, reporting in *Metronome*, noted that it was "more like a French imitation of Igor than the great man himself. . . . Rhythmically, tonally and melodically it is as dry as dehydrated eggs and far less palatable."

Woody plays, Stravinsky conducts.
Others: *pianist Tony Aless, guitarist Billy Bauer, drummer Don Lamond,
bassist Chubby Jackson, saxists Flip Phillips, John LaPorta, Sam Marowitz*

Woody, who didn't always agree with certain critics, Ulanov included, and who seldom hid his feelings, reacted bitterly to Barry's comments. "I think it's a complete gem, a work of art," he recently asserted. "It's now being used as an academic piece in music schools throughout the country. But we had no more right to play it than the man in the moon had. For Stravinsky it was a challenge to write for this ridiculous combination of instruments. He had no desire to write jazz or anything like it and the work should never have been judged a jazz piece."

As the band began growing more and more successful, not only critics but managers, agency men and even sponsors began telling Woody what to do. He could go just so far, they kept insisting, and no farther unless he broadened his appeal. Possibly because the constant conflicts were starting to wear him down, Woody, who usually made his own decisions, began accepting too much advice. He had the band play more pop tunes. He added a vocal group. And when the writer of his radio series wrote Woody some inane lines, Woody, instead of rebelling, read them—and sounded like an idiot.

He probably was unaware of it, but the strain of keeping a band on top was beginning to tell on him. The men were showing signs of discontent with having to share the spotlight with some rather mediocre singers. They played some good new instrumentals, including Ralph Burns's attractive "Summer Sequence," which Woody readily admits had Ellington overtones ("That's the band we always admired most"). And they also recorded a new version of

Woody and Ralph Burns

the constantly requested "Woodchoppers' Ball," by now an old-fashioned opus of which Woody, expressing not only his opinion but also that of his men, says, "I've been sick of it for twenty years. But it's been such a big number for us that I really shouldn't knock it."

Other outsiders tried to horn in. Recording men and personal managers, according to Herman, "would steam up some of the men and try to get them to go out on their own with new bands." The result—uncertainty, mistrust, dissension and unhappy prima donnas. "Everything would have been all right if they had left us alone. We had no internal problems. Every once in a while Chubby would round up some of the men and they'd start making plans about leaving, but then they'd see how senseless it was, and we'd go on just as before."

Woody used wise tactics in dealing with those who were thinking about cutting out on their own. He would talk patiently with them and give them his advice. He would tell them that whatever they did, they would have his blessings. He would even offer them some arrangements for their new bands. "Only one thing," he would say, "don't ask me for any money!" Generally at that point the men would decide to stay with the band.

For ten years Woody had been struggling as a bandleader. Now he could afford his first vacation in eight years, and so he and his pretty, patient and charming wife, Charlotte, took a nine-day trip to Bermuda. Shortly thereafter they bought Humphrey Bogart's attractive home high in the hills above Hollywood's Sunset Strip.

By now Woody had just about everything he'd always wanted: a fine home and security for himself, his wife and their daughter, Ingrid, plus the realization that he had created and brought to the top one of the most popular and still one of the most musicianly big bands of all time.

Then one night in December of 1946 after a dance at the University of Indiana he announced his big decision, a decision influenced by his desire to spend more time with Charlotte and Ingie, and by the realization that, having reached the top, there would henceforth be only one more way for him to go —down. That's when and why Woody dropped his bomb: he was giving up his band!

Metronome heralded the passing of The Herd with a lead editorial titled "Obituary in Rhythm." Even though seven other bands—those of Benny Goodman, Tommy Dorsey, Harry James, Les Brown, Jack Teagarden, Benny Carter and Ina Ray Hutton—had all given up during the same month, it was Herman's disbanding that was felt most acutely.

"Only once before," noted the obituary, "was a band of such unequivocal standards and evenness of musicianship organized. That was the Ellington band. It still is, but Herman is not. . . . Woody Herman's magnificent band is dead. Requiescat in pace."

Woody tried hard to rest. He played golf. He tried being a disc jockey, but he didn't like it much. He made a few relaxed records with a pick-up group, but they didn't satisfy him, either. He yearned to have a really good band again. And so, a year later he started The Second Herd, the one with Stan Getz and Zoot Sims and the other famous Four Brothers.

The Herds kept coming. The Third followed the Second, the Fourth followed the Third, and so on. In the early sixties he was fronting still another Herd. Don't ask me what number this one was. All I know is that it too was great, one of the most startlingly exciting outfits I'd ever heard. And in 1966 he was fronting an entirely new Herd, composed completely of young unknowns, one so great that it received an ear-splitting, rip-roaring standing ovation at the Newport Jazz Festival. And he continued to come up with even more unknowns, adapting his music, more than any other leader of the so-called big band era has ever done, to the current tastes. He used electronic instruments, and he produced arrangements by young, talented writers that may have turned off some of his old fans, but which brought rip-roaring responses from thousands of equally enthusiastic new ones.

To those of us who had followed Herman's Herds through their thirty years, including the twenty years since the end of the Big Band era, finding Woody still swinging so strongly was no shock. True, there had been shaky times when he had limited himself to just a small group, but we always had a hunch that soon he'd be fronting another one of this big, wildly swinging Herds— full of young, dedicated and appreciative musicians, following the inspiring direction of a man as young at heart and in mind as any one of the spirited kids he was leading.

And that's exactly what he was still doing as he and his newest Young Thundering Herd roared into the 1980s!

"Requiescat in pace." My eye!!!

Earl Hines

EARL (FATHA) HINES was firmly ensconced in Chicago's Grand Terrace Café when the big band boom got under way in the mid-thirties. He'd become a fixture there, after having starred in the same club with Louis Armstrong's band, with which he made numerous recordings.

Handsome, gregarious, a chain-smoker of cigars, Earl Hines must go down in jazz history as one of the greatest and most influential of all pianists. His full, rich, driving, two-handed style sounded more like that of a band than of a piano soloist. With his right hand he punched out melodic lines much in the manner of a trumpet section, while his full left hand beat out rhythm figures that might have been blown by the rest of the band.

The Hines style had been drilled into me during my college days by two pianists, Carleton Bates and Olie Neidlinger, who played in the band I led in college. Each was obviously a Hines devotee, for each emphasized the "Fatha's" hard, rock-bottom, driving style, which for a band with a drummer as rhythmically immature as I was, proved to be quite a blessing.

The Hines band recorded some exciting sides in those days, including one of Earl's most famous songs, "Rosetta," which featured a great vocal by Walter Fuller, who, with Herb Jeffries, was then singing with the band. Trummy Young, who later gained great fame with Jimmie Lunceford and Louis Armstrong, was a trombonist, and many of the arrangements were written by tenor saxist Jimmy Mundy, who was soon to go with Benny Goodman.

For several years after the start of the big era nothing very exciting happened to Earl, and the great pianist seemed to be turning into one of the forgotten jazz stars. Then in 1940 the boogie-woogie piano craze swept the country. Earl latched on to this and came up with a smash hit recording of "Boogie-Woogie on St. Louis Blues."

Featured in the band at that time was a handsome baritone named Billy Eckstein, whose career was launched when he sang on several more Hines hits, notably "Jelly, Jelly" and "Stormy Monday Blues." Arranging at this time was tenor saxist Budd Johnson. Billy and Budd had both been listening to some of the newer jazz sounds emanating from Minton's in Harlem, and together they convinced Earl that he ought to try using them in his big band.

Earl took their suggestion, and so the Hines band became the first and in many ways the most successful of the early big bop outfits.

Johnson talked Hines into taking an amazingly creative, if somewhat unreliable, saxist from Jay McShann's band. This was the late Charlie (Yardbird) Parker. Billy had also found what he considered one of the truly great girl singers of the day, Sarah Vaughan, and induced Earl to hire her. Dizzy Gillespie was playing trumpet in the band by then, too, and it has been reported that some of the duets he and Sarah produced were positively stupendous. And, according to Benny Harris, who played trumpet in the band, "the whole brass section used to try to play like Diz. And when Earl went offstage, Diz would jump right out of the brass section and sit in on piano."

Unfortunately much of the great music that the band was playing in the early forties, including those Vaughan-Gillespie duets, was heard by all too few people, because the recording ban was in effect. By the time Petrillo had rescinded it, many of the key men had departed—in fact by September, 1943, instead of featuring his great array of modern jazz stars, Hines was sporting twelve violins! "I'd always had a funny ambition to do something like Waring and Whiteman along jazz lines," he confessed later.

Earl may have realized his ambition, but no band of his ever again attained the high degree of musicianship or the commercial success of the one he led during the early forties. By 1947 he had given up his career as a big band leader, and in 1948 he returned to play with his old boss of the twenties, Louis Armstrong. Earl stayed with him for three years, then settled down to perform mostly as a single attraction. In the mid-sixties a Hines revival boom began, and for the next decade and a half jazz fans in America and many foreign countries, including Russia and Japan, through which Hines toured, thrilled to his powerful, pulsating piano.

*The Earl, his cigar
and his piano*

Hudson-DeLange

WILL HUDSON and Eddie DeLange led one of the gentlest swing bands during the middle half of the thirties. Known as the Hudson-DeLange Orchestra, it played many successful engagements, principally in eastern colleges, and recorded some very fine sides for Brunswick.

Both Hudson and DeLange were songwriters. Will wrote melodies and Eddie wrote lyrics. Will was a very serious-looking man with glasses who could easily have passed for an accountant. Eddie, on the other hand, was a big, hearty redhead, full of life and energy, sometimes playing the clown, other times as serious as he must have been when he was awarded his Phi Beta Kappa key at the University of Pennsylvania.

It was Eddie who actually started the band early in 1936. But after a few weeks, he realized he'd need many more arrangements, so he contacted Will, with whom he had written some songs, and offered him a partnership in return for his arranging. And that's how the band continued—Eddie as leader, Will as behind-the-scenes musical director who would travel with the band approximately one week per month.

Hudson's arrangements were simple, direct, yet always musical and in good taste. Generally they were of two distinct kinds: light, uptempoed swing numbers and relaxed, moody ballads that emphasized numerous unison reed passages. They were well played by some of New York's better junior musicians, several of whom, like clarinetist Gus Bivona, trumpeter Jimmy Blake, guitarist Bus Etri, bassist Doc Goldberg and drummer Nat Polen, were to gain greater recognition with the bands of Tommy Dorsey, Charlie Barnet, Glenn Miller or Les Brown.

DeLange whispered some of the ballads in a whiskey sort of way. More impressive, however, were the vocals by the girl singers who worked with the band, especially Ruthie Gaylor, Nan Wynn and Fredda Gibson. Fredda, who made a whale of a record of a tune called "If We Never Meet Again," later changed her name to Georgia Gibbs and became a radio and recording star.

DeLange wrote the lyrics for a number of the ballads, including "Deep

Will Hudson (left), Ruthie Gaylor and Eddie DeLange

in a Dream," "Heaven Can Wait," "Remember When," and the team's most successful collaboration, "Moonglow." Hudson also penned a batch of instrumentals including "Organ Grinder's Swing," "Sophisticated Swing," "Monopoly Swing," plus such semi-swing novelties as "Hobo on Park Avenue," "Love Song of a Half Wit" and "Eight Bars in Search of a Melody." The band recorded all these tunes; in fact, much of its output was written by Hudson and DeLange with additional credits on many songs going to their wealthy publisher, Irving Mills, who also owned not only Master Records, for whom they recorded for a while, but also an interest in the band itself!

But it wasn't long before Will and Eddie, so opposite in their personality and outlook, found it harder and harder to get along with each other. Thus, in the early part of 1938, under rather unpleasant circumstances, they dissolved their partnership. Will claimed that patrons often asked for him, hoping to see the writer and arranger of the tunes they admired, and were disappointed when he didn't show. Since the band couldn't be fronted by two men, Hudson offered to buy out DeLange.

Eddie's story was quite different. He claimed that Will suggested dissolving their partnership so that they could get out of their booking contract. After this had been done, according to Eddie, Will asked if he could keep the band for himself, and when Eddie demurred, they put it up to a vote by the musicians, who, appreciating Will's contributions as their arranger, selected him.

Each then fronted his own band. Neither was successful. So, in 1941 they decided to try again as a team, but the venture fizzled. Each continued writing on his own. Will arranged for Glenn Miller's Army Air Forces Band during the war, and Eddie in the late forties settled in Hollywood to write for the movies, a career that ended when he died in the summer of 1949.

Ina Ray Hutton

WITHOUT a doubt, the sexiest of all the big bandleaders was Ina Ray Hutton. Fortunately for her sake and that of the rest of the band she had a good deal more to offer. For Ina Ray was a warm, gracious, intelligent and talented gal.

Ina Ray

The early part of her career had been spent fronting an all-girl orchestra, one that never achieved any great musical heights but which, just because it was an all-girl orchestra, received some commercial acceptance. But, since she couldn't find enough topnotch female musicians to satisfy her tastes, she decided to organize one composed entirely of men instead.

The band at which Ina Ray began waving her long baton in a languorous, seductive sort of way in 1940 was composed of several good jazz musicians, with one, guitarist Jack Purcell, truly outstanding. It played well, if usually too loudly, but with Ina Ray weaving her torso in her magnificent, undulating manner, it managed to attract many customers. And it held them with its good dance music.

Chief musical light in the band was a tenor saxist and arranger named George Paxton, a relaxed, witty man with a great flair for writing commercial arrangements and a great and reciprocal flare for Ina Ray. As the band's career progressed, Paxton began to play a more and more important part, until he eventually emerged as its musical director and, insofar as most of the musicians were concerned, its apparent leader. Later Ina Ray married trumpeter Randy Brooks and Paxton did rather well for himself with his own band.

One of the most pleasant musical attractions within the band was a handsome, dark-haired baritone who went by the name of Stuart Foster and who, besides having a great voice, knew how to make sense out of lyrics. (Foster wasn't his real name, he was an Armenian, and a wonderful guy, by the way. But then, Ina Ray, whose ancestry was Italian, as I recall it, wasn't using her real name either!)

By 1943 the band, which continued to get better and better, took on even more of an international flavor with the addition of the Kim Loo Sisters, a good vocal trio, one of whose members later became Mrs. Stuart Foster. Purcell, meanwhile, had developed into an even more exciting jazz guitarist, while newly added Hal Schaefer turned out to be an excellent jazz pianist.

But the paramount attraction remained Ina Ray. Good as the band was musically, it probably would have remained just another outfit with the public if this mighty attractive lass hadn't stood (which, come to think of it, is much too inactive a verb in this case) in front of it. With all her charm, looks and talent, it always amazed me that the movies never latched on to her.

Harry James

IT WAS on a day in mid-September of 1936 that Glenn Miller and Charlie Spivak invited me to go with them to hear a recording session of a band by their former boss, Ben Pollack. He had just arrived in town to do a date for Brunswick, and Glenn, who had always been telling me what a great drummer Pollack was, said, "Now you can hear for yourself."

The band was composed of young musicians, the good kind that Ben had a knack for discovering (he had started Miller, Spivak, Benny Goodman, Jack Teagarden and many other stars). Pollack, I soon found out, was a helluva drummer, and the young, fat man in the reed section, Irving Fazola, was a magnificent clarinetist. And then, of course, there was the long, lean, hungry-looking trumpeter whom I'd raved about in a column a few months earlier—without even knowing his name—after having heard a Pollack band broadcast from Pittsburgh, and whose rip-roaring style proved to be even more exciting in person. The session became quite something, with Miller and Spivak joining the band and later both spouting raves about the new kid trumpeter.

He, of course, was Harry James, and his playing on these records drew another rave notice from me. "Irving Goodman, Benny's brother, read it in *Metronome*," James revealed years later, "and he started listening to me. Finally he convinced Benny he ought to get me into his band." In December, 1936, James joined Goodman, replacing Irving.

Harry was only twenty years old then, but he already had had as much experience as many of the band's veterans, having blown his horn in dance bands since he had been thirteen. His impact on the Goodman band in general and its brass section in particular (he played both lead and hot) was immense. What's more, his unfailing spirit and enthusiasm seemed to infect the other musicians—he was extremely well-liked and respected, despite his age. And obviously he enjoyed his new environment. Even after he had been with the band for a year and a half and reports persisted that several of the Goodman stars would follow Gene Krupa's move and start their own bands, Harry remained steadfast. "Benny's too great a guy to work for!" he exclaimed in the spring of 1938, insisting that he wouldn't even consider leaving for at

least a year. It turned out to be a very short year. In January, 1939, James left Goodman to start his own band.

Benny didn't seem to mind. He gave Harry his blessings and some cash in return for an interest in the band. Eventually James paid him back many times that amount in return for his release.

The new band's first engagement was in Philadelphia at the Benjamin Franklin Hotel. It opened there on February 9, and the March, 1939, issue of *Metronome* carried this capsule review with the heading "James Jumps."

> Harry James' new band here in the Ben Franklin sure kicks—and in a soft way, too. Outfit gets a swell swing, thanks mostly to great arrangements by Andy Gibson, to Dave Matthews' lead sax, Ralph Hawkins' drumming and Harry's horn.
>
> Hotel management insists upon unnaturally soft music. Band complies, producing stuff reminiscent of the original Norvo group. However, in last supper sets it gives out and really rocks!
>
> Some rough spots still obvious: brass intonation varies; saxes, brilliant most of the time, not yet consistent. Missed: a good hot clarinet and ditto trombone. Personalities of Harry as leader and Beatrice Byers, warbler, fine.—Simon

Also in February, on the twentieth, the new band cut its first records for Brunswick, for whom Harry had previously made several sides with pickup bands that usually included some of Count Basie's men. The new sides by his own big band weren't very impressive at first, but even the best groups suffered acoustical malnutrition from the company's woefully small, dead-sounding studios.

The band, however, did impress its live audiences and radio listeners, and James seemed happy. "No, I don't think I made any mistake when I left Benny," he said. "When I was with Benny, I often had to play sensational horn. I was one of a few featured men in a killer-diller band. Each of us had to impress all the time. Consequently, when I got up to take, say, sixteen bars, I'd have to try to cram everything into that short space."

Right from the start, James began to feature himself more on ballads— tunes like "I Surrender, Dear," "Just a Gigolo," "I'm in the Market for You" and "Black and Blue." "Playing what you want to play is good for a guy's soul, you know," he explained.

As for the band itself he insisted: "I want to have a band that really swings and that's easy to dance to all the time. Too many bands, in order to be sensational, hit tempos that you just can't dance to." Maybe it's just coincidental, but just at the time James made this statement, Glenn Miller's band, with its extremely fast tempos, had started coming into its own. "We're emphasizing middle tempos," Harry continued. "They can swing just as much and they're certainly more danceable."

The band provided much color, even with its uniforms. Harry had been brought up in a circus, and his tastes often showed it. His men were attired in red mess jackets, and with them they wore white bow ties and winged collars that went with full dress outfits. Harry had a flashy way of playing his horn, too, visually (he'd puff his cheeks so that they'd look as if they were about to pop) as well as aurally, so that you couldn't help noticing him and his band.

He was in those days—and he continued to be, for that matter—a refreshingly straightforward, candid person. His personal approach was much more informal than his band's uniforms, and he succeeded in creating and retaining a rapport with his men that must have been the envy of many another bandleader.

One of his closest friends turned out to be a young singer James says he heard quite by accident one night on the local radio station WNEW's "Dance Parade" program in New York. (Louise Tobin, who was then married to James, insists that she had first drawn his attention to the voice.)

As Harry recalls, it happened in June, 1939, when his new band was playing at the Paramount Theater in New York. James, lying in bed, listening to Harold Arden's band from the Rustic Cabin in Englewood, New Jersey, was immensely impressed when he heard the band's boy vocalist sing. But Harry failed to note his name, so the next night, after his last show, he traveled over to the Rustic Cabin to find out. "I asked the manager where I could find the singer," he recalls, "and he told me, 'We don't have a singer. But we do have an MC who sings a little bit.' "

The singing MC's name turned out to be Frank Sinatra. He crooned a few songs, and Harry was sufficiently convinced to ask him to drop by the Paramount to talk more. "He did, and we made a deal. It was as simple as that. There was only one thing we didn't agree on. I wanted him to change his name because I thought people couldn't remember it. But he didn't want to. He kept pointing out that he had a cousin up in Boston named Ray Sinatra and he had done pretty well as a bandleader, so why shouldn't he keep his name?" Even way back then, Sinatra was a pretty persuasive guy!

The new vocalist recorded his first sides with the band on July 13, 1939. They were "From the Bottom of My Heart" and "Melancholy Mood," and though they were musical enough, they sounded very tentative and even slightly shy, like a boy on a first date who doesn't quite know what to say to his girl.

In those days Sinatra, despite an outward cockiness, needed encouragement, and he got it from James, with whom he established a wonderful rapport.

The Harry James band (summer, 1939)
Front row: *drummer Ralph Hawkins, trombonist Truett Jones, girl vocalist Connie Haines, James, boy vocalist Frank Sinatra, saxist Dave Matthews, trumpeter-singer Jack Palmer*
Second row: *trumpeter Jack Schaeffer, bassist Thurman Teague, saxist Drew Page, trombonist Russell Brown, trumpeter Claude Bowen, guitarist Red Kent.*
Back row: *saxist Claude Lakey, pianist Jack (Jumbo) Gardner, saxist Bill Luther*

The first indication I had of Frank's lack of confidence came in August when I dropped into the Roseland to review the band. As I was leaving, Jerry Barrett, Harry's manager, came running after me to find out what I thought of the new singer. "He wants a good writeup more than anybody I've ever seen," he said. "So give him a good writeup, will you, because we want to keep him happy and with the band."

The writeup commended Sinatra for his "very pleasing vocals" and his "easy phrasing," praise that was nothing compared with that I had for the band itself: "a band that kicks as few have ever kicked before!" In addition, it did what Harry had said he wanted to do: it played exceptionally well for dancing, producing even waltzes, tangos and rumbas. It also spotted several fine soloists, including Dave Matthews on alto sax, Claude Lakey on tenor sax, Dalton Rizzotti on trombone and Jack Gardner on piano.

The band was doing well around New York. But after Roseland it went out to Los Angeles and into a plush restaurant called Victor Hugo's. "The owner kept telling us we were playing too loud," Harry recalls. "And so he wouldn't pay us. We were struggling pretty good and nobody had any money, so Frank would invite us up to his place and Nancy would cook spaghetti for everyone."

After the West Coast debacle, the band went into the Sherman Hotel in Chicago. The future wasn't looking so bright anymore. What's more, Frank and Nancy were expecting their first baby, who turned out to be little Nancy.

Meanwhile—nearby at the Palmer House—Tommy Dorsey was having boy singer problems. He was told about "the skinny kid with James," heard him and immediately offered him a job. Frank talked it over with Harry. Aware of the impending arrival and the necessity for a more secure future, James merely said, "Go ahead." And Sinatra did.

Sinatra's contract with James still had five months to run. "Frank still kids about honoring our deal," Harry recently noted. "He'll drop in to hear the band and he'll say something like 'O.K., boss'—he still calls me 'boss'—'I'm ready anytime. Just call me and I'll be there on the stand.'"

Sinatra's voice had become an important one in the James band. Jack Matthias had written some pretty arrangements for him, including some in which the band sang glee club backgrounds in a strictly semiprofessional way. For me the two best vocals Sinatra sang with James were "It's Funny to Everyone but Me" and "All or Nothing at All," which was re-released several years later and only then became a bestseller. Possibly the worst side he *ever* recorded was the James theme, "Ciribiribin."

With Sinatra gone, James naturally began looking for a replacement. He found him quite by accident one afternoon when the band was rehearsing in New York at the World Transcription studios at 711 Fifth Avenue. Larry Shayne, a music publisher, had brought along a young songwriter to audition some tunes. Harry listened, then turned to Shayne and said, "I don't like the tunes too much, but I sure like the way the kid sings." The kid was Dick Haymes.

James and new boy vocalist Dick Haymes

If ever there was a nervous band singer, it was Dick Haymes. The son of a top vocal coach, Marguerite Haymes, he was incessantly aware of all the problems that singers faced: stuffed-up nasal passages, sore throats, frogs, improper breathing, wrong stances, etc. As a result he looked completely self-conscious whenever he prepared to sing. I still have visions of his routine at the Fiesta Ballroom, at Broadway and Forty-second Street, where the band was playing shortly after Dick joined. As he prepared to sing, he'd clear his throat a couple of times and then invariably take his handkerchief out of his breast pocket and put it to his mouth for a second. Then he'd approach the mike with long steps, look awkwardly around him, take a deep breath and start to sing.

And how he could sing! There wasn't a boy singer in the business who had a better voice box than Dick Haymes—not even Bob Eberly, whom Dick worshiped so much and who amazed Dick and possibly even disillusioned him by doing something no highly trained singer would ever do: smoke on the job! Haymes sang some exquisite vocals on some comparatively obscure James recordings of "How High the Moon" (as a ballad), "Fools Rush In," "The Nearness of You" and "Maybe." They appeared on a minor label called Varsity, with which Harry had signed early in 1940 after his Brunswick and Columbia sides (the two labels were owned by the same company) had shown disappointing sales.

But though his records may not have been selling sensationally, James continued to hold the admiration of his fellow musicians. In the January,

1940, *Metronome* poll he was voted top trumpeter in two divisions: as best hot trumpeter and as best all-round trumpeter.

During this period the band returned to New York's Roseland, where it sounded better than ever, swinging sensationally throughout the evening. But Harry was thinking ahead. He wanted to be able to play more than just ballrooms and in the too few hotel spots that didn't boycott high-swinging bands. "You know what I want to do?" he confided to me one evening. "I'm going to add strings and maybe even a novachord. Then we'll be able to play anywhere."

My reactions, like that of any jazz-oriented critic who couldn't see beyond the next beat, was one of horror. James add strings? What a wild, scatter-brained idea! "You're out of your mind," I told him. A few weeks later he announced he was giving up the idea, explaining that he'd planned it only because he figured that was how he could cop an engagement in a class New York hotel spot. But when the hotel operator insisted upon owning a piece of the band too, Harry shelved his plans.

During the summer of 1940 the band appeared at the Dancing Campus of the New York World's Fair. It had begun to settle into a wonderful groove, with the ensemble sounds matching those of such brilliant soloists as James himself, Dave Matthews on alto and Vido Musso and Sam Donahue on tenor saxes. In a fit of critical enthusiasm that caused Benny Goodman to appear in my office to ask incredulously, "Do you *really* think so?" I had noted in *Metronome* that "strictly for swing kicks, Harry James has the greatest white band in the country, and, for that matter, so far as this reviewer is concerned, the greatest dancebandom has ever known. And that's leaving out nobody!"

But Harry never seemed to be quite satisfied. In the fall he made several personnel changes, explaining that "the boys need inspiration, so I decided to call in some fresh blood." One of the most surprising moves was installing Claude Lakey, who had joined the band on tenor sax and then had switched into the trumpet section, as new leader of the saxes in place of Matthews.

But the most important move was still to come. Harry had finished his contract with Varsity Records (if you think the Brunswick sound was bad, listen to some of the Varsity sides!) and had returned to Columbia, which by now was getting some great results out of its large Liederkranz Hotel studio. The company had a very astute A&R producer named Morty Palitz who, Harry recently said, "suggested I add a woodwind section and a string quartet. I settled for the strings."

Remember how those of us who knew everything had warned Harry against such a move less than a year before? Harry just didn't have sense enough to listen to us, though. He added the strings and recorded such trumpet virtuoso sides as "The Flight of the Bumble Bee," "The Carnival of Venice" and the two-sided "Trumpet Rhapsody" all complete with a string section. And on May 20, 1941, he recorded "You Made Me Love You," his schmaltzy trumpet backed by the dainty sounds of his strings. Despite our grave warnings, the record proved to be a smash hit, and the James band was on the way to stardom.

He recorded the tune for a very simple reason: he loved the way Judy Garland sang the song. I remember his raving about her during those very quiet nights when he and I used to sit in the Blue Room of the Hotel Lincoln, where the musicians would sometimes outnumber the customers. In addition to music, we shared another passion, baseball and, at that time, the Brooklyn Dodgers in particular. (For the sake of the record it should be noted that James eventually became a staunch fan of the St. Louis Cardinals, for whom he still roots today.) It was a curious routine that we followed: we'd sit in the Lincoln all night and talk about baseball and then during the afternoons we'd go out to Ebbets Field to watch the Dodgers. And what would we be talking about out there? Music, of course.

In June, James recorded a swinging salute to his favorite team, "Dodgers' Fan Dance." He also tried to emulate them literally by playing ball with his team in Central Park on almost every clear afternoon. There was an unconfirmed rumor that before James would hire a musician, he'd find out how well he could play ball—after which he'd audition him with his instrument. Certainly he had some athletic-looking guys in his band during those days.

"Dodgers' Fan Dance" wasn't much of a hit. But "You Made Me Love You," of course, was, and from then on the character of the James band changed for good. It still played its powerful swing numbers, but it began interspersing them more and more with many lush ballads that featured Harry's horn, blown, as I noted in a *Metronome* review, "with an inordinate amount of feeling, though many may object, and with just cause, to a vibrato that could easily span the distance from left field to first base."

Ironically, "You Made Me Love You" wasn't released until several months after it had been recorded. Perhaps the Columbia people agreed with some of the jazz critics. But they were wrong, too.

The hit was backed by one of the greatest of all James ballad sides, "A Sinner Kissed an Angel," which proved once again what a great singer Haymes had become. During this period Dick also recorded several other outstanding sides: "I'll Get By," "You Don't Know What Love Is" and probably his greatest James vocal of all, "You've Changed."

With singers like Sinatra and Haymes, Harry apparently felt he didn't need to feature a girl vocalist. Previously he had carried several, Bernice Byers and then Connie Haines during the band's earliest days. And in May, 1941, he had hired Helen Ward, Goodman's original singer to make a recording of "Daddy." Then later, for a while, he spotted a very statuesque show-girl type named Dell Parker, who in July, 1941, was replaced by petite Lynn Richards. But few sang much or sang well. Definitely the best was yet to come.

The best turned out to be Helen Forrest, who'd recorded some great sides with Artie Shaw and Benny Goodman but who suddenly quit the latter, "to

James and Helen Forrest

avoid having a nervous breakdown. Then just on a hunch," Helen recently revealed, "I decided to contact Harry. I loved the way he played that trumpet, with that Jewish phrasing, and I thought I'd fit right in with the band. But Harry didn't seem to want me because he already had Dick Haymes to sing all the ballads and he was looking for a rhythm singer. Then Peewee Monte, his manager, had me come over to rehearsal, and after that the guys in the band took a vote and they decided they wanted me with them. So Harry agreed.

"I've got to thank Harry for letting me really develop even further as a singer. I'll always remain grateful to Artie and Benny. But they had been featuring me more like they did a member of the band, almost like another instrumental soloist. Harry, though, gave me the right sort of arrangements and setting that fit a singer. It wasn't just a matter of my getting up, singing a chorus, and sitting down again."

What James did, of course, was to build the arrangements around his horn and Helen's voice, establishing warmer moods by slowing down the tempo so that two, instead of the usual three or more choruses, would fill a record. Sometimes there'd even be less; many an arrangement would build to a closing climax during Helen's vocal, so that she would emerge as its star.

Helen, who was just as warm a person as she sounded, blended ideally with the schmaltzier approach that was beginning to turn the James band into the most popular big band in the land and that helped Helen win the 1941 *Metronome* poll. True, there were times when she tended to pour it on a little too thick with a crying kind of phrasing, but then she was merely reflecting the sort of unctious emotion that Harry was pouring out through his horn. It may not have been what his real jazz fans wanted, but Harry was beginning to care less and less what they thought and more and more about the money and squarer customers who kept pouring in.

Helen turned out a whole series of excellent ballad sides that helped the band's stock soar. Many of them, beginning with her first vocal, "He's 1-A in the Army and He's A-1 in My Heart," dwelled upon the-boy-in-the-service-and-his-girl-back-home theme. Thus came such recordings as "I Don't Want to Walk Without You," "He's My Guy," "That Soldier of Mine" and "My Beloved Is Rugged," plus plain but equally sentimental ballads, like "Make Love to Me," "But Not for Me," "Skylark," "I Cried for You," "I Had the Craziest Dream" and "I've Heard That Song Before."

The band personnel began to improve, too. A young tenor saxist, who was still a guardian of another bandleader, Sonny Dunham, joined and became one of the James fixtures for the next twenty-five years. This was Corky Corcoran, a great third baseman, who was released by Dunham upon Harry's payment to him of the costs of the seventeen-year-old saxist's recent appendicitis operation. The reeds had already been bolstered by the addition of two excellent alto saxists, Sam Marowitz in the lead chair, and Johnny McAfee, who, after Haymes left at the end of 1941, contributed some very good vocals. James had also featured another singer, Jimmy Saunders.

An indication of what lay ahead appeared when the band entered the select winner's circle of the Coca-Cola radio show, which spotted the bands with the most popular records. Previous victors had been Glenn Miller, Tommy Dorsey, Freddy Martin and Sammy Kaye, all Victor artists. Then, in March, 1942, the James band broke their hold with its recording of "I Don't Want to Walk Without You." What's more, two months later the band and the record copped honors for the show's favorite recording of all!

The new formula of Harry's schmaltzy horn and Helen's emotional voice, with swing numbers interspersed, was certainly beginning to pay off. In the spring of 1942 the band broke records on two coasts—at the Meadowbrook in Cedar Grove, New Jersey, and at the Palladium in Hollywood, where it drew thirty-five thousand customers in one week and eight thousand of them in a single evening!

To those of us who had been enraptured by the band's tremendous free-swinging drive, the change in musical emphasis was disappointing. In a review of a radio program during its record-breaking Palladium stay, I concluded, after deploring the band's muddy-sounding rhythmic approach, that "it would be a shame to discover that the Harry James band had really lost that thrilling drive that sparked its performances for such a long time."

But the band just kept going on to bigger and bigger things. In the summer of 1942 it won Martin Block's "Make Believe Ballroom" poll, unseating what most people considered the number-one band in the country, Glenn Miller's. And then, when shortly thereafter, Glenn enlisted in the Army Air Force, his sponsor, Chesterfield cigarettes, selected James to replace him. By then, the band was appearing on commercial radio five nights a week—three times for Chesterfield, once for Coca-Cola and once again for Jello as part of "The Jack Benny Show" emanating from New York.

While in the East the band again played the Meadowbrook. And it also repaid a debt to Maria Kramer, owner of the Lincoln Hotel, where it had spent so many of its earlier nights, by playing the spot at quite a loss in income.

But it left the engagement early when it was summoned to Hollywood to appear in the movie version of *Best Foot Forward*.

Barry Ulanov, who preferred jazz to schmaltz, summed up the reason for the James success in a December, 1942, *Metronome* review that began:

> Rarely has the public's faith in a band been so generously rewarded as it has in the organization headed by Harry James. Of the number one favorites of recent years, Harry's gives its fans the most for its money. . . . His taste is the public's taste, and his pulse runs wonderfully right along with that of the man in the street and the woman on the dance floor. . . .
>
> Whether or not you agree with or accept Harry James' taste doesn't matter in appraising this band. It's not the band of tomorrow. It's not an experimental outfit. It's not even the brilliant jazz crew that Harry fronted a couple of years ago. It's just a fine all-around outfit that reflects dance music of today perfectly.

One further indication of the band's commercial success: the day it was to open a twelve-thousand-five-hundred-dollar-a-week engagement at New York's Paramount Theater was a nasty, rainy one. The doors were to open at a quarter to ten. At five in the morning the lines began forming, and if a batch of extra police hadn't arrived, there could have been a riot.

And still another sign: Columbia Records announced in June, 1942, that it was running into a shellac famine because of James. That band's version of "I've Heard That Song Before" had become the company's all-time biggest seller at 1,250,000 copies! "Velvet Moon" and "You Made Me Love You" had passed the one million mark. And "All or Nothing at All" and "Flash," the former featuring Sinatra, the latter a James original, a coupling that had sold 16,000 copies when it had been released three years earlier, had been reissued and had sold 975,000 copies to date!

Meanwhile the band was signed to appear in two more movies, *Mr. Co-Ed* with Red Skelton and *A Tale of Two Sisters,* as Harry kept growing closer and closer to the movie scene, and particularly to one of its most glamorous stars. She was Betty Grable, who occupied a table every night at the Astor Roof when the band appeared there in the spring of 1943.

During that engagement it became increasingly obvious that Harry was far more interested in pleasing his public, and in Miss Grable, then he was in playing any more outstanding jazz. The band performed its ballads as well as usual, but the men seemed to be blowing listlessly. "The stuff instead of sounding solid, sounds stolid, on the pompous side," I noted in my July, 1943, review. "You get the feeling that the men are plodding through the notes. . . . I don't know whether it's because they are living too well, or because they just aren't capable of playing more rhythmically. . . ."

Mr. and Mrs. Harry James

Perhaps my thoughts were going back too much to those early days when the band had such tremendous spirit, when it was filled with laughs and good humor and ambition and a healthy desire to play and swing and succeed. Now success had come, but the inspiration seemed to have disappeared.

Harry, himself, seemed far less interested in his music. Of course, with someone like Betty Grable around, most of us could hardly blame him.

But Harry had worries, too. The armed services were taking some of his best men. And, what's more, they were constantly beckoning in his direction too.

On July 5 in Las Vegas, Nevada, Harry James married Betty Grable. One month later his draft board classified him 4-F.

But his draft problems were by no means over. Rumors kept persisting that he would be reclassified 1-A. On February 11, 1944, he took his pre-induction physical. Then Harry put his entire band on notice with an invitation "to stick around and see what happens." There really wasn't much to stick around for because his radio series sponsor announced that the band would be dropped from the program in March.

And then it happened: at the very last minute, James was reclassified 4-F because of an old back injury. Quickly he called together some of his old men. He had been featuring Buddy DiVito and Helen Ward (Helen Forrest had begun her career as a single late in 1943) as his singers, but the latter was replaced by Kitty Kallen when the band returned to the Astor Roof on May 22. Juan Tizol, meanwhile, had come over from Duke Ellington's band to fill a James trombone chair.

The band's success continued. After its Astor engagement, where an improved rhythm section was noted, it went on a record-breaking tour, highlighted by a sixty thousand throng at the Rubber Bowl in Akron, Ohio, and terminating in California, where it began another healthy schedule on Coca-Cola's Spotlight Band radio series, and where Harry broke something other than a record—his leg. How? Playing baseball, of course.

The James band had not made any good new recordings for more than two years; the AFM ban saw to that. Finally, on November 11, 1944, the companies and Petrillo ended their war. Immediately James went into Columbia's New York studio to record four sides, including a fine version of "I'm Beginning to See the Light," featuring his pretty, new vocalist, Kitty Kallen, plus his first jazz combo opus in many a year, "I'm Confessin'," which spotted the great Willie Smith, Jimmie Lunceford's former alto saxist, who had just joined the band, and a brilliant pianist named Arnold Ross.

When the band returned East to play at Meadowbrook, Barry Ulanov noted a stronger emphasis on jazz, praising James for playing swinging things instead of merely playing it safe. "He has taken advantage of his unassailable commercial position to play good music, to diminish the amount of tremulous trash which formed the bulk of his sets when he was coming up. Now, if he will just drop those meaningless strings. . . ."

But Harry wasn't listening. He increased his string section to two full dozen. "With a section as big as that," I wrote in July, 1945, "somebody ought to be able to produce impressive sounds." But nobody did.

The more I saw Harry in those days, the more I realized he had become less and less interested in his music. He had broadened his career as an entertainer when in January, 1945, he had been signed for the Danny Kaye radio series, where, in addition to leading and blowing his horn, he also acted as a stooge and a comedian of sorts. And he seemed to like his new roles—perhaps even more than his music.

He developed other consuming interests. With his wife, he devoted a great deal of his time to horseracing, running his own nags and spending much time at the tracks. He became so successful that he could choose the spots he wanted to play with his band, and, if he felt like concentrating on affairs apart from music, he'd do so.

But in 1946 the bottom began to fall slowly out of the band business. The big-paying steady dates were disappearing. James, who had refused to play one-nighters for almost two years, ostensibly because he wanted to remain where the action was, announced in February that he would again tour with his band.

His financial overhead was high. But Harry was not drawing his usual big crowds. It must have been a big blow to him and his pride. In December, 1946, just ten years after he had joined Benny Goodman's band, Harry James announced that he was giving up. Ironically, Goodman made a similar announcement that very month.

But then something—nobody knows just what—changed Harry's mind. A few months later, he was back again with a brand new, streamlined band. It jumped. He jumped. And there were just four fiddles, and they had very little to do.

How come the sudden change? A healthy and happy-looking Harry James talked about it in the summer of 1947: "First of all, I've settled a few problems in my mind, problems nobody ever knew I had and which I didn't bother telling anyone about. But when you're worried and upset, you don't feel like playing and you certainly can't relax enough to play anything like good jazz."

It was like the old days in more ways than one. James cut his price in half; he played one-nighters everywhere and on every one of them he blew his brilliant jazz, just the way he had when he first started his band.

And then there was the new group's contagious enthusiasm. "The most important thing that makes me want to play," he said, "is this new band of mine. You know what I've had in the past. Well, now I've got me a bunch of kids and their spirit kills me. They're up on the bandstand wanting to play all the time, so how can I possibly not feel like blowing! I haven't had a bunch like this since my first band."

Harry made that statement thirty years ago. And, with just a few short time-outs, he has been leading a group ever since, at times only a small one, but most of the time a big, swinging band with a booting brass section and a swinging sax section and rhythm quartet to match—and with no strings attached!

It has played mostly in Nevada—forty weeks out of each year, to be precise. In 1966 he brought his band back to New York for a few weeks, and a wonderfully swinging outfit it was, too, with some youngsters, and some veterans like Corky Corcoran and Louis Bellson, who had just replaced Buddy Rich on drums. And there were some of the old arrangements and there were some new swinging ones.

But most of all, there was Harry James, happy, effervescent, boasting without reservations that "this is the best band I've ever had in my life! These young musicians, they're getting so much better training and they can do so much more!"

It was the Harry James of old, enthusiastic about his music, anxious to please and to be appreciated. He looked about thirty pounds heavier, with a few gray hairs here and there, but he was still blowing his potent horn, still getting and giving his musical kicks via one of the country's greatest bands.

It was quite a sight to see and quite a sound to hear!

Isham Jones

"THE other night I spent a few hours at the radio, listening to dance bands. I heard 458 chromatic runs on accordions, 911 'telegraph ticker' brass figures, 78 sliding trombones, 4 sliding violas, 45 burps into a straw, 91 bands that played the same arrangement on every tune, and 11,006 imitations of Benny Goodman."

So began an article by famed arranger Gordon Jenkins in the September, 1937, *Metronome*. Gordy had arranged for the Jones band for many years and, like many of its ex-members, had come to know, respect and love its music with a loyalty matched by very few big band alumni.

"These figures," Jenkins admitted, "are slightly exaggerated, but that was my personal impression. Slightly nauseated, I went to bed and lay for some time thinking about the 'good old days' and the Old Jones band. That, gents, was a band . . . writing for that band was fun, not work."

For pure, ungimmicked music and musicianship, there were few bands to match the one led by Isham Jones, a somber, long-faced gent who looked more like a strict manual arts teacher than a leader of one of the most romantic-sounding bands of all time.

As a kid I used to listen to the Isham Jones records of the twenties, and I'd been enthralled by their wonderfully rich ensemble sounds. In the mid-thirties the Jones band ranked as one of the most popular and polished of all the big bands, spotting in its personnel such future stars as trombonists Jack Jenney and Sonny Lee, trumpeters Peewee Erwin and George Thow, pianist Howard Smith and a lean saxist-vocalist named Woody Herman.

Woody was a part of the band the first time I heard it in person in New York's Lincoln Hotel in 1935. But he wasn't the most impressive part. What thrilled me was the pure, rich ensemble sound that had permeated so many of its recordings. Jones had a way of getting his men to phrase in long, flowing lines, so that they sounded as if they never inhaled. This warm, broad barrage was led by a magnificent trumpeter named Johnny Carlson, one of the truly great lead men, whose powerfully persuasive tone and phrasing carried the entire band. The full, robust ensemble effect was further enriched by Saxey Mansfield's big-toned tenor sax doubling the lead an octave below the trumpet, so

277

Isham Jones and His Orchestra. Jones is standing at extreme left; arranger Joe Bishop third from left, then trombonists Sonny Lee and Red Ballard and trumpeters Clarence Willard and Johnny Carlson. Featured tenor saxist, Saxey Mansfield, is seated second from left. Featured vocalist, Eddie Stone, is seated at far right.

that, in a way, the result was a gutsier, more masculine version of the Glenn Miller ensemble sound, which used a similar doubling technique.

Jenkins wrote many of the arrangements. Joe Bishop, who played tuba, penned some scores, too, plus several original songs, including "Blue Prelude." But the outstanding composer in the band was, of course, Jones, himself, a prolific songwriter responsible for a whole slew of hits, including "I'll See You in My Dreams," "It Had to Be You," "The One I Love Belongs to Somebody Else," "On the Alamo," "Swingin' Down the Lane," "You've Got Me Crying Again," "There Is No Greater Love," and the band's lovely theme song, "You're Just a Dream Come True." Jones had a fine ear for other writers' tunes: even before the song had any lyrics, he waxed the first hit version of Hoagy Carmichael's "Stardust."

Vocalists were important to any band that dealt so much in ballads, and Isham had some good romantic singers—Frank Sylvano, Frank Hazzard, Joe Martin and Woody. But by far the most important and distinctive voice in the Isham Jones band was that of Eddie Stone, whose cute, infectious, impish way of singing, a sort of "what-you-did-to-me-really-hurts-but-I'm-going-to-have-a-ball-anyway" approach, captivated the band's listeners both on records and in person. He remained with Jones for years and was one of the two singers in the band when I reviewed it in 1935.

Woody was the other one, and good as he was, he wasn't as impressive as little Eddie. To the best of my memory, Stone supplied the evening's only personality spark. Certainly none came from Jones, who waved a baton effectively but austerely, and who seemed to have difficulty communicating with both his audience and his men.

Even today his alumni speak of him with great reverence as a musician and as a bandmaster. Yet few ever felt really close to him, and some didn't like him at all. As Jenkins reports, "There was a musical affinity between Jones, the boys and myself that is far too uncommon today. . . . The picture of that big farmer standing up there, molding seventeen boys (half of whom probably weren't speaking to him at the time) into one gorgeous unit, was something I'll never forget."

And the band, itself, was one that other bandleaders didn't forget either. Often I'd hear one of them, who was having second thoughts about going too far out as a swing band, say such things as "What we really should do is try to sound like the old Isham Jones band." Gene Krupa was emphatic about trying; so was Lionel Hampton. Neither one could bring it off, however. Probably the closest were Horace Heidt (for a while), Dick Jurgens, George Paxton, Eddy Howard and, naturally, the Jones Alumni Association, the Woody Herman band, when it first started.

Woody's achieved the sound because it had as its lead trumpeter Clarence Willard, who had played alongside Johnny Carlson in the Jones band and had learned Carlson's phrasing and unique use of the vibrato. Also, for a while the alumni played the Jones-styled arrangements of Joe Bishop. And, of course, there were Woody's vocals.

Some years after disbanding in 1936, Isham came out of his self-imposed retirement and decided to try again. But his band of the early forties was not in a class with the one he had led before, and it made little musical or commercial impression. Thus, "Ish" (pronounced with a long "I"), who passed away on October 19, 1956, at the age of sixty-two, is best remembered for his lovely songs and for his orchestras of the early thirties, which Gordon Jenkins once called "the greatest sweet ensemble of that time or any other time."

The Isham Jones Orchestra at Denver's Elitch's Gardens in June, 1931.

ISHAM JONES AND HIS ORCHESTRA
ELITCHS GARDENS
JUNE 1931

Dick Jurgens

ONE of the most attractive and certainly one of the most musical of the many bands that used to play the mickey-mouse oriented Aragon and Trianon Ballrooms in Chicago was that of a handsome second-rate trumpeter out of California named Dick Jurgens.

The difference between his band and most of the others that dispensed the rather infantile-sounding music that usually filled those Chicago ballrooms was that Dick's played good music. Only occasionally did it spew forth the kittenish little novelty gimmicks required to satisfy many of the unsophisticates who frequented Andrew Karzas' two immensely successful dance emporiums. The Jurgens band maintained its musical integrity, refusing to splatter its sounds with any whining saxes, slurping trombones or spastic trumpets. Instead, Jurgens, who first attracted attention in San Francisco, concentrated on pure, rich ensemble sounds.

His band was blessed with a wonderful trumpeter named Eddie Kuehler, whose great tone and facile command of his horn enabled the band to achieve

Dick Jurgens

some especially attractive dynamics. In this it was abetted by the consistently good, if never overly stimulating arrangements of pianist Lou Quadling.

It was a romantic-looking band. Jurgens, who sometimes played a fourth trumpet and who had a tendency to overact as a comedian, was handsome, athletic, collegiate-looking, and his men deported themselves well. It was also a romantic-sounding band; its lush ensemble phrasings served as good emotional and dynamic contrast for its warm, often intimate-sounding vocalists.

One of these was Eddy Howard. He wasn't a romantic-looking sort—he had the cheery, pink-cheeked vanilla appearance one might expect of a clerk in a country store—but he sang with tremendous warmth and expression. His was a crooning style, a sort of modernized, non-nasal version of Rudy Vallee, that enthralled his listeners, including many who preferred jazz to ballads but who nevertheless recognized a goodly amount of musicianly feeling and phrasing in Eddy's work. His big hit with Jurgens was a sentimental ballad called "My Last Goodbye," but he also sang numerous other, lighter and sometimes swinging songs quite well.

After Eddy left to start his own band, Jurgens began featuring a different type of singer—a tall, handsome, virile, curly-haired baritone whom Perry Como had recommended vociferously to Dick. This was Harry Cool, who sang out in a ringing, masculine, semilegitimate voice but succeeded in projecting, because of his well-controlled dynamics, the aura of intimacy required of pop ballad vocalists. There was another featured singer in the band, too, a grinning, seemingly ever-joyous guitarist named Buddy Moreno, who on novelty and uptempoed tunes projected a pleasant personality and voice to match. Like Howard, Buddy also left to start his own band, eventually settling down in St. Louis, Missouri, to pursue a successful radio career.

In a way, Jurgens became responsible for one of the era's most popular songs. It seems that while Dick was working at the Aragon Ballroom in Chicago, he'd drop by at noon to answer fan mail. One day he heard a song that sounded like "If I Could Be With You" coming from the bandstand piano. He investigated and found that a young mortician, who worked next door, had received permission to use the piano during his lunch hour. His name was Elmer Albrecht, and Dick became so enamoured of the tune he was playing that he had it arranged for his band. It had no lyrics, so they called it simply "Elmer's Tune." Jurgens, now living in Sacramento, California, recalls that "one day I got a call from Glenn Miller. He said he'd heard the tune, wanted to record it and asked if it had any lyrics. I told him 'No,' but I'd have some written." So Jurgens called in Sammy Gallop, a well-known lyricist living in Chicago, who immediately came up with a set of lyrics that Miller recorded and helped turn the tune into a huge hit that remained on the Hit Parade for seventeen weeks.

Aside from its music, the Jurgens band also went in for some pure hokum, split-second timing comedy effects less suited to dance dates than to its theater appearances. Had Jurgens invested as much time and money into his music as he did into his novelties, he might have had himself a consistently top-notch musical band—in which case he probably wouldn't have been so consistently welcome in the Aragon and Trianon. And who's to fault the man for putting that sort of security above artistry?

Sammy Kaye

THE first time I ever had anything to do with Sammy Kaye was at three o'clock one morning in 1936 when he startled me and my entire family out of our sleep with a phone call. Sammy and I had never met, but somebody had told him I knew of a good girl singer and he wasn't about to let a mere night's sleep deter him from immediate action.

Such an inconsiderate attack on my dreams could have prejudiced me forever against Kaye's music. But it didn't. It didn't have to. Just listening to his band was enough.

In those days, taking potshots at Sammy Kaye was considered both fun and the right thing for any self-respecting jazz musician or critic to do. For his was one of the foremost examples of what we sneeringly referred to as mickey-mouse music. Where the phrase came from, I don't know, except perhaps that the music sounded as manufactured and mechanical as Walt Disney's famous character—and projected just about as much emotional depth!

From the start, Kaye proved himself to be, above all, an astute businessman. He'd gained a degree in Civil Engineering at Ohio University and, after establishing his band in Cleveland, had engineered an uncivil attack on the reputation of swing with his catchy though inaccurate slogan, "Swing and Sway with Sammy Kaye."

At that time, the slogan was better than the music. "The 'swing' of Sammy Kaye," I wrote in November, 1938, after having heard the band during its New York debut at the Commodore Hotel, "can truthfully be described as follows." There ensued a blank space of several inches, plus a sarcastic notation: "End of description of Sammy Kaye's swing." Then the article pointed out that "not a thing is left to imagination or inspiration, the total result being a magnificently trained and exceedingly unoriginal group of musicians."

Musical specifics followed: the exaggerated vibrato of the first trumpet, the gnawing glissing of the trombones, the mechanical crunch of the rhythm section and the individual defects of several of the musicians. The review also blasted the band's appearance—"stiff mess jackets which had gone out with laughing saxophones"—and the lack of showmanship—"the band runs through everything very mechanically with long faces, never seeming even to enjoy its own music."

The last observation might have been quite true, because not many self-respecting musicians enjoyed playing in mickey-mouse bands—that is, if they were at all capable of playing better. Now, more than a generation later, as I look back from the vantage point of a more mature person, able to evaluate things in a broader perspective, I realize one thing about all those nasty comments: I was absolutely right!

But as horrendous as the band sounded from a musical point of view, its commercial appeal cannot be denied. For this it had just one person to thank: Sammy Kaye, even though some people insisted that Kay Kyser also should be thanked, because Sammy was using the same sort of singing titles and

segues into vocal choruses that Kyser had been featuring for several years.

But Sammy's success can be laid to more than mere gimmicks. For Kaye always kept his ear attuned to the times and to the dancers. He was adept at setting ideal tempos for dancing, at mixing his selections to get the most out of his sets, at pacing each set so that there would never be a lull between numbers, at fronting his band with grace and charm, and at supplying satisfying sounds for those unable to appreciate and/or comprehend what the more musical bands were playing.

It was as a stage band that his was especially successful, and here again Sammy gets the credit. He was never content merely to play one number after another; instead, he constantly worked up new production routines that would bring him and his band into closer contact with his audiences.

His major success in this endeavor was his "So You Want to Lead a Band" series, which began in theaters and eventually reached television. Members of the audience were invited to conduct the band—and make fools of themselves as they competed for such fabulous prizes as Sammy Kaye batons!

Sammy was smart in another way. Though he played clarinet, he didn't feature himself on the instrument, for a Benny Goodman or an Artie Shaw he definitely was not. In fact, he seldom spotted any instrumentalists, leaving almost all solo honors to his horde of vocalists. At one time, in 1941, Sammy featured a total of six singers: George Brandon, Maury Cross, Marty McKenna, Tommy Ryan, Charlie Wilson and Arthur Wright. One of Sammy's singing mainstays, Jimmy Brown, had left the band by then, claiming to be fed up with mickey-mouse music and to want to sing with a swing band. Whom do you think he joined? Blue Barron!

During 1941 the Kaye band played a highly successful engagement at Frank Dailey's Meadowbrook. Swing was as big as ever, and again Sammy was smart enough to make the most of a good situation. For his "Afternoon at Meadowbrook" concerts he brought in several outstanding swing stars, including Gene Krupa, Roy Eldridge and Teddy Wilson. Some years later he also hired Milt Buckner, Lionel Hampton's swinging pianist-arranger, to contribute a few scores to the band's library. Moreover, Kaye notes that he didn't always box himself in with his highly stylized routines. "On our three biggest record hits," he points out, referring to "Daddy," "Harbor Lights" and "It Isn't Fair" (which featured the pulsating, well-greased voice of Don Cornell, the band's most illustrious graduate), "we didn't even use any of those singing intros. We were really more versatile than many people realized."

It has been reported that once, when Benny Goodman and Sammy Kaye were playing in the same city, Benny visited Sammy backstage and suggested that the two of them play some clarinet duets together. How well they fared, or whether Sammy even accepted Benny's invitation, has never been confirmed. But it is interesting to note that, despite the vast difference in their approach to music, Kaye and Goodman did have certain common traits:

Sammy

both were completely self-made men and as such men usually do, each demanded and expected a great deal from those who worked for him.

Making mickey-mouse music was serious business for Sammy. For those of us who scoffed at this style, this may have been hard to believe, but Marty Oscard, an excellent musician who played lead sax in the Kaye band for several years, points out that the precision of the outfit was tremendous. "Sammy knew *just* what he wanted and he worked like a dog to get it." The band held arduous rehearsals, and at least some of the musicians took great pride in the results. "I remember sitting there in the saxes," adds Oscard, "and just waiting for Dale Cornell, the lead trumpeter, to make a mistake. Once I sat there for a week and he never hit a single bad note!"

Such intense devotion to precision could, of course, have been one of the reasons for the band's stiff sound. Oscard was right, Sammy did work hard. And so did his men. I recall attending a rehearsal backstage at the Capitol Theater in New York and being utterly amazed by the manner in which Sammy, wearing a silk dressing gown and sporting a long cigarette holder, barked orders at his men. With the possible exception of Fred Waring's, his was the most dictatorial attitude I'd ever witnessed on the part of any band-leader, a factor that might explain why several years later almost the entire band left Kaye as a unit and attempted to carry on by themselves.

The move proved to be disastrous—for the men. They needed Kaye even more than he needed them. For Sammy had brought to the band world a highly developed business acumen and an amazing ability to win over people to his music. No doubt about it, he was a topflight businessman, who had sense enough to pay his men well, who always traveled first class (as did his musicians), and who was very much aware of what was going on outside the world of music.

My respect for Kaye as a businessman was reaffirmed in the late fifties when I was asked to serve as writer-producer of his television series. There I saw firsthand how shrewly he operated. But, more importantly, I found him to be much more vital, flexible and admirable than his music. I was especially impressed during one of those frequent staff meetings that plague most TV series when the show's packager, in a typical pep talk, tried to explain to us why we should do even better than Lawrence Welk. One of the so-called selling points was that Sammy's American lineage would be much more attractive to the general public than Welk's obviously foreign ancestry. "Hardly," commented Sammy quite candidly. "You see, I'm first generation Czechoslovakian."

Recently Sammy elaborated further to me about his foreign lineage. "I had an accent too," he explained. "In fact, it was so bad that back in Cleveland, when we started out at the Statler Hotel, a man named Mr. Henderson, who was the manager, took me aside and said he didn't want to hurt my feelings or anything like that, but he wondered, if he agreed to pay for them, whether I'd take elocution lessons. I did, and they helped me a lot. But now sometimes I wonder, when I look at Welk's success, if I really didn't make a mistake taking those lessons!"

Over the years Kaye had really mellowed. Through smart investments in publishing, bowling alleys and other businesses, he had become wealthy and he could afford to relax. Perhaps that was why he offered surprisingly little resistance when several of us on the production staff, whom he treated most respectfully, kept suggesting better quality music in place of the rigid mickey-mouse diet. By the time the forty-week series had been completed, the Sammy Kaye band was beginning to play some surprisingly good dance music.

This must have opened Sammy's ears, because from then on his recordings began to veer farther and farther from his ricky-tick style. He began to use voices and strings and to produce thoroughly legitimate musical sounds. And his records began to sell better than they had in years, even though most of them didn't bear the slightest resemblance to "Swing and Sway with Sammy Kaye."

Come to think of it, some of them even swung!

Hal Kemp

ONE of the greatest sweet bands of all time started out as a jazz band. This was Hal Kemp's orchestra, whose style during and directly after its under-graduate days at the University of North Carolina bore little resemblance to the soft, soothing sounds that made it the most popular of sweet bands during the opening days of the big band era.

Despite a couple of brilliant jazz trumpeters in Bunny Berigan and Jack Pettis and a corps of dedicated, hard-working musicians, the band converted comparatively few people during its first years. One of its most influential rooters in America was another ex-collegian-turned-leader, Fred Waring, who

The Hal Kemp Band in the early thirties
Front row: Kemp, Harold (Porky) Dankers, Ben Williams, Saxey Dowell
Second row: John Scott Trotter, Skinnay Ennis, Earl Geiger,
Fred Train, Gus Mayhew
Back row: Eugene (Pinkie) Kintzel, Paul (Pappy) Weston

lent the band financial and spiritual support. And across the sea, an even more influential fan became a staunch convert when the band toured his country during the early thirties. He was then Prince George; soon thereafter he became King George of England.

It wasn't until 1934, however, when it played a lengthy engagement in Chicago's Blackhawk Restaurant and developed its highly intimate and individualistic style, that Kemp's band really began to catch on in America. From Chicago it returned to New York, where it had once played with fairly successful results at the Hotel Manger (now the Taft). This time, however, it went into the Madhattan Room of the Hotel Pennsylvania, and there it scored a tremendous triumph.

It was a wonderfully smooth, sophisticated-sounding outfit that twice was voted Best Sweet Band by *Metronome*'s readers. It played more softly and more sensuously than any other band of the times, and its mellow, intimate, romantic moods mesmerized the college kids who swarmed into the Pennsylvania's low-ceilinged basement room. But unlike other sweet bands of the day whose music was either dull or unmusical, Kemp's produced some unusually colorful and attractive sounds.

Its style was deceptively simple, and for a good reason. John Scott Trotter, who created that style, and Hal Mooney, who followed him as chief arranger, agreed that the Kemp band, though a happy group (Trotter called it "a traveling fraternity"), was by no means bursting with topflight musicians. According to Mooney, "there were only two good readers in the band, Kemp and Trotter. Many times they'd have to sing the parts to the musicians so that they could learn them."

Part of the style centered around the muted trumpets, which played many staccato triplets. "Now I can see why they played that way," reasons Mooney. "The guys didn't have really good, legitimate tones, and they couldn't sustain notes too well." Trotter stated it even more eloquently and more positively: "The band created and kept its style because it was limited by its musicians' limitations."

The clipped phrasing of the trumpets (Johnny Mercer accordingly referred to Kemp's as "the typewriter band") was just part of a style that also emphasized a series of simple, sustained, unison clarinet notes. These notes were often blown through large megaphones. The men would put their fingers through holes in the sides, a gimmick Trotter credited to one of the band's earliest saxophonists, Joe Gillespie, play extremely softly, and out would come some lovely, round tones that contrasted effectively with the muted brass.

The clarinet's languid sounds fitted in with Kemp's personality. Hal, who played reeds, was long and lanky—and languid, too. He always struck me as being especially easygoing, though Trotter once pointed out that Hal had a strong but controlled temper. He projected a pleasant, stereotyped southern charm, complete with a smiling "Hi ya'll" plus plenty of slaps on the back. Kemp was able to concentrate on winning friends because he could leave the less pleasant tasks to his especially able manager, Alex Holden, thus avoiding the risk of tarnishing his "friendly neighbor" image.

Kemp's relaxed and casual air was reflected by the band's most popular vocalist, Skinnay Ennis, who doubled on drums, which he'd leave, with little appreciable harm to the rhythm, to come down to the mike and sing. Skinnay's style was both haunting and sexy. Actually, he talked more than he sang his lyrics, delivering them like a shy little boy who became breathless at the very thought of having to mention such a word as "kiss" or "love." Yet convincing he most certainly was, and, along with Casa Loma's Kenny Sargent, he ranked as one of the best of the early big band swooners.

Skinnay, who was well nicknamed, was featured on a batch of the band's best Brunswick sides, such as "Hands Across the Table," "You're the Top," "Heart of Stone," "The Touch of Your Lips," "Lamplight," "It's Easy to Remember," "Got a Date with an Angel," the band's opening theme (the closer was "How I Miss You"), which began with the familiar "Climbing up the ladder . . . of love . . . to find . . . the one . . . w-h-o . . . w-a-i-ts . . . f-o-r . . . m-e-e-e-e."*

The Kemp band, according to Trotter, "seemed for some reason or other to be inspired by show tunes." It played many of them, for, as Hal Mooney pointed out, "publishers kept giving them to us first." It also played occasional novelties, such as Reginald Forsythe's "Serenade to a Wealthy Widow" and several items of dubious distinction, like "Three Little Fishes," written by Saxey Dowell, the band's jolly, rotund tenor saxist, who sang most of the novelty songs.

There were several other good vocalists with the band in the mid-thirties— Bob Allen, who sang romantically in a more legitimate manner than Ennis, and Maxine Gray, an attractive brunette, whom Trotter described as being

* Lyric by Ramond Klages, melody by Jesse Greer. Copyright 1926 (copyright renewal 1954) Robbins Music Corp., New York. Used by permission.

Kemp with vocalists
Bob Allen and
Maxine Gray

like "the prettiest high school girl in a town of fifty thousand people" and who sang effectively if somewhat a bit too melodramatically, and another girl, a redhead, named Deane Janis.

The band also featured a couple of very good musicians. One of these was the very important, in fact irreplaceable, lead trumpeter, Earl Geiger, who phrased softly yet with tremendous warmth and emotion, producing a fascinating feeling of positive passive persuasion. The other was a brilliant trombonist named Eddie Kusborski, who played many fine solos.

The second trombonist, Gus Mayhew, doubled as arranger along with Trotter, who also played piano. But John Scott left in January of 1936, and with him went much of the relaxed charm of the band. Exactly what caused the change, almost imperceptible at first, is hard to determine. It could have been that Kemp needed Trotter's impeccable taste more than he realized, or it might have been that with bands like Goodman's and Shaw's attracting the kids, Kemp wanted to prove that his, too, could swing. Unfortunately it seldom did.

The departure in 1936 of the fast-living "passive persuader," Earl Geiger, left a deep void. His replacement, Clayton Cash, a better all-round musician than Geiger, tried very hard to duplicate Earl's gentle trumpet style. But nobody, not even someone as good as Cash, could play so delicately, yet so surely, as Geiger did. Geiger was simply unique.

In the later thirties the band grew less and less stylized, though its new arrangers, Hal Mooney and Lou Busch, did retain some of the distinguishing gimmicks. But they also went after a fuller, more legitimate big band sound. Instead of four muted brass they used five open horns. Instead of subtone clarinets they featured harder-blowing saxes. And when Skinnay departed to start his own band, Kemp lost one of his most important identifications.

Ennis left with Kemp's blessings, and Saxie Dowell soon followed suit. Ironically, Skinnay appeared shortly thereafter as leader of the orchestra on the Pepsodent radio series with Bob Hope, which was on the air at precisely the same time that Hal and his band broadcast for Chesterfield.

The band vacillated thereafter between being a swing and a sweet band. There was one spell when it seemed to be making a serious attempt to recapture the moods and the fans of its mid-thirties era. For a while it enlisted the support of a very soft, soothing singer named Nan Wynn, and she helped. But soon thereafter it began to veer more toward extrovertism at the same time hiring a talented singer, soon-to-turn-actress, who projected more than other Kemp singers had. Her name was Janet Lafferty. It was Alex Holden who changed it to Janet Blair.

By the summer of 1940, Janet had departed. In July, two of the band's most dependable veterans, trumpeter Cash and trombonist Eddie Kusborski, also left. *Metronome*, in whose sweet-band poll Kemp finished ninth that year (never before had he finished lower than third), announced the changes with a headline that read "Kemp Plans New Blood," with the ensuing article noting that "stars leave in move to freshen up the style of the outfit that was once voted America's finest sweet band. The morale of the band," the article concluded, "was known to have been at a low ebb. Kemp apparently feels that new, eager talent will give his outfit a much-needed spiritual lift."

Unfortunately Hal had very little time left to improve either his band's morale or its music. On December 19, while driving from one engagement in Los Angeles to another in San Francisco, his car and another collided head-on near Madera, California. Kemp suffered eight broken ribs, one of which pierced a lung. Pneumonia developed, and two days later Kemp died.

Ennis and Trotter rushed to San Francisco to help out with the band. Bob Allen stepped in for a short time as leader. But no one could replace Hal, and shortly thereafter the band broke up. A few months later, Porky Dankers, one of the original saxophonists, reassembled many of the men, and they tried making a comeback under the leadership of singer Art Jarrett. But the experiment didn't work out, and the Hal Kemp band passed forever from the big band scene, with only its many wonderful recordings to preserve the memory of some of the prettiest and most tasteful dance music of all time.

Hal with saxist-singer Saxie Dowell and petite singer Judy Starr in May, 1938.

Stan Kenton

TALK to a baseball fan about Stan the Man and he'll know you're referring to Stan Musial. But mention Stan the Man to any jazz buff or big band enthusiast outside St. Louis and he'll know you're talking about Stan Kenton.

Stan happened to be quite a man, too—six and a half feet of him. Six and a half feet of nervous, exhausting energy that once produced some of the most thrilling, some of the most aggravating, some of the most impressive, some of the most depressive, some of the most exciting, some of the most boring and certainly some of the most controversial sounds, music and/or noise ever to emanate from any big band.

A friend of mine, an arranger named Ralph Yaw, had tipped me off on the Kenton band when it was still an unknown infant. In March of 1941 he had written in a letter from Los Angeles:

> Been meaning to write ever since getting here, but you know how it is.
>
> The reason is in connection with a band I'm working with. This band is something quite special and different. Stanley Kenton is the leader and I am working with him. We do the arranging and I think we have cooked up something new in style.
>
> However, I will not take time to try to describe it, but only say that a swell new treatment of saxes and a couple of other style tricks do it. The saxes are treated to my mind in the right way for the first time. It really scares me.

The band debuted a few months later—Memorial Day—in Balboa Beach, where seven years before young Stanley Kenton had been playing piano in Everett Hoagland's then swinging band. When I arrived in L.A. in the summer of 1941, one of the first things I did was to look up the Kenton band. I found it in the KHJ radio studio, where it was doing a live broadcast, which the announcer kept telling his listeners was actually emanating from Balboa Beach! Several nights later I drove out to Balboa to spend the first of several evenings listening to the band and to gather material for its first major review, a well-reserved rave—for the most part.

"Within the Stan Kenton band," the review noted, "nestles one of the greatest combinations of rhythm, harmony and melody that's ever been assembled by one leader." Then, after crediting Kenton for most of the band's good points, including his arrangements, while also extolling several of the young musicians, especially bassist Howard Rumsey, lead trumpeter Frank Beach and also saxist Jack Ordean, I faulted the band for "continual blasting. It's great to screech with complete abandon," the review said, "but you've got to screech at the right time." It also suggested that Stan "curb his gesticulative enthusiasm" and in general recommended "greater restraint."

One thing I found out immediately: there's nothing more vociferous than a Kenton fan. The mail started coming in at once, faulting me for faulting the band. Stan himself, I understood later, also objected to my criticism, and our relationship became tenuous, with only slight variations ever after. I must admit once and for all that I have never become a complete Kenton band convert, for no matter how great his bands have been musically, their emotional impact has for me too often been blunted by an air of self-consciousness, sometimes combined with pompousness, and too often an inability to swing freely. Never, though, have I failed to admire Kenton for his courage, his tenacity, his sincerity, his thoughtfulness and his complete belief that what he is doing was right.

Kenton's unbending approach always made him quite susceptible to some rather caustic criticism. Thus in 1941, in his first radio review of the band,

Barry Ulanov admitted that it had "that combination of heavy voicings and staccato phrasings down pat. But there's no reason why so formidable an organization must always sound like a moving-man grunting under the weight of a concert grand."

The Kenton style was indeed heavy and ponderous, especially on ballads. Some people, including some critics, insisted that Kenton's projected the swinging approach of the Jimmie Lunceford band. Both, they pointed out, played heavily accented music. I think this evaluation misses the one basic difference: the Lunceford band always played and sounded relaxed, rolling along easily with the beat instead of fighting and trying to push it ahead, as Kenton's did. One band moved like a fleet halfback, the other like a muscle-bound lineman.

In his *Treasury of Jazz* Eddie Condon wrote that "every Kenton record sounds to me as though Stan signed on three hundred men for the date and they were all on time. Music of his school, in my opinion, ought only to be played close to elephants and listened to only by clowns." But, Condon admitted, "It's a real accomplishment to take that many men and make them sound ruly."

Kenton's musicians have sounded "ruly" because they not only believed in his music, but also believed in him as a leader. Consequently, they worked especially hard for him. Few leaders have been accorded as much love and respect as Kenton achieved, not only because of his dedication and his talent, but also because of the consideration he accorded his musicians.

Shelly Manne, who for several years handled probably the most difficult assignment of all musicians in the Kenton band, that of trying to swing it from the drums, emoted words of high praise several years after he had departed the group, words that undoubtedly express the feelings of many other men who played for Kenton. Said Shelly: "He was so personal, always one of the fellows and yet nobody ever lost any respect for him. If the guys needed money, Stan would lend it to them. Everybody really wanted to work for what he was working. And the spirit of the band was wonderful. It was such a clean atmosphere. You always felt that you were working for something that mattered instead of just jamming 'Tea for Two' or 'Perdido.'

"The way Stan encouraged everybody was so wonderful, too. He was always encouraging young arrangers. If a guy joined the band, he'd never judge him on first appearances, the way most leaders do. He'd let him play for a while until he settled down. Then Stan would make up his mind.

"And he was so wonderful with the public, too. He never fluffed anybody off."

But Stan wasn't without faults. During his early days especially he showed great stubbornness, often refusing to face certain harsh realities and insisting upon doing only what he, in his idealistic way, believed he should do, regardless of what anybody else thought or felt.

This attitude, of course, tied in directly with a certain obstinacy that he admitted to as a youth when his mother wanted him to learn piano and he

The Kenton Band in the Café Rouge of the Hotel Pennsylvania (1946):
guitarist Bob Ahern; bassist Eddie Safranski; drummer Shelly Manne;
trumpeters Johnny Anderson, Buddy Childers, Ray Wetzel, Ken Hanna,
Chico Alvarez; trombonists Skip Layton, Harry Forbes, Kai Winding,
Milt Bernhart, Bart Varsalona; saxists Red Dorris, Boots Mussilli, Al Anthony,
Bob Gioga (also road manager), Bob Cooper

insisted on playing ball instead. It took a lengthy visit from two cousins who played jazz at his house to convince him that music was after all what he really wanted to do.

Like any good man, Kenton was quite willing to admit his mistakes. In 1947, after he had reorganized, he told me, during a lengthy interview what he thought had been wrong with his last band. "It was much too stiff," he said. "Some people with lots of nervous energy could feel what we were doing, but nobody else could. Our music seemed out of tune with the people; we just had no common pulse. I guess I just had the wrong goddam feel for music."

Kenton, who once threatened to quit the music business to become a psychiatrist, may have been unduly hard on himself, for his band had made a fantastic number of converts, many of them through his popular recordings, which began in late 1941 with "Adios," and "Taboo" and "Gambler's Blues," the last a rehash of "St. James Infirmary" on which Stan "sang." Even more popular were his 1943 recordings of his theme, "Artistry in Rhythm," and "Eager Beaver," one of his most swinging sides. New, more experienced, not completely Kenton-indoctrinated personnel had dispelled much of the band's stiffness by then; only three men remained from the unit that had been formed just a little over two years earlier.

But the band's swingingest sides were still to come. In the spring of 1944, Anita O'Day joined Kenton and during the same period Dave Matthews and Stan Getz came in on tenor saxes, with Dave also writing some of the arrangements. In May, with Anita singing, the band recorded one of its most famous and infectious-sounding sides, "And Her Tears Flowed like Wine," and a swinging "Are You Livin', Old Man?"

Anita stayed with the band for less than a year. She was followed by a cute blonde whose singing resembled Anita's, though it lacked both Anita's sparkle and intonation. This was June Christy, bright, friendly and very well-liked by her compatriots, who recorded such commercial sides as "Tampico" and "Willow Weep for Me." A young tenor saxist, Bob Cooper, also joined Kenton around this time; later he and June were married.

As the war ended and more musicians became available, the Kenton music improved even more. So did its popularity. It scored a big hit at the Sherman Hotel in Chicago, the first really great reception it had received in a major room outside Los Angeles. In September the band returned to New York and registered just as impressively at the Paramount Theater and at the Pennsylvania Hotel, where Barry Ulanov reviewed it. "Stan had been wandering musically," he noted, "playing more and more ballads, going in for more and more production numbers, and, consequently, playing less and less of the kind of galvanic jazz which was first associated with his name. The wandering years are over. Stan is back to the kind of jazz he knows, feels and is best able to play . . . and his band swings more subtly now and, as a result, connects."

Stan and June Christy

Eddie Safranski had joined the band by then on bass, and his playing made a big difference. Vido Musso and his tenor sax were also there, and they played important roles on one of the band's biggest hits, "Artistry Jumps." And soon came more stellar musicians, like trombonist Kai Winding, drummer Shelly Manne and arranger Pete Rugolo, pushing the Kenton band toward musical heights it had never been able to attain previously.

Rugolo, serious, bespectacled and highly imaginative, made the biggest difference. Not only did he write distinctive arrangements, giving the band an ever clearer identity, but he also took a good deal of the load off Stan, with whom he became very friendly, establishing a relationship similar to that of Duke Ellington and Billy Strayhorn.

In January, 1946, Kenton was declared Band of the Year by the editors of *Look* magazine. Twelve months later, *Metronome*'s editors, who had never been complete Kenton converts, accorded the band the same honor.

In the same issue they ran an article headed "Bands Busting Up Big" and listed eight top dance orchestras (Stan's not included) that had decided to disband during the preceding months.

But Stan wasn't discouraged. Perhaps the era of the big bands that played for dancing and strictly for the public may have ended, but Stan's wasn't one of those bands. He continued to have faith in his more specialized, modern approach. "Soon there'll be no more 'in the middle' bands," he predicted at the time, "no more of those that try to play something new for a few minutes and then settle back into the old way because it's commercial. The pace is much too fast for that sort of thing. . . . Quite frankly, I think that

*Stan and
Pete Rugolo*

if the commercial bands try to compete with the more modern bands, they'll wind up making asses of themselves."

Stan often came on strong like that. He was thoroughly convinced that what he and his men were doing was the right and perhaps the only thing, and he spoke out all over the country for what he believed in. Spoke out and spoke on and on and on. I can't recall any bandleader who ever did a greater selling job for his music than Stan Kenton did. He was a press agent's delight, a constant joy to his equally voluble, omnipresent PR man, Milton Karle. He was forever visiting disc jockeys, dropping in at record shops and granting interviews anywhere, anytime with anyone who would listen to his impassioned diatribes. His highly contagious and often overpowering enthusiasm frequently carried him away too, as he rambled on about his music, his philosophy and various other subjects. Many of his interviews turned into monologues as the sentences poured out, seemingly without any punctuation except exclamation points, which he'd drop in all over the place.

He knew he had a selling job to do, and he relished it. "If you ask any ten people on the street," he pointed out, "if they have ever heard of Stan Kenton, only a couple of them will say 'yes.' We have to try to get the other eight. And the only way I can see to do it is to make myself a personality and take my band along."

The big bands as a group may have started to fade away in 1947. But not Stan Kenton's. He kept building bigger and more complex units, which played bigger and more complex works. He veered more and more from the dance band field and began concentrating almost exclusively on concerts, bringing greater satisfaction not only to himself but to those who came to listen but seldom to dance.

There were times when he was successful; there were times when he failed. But always he kept up that indomitable spirit. Perhaps his enthusiasm was not as intense and as pervasive as before. Perhaps he listened more as the monologues ebbed and the dialogues flowed.

In the sixties, he and I participated in a dialogue. Looking back at his music, especially his ballads, he said, "There was just too much tension, but I'm rid of that now. . . . At my age [he was then nearing fifty] I've finally found out what is and what isn't important. I used to try to prove every point. Now I'm concentrating on those that really mean something to me.

Concentrate Stan did, as hard as he possibly could, for almost two decades more. His spirit never flagged, as he kept trying to prove all the musical and philosophical points that mattered to him. The pace was literally killing. In 1977, after an engagement, he fell in a parking lot and suffered a severe skull fracture that required a lengthy hospitalization. Upon his release, he was warned to slow down. He never heeded that warning, and on August 17, 1979, he suffered a terrible stroke. He lingered for just eight days more, and one of the big bands' greatest innovators was gone.

Wayne King

THE kids may have wanted Glenn Miller; the swingers Count Basie; the squares Sammy Kaye; and the bluebloods Meyer Davis. But for the Sixty-Five-and-Over Clubs the big band had to be Wayne King's. The gout, arthritis, varicose veins and even bunions seemed to disappear whenever the Waltz King emitted those lovely, soft, satiny sounds that brought back the reassuring aura of the wondrous yesteryears—brought it back simply and gracefully and with all the color and excitement of a bowl of stewed prunes.

It hadn't always been thus for this bright, self-assured saxophonist. In the late twenties and early thirties King had led a good, all-round dance orchestra, which featured a refreshingly light beat—this time in straight four-four tempo —and an attractive sax section led by his facile alto. The group played regularly at the Aragon Ballroom in Chicago, and it was there that Wayne developed his attachment to the waltz.

Lady Esther's King

During the early thirties, according to big band buff Gary Stevens, a brother and his sister were manufacturing cosmetics in the back of their house. To advertise their product, they hired King and his orchestra for a weekly radio show for which the band, including its leader, was purportedly paid a cool five hundred dollars per show. Four years later "The Lady Esther Serenade" had emerged as one of the nation's top radio programs; the brother and sister had a large factory, and King was earning around fifteen thousand dollars a week from his top radio series.

The program was ideal for the client. Kids in those days used makeup sparingly, but the oldsters poured it on. King's schmaltzy music, interspersed with poetry readings, first by Phil Stewart and later by Franklyn McCormack, was made to order for elderly spinsters and matrons who bought large doses of the sponsor's powdered sunshine to spread over their fading faces.

Always and generously featured was King's soft, reassuring sax. Had he any desire to revert to the more lively music he had once played, he managed to suppress it sufficiently to sustain his new image. He was a good musician; his band was strongly disciplined; and he could afford to pay his men enough to stay with him, despite any musical or personal differences. Such a steady personnel made for excellent consistency, if nothing else.

King spent very little time in New York, perhaps because his ultra-homey style had less appeal for the more sophisticated dancers. But he did appear in many of the major hotels and ballrooms in other parts of the country, often attracting mature, well-heeled patrons. Having invested wisely in real estate and cattle, he soon became an immensely wealthy man.

During the war, King became an Army officer stationed in the Chicago area. Bob Eberly sang in his unit. So did Buddy Clark, who also made some records with King's band. After the war, Wayne remained quasi-active as a bandleader, his career reaching an emotional climax in 1964 when he returned to Chicago's Aragon Ballroom, where he had established such a fervent following, to lead his orchestra on that lavish dance emporium's shuttering night.

It was, according to a UPI dispatch, "a bitter-sweet farewell. . . . Grandmas and grandpas who did their courting under the Aragon's make-believe stars swayed to the strains of the Waltz King's theme song, 'The Waltz You Saved for Me.' "

It was just too bad that all of *their* grandmas and grandpas couldn't have been there too!

Andy Kirk

HE WAS a gentle man, a kind man, a happy man, an intelligent man and a talented man. He was Andy Kirk, who led one of the better swing bands, one that at times threatened to achieve greatness but which never quite reached the pinnacle it seemed to be constantly approaching.

Called "Andy Kirk and His Clouds of Joy," it was a band composed of good musicians, a band that for several years played outstanding arrangements, but a band that could be wonderful one minute, mediocre the next, wonderful again, only fair for a while and then suddenly wonderful once more.

Perhaps Andy was too lenient. Perhaps had he driven his men harder, they might have played better more often. But such an approach might also have destroyed the warm and relaxed rhythmic feeling that pervaded so much of the band's music.

The first time I heard the band in person, early in 1937 in Harlem's Savoy

Kirk, Pha Terrell,
Mary Lou Williams

Ballroom, I was greatly impressed by its simple swinging riffs both in ensemble passages and as backgrounds for soloists, of whom the most impressive was a girl, Mary Lou Williams. One of the most brilliant jazz pianists of all time, serious-looking, with long hair, a shy smile and surprisingly attractive buck teeth, she played in an Earl Hines manner, her solos mirroring phrases that the full band played in its arrangements—arrangements which she herself had written. There was also a good tenor saxist, Dick Wilson, a fine trombonist, Ted Donnelly, whom I always considered to be one of the most underrated of all musicians, and a steady, heady drummer, Ben Thigpen, whose son, Ed, years later, was to drum in the Oscar Peterson Trio.

The band had arrived in New York about the same time that Count Basie's had, but with much less ballyhoo. Organized in 1929 in Oklahoma, it had, like the Count's, established itself in Kansas City. It began to blossom there after 1933, when Mary Lou became a regular member. Married to Johnny Williams, a saxist with Kirk, she had occasionally sat in with the band and seemed so eager to play at all times that Andy nicknamed her "The Pest." Then, one day in 1933, the regular pianist showed up for a recording date reportedly in no condition to play. In desperation, Andy called for Mary Lou, and from then on "The Pest" remained seated on Kirk's piano bench until the middle of 1942, when she finally decided to seek a career as a solo performer.

Some of the band's greatest recordings featured Mary Lou, sides like "Froggy Bottom," "Walkin' and Swingin'," "Cloudy," which it recorded three different times, and "The Lady Who Swings the Band," which was a much more accurate identification tag for Mary Lou than "The Pest." She also wrote one of the most popular instrumentals of the period, "Roll 'Em," a boogie-woogie type of opus, which Benny Goodman's band parlayed into a hit.

Kirk also featured a singer named Pha (pronounced "Fay") Terrell, who sang the vocal on the band's most commercial record, "Until the Real Thing Comes Along." Pha was a rather unctuous singer (some of us used to call him Pha "Terrible"), but he knew how to sell a song. Less commercial but much more musical was another Kirk vocalist, Lunceford alumnus Henry Wells, who also played trombone and arranged, and who, for me, was one of the truly outstanding band singers of all time. (His "I'll Get By" and "Why Can't We Do It Again?" were especially outstanding.) His was a very smooth, musical style, and what he may have lacked in showmanship, he more than made up for in his phrasing. Barry Ulanov, with whom I didn't always hear ear-to-ear on singers, described Wells in the November, 1941, *Metronome* as "a remarkable, indeed a unique singer, quite unlike any other in popular music. He sings softly, gets a crooning tone, but Henry doesn't croon. He sings with all his voice, he's always got the control for the subtle dynamics of truly rich singing. . . . He is an expressive singer with a lovely voice, a smart musical head . . . who's absolutely untouched in the business." I agreed completely.

Henry Wells,
June Richmond,
Floyd Smith

Kirk varied his fare between ballads and jazz. The latter department was strengthened considerably both musically and commercially in 1939 by the addition of guitarist Floyd Smith, whose sensuous, insinuating version of "Floyd's Guitar Blues" became one of the band's most attractive assets. Andy also brought June Richmond into the band at about the same time, and the vivacious, carefree, ever-rhythmic singer added much aural and visual color.

The band was especially impressive in theaters. Here it would run through its well-prepared routines in truly professional fashion, with Kirk, who paced his programs exceedingly well, presiding over the festivities like a father immensely proud of his brood—happy, somewhat reserved, but definitely in charge at all times.

Musicians enjoyed playing for Kirk, and it was no wonder that some of the younger, better stars worked for him even though the pay could never have been very high. When Mary Lou left in 1942, Kenny Kersey took her place. Don Byas and later Al Sears came in to fill Dick Wilson's tenor chair, while several future trumpet stars, Hal (Shorty) Baker, Howard McGhee and Fats Navarro, all played in the Kirk brass section.

Andy was generous in the way he featured his men. Perhaps he was a bit too generous, a bit too lenient, believing, as he must have, that the best music comes from relaxed musicians. The potential for one of the great bands remained with the group throughout the years, and yet Kirk never quite realized that potential, perhaps because he could never quite create the musical militancy that in one form or another drove the most successful bands to the top.

When big bands started to fade from the scene, Andy went with them. But, unlike many other leaders, he found various other things to do. One of the most respected men in his community, he managed Harlem's Hotel Theresa for many years, settled into real estate for a while, then became a pillar of New York's musicians local. Throughout it all, he remained the same gentle and kind man whom we all admired so much.

Who said "Nice guys finish last"?

Gene Krupa

THINGS weren't going too well between Benny Goodman and Gene Krupa in early 1938. The drummer, who'd been with the band for almost three years, and his boss had not been agreeing on matters musical. And there had also been some personality clashes.

"Chances are you'll be hearing all sorts of rumors that Gene is planning to leave Benny tomorrow or the day after," I wrote in the March, 1938, *Metronome*. "The chances are even greater that these rumors won't be true and that Gene will continue to chew gum in the back of Benny's stand for a while to come," I added reassuringly.

A sad seer I proved to be: the day after the issue hit the stands, Gene Krupa left Benny Goodman after a blowup at the Earle Theater in Philadelphia.

By mid-April Gene, who had been saying that he'd like to lead a band someday, had whipped his new outfit into shape for its opening on the Steel Pier in Atlantic City. Convinced, despite my poor reporting, that Gene really did have a band, I showed up to hear what it was all about. And, as my May *Metronome* eye- and ear-witness report attests, I wasn't alone:

> About four thousand neighborhood and visting cats scratched and clawed for points of vantage in the Marine Ballroom of Atlantic City's Steel Pier on Saturday, April 16, and then, once perched on their pet posts, proceeded to welcome with most exuberant howls and huzzahs the first public appearance of drummer-man Gene Krupa and his newly formed jazz band. The way the felenic herd received, reacted to and withstood the powerful onslaughts of Krupa's quadruple "f" musical attacks left little doubt that Gene is now firmly entrenched at the helm of a swing outfit that's bound to be recognized very shortly as one of the most potent bits of catnip to be fed to the purring public that generally passes as America's swing contingent. . . . Throughout the evening the kids and the kittens shagged, trucked, jumped up and down and down and up, and often yelled and screamed at the series of solid killer-dillers.

Seldom had any band started off so well. Gene had been handed expert advice and assistance from two astute managers, Arthur Michaud and Johnny

Gluskin. And who were Arthur Michaud and Johnny Gluskin? They were the managers of Tommy Dorsey, Benny Goodman's big rival.

The association certainly didn't help close the Goodman-Krupa rift. It did, however, bring Gene two guests appearances on Tommy's radio commercial. He got none on Benny's. However, the former bandmates did get together some weeks later, again in Philadelphia, when Gene, whose band was playing at the Arcadia Restaurant, invited Benny and his group, which was appearing at a local theater, to drop by after work as his guests. There at the Arcadia, Benny, on the bandstand, publicly wished Gene the best of luck. A couple of days later the Goodman band played the Krupa band in baseball—just to prove there were no hard feelings. Or were there? The final score: Goodman, 19, Krupa 7!

Gene, who had cut some sides for Victor, left the company (Benny was still recording for it) and signed with Brunswick, where he proceeded to record several instrumentals, including "Blue Rhythm Fantasy," "Wire Brush Stomp" and "Apurksody," the band's theme. The title was a combination of "Krupa" spelled backward and the second half of "rhapsody."

A couple of Goodman alumni joined Krupa, Helen Ward for the first recording date, and Jimmy Mundy to head an arranging staff that for the following few years included Chappie Willett, Elton Hill and Fred Norman. The girl singer at the Steel Pier opener was a statuesque beauty named Jerry Kruger, who tried hard but unsuccessfully to sound like Billie Holliday. The only male vocals during the band's first year or so came from Leo Watson, who sounded like nobody but Leo Watson. His was probably the wildest of all "scat" singing styles—completely uninhibited, full of crazy nonsense syllables delivered at a fantastic pace in what sounded like nothing else but musical shorthand. And what's more, Leo looked and acted as wild as he sounded.

Gene was quite a showman too, with his gum chewing and his hair-waving and his grimaces and his torrid drumming. But this was merely Gene Krupa the showman. Gene Krupa the man was something else again, a sober, serious, self-disciplined gentleman, never to the point of stuffiness but at least to the point of handing the lie to those who thought of him as the wild, unreliable jazz musician stereotype. As a matter of fact, I have known few musicians as reliable and trustworthy as Gene. This knowledge is firsthand, because I worked with him on all four of the Timex All-Star Jazz TV shows and on every one of them he was not there merely *on* time but *ahead* of time, completely prepared for what he was to do and eager to make any further contributions that might be asked of him. His was the sort of sense of responsibility that has been all too rare—both in and out of the music field.

Krupa has always been very serious about his drumming. I recall our first interview in 1935. He had asked me to come up to his apartment in the Whitby on New York's West Forty-fifth Street. There in the small living room, in addition to the regular drum set, was a xylophone. And into the even smaller bedroom he had managed to cram two tympani. Obviously drumming meant much more than mere banging to him—it meant music in the strictest sense.

Years later he expounded his musical approach to drumming. "I'm concerned with all aspects of music," he said, "not just pure, plain driving rhythm. I try to produce sounds that blend with what's going on." Then he proceeded to explain how hitting different cymbals different ways, with the tip or the side of a stick, on the edge or near the center, can produce all-important musical nuances. And then he went on to reveal what most big band fans probably never suspected existed: a philosophy for playing a drum solo!

"Drum solos must have substance and continuity. Before I begin one, I try to have a good idea of what I'm going to play. Then, while I'm playing, I'll hum some sort of thing to myself, something maybe like 'boom-did-dee, boom-did-dee, boom-did-dee, boom' and follow that with another phrase that relates to the one I've just played. At the same time I keep on humming to myself so that each syllable becomes not only a separate beat but also a separate sound. That's very important, because drums, if they're to be musical, must produce sounds, not just noise. So a 'boom' could be a deep-sounding tom-tom, and a 'dang' a rim shot, and a 'paaah' could be a thin cymbal."

Gene always wanted his band to be a musical one. He hired some of the better young musicians around, like trumpeters Shorty Sherock and Corky Cornelius and saxists Sam Donahue, Sam Musiker and Clint Neagley. Cornelius and Donahue were to carry on a big romantic rivalry for Irene Daye, the very pretty and able girl singer who joined the band and was featured on some of its better recordings, such as the very swinging "Sweetheart, Honey, Darling, Dear" and the famous "Drum Boogie," which Gene has called "our most requested number through the years." Eventually Cornelius won out over Donahue, and when Corky left to join the Casa Loma Orchestra, Irene went with him.

Immediately Gene went from Daye to O'Day. Anita had been singing with a group in Chicago—and also playing some drums—and as soon as she joined the band a whole new Krupa era began. Anita was an outstanding stylist and a most definite personality. "She was a wild chick, all right," Gene recalled, "but how she could sing!" (Barry Ulanov, upon hearing her for the first time, commented in *Metronome*: "Anita O'Day should clear her throat.")

Her rhythmic, gutty, illegitimate style first confused but soon converted many listeners. Whereas most band girl singers had projected a very feminine or at least a cute girl image, Anita came across strictly as a hip jazz musician. She would dress in a suit similar to those of the musicians, and when she'd sing she'd come on strong, full of fire, with an either-you-like-me-or-you-don't-but-if-you-don't-it's-your-loss attitude.

Before she joined, the band's over-all approach had been fairly conservative. It had played a fair amount of jazz during personal appearances. But too often on records it produced just plain dull sides; in fact for a time, instead of creating something of its own, it tried cashing in on other artists' hits. Thus it recorded "I'll Never Smile Again" (Tommy Dorsey), "Yes, My Darling Daughter" (Dinah Shore), "Moonlight Serenade" (Glenn Miller) and "Tuxedo Junction" (Miller and Erskine Hawkins).

Anita provided the band with a new spark. But one every bit as brilliant came when Gene, much to his surprise and joy, landed one of the most electrifying trumpeters of all time, Roy Eldridge, "I used to follow him all the time," Gene told me several years ago. "He had a great little band, and I figured he was all set for good. Frankly, much as I loved him, I never dreamed he'd go with me. But one night in Chicago we were sitting and talking, and all of a sudden he said, 'Hey, I'd like to play with your band.' I said, 'Would you?' and he said, 'Yeah, I would.' It was a simple as that."

Eldridge gave up his little group, joined Gene, and became one of the band's most important members. He not only played sensational trumpet, he also sang, and on occasion, when Gene wanted to lead, he'd play drums— and exceptionally well, too.

With Roy and Anita, the Krupa band made its greatest recordings and enjoyed its greatest popularity. Anita cut several marvelous sides that still

Anita and Roy

stand up wonderfully well and show clearly what a much better singer she was than the other girls (June Christy, Chris Connors, Jerri Winters and more) who were so influenced by her. Few band vocals can compare with her renditions of "Georgia on My Mind," "Green Eyes," "Thanks for the Boogie Ride," "Murder, He Says" and "That's What You Think," the last a slow, swinging, totally infectious, almost wordless opus in which, as Gene points out, "you can hear how much she sounds like a jazz horn."

Together, Anita and Roy recorded one of the band's all-time hits, "Let Me Off Uptown," complete with Roy's famous plea of "Anita, oh Anita! . . . say, I feel somethin'!" followed by his sensational trumpet passage. Roy would sing occasionally, in a cute, jazz-tinged voice, and made quite an impression on "Knock Me a Kiss." But it was his brilliant trumpeting that stood out most, especially on recordings like "After You've Gone," played at an unbelievably fast tempo, and the exciting version of Hoagy Carmichael's "Rockin' Chair." Gene recalled the time they made that recording: "It was a rough date. We were playing at the Pennsylvania Hotel, and we had to make quite a few takes. You can imagine how hard it was on Roy's chops. He finally made it, though. But to show you how conscientious a guy Roy was, we played the tune again that night at the hotel and this time Roy missed the ending. I looked at him and I could see big tears in his eyes. Then I looked at his lip—it looked like a raw hamburger!"

The Eldridge-Krupa relationship was one of the most understanding between sidemen and leader. Roy once expressed his appreciation of Gene, based, conceivably, on incidents like that night at the Pennsylvania when he had missed that last note. "Man," he said, "Gene never turns or glares at you if you have a bad lip or hit a bum note. He just lets you play the way you know best. He never drives you."

Roy's relationship with Anita proved to be more fragile. For some reason that was never revealed publicly, ill feeling developed between the two, and it soon became quite obvious that they no longer wanted to work with each other. The feuding affected the spirit of the entire organization, and eventually Anita left the band to marry a golfer named Carl Hoff, not to be confused with the orchestra leader of the same name.

Ray Eberle, who had left Glenn Miller, came in for a short while. He had been preceded by Johnny Desmond, who himself had been preceded by Howard Dulany. Desmond was the most impressive of the three boy vocalists, though none of them ever achieved the popularity of an O'Day or even an Irene Daye.

A few months after Anita's exit, Gene left the band. He had been arrested in California on a marijuana possession charge, one that some believed was inspired less by the facts of the case than by the publicity that accrued to those who prosecuted and, we felt, persecuted him. Eventually, the chief witness for the prosecution, a valet Gene had recently hired, recanted his testimony and the charge was dropped, but only after Gene had been forced to languish in jail for a number of weeks.

His popularity didn't diminish in the slightest. In January, 1944, he was again voted the country's outstanding drummer, capturing more votes than the combined total of the next ten drummers. When he appeared one night, unannounced, in Tommy Dorsey's band on the stage of New York's Paramount, a wave of spontaneous cheering filled the theater.

Tommy's band had a big bank of strings in those days, and when Gene left after several weeks to start his own new outfit, he decided to go the violin route too. The results were pretty nothing. With the recording ban still in effect, he decided to record for us on V-Discs, and the few sides he made were dull and stodgy-sounding. "I guess I must have had the idea that I was a Kostelanetz or something," he said in retrospect. "Do I regret it? Financially, yes. But it was a good experience."

But it was a tremendously disappointing experience for his fans, who had to take large doses of the new Krupa band with Gene concentrating on his new role of conductor. He played drums infrequently and generally unswingingly, concentrating almost entirely on showmanship—fast technical stuff, complete with wild visual effects including dramatic lighting gimmicks and tom-toms for all his sidemen to bang on with pseudo-dramatic passion. Horace Heidt would have loved him.

Gradually Gene switched back to the kind of music that suited him best. He recorded a jumping instrumental called "Leave Us Leap," written by his new, modern arranger, Eddie Finckel, and an ingenious, scat-vocal duet called "What's This?," which featured two fine singers, both since deceased, Buddy Stewart and Dave Lambert of Lambert, Hendricks and Ross fame.

Tenor saxist Charlie Ventura, who had just started coming into his own when Gene had given up the band, rejoined, and he and pianist Teddy Napoleon and Gene formed a trio that played self-conscious, heavily stylized, seldom swinging renditions of tunes like "Dark Eyes" and "Body and Soul." The band's swinging stock soared higher when Anita O'Day returned and recorded Sy Oliver's "Opus One" as well as "Boogie Blues," in which the band definitely returned to its swinging ways, sounding at times more like Lionel Hampton's than like Krupa's crew.

As the forties passed their midpoint, bop was emerging as a major jazz influence, and Gene, who tried to keep up with the times, quite willingly began featuring some of the younger, bop-influenced musicians. His style of drumming did not fit in well with the music that men like trumpeters Red Rodney and Don Fagerquist or saxists Buddy Wise and Charlie Kennedy were playing, but Gene tried to adjust, and generally the results were quite satisfactory.

Ventura, whose jazz roots went deeper, and Krupa hit it off quite well. So did Gene and a young, swinging clarinetist from Philadelphia. This was Buddy DeFranco. It was in this period that a fourth Philadelphian, young Gerry Mulligan (Ventura and Rodney also were from the City of Brotherly Love), began writing some especially good arrangements for the band, including an original instrumental called "Disc Jockey Jump," which Gene pointed out "was good both musically and commercially. We always had a lot of requests for it. What was Gerry like in those days? As I recall him, he was sort of a temperamental kid who always wanted to expound on a lot of his musical ideas."

Gene continued trying to keep up with the times, giving opportunities to young musicians and arrangers who could find few big bands interested in their new ideas. He may not always have agreed with or appreciated what some of these much younger men were trying to prove, but it is to his credit that he remained ever tolerant and always the gentleman.

In looking back at his career, Krupa once told me, "I'm happy that I succeeded in doing two things: I made the drummer a high-priced guy, and I was able to project enough so that I was able to draw more people to jazz." He was also grateful that so much of his band's music had been preserved on recordings, many of which he often played. He once said, "They stir up many wonderful memories, so that suddenly you begin to remember so many things, and the past becomes alive again, and it makes being alive today seem even more worthwhile than ever!"

In the mid-sixties, Gene suffered a heart attack, and from then on he began to work less. By the early seventies, his health was getting progressively worse, and he spent most of his time inside his Yonkers home (when he wasn't in the hospital). That home, of which he was immensely proud, was almost completely destroyed by fire, but Gene remained in it. "Come visit me in my kitchen," he once suggested to me. "It's the only room that's still livable. Also, if you can, would you get me some new copies of your books. I had them all, you know—even that first one you wrote, *Don Watson Starts His Band*, but the fire destroyed them." I was both touched and flattered, and the next time I saw Gene, in the summer of 1973 on a lawn in Central Park, just before a bunch of fellow-drummers were to honor him on a hot summer's day during a Newport Jazz Festival program, I gave him the books. He looked terribly tired. Walking was extremely difficult, and I remember having to help him get backstage. It was the last time I saw him alive.

Gene died of various illnesses on October 16, 1973. At a memorial service a few days later I was asked to deliver a eulogy. I couldn't have spoken for a nicer guy.

Kay Kyser

SHORTLY after Kay Kyser moved into Chicago's Blackhawk Restaurant late in 1934, the actors' union clamped down on a local radio show that had been emanating from the room every Saturday night. The reason: the professional talent which was avidly seeking exposure wasn't being paid.

This was a blow for the Blackhawk and especially for Kyser, whose band, which was being paid, had begun to create a sensation in the Windy City. For it too needed the program's great exposure. So Kyser, intelligent and quick-witted, a man who once had studied to become a lawyer, came up with his own solution: forget about the pros and utilize the Blackhawk's patrons instead. How? It was simple: play a game about songs; see if the amateurs can guess the titles, and when they do, give them prizes. Thus was born Kay Kyser's College of Musical Knowledge.

Kay

According to Paul Mosher, who for many years was Kyser's publicist and later became his band manager, "The show was too slow at first. The timing was all wrong. But Kay worked hard at it, and soon it became a big hit."

Kyser then began to feel that the show belonged on more than just a local station and suggested to his agency, MCA, that it try putting it on a network. (Larry Barnett, who worked for MCA, believes that the show was created by Lew Wasserman, then the agency's publicity director, now its chairman of the board.) But reportedly the MCA radio department demurred. Kyser argued. MCA continued to demur. Meanwhile the radio audience's mail, bearing suggested questions for the Blackhawk's patrons to answer, kept pouring in. "Kay was smart enough," Mosher relates, "always to read over the air the name of the person who submitted the questions. This made people want to write in—just to hear their names." In a desperate and ingenious move to convince his agency, Kyser hired four bellhops and had them deposit sacks of mail (Mosher estimates in the neighborhood of a million letters) on and around the local MCA chieftain's desk.

A few weeks later MCA had sold the program as a network series to the American Tobacco Company, and Kyser's future was assured.

His start had been even more difficult. He had formed his band at the University of North Carolina but had become so petrified on the first date that a friend, songwriter Johnny Mercer, had to front the group. Once over his initial stage fright, however, Kyser developed into a topflight leader. In September, 1934, he followed Hal Kemp, another UNC alumnus, into the Blackhawk. The following June he busted Kemp's all time attendance record there.

Kyser brought with him into the Blackhawk one of his most commercial gimmicks: the singing song titles, which he had introduced during the previous summer at the Miramar Hotel in Santa Monica, California. It was simple but it immediately attracted much attention, this playing of a few bars of music near the start of each selection in which a vocalist would sing just the words of the title (Kyser claimed this also served a more utilitarian purpose: it saved spoken-introduction time on radio shows.) Then for further identification, the band would vamp a few bars of its theme, "Thinking of You," as Kyser announced the vocalist's name just before his or her chorus. It was a unique and ingenious image-building device. Imagine Kyser's surprise when, arriving in New York for his first lengthy engagement a few years later, he was accused of imitating Sammy Kaye, already in town, whose band was using the same tricks. Kyser reacted bitterly, pointing out that Blue Barron, who was also introducing songs in this way, "at least told me that if he's a success, he'd owe me ten per cent!"

It wasn't surprising that Kyser spoke out as directly as he did. George Duning, the chief arranger throughout the band's career, once wrote that "Kay has many decided likes and dislikes, which unfortunately he cannot conceal, especially when contacting people."

Duning further described Kyser as a southerner but certainly not a slow-moving one. Kay insisted upon getting things done quickly. "Procrastination," he would say, "is the condemnation of the world." He also could be very homey in his speech; when urging his men into action, for example, he would call out, "Hoppy, jumpy, skippy."

Duning also described Kyser as "a man of contradictions and extremes. On the bandstand he can be the soul of dignity or buffoonery, either one. But off the bandstand Kay is a practical but shrewd businessman, an unassuming person leading a normal life of clean habits and simple tastes."

Duning further noted that Kyser was especially interested in filling the band with gentlemen. "You might make a musician out of a gentleman," he used to say, "but you cannot always make a gentleman out of a musician."

Personnel changes in the band were infrequent, for Kyser picked his men carefully and remained loyal to them. When I first caught the band in Chicago many of its original members were going on their twelfth year with Kyser. But their sophomoric antics distressed and confused me. "There is so much kidding going on," I reported, "that when they settle down to playing music you don't know if they're still kidding."

One reason for my doubt was the odd mixture of bad and good music. Enamoured of Lombardo's band at the time, Kyser affected a mickey-mouse approach, with sugary, simpering saxes and clippety-cloppety brass tickings which were far from impressive musically. But the band did perform some cute novelties, especially when "Ishkabibble" (a good trumpeter whose real name was Merwyn Bogue) performed. And it produced some good glee club sounds, imitative of those of Fred Waring, whom Kyser also admired.

There was no doubt about it, Kyser did have a splendidly routined outfit; its hokey novelties and a professional approach, which allowed for no stage waits and a maximum of music in a given period, helped to attract the dancers to the bandstand and to make Kyser's "College of Musical Knowledge" an immensely successful radio series. Kyser himself wrote many of the early shows. Incidentally, one of the young men running through the audience in those days was an NBC pageboy named David Susskind.

Gradually the band became more and more musical. The novelties continued, with Kyser, "Ishkabibble" and another original member, Sully Mason, supplying the laughs for such magnificent minuscules of mature American musicana as "Three Little Fishes," which rivaled a couple of later offerings, "Who Wouldn't Love You" and the wartime "Praise the Lord and Pass the Ammunition," as the band's most famous recording.

"Praise the Lord," recorded on one day's notice, exemplified Kay's disdain of procrastination. According to Mosher, Frank Loesser, the composer, phoned Kyser in Detroit when he learned Kay was due to record the next day. He sang the song to him; Kyser was impressed (which comes as some sort of minor miracle to those of us who ever heard Loesser sing) and put arranger Duning on the line. The latter wrote down words and music as Loesser

Ishkabibble (Merwyn Bogue)

Harry Babbitt and Kay Kyser

Kay, Ginny Sims, Sully Mason with Eddy Duchin

repeated the singing, and the next day the band actually recorded the song.

By this time Kyser's band was devoting all its appearances to service camps. Kay refused to accept any other engagements, and, points out Mosher, "he played over 580 service installations—camps and hospitals. I'll never forget right after the Battle of the Bulge when we were playing hospitals and some of the patients were in such bad condition that several times some of the guys in the band just couldn't take it, and right in the middle of a number they'd have to leave the stand to go backstage to cry it out."

Working with Kay in the early forties were his two best-known vocalists, Harry Babbitt, a handsome man with an ingratiating grin, who never sang in any especially identifiable style but who always sang well, and Ginny Sims, an especially attractive girl who sang very smoothly, while making more sense out of lyrics than did most other vocalists. For many years there were rumors of a romance between Kay and Ginny. She, it has been reported, wanted to marry him but he wasn't ready; later he wanted to marry her, but by then, according to further reports, she had changed her mind. In September, 1941, she also changed her job, leaving the band with Kyser's blessings, to star on the Kleenex radio series.

The Dean of the
College of Musical Knowledge

A succession of singers soon entered and left the band—Dorothy Dunn, Trudy Erwin, Julie Conway, Gloria Wood, Lucy Ann Polk and her sister and two brothers, and eventually, after Babbitt went into the service, a handsome tenor named Michael Douglas, later to become even better known as Mike Douglas, star of his own TV series.

By 1942 the band had developed into an outstanding musical unit. Kyser had hired Van Alexander to write, in addition to Duning, and had also tapped such top jazz-tinged musicians as lead saxist Noni Bernardi (now a prominent California politician and businessman), tenor saxist Herbie Haymer and guitarist Roc Hillman. During this transitional period drummer Eddie Shea, who had worked with the band for years, went into the service. I remember the situation well, because Kyser dropped in one night at Nick's in Greenwich Village to hear some dixieland jazz. After one of the sets, he summoned over a drummer who had been sitting in, told him he liked his playing, and asked him whether he belonged to Local 802 and what he was doing those days. When I replied that, despite my having given his band a none-too-good review a few years earlier, I was still writing for *Metronome,* Kyser threw me one of those oh-you're-the-guy! looks and began searching elsewhere for another drummer.

The band also cut several excellent sweet sides. Its Lombardo-like sound had disappeared completely. Instead it produced some legitimate and very mellow musical effects, so good, in fact, that the jazz-oriented review board of *Metronome* selected the band's dreamy version of "Can't Get Out of This Mood" as the most musical side of December, 1942.

Several years later, Kyser discovered that he himself couldn't get out of a certain chronic mood—love. The chief cause was a breathlessly beautiful, well-bred Hollywood model named Georgia Carroll, who was singing with his band. One night, Paul Mosher relates, she and Kay were speeding through Nevada when they were stopped by a state trooper. After identifying himself and Miss Carroll, Kyser pulled out of the blue the explanation that they were rushing to get married. The idea, of course, was not new to either one of them, and the desire of avoiding a traffic ticket and its attendant publicity proved to be the final push toward the big plunge. So they awakened a Justice of the Peace, got married, tipped him ten dollars to keep the news quiet and the next day continued back to Hollywood with their secret. Secret? Little did they know that the ten bucks they tipped the Justice didn't nearly match the bigger tips that wire services paid Justices for scoops!

The marriage, which produced three children, was a huge success. Though Kay continued his band for a few more years—he even brought his "College of Musical Knowledge" to television with minimal success—he became far more involved with Christian Science. He returned to North Carolina and became a practitioner, then moved to Boston to serve as national head of the church's film and broadcast division, and by the 1980s had returned to his native state, reportedly a contented and wealthy man.

Elliot Lawrence

ELLIOT LAWRENCE started his band career when many of the top leaders were thinking of giving theirs up. A recent graduate of the University of Pennsylvania, where he had gained a degree in three years, conducted the football band and been named for the Art Achievement Award (the second time in the university's history that this award had been given in the field of music), Elliot took over late in 1944 as musical director at radio station WCAU, of which his father was general manager. Immediately he began whipping into shape the greatest studio band in the country.

I happened to catch it quite by accident one night while listening to the radio, and I was so impressed that I gave the band a huge rave in the March issue of *Metronome*. Shortly thereafter I went down to Philadelphia to see if the band was really as good in person. I was delighted to find that it was.

I was also delighted to find in Lawrence one of the most refreshing personalities to appear on the big band scene in a long time. Immensely enthusiastic, deeply dedicated to good music, yet charmingly naive in his faith in everyone, Elliot had obviously won the respect and admiration of his musicians, despite his being the Boss's son.

At times the band sounded like Claude Thornhill's, especially when Lawrence played his delicate piano solos and fill-ins and the arrangements spotted his very good French-horn player. But the band also had a great deal of rhythmic sparkle, some of it attributable to the scores (Gerry Mulligan was one of the arrangers, Lawrence was another) and some to the tremendous drive of the trumpet section. Everything the band played sounded musical, for Lawrence was an expert conductor who had studied under one of the world's leading teachers, Leon Barzin, and had done so well that Barzin had offered him a job as his assistant.

By the early part of 1946 Elliot figured he was ready to leave Philadelphia. With the help of his father, Stan Lee Broza, who gave up his lucrative long-time job at the station to become his son's manager, Lawrence migrated from the local to the national big band scene. He opened at the Café Rouge in New York's Hotel Pennsylvania, where he scored a big hit. He expanded his radio coverage and began recording for Columbia.

Elliot's faith in people, his desire to please and an apparent lack of self-assurance raised some problems. He could be overly polite, overly receptive. On his record dates, instead of calling Columbia's recording director "Mitch," the way all the other artists did, Elliot would address him as "Mr. Ayres." So anxious was Elliot to please and to succeed that he would listen patiently to all kinds of advice, much of it conflicting. As he explained later: "One man would say 'play your slow numbers slower and your faster numbers faster. I know. I've been in the business fifteen years.' Then another would say, 'Play your fast numbers slower and your slow numbers faster. I know. I've been in the business fifteen years.' What would you have done?"

Eventually it dawned on Elliot that he had matured enough to make up his own mind. That's when his band began making even more impressive sounds. "For a long time," he said while recalling this awakening process, "just about the only thing I'd think of when making a score was 'I wonder what the critics will say.' Then it dawned on me that even all the critics don't think alike, so why not do what *I* felt was best?"

He continued to play sweet music at the right times, complete with vocals by Roz Patton and Jack Hunter, but more and more his band started to jump. In those days it didn't feature any really great soloists except for young Red Rodney and for a while Mulligan and then Alec Fila, who under Lawrence began to show that he could play good jazz as well as great lead trumpet. But as a group the band's musicianship was always outstanding, and Elliot, who continued to retain his wide-eyed admiration for the best jazz arrangers, began to make even more interesting sounds after he commissioned fine young writers like Johnny Mandel, Al Cohn, Mulligan and Tiny Kahn to write for him.

Elliot

By this time the popularity of big bands had begun to wane considerably. Lawrence, however, continued to work for many years—on weekdays in television and radio, on weekends mainly in schools and colleges. For these occasions he stocked his personnel with musicians he especially admired—trumpeters like Nick Travis, Bernie Glow and Ernie Royal, Urbie Green on trombone, Cohn, Hal McKusick and Sam Marowitz on saxes and Kahn or Sol Gubin on drums. These top studio men, in turn, admired and respected Lawrence and responded with enthusiastic readings of the always musical and interesting arrangements.

Elliot continued to arrange and often to conduct for several television programs. Eventually he became musical director of such hit Broadway musicals as *Bye, Bye Birdie, Golden Boy* and *The Apple Tree.* To the theater he brought a rare combination of musical maturity and boyish enthusiasm, a reflection of the spirit that had pervaded his and other swinging big bands.

Other portions of the commercial music world turned to him. For many years he became very active in jingles and other aspects of radio and television advertising, serving as consultant for N. W. Ayer, a major agency, where his sharp business sense coupled with his innate good taste and ever-present enthusiasm brought him both respect and a considerable income.

Guy Lombardo

ONE of the most listened-to, talked-about and imitated big bands of all time was that of Guy Lombardo and His Royal Canadians. Why? For a time even its leader couldn't answer that question. "We didn't know what we had," Guy once told me during a discussion of his band's early days. "We had to ask people what it was they liked about the band."

They did not have to ask for long. It soon became evident what it was that people liked about "The Sweetest Music This Side of Heaven": Carmen's lead saxophone and singing, Lebert's lead trumpet and Guy's leading of the band as a whole. And, as I noted in a review in the February, 1942, *Metronome*, the band had more commercial assets:

> It hits superb tempos, and though it doesn't produce a rhythmically inspiring beat, it produces a succession of steady, unobtrusive beats that make it a pleasure to take your girl out on the floor and move around to the best of your ability. If you can dance at all, you can dance to Lombardo's music. . . .
>
> Lombardo's band is also a wonderful band to talk to. It never plays so loudly that you've got to say 'what?' whenever somebody asks you a question. If you catch it at dinner sessions, you can even hear a mashed potato drop. . . .
>
> And Lombardo plays wonderful tunes. . . . For Lombardo, with his years and years of experience, knows how to select tunes that create a mood, an intimate, cozy mood.

Of course, many of us, even though we may have understood Lombardo's appeal, were less than knocked out by his music, especially, as the review indicated, by "the exaggerated sax vibratos, the clippety brass phrases with their illegitimate tones, the little use made of the five rhythm instruments, and the style of singing that lets you hear all consonants and no vowels."

Musically adventurous, or musically satisfying to serious buffs of the big band scene, the Lombardo outfit most certainly was not. Many musicians ridiculed its addiction to a style that they felt was about as artistically creative as the average comic book. But Lombardo believed implicitly in his music, and he succeeded handsomely in selling it to two generations of dancers.

More than any other band, Guy Lombardo's based its success, purely and simply, on a securely set style. "The big trick," Guy admitted, "is to be recognized without an announcer telling you who it is." The Lombardos most certainly mastered *that* trick!

They started developing the formula in the early twenties in their hometown of London, Ontario, and never changed it as they made successive—and successful—stops of several years apiece in Cleveland and Chicago and then finally the Roosevelt Grill in New York City.

It was always a tightly knit group, built around brothers Guy, Carmen and Lebert, who owned the band and who sometimes fought almost passionately among themselves. Later young brother Victor joined them on baritone sax, along with several steadfast stalwarts—saxists Fred (Derf) Higman and Mert Curtis, mellophonist Dudley Fosdick, pianist Fritz Kreitzer, (for years one of the two famous "Twin Pianists"), drummer George Gowans and vocalist Kenny Gardner.

Ostensibly, Carmen, the band's musical director until he died in April of 1971, and Lebert owned the band with Guy. But it was Guy who throughout assumed and retained the leadership, visual as well as spiritual. According to Decca Records' Milt Gabler, who supervised many of the band's biggest hit records, "Guy was the complete boss. No matter what anybody else said or thought, if Guy felt strongly about something, that was it."

The respect that Lombardo generated from people who had been associated with the band was tremendous. As Gabler once emphasized: "Guy is just a sensational person—as a human being and as a man to work with." One of the most prominent talent agency executives, Larry Barnett, who handled dozens upon dozens of top stars, once stated: "Guy Lombardo is the nicest man that's ever been in the music business."

And Lombardo finished first in more than just personal popularity polls. His band sold more records than any other dance band. In addition, it played for more Presidential Inaugural Balls than any other organized name band. What's more, it created more hit songs than any other band: "Boo Hoo," "Coquette," "Sweethearts On Parade" and "Seems Like Old Times," all written by Carmen; "Give Me a Little Kiss," "You're Driving Me Crazy," "Little White Lies," "September in the Rain," "Little Girl," "Annie Doesn't Live Here Anymore," "Everywhere You Go," and so many more. Many people who listened to the band's annual New Year's Eve broadcasts for so many years must have assumed that the Guy Lombardo orchestra had also introduced "Auld Lang Syne!" Not true.

The band also set numerous all-time attendance records, including one, believe it or not, at the Savoy Ballroom in Harlem. Guy appeared very proud of his acceptance among blacks. One of his band's most avid fans was Louis Armstrong, who once described the Lombardos as "my inspirators!" Insisted Guy, "Lots of colored bands imitated us." But certainly no musicians did so to more absurd effect than Armstrong's saxists. What an incongruous sound it was, that virile trumpet backed by those simpering saxophones! Shades of Sir

Front row: *Fred Higman, Larry Owen, Carmen and Guy Lombardo*
Middle row: *Ben Davies, Victor Lombardo, Frances Henry,*
Lebert Lombardo, Jim Dillon
Back row: *Hugo D'Ippolito, George Gowans, Fred Kreitzer*

Laurence Olivier reciting Shakespeare against a musical backing by Lawrence Welk's Champagne Music!

What was the Lombardo sax appeal? For one thing, "Carmen's vibrato always had a lot of soul," reasoned Guy. Sometimes the band would step out of character in an attempt to please the dancers even more. But it didn't always work. "I remember once when we played at a large armory in the Negro section of Chicago. We were doing fine until we started playing things like 'Tiger Rag' and 'St. Louis Blues.' They didn't like that at all. No, it was strictly our sweet music that they wanted to hear."

Though the band occasionally did try other novel approaches, such as calypso and country and western music, its success was always basically predicated upon its set style. "We really never changed," Guy used to say with pride. "We improved, yes. But we never changed."

The consistency also obtained in the band's businesslike approach to everything it did. It seldom shortened its rehearsal schedule, and seldom diminished its pride in its work. And through all those years, the Lombardos continued to project an almost adolescent enthusiasm, like that of a high school band that had suddenly discovered the thrill of being able to sound like real, honest-to-goodness, grown-up musicians.

Said Gabler, "It was the most completely responsible band I ever knew. The men were always punctual, and they were always strictly business. They would arrive on each recording date with their complete library, and each man would carry in and be responsible for his own book. So far as I could find out, they never had a band boy. They worked very hard on every

Guy, Carmen, Lebert, Victor

date and insisted that everything come out just right. Sometimes Guy worked with me in the control room, but I noticed that when he was out there in front of the band, waving his stick, the men played better. As soon as they finished, each man would pick up his own music and his own instruments. I've never seen a band leave a studio quicker—or cleaner.''

The Lombardos had always been noted for the same sort of dependability during personal appearances. For years at the Roosevelt Grill they followed Guy's instructions: "No drinking until midnight." Inasmuch as the band finished playing an hour later, a stoned Lombardoan was a notable rarity among working dance band musicians.

Though others may not have imitated the band's personal habits, numerous bands did imitate its music. Did Guy mind? "There was nothing we could do about it,'' he once said. However, he did resent those "who exaggerated everything we did and didn't give the true picture. They moaned and groaned like we never did. What they did made us sound cheap, and of course we didn't like that."

Cheap is one thing Lombardo could not be accused of—though there was a time when brother Victor must not have agreed. That was in the late forties when he quit and started his own band because, according to reports, Guy had refused him a twenty-five-dollar-a-week raise. But Victor didn't make it on his own and eventually returned to the fold.

As Guy became more and more successful he began to pursue numerous other activities: speedboat racing, in which he won the Gold Cup races, the sport's highest honor; his Jones Beach Marine Theater productions on Long Island, in which he was joined in 1966 by Louis Armstrong and his band; and restaurant ownership, with the successful Guy Lombardo's East Point House in Freeport, Long Island, and the Port O' Call on Tierra Verde in Tampa Bay, Florida. In addition, he kept drawing large royalties from music publishing ventures and large crowds all over the country wherever he and his Royal Canadians appeared. In fact, they appeared to be America's most permanent fixtures. "I'll keep on working forever," he told Frank Meyer of *Variety* in the late 1970s. "The only thing I dread is a night I don't have to work. There's nowhere to go. I hate a night off."

His manager, Saul Richman, revealed in 1977 that the band had received an offer for an engagement no less than four years away. "You see," he said, "people just will not believe that there won't always be a Guy Lombardo."

But later that year they had to believe it. On November 5th in Houston, Texas, where his band was playing, Guy was felled by a mammoth heart attack. For a while the band continued under Lebert and then under Lebert's son. But it just didn't work out, and Guy's dreaded nights off became a permanent reality for his loyal Royal Canadians.

Johnny Long

ITS best-remembered work is its glee club's swinging version of "A Shanty in Old Shanty Town," but actually the Johnny Long band stood out as one of the most musical of all sweet outfits. It played many of the leading hotel rooms, most of them in the East and Midwest, where its pleasant, subdued but always danceable sounds ingratiated the band with its dancers.

Long himself was especially charming. A graduate of Duke, where his band had followed Les Brown's as the campus's standout crew, he had a soft, mild manner (he looked like "that polite boy" every mother would like her daughter to date), a warm smile and a knack of getting along well with people in and out of his band. He himself played a violin, left-handed, which was cause for some comment but which never figured very much in his band's musical style.

*Johnny Long
and Helen Young*

The orchestra featured several other good vocalists in addition to the glee club. Helen Young, a pretty, well-mannered girl was a fixture for years. So was Paul Harmon, who sang the novelties. Throughout its career the band also featured numerous male ballad vocalists; of the bunch the most impressive was Bob Houston, a Crosby-type crooner who later became a member of Glenn Miller's AAF Band.

Sometimes the band tried to play jazz, seldom with notable success. Throughout its career it boasted few good jazz soloists, while its five brass and four saxes couldn't deliver enough punch to carry out jazz ensemble assignments effectively. What's more, until pianist Junie Mays began producing some fine arrangements in the mid-forties, the band lacked any distinctive musical style. Then, with seven saxes and seven brass to work with, Mays delivered a batch of interesting scores. However, the band's forte still remained pleasant, danceable but never especially exciting dance music.

Long never quite made it as big as some observers thought he would. Perhaps Johnny was too easygoing, too nice a guy. Several times the critics concluded a review with words about how the band was "knocking on the door of success." But Johnny just never drove hard enough to force that door open wide.

Still, he kept trying. During the sixties he was fronting a band, but finally gave up and started a career as an English teacher. But his health was poor and life wasn't too happy for him, and it all ended on October 31, 1972.

A left-handed fiddler
trying to look right-handed.

Jimmie Lunceford

WHAT must go down in dance band history as the greatest gathering of the clan took place in New York's Manhattan Center on the night of November 18, 1940, when Benny Goodman, Glenn Miller, Count Basie, Glen Gray, Les Brown, Guy Lombardo, Will Bradley, Sammy Kaye and twenty other big bands wowed six thousand enthusiastic fans without a letup from eight in the evening until four the next morning.

In this marathon, MC'd by disc jockey Martin Block, all the bands were scheduled to play fifteen-minute sets—and all except one of those twenty-eight bands got off the stage when it was supposed to. But that one couldn't, for the simple reason that along about midnight it broke the show wide open, to such hollering and cheering and shouting for "More!" that no other band could get on stage until Jimmie Lunceford's was allowed to play some extra tunes.

That this fantastic outfit could top all the others in a show of this sort came as no surprise to those of us who had seen it in action before, and probably comes as no surprise to any reader who ever caught the band during its heyday. For Jimmie Lunceford's was without a doubt the most exciting big band of all time!

Jimmie

Trummy Young (at mike) backed by singers Eddie Tompkins,
Joe Thomas and Willie Smith

Its music was great, but not that much greater than that of several other top swing bands' and, in fact, not as consistently brilliant, perhaps, as one or two others'. But the Lunceford band was so far ahead of all the rest in one department—showmanship—that when it came to any battle of the bands, none could touch it.

It was the sort of band that no one with even the slightest feel for swing could stand in front of and stand still. It propelled a fantastically joyous swinging beat, and the musicians projected it with uninhibited, completely infectious enthusiasm.

It was not a band that relied on star soloists, though it did have several outstanding jazz men. Instead, it emphasized ensemble sounds, brilliant brass, sweeping saxes and a wonderfully buoyant rhythm section, all playing some of the swingingest arrangements of all time.

There was constant aural and visual interplay among the musicians. The trumpets would throw their horns in the air together; the saxes would almost charge off the stage, so enthusiastically did they blow their horns; the trombones would slip their slides toward the skies; and throughout the evening the musicians would be kidding and shouting at one another, projecting an aura of irresistible exuberance.

In front of all this stood Lunceford, a big, impressive-looking man with a huge smile and baton to match, supervising and controlling the entire proceedings. He may not have displayed the flash of a Goodman or a Dorsey or an Ellington or a James, but as Sy Oliver, the man responsible for so much of the band's music, recently emphasized, "Make no mistake about it, Jimmie definitely was a leader. He was a strict disciplinarian, like a teacher in a schoolroom, but he was consistent in everything he did, and that gave the fellows in the band a feeling of security."

Lunceford had started out as an athletic director at a Memphis, Tennessee, high school; in fact, he had coached some of the musicians who later worked in his band. He had been graduated from Fisk University and had also taken graduate courses at the City College of New York. The band, organized in Memphis in the late twenties, began developing into a mature unit during annual summer engagements in Lakeside, Ohio.

After establishing a name for itself in Buffalo, it came to New York City in 1933, appearing at the Cotton Club. It recorded several numbers that, as Oliver now points out, were not at all typical of the band's music. Such racing flag wavers as "White Heat" and "Jazznocracy" were written for the band by Will Hudson, a white arranger who was working for Irving Mills, the influential music publisher, who was helping the band and who wanted to get his firm's music, which included Hudson's originals, performed on records and on the air.

The *real* Jimmie Lunceford music was far more relaxed. Its style has often been referred to as "the Lunceford two beat," a light, loping, swing, created and developed by Oliver. Sy, a bright, broad-faced, intelligent trumpeter, who never studied arranging in his life, came from a musical family. Orig-

Arranger Oliver

inally his parents had wanted him to study piano, but athletics intrigued him more. Finally, he acquiesced sufficiently to take up the trumpet and, after his father died, played seriously enough to land a job in Zack White's band, for which he also began to arrange, picking up his own technique. "One day in Cincinnati," he recalls, "I heard the Lunceford band rehearsing. I was so impressed, because Jimmie was so careful about every single detail, that I asked him if I could try writing for the band." Lunceford said yes, so Oliver wrote several arrangements for him. Soon thereafter came an offer to join the band. Sy grabbed it.

Right from the start, Oliver began turning out brilliant scores, many of which have survived through the years as the most outstanding in the Lunceford library—"Swanee River," "My Blue Heaven," "Four or Five Times," "Organ Grinder's Swing," "On the Beach at Bali Bali," "For Dancers Only," "Margie," "Cheatin' on Me," "Dream of You," a tune that Sy wrote, plus his own favorite arrangement of "By the River St. Marie." The band recorded it for Decca, but, Sy says, "We never did get to do the full arrangement of 'St. Marie' because it ran six minutes and that was too long for those old seventy-eight sides." Oliver also wrote another tune, which he liked very much but which Lunceford apparently didn't. Jimmie may have turned it down, but Tommy Dorsey, for whom Sy later arranged, didn't. He recorded and made a big hit out of "Yes, Indeed!"

Though praised by many musicians, Oliver's arrangements were curiously deprecated during an interview I had early in 1946 with none other than Sy Oliver himself. "Those arrangements," he insisted, "they were all just alike. I couldn't write. It's just that those guys played so well. Anybody could have written for that band."

The point, of course, is that nobody else did write like that for the Lunceford band, nor for Dorsey's band, nor for Billy May's band, nor for Sam Donahue's, nor for any of the many others which paid Oliver the supreme compliment by basing their styles on his.

Not that everything Sy did was always accepted. Jimmie Crawford, the great drummer, whose simple but always swinging playing inspired the Lunceford band for such a long time, at first wasn't completely sold on Oliver's penchant for emphasizing two instead of four beats in each measure. "Sy

Drummer Crawford

would say 'Drop it in two,' and I'd maybe show I didn't agree with him, and so he'd say, 'What's wrong with two beats?' and I'd answer, 'Well, there are two beats missing, that's all.' I felt that if you were really going home in those last ride-out choruses, then you should really go home all the way, full steam and stay in four-four instead of going back into that two-four feel again. Oh yes, Sy and I would have some terrific arguments all right, but then we'd kiss and make up right away." Apparently Sy and Jimmie hear better ear-to-ear these days, because on almost every recording date Sy now conducts, he uses Jimmie on drums. Crawford, by the way, is one of today's most sought-after drummers for Broadway musicals: his drive and his spirit remain as contagious as ever.

Oliver wasn't the only arranger in the band. Several other musicians wrote scores, and one of them, pianist Edwin Wilcox, has been tabbed by Sy as "one of the most underrated musicians in the business. People don't realize how much he contributed to the band. He did as much as I did, and he definitely was the man responsible for all those beautiful sax ensemble choruses that we used to play. Don't ever overlook him, please!"

The sax choruses were blown by a section led by a fine alto man, the late Willie Smith, who also sang some cute vocals, and who later became a mainstay of the Harry James, Charlie Spivak, and in the mid-sixties the Charlie Barnet sax teams. Playing with him were Joe Thomas, a fine tenor saxist, considered by many to have been the outstanding soloist in the band, who also sang; Earl (Jock) Carruthers, an especially spirited baritone saxist; and Dan Grissom (called "Dan Gruesome" by his deprecators), who for many years was also the band's chief ballad vocalist.

The trumpets, in addition to Oliver, spotted a great lead man in Eddie Tompkins and, in the early years, a high-note screecher named Tommy Stevenson, who was replaced by an equally stratospheric trumpeter named Paul Webster.

The trombonists featured a very funny fellow named Elmer Crumbley, an outstanding, soft singer, Henry Wells, who also arranged, and, for a while, a good jazz soloist, Eddie Durham, who doubled wonderfully on electric guitar, an instrument seldom heard during the mid-thirties. Later James (Trummy) Young joined the band and provided it with some of its outstanding jazz trombone and vocal moments.

After Oliver left, Trummy replaced him in the vocal trio which had previously projected such a wonderfully light, free-swinging sound on "My Blue Heaven" and "Four or Five Times." According to Oliver, "nobody in the group could really sing, but yet no group could sound like that."

Both in regard to the vocal trio and to the band as a whole, it is Sy's contention that "the whole was three times as great as the individual components. The band played way over its head simply because of its tremendous spirit. The guys were all individualists. They were all characters in their own fashion. And each one of them was a definite personality."

The characters and their personalities were always there for all to see and hear. This, according to Lunceford, accounted for much of the band's success. "A band that looks good, goes in for a better class of showmanship, and seems to be enjoying its work," he said in the early forties, "will always be sure of a return visit wherever it plays."

"We did have a barrel of fun," Oliver says. "Jock Carruthers was really the playmaker of the band. He was always up to something. I remember one night after we'd finished work around two in the morning and we'd all gotten nice and settled on the bus and suddenly this alarm clock went off. We couldn't figure out where it was coming from. Finally we located it in the bottom of the luggage—in Carruthers' bag. He'd set it to go off at six in the morning!

"So then Paul Webster decided he'd go Jock one better, and one night he put *two* alarm clocks in his bag, and just to make sure everybody'd hear them, he put them in *two* pie plates. What a racket that made!"

Traveling was something the Lunceford band did a great deal of. Jimmie recapped some statistics in 1942 as follows: "We do a couple of hundred one-nighters a year, fifteen to twenty weeks of theaters, maybe one four-week location and two weeks of vacation. All in all, we cover about forty thousand miles a year!"

The men got along together surprisingly well, considering the conditions under which they were forced to work. Other top (white) outfits could stay in big cities for weeks at a time, and therefore could benefit by playing the name spots and getting exposure through radio shots. But Lunceford, apparently resigned to the facts of life, rationalized that air time, of which the band still had some, was not that important. He indicated that recordings were more powerful, and he'd point out that if you made a mistake on records, you could try again, but when you made one on live broadcasts, there was nothing you could do about it.

Pride and internal competition buoyed the band's spirits. The brass and sax teams kept trying to outplay each other. If one section made a mistake, the other gloated—often to the accompaniment of stomping feet. "But Jimmie finally stopped that," relates Oliver. "He claimed all those feet stomping ruined the broadcasts."

One exciting bit of showmanship the brass introduced was the waving of derby hats, an effect Glenn Miller picked up and utilized so extensively with his band. Says Oliver: "That was Stevie's idea. [Stevie was Tommy Stevenson.] He was full of ideas like that. The only trouble was that Eddie [Tompkins] and I would remember them, and then he'd be the one who'd forget what to do!"

And something else in the trumpet section bothered Oliver: "I was a lousy trumpet player. If I'd been a leader, I would never have hired me for a record date." However, Sy's opinion of his playing doesn't jibe with that of many others. He was, I always felt, the most interesting trumpet soloist in the band—not as flashy as the others but very musical and warm and emotional. What none of us realized, though, as we listened to what we thought were such great extemporaneous jazz passages, was that Sy had prepared every one in advance. "I could never ad-lib the way the others did. The way I worked it, I'd write out my chorus and then I'd start building my arrangement around it. It was like taking a mediocre picture and putting it in a good frame so that it seems better than it really is. And you know what? I still use the same formula when I arrange for mediocre singers today.

"Another thing I used to do when I wrote for the band was to write with the various guys' limitations in mind. That way there'd be a minimum of trouble."

When I first reviewed the band in 1936 at the Larchmont Casino just outside New York City, I found it had some surprising limitations. Before then I'd heard it only on recordings. On location I was quite shocked to discover that the saxes especially sounded very ragged on some of the tunes they had not recorded. "Sad displays of out-of-tune slop" is how I described it. Two years later though, such deficiencies had pretty well disappeared and the band had developed a consistency that was truly remarkable. I can't recall any succession of evenings more exciting than those I spent listening to the Lunceford band, night after night, during its stay in the summer of 1940 at the Fiesta Danceteria above the Rialto Theater in New York's Times Square.

Its style had changed somewhat by then. It still played many of Oliver's famous arrangements, but it also performed some by Billy Moore, who had taken over as chief writer and who contributed the score for the band's big hit recording, "What's Your Story, Morning Glory?"

Sy had left the band for no better reason than, as he said it, "I'd grown tired of traveling. I felt I was going out of the world backwards. I wanted to stay in New York and study and write. But Jimmie didn't want me to go until he could find another trumpet player to take my place. He kept me in the band until I just quit one night, and then I found out that he had had Gerald Wilson waiting in New York all the time, ready to come in as soon as I cut out." That's when Oliver joined Tommy Dorsey.

The Lunceford band continued to sound good for a while longer. Late in 1941 I heard it at the Paramount and found it to be great, with the trumpet section of Wilson, Webster and Snooky Young especially impressive and Dan Grissom a vastly improved singer.

About a year later I caught Lunceford again at the Apollo Theater in Harlem, and I was so thrilled that I sat through several shows, just as one would sit through several sets if the band were playing in a regular spot—something it was doing distressingly seldom during those days. Some more new members impressed me too: Freddy Webster, a brilliant young trumpeter, and Truck Parham, a stronger bassist than Mose Allen had ever been, though no bassist could match Mose for contagious spirit.

But the great over-all Lunceford band enthusiasm was beginning to fade. "Most of the replacements were better musicians," Oliver agrees, "but they didn't bring the same spirit into the band. That could never be duplicated."

Jimmie Crawford cites another reason for the band's eventual deterioration. "We never created anything new. It was always the same old stuff. Jimmie wouldn't spend money on enough good new arrangements."

The sad part of it all, as Crawford found out in later years, was that Lunceford was not in control of the band's finances. "We thought so all the time we were working for Jimmie. But then we discovered that Jimmie was working for Harold Oxley, that Oxley owned the band and we were working for him too, and that Jimmie was just getting a salary like the rest of us."

Soon Crawford and Willie Smith and Paul Webster and Trummy Young and Freddy Webster and others had left. Eddie Tompkins, who had gone into the Army, had been killed during war maneuvers. Al Norris had been drafted. When I caught the band during a very desultory theater engagement in the summer of 1944, only Carruthers, Thomas, Wilcox and trombonist Russell Bowles were there as reminders of the brilliant crew that had once created such sensational music.

"Jimmie made one mistake," notes Oliver in assessing the causes of the band's decline. "He kept looking for good musicianship, good character and intelligence, and he found it all. But so many of the guys were so intelligent that, as they matured, they realized there were other things in life more worthwhile than traveling all year and living in bad hotels."

For several more years the Lunceford band kept plugging away, continuing to travel—and to live in depressing places. But it was never the same. It remained a splendidly routined band (I recorded it for V-Discs and it cut six sides in one hour, which was some sort of record for efficiency), for Jimmie was, to the end, a first-class leader. "The end" came on July 16, 1947, when the band was once again on the road—this time in Oregon, where Jimmie suffered a fatal heart attack.

The band tried carrying on under Edwin Wilcox and Joe Thomas, two of its great stalwarts, but the attempt failed and it wasn't long before the Jimmie Lunceford band passed from the scene for good.

But what great music it left! For many it remains, pressed in the grooves of all the fine Decca and Columbia records it made. And for those of us lucky enough to have caught the band in person it has also left memories of some of the most exciting nights we ever spent listening to any of the big bands!

Freddy Martin

DUKE ELLINGTON'S famed alto saxist Johnny Hodges used to call him "Mr. Silvertone." Chu Berry, one of the great jazz tenor saxists of all time, listed him as his favorite man on his own instrument. And when Eddie Miller, later recognized as the jazz tenor saxist with the most beautiful tone, decided he'd like to switch from alto to tenor sax, he asked his boss, Ben Pollack, for the night off. "What for?" asked Pollack. "Before I start playing tenor," Miller answered, "I want to spend an evening listening to Freddy Martin and try to figure out how he gets that tone." "Go ahead," Pollack told him. "You're going to hear the right man."

Freddy Martin, even though his saxophone sound has been so admired by leading jazz stars, has never tried to be a jazz musician. He has always led a strictly sweet band, one in which his "silver tone" has always played an important role, not merely on solos but also on ensembles, where its warmth has provided the rich, lower-register tonality that has distinguished Martin's as one of the most musical and most melodic of all sweet bands.

Freddy had his own idols before his professional career really got under-way in his native Cleveland. They were the Lombardo Brothers, and Freddy, working after school hours for a musical instrument company, was trying to sell them new saxes with absolutely no success. But, says Martin, "I had a high school band in those days, and Guy heard it a couple of times and kept encouraging us. Then one night his band had to play somewhere else so he asked us to fill in at his regular spot." The Martin team did very well that night, and Freddy's commercial career was launched in earnest.

For several years he fronted one of those typical hotel-room bands, built around three tenor saxes that mooed all night long. It played at the Bossert Hotel in Brooklyn, performed well but, as Martin notes, "after a while I realized I'd have to get rid of that muddy sound and get more color into the band." He did and soon he graduated to the Roosevelt Grill in Manhattan, the same spot that Lombardo had been making famous.

One source of the color Freddy added was Russ Morgan. "We'd played together years before, but I hadn't seen him in a long time," Freddy explained. "One night while we were at the Roosevelt he came around. I didn't recog-nize him, because he'd had an awful automobile accident, and the Roman nose he used to have was no longer there. He was in pretty bad shape. He wanted a job, but I had no use for a trombone then. 'I play piano, too, you know,' Russ said. Luckily I had just let one of my piano players go. So Russ joined us."

Morgan soon brought along his trombone, too, and started injecting it into some of the arrangements he wrote. "One night," Freddy recalls, "when nobody was in the room, he started fooling around with some trumpet mutes and making funny 'wah-wah' sounds. He was just kidding, but when he did it for some of the dancers, the reaction was so great that we decided to play it for real."

Eventually Morgan left the band to take a recording job that Martin had turned down. "I'd always wanted him to record those 'wah-wah' songs like 'Wabash Blues' and 'Linger Awhile' when he was with us. But his lip always seemed to go bad at the 'right' time. As soon as he left, though, he began recording those 'wah-wah' sounds with his own band. And they brought him two quick hits—'Wabash Blues' and 'Linger Awhile.' " From then on the "wah-wah" effect became a basic part of Morgan's style.

Martin and Morgan, somehow or other, have always remained friends, even though Russ, when he and his band finally got a job in a New York hotel, the Biltmore, played many of the Martin band's arrangements. Russ went even further; when he finally landed a radio series, he used the tag "Music in the Morgan Manner," even though Freddy had been using "Music in the Martin Manner." Freddy just let it pass. Larry Barnett, Freddy's good friend at MCA, was probably right when he recently told me, "Freddy Martin is such a nice man; he's almost too nice for his own good."

Morgan had wanted to sing when he was with Martin. But in those days Freddy already had a good jazz-tinged vocalist named Terry Shand, who

The Freddy Martin band on New York's St. Regis Roof (1934).
Vocalist Elmer Feldkamp is third from left in rear;
trombonist Russ Morgan at far right in rear;
pianist-vocalist Terry Shand at far right in front.

Freddy with violinist-vocalist Eddie Stone and violinist Eddie Bergman

doubled on piano, and a saxist whose singing sounded even more beautiful than his name—Elmer Feldkamp. So Russ seldom emoted. Freddy also featured Helen Ward, before that wonderful singer joined Benny Goodman. Helen was the only girl ever to work regularly with Freddy's band. "I never wanted to mix business with pleasure," he admits.

Probably the most consistently impressive ballad singer Martin ever had, excluding Merv Griffin, who sang, and sang well, too, and played piano with the band in the fifties, and Buddy Clark, who recorded with the band in the mid-thirties was a tall, handsome baritone named Stuart Wade. Remember that homecoming father who tripped over his kid's tricycle, lost his temper completely and then, after a soft "Control yourself!" and a quick dose of Anacin, abruptly began to love the whole world around him? That was Stuart Wade.

For years Martin also spotted a different sort of singer, an impish-sounding man with a great grin. This was Eddie Stone, who had been a part of the Isham Jones outfit for many years, and who recorded many good sides with Freddy's band, including two of its biggest hits, "The Hut Sut Song" and "Why Don't We Do This More Often?"

According to Freddy, Allie Wrubel and Charlie Newman, composers of "Often," objected strenuously when they learned that their song was to appear on the back side of a certain instrumental. "That classical piece," they felt, would never attract record buyers. And what was "that classical piece"? Merely Tchaikovsky's Piano Concerto, later called "Tonight We Love," one of the biggest record hits of all time.

"I happened to record this quite by accident," Freddy reports. "One Saturday night, just before going to work, I was listening to the radio. I heard Toscanini and the NBC Symphony—we were three hours earlier on the Coast—and I heard this beautiful theme out of Tchaikovsky's Piano Concerto. On Monday I went out and bought Artur Rubinstein's recording, listened to it a few times, and then called in Ray Austin, our arranger. He brought in three different versions before we hit on the right one. I knew it was the right one, too, because we would try out various numbers on the dancers in the room and the reaction to this thing was tremendous. Jack Fina was our pianist in those days, and he did a helluva job on it."

Eddie Heyman, who'd written "Body and Soul" and many other hits, was asked to do a lyric. "He wrote a beautiful one, too," Freddy recalls. "But Eddie was an ASCAP writer and this was 1941 when ASCAP wouldn't allow its songs to be played on the air. So I had to call in a BMI writer, Bobby Worth, and he came up with the title and lyrics of 'Tonight We Love.' Incidentally, before we could come out with our record, Claude Thornhill, who used to play piano for us back in 1934, came out with his own recording of the same melody. He called his 'Concerto for Two.' "

So huge was the success of the Piano Concerto that Martin began to concentrate on this concertized approach to dance music. Next came the Grieg Concerto, which he called "I Look at Heaven," and then "Intermezzo." Fina had left, so Freddy began featuring Murray Arnold and then another exceptional pianist, Barclay Allen, whose brilliant career was cut short by a horrible auto accident.

The approach was commercial, though rather pedantic, and brought the comment of "much pomp but very little circumstance" from one of the more caustic critics. But the approach assured Martin's success. Freddy found a home for himself in the Cocoanut Grove, leaving at times to play other spots and to do his regular Lady Esther show, a sequel to Wayne King's famous radio series. So good were his musicianship, his taste and his manners that he had few worries thereafter. Perhaps he would have made more money had he been more aggressive or had he been able to follow the advice of Larry Barnett, "who kept telling me to invest a little of my money each week in IBM stock. The only trouble was I wasn't making as much as Larry was. That's why *he* is now a millionaire."

Today Martin is still a happy and well-liked man. Unlike many leaders, he has succeeded in keeping his band, his musical reputation and his respect intact. He has appeared on several TV series, and during the early seventies his band became the nucleus of two long series of one-nighters that played concerts and dances as "The Big Band Cavalcade." Margaret Whiting, Bob Crosby, Frankie Carle, Buddy Morrow, Art Mooney, and George Shearing also participated. And when those tours were all over, Freddy returned to the West Coast to continue doing what he obviously enjoys most: leading one of the most pleasant, most relaxed dance orchestras that ever flowed across the big band scene.

Hal McIntyre

THE first time I ever saw Hal McIntyre he was wearing a big, happy grin and driving a Model A Ford convertible roadster with its top back—in sub-zero, snowy weather! It was early 1937. The place was Cromwell, Connecticut, and Glenn Miller, who was just starting to organize his band, had driven up, at John Hammond's suggestion, to audition Hal and some of the members of McIntyre's young group. The others never made it, but Glenn was so impressed by Hal's playing that he hired him right then on that cold wintery night. Miller still wasn't too sure just where he was going, but he was sure that, wherever it was, he wanted Hal with him.

Hal

Glenn was won over completely, not only by Hal's musicianship—he played even more clarinet in those days than he did alto—but also by his friendly enthusiasm. He was then, and always remained, one of the most charming and genuine men in the whole dance band field, and when he left the Miller band, late in 1941, I always felt that a vital part of the band's personality went with him.

He and Glenn became very close friends, often rooming together on the road during the band's earlier days. He was the first musician Miller hired, and even though Glenn's band underwent numerous wholesale changes thereafter, including one complete breakup and another "almost," Hal continued to stay on. Eventually, when Glenn and Hal agreed that it was time for Mac to start out on his own, Miller backed him financially and spiritually.

Like Miller's, the McIntyre band was a very musical one. But its style was far removed from Glenn's. It was more like Duke Ellington's, and for this Dave Matthews, the band's arranger, was directly responsible. Dave, who wrote many Ellingtonian arrangements for Woody Herman's band, has freely admitted the Ellington influence, which went as far as cribbing whole passages from his arrangements. Said Dave: "My only reason for using such music was for the musical pleasure it gave me on hearing it played in arrangements—nothing more!"

The McIntyre band had a colorful sound, thanks not only to the Ellington imitations but also to other voicings that Matthews and, later, arranger Howard Gibeling employed. Hal, who by now was sticking strictly to his alto sax, was featured on several Johnny Hodges-like passages, but it was always my feeling that had the band been built more around Hal's horn and less around the musical but not always identifiable arrangements, the McIntyre band might have been much more successful. Still, it played many of the top spots, including Glen Island Casino and the Hollywood Palladium and numerous hotel rooms and ballrooms in between. It also played at President Roosevelt's Birthday Ball at the Statler Hotel in Washington on January 30, 1945.

Matthews was also an impressive tenor sax soloist. But the most exciting sideman in the band was a young bassist named Eddie Safranski, whose virtuoso technique astounded many of us and who was to become a mainstay of Stan Kenton's famous outfit several years later.

In addition to Matthews' jazz instrumentals Hal played many ballads. On those he featured various vocalists, including Al Nobel, Carl Denny, Gloria Van, Ruth Gaylor and Helen Ward, Benny Goodman's great ex-singer, who had tired of her housewifely duties and wanted to return to the singing wars.

In May of 1945, Hal and his band started on a memorable trip overseas to entertain the troops. Because some of his men could not meet all the Army and USO requirements, Hal was forced to reorganize his band quickly and drastically. Thus, the music with which he entertained in enlisted men's clubs, in improvised theaters and in open fields may not have been up to McIntyre's top standards. Nevertheless, its reception everywhere was tremendous as it provided our fighting men with some of their greatest musical and emotional happiness.

By the time the band returned, it was again in good musical shape, and Hal continued his career where he had left off. "I was warned the trip might kill my future," he stated, "and I knew it might. But George Moffatt [his manager] and I both felt we had a really important contribution to make, and we wanted to make it."

When the big bands began fading from the scene, Hal McIntyre's did too, even though his worked more regularly than some of the bigger names during the fifties. But in the latter part of the decade Hal experienced distressing difficulties. He was separated from his wife and children, and he moved to California. When I last saw him, in 1955, the innate warmth and the big grin were still there, but the spirit had begun to wane. In 1959 tragedy struck: apparently it was a carelessly discarded cigarette that started a bedroom fire that snuffed out the career and the life of Hal McIntyre, one of the really nice guys of the big bands.

Ray McKinley

RAY McKINLEY was always an amazing drummer. He propelled a swinging beat, very often with a two-beat dixieland basis, that inspired musicians to play better. He spent more time on getting just the right sound out of his drums than any other drummer I can recall. He had a wild, zany sense of humor, which he often expressed through his instrument. Extremely bright, articulate and sensitive, he sometimes hid his true nature beneath a veneer of sarcasm. Incompetence and fakery bugged him, and he'd show it. True talent and candor pleased him, and he'd show that too. Few musicians have acted as blunt, as independent and as honest as this sometimes hard-nosed, more often softhearted, Texan.

Long before he ever had his own band, he was sparking those of others. Ever hear of Savage Cummings or Larry Duncan? McKinley did. He was their drummer down Fort Worth way before he joined Smith Ballew's band, some of whose members later became an integral part of the Dorsey Brothers' and then Jimmy Dorsey's organizations. Then Ray became a co-bandleader with Will Bradley, but the two maestri failed to agree on many musical matters, so early in 1942, Ray set out to organize his own outfit.

First he took several trips, looking for young musicians, and when he had found what he wanted he hid away in Patchogue, Long Island ("so no other leaders could steal my men," he explained), and began rehearsing.

In April the band appeared in the New York area—at the Commodore Hotel and at Frank Dailey's Meadowbrook. It was a swinging outfit, featuring Mahlon Clark, the brilliant clarinetist who had followed Ray from Will's band, a fine seventeen-year-old trumpeter named Dick Cathcart, a swinging young pianist named Lou Stein, a very pretty and very good singer named Imogene Lynn, and two veterans: trombonist Brad Gowans and tuba player Joe Parks, who, instead of burping with the rhythm section, played right along with the brass, to which he added an unusually full, rich sound. "The band really swung," Ray recalls. "But it couldn't play ballads worth a four-letter word."

The outfit lasted less than a year, during which it made some joyful jazz sounds on Capitol Records, the most successful of which was "Hard Hearted Hannah," which featured one of several rhythmic McKinley vocals. Its most

Ray

successful dates were in California, where it made a movie, *Hit Parade of 1942*, which also featured Count Basie and Tony Martin.

"We were at a big ballroom in Southgate, California," McKinley remembers, "when we heard that the Marines at Camp Pendleton were looking for a band. Everybody was being drafted then, so we decided to enter as a unit. But the Marines were pretty busy those days in places like Guadalcanal, and I guess orchestras must have been running a poor second in their thoughts right then. Anyway, there was a long delay, and a lot of the guys in the band were getting their draft notices, and finally I got mine. That was when I contacted Glenn about joining him." Captain Miller grabbed rookie McKinley at once.

Glenn Miller and Ray McKinley had been close friends since the Smith Ballew days, and the role that Ray was to play in Glenn's band was something neither he nor anyone else ever expected. But that's another story.

After the war, McKinley started the kind of band few ever thought he'd front, a highly sophisticated musical outfit. At the suggestion of band booker and builder Willard Alexander, Ray joined forces with one of the most progressive of all arrangers, Eddie Sauter, about whom Glenn Miller had once exclaimed admiringly, "Eddie Sauter is just about ten years ahead of every other arranger in the business."

Sauter's wonderfully inventive scores were musically superb. But they were difficult to play, requiring intensive rehearsing and concentration. The results were sometimes good, sometimes not so good, as I noted in my April, 1946, review of the band, which began: "Ray McKinley's new band is new in age, maturity and ideas. Therein lies its assets and liabilities with the former far exceeding the latter."

Ray, I remember, seemed disappointed with the review. At first I couldn't quite figure out why. I thought it was quite favorable. But then one day I happened to glance at the issue of the magazine, and directly opposite the McKinley review had been one of Elliot Lawrence. Mac's band had received a B plus rating. But Elliot's had drawn an A minus. Shortly thereafter we stopped all band ratings at *Metronome*.

As the McKinley band mastered the magnificent Sauter arrangements, it developed into one of the most musically exciting groups of all time, one that combined artistic creativity, color and wit with a true swinging beat. It created a batch of great Sauter instrumentals for Majestic, most of which, unfortunately, were badly recorded. But musicians still rave about sides like "Hangover Square" (for me one of the greatest of all time by any band!), "Sandstorm," "Tumblebug" and "Borderline," which featured a brilliant young McKinley discovery, trombonist Vern Friley. The new band also housed several other excellent young musicians: guitarist Mundell Lowe, who was followed by Johnny Gray, clarinetist Peanuts Hucko and trumpeter Nick Travis.

Ray developed his commercial appeal too. Both Sauter and arranger Deane Kincaide produced many novelties, which Ray sang. Most successful: "Red Silk Stockings." There was also a number that Ray recorded with just a small group for RCA Victor, "You've Come a Long Way from St. Louis," which proved to be the band's biggest hit.

After the big band era, McKinley continued his band for a few years, then switched to radio and TV work as a swinging singer and glib disc jockey. In 1956 he accepted an appointment from Helen Miller, Glenn's widow, with whom he had remained on very friendly terms, to take over the Miller band. This he did with great success, touring all over the world. In 1965 he finally called it quits so he could settle down with his wife and daughter in their Stamford, Connecticut home. For ten years or so he hit the road with small jazz groups or semi-big bands which were organized for him in strategic spots, spreading his infectious charm and rhythm to the delights of groups of all ages. In the mid-1970s he called it quits for the north and migrated to Largo, Florida, continuing to play gigs while also enjoying golf and other forms of relaxation and generally living the sort of relaxed life that typified his personality.

Glenn Miller

OF ALL the outstanding popular dance bands, the one that evokes the most memories of how wonderfully romantic it all was, the one whose music people most want to hear over and over again, is the band of the late Glenn Miller.

This was a band of great moods, of great contrasts, of great excitement, all put together by a man who, I felt, knew better than any other leader exactly what he wanted and how to go about getting it. For Glenn Miller, for all the appearance he presented of a stern, stolid, straight-ahead-looking

Glenn with leader Ray Noble and his favorite trombonist,
Wilbur Schwitchenberg (Will Bradley)

schoolteacher, was a man of human and artistic sensitivity and great imagination. What's more, he was an exceptional executive. He made decisions easily, quickly and rationally. He was strong-willed, but that strong will almost always had a clear purpose. He was stubborn, but he was fair. He had intense likes and dislikes, though he'd admit it when he was proved wrong.

He displayed great confidence in himself. His attitude was that if he couldn't run a band properly, then he had no business having one. Yet he was never cocky. He was, in fact, a man of natural reserve. At first, he was extremely uncomfortable fronting a band. He felt that people wanted him to be a glamour boy, but he couldn't fake that sort of front. In fact, the only way Glenn knew how to fake was on his trombone.

Long before he'd ever led a band, he'd done very well as a jazz trombonist, playing with top jazz stars on numerous recordings in the late twenties and early thirties, as well as arranging jazz for the bands of Ben Pollack, Red Nichols, the Dorsey brothers and Ray Noble.

It was while he was a member of Noble's band that he decided he'd finally like to start his own outfit. He did so in 1937 and for the next two years struggled desperately just to survive. In the spring of 1939 the band suddenly caught on, and from then, until September, 1942, when he disbanded to accept a commission in the Army Air Force, Glenn Miller's remained the most popular of all the country's dance bands. Nine months later his new and enlarged all-soldier orchestra was again regaling America via coast-to-coast broadcasts, and a year after that it began playing its music for American G.I.'s fighting in Western Europe.

The entire career of the Glenn Miller band lasted just eight years. The last six were glorious; the first two were horrendous.

I remember those first years. I remember them well. I remember the night Glenn and I were listening to records at my house and he confided in me that he was planning to start a band. I was impressed, and the more he spoke, the more impressed I became, so much so that in the March, 1937, issue of *Metronome,* in a short piece headed "The Country's Newest Coming Band?!" I predicted, rather rashly, that "Miller, besides great talents as an arranger, possesses other attributes which should help him nicely in what already looks like a pretty easy climb to the top." I didn't mention his ability as a trombonist because in those days he adamantly refused to feature himself. "I can't compete against Tommy Dorsey," was his explanation.

I remember those years, because for a couple of them it looked as if I might have made one of the worst predictions of all time. I remember them, too, because Glenn asked me if I'd help him in his search for new, young musicians, and after we had found Hal McIntyre in a small town in Connecticut, we'd drive to various other places trying to discover other worthy unknowns. It was exciting, too—like the night we got tossed out of a very unswank West Forty-second Street hotel for not drinking.

We'd heard about a Texas tenor saxist named Johnny Harrell, who was playing there. After we'd ordered a couple of sandwiches and cups of coffee, the waiter left us to MC the floor show. When it ended he came back to the table (I don't think there were more than a half-dozen couples in the room) and asked us what we'd like to drink. We answered, "Two more coffees." "No, I mean *drink*," he said. When we told him we didn't want to drink, he told us we had to get out. So we did—and we took Johnny Harrell with us.

Glenn worked hard rehearsing his young musicians. They met every day in a two-story walk-up in a place called the Haven Studios on West Fifty-fourth Street, and there he'd drill them. His patience was immense. If a section couldn't get the correct phrasing of a certain passage, he'd bring over his trombone, sit down and play the passage over and over exactly the way he wanted it to sound until the guys had mastered it.

In March, 1937, he landed a record date at Decca, with Dave Kapp, later head of Kapp Records, as supervisor. Glenn must have felt that some·of his young musicians were not yet ready, because he augmented the band with some top veterans, all close personal friends. Thus Charlie Spivak, Sterling Bose and Manny Klein, the last then considered the best all-round trumpeter in town, were on trumpets; Dick McDonough strummed guitar, and Howard Smith played piano. Inasmuch as I had been sitting in at rehearsals on drums, because neither of us could find a drummer Glenn liked, he asked me to make the date too.

The results weren't great, but they were by no means bad, even though I was so nervous that I must have been playing uncontrolled triplets throughout. There were five sides arranged by Glenn, of which "Moonlight Bay" and "Peg o' My Heart" were probably the best, and a sixth side, "I'm Sittin' on Top of the World," arranged by and featuring McIntyre on clarinet, an instrument he played quite well but on which Glenn seldom used him thereafter. The style, however, was entirely unlike that of the Miller band as most people remembered. It was semi-dixieland, but there were some of the repeated riffs, especially on "Moonlight Bay," that had characterized Glenn's writing with the Dorsey Brothers and that he would bring into some of his own band's scores during its most successful years.

A month or so later the band played its first engagement, a one-night fill-in at the Hotel New Yorker. Seymour Weiss, President of the Roosevelt Hotel in New Orleans, heard about the band and booked it for his hotel's famed Blue Room early in June for two weeks. "Five weeks was the record length any band ever stayed," Glenn wrote me on August 8, 1937, "and when we finish here, which is August 25, the boys will have been here ten weeks," he added proudly. From there it played several more hotels, including the Adolphus in Dallas and the Nicollet in Minneapolis.

But the customers in those cities weren't very satisfied with Glenn's band, and Glenn, in turn, was becoming increasingly dissatisfied with his personnel. So he kept making constant changes. Most troublesome of all was the drummer's spot. On October 12, 1937, he wrote from the Nicollet:

> We are getting a new drummer (thank God), about two hundred and fifty pounds of solid rhythm, I hope. This boy we have is pretty bad and MacGregor [Glenn's close friend and pianist, who was to remain with him throughout his civilian years] says outside of being a bad drummer he has a quarter beat rest between each tooth which doesn't enhance the romantic assets of the band. . . .
>
> I don't know just where we are going from here—I guess no one else does either. We are hoping for some sort of a radio setup that will let more than three people hear us at a time. If this drummer only works out, there will be nothing to stop us from now on.

Late that fall, when it played the Raymor Ballroom in Boston, the band finally began to broadcast coast to coast, and to many more than three people at a time. It was on those programs that Glenn experimented with a few bars of the clarinet-lead style that eventually became his musical trademark.

During his days with Noble, Glenn had written several arrangements that had featured trumpeter Peewee Erwin doubling lead an octave above another lead line played by the tenor sax. But after Peewee left, his replacement didn't have a strong enough lip for those high parts. As an experiment Glenn assigned the trumpet part to Johnny Mince on clarinet (both horns are B-flat instruments) and used a violinst who doubled on sax as a fifth voice in the reed section. Out came the unique voicing that someday was to win fame as "The Miller Sound."

But that "someday" was still quite a long way off. Numerous replacements had helped a bit. One of these, Irving Fazola, owner of one of the most gorgeous clarinet sounds of all time, was the particular apple of Glenn's ear.

Undoubtedly his presence had contributed much to Glenn's experimenting with his unorthodox clarinet-lead idea. But Miller still couldn't afford to hire enough pros as talented as Faz.

His musicians' inexperience hurt. Bolstered by several top studio musicians, the band had been able to complete six sides in three hours on its original Decca date; now, early in December, 1937, his much greener group took five hours to cut just two sides for Brunswick—and they weren't very good.

The band's morale wasn't very good either. Glenn was saddled with several ever- and overimbibing trumpeters. One could never get to sleep until he'd had so much to drink that he would roll off his bed and sleep on the floor. Another wrecked one of Glenn's cars.

Even people outside the band seemed to be against him. I remember his first theater date in Newark, New Jersey. Glenn had prepared a lovely, moody arrangement of "Danny Boy" which started with muted brass placed around one mike in front of the stage and the reeds grouped around another one. The number began in total darkness. The light man had instructions that on the opening notes, to be played by the brass, he was to put a pinspot on them. Glenn gave the downbeat, the brass started playing softly, and immediately the light man put the pinspot, not on the brass, but on the reeds—who were just standing there, waiting for their parts to come along!

Glenn was afflicted with personal problems too. His wonderful wife, Helen, underwent a serious operation. Throughout all their years together, she was a stalwart companion and confidante; in fact, I can't recall any two people in the field more devoted to each other than Glenn and Helen Miller. The 1953 movie of Glenn's life may have contained several inaccuracies, but the tender rapport projected in the film by June Allyson, who reminded me so much of Helen, and by Jimmy Stewart, who reminded me so very much of Jimmy Stewart, was entirely authentic.

The band's career hit bottom on a road trip through Pennsylvania during the especially snowy 1937 Christmas season. Everything went wrong. Several of the band's cars broke down. So did several of the musicians. The lone bright spot was the arrival of Maurice Purtill, whose drumming inspired the band—but for just one night. On the very evening that Purtill arrived, Glenn received a frantic phone call from his close friend and supporter, Tommy Dorsey, asking him please to send Purtill back to New York. Davey Tough had once again failed to show up, and Tommy desperately needed Purtill for an important date. So back went the band's one-day inspiration.

Conditions grew so bad that by the middle of January, 1938, Glenn decided he'd had it as a bandleader. He told the musicians to take a rest, that he'd call them when he needed them again. Almost immediately the better ones found jobs. Kitty Lane, a pretty vocalist with a gorgeous figure who had sung especially well on a record of a tune called "Sweet Strangers" (at times she sounded a bit like Mildred Bailey), joined Isham Jones. Fazola went back to Ben Pollack. Glenn's star trumpeter, Les Biegel, returned to

An early Miller band contract—note the hours and the price!

the Midwest. Tenor saxist Jerry Jerome, one of Glenn's favorites, joined Red Norvo.

I remember the Jerome incident well because it showed me for the first time how stubborn Glenn could really be. I had discovered both Jerry and lead saxist George Siravo, who later became one of the country's top arrangers, in Harry Reser's band. I had told Glenn about them, and he'd hired them both. Then, when Glenn broke up the band, I told Red Norvo about Jerry, and Red hired him. Suddenly my relationship with Glenn changed completely. He seemed to go out of his way to avoid me. I couldn't figure out why.

Finally I cornered him one afternoon at a Tommy Dorsey radio rehearsal (Glenn was doing Tommy's show during the lay-off) and asked him point-blank what was eating him. Only then did I discover that he felt I'd been disloyal in recommending one of his musicians to Norvo. When I reminded him that he'd given Jerry no assurances that he still had a job, that Red and Jerry were friends of mine too, and that Jerry still had to earn a living, Glenn's attitude softened. How much simpler it would have been if he'd just told me at the outset what was eating him instead of going through that polar routine. But then, as I mentioned earlier, Glenn was stubborn. He was also possessive and reserved.

Glenn was wrangling with others, too. He split with his manager, Arthur Michaud, who also handled Tommy Dorsey, and signed with a big, hearty and very influential Bostonian named Cy Shribman, who had been a tremendous help to Artie Shaw and Woody Herman.

In March, Glenn decided to try again, so he began a new series of rehearsals with a batch of new, young musicians, plus four holdovers from the first band —McIntyre, MacGregor, bassist Rolly Bundock and lead trumpeter Bob Price.

On lead clarinet Glenn put a young New Jerseyan named Wilbur Schwartz. Wilbur, who looked like a kewpie doll, had been playing in Julie Wintz's band, and with the addition of his wonderful tone the sound of the Miller band became one that none of its imitators could ever reproduce. From Philadelphia Glenn brought in an exciting jazz trumpeter named Johnny Austin, who brought along a friend, Bob Spangler, who turned out to be the best drummer the band had up to that time.

And Glenn went even farther out of town to get a tenor saxist who he always swore was "the greatest." Others may have preferred Coleman Hawkins or Bud Freeman or Lester Young or Chu Berry, but Glenn remained ever loyal to his Gordon (Tex) Beneke.

I could never really decide whether Glenn was completely convinced himself when he came on so strong about certain men in his band. Beneke was one. Another was singer Ray Eberle. The hiring of Ray was surprisingly simple—almost naive. One night in a restaurant Glenn ran into Ray's brother Bob (who later switched the final "e" to a "y"), whom he'd known and admired since their Dorsey Brothers days. According to Bob, Glenn asked him if he had any brothers at home, and when Bob said he did, Glenn simply said, "If he's your brother, he must be able to sing. I'll give him a job." Actually, Ray had had no professional singing experience at all. But Glenn worked with him, and it wasn't long before he was proclaiming, and I think truly believing, that Ray was better than Bob. "And he doesn't sing so far behind the beat either," he'd keep telling me. I was never convinced.

Glenn and I disagreed about other musical matters. One of these concerned his use of his rhythm section. He kept insisting that the bass play a steady four beats to the bar. This used to bug me. "It makes everything sound so stiff," I'd argue. "Besides, it makes it much harder to dance to."

Glenn and Ray Eberle

To which he'd snort, "The trouble with you is you don't know how to dance. All you do is wheelbarrow your gal around the floor, just like Smith Ballew used to do." I'd never seen Smith Ballew dance, so again I wasn't convinced.

The emphasis upon a steady four-to-the-bar was a change for Glenn, because when I first knew him he'd been primarily a two-beat dixieland fan. Even after he had switched away from that, his favorite band had become Jimmie Lunceford's, which played so many of its numbers in an easy, relaxed, two-beat style. But as the Basie band with its swinging four-beat, riff-filled style began to emerge on the scene, Glenn became one of its most devoted fans. Soon the Basie approach became the Miller approach—except, of course, that the Count's always remained much looser and freer and swingier.

The Miller band played quite a bit of jazz in those days. Some of it was appreciated in ballrooms, especially around Boston, where it appeared often. But it was completely lost on the customers of the band's semi-steady New York spot, the Paradise Restaurant, a typical Broadway nightclub that catered to out-of-town salesmen and even gave Miller second billing to Freddy Fisher and his Schnickelfritzers, a bunch of musicians who purposely played corny. There Miller played mostly for floor shows, and his musicians were so tired and brought down by all those dull arrangements for the acts that by the time they got to do radio broadcasts, their own music sounded tired and uninspired.

The sidemen weren't any happier with the setup than Glenn was. The only difference was *they* could leave the band when they wanted to. And quite a number of them did, including vocalist Gail Reese, an attractive lass who could sing well. But her departure was Glenn's doing. For while he had been in Boston he had heard two sisters, Betty and Marion Hutton, singing with the Vincent Lopez Orchestra. Everyone was raving about how great Betty was, but Glenn figured, he told me later, that Marion would be easier to handle than Betty. And so in September, 1938, Marion joined the band.

Glenn was right about Marion. She was a joy in every way. She brought into the band a new, light, bright spirit that it had never known before. But that still wasn't enough.

*Glenn with Marion Hutton
and Tex Beneke*

In February, 1939, Miller took a trip down to North Carolina. Marion and Tex and a brand new trombone player, a lanky, slow-moving fellow named Paul Tanner, who's now a professor at UCLA, and I rode down together. We had lots of laughs on the way. But that was before the band performed. By the time the short trip was over, Glenn was completely discouraged. The brass, which had recently undergone another of its periodic changes, was awful. The rhythm section wasn't much better. "I guess," he told me as we drove back to New York, "I may as well give it all up and go back in the studios and just play trombone."

But Glenn never quite made it back to those studios—at least not as a sideman. For on March 1, 1939, on Glenn's thirty-fifth birthday, at the old, reliable Haven Studios, while the band was rehearsing once again (probably trying to break in another brass section!) the Miller career got its most important shot in the arm. That was the day the word came in from GAC, Miller's booking office, that the famous Glen Island Casino had selected the band for the coming summer season. And the surprising part of it was that the band had been selected on the basis of its Paradise Restaurant performances, of which Glenn had been somewhat less than even half-proud!

Being chosen to play Glen Island was as important to a band's success as a dozen consecutive appearances on Ed Sullivan's TV show would have been to one of the singing groups of the sixties. Frank Dailey at the Meadow-brook immediately got into the act and offered the band a lengthy stay at his spot before the Glen Island Casino opening.

At Dailey's, Glenn really whipped the band into shape. I recall one night catching one of its broadcasts (it did ten per week, thereby getting fantastic exposure) and hearing it jump as it never had. I couldn't believe it was the same drummer. The next day I phoned Glenn and asked him how come the man had improved so much. "It wasn't him," Glenn explained. "It was Moe Purtill. He came in to sit in a few nights ago and he got such a kick out of working with us that he's going to stay." To do so, Purtill, a bright, exuberant drummer, had given up a teaching career that had already netted him a sizable array of students.

Seeing broad daylight ahead, Glenn started investing more time and money in his band. He had already received much needed and much appreciated help from Cy Shribman, but now he decided to go for broke. In addition to restoring the guitar, he added a trumpet and a trombone—making his the first major band with an eight-man brass team. He also began to introduce many new arrangements, including some very good ones by Bill Finegan.

With success apparently coming his way, more people began to latch on to the Miller bandwagon. But Glenn knew he was not yet out of the woods. He was playing Glen Island Casino at a loss, as bands so often did in order to get the air time and the promotional value that the place offered. And he began to show resentment when certain people tried taking advantage of him.

One evening one of the most influential critics in the trade came into the Casino with a party of six. They had cocktails, dinner and then stayed on, ordering more drinks. When the waiter brought them their check, which amounted to more than seventy-five dollars (equivalent to a hundred and fifty today), the critic told him, "Mr. Miller will take the check." So the waiter brought the check over to Glenn, who looked at it, then brought it over to the critic. "I'm sorry," Glenn said, "but if this is what it's going to cost me to get a write-up, I can't afford it." And he handed the check back.

Glenn had guts. He could also spot phonies, whom he truly detested. If you were straight with Glenn, he'd give you at least the time of day. But if you weren't, he wouldn't even give you the time of night.

There was a columnist in that era who also wrote songs. They were usually pretty corny, but bands often played them hoping they'd get a good write-up. He dropped into the Casino one night, and a friend told Glenn he was there. Glenn made some sort of a remark about how little he thought of the guy. "But you've got to admit," said the friend, trying to placate Miller, "that the man's got a pretty good sense of humor." "Sure, he must have," muttered Glenn sarcastically, "to be able to write songs like those!"

There was no doubt about it: the Glen Island Casino engagement really made the Miller band. Within a month after it closed there in 1939, it began to break attendance records almost wherever it went. At the Capitol Theater in Washington it did the best business the house had done in three years, twenty-two thousands dollars' worth. At the Hippodrome in Baltimore it achieved the highest theater gross in the city's history, nineteen thousand dollars. In Syracuse it set a record for the largest crowd ever to attend a dance there. In Hershey, Pennsylvania, it broke a Guy Lombardo record that had been standing since 1931. And at the State Theater in Hartford it broke the house record—with only Glenn's name, not even that of the movie playing, appearing on the marquee!

And while he was smashing records, he was also making them. Late in 1938 he had switched from Brunswick to Victor's thirty-five-cent Bluebird label. One of his earliest and eventually most important couplings had Frankie Carle's theme, "Sunrise Serenade," on one side and Glenn's own theme, "Moonlight Serenade," on the other.

"Moonlight Serenade" hadn't always been "Moonlight Serenade." Glenn had written the melody during his Ray Noble days as an exercise in a course in arranging which he was taking with Joseph Schillinger. The first time I ever heard it was when Al Bowlly, Noble's sentimental and sensitive singer, cornered me backstage at the Rainbow Room, where Ray's band was playing, and in an emotional voice softly crooned what he seemed to consider the most beautiful song ever written.

I must admit I was tremendously impressed—not merely by the melody, not merely by the way Bowlly sang it, but also by the words written by Eddie Heyman, Johnny Green's collaborator on "Body and Soul." He called the Miller melody "Now I Lay Me Down to Weep," and to this day I still can remember the original lyrics:

> Weep for the moon, for the moon has no reason to glow now,
> Weep for the rose, for the rose has no reason to grow now,
> The river won't flow now,
> As I lay me down to weep.
>
> You went away, and the break in my heart isn't mending,
> You went away, and I know there is no happy ending,
> There's no use pretending
> As I lay me down to weep.
>
>> When you were mine, the world was mine,
>> And fate constantly smiled.
>> Now in its place, I have to face
>> A pillow of tears, all through the years.

Though you are gone, I still pray that the sun shines above you,
Time marches on, yet I know that I always will love you,
I'll keep dreaming of you
As I lay me down to weep.*

Glenn wanted to use this as his theme song. But he was advised, and convinced, that Heyman's words were too sad for a theme, that it needed something more romantic and hopeful. I had also contributed a set of lyrics called "Gone with the Dawn" (some writers have erroneously reported that the tune was once called "Gone with the Wind"), but they also were considered too depressing. Eventually Glenn contacted Mitchell Parrish, who had written the lyrics for "Stardust" many years after Hoagy Carmichael had written the original melody, and Parrish came·up with "Moonlight Serenade."

A few weeks after the record of the two themes came out, Bluebird issued one of the band's most important hits. This was Bill Finegan's swinging version of "Little Brown Jug," which viewers of the motion picture *The Glenn Miller Story* will recall was romanticized as Glenn's *final* recording. But after all, didn't Hollywood also try to tell us that Glenn was like Jimmy Stewart?

During the summer of 1939 the band recorded an average of four sides every two weeks. Two of these featured a brand new girl singer who had replaced Marion Hutton for a short time when late in July she collapsed on the bandstand from overexhaustion. The sub, who sang on two sides, "Baby Me" and "Love, with a Capital You," was young Kay Starr, who in some ways was a better singer than Marion, but who couldn't compete with her when it came to the "All-American Girl Next Door" impression that Marion projected so well. As a matter of fact, when Marion first joined the band, Glenn had changed her name for a short time to Sissy Jones. One step further, and he might have been featuring the only girl singer wearing a Girl Scout uniform!

On August 1, 1949, the band recorded its biggest hit of all time, "In the Mood," complete with the tenor sax exchanges between Beneke and Al Klink, whom a number of the band's musicians, including arranger Billy May, considered the more interesting soloist of the two. Billy even tried to give Al solos in his arrangements, but Glenn invariably turned them over to Tex. Today Klink is one of the most sought-after saxists in the New York studios and often appears with Benny Goodman and other top jazz leaders.

"In the Mood" had an interesting history. It was written by a musician-arranger named Joe Garland who had originally submitted it to Artie Shaw. Artie appreciated the catchy riff piece, and he played it quite often on the job. But the Garland arrangement ran something like eight minutes, and in those days eight minutes was much too long for a recording. So, after Shaw had decided he couldn't do very much with the piece, Garland brought it to

Miller, and Glenn, with his savvy as an arranger, made appropriate cuts, whittling it down to a length that would fit on one side of a record.

Wherever the band played, the kids would scream for "In the Mood." And Glenn always responded with quite a show, winding up with the trumpets waving their derbies and the trombones whirling their horns high toward the sky. It was the sort of showmanship that Glenn had always admired in the Jimmie Lunceford band, to which he always willingly gave credit.

"In the Mood" also utilized a typical Millerian device—that of the riff repeated over and over again, fading away and almost disappearing, then suddenly blasting back again with the entire cycle repeated. It was an ear-catching trick he had used often in the Dorsey Brothers band, a sort of musical cat-and-mouse teaser that was a cinch to rouse a crowd.

About this time Glenn also hired two more good jazz musicians, Ernie Caceres, who played clarinet and baritone sax, and John Best, who blew an especially warm-sounding trumpet.

By the beginning of 1940 the Miller band was such a success that it couldn't fill all the dates proffered it. On October 6, 1939, it had shared the Carnegie Hall stage with the well-established bands of Benny Goodman, Fred Waring and Paul Whiteman. On December 27, 1939, it had replaced Whiteman on the Chesterfield show. On January 5 it opened at the Café Rouge of the Hotel Pennsylvania, and shortly thereafter it also played the Paramount Theater.

That was quite a schedule! Three radio programs a week, complete with rehearsals. Two sessions, totaling five hours of music per night and six on weekends, at the hotel. And four and sometimes five shows a day at the Paramount! (While Glenn was at the theater, he brought in Charlie Spivak's brand new band to substitute an hour or so a night for him at the hotel.) In addition, during the first two months of 1940, the band recorded close to thirty sides, including "Tuxedo Junction," which Glenn had picked up from the Erskine Hawkins band, and "I'll Never Smile Again," a record that meant absolutely nothing to Glenn, did nothing for the song, and proved, via Tommy Dorsey's successful recording of the same tune several months later, that Miller was totally fallible.

Glenn, according to himself in those days, was worse than just fallible, as he confided to me one day in his dressing room at the Paramount: "I don't quite know how to handle it," he said. "I'm really beginning to be one hell of a [I forget just what he did call himself]. I can't help it, though. So many people are asking me to do so many things and I really want to do some of them, but I just don't have the time. It's murder. I find myself doing things I'm ashamed of doing, and yet I know people would never understand if I told them the plain, simple truth. I'm not the kind of a guy I really want to be."

One thing Glenn had very little time for in that period was his arranging. Fortunately, his friend Tommy Dorsey had sent over a young arranger who took over most of the duties and who, Glenn told me some years later, was the most creative writer who ever worked for the band. This was Bill Finegan, an imaginative, witty man with a dour expression that did not at all reflect the spirited manuscripts with which he supplied the band. It was Finegan who had written the "Little Brown Jug" arrangement, and it was Finegan who was to pen hundreds more, some for Glenn's band, some for Tommy's and, in later years, for the Sauter-Finegan Orchestra, which he co-led with Eddie Sauter.

Finegan wasn't the only one to supply swinging arrangements for Miller. When Artie Shaw's band suddenly broke up late in 1939, Glenn offered Artie's arranger, Jerry Gray, a job. His writings may not have been as startlingly creative as Finegan's, but he did bring in some thoroughly commercial yet very musical arrangements.

"I was happier musically with Artie," Jerry once admitted. "But I was happier personally with Glenn. One thing that Glenn did, he encouraged me to write." One of the first hits Gray turned out for the band was a simple rhythmic opus called "Pennsylvania Six Five Thousand" (the Hotel Pennsylvania's phone number), which, Jerry points out, "was based on a riff from Larry Clinton's 'Dipsy Doodle.' "

As Glenn left the arranging chores more to others (he never stepped out of that picture completely, especially with Gray, with whom he often sketched ideas that Jerry would then carry through), he became more and more involved in the commercial aspects of leading a band. I hadn't realized how deeply immersed he had become until one day when he phoned me and asked me to meet him at one of his favorite places, the Victoria Hotel Barber Shop, where he could transact business without being interrupted by phone calls, etc.

When I arrived he came right to the point. "How would you like to write my biography?" he asked. I was knocked out. Here was a story I felt I could really tell—the tale about the musician who believed so deeply in his music, who was going to prove to the world that, despite all the hardships and the heartaches, despite all the overly commercial parasites who had infested the music world, good music would emerge triumphant! What a great object lesson for every dedicated, aspiring musician!

"I have the title already," Glenn said from the barber chair. "Listen. It's 'My Dance Band Gave Me $748,564!' " I don't recall the exact figure, but it was somewhere in that neighborhood.

What I do recall, though, is that I felt terribly let down. In those days I was still quite an idealist, and I guess I must have thought that Glenn was too. But, as I learned so well that afternoon, he had become a realist long before I had.

Nevertheless, Glenn continued to improve his band. In September, 1940, he brought in a young, spirited bass player from Alvino Rey's band. Herman (Trigger) Alpert. "I used to complain to Glenn about the rhythm section," Jerry Gray recently said, "but the minute Trigger joined the band it was the difference between night and day!"

The Glenn Miller band in the Café Rouge of the Hotel Pennsylvania
Front row: *Ray Eberle, Billy May, Al Klink, Willie Schwartz,*
Jack Lathrop, Marion Hutton, Ernie Caceres, Hal McIntyre, Tex Beneke
Second row: *Jimmy Priddy's eyes, Frank D'Annolfo's ear, Glenn*
Back row: *Johnny Best, Ray Anthony, Mickey McMickle,*
Maurice Purtill, Trigger Alpert, Chummy MacGregor

A few weeks later two trumpet replacements arrived and immediately the
brass section began to spark, crackle and pop as it never had before. Young
Ray Anthony, with a warm lower register, played a good fourth trumpet,
but the real excitement came from the horn of big, broad-shouldered-and-
bellied Billy May, who not only played excellent lead but also emoted some
of the best jazz that ever came from the Miller ranks. And on top of all that,
May, who had done so much for Charlie Barnet's band, proceeded to write
some wonderfully relaxed, swinging arrangements for Miller.

Amy Lee, never one of the band's biggest boosters, noted in the December,
1940, *Metronome* that "something is happening to lighten the Miller music's
tendency to heaviness. Maybe it's the presence of ex-Charlie Barnet trumpeter
Billy May." But then she reverted to the complaint often expressed by those
who felt the band had become too mechanical. "Glenn's is an appeal to the
head rather than to the heart of the listener. As an aggregation that has been
rehearsed until every bar of every tune is letter perfect, the Miller men probably have no rivals. For precision, attack, shading and blend, the band cannot be topped.

"But," she asked in conclusion, "is letter-perfect playing worth the inevitable sacrifice of natural feeling?"

Glenn's reaction to this sort of criticism—and there was a great deal of it—
was direct, if seemingly contradictory. He never wavered in his admiration
of the most swinging bands—Basie's especially. He realized that for his band
to retain its spirit, it too had to remain loose. But he remained acutely aware
that much of its success was based purely and simply on the magnificently

disciplined organization that he had created, and that if he allowed its superb pacing and exciting, machinelike precision to slacken, he would lose much of his commercial appeal.

He never strayed, therefore, from his strict, disciplinarian approach, even though it was resented by some of the band's sidemen who felt that their jazz should have been featured more often. But to front the world's greatest jazz band was not Glenn's big ambition.

In early 1941, to add more musical and visual variety, he hired the Modernaires, an outstanding vocal quartet—Chuck Goldstein, Hal Dickenson, Ralph Brewster and Bill Conway—which had once been featured in Charlie Barnet's band and had recently been working with Paul Whiteman's. And he also, but this time not of his own volition, replaced Marion Hutton with another vivacious singer, Dorothy Claire.

Marion's exit, even though temporary, was unfortunate and at the time unnecessary. Somehow a gossip columnist had learned that Marion, then married to Jack Philbin, then a music publisher and later for many years executive producer of the Jackie Gleason TV series, was going to have a baby. She could easily have sung with the band for a few more months, but the scoop embarrassed her and so she resigned. When Glenn took Dorothy from Bobby Byrne's band, a feud started between the two leaders, but it all blew over when Glenn eventually decided that Dorothy wasn't what he wanted after all and let her return to Byrne. He then hired Paula Kelly, who had been singing with Al Donahue's band, and who soon married Hal Dickenson of the Modernaires, with whom she sang for awhile.

Most famous of all the Modernaires' recordings with the band was, of course, "Chattanooga Choo Choo," which they sang with Beneke, not only on the recording but also in the band's first of two movies, *Sun Valley Serenade,* filmed in 1941. As band pictures went, it came off well, principally because it revolved around the orchestra and presented Glenn in a tasteful manner; and it didn't go off half-cocked, as so many other swing and band films of the times did, in a mad attempt to show musicians as they weren't. Undoubtedly Glenn's firm hand had a part in this and in his second and even more believable movie, *Orchestra Wives.*

Marion returned in August at about the same time that Glenn, at Cy Shribman's suggestion, hired Bobby Hackett. This was a surprising move, because Bobby was not a great section man. He was, however, a beautiful, soulful cornet player, a sort of modern-day Bix Beiderbecke, whose playing was revered by jazz fans throughout the world. "What a great idea!" they exclaimed when they heard of Miller's move. But what a shock they got when they discovered Bobby not among the brass, but in the rhythm section, strumming a guitar, an instrument he played with adequate mediocrity. The fans howled. What they didn't know was that Bobby Hackett had just completed dental surgery, was having trouble blowing his horn, and was sitting it out on the guitar chair until his gums had healed. "It was the only way Glenn could sneak me in," Bobby recently told me. "Besides he liked the other four trumpets so much." When Bobby eventually took up his horn again, he contributed some gorgeous solos, including one on "Rhapsody in Blue" which will go down as one of the most beautiful passages ever to grace a recording.

Meanwhile the band continued to feature many ballads, all with those clear reeds, so liquid and long-phrasing that one felt that the section never inhaled. And most of the ballads continued to emphasize vocals by Ray Eberle, who, shortly before he left the band, was featured on two of its most successful sides, "At Last" and "Serenade in Blue."

Eberle's departure was unfortunately unpleasant. For years a warm relationship had existed between him and Glenn, and though friends had often complained to Miller that Eberle, whom his leader fondly called "Jim" for no particular reason, was dragging down the band's musical level, Glenn invariably defended him vigorously. But after Miller had let him go, a trade paper printed an Eberle blast in which he stated that he had grown sick of Miller's gab and that he hadn't been getting paid regularly.

Glenn, who usually controlled his temper, blew his stack. He gave out his side of the story, that Eberle had too often been in no condition to sing and that finally he'd just had enough of his undisciplined attitude. Chummy MacGregor later revealed that the actual firing resulted from a tardy appearance that wasn't Ray's fault. The band was in Chicago at the time and was doubling between two engagements, one of which was its radio show. On the way to the studio, Eberle dropped off for a quick refreshment, then continued to the rehearsal. But one of the bridges that span the Chicago River got stuck, traffic piled up, Ray was caught in it, and arrived at the studio late. Glenn sacked him right then and there with no questions asked.

Skip Nelson, a good, all-round musician, replaced Ray, who soon joined Gene Krupa's band. Nelson cut several sides, including a good "Dearly Beloved," one of thirteen tunes recorded in three days by the band as it tried to squeeze in as many sides as possible before Petrillo was to call his recording strike.

Ironically, one of the last records Glenn's civilian band ever made was called "Here We Go Again." But go again on records it never did. Instead, on September 27, 1942, the band just plain went—forever.

I was there backstage that night at the Central Theater in Passaic, New Jersey, just as I'd been present at the band's first rehearsal at the Haven Studios, its first recording date at Decca, its first engagement at the Hotel New Yorker, its first theater date at the Adams in nearby Newark, and its Glen Island Casino opener. Those had been occasions filled with hope, hope for the future of a band that was just starting, hope for the future of a band in which so many of us had so much faith.

But this was so very different. This, we knew, was the end, and no matter how much faith we may have had, so many of us feared that it might never be the same. For Glenn, like so many others, was going off to war. It was a

Captain Miller

sad occasion. The emotional musicians tried their best to put on one great last show, without letting anyone know how they felt. But poor Marion Hutton couldn't go through with it; she wept uncontrollably and unabashedly.

Glenn wasn't obliged to go. He was too old to be drafted. But he insisted on going. He was filled with patriotic spirit, and he said so in a public statement: "I, like every American, have an obligation to fulfill. That obligation is to lend as much support as I can to winning the war. It is not enough for me to sit back and buy bonds. . . . The mere fact that I have had the privilege of exercising the rights to live and work as a free man puts me in the same position as every man in uniform, for it was the freedom and the democratic way of life we have that enabled me to make strides in the right direction."

Before Glenn received his commission he became quite ill at his new home in Tenafly, New Jersey, and for a while pneumonia, with all its possible complications, was feared. But Glenn recovered, and by early 1943, he was actively engaged in his Air Force duties.

Actively engaged? Well, as actively as the Air Force would let him. Glenn had all sorts of plans built around creating a batch of wonderful service bands throughout the country, bands that could play not only marching music but could also entertain the troops.

His plans never materialized.

Throughout his career in the service, Glenn was forced to buck bureaucracy. He was a man used to getting things done, quickly, directly, his way. But other officers, who for various reasons, ranging from legitimate protocol to morbid fear, to outright resentment of any non-regular Army men telling them what do, succeeded in raising all sorts of road blocks.

Eventually, Glenn was assigned to the Army Air Forces Technical Training Command, which, so far as I could figure out, consisted of all of us who didn't go up in the air. For this outfit he did organize what was surely one of the greatest musical units of all time.

Many of the soldier-musicians took their basic training in Atlantic City, New Jersey, and after they'd proved that they could march in step and shoot a gun, all those whom Glenn finally selected were shipped up to Yale University in New Haven, Connecticut. There Miller began whipping his unit into shape. (I recall spending several evenings walking the Atlantic City boardwalk with one quiet and rather lonely musician who must have assumed that he, too, would soon be going up to Yale. Perhaps Glenn didn't know enough about his talents to realize how valuable he would be. In any case, Henry Mancini was never called to New Haven.)

The group that arrived at Yale between March and May of 1943 consisted of some of the big bands' top players. Glenn's old pal Ray McKinley was there as head drummer. The civilian Miller band's first trumpeter, Zeke Zarchy, became the Army Miller band's first sergeant. Other alumni, arranger Jerry Gray, bassist Trigger Albert and trombonist Jim Priddy, also rejoined their boss.

From Benny Goodman's band came pianist and arranger Mel Powell and trumpeter Steve Steck; from Artie Shaw's, trumpeter Bernie Privin and saxist Hank Freeman; from Harry James's, saxist Chuck Gentry; from Tommy Dorsey's, guitarist Carmen Mastren; from Will Bradley's, saxist-clarinetist Peanuts Hucko; from Jan Savitt's, saxists Jack Ferrier and Gabe Gelinas, and from Vaughn Monroe's, trumpeter Bobby Nichols.

There were many other musicians, too, including a batch of string players from various symphony orchestras (a bloc came from the Cleveland Symphony) and from the recording studios, most of whom doubled on drums in the marching band with untelling effect.

Nevertheless, that marching band was terribly exciting. In addition to its superb muscianship (how those trumpets could blow!), it performed some swinging arrangements that really inspired the Air Force Cadets up at Yale to parade with unmitigated zest.

But the Commandant of Cadets, apparently steeped in tradition, reportedly objected to those superbly effective marching arrangements of favorites like "St. Louis Blues" and "Blues in the Night," on which Miller, McKinley and Gray had collaborated so skillfully. The result: a showdown between the Commandant and Glenn in the Post Commander's office.

After listening patiently to the Major's protocol-inspired argument—"We played those Sousa marches pretty straight in the last war and we did all right!"—Glenn finally popped off. "Tell me, Major," he asked contemptuously, "are you still flying the same planes you flew in the last war too?"

The Miller band continued to play "St. Louis Blues March" and "Blues in the Night March."

Glenn had bigger plans than playing primarily for reviews and retreats. He wanted to take his band overseas, but for various reasons, many of which never seemed to be too clear to him, he was kept in New Haven. While there he whipped into shape his impressive AAF orchestra, which in the spring of 1943 began a series of weekly coast-to-coast Air Force recruitment radio broadcasts. Emanating from New York, they featured the orchestra's huge horde of musicians, plus singers Tony Martin, Bob Carroll, Bob Houston (Johnny Desmond eventually replaced Martin when he went to Officers Training School), arrangements by Gray, Norman Leyden, Ralph Wilkinson, Perry Burgett and Powell, plus regular dramatic sketches enacted by a cast headed by Broderick Crawford.

The series lasted a year and all through that year Glenn was chafing at the bit, waiting to take the large unit overseas. And the more he chafed, the more irritable he became. Those of us who had been close to him found him far less predictable. At times he'd be his charming, friendly, self-assured self; at other times he'd play the part of "The Officer" to the hilt—much to the dismay of his old friends.

For example, he ordered all the musicians in the band to shave off their mustaches, ostensibly so that they would look more like soldiers. This proved to be quite a hardship, not only for the egos of certain men who had sported mustaches for years, but also for the embouchures of the brass and reed players, for whom such drastic changes in the area of their lips were bound to bring both spiritual and physical discomfort.

Finally, in the spring of 1944, the orders came for the unit to go to England. Some of us, especially those who weren't the greatest musicians in the world, remained behind. But it was still a large group that shipped overseas: twenty string players, five trumpets, four trombones (not including Glenn), one French horn, six reeds, two drummers, two pianists, two bassists, a guitarist, three arrangers, a copyist, five singers, two producers, an announcer, two administrators, two musical instrument repairmen plus Warrant Officer Paul Dudley and First Lieutenant Don Haynes, who had been Glenn's personal manager in his civilian band days.

As soon as the outfit arrived in London it knew it wasn't in New Haven. For this was buzz-bomb season. Some of the men took it lightly and on their first night in London went to the roof of their building to see the display. In a few seconds they were back down again.

But to Glenn the situation was very serious and called for immediate action. He hadn't spent all these months and all this effort putting together such a magnificent outfit only to have it blown to bits as soon as it arrived overseas.

For once Glenn found a quick scissors to cut the red tape that would have held the group there for several days while trucks were being requisitioned through regular channels. For in England, in addition to our AAF, there was also England's RAF, and it was to them that Glenn went with a deal in mind: move the band out immediately to Bedford, a town outside the range of the buzz bombs, and the musicians would play a special concert for the RAF.

Glenn refused to waste a day. The next morning, a Sunday, despite the gripes of those of his men who wanted to take it easy, Glenn insisted that they move out. So the entire day was devoted to packing paraphernalia into the waiting RAF trucks.

That night the band was in Bedford.

On the following morning a buzz bomb scored a direct hit on the band's vacated London headquarters, demolishing it completely.

Working out of Bedford, the band began a year of backbreaking, lip-leveling, superbly satisfying activity, playing in England for five and a half months, broadcasting over the BBC several times a day with various groups (the big orchestra, the dance band, the jazz group, the strings), and, of course, appearing in service camps everywhere. For example, on August 14 it played before ten thousand enlisted men and officers at Wharton; on the next day it played two concerts in Burtonwood for a combined audience of seventeen thousand more!

One of these GI's sent a letter to *Metronome* in which he complained about the band's lack of jazz, closing his missive with, "No doubt it is one of the best service bands ever, but here is one lad who is eagerly awaiting a chance to hear a second service band now in England, the Navy band led by Sam Donahue. Then he hopes to get some real musical kicks instead of a repeti-

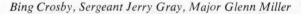

Bing Crosby, Sergeant Jerry Gray, Major Glenn Miller

Somewhere in England

tion of arrangements that have been played and replayed, all in the same precise, spiritless manner that has characterized Miller bands since he first attained commercial success."

Glenn reacted in typical Miller fashion. This was, he felt, entirely unjustified criticism, but, perhaps even more, he resented bitterly any attack on a group of musicians who had worked and trained so hard to do the kind of a job he and they felt needed to be done. Late in October he wrote me about how he felt!

> We [the band] didn't come here to set any fashions in music—we came merely to bring a much-needed touch of home to some lads who have been here a couple of years. These lads are doing a hell of a job— they have been starved for real, live American music, and they know and appreciate only those tunes that were popular before they left the States. For their sake, we play only the old tunes. You know enough about musicians to know that *we* would enjoy playing new tunes and plenty of them. I expect the "critic" who wrote the article expected to hear mainly new arrangements featuring a bunch of guys taking choruses a la Town Hall Concerts. . . .
>
> This lad missed the boat completely on the conditions and our purpose for being here. I'm surprised that the *Metronome* editorial staff printed the things they did, because they should realize the needs over here, even though this "hot soldier" over here doesn't seem to. While he listened for things which he opined were musically "wrong," he failed to hear the most important sound that can possibly come out of such concerts— the sound of thousands of GI's reacting with an ear-splitting, almost hysterically happy yell after each number. That's for us, Brother, even if it doesn't happen to be for *Metronome*. . . .

What they print about any civilian band of mine is O.K. with me, and they are certainly entitled to print anything they like without my taking any action to defend my position, but when they take cracks at a wonderful bunch of GI musicians who are doing a great job, that's too much. . . .

I am so firmly convinced that these boys over here ARE great that, should I have a band after the war, and should any of them desire a job, I would gladly give it to him regardless of his musical proficiencies.

Unfortunately Glenn never had a chance to give any of his men any job after the war. On the afternoon of December 15 he set out in a small plane over the English Channel to set up arrangements for his band's arrival in Paris a few days later. The plane took off, and neither it nor any of its three occupants were ever heard from again.

During the weeks and months that followed, all kinds of reports were circulated about the flight. But, "regardless of all the rumors," Don Haynes wrote me a few months later, "there's been no trace of Glenn, the other passenger [a colonel in the Air Forces], the pilot, or the plane since that foggy afternoon I alone saw them off. . . .

"Glenn took the trip that I was to make—decided to the day before—and as I had made all the arrangements, it only necessitated canceling the orders that had been cut for me, and getting orders cut for him. I brought the outfit over three days later (after having been 'weathered in' for two days), only to find that Glenn had not arrived. Our trip was uneventful, but not his."

Jerry Gray later revealed that he, too, was supposed to have gone on the same trip. "Glenn was in my room the night before and asked me if I'd like to go. But I had caught a pretty bad cold, and they decided maybe I'd better come over a few days later with the rest of the men."

The exact fate of Glenn and the plane will undoubtedly never be known. There is even a chance that it may have been shot down not by the enemy but by our own ack-ack, because the three men took off informally, on an unchartered flight, one that could quite conceivably have had no clearance of any sort, under weather conditions so atrocious that none of the AAF transport planes were flying.

Why Glenn, who had a real fear of planes, decided to risk a trip under such adverse conditions has never been determined. He was, of course, strictly a do-it-yourself guy, which could have accounted for his taking Haynes's place at the last moment. But he was also a rather frustrated man in those days, because, just as he had to unravel so much red tape to get his unit from New Haven to England, so was he experiencing the same sort of trouble in trying to get his men closer to the fighting front, where he wanted to be.

It's quite probable that taking off was not Glenn's idea. Those of us who had known him well during his civilian years had never found him to be in the least reckless. But it's entirely possible that the Glenn Miller at the airfield was not the same Glenn Miller we had grown to know; that this Glenn Miller, frustrated, impatient and harried, may have been in no frame of mind to turn down any dare to fly that could easily have been tossed his way on that foggy afternoon.

But we'll never know for sure.

Meanwhile, after its arrival in Paris, the band carried on as best it could. But the job grew more difficult. Glenn had always been the "compleat" leader, spiritually as well as musically. Haynes, assisted by Dudley, who was especially well liked, took over as administrative head. Jerry Gray conducted the large orchestra. Ray McKinley led the dance band. Mel Powell headed a small jazz group; George Ockner a string unit. Johnny Desmond, featured often, gained great popularity and a reputation as "The Creamer."

It was McKinley who, according to many of the men, eventually emergéd as the outfit's new spiritual leader. It was to him that they looked whenever things got roughest. Like Glenn, Ray found ways of cutting through official uninterest or inefficiency. For example, there was the time when all routine attempts to get the band some much-needed wood to heat its bitter-cold quarters had failed. And so, when an important general came up to Ray at an officers' dance and asked in a routine manner how everything was going, Mac didn't give him the expected enlisted man's response of "Just dandy, sir." Instead, he retorted, "Like ————, General," and then proceeded to tell him all about the wood the band couldn't get. Bright and early the next morning enough wood arrived to heat the quarters until spring!

The band, originally scheduled to remain on the Continent for six weeks, made such an impression that it stayed for six months instead. A review of its official Monthly Activity Reports shows that in the less than one year that the group was overseas, it engaged in more than eight hundred musical activities, including five hundred radio broadcasts, live or transcribed, heard by many millions of servicemen in the European Theater, plus three hundred personal appearances—concerts, dances, etc.—played to a total attendance of over 600,000 men!

Major Miller with Sergeant Ray McKinley,
who took over the dance band, and Sergeant Mel Powell, who headed the jazz group

Quite obviously the band had done one helluva job—just as Glenn Miller had intended it to do.

When the men returned in July, too late to participate in a nationwide Glenn Miller Day, they were granted a thirty-day furlough. There was some discussion of assigning the band other tasks, but some of the men had already applied for and were about to be granted their discharge. They made one major appearance as a unit in Washington, D.C., at a special function. Then the group slowly disbanded.

Many of the newly activated civilians were reassembled at Don Haynes's behest, and with the blessings of Helen Miller, for an engagement at New York's Capitol Theater. Tex Beneke, who had been recently discharged from the Navy, was engaged by the Miller estate to front the band.

It was called "The Glenn Miller Band with Tex Beneke," and its date at the Capitol, was, according to my March, 1946, review "a smart affair—slick strings, powerful brass, a well-blended, rhythmic sax section, plus, of course, the well-known clarinet lead, a rhythm section that jumps and a handful of entertaining singers—all presided over with fine taste by Tex Beneke, Glenn's discovery and pet sideman."

The band did great for a while—for the first and possibly the second time around. But it was not a well-run outfit. Tex, attractive as he was, was not a leader of men. He seemed indefinite and unsure of himself, possibly because he knew too well that he actually was leader in name only. The real leader was Miller's sidekick Don Haynes.

Now Haynes was excellent at selling bands, but he was not a musician and he had less musical know-how than Beneke and hardly a fraction of the musical wisdom, intuition, imagination and experience of a Glenn Miller. Tex began to complain vehemently. He felt, as many others did, that the band should be doing more than just standing still. Glenn, he was sure, would have tried new things in a new world. But Haynes and Eli Oberstein, who recorded the band for Victor, kept telling him, he insisted, to play just the way the band had always been playing.

It didn't work.

Without a single, knowing leader empowered to make policy decisions, the band began to disintegrate. Eventually the Miller estate and Tex split, and Beneke went ahead on his own, with no official Glenn Miller connections.

But the Miller music continued to flow forth via reissues of records Glenn had made years before. Inspired by such sales, several other leaders began to emulate the Miller sound: Ralph Flanagan, who had never been associated with the band; Ray Anthony, who had been with it for a few months, and Jerry Gray, writer of many of its arrangements, who later was to lead a non-Miller type band in Dallas before a fatal August, 1976 heart attack.

Including Beneke's, four such bands were simultaneously trying to cash in on the Miller sound. Teddy Powell, one of the most sensitive, if not always the most articulate of bandleaders, reflected the feeling of many who were disturbed by such bold intrusions. "You know," he told me quite seriously, "if Glenn Miller were alive today, he'd be turning over in his grave!" Awakened, no doubt, by the scavengers pecking away at his tombstone!

Eventually, in 1956, the official Glenn Miller band was revived when Helen Miller and David McKay, the lawyer in charge of the Miller estate, selected Ray McKinley, a long-time Miller friend and associate, to re-form and lead a new group. Theirs was a smart move, one that was to bring back a great deal of interest in and respect for the music of Glenn Miller.

For almost a decade Ray led the band throughout America and through various other parts of the world. While retaining much of the Miller sound (Ray could never play a date without having to trot out at least a dozen of the old band's biggest hits), he also injected new spirit and discipline into the outfit, while at the same time giving it the benefit of his musical wit, know-how and experience. Glenn would have been proud of him.

After almost ten years of traveling with the band, McKinley hung up his baton. With the style focused so strongly on the clarinet, the Miller estate decided to invite one of the world's greatest clarinetists, Buddy DeFranco, to front the band. He accepted, staying on as leader, until January, 1974, when he was succeeded for a comparatively short time by Peanuts Hucko, star clarinetist of Miller's AAF Band, then by trombonist Buddy Morrow, after that by a lesser-known west coast trombonist, Jimmy Henderson, and in June of 1981 by trombonist Larry O'Brien.

Now, almost two full generations later, he retains the most loyal group of fans ever associated with any bandleader. His recordings continue to outsell those of all others, and the Glenn Miller Society, based in England with a branch in the United States (c/o Ralph Monsees, 170 Summit Avenue, Tappan, NY 10983), seems to keep on growing.

His two adopted children have become more involved with his music, and the executor of his estate, upon David Mackay's death in 1980, became Polly Haynes, Don's widow, Helen Miller's closest friend and Glenn's loyal assistant for so many years.

People have often wondered—many times out loud—what Miller might be doing if he were with us today. Paul Dudley told me some years ago that Glenn had told him in Europe that he had been making broad and exciting plans. He wanted to expand his operations after the war to include more than just leading a band. He would publish songs on a larger scale. He might possibly go into personal management. And almost certainly he would have entered the field of radio production, in which he had done so well in the States, and overseas as head of his AAF unit. Quite conceivably he would have gone into recording and television production as well.

For Glenn Miller was never a man who would or could stand still. Beneath that serene but stern exterior there whirled an active, probing, intelligent mind —one that understood so well and respected so much all that was good in music and in human beings—the mind of a strong but sensitive man who had accomplished so much in such a short time, and who almost certainly would have accomplished so much more—if he had only been given the chance.

Vaughn Monroe

VAUGHN MONROE was one of the most romantic-looking leaders of the big band era. A large, handsome man with a great smile, he still managed to project a bashful, little boy image that appealed not only to the teen-agers of the mid-forties but also to their older sisters, their mothers and even their grandmothers.

The band itself was never brilliant, even though it improved greatly after its big-time debut at the Meadowbrook in the spring of 1941. In a review headed "Monroe More Impressive Than His band," I pointed out that

> "The Rapid Rise of Vaughn Monroe," or "A Press Agent's Dream," is certainly the current phenomenon of dancebandom. Seldom has any band come up so quickly, and clicked so heavily with the audiences it has had to face.
>
> The primary cause is obvious. For, despite all managerial push and tremendous pressure from press agents, the group would never have had a chance to score so brilliantly were it not for that one cause—Vaughn Monroe himself.
>
> Here is a dynamic personality. It's around him, not his band, that the girls flock. It's when they hear his voice, not his band's playing, that they go girlishly ga-ga. His smile sends romantic, not musical, shivers down spines that are just beginning to harden. Here is the modern generation's Rudy Vallee. [A better and more modern comparison: he was the Robert Goulet of his day.]

The review found the band dull, except for a seventeen-year-old trumpet find named Bobby Nichols, a very good girl singer named Marylin Duke and a comic vocalist named Ziggy Talent. "But were it to stand strictly upon its own musical merits, chances are it never would have done better than remain a territorial favorite."

Vaughn's band had been a smash hit in the Boston area when Willard Alexander brought it to New York to build it into a national attraction. Vaughn had been performing as quite a respectable trumpeter, an instrument on which he began to concentrate during the Depression, when lack of funds curtailed his operatic coaching and ambitions.

Vaughn's singing was always a bone of contention among those who heard it. The girls, of course, loved it. His coterie thought it was magnificent. But the critics, almost to a man, felt different. "He is a baritone who tries too often to sing bass with tenor accents," wrote Barry Ulanov. I was more caustic, pointing out that if Monroe would only open his mouth a little more, less of the sound would be forced to come out his nose.

My lack of appreciation of his singing (opera singers and even would-be opera singers take their voices quite seriously) made it difficult for me to get to know Monroe more than perfunctorily. This, I was told by those close to him, was my loss, and I believe they were probably right. Barbara Hodgkins once described him, after an interview, as "one of the most polite, pleasant and peaceful citizens in the music business—a very normal person in a very crazy world."

"Racing with the Moon"

In that interview, Monroe revealed his bandleading philosophy. "The band business," he stated, "isn't an artistic thing. It's a business. I could name four or five bands that aren't doing very well today because they don't do what people ask for. I can't feel sorry for them. You've got to justify what you're doing; you can't fool a promoter more than once or twice. And you've got to be right in there working all the time."

"In there working all the time" is precisely what Vaughn did after he brought his band to New York. He must have known that the group wasn't as great as his press agents made it out to be, for during the first six months he made eight important personnel changes. He also hired for a time a fine lead trombonist and arranger. His name: Ray Conniff.

Much of the band's musical emphasis was on singing—not only on Vaughn's, which continued to improve, but also on that of his groups—the Murphy Sisters, the Moonmaids ("Monroe" and "Moonmaid" were alliterative; besides, the band had a theme called "Racing with the Moon")—and, at one time, that of a whole bunch of his musicians who also sang—few of them well. For a while the band gave the impression, according to one critic, of performing like "a kind of legitimatized Sammy Kaye."

The end of the big band era by no means meant the end of Vaughn Monroe. If anything, his band, built as it was around so much singing, grew more popular than ever, while so many other, more instrumentally oriented outfits lost ground drastically.

Monroe became very big on radio, especially via his Camel Cigarettes commercials. He continued to handle himself beautifully. His recordings kept on selling well, built, as they were, around his voice—a situation that did not make him completely happy. "Don't think I like the idea of making all those vocal records," he revealed. "We have plenty of good jazzmen in the band, and I'd like to do some instrumentals. But Victor tells me to keep right on singing."

And so right on singing he did—not only *on* Victor records, but also *on behalf* of the RCA organization when he became the mammoth corporation's star image on its long series of RCA television commercials. Eventually Vaughn Monroe's Orchestra disappeared completely from the scene. But Vaughn continued to sing, opening his mouth perhaps a bit more widely, straining less to sound operatic, but always projecting the personality of a solid, fairly musical and well-respected citizen. By the end of the sixties, he was spending most of his time in his Florida home. I last saw him during a rare New York public appearance in the early seventies, and to me he sounded as good as, if not better than ever. But I was never to see him again, because Vaughn died on May 21, 1973, after a lingering illness.

Russ Morgan

"I WANT to retire as quickly as possible, before the music business gets me. If I were given a million dollars tomorrow, I would not only retire, I would get lost."

That was Russ Morgan talking—not this year, not last year, but all the way back in 1936 at a time when he was in New York leading one of the better musical bands. He had already put in more years in music than almost any of the other name bandleaders around; in fact, if ever a musician had paid his dues, it was this husky, garrulous, talented former coal miner from Pennsylvania.

Morgan is best remembered for his trombone playing, especially for that identifiable, much-too-corny-for-his-talents "wah-wah" style. It was a trick he had come across while playing in Freddy Martin's band, a trick that he was smart enough to realize could probably bring him more money than anything he had previously done in music.

And he had done a lot. He had started early as a pianist, had broken his arm and, in order to get back strength in the limb, had taken up the slide trombone. He also played sax, guitar, vibes and organ.

When he was only twenty-one, he had been arranging for John Philip Sousa and Victor Herbert. Later he had become a member of the Detroit Symphony, arranger and trombonist in the famed Jean Goldkette Orchestra, musical director of radio station WXYZ in Detroit, recording director of the American Record Company (Brunswick was its big label), an NBC staff conductor and finally musical head of the Lifebuoy and Philip Morris radio series.

With such a background it was little wonder that the band he led in 1936 at New York's Biltmore Hotel was a good one. Its music was soft, loose, easygoing, well-blended and had an infectious, light lift. It played a batch of excellent arrangements by Morgan, but it did have one obvious failing: it was poorly routined. "At times this [condition]," noted my review, "tends to approach the ridiculous, for, after all, the entire band should at least have the same conception of what chorus of what tune is coming next in what key!"

On location, Morgan, who had a wild sense of humor and, like his close friend Joe Venuti, dug practical jokes, may have played it loose. But when it came to more important business it was a different matter. "He wouldn't stand for carelessness," emphasizes Milt Gabler, who supervised Morgan's recordings in the forties and fifties. "He'd yell at the guys when they made mistakes, and I'd say about 25 per cent of it was kidding but 75 per cent was dead serious." It is Gabler's further contention that Morgan, who had "so much soul and melody in him, should have gone into the studios and become a conductor there. He certainly had all the necessary equipment."

But so long as Russ was staying in music, he wanted to be seen and heard. There was in him a certain happy, hammy streak that came out most obviously in his constant desire to sing. He really didn't have much of a voice, but he had a style and he knew how to make sense out of lyrics. And, of course, he could also draw people's attention with that trombone "wah-wah" gimmick.

Morgan always had a good feeling for what the public wanted. Those musicians who thought he was burying a superior talent beneath commercial gimmicks may have been distressed, but it paid off for him. This was especially true in his songwriting. His tunes weren't startlingly inventive, but he surely did reach the average listener with originals like "Does Your Heart Beat for

Me?," "Somebody Else Is Taking My Place," "You're Nobody Till Somebody Loves You," and "So Tired," which he made into a hit record as late as 1948.

The post-big band years were good ones for Morgan; in fact, at one time he had four recordings among the Top Ten: "So Tired," "Cruising Down the River," "Sunflower" and "Forever and Ever." On the last selection he uncovered a vocal quartet that was just starting out and that later became famous as the Ames Brothers.

Russ was undoubtedly even more thrilled some years later when two other brothers joined his band: his own two sons, Jack and David, who played trombone and guitar. With his kids around he could have been thinking in terms of either of two of his big hits, "Forever and Ever" or "Somebody Else Is Taking My Place." As a matter of fact, after Russ died on August 8, 1969, son Jack did take over the band and forged quite a nice career for himself as he continued to play the sort of music that his dad had created, perhaps never truly indicative of his true musical talents, but certainly an example of some of the shrewdest marketing of a sound in the history of the big bands.

Ozzie Nelson

TELL your teen-age kids that both Ozzie and Harriet Nelson were much better singers than their son Ricky ever was, and they're likely to look at you scornfully and mutter, "What's the matter with you—are you some kind of nut or something?"

Well, maybe you are—to them. But just about anyone who spent much time listening to Ozzie Nelson and His Orchestra will attest that two of the most musical and attractive band singers of the early and mid-thirties were Ozzie Nelson and his girl singer, Harriet Hilliard.

The band itself was musical, well disciplined but quite unexciting. Its leader was a pleasant, passive gent—intelligent, articulate with a sort of subdued, rah-rah collegiate manner. He had been graduated from Rutgers University, where he played on the football and lacrosse teams and had swum and boxed. From there he had gone to New Jersey Law School and might have settled down at the bar if his band hadn't become such a big hit.

It made its first impression nationally when it played at Glen Island Casino for the 1932 summer season. I first heard it in 1935 at the New Yorker Hotel and found it an exceptionally pleasant and musicianly, if never very inspiring, outfit. It featured two pianos, a rich, warm brass team and a full-bodied sax section that concentrated a great deal on the lower register, thereby enriching the band's ensembles.

Ozzie, whose real name is Oswald George Nelson, married Harriet Hilliard on October 8, 1935. I remember her as an exceptionally pretty and charming girl who sang very well. She and Ozzie sang numerous duets, often filled with lovey-dovey bits of light humor. These duets were more effective than those Ozzie sang in later years with such successors of Harriet's as Shirley Lloyd and Rosanne Stevens.

Ozzie himself sang in a slightly hip Rudy Vallee manner. His sound was just as nasal, his phrasing more musical, his style just as relaxed. Falling asleep in the middle of a Nelson vocal chorus was by no means an impossibility. Sometimes I wondered if Ozzie would ever do it himself.

The last time I heard the band was late in 1941 in California, and I wasn't surprised to find that it hadn't changed much. Ozzie, it seems, was

*Ozzie and Harriet
(early 1930's style)*

always playing it safe. "If you're looking for a quiet, comfortable evening, bordering very much on the Babbitt," I wrote, "you couldn't find a more suitable organization. It produces staid, stereotyped music that'll never hurt anybody and never do anybody much good, including Mr. Nelson."

Everything the band did it did well, but it did little but play middle tempos that featured full ensembles with a good blend, good phrasing, good intonation and, very infrequently, an individual solo. Perhaps the best tipoff was the change that had come over trumpeter Bo Ashford, who, in 1935, had played some exceedingly impressive Beiderbecke-like jazz choruses. By 1941 Bo's playing had become just plain dull as he stuck very close to the melody, seemingly afraid of startling anyone, including, perhaps, his leader.

Eventually, of course, as most of us know, Ozzie drifted more and more into the Hollywood picture, achieving his greatest fame as headman and producer of his long-lived "Ozzie and Harriet" TV series.

An aside to viewers who never knew the real Ozzie: He was really much, much brighter than the show ever let him appear to be.

Red Nichols

MOST people remember Red Nichols as leader of the Five Pennies, an exceptionally good, loosely organized and totally impermanent jazz group that included at various times such stars as Benny Goodman, Jack Teagarden, Gene Krupa, Glenn Miller, Jimmy and Tommy Dorsey, Joe Venuti and Eddie Lang and other top jazzmen. It made a flock of classic jazz records during the late twenties and early thirties. Seldom, though, was there just a nickel's worth of Pennies. "That was only a number we tied in with my name," Red confessed shortly before he died on June 28, 1965. "We'd generally have eight or nine, depending upon who was around for the session and what we were trying to do. I'd always try to get the best men I could each time."

Nichols played a very melodic-sounding cornet in a dixieland sort of way. He readily admitted Bix Beiderbecke's influence, and he did a good job of playing that style. Perhaps he wasn't as startlingly creative as the men he featured, but his role was equally important. "I was the businessman in the group," he pointed out.

When the big band era got underway, Red had already migrated into radio. He was starred, along with Ruth Etting, on a regular series for Kellogg's Corn Flakes. His band was composed of topflight musicians, one of whom, Charlie Teagarden, was featured on trumpet more often than Red was. Before then Red had led another group for the Gershwins' *Strike Up the Band* on Broadway and had fronted a full-sized band that broadcast regularly from the Golden Pheasant Restaurant in Cleveland and featured several good singers, Frances Stevens, Ernie Mathias and Tony Sacco, plus a haunting theme song called "Wailing to the Four Winds."

When so many of the stars who had played for Nichols were leading their highly successful bands in the very late thirties, Red, whom most of us had relegated pretty much to the past, suddenly burst upon the scene with a tremendously impressive big band composed of a batch of young, eager, well-trained musicians. Its style was primarily dixieland; its sound a mixture of the bands of Bob Crosby and Will Bradley.

I first heard his new band early in 1940 at the Famous Door, where it made its New York debut. It was an exciting outfit ("The Surprise of 1940," I called it) that featured a driving pianist, Billy Maxted, who wrote many of the arrangements; a fine, relaxed drummer, Harry Jaeger, who also sang; a brilliant clarinetist named Henie Beau, who eventually was starred with Tommy Dorsey; and an emotional singer with an uncontrollable vibrato, Bill Darnell.

And, of course, there was Nichols, whose relaxed, gentlemanly horn blowing must have seemed almost like a novelty to the big band fans, most of whom had been weaned on the more aggressive, blaring styles of Harry James, Bunny Berigan, Ziggy Elman and the rest of the spectacular stylists featured with the era's top swing bands.

This edition of the Nichols band recorded several fine sides for Bluebird ("Poor Butterfly" was an especially good example of its sophisticated, often humorous approach to dixieland jazz) but then began fading from the scene. When I heard it again, about a year later, it was playing in Boston with an entirely different personnel, and Red, who had seemed so relaxed and satisfied in front of the band at the Famous Door, was trying to exhort his new set of youngsters to musical heights they seemed incapable of attaining. To show you just how hard Red was trying to impress, he even featured a singer, Penny Banks, who did little more than sound like Wee Bonnie Baker—quite a switch for a man who had made a name for himself starring only the best in music!

Nichols gave up leading a big band shortly thereafter. For a while he played with Glen Gray and the Casa Loma Orchestra, then settled down on the West Coast leading a small jazz group. Possibly not much more would have been heard from or about him if Hollywood hadn't latched onto the idea of making a movie about his life. Called *The Five Pennies,* it featured a few of the musicians with whom he had been connected, plus some disconnected actors playing parts—in typical Hollywood stereotype performances—of others. It emphasized sentimentality, concentrating a good deal on Red's daughter and the effect of her serious illness on Red's career. In between it spotted some good musical moments including some fine blowing by Louis Armstrong, but lost those of us who had known Red by casting Danny Kaye in his part.

But the movie helped Nichols tremendously. Soon he was back leading his Pennies again, playing many of the country's leading supper clubs. When I last saw him in 1962, he seemed to be a very happy man, delighted to be back blowing his tasty horn, a horn that was stilled shortly thereafter when Red Nichols passed peacefully away.

Ray Noble

OVER in England during the early thirties, Ray Noble was leading one of the greatest sweet bands of all time. But it wasn't really his; its musicians were actually members of other leading London orchestras, many of them from Lew Stone's band, who would assemble in a studio to record for Noble. Their job completed, the British all-stars would return to their home units.

They produced some notable dance music, excellently recorded and exquisitely played, that included several lovely ballads written by Noble: "The Very Thought of You," "By the Fireside," "Love Is the Sweetest Thing" and "Love Locked Out." The records became hits in America, creating a demand for personal appearances here. And so, late in 1934, Ray arrived on these shores.

But this time he didn't organize another all-star band. Instead, he let Glenn Miller do it, the theory being that the man who had already put together bands for Smith Ballew and the Dorsey Brothers would know just where to find the right musicians.

Which is precisely what Miller did. He selected Charlie Spivak and Peewee Erwin as trumpets. He picked Will Bradley (then known as Wilbur Schwichtenberg) as his fellow trombonist. He created a sax section that included the famous Chicago tenor man Bud Freeman, and a young Long Island clarinetist Johnny Mince, who was to gain greater fame in Tommy Dorsey's band later on. For the rhythm section he chose Claude Thornhill on piano, George Van Epps, the best around in those days, on guitar, and Delmar Kaplan, a bassist with a gorgeous tone who had worked with Glenn in the Dorsey Brothers band. Noble had brought along two compatriots he wanted in the band. One was his flashy though not very swinging drummer-manager, Bill Harty. The other was his vocalist, Al Bowlly, who had already attained a large following in this country via his emotional but always musicianly singing.

Noble was having difficulties with the American musicians' union when he arrived, so he went out to California to write songs while he waited for the problem to be settled. When it was, he turned to New York to front the band that Miller had put together for him.

Thanks to Glenn's work, plus Noble's good musical taste, it turned out to be a superbly musical outfit. But it wasn't an especially relaxed group,

The Ray Noble orchestra in the Rainbow Room
Front row: *Al Bowlly, Fritz Prospero, Nick Pisani, Danny D'Andrea,*
George Van Epps, Claude Thornhill
Second row: *Glenn Miller, Wilbur Schwitchenberg, Charlie Spivak, Peewee Erwin,*
Jimmy Cannon, Johnny Mince, Milt Yaner, Bud Freeman
Back row: *Bill Harty and Delmar Kaplan*

because several of the musicians appeared to admire and trust Miller more than they did Noble and Harty. Thus an unpleasant uneasiness often pervaded the band.

Noble, according to Will Bradley, tended to stand somewhat in awe of all these great, established musicians. Says Will, "I remember one night when I wasn't feeling too good, and on a radio broadcast I went for a high last note on an arrangement—I think it was high D. I missed it. Only air came out. I tried again. Again only air." But apparently Noble respected Bradley's ability so much that, instead of blowing his stack, he merely sputtered incredulously, "I say, ol' boy, did you lose one of your relatives?"

Mistakes and missed notes were rather rare in this band. Both Noble and Miller were musical perfectionists, and they'd rehearse numbers constantly and carefully. They were especially finicky about what the band did on its recording dates, spending hours to make sure that it achieved exactly the right sound and effects. In fact, there was one date with which they were so dissatisfied that they scrapped everything they'd recorded on it.

The American records, though never as well recorded as those the band had made in England (the latter were considered the best recorded sides of the early thirties), did offer something that the earlier records lacked. This was good jazz, with arrangements by Miller and performances by soloists Freeman, Mince, Erwin, Van Epps, Thornhill and, occasionally, by Miller himself. Two sides especially, "Way Down Yonder in New Orleans" and "Dinah," projected some very satisfactory jazz sounds.

But the band's forte remained ballads, with special emphasis on Al Bowlly's singing. He had a particularly persuasive way of crooning—soft, intimate, sexy, complete with a charming South African accent, which came across especially well on such Noble recordings as "Yours Truly Is Truly Yours" and Ray's own song "The Touch of Your Lips." When Al left late in 1939 to return to England to resume his career as a soloist, the orchestra lost much of its musical identity. And when Bowlly was killed in his London flat by a buzz bomb during an air raid in April, 1941, music and the world lost a truly nice person.

Noble occasionally also sang, in a talking manner, contributing some droll foolishness to the proceedings. Seemingly both vague and charming, he reminded me of the guy in a terribly British "B" movie who never quite got the girl because he always kept falling into the swimming pool. Of course, much of Noble's manner was an act, as many of his men discovered when they did business with him.

The band played in New York's swankiest spot, the Rainbow Room, "sixty-five stories near the stars," as the announcers used to say, located atop the RCA building at Radio City. Its schedule was a rough one—from 9 P.M. until 3 A.M. seven nights a week.

Once in a while, when business was slow, the men could get off earlier. On one particular night after they'd been dismissed at two instead of three, and were already changing into their clothes down on the sixty-fourth floor, Bill Harty came in and announced that an important customer had arrived and that the band was wanted back to play the last hour. So the men put on their tuxedos again and back they went to work. Noble was about ready to give the downbeat when he noticed that Claude Thornhill wasn't at the piano. He waited a short while. Finally the band started to play without Claude. But hardly had it begun when into the Rainbow Room walked Thornhill, immaculately dressed in his tuxedo jacket, shirt and tie. Only one thing was missing—his trousers!

Obviously, the job was beginning to get some of the men down.

The important customer who caught Thornhill with his pants down—or off—was Nelson Rockefeller, later Governor of New York. It's interesting to note that the Rockefeller family continued for the next twenty years to be good friends and admirers of—no, not Ray Noble, but of Claude Thornhill. (There must be some kind of moral here somewhere!)

Thornhill and quite a number of the stars began drifting away from the band during 1936, and by the time Noble closed his second season at the Rainbow Room, much of the brilliant musicianship had disappeared. In the following year, after some angry exchanges with their musicians, Ray, along with his sidekick Bill Harty, migrated to Hollywood, where Ray began a very successful career in radio as musical director and stooge on the Edgar Bergen series. He continued to write music, but eventually left America to settle down, supposedly forever, on the Isle of Jersey. But apparently California's call was too potent and around 1970 he returned to live in Santa Barbara where he remained until his death in 1977.

Red Norvo

FOR real listening thrills, few bands could match the one that Red Norvo
fronted during the fall of 1936. It was only a small band, ten musicians plus
Red, and it wasn't a very famous one then. But the way it swung in its soft,
subtle, magnificently musical way, insinuating rather than blasting itself into
one's consciousness, gave me one of the most remarkable and satisfying
listening experiences I have ever felt.

I use the word "felt," purposely, because this was a band with an under-
lying sensuous as well as musical appeal. Unlike swing bands that overpowered
its listeners, this one underplayed its music, injecting into its unique Eddie
Sauter scores a tremendous but subdued excitement—the sort of excitement
one experiences not during the culmination of something great but in anticipation of something great. It would swing so subtly and so softly and so
charmingly through chorus after chorus of exquisite solos and light, moving
ensembles, always threatening to erupt while holding the listener mesmerized,
until at long last, when he was about ready to scream "Let me up!" it would
charge off into one of its exhilarating musical climaxes. There was never a
band like it.

Featured, naturally, was Norvo himself, a magnificent xylophonist of exquisite taste, with a volatile, smoldering rhythmic beat, a great ear, a remarkably deft touch and pixie-ish sense of humor, plus an ability to keep his playing always attuned to the times. He was great in those days, he had been great before those days, and he is great today. Of all the musicians in jazz he has remained for me, through the years, the most satisfying of them all; in short, he remains my favorite of all jazz musicians.

The band that I went to hear for several nights in a row during its debut at the Syracuse (New York) Hotel was far ahead of its time. The room in which it played was small and intimate, well suited to Norvo's soft, simmering style. But alas, there were very few such rooms that set it off so well. Within a few months, as more and more ballroom and nightclub managers kept wondering aloud, "Hey, can't youse guys play no louder?" the band's unique, warm, soft, subtle charm began to disappear.

Underplaying had always been part of Norvo's style, way back when he had appeared as a soloist with Paul Whiteman and later, in 1935, when I first heard him at the Famous Door in New York with a sextet that swung gorgeously even without drums. Dave Barbour played guitar in that group, Stewie Pletcher was the trumpet, and Tony Zimmers, soon to be replaced by Herbie Haymer, played tenor sax. Pete Peterson, who stayed with Norvo longer than any other musician, was the bassist.

The big ten-piece band that too few of us heard in Syracuse was actually an extension of the sextet. During its long stay at Chicago's Blackhawk Restaurant, it began to gain national recognition. For a while it was able to retain its soft, swinging ways. But the Blackhawk was a big room, and gradually the band was forced to blow more blatantly and obviously for the larger and generally squarer customers. "Red is offering," I wrote rather sadly in 1937, "more and more slam-bang arrangements with much gusto and forte."

In Syracuse the band had featured a very attractive young singer named Nancy Flake, who later married Red's drummer, Moe Purtill. But during that engagement Mildred Bailey, Red's wife and one of the truly great singers of all time, came up to visit, and shortly thereafter she took Nancy's place. From then on Red and Mildred were billed as "Mr. and Mrs. Swing."

Mildred changed the character of the band somewhat. A warm, witty, often charming, sometimes alarming extrovert, she provided the group with a flash and musical excitement it had never known before. There is absolutely no denying that more than any other element her great singing and showmanly finesse were responsible for the band's commercial success.

But Mildred, an extremely overweight woman (although she had, I noticed, two of the most beautifully shaped ankles and tiniest feet I've ever seen), was not always easy to get along with. Tremendously talented, with a fantastic musical ear, she was, nevertheless, unhappily insecure. As a result she often asserted herself too emphatically, creating tensions that were anathema for a band that relied so much on a relaxed approach.

Most affected of all was Red, one of the most pleasant, unselfish and unphony men I have ever known. Mildred could bring him way down, and when she did, Red's sensitive, outgoing personality would be stifled, and so would his and the band's musical enthusiasm.

At the big Blackhawk the band suffered from the size of the room and the corny tastes of some of its customers. (Once some cornball actually offered Mildred a dollar tip to sing his favorite song!) But on its Brunswick records it continued to impress—despite the ridiculously small, antiquated studios that gave the records a pinched sound. The band made several outstanding instrumentals, all scored by Sauter: "I Would Do Anything for You," "Do You Ever Think of Me?" and, best of all, a smoldering version of "Remember."

And there were also the fine sides on which Mildred sang—"It All Begins and Ends with You," "A Porter's Love Song to a Chamber Maid," "It Can Happen to You," "Everyone's Wrong but Me" and "Smoke Dreams," the last a rather harmonically far-out affair arranged by Sauter, with an especially difficult modulation right before the vocal. "I made it hard on purpose for Mildred," Eddie once revealed, "because I was mad at her then. But, you know, her ear was so good that she got it on the very first run-through!"

Eddie, quiet and shy, played trumpet with the band for a while, then began to concentrate on arranging, launching a career that has for thirty years brought him scores of accolades from musicians and fellow arrangers. Through those three decades he has never stopped progressing, creating many great sounds via his imaginative, unique voicings, harmonies and rhythms, while always retaining his exquisite taste.

No one was more of a Sauter fan than Mildred Bailey. "When I hear a new song," she once told me, "I immediately get a definite idea of how I want to sing it and how the entire arrangement should sound. And without fail, Eddie comes through with just the kind of an arrangement I'd been dreaming of—only better!" In the sixties, another big Sauter fan, Stan Getz, was so grateful to Eddie that when he, Stan, won a coveted Grammy, he turned it over to Sauter in appreciation of his arrangement.

In addition to Norvo, the band had several other standout soloists. Pletcher, recently graduated from Yale, blew a far-out, often humorous trumpet; Haymer a booting but invariably tasteful tenor sax; while clarinetist Hank D'Amico, whom Red had discovered when the band played Syracuse, provided the most brilliant passages. And the saxes were blessed with one of the truly great lead men, Frank Simeone, whose soft, undulating alto made the reeds one of the outstanding sections of all time.

Gradually the personnel and the mood of the band began to change. When it opened at New York's Commodore Hotel early in 1938, Jerry Jerome had replaced Haymer; George Wettling had come in on drums, bringing with him some dixielandish rhythmic effects that didn't always suit the band; young Allan Hanlon, a slightly built lad with a good, strong beat (he was so excited on opening night, his first with a name band, that he fainted dead away!)

*Mr. and Mrs. Swing. Tenor saxist Jerry Jerome is between trumpeters
Zeke Zarchy and Jimmy Blake.
Allan Hanlon is the guitarist, George Wettling the drummer,
Pete Peterson the bassist.*

joined on guitar; and the band took on its first boy singer, Terry Allen, one of
the most musical of the era's male vocalists.

But by the following October the group had undergone even more drastic
changes. Of its original personnel, only Pete Peterson remained. In discussing
the "soft, subtle swing of Red Norvo," I noted then that "the 'soft' had disappeared; the 'subtle' had been minimized, and now only the 'swing' remains."
After all, it would have been absolutely impossible for any band in which
Red Norvo played not to swing at least some of the time.

A few months later, though, there was no Red Norvo band to swing or to
do anything else. While playing at the Famous Door in New York, so many
of its members became ill with colds that Red was forced to disband, simply
because he had no group to field. But not everyone was satisfied with Red's
excuse. One trade paper insisted that Mildred's temperament had wrecked the
band, for which the publication was promptly sued for fifty thousand dollars.

This was by no means the end of Red Norvo's band. He reorganized, and
during the spring and summer of 1939 played at Murray's in Tuckahoe, New
York, from which he broadcast regularly. But the pay was terrible, and once
again, this time amid rumors of financial problems, the band broke up.

Red decided to stay in New York and study at Juilliard. Meanwhile,
Mildred accepted a job as featured singer on the Camel Caravan radio series,
on which Benny Goodman led the band, and from then on, except for occasional reunions with Red on recordings, the great singer, with the wonderful
vibrato and innate feeling for everything good in music, continued as a
single attraction, just as she had been doing for years before joining her
husband's band. Her career lasted until December 12, 1951, when after
having recovered from a serious illness, Mildred died, and the musical world
lost one of its most musicianly voices.

Red came back with another ten-piece band in the spring of 1940. This one featured two brilliant young trumpeters, Conrad Gozzo, who later led both the Herman and Kenton brass sections, and Rusty Dedrick. It produced the same sort of soft, subtle swing that his 1936 group had—which in a world geared to the tensions of war could have accounted for its quick demise.

Late in 1941, Red organized his biggest and final dance band. There were six brass and five saxes, plus Red and a rhythm section (sixteen musicians in all), a girl vocalist, Linda Keene, for personal appearances, and Mildred Bailey for recordings. It also had a very good arranger, Johnny Thompson. But it made just two recordings, both good ones—"Jersey Bounce" and "Arthur Murray Taught Me Dancing in a Hurry"—before the Petrillo recording ban went into effect.

Red's timing couldn't have been less fortunate. In addition to no recordings, there were increasingly fewer musicians to replace those being drafted, and fewer ways of transporting his band. So what could have been Red Norvo's most succesful group never got very far off the ground.

Red went back to a small jazz group, in which he introduced several "finds" —trumpeter Milton (Shorty) Rogers, trombonist Eddie Bert, clarinetist Aaron Sachs and, a short while later, pianist Ralph Burns. It was a fantastically exciting unit. Several of the musicians wrote arrangements. But only those aficionados who caught the group on its few New York appearances ever had a chance to hear this swinging octet. (I was more fortunate, because the guys spent two long afternoons down at my house in Greenwich Village recording about a dozen of their best works.)

Again the draft caught up with Red's music, and so he finally decided to let another leader do the worrying. He switched from xylophone to vibraphone, on which he displayed an amazingly deft touch. Then he joined Benny Goodman, and along with Benny, Teddy Wilson and Slam Stewart, formed one of the most delightful quartets ever to grace the jazz scene. In the following year, another leader bid for and won Red's services, Woody Herman, for whom Norvo organized a band within a band, the Woodchoppers, which cut eight memorable sides. Red also played several solos with the large outfit.

When the big band era ended, Red continued to lead small groups, devoting much of his time to trios. One of these was a remarkable outfit that included two tremendously talented and especially empathetic musicians, guitarist Tal Farlow and bassist Charles Mingus. Eventually Red settled down on the West Coast, married Eve Rogers, Shorty's sister, and divided his time between his family and numerous recording dates, and regular excursions to Las Vegas, where he led yet another great group and where he spent much time after Eve's tragic death in the early seventies. Much too seldom he migrated to other parts of the world, but whenever he did, he continued to project the tastiest, swingingest music extant, plus all that warmth and kindness that have made Red Norvo one of our truly great humans.

Tony Pastor

WHEN Artie Shaw suddenly forsook his band late in 1939, the logical man to take over the leadership was his old pal and sidekick, the band's featured singer and tenor saxist, Tony Pastor. But Tony had other ideas.

Under the new setup, the band was scheduled to turn into a cooperative affair. "I had a chance to go out with my own band, so who needed a whole band full of partners?" Tony said recently as he revealed that Cy Shribman, the famed Boston band booker who had angeled so many orchestras, had a year earlier offered to put up fifty thousand dollars so that Pastor could start his own outfit. "But Artie screamed to high heaven then. 'You can't do that to me,' he said, 'You've got a contract with me.' So I told him, 'All right, I'll stay, but I'll play and sing out of tune all night long.' Of course, I never would have done that to Artie; we'd been friends for much too long."

The Shaw-Pastor friendship had begun back in 1927 in New Haven, Connecticut, where both had been raised. Tony was three years older and he remembers that "Artie used to hang around the John Cavallaro band in which I was playing—Rudy Vallee played sax, too—and he'd carry my horn down to the railroad station for me. You see, I could play a whole tone scale in those days, and I guess Artie must have thought I was a genius or something." Later, Pastor played with the Wesleyan Serenaders, a group that included trombonist Andy Wiswell, now one of RCA Victor's top record producers, and then, along with Shaw, blew sax for Irving Aaronson and his Commanders and for Austin Wylie's orchestra.

When Artie formed his first permanent orchestra in the summer of 1936, he asked Tony to join him as the group's only saxophonist. There he stayed for three years. Then, when Shaw ran off to Mexico, Pastor phoned Shribman in Boston to take him up on his offer.

Within a few weeks the Pastor band was good enough to accept engagements, though hardly good enough for one of the first dates on which manager Shribman booked it. "It was a battle of music with Duke Ellington's band!" Pastor retrembled. "All we had in our books were eight special arrangements and a bunch of stocks. Soon after that, Cy booked us for another battle, this time with Count Basie. Now we had a nice little band, but we weren't in *that* league!"

Shribman, though, had faith in Pastor, just as he had had in Shaw, Glenn Miller, Woody Herman, Claude Thornhill, Hal McIntyre and other bands which he had backed with bookings and with cash. For the big bands, Si was, in Tony's words, "definitely the greatest angel who ever lived."

Because of Shribman's support, Pastor could afford to take a lengthy engagement in the Blue Room of New York's Hotel Lincoln. "We had eighteen air shots a week, so everybody could get to hear us. But the place wouldn't pay for the radio wire, so Si loaned me the forty-five thousand dollars it cost us." Eventually Pastor was able to pay it all back—out of commissions.

I first heard the band at the Lincoln and liked it. One of its greatest assets was its friendly, unpretentious approach. Tony's infectious, impish, pixieish personality, plus his good will and humor, permeated the entire band, and it was obvious his men liked him immensely. The group's musical standouts were Tony with his warm-toned tenor sax and singing; the excellently blended sax quintet, led so superbly by Johnny McAfee, who also sang ballads with great feeling; and an old Pastor friend, Maxie Kaminsky, who had brought his tasteful dixieland trumpet into the band. By this time (January, 1941) the band had amassed a good, original library, most of it written by Tony's stalwart guitarist, Al Avola.

The new band had several singers in addition to Pastor and McAfee: a handsome blond named Dorsey Anderson, and Kay Little, the first of several girl singers who were to grace a Pastor bandstand that later showcased the gorgeous and very talented Eugenie Baird, who became one of the top jingle singers; the vivacious Virginia Maxey, now married to singer-composer Matt Dennis; pretty Dolores Martel, who married Joe D'Imperio, an RCA Victor vice-president; and the most famous of all Pastor alumnae, Rosemary Clooney, who married José Ferrer.

Rosemary sang mostly as part of the Clooney Sisters. She and her sister, Betty (she also got married—to Latin maestro Pupi Campo), had been recommended to Tony by bandleader Barney Rapp when they were appearing on the mood-filled "Moon River" radio program over Cincinnati's WLW. Says Tony in restrospect: "They were smart kids, but they were only babies then. [Then was 1947.] Betty was fifteen and Rosey was seventeen, and they had good ears and some corny arrangements of their own. But Ralph Flanagan, who was writing for us, gave them some good new arrangements." On many of these, Tony joined forces with the Clooneys, who impressed me as two very attractive, musical girls.

The most distinctive and most commercial singer the band ever featured, though, was Pastor himself. He always had a delightful way of emoting, a sort of let's-see-how-far-I-can-go-without-getting-my-face-slapped approach, during which he'd squinch up his eyes and grin through the lyrics of songs like "Let's Do It," "Makin' Whoopee," "I'm Confessin'" and "'A,' You're Adorable." He freely admits that his singing style was shaped by his years of listening to one man, "My idol, Mr. Louis Armstrong. Is there anybody better than that?"

Tony

During the mid-forties, the band concentrated more on jazz, with Budd Johnson and Walter Fuller, who wrote in a modern vein, supplying most of the arrangements. "I bought eighteen thousand dollars' worth from Budd alone," Tony has said. "The band was real good then."

In addition to his own tenor, Tony was also featuring the very fine, Berigan-like trumpet of his younger brother, Sal, who soon became one of the band's leading attractions and remained with the band for several years, the beginning of loving nepotism in the career of Tony Pastor, who succeeded in sustaining a big band longer than most of his peers did.

But by 1957 Pastor realized he couldn't buck the trend any longer. So he organized a small group that started a lengthy stay in Las Vegas. Featured with him were two fine young singers, his two sons, Guy Pastor and Tony Pastor, Jr. Since then, both have ventured forth on their own. A third son, Johnny, decided to concentrate on the flamenco guitar, and might even have joined his father as an accompanist. But late in the sixties, Tony grew very ill. He remained almost in seclusion in his Connecticut home until he passed away on October 31, 1969, five days after his 62nd birthday.

Teddy Powell

ONE of the most impressive dance bands of the mid-forties was one that too few people ever heard. The reason? The recording ban imposed by the musicians' union. The band? Teddy Powell's.

Powell, a former violinist and guitarist with Abe Lyman's band and also a successful songwriter, embarked on his bandleading career late in 1939. It was a flamboyant beginning. A nervous, impatient, but big hearted and completely lovable character, he tried starting off right at the top. He hired a high-pressure press agent and some of the country's most outstanding musicians and made his big-time debut with a very green outfit at New York's Famous Door.

It was a good band that could have sounded much better under a more knowledgeable leader. But Teddy's ambitious optimism couldn't overcome his inexperience. Very much in awe of his great sidemen, he kept trying too hard to please them. One report insisted that when Powell counted off tempos for a tune he would look hopefully at guitarist Benny Heller (one of four Goodman alumni in the band) as he called out apprehensively, "One! . . . two??"

Powell's band was received so well by the Famous Door's hip patrons that Teddy immediately proclaimed to the world what a great band he had, boasting that he had accomplished in six weeks what it had taken Goodman and Dorsey years to do. But poor Teddy was in for a rude awakening, for once his band hit the less hip hinterlands, nothing happened. "I thought with the Famous Door buildup, I'd clean up on one-nighters," he related afterward. "But I sure learned a lesson—it can't happen that quick."

In less than a year Powell had lost thirty-five thousand dollars of his own money. But also in less than a year he was booked back into the Famous Door. Then one of several career tragedies hit him. A few weeks after the start of his second engagement there, the club folded. The owners had gone broke.

But Teddy, forever the optimist, wouldn't be deterred. If those guys couldn't run the club, he would. He raised more cash and bought it, installing his band as the first attraction under his management.

The second tragedy struck in October of 1941. Teddy had built himself another good band by then, one that eschewed much of the jazz his first group had played, concentrating more on musical ballad sounds. It was, as one writer put it, "today's Isham Jones band." *Metronome* tabbed it "The Surprise of 1941."

Teddy was playing at the Rustic Cabin, just across the George Washington bridge in nearby New Jersey. One Saturday morning I was down at the printer's, putting the magazine to bed, when I received a phone call that the Rustic Cabin had just burned to the ground. I immediately contacted Teddy at home. "Really?" he said. "You know, somebody called me a couple of hours ago and told me about it, but I thought it was just a gag so I went back to sleep."

The two of us drove out there together. What a sight! The place was totally destroyed. All the band's instruments and music had been burned. Teddy was completely crushed. The only visible evidence of anything musical was the cast iron frame of the piano, which had fallen down into the cellar.

As we were standing there, a little man emerged from a car that had just driven up. He was carrying what looked like a doctor's bag and wearing a very bewildered look. He saw us and came over. "Pardon me, gentlemen," he said, "but I'm wondering if you can help me. I'm the piano tuner. I came to tune the piano."

Fortunately for Powell, not everything was lost. In a trunk in his office he still had the original scores of all his arrangements. With the help of friends, new copies were made, and after a few months, Teddy was in business again.

This time he landed a job in another Cabin, the Log Cabin in Armonk,

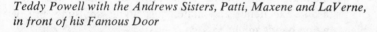

Teddy Powell with the Andrews Sisters, Patti, Maxene and LaVerne,
in front of his Famous Door

New York, and there he presented one of the finest dance bands of the times. It set magnificent moods. It played consistently good music. It used a batch of fine new arrangements, many of them written by Henry Wells, of Andy Kirk and Jimmie Lunceford fame. And it featured great soloists like Irving Fazola on clarinet, Jack Satterfield, who later became the first trombone player in the New York Philharmonic, and a brilliant young jazz trumpeter named Dick Mains. It also had an exceptionally fine ballad singer in Peggy Mann and a better-than-average boy singer in Tommy Taylor.

By this time, with the help of his band manager, Peter Dean, Powell had learned that there was much more to leading a band than merely standing in front of it—that it was necesary not only to create but also to sustain moods for dancers. Most leaders, fearful of monotony, varied their tempos as much as posible. But Teddy, when he noticed that the dancers were in a romantic mood, would play several ballads in a row. The crowds loved it. "The Surprise Band of 1941," wrote Barry Ulanov, "has turned into a great band in 1942."

But the recording ban allowed few people to hear much of Teddy's outfit, most of whose members were soon swallowed by the draft. (It had recorded one novelty for Bluebird, "Serenade to a Maid," which had created some fuss among fans and censors alike.) Teddy soon organized another group, which drew this rave opening in my January, 1943, *Metronome* review:

> It's amazing how this Teddy Powell man does it! He's not a great arranger. He's not a great instrumentalist. He's not a great singer or showman. You couldn't call him a great musician. And he's by no means a strict disciplinarian.
>
> And though he's none of these, any combination of which might make for a great bandleader, he still manages to turn out dance music that for musical taste and excellence can match just about anything any of the even bigger name bands might toss your way.

A year and a half later, Powell had yet another outfit—and still another great one at that! Only vocalist Peggy Mann remained. But Teddy had uncovered several budding stars, including tenor saxist Charlie Ventura and trumpeter Pete Candoli. But again, few people had an opportunity to hear the group, for it didn't last long enough to make any impressive recordings. Teddy was soon forced to give up his band for about a year, settling down in nearby Connecticut, where he had an opportunity to reappraise his position.

There was no doubt about it: he had created some very musical bands. But he had never been able to cash in on their musical worth. Wouldn't it be simpler to have a band without stars, one that didn't try to prove anything musical but instead could work steadily in hotels throughout the country?

Teddy's answer apparently was a strong "yes," because he soon had built himself a very good, hotel type orchestra. It had no star soloists, but it could satisfy and, in one particular instance, much to Teddy's chagrin, completely fool the customers.

Powell laughed when he told the story to writer Bill Coss, a tale that summed up neatly the frustration and comparative anonymity that hounded him throughout his bandleading career. He had been appearing for a couple of months at the Roosevelt Grill while Guy Lombardo and his band, the perennial incumbents, were touring the country. "One night, just about closing time," Powell related, "a young couple came up to the bandstand. They explained that they had always admired my music and during their trip from Canada they were happy that they could finally get to see and hear me. Then they said, 'Could we have your autograph, Mr. Lombardo?' I didn't have the heart to tell them who I was, so I just signed Guy's name and sent them away happy."

Teddy and singer Peggy Mann.

Boyd Raeburn

SO FAR as musicians were concerned, one of the truly great bands of the mid-forties was Boyd Raeburn's. But so far as the public was concerned it was just another modern-sounding outfit that wasn't very good to dance to and emitted sounds that few of them could understand.

Boyd, who'd begun his career in the thirties as a mickey-mouse bandleader and by 1942 had improved to the point of leading a swing band of dubious distinction, started impressing jazz fans in 1944 with a bright new outfit that included a group of Sonny Dunham refugees who had refused to sign long-term deals. The Boyd outfit played some startlingly good arrangements by Ed Finckel and featured a batch of young, eager musicians like trumpeters Sonny Berman and Marky Markowitz, trombonist Earl Swope and drummer Don Lamond, all of whom were to gain greater fame a few years later in Woody Herman's band, plus saxist Johnny Bothwell and trombonist Tommy

Boyd with wifely singer Ginny Powell

Peterson. Emmett Carls, the tenor saxist, who had been the ringleader of the ex-Dunhamites, also brought in a young arranger, Johnny Mandel, to contribute some scores. Carls even got Dizzy Gillespie to sit in occasionally.

Boyd himself played various saxes—first tenor, then baritone and finally the seldom-heard bass sax. He was a bright, direct, enthusiastic person, wiry and handsome, a good frontman who was respected by his musicians.

His 1944 band was ahead of the times. Perhaps the times would have caught up with the band. But before there was a chance, a fire at Palisades Amusement Park in New Jersey destroyed the band's music, some of its instruments and most of its momentum.

In 1945 Boyd organized another group and, to make sure that the times couldn't catch up to him, he began featuring even more modern sounds. Most were George Handy's, who had worked with Boyd during the latter part of 1944, after Finckel had left. The new scores emitted flashes of Stravinsky, Bartok, Debussy and Ravel. To musicians such deployments on classical Modernists and Impressionists were completely dazzling. But the public was completely dazed.

"The enthusiasm of the Raeburn band," wrote Barry Ulanov, its biggest booster, in September, 1945, "matches the fervor of their leader and the imagination of their arranger. . . . There are no limits to their imagination and their daring." Singled out for special credits were saxists Hal McKusick, trombonist-arranger Mandel (years later he wrote "The Shadow of Your Smile") and singer David Allen.

Ulanov, in another burst of exuberance, summed up the band's assets and liabilities several months later: "This Raeburn band is by no means a dance organization. The music it plays is designed for listening; it's modern music, cast in new molds out of classical forms and jazz rhythms and harmonies. . . . This is the way music will be played from now on by the really hip and talented and profound and musically healthy." "But not," he might have added, "by the wealthy."

Still, so many people had so much faith in Raeburn, that, despite his uncommerciality, he was able to sustain for a number of years. Musicians enjoyed working for him, for his music was a challenge to them, and many willingly gave up more lucrative jobs to play in his band. Reportedly, Duke Ellington was so impressed with what Boyd was doing that he not only encouraged Boyd verbally but supported him financially.

Raeburn enjoyed one post-big band era spurt in the late forties, with Johnny Richards this time writing the advanced and again highly provocative scores. By 1950, however, Boyd and his pretty wife and vocalist, Ginny Powell, a lovely person who died in 1959, had settled down, first in New York, then in Nassau. Boyd continued to be pretty well removed from the music business for the rest of his life, which ended on August 2, 1966, when he suffered a fatal heart attack.

Alvino Rey

"THEY'RE out to have fun and at the same time to give you a good time. As a result, you feel as if you've busted into a big family group, composed completely of kids who are just awfully happy to have you with them."

Sounds like a review of the famous King Family television series, doesn't it? Actually, it comes from my first review of the Alvino Rey band with the King Sisters, which I wrote in April, 1941, when they were playing at the Rustic Cabin in Englewood, New Jersey. Calling it "The No. 1 'Never-a-Dull-Moment' Aggregation of Dancebandom," I proceeded to laud not only its showmanship, which revolved around the Kings and two very funny but good musicians, saxist Skeets Herfurt and guitarist Dick (Ickey) Morgan, but also its musicianship, especially that of Rey, Herfurt, Morgan and a young pianist who was to go on to greater things on his own, Buddy Cole.

Alvino, who could play excellent rhythm guitar, was featuring his electrified instrument, complete with glisses and Hawaiian sounds, which he used tastefully and discreetly. For the band's opening theme, he also employed a weird effect that sounded like a bunch of electrified voices. This, actually, was a gimmick, which he has steadfastly refused to reveal in technical detail, whereby Louise King, his wife, would solo into a mike that led to the amplified guitar, which, in turn, Alvino fingered so as to produce the eerie, multivoiced sound that became the band's trademark.

Rey, whose real name was Al McBurney ("I'm from Scotch-Irish ancestry and I hate Latin and Hawaiian music!"), was bright, warm, witty, and extremely well liked by his musicians. During their several months at the Rustic Cabin engagement, almost the entire band was ensconced nearby in a large house, which Alvino referred to as "The Chateau." It, said he, "belonged to some bootleg king, but the guys in the band were only making thirty-five dollars a week, and the Sisters and I were getting only thirty, so to save the commuting money to New York, most of us lived there."

The group was a happy one, and Alvino, with his kooky sense of humor, helped keep it so. Its heavy schedule included a weekly Sunday broadcast at a ridiculous hour—twelve noon. One Sunday, some of the musicians were rudely awakened by the sound of the band's opening theme and an announcer's voice giving details about the noon broadcast. Alarmed that the show had

Alvino and the King Sisters: Yvonne, Donna, Louise and Alyce

started without them, they jumped out of bed, only to discover that Alvino had recorded the previous week's program and was playing it back full volume to awaken them.

Rey had formed the band late in 1938 when he and the King Sisters left Horace Heidt. They settled in California (the Kings came from Utah, and Los Angeles was a lot closer than New York), where station KHJ, aware of their reputation through the Heidt performances, suggested to Alvino that he form a studio band. Assured of work, Alvino sent for Frank DeVol, a former saxist and arranger in Heidt's band ("Frank wrote a lot of good arrangements, but Heidt never used them") to create a new library. He also suggested to his old friend, Herfurt, that he leave Tommy Dorsey and join him. "Skeets was playing fourth tenor with Tommy, and when I told him he'd be playing lead alto for us he came."

Alvino was quite proud of his band. It broadcast regularly and recorded a batch of transcribed radio shows. "We wanted to go with MCA, and Larry Barnett came from their office to hear us and said, 'It's a nice band,' but that he couldn't use us. So we went ahead and started to book ourselves. The first big job we landed was at the Pasadena Civic Auditorium, and on the first night, four thousand people showed up. We were a big hit. More people than we realized must have been listening to our KHJ broadcasts and our transcriptions."

Duly influenced, MCA then "discovered" the band and booked it into the New England territory, where nobody knew it. Business was awful. But for some inexplicable reason, the band did very well in Detroit. Hugh Mulligan, manager of New York's Biltmore Hotel, heard about Rey's success and booked him into his spot.

"We went in with mutes in all the horns and with yellow jackets to match the color of the hotel's tablecloths. Everything was going along fine until one night somebody asked us to play some jazz. So we took out the mutes. Just then Mulligan came roaring in and told us to get out. So from then on we started playing the kind of music we wanted to play—elsewhere!"

The Biltmore engagement, though, bore fruit. On the strength of its broadcasts the band was asked to sub at the Paramount Theater for Dinah Shore when she was ill. "We were amazed at the great response. We had no idea we would be so well accepted. But enough people had heard all those radio broadcasts from the Biltmore so that they knew us and, I guess, liked us."

Soon thereafter the band opened at the Rustic Cabin, where it broadcast more than ever. "I remember one time when everybody was snowbound," Alvino has said. "We had already gone to work, but the engineer and announcer couldn't get out to do the air shot." Alvino, though, through his amplified guitaring, had learned basic electronics, enough "so that I could set up the equipment, and we did the broadcast ourselves. I turned out to be both the engineer and announcer."

The band was contracted to go back in the following winter. By then its fame and price had risen considerably, and when the Rustic Cabin was destroyed by fire, burning Rey's contract along with everything else, Alvino wasn't entirely unhappy. "It finally gave us the chance to go into Meadow-brook," a more prestigious spot, and one that didn't book bands that also played at the nearby Cabin.

In his February, 1942, review of the band at Meadowbrook, Barry Ulanov tabbed it "the finest of all show bands." He also commended it for its musicianship, drawing attention to the arrangements by Jerry Feldman, who later became more famous as Jerry Fielding.

Later that year, Rey started what he called "the best band I ever had." But, like other "best bands," this one, thanks to James Caesar Petrillo's murderous ban, was never recorded. It played great arrangements by such future stars as Neal Hefti, Ray Conniff, Johnny Mandel and Billy May, and it sported many fine jazz musicians.

"It was a huge band," says Rey. "I guess we wanted to outdo Stan Kenton. We had six saxes and ten brass, with four bass trumpets, and seven vocalists, including Andy Russell, who played drums with us for a while." From time to time, Rey hired some even better drummers: Don Lamond, Irv Cottler, Nick Fatool, Mel Lewis and on transcriptions, some released years later on Hindsight Records, Rey used his all-time idol, Davey Tough.

In February 1943, Alvino took a war-plant job with Vega Aircraft in Los Angeles, where he inspected radio parts for Flying Fortresses and lined up a number of factory jobs for his musicians. They worked the night shift. from 12:30 A.M. to 7 A.M. The rest of the time they were free to do what they wanted. What they wanted to do, of course, was keep the band going, and this they did through a regular weekly sustaining broadcast, soon to be followed by a commercial show, plus irregular personal appearances.

The band got better and better. May was contributing most of the arrangements, with others coming from a newcomer, Nelson Riddle, and "a kid whose father came up to San Francisco where we were playing and took him by the hand and said, 'Come on home, son.'" The "son" was George Handy, soon to develop into one of the most creative arrangers of all time.

Early in 1944 the band broke up when Alvino entered the Navy in which he formed an excellent service group. Late in 1945 he was discharged and formed another band. But he soon grew discouraged. "After the war," he recently told me, "forget it. Everybody was in it for the money. The guys were always fighting. It was the boppers against the others. The fun was all gone."

Alvino today plays occasionally but spends more of his time producing records and TV shows. Looking back at his career and reflecting on the course he'd take if he had it to do all over again, he says: "I'd keep the small band, the one with six brass, five saxes and rhythm. The big band I had later had some musical kicks, but it never did swing. The operators kept telling us we were too big and too loud, and the trumpets always kept trying to play an octave above one another."

Rey, who started off in his native Cleveland as a jazz guitarist ("I met Eddie Lang there and always idolized him."), was orginally attracted to the Hawaiian sound, which he later learned to abhor, and eventually the electronic one, "after I heard Andy Sanella play." With Heidt, Rey had developed his distinctive sound, and gradually he became to be recognized as one of the most inventive of the electronic guitarists.

Recently asked how he felt about today's strange-sounding uses of an instrument he worked so hard to develop and popularize, Alvino looked skyward with an expression of helplessness mixed with embarrassment. "I don't know what to say. But," he quickly added to prove that he didn't create only monsters, "my son, Robby, is a big jazz fan. He idolizes Charlie Mingus!"

Buddy Rich

THEY called him "Baby Traps" when he played vaudeville at the age of seven. The first time I ever saw him he was tap dancer and MC for a show on an afternoon excursion boat. The next time I saw him he was playing drums for Joe Marala's Sextet in New York's Hickory House. After that it was in Bunny Berigan's band. But it was when he started making the Artie Shaw band jump as it never had before that he really began to thrill me.

This was Bernard (Buddy) Rich, the most brilliant and dynamic drummer of all time, who soon went on to fire up the Tommy Dorsey band and to fight with just about everybody, including its featured singer, Frank Sinatra. Buddy was always a swinger, whether it be with his sticks or his fists. "It used to be," wrote Bob Bach in *Metronome,* "that you almost had to stand in line to be able to get a sock at him. He was cocky, rashly outspoken and brutally sarcastic."

Buddy

But oh, what native talent—as a fleet dancer, a fantastic drummer and also as an insinuating, thoroughly convincing singer. "Frank Sinatra once heard me singing 'Aren't You Glad You're You?' at one of my band's early rehearsals," Buddy recalls, "and he suggested that I sing more often." And what was Sinatra, with whom Rich had feuded so often, doing at one of his rehearsals? He merely had so much faith in Buddy's ability that he decided to back his new band.

Buddy flanked by backer Frank Sinatra and booker Sonny Werblin

The band which didn't get started until the Big Band Era was nearing its end, was an impressive one when I caught it during its first major engagement in January, 1946. It sported a batch of excellent, modern arrangements by Ed Finckel, Tad Dameron, Turk Van Lake and Billy Moore, Jr., and some fine sidemen in trombonists Earl Swope and Johnny Mandel, trumpeter Lou Oles and clarinetest Aaron Sachs (Tony Scott replaced Sachs, fought with Buddy and left after four days). But by far the outstanding man in the band was Rich himself. His drumming, as always, was astounding. His singing, especially of "Baby, Baby All the Time," was delightful. And thanks to his years of experience in show business, he knew how to handle a crowd better than any other brand new bandleader did.

For a while things went well. The band secured such choice bookings as the Palladium in Hollywood and the Hotel Sherman in Chicago. But more and more, Buddy seemed to want to play jazz. "I like ballads with a beat," he announced. But not enough people seemed to feel the same way, not only about Buddy's band in particular but about big bands in general, and after a little more than two years as a bandleader, Rich joined the touring Jazz at the Philharmonic troupe.

Buddy has never ceased to amaze me, and not merely as a performer (no drummer has ever matched his rhythmic fire and excitement). Outwardly cocky and often intensely insulting, he can also be a thoroughly charming, thoughtful human being. He respects talent but abhors phonies. His attitude toward people is as direct and sometimes as volatile as his drumming. Unpressed, he can be a delight; pressed too hard, he can become a disaster.

Long after the Big Band Era had ended, various maestri sought out Buddy to help them with their bands. For no other big band drummer has ever been able to fire up a crew the way Rich has. In the early fifties he joined Harry James, went back with his old boss, Tommy Dorsey, for a while, then kept going in and out of Harry's band. Late in 1966 he finally organized his own band again, a tremendously exciting, swinging outfit, made so in part by some excellent, modern, swinging arrangements, a batch of good sidemen, but most of all by Buddy's dynamic and consistently inspiring drums. In the summer of 1967 its career received a tremendous shot in the arm when the band was selected by Jackie Gleason as a regular on his summer replacement TV series, and by a one-time Rich antagonist and long-time Rich admirer, Frank Sinatra, to accompany him on a concert tour.

During the late sixties and through the seventies, Buddy brought in more modern-sounding arrangements, many of them with rock overtones. Obviously he wanted to catch the ears of a younger public, and in this he was quite successful. His band began to appear in rock clubs where it received resounding and often standing ovations. Soon he was being "discovered" by fervent fans who greeted him even more boisterously than had those of a generation or more earlier.

Buddy also became known as a personality, primarily because of his frequent appearances on Johnny Carson's "Tonight" TV show, during which he issued brash and often insulting pronouncements, creating the sort of shock effect admired by both young and Las Vegas type audiences.

Warned by doctors to take it easier, because of a heart condition and back problems, he reduced his band to a sextet in the mid-1970s. When his condition improved, aided by an intensive physical build-up program that included the art of karate, he formed another big band, staffing it with young, eager musicians from whom he sometimes demanded more than they were willing or able to give. For keeping up with Buddy Rich had always been in more ways than one a difficult chore as he continued right into the 1980s to maintain a torrid pace that few other big bandleaders had ever before attained and certainly seldom maintained.

Jan Savitt

AT a time in the mid-thirties when most radio studio dance bands sounded as if they were stocked with a bunch of disgruntled, disillusioned musicians, big band fans were surprised and delighted by some crisp, modern, exciting sounds coming from the studios of Philadelphia's KYW. The band: Jan Savitt and His Top Hatters.

The Top Hatters played ballads tastefully and with feeling, and, wonders of studio wonders, they also swung via a propulsive, though somewhat restricting beat called shuffle rhythm. Built around a piano playing at double time, it was an attracting device and soon Savitt, who a few years before had never dreamed he'd become a swing bandleader, was receiving offers from top spots throughout the country.

Originally Jan had planned and pursued a career in the classical music field. Born in Russia, the son of a drummer in the Imperial Regimental Band of the Czar, he was, at the age of six, hailed as a child prodigy on the violin. At the age of fifteen, after his family had migrated to America, he won three scholarships for playing and conducting at the Curtis Institute in Philadelphia and soon became the youngest musician ever to play in the Philadelphia Symphony. A few years later he had graduated to the rank of concert master for Maestro Leopold Stokowski.

By 1926 young Savitt had organized his own string quartet, which bore his name, and won the Philharmonic Society's Gold Medal Award, plus a coast-to-coast radio series on CBS. Philadelphia's local network station, WCAU, was so impressed that it hired Jan as its musical director. So successful were his programs there that rival station KYW offered him an even better job—and that's when the Top Hatters began attracting a national audience.

My first major impression of the band was based on its early 1939 appearance in New York's Hotel Lincoln. It was, I thought, a good band, but it played, consistently and annoyingly, too loud, as though it were trying too hard to prove to the public and to itself that it really was a swing band. Such overblowing wasn't necessary to produce good swinging sounds, a fact that Jan, who was not a jazz musician, conceivably still had to learn.

Not only was Jan talented, he was also very enthusiastic, which might have accounted for his going overboard at the start of his first major New

Bon Bon and Savitt

York engagement. However, he was also very bright, well-informed and eager to discuss his music, so that he soon learned what jazz and swing were all about. And so it wasn't long before his band settled into a much more relaxed groove.

According to Jack Hansen, the trumpeter who played with Savitt for many years, the band always maintained an excellent spirit. The men admired and respected Jan, even though they may not always have agreed with his ideas about jazz. And they got along well among themselves. "There were no factions, like the drinkers versus the nondrinkers, the way there were in some bands, and there was very little 'cutting' going on among the guys." (In fact, there were very few jazz soloists who were inclined to cut one another.) However, Savitt did have two exceptional singers, Carlotta Dale and Bon Bon.

Carlotta's was a very emotional and very musical style of singing. She was one of the few girl singers I ever heard who could sound dramatic without resorting to melodramatics. She sang with conviction and with taste and in tune. She was an exceedingly attractive girl, but her beauty and career were sadly affected by a tragic accident in which she fell from a moving car driven by Savitt.

Bon Bon was the band's prime attraction. A handsome man, with a jubilant face, he had been leading his own vocal trio, The Three Keys, when Jan picked him as his featured vocalist. He was one of the first blacks ever to work with a white band. His true name was George Tunnell, and, according to Hansen, he was articulate, intelligent and sensitive.

He and the band had to face various racial problems that existed quite overtly in those days. So that he could stay in the same southern hotels with the rest of the men, Hansen reports, Bon Bon would sign in as the band manager's valet. But that was as far as he would compromise. He was, Hansen recalls, a man of great pride and loyalty. One night, for example, while standing at a soda stand in the back of a Kentucky ballroom before a job, he was refused service. And so, for the next two and a half hours, Bon Bon refused to come on stage. Only when the band played a remote broadcast did he appear to sing his numbers. The crowd immediately let out a tremendous cheer of welcome. But as soon as Bon Bon had done his bit for his band, off the stand he went, refusing to sing any more for the people who had snubbed him.

Bon Bon was featured on many Savitt recordings, notably "It's a Wonderful World" and "Vol Vistu Gaily Star." But of all the band's numbers, the most requested remained an original by arranger Johnny Watson, "720 in the Books," so called because that *was* its number in the Savitt library and nobody could come up with a better title. So popular did the melody become that lyrics were eventually added.

After several years with the band, Bon Bon returned to Philadelphia to head The Three Keys again and to embark on a successful business career. Jan used numerous vocalists thereafter, boys and girls, the most famous of which was a budding young movie star who recorded several sides with the band. Her name: Gloria DeHaven.

In the latter part of his band's career, Jan made several stylistic changes. For a while he patterned his music after that of the Jimmie Lunceford band, and did a good job of it, too. By 1942, when Tommy Dorsey and Harry James were sporting string sections, Jan decided that he should have one also. But, whereas Tommy and Harry led big units, Savitt limited himself to five strings plus himself. Yet so good was this small section (three men from Curtis Institute, one from Juilliard, with the fifth chair filled by vocalist Joe Martin), and so expertly was it used, that to discerning listeners the Savitt strings sounded more impressive than those in any other dance orchestra.

In 1944 Jan increased his string section to a dozen and a half players, as he expanded his orchestra for a theater tour on which he conducted for Frank Sinatra (even in those days, Frank did things on a big scale).

Devoting much of his time to activities on the West Coast, Savitt worked regularly for the next few years. But soon the big bands were beginning to call it quits, and chances are Jan would have, too, if he hadn't found himself faced by a large tax debt, incurred, according to reports, when one of his former associates absconded with the band's tax deductions. In order to pay that debt, Jan embarked on what he hoped would be a highly successful one-nighter tour. But late in 1948, while traveling to an engagement in Sacramento, California, it all ended. Jan Savitt, not yet forty years old, suffered a cerebral hemorrhage, and the career of one of the most complete musicians ever to lead a big band came to a sudden end.

Raymond Scott

RAYMOND SCOTT enjoyed his greatest popularity before he led his big band. That was in 1937 when he fronted a sextet that played regularly on CBS and made several Brunswick records of Scott originals with such titles as "Twilight in Turkey," "Dinner Music for a Pack of Hungry Cannibals," "The Toy Trumpet" and "War Dance for Wooden Indians."

The group displayed a naive charm, which was probably appreciated more by grade school music teachers than by jazz fans and musicians. Years later Scott admitted that it "never jumped, primarily because we didn't have the musicians who knew how. They were fine studio men, but that was all."

Scott, bright, inventive, quite intense, sometimes stubborn and often self-conscious, at times experienced difficulty in communicating with some of his musicians on their level. He was an introvert, a dreamer, and he loved to experiment. He tended to act more like an absentminded college professor or like a member of a classical string quartet than like a leader of a "jazz" sextet.

His real name was Harry Warnow. His older brother was Mark Warnow, who led the Lucky Strike Hit Parade Orchestra for many years and helped Ray become established at CBS. There Ray made his musical home until mid-1940, when he began a series of personal appearances heading a new thirteen-piece band.

It wasn't an overly impressive outfit, chiefly because getting a big group to play so many tricky passages was almost impossible. At its best, the kittenish, pseudo-jazz approach made fairly interesting listening. But as music for dancing, it was too choppy and unrelaxed.

The musicians were given little freedom, because Scott insisted upon absolute accuracy. He wanted to achieve, he said at the time, "an inspired precision machine, not a mechanical one." The one time I reviewed it, I was depressed by its lack of feeling, though I had to admire Scott for his "push-button discipline."

His big band lasted a couple of years; then Ray returned to CBS and organized a new and much better sextet which was distinguished also for mixing black and white musicians. Originally, Scott had hoped to acquire Cootie Williams and Johnny Hodges from Duke Ellington's band (Cootie

*Pianist-composer-
conductor-arranger-
inventor-dreamer
Raymond Scott*

joined Benny Goodman instead) as well as Benny Carter, but when these deals
fell through he still wound up with an impressive lineup that included trumpeter
Emmett Berry, saxist Jerry Jerome, pianist Mel Powell and drummer Cozy
Cole.

Eventually Ray expanded the group, and by 1944 he was heading one of
the finest of all studio bands. Also a mixed group, it featured at one time
Ben Webster on tenor sax, Les Elgart and Charlie Shavers on trumpets,
Benny Morton on trombone, Tony Mottola on guitar, Israel Crosby on bass
and Specs Powell on drums.

Ray drove his men hard. He was, he admitted to me later, a perfectionist,
much like one of his idols, Glenn Miller, whom Ray described as "the one
great genius we have had among leaders of dance bands."

Ray made another revelatory comment at the time. "The trouble with me,"
he said, "is I want what I want so badly." But he continued to find it difficult
to communicate with his musicians. His idol, Miller, could do it with his
horn. But the piano, which Ray played—and not especially well at that—
is, so far as phrasing is concerned, a much more limited instrument. And
since Ray couldn't express himself very well verbally, the men sometimes
began to look upon him as an eccentric.

But Ray knew what he wanted, even though his methods were at times considered rather peculiar. For example, he insisted that an orchestra should train mechanically, just like a football team, with its members practicing breathing exercises together, even studying together. Once, to implement this theory, he suggested to his entire group that they enroll for classes at the Juilliard School of Music. (Afterward, drummer Cozy Cole made one of his classic remarks: "Man, I went up there to Juilliard to register, like Mr. Scott suggested, and, you know, I looked around me and, man, I suddenly realized I knew half them cats up there already!")

Ray had another pet theory, one that could have explained why some musicians thought he was crazy: "Too often, if they can't play something right, they'll blame their leader. They try their damndest, but then when they've failed, they become obsessed with that old 'evil forces are at work' idea, and then they start to feel they're being needled by the leader. That's when they begin resenting him, swearing he's the hardest man they've ever worked for, and eventually they rationalize and say, 'He's crazy. Why should I try to please a crazy man?' "

One person who obviously learned to understand Scott was his young singing discovery, Dorothy Collins, who for quite a while lived with Ray and his wife as a kind of "adopted daughter." But the "daughter" soon blossomed into an attractive woman who later became the next Mrs. Raymond Scott. Raymond and Dorothy appeared together publicly often—most memorably in their roles as conductor and featured singer of the "Lucky Strike Hit Parade" series. Years later they were divorced. Dorothy moved to the west coast and remained there for a long time. Ray stayed on Long Island, though later he also migrated west, bringing with him his magnificently outfitted electronic workshop with which he continued to forge ahead in his persistent campaign to mate mechanics with music.

Some of the originals Ray had written for his mid-forties group had sounded pretty far out then. So had their titles, especially one called "A Dedication Piece to the Crew and Passengers of the First Experimental Rocket Express to the Moon."

Come to think of it, just how crazy was this guy, Raymond Scott, in the light of what eventually was to take place not only with our space program but also with the preponderance of electronic sounds in all forms of modern music? Who knows, maybe they'll be playing his music some years from now over the PA system for the crew and passengers of that Rocket Express to the moon. And maybe over that PA system, they might also hear, "Good afternoon, everybody, this is your pilot, Raymond Scott speaking!"

Artie Shaw

"WE'LL find an identity. Perhaps it would be fairer to say I'll find one. Sooner or later all bands that stick find an identity, and find it through their leader. All the sounds—the creative arrangements, the pop tunes and the originals—must be channelized through the leader."

Thus spake Artie Shaw in 1949, when he was about to start another band. But he could just as easily have said it—and meant it—in 1936 when he formed his first group, or in 1937 when he formed his next one, or in 1940 when he formed another one, or later in 1940 when he formed still another one, or in 1941 when he formed another one, or in 1942 when he transformed another one, or in 1943 when he started his Navy band, or in 1944 when he formed another civilian band, or in 1949 when he formed a bop band, or in 1953 when he put together his final group.

For Artie Shaw was a searcher, a man looking for something new, something different, something with which he could identify and which he could identify as his own. He was a thinker, a much deeper thinker than most bandleaders, a man concerned with and constantly analyzing his place and the place of his music in society. "I'm cursed," he once said, "with serious-mindedness. And I know you can take yourself too seriously. Unless you have a desire to live, to live a good deal apart from yourself, from that overbearing self-concern, you can't play."

Artie was both serious and searching when, in 1935, Joe Helbock, a night-club owner about to stage a swing concert, invited him to participate with a group of his own. Shaw, even then attempting to establish his own identity, put together an outfit that featured a string quartet along with his clarinet. It made such a great impression that Tommy Rockwell, head of Rockwell-O'Keefe, the booking agency that didn't have a band to compete with MCA's Benny Goodman, kept after Artie to form a permanent group. This he did in 1936, ending his career as one of the most successful studio musicians, a career that had included playing alongside such future rivals as Goodman, the Dorseys, Bunny Berigan, Jack Teagarden and Artie's close friend Claude Thornhill.

Shaw debuted at the Lexington Hotel late in the summer of 1936, succeeding Bob Crosby and his dixieland-styled band. Artie's, too, had a dixie-

Shaw: "I'm cursed with serious-mindedness."

land jazz approach, which featured his clarinet, Lee Castle's trumpet and Tony Pastor's tenor sax. But the total effect was softened by the inclusion of a string quartet, resulting in what my review termed "a soothing, syrupy swing."

Many of the arrangements were written by the band's pianist, Joe Lipman, who had recommended a fellow Bostonian to Artie to lead the strings. This was Jerry Gray. "I didn't know what it was all about when Joe called me," Jerry recalled. "I thought I was supposed to audition for some society job, so I brought along my accordion too." Gray, who bowed good jazz fiddle, was one of the first of the jazz accordion players, and he had made quite a name for himself on both instruments in Boston.

The band had a unique sound. But it wasn't powerful enough to please a public that had become captivated by the more blatant approaches of Goodman, the Dorseys, Charlie Barnet, Bunny Berigan and other bands that featured bigger and more blasting brass sections. So, early in 1937, despite some impressive recordings by "Art Shaw and His New Music," the string quartet approach was discarded.

"It broke my heart," said Gray. "It was such a good band." But Shaw was a realist. "I just want a good, orthodox, sock swing band," he said at the time. "Personally, it'll be a relief."

Pastor, who doubled as the boy singer, and Peg La Centra, one of the finest of all girl vocalists—she had a unique, thin quality that emphasized a captivating vibrato—stayed on in an outfit that featured the standard three trumpets, two trombones, four saxes and four rhythm. Many of the arrangements were written by trombonist Harry Rodgers, who through those early years contributed some fine scores to the band's library. Gray continued to arrange for Shaw, while playing violin in Sonny Kendis' society band. Eventually, Jerry could no longer take that kind of music and so he returned to Boston.

Meanwhile Shaw and his band had migrated to Boston too. They had cut a batch of new sides for Brunswick, none of which really satisfied Artie. So he decided to settle down in the Roseland-State Ballroom, which was owned by Si Shribman, the magnanimous and farsighted booker and manager, who proceeded to give the same sort of encouragement and assistance to Artie that he had given many other struggling young groups.

Shaw and Gray got together again in Boston. This time Jerry stuck close to the band. One night he and Artie were discussing tunes to do and they hit upon an old Cole Porter number, "Begin the Beguine," a tune that Tony Pastor recalls the guys liked to play at jam sessions. Artie told Jerry to arrange it. "I felt I had to get the attention of the dancers in the ballroom,"

Peg La Centra and Shaw. Jerry Gray fiddles in lower right hand corner.

Jerry explained, "and that's why I wrote that hard intro." Soon thereafter the band started to record for Bluebird, and the first tune on its first session was its first big hit, "Begin the Beguine."

"After that it was a whole different world," pointed out Gray. Shaw's broadcasts from Roseland-State had already begun to draw attention to the band. And soon came a series of such Bluebird hit sides as "Indian Love Call" (the back of "Beguine"), the swinging "Back Bay Shuffle" and "Non-Stop Flight," "Yesterdays" and Artie's mournful theme song, "Nightmare," which, according to Pastor, was born when "Artie started noodling around one night in his hotel room. It sounded just like a nightmare, too!"

The public loved those sides. But the record many musicians still rave most about is that of a pop tune called "Any Old Time." The reason: a superb vocal by Billie Holiday, the magnificent jazz singer who sat on the Shaw bandstand at Roseland-State for a lengthy period, during which, unfortunately, the band made few recordings. By the time the band was ready to resume recording, Billie was about to leave.

During the Roseland-State stay, Artie brought in another girl singer, a fine one who had been performing on CBS as Bonnie Blue. In reality she was Helen Forrest, and she turned out to be the most important singer the band ever had.

Helen recalls vividly and fondly the nights she sat on the bandstand with Billie. "She was so wonderful to me," Helen said of the great stylist whose talents she admired so tremendously. "She was always trying to help. I can remember what she used to tell Artie: 'Why don't you let that child sing some more? Go ahead. And make her some more arrangements, too!' She was really a great person!"

With its records selling and its radio broadcasts reaching millions, the Shaw band was well on its way. A Boston writer, who had faulted the band for playing a thirty-five-minute version of the blues, accused Artie of claiming he'd be King of Swing within a year, a statement Shaw vehemently denied in a revealing letter to *Metronome:*

> My personal craving for success and the contributions I want to make to swing music certainly do not hinge upon my being crowned "King." There is room for twenty, even fifty swing bands, and I say more power to any contemporary leader who makes an outstanding success. If I were writing a novel I wouldn't particularly want to be known as the greatest novelist. I'd have satisfaction enough if my book were judged a success on its own and not on a basis of comparison . . . and that's how I feel about my music. I want the public to recognize me, naturally, but I gain plenty of personal satisfaction without necessarily bowling over all rival orchestras.
>
> I'd like to deny that statement [the one attributed to him by the Boston writer] because I personally would have contempt for any individual who made such a pompous, bombastic announcement.

Knowing Artie as I have through the years, I'm convinced that he never made such a statement. Certainly the rivalry between him and Goodman was already building into gigantic proportions, but it was those associated with Shaw, rather than Artie himself, who were really pushing and pulling and sometimes resorting to tactics of which I'm sure he never would have approved.

This became patently clear to us at *Metronome* during one of our Best Swing Band contests. We had a pretty good idea of our readers' tastes, and it surprised us when all of a sudden the Shaw band pulled in a tremendous batch of votes, many of them often arriving on the same day. We became suspicious and began analylzing the ballots. When we thought we had uncovered some telling evidence, we took the questionable ballots to a handwriting expert. Sure enough, many of them were written by the same person, and almost all of those that were typewritten had been typed on the same machine. Shaw won several important contests that year, but not *Metronome*'s.

Since Goodman was already known as "The King of Swing," Shaw's men named him "The King of the Clarinet." This, of course, resulted in endless arguments among fans on both sides. In a sense, the two titles were rather accurate, for Goodman certainly was a more swinging musician than Shaw, while on the other hand Artie, according to other clarinetists, drew a much better and fuller tone from his instrument.

The rivalry, the backbreaking schedule and the resultant strain were beginning to tell on the high-strung Shaw. On September 16, 1938, while battling Tommy Dorsey's band in New York, Artie suffered the first of several collapses. He was helped off the stage and rushed home to bed and a doctor's care.

On October 26 the band began its first big-time New York engagement. This was in the Blue Room of the Hotel Lincoln, where Tommy Dorsey had first gained recognition and where Harry James, Jan Savitt and Tony Pastor were to get their starts.

In my review of the band, I raved about its great tempos and especially its great spirit. "If Shaw can maintain that," I wrote, "he'll be swinging years hence, too."

Years hence Artie and I were listening to tapes of the broadcasts he made from the Lincoln. "It's hard to realize," he remarked with both fervor and amazement, "that those guys played with such spirit!" Looking back at those times, he said, "I guess I had the healthiest attitude when I was first coming up. All I cared about was that the band sounded good to me."

Good and spirited it certainly did sound, not only to Artie but to all of us who'd crowd into the Blue Room to hear it. Much of the excitement came from the drums of young Buddy Rich, who had just replaced George Wettling, who had replaced Cliff Leeman. Though he tended in those exuberant years to overplay his drums, Buddy nevertheless projected such a propulsive beat

The Artie Shaw band (1938):
saxists Ron Perry and Les Robinson, drummer Cliff Leeman,
trumpeter Claude Bowen, trombonist George Arus,
saxist-vocalist Tony Pastor, Shaw, trumpeter Chuck Peterson, pianist Les Burness,
trombonist-arranger Harry Rodgers, trombonist Russell Brown, bassist Sid Weiss,
saxist Hank Freeman, trumpeter Johnny Best

that it inspired the other musicians to greater heights. In addition to Shaw and Pastor, who was still in the band, there were several other outstanding soloists: Georgie Auld and his kicking tenor sax; Johnny Best and his lovely, Armstrong-like trumpet; Bernie Privin and his biting trumpet; George Arus and his booting trombone and Les Jenkins with his easy, bluesy, relaxed style about which Tommy Dorsey remarked enviously, "If I could only play jazz like Les Jenkins!"

Helen Forrest was with the band, and so was a young Harvard graduate, Bob Kitsis, who played fine piano. One good record followed another, many of them outstanding show tunes: "Lover, Come Back to Me," "My Heart Stood Still," "Rosalie," "Bill," "The Carioca," "Alone Together" and many more. RCA Victor was so happy with the band's Bluebird sides, that when Eli Oberstein, who had guided Shaw's recording career, announced he was leaving the company to start his own firm, Victor, to insure against Artie's following Eli, immediately offered Shaw an almost unheard-of guarantee of $100,000 minimum over a two-year period. Artie accepted at once.

Shortly thereafter in Hollywood, where the band had gone to appear at the Palomar, to start work on its first movie, *Dancing Co-Ed,* and to continue its regular Old Gold radio series with Robert Benchley, Shaw collapsed again. He was rushed off the Palomar bandstand and into a hospital, and was reported seriously ill, "suffering," according to his lawyer-manager, Andrew Weinberger, "from a usually fatal and rare blood disease called malignant leucopenia or agranulocytosis." For days his temperature was 105 degrees, and he was not expected to live.

The band carried on without him. Jerry Gray conducted on its radio show and Tony Pastor took over at the Palomar. Eventually Shaw returned and with him brought a bombshell. "You guys take the band," he told Gray and Pastor. "I don't want it." According to Jerry, he and Tony pleaded with Artie, who finally agreed to stay on. "Artie must have felt," Jerry surmised, "that the guys weren't for him."

If Artie did feel that way, he wasn't entirely wrong. He knew as well as anyone that he wasn't the easiest man in the world to get along with. He had a tendency to look down on musicians, not for reasons of musicianship (although he was quite a perfectionist) but for their lack of intellectual interests. Artie was an avid reader, a man interested in many arts and many causes, and he liked to mingle with people who could discourse with him on the many subjects that interested him. This few, if any, of his sidemen could do, and so it was only natural that some of them should resent him as an intellectual snob.

Not all his public was completely enamored of Shaw, either. Many resented his obvious aloofness as well as his several rather vitriolic outbursts about jitterbugs, annoying fans and people who didn't know much about music.

What irked Artie especially was any intrusion on his private life, which encompassed a rather full marital schedule and which caused one wag to suggest that after Glenn Miller had completed his movie called *Orchestra Wives* Shaw should make one called *Orchestra Leader's Wives* with a cast to include Lana Turner and Ava Gardner, both of whom he had married and divorced.

Upon its return from the West Coast, the band opened in the Café Rouge of the Hotel Pennsylvania. It sounded better than ever. And Artie began to sound off more than ever.

The night after his Pennsylvania opening I spoke with him in his room. The New York *Post* had recently printed an interview by Michael Mok in which Artie had teed off on jitterbugs.

"Sure, I don't like jitterbugs," he told me. "I don't like the business angles connected with music. I can't see autograph hunters. I thought the Old Gold program was lousy for my music. And I don't like prima donna musicians."

Referring directly to the *Post* article, Artie continued, "Everything I said, I feel. Frankly, I'm unhappy in the music business. Maybe I don't even belong in it. I like the music—love and live it, in fact—but for me the business part plain stinks."

Shaw had gone on to point out that when he had started his band he had been an idealist and had pictured himself rising to the top while always playing only the music that appealed to him. "But it's not like that at all," he confessed. "Two years ago we used to love playing; we made up tunes on the stand. Now it's all business. I'm a musician, not a businessman. If I wanted to go into business, I'd enter Wall Street and at least keep regular hours."

After lambasting the Old Gold show because "it turned into a comedy show which wasn't doing the band any good," Shaw announced that henceforth he was "going to pay strict attention to music. The band's morale is still high, thank God, though there are a couple of guys who feel they're too important. That'll have to change. No prima donnas in this band!

"You know," he concluded, "I'm not sorry this has happened. There's been some tough publicity—in fact, I'm sick of being asked what I really think of jitterbugs—but it puts me straight with the world. I want everybody to know that all I'm interested in is making good music. If they like it, they can have it; if they don't, they can keep away from it. But let 'em concentrate on my music and not on me."

The guys in the band readily sensed their leader's touchiness. Rumors began spreading that he was going to quit. Buddy Rich jumped when an offer came from Tommy Dorsey. Tony Pastor denied stories that he was cutting out too.

Conditions grew worse. One night Artie walked off the bandstand and didn't return for the rest of the evening. The band suspected that his old illness was recurring. But his doctors gave him a clean bill of health. Artie did admit to close friends that he feared his trouble was more emotional than physical. He was worried. So were they. So was his band.

Then on November 18, Artie lowered the boom. He summoned his entire band to his hotel room and told them that of right then and there he was through. He was cutting out, going away for a long vacation, and, so far as he was concerned, the band was theirs. That night he left with Frank Nichols, the band's assistant manager, for Mexico.

The men held several meetings. They decided to incorporate as a group, and they invited Pastor to lead them. But Tony had already made other plans, so Georgie Auld became the new front man of an outfit that was known as "Georgie Auld and His Artie Shaw Orchestra." Within three months, realizing they couldn't make it on their own, the men took jobs with other big name bands, and this edition of the Artie Shaw band was gone forever.

Meanwhile in Mexico City and Acapulco a restless Shaw started collecting Mexican songs, jammed with local musicians and reportedly broke a kneecap in five places. By January he was back in the United States, telling people in Hollywood that he was going to have a sixty-five-piece orchestra that would play concerts. He was also working on *Second Chorus,* the movie version of his career.

The sixty-five-piece orchestra never materialized, but early in March, Artie recorded with exactly half that number—thirty-two musicians plus a half for the girl singer, Pauline Byrne, who sang on three of the six sides. She did very well on "Gloomy Sunday" and "Don't Fall Asleep," but the hits of the session were two Latinesque tunes, "Adios, Mariquita Linda," which Artie had uncovered in Mexico, and "Frenesi," which became one of the band's biggest hits.

The orchestra had been staffed by Hollywood studio men. But when Artie decided late in the summer to resume his career as a full-time bandleader, he had to organize a permanent group. This one was a beaut.

Part of its nucleus was the sextet that became known as Artie Shaw and His Gramercy Five (Gramercy Five was a New York telephone exchange), which included Artie's clarinet, Billy Butterfield's trumpet, plus a rhythm section that featured Johnny Guarnieri on harpsichord and waxed four of Shaw's most famous sides, "Special Delivery Stomp" (Bob Crosby had waxed "Air Mail Stomp" a year earlier), "Summit Ridge Drive," "Keepin' Myself for You" and "Cross Your Heart."

In the new big band, which opened at the Palace Hotel in San Francisco on September 12, Shaw also featured trombonist Jack Jenney, whose magnificent solo highlighted a memorable recording of "Stardust," and later a young trombonist who also arranged, Ray Conniff. The band also showcased nine strings plus Anita Boyer as vocalist.

But again Shaw grew restless. The band garnered great critical acclaim, and it recorded a flock of good sides, but apparently Shaw was dissatisfied, not so much with his orchestra as with himself. Shortly after the start of 1941 he disbanded (several of his men transferred into Goodman's band) and returned to New York. There he began improving himself musically by studying orchestration under Hans Burns, former conductor of the Berlin Opera.

Artie continued to play jazz however. He recorded twice, once with a group of studio musicians and once with several jazz greats, saxist Benny Carter, trumpeter Henry (Red) Allen and trombonist J. C. Higginbotham, plus a string section.

In the fall of 1941 he organized another group—another great one—which included a whole host of brilliant musicians: Jenney, Conniff, Guarnieri, drummer Davey Tough, and four alumni from his earlier bands, saxists Georgie Auld and Les Robinson and trumpeters Lee Castle and Maxie Kaminsky. There was also another trumpeter, Hot Lips Page, a brilliant musician and a colorful performer whose vocal on "Take Your Shoes Off, Baby, and Start Runnin' Through My Mind" became one of the high spots of all Shaw recordings.

There were three good vocalists, too: first Bonnie Lake, who was Jenney's wife, then Paula Kelly and then Fredda Gibson, who later became better known as Georgia Gibbs.

Originally, Shaw had planned to put together an orchestra of fifty-two pieces, but he was forced to cut out twenty of these when his managers discovered there weren't enough spots sufficiently large to hold the number of customers required to permit the band at least to break even financially. Nevertheless, they still billed the attraction with the pretentious title of "Artie Shaw and His Symphonic Swing."

It really wasn't symphonic at all. It was simply a fine dance band, with strings and an ability to play exceptionally good jazz and ballads. There have been few bands that have matched it for sheer musical ability and good taste, and it could have caused even more of a general furore had it lasted long enough.

But in January, Shaw reported sick again, and that was the end of that edition. After a couple of months he did return with a band—not his but Lee Castle's—but only to fulfill some theater bookings he couldn't get out of, after which he went into something even bigger that he also couldn't get out of—the United States Navy.

Shaw wasn't drafted. He enlisted in April, 1942, completed boot training, was stationed on Staten Island in New York harbor and served for a couple of months on a minesweeper. Until then there had been no music, just straight apprentice-seaman training. And so far as any attempts by Artie were concerned, there seemingly would be no change.

But the Navy had different ideas. After he had been transferred to Newport, Rhode Island, he was put in charge of a pretty miserable band, and his rank jumped all the way to Chief Petty Officer. But if he was going to lead a band, he reasoned, it ought to be a worthwhile one. So he traveled to Washington, succeeded in reaching some influential ears and requested permission to form a really good band to take out into the battle zones. Permission was granted.

Artie put together a terrific band. It was sparked by a brilliant trumpet section of Conrad Gozzo, Frank Beach, Johnny Best and Maxie Kaminsky. Sam Donahue stood out among the saxes; Davey Tough played drums; Claude Thornhill played piano and wrote some of the arrangements along with Dick Jones and Dave (not David) Rose.

The band saw plenty of action—all in the Pacific Theater. It played in jungles, in airplane hangars, on decks of ships and even in outdoor areas camouflaged for protection from enemy attack.

Conditions were grim. Nearby, boats were being torpedoed. "Was I scared? You bet I was," Shaw told Mike Daniels in a January, 1944, *Metronome* interview, shortly after returning to the States. "You just quake and wonder if it's you or the next guy who got hit. You take your battle station and you do your job." Altogether the Shaw band survived seventeen bombing attacks from Japanese aircraft trying to hit the warships that were transporting the band from island to island.

"We hitch-hiked everywhere," Shaw explained. "Sometimes on a large ship, then on a small one, and sometimes by airplane. We traveled any way we could."

The band not only traveled but also played under all sorts of handicaps. Even their instruments were under attack—by the weather. "I found it not unusual to be playing a solo and have a pad drop right out of my clarinet," Shaw said. In addition, reeds were impossible to come by; the guitar and brass strings were continually snapping, and most of the time there wasn't any PA system, so the guys had to blow their brains out to be heard.

When Shaw had the band it played many of his old arrangements. "It's amazing how the kids out there are familiar with the band," he said. "And they get so excited when we show up on some godforsaken island unexpectedly. Some of them throw gifts at the band. Others cry. Most of them just listen, devouring everything we kick off."

Shaw also reported hearing Radio Tokyo playing his records and announcing that the band was appearing at the St. Francis Hotel in San Francisco. "The idea was to make the American boys homesick," he pointed out. "Out there on a tiny island, thousands of miles away from the mainland, the boys and I got quite a kick out of that spiel."

But the strain told on the high-strung Shaw, and he soon received his discharge. When he returned from the Pacific in November, his friends reported him to be unusually nervous. Davey Tough had received his discharge. Maxie Kaminsky was reported in bad shape. The band had turned in a superb job, but, according to some of the men, there had been a good deal of friction, and several of them had rather unkind words to say about Artie—which was not surprising. Throughout his career, not many of his musicians were able to penetrate his façade very deeply; consciously or unconsciously, he was adept at parrying personal approaches. At least in civilian days Artie had found it relatively easy to withdraw from his musicians. In the Navy such seclusion had become virtually impossible.

The band Shaw had formed continued under Donahue and emerged as one of the great units of its era. It dispensed with the Shaw book entirely, built up its own library and eventually was transferred to the European Theater, where it provided some magnificent music that rivaled the Glenn Miller band both in quality and, at least with the hipper servicemen, in popularity.

Artie, married at the time to Betty Kern, daughter of the famed composer, relaxed in Hollywood, where he grew to know their tiny son. Gradually his health returned, and by the fall of 1944 he had organized another band, this a seventeen-piecer without strings which featured stars like Roy Eldridge on trumpet, Ray Conniff on trombone (he and Harry Rodgers wrote most of the book), Dodo Marmarosa on piano and Barney Kessel on guitar.

In an interview with Barry Ulanov, Shaw insisted that he didn't want to get mixed up again in all the turmoil of the band business. He said he preferred to confine his activities to radio, movies, recordings and a yearly theater tour. "I don't want to do a lot of theaters," he stated. "A guy who plays theaters must hate music. He must."

But, according to critic Leonard Feather, the band was quite impressive on the stage. After complimenting it for its high-level musicianship, especially Conniff's arrangements and solo on "S'Wonderful," Feather added that the band exhibited "a refreshing lack of bad taste and bombast."

"S'Wonderful" turned out to be one of the best of a batch of sides the band recorded—eighteen sessions in six months, or an average of three a month. Most of the sides turned out to be pretty good, too, despite Artie's expressed disdain for the majority of recording executives, who "don't permit jazzmen to record their best. Louis [Armstrong], for example, leaves much of his greatness on records, but not enough."

Shaw in a jam session with Pat McNaughton, Tony Faso, Tommy Mace,
Roy Eldridge and Ray Conniff

One of the greatest of all Shaw sides was his last one for RCA Victor,
a delightful Eddie Sauter opus called "The Maid with the Flaccid Air." Soon
thereafter he switched company affiliations and signed with a new label called
Musicraft Records. Back came the strings, fifteen on one date, twenty-three
plus eight woodwinds on another. In came some exceptionally good singers,
Kitty Kallen, who recorded an outstanding version of "My Heart Belongs to
Daddy," and a young Chicagoan and his vocal group, Mel Torme and the
Meltones, who provided some brilliant singing on several more Cole Porter
tunes, "Get Out of Town" and "What Is This Thing Called Love?"

The Musicraft sides produced Shaw's final important contributions to
the Big Band Era. For a while he continued with the band, but halfheartedly;
then he gave it up. But in 1949, during the post-big band days, he reappeared
with a brand-new outfit.

Again talking with Barry Ulanov of *Metronome,* Artie said that he planned
to play three-quarters of the time what the public wanted and one-quarter
of the time what he wanted. Then he began to philosophize:

> There are two fundamental disciplines to which we are subject in this
> business. One is the business itself, the commercial discipline. That's
> outside the bandleader; there's nothing much he can do about it; it's
> firm, fixed and unyielding. For me it means playing music that's been
> summed up as 'Frenesi–Begin the Beguine–Stardust.' I know that music
> is still attractive to lots of people. I have what you might call docu-
> mentary proof: my royalty checks.

The inner discipline is something else again. It's a great deal less certain, though it's less demanding. Today, I think I am more responsive to it, both in myself and in others. . . . I can give musicians a free rein now. I'm free. I've been analyzed.

I used to have too much of a set idea of what I wanted. And at least in one band I got what I wanted, but in that band I also think I got what the musicians wanted. This new band can't be a stylized band. At least not at first it can't be. Style? I'll try anything.

And Artie meant it. He was willing to try anything. He proved it in his music: he even led a bop group in 1949. He proved it in his series of marriages that included such glamour figures as Lana Turner, Ava Gardner, Kathleen Windsor, Doris Dowling and his current wife of many years, Evelyn Keyes. And he proved it in the series of successful careers that he pursued after he finally decided the music business wasn't for him—as a farmer, as a gun expert, as a writer (his autobiographical book, "The Trouble with Cinderella," offers an illuminating insight into Shaw and his relationship to the band business) and most recently as a distributor of motion pictures.

Artie Shaw, who years ago kept talking about finding an identity, found quite a few of them. There was a time when his band career featured "Artie Shaw and His New Music." But that's nothing. His entire personal life could well be described as "Artie Shaw and His New Artie Shaw!"

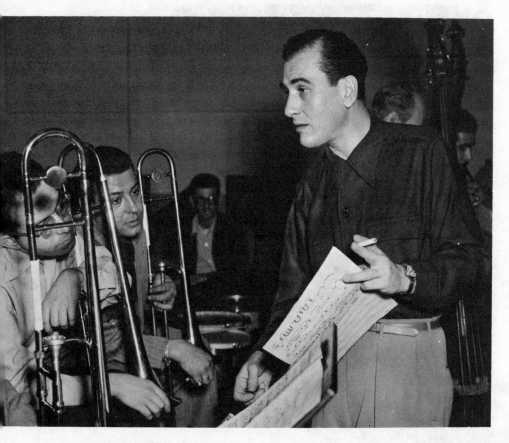

Charlie Spivak

"CHEERY, Chubby Charlie Spivak" is what they used to call him. A rotund, well built man with a bright smile, he had made a reputation as one of the truly great lead trumpeters while playing in the bands of Ben Pollack, the Dorsey Brothers, Ray Noble, Bob Crosby, Tommy Dorsey and Jack Teagarden before he organized his own band early in 1940.

Encouragement and financial aid came from another leader and close friend, Glenn Miller, who felt, as many of us did, that there was room for a band led by a trumpeter with a sound as pure and beautiful as Charlie's. (Most other trumpeting leaders played either jazz or else tricks.) And to make sure that the group had something to do other than rehearse, Glenn saw to

Charlie Spivak (right)
and Lee Castaldo

it that Charlie and his boys substituted for him when the Miller band took time off from its Hotel Pennsylvania gig to play its Chesterfield broadcasts and/or its Paramount Theater engagements.

The first Spivak edition had a pretty sound but little *esprit de corps*. Spivak, long a sideman but never a leader, found it difficult to adjust to his new role. He seemed unsure of himself. Basically a warm person, but a worrier, he seemed to become preoccupied with how to project his own image. This the men in his band, many of them good soloists themselves, resented. A chill developed, and after a few months the band broke up. The men announced that they wanted to stay together as a group (which they didn't), and Spivak took over a Washington outfit that had been formed and led by Bill Downer.

Employing a much broader musical approach that included arrangements by a former bandleader, Sonny Burke, and a new trombonist, Nelson Riddle, and playing some good jazz as well as pretty ballads, Charlie's new outfit made such a good impression that when Glen Island Casino, flushed with the success of Glenn Miller's and Bobby Byrne's summer seasons, decided to remain open for the winter, it hired the new Spivak band. (Could be that the fine Miller hand had been at work here too?)

The band sounded good, but to the vast disappointment of many listeners, there was one thing missing—the brilliant Spivak open horn. Charlie propounded a theory that many of us didn't buy. He wasn't sure that people would like the brilliance of an open trumpet; perhaps it might even drive them away. Therefore, he was trying to achieve the same intimacy on trumpet that Tommy Dorsey had projected so successfully on trombone. Accordingly, Charlie did almost all his blowing through a specially designed mute, which emitted a very soft but not particularly distinguished sound.

Had Charlie been surer of himself he might have captured some of the attention that Harry James grabbed shortly thereafter with his wide-open trumpet blowing of ballads. Once Harry had paved the way, Spivak began to take out his mute more often. The result: some of the most beautiful and thrilling sounds ever to emanate from any dance orchestra. Unfortunately for Charlie, Harry, whose tone couldn't begin to match Spivak's but who got there first, drew the most attention, the most plaudits and the most money.

During the 1941–42 winter Charlie made several personnel changes. He bolstered his rhythm section, which already had a magnificent bassist in Jimmy Middleton, with the addition of drummer Davey Tough. He changed singers, bringing in a good boy vocalist, Garry Stevens, and an exceptionally fine quartet, the Stardusters, whose lead singer, June Hutton (Ina Ray's younger sister), still stands out for me as the greatest lead voice ever to have sung with any vocal group. Later, June replaced Jo Stafford in the Pied Pipers—remember their record of "Dream"?—then married Axel Stordahl, with whom she made some exquisite Capitol sides.

June's singing helped the band achieve even greater musical warmth. And Charlie, backed by a strong trumpet section led by Les Elgart, proceeded

The Charlie Spivak band (1942)
Front row: *June Hutton and three other Stardusters; Spivak; saxists Fran Ludwig,*
Artie Baker, Charlie Russo, Don Raffel, Jerry Florian, vocalist Garry Stevens
Second row: *trumpeters Buddy Yaeger, Les Elgart, Lee Knowles;*
guitarist Kenny White; pianist Dave Mann
Back row: *trombonists Nelson Riddle, Joe Ortolano, Bill Mustarde;*
drummer Dave Tough; bassist Jimmy Middleton

to blow more beautiful open horn during both his 1942 and 1943 sessions in
the Café Rouge of the Hotel Pennsylvania.

For a while he affected a James-like vibrato that detracted from the musical
quality as well as the individuality of his horn. But this nanny-goat effect
had pretty well been discarded by the time I reviewed the band in July, 1943,
although Spivak still insisted on playing his muted horn too often. "Charlie
with a mute is like Coleman Hawkins with a flute," I wrote. The band was
helped considerably by the addition of Willie Smith, Jimmie Lunceford's
great sax man, on alto, and by the Glenn Miller trombone trio, which had
migrated to Spivak when Glenn had gone into the service.

That year two important events affected the band in California: (1) it
was selected to appear in *Pin-Up Girl,* with the armed forces' favorite p.u.g,
Betty Grable, and (2) June Hutton and the Stardusters left and Charlie
hired Irene Daye, Gene Krupa's former singer, who had retired after marrying
Corky Cornelius and giving birth to their child. But Corky had died, and
Irene was anxious to get back to work. Charlie liked her singing; in fact,
as it turned out, he liked her sufficiently as a person so that some years later,
after he and his attractive and popular first wife, Fritzie, had been divorced,
Charlie married Irene.

It would be pleasant to report that everything was just great from 1943 on.
But it wasn't. Irene sang very well with the band, and the band continued

to make some rather pretty sounds. However, by late 1945 it was turning into a pretty bland outfit. It had "little semblance of a common, live beat, nor much enthusiasm for one." A year later it was even worse, dispensing "some of the dullest music played by any so-called topflight band," as I noted in a review of the band again when it was at the Café Rouge. "Spivak has, in his trumpeting, one of the greatest musical and commercial attractions in captivity. His waste of such talent behind a screen of old-fashioned, colorless arrangements is a shame. . . . There is little or no attempt to create much of an emotional mood and only once in a while is there anything of intellectual interest." Then, after noticing that "the brilliant-toned Spivak fluffs much too often," I surmised, perhaps correctly, that "maybe he's discouraged."

Certainly those were discouraging times for a musician who was as much of a purist as Charlie Spivak. The boppers and the blasters were taking over, and the play-it-straight musicians, no matter how good they may have been, were finding the going rougher and tougher.

Charlie had carved a niche for himself, a deep and attractive one, but one from which a musician as set in his ways as he was could not easily escape. Eventually, like so many other leaders, he realized that the good old days were gone. He and Irene moved to Florida, where he fronted a small group for several years. He was a very sick man for a while, but he recovered, and later moved to Greenville, South Carolina, where he organized a small group featuring his horn and Irene's voice that played regularly in a local restaurant. Irene died in 1971, and three years later Charlie married Dubby Hayes, who also sang with his group. As the big band boom broadened in the early 1980s, Spivak, living "in Mountain Lake Colony, just above Cleveland, South Carolina, near Ceasar's Head," assembled a seventeen piece outfit that featured both his old and some new arrangements which, he explained, "stay within my character." This meant, of course, that they focussed on his beautiful trumpet, open rather than with a mute, evidence of his admission to *New York Times* writer John S. Wilson that even though Glenn Miller years ago had kept insisting that he would be better off blowing his horn into a mute, perhaps George Simon, who instead had been encouraging to forget the mute and to concentrate on his gorgeous open-horned tone instead, may have been right after all!

Jack Teagarden

BECAUSE he was just the way he sounded—relaxed, warm and wonderfully creative—Jack Teagarden was one of the most beloved and most admired musicians in all of jazz history. He brought to music his own very personal, languid style, singing or swinging the blues on his trombone with a minimum of effort and a maximum of emotion. His admirers spanned two generations, beginning with fellow musicians like Benny Goodman and Glenn Miller and the Dorseys during the twenties and extending well into the sixties when a comparative youngster, Gerry Mulligan, proclaimed "He has everything a great jazz musician needs to have—a beautiful sound, a wonderful melodic sense, a deep feeling, a swinging beat, and the ability to make everything, even the most difficult things, sound relaxed and easy."

Jack's career as a big bandleader was a short and relatively unsensational one. Yet it was always musical and often quite inspirational. He started his first big band in the beginning of 1939, right after his long contract with Paul Whiteman had expired, and ten years after he had been starred in the Ben Pollack band.

"Tonally, it's beautiful. Rhythmically, it's highly danceable. Spiritually it offers rare bits of inspiration." So started my review of the brand new Teagarden when it appeared early in 1939 at New York's Roseland Ballroom. Jack had formed the band in quasi-partnership with Charlie Spivak, who played a glorious lead trumpet. There were other good musicians too: saxist Ernie Caceres, jazz trumpeter Lee Castaldo (Castle), guitarist Allen Reuss and a fine young clarinetist named Clint Garvin. Teagarden, always a generous man, paid them well—too well, in fact, because before the year was over his high financial overhead had taken its toll and he was forced to reorganize with lower-priced musicians.

That first edition, distinguished by Jack's warm horn and vocals and by Spivak's brilliant trumpet, made some excellent recordings of such standard tunes as "The Sheik of Araby," "I Gotta Right to Sing the Blues" (his theme), "Aunt Hagar's Blues," "Peg o' My Heart," "Somewhere a Voice Is Calling" and the most popular of its recordings, a swinging arrangement of "Red Wing." And, of course, Jack was often called upon to sing his famous version of "Basin Street Blues," complete with its special "Won't You Come

Along With Me" patter written years before especially for him by his good
friend Glenn Miller.

There were two other good singers in the band, the wonderful Dolores
O'Neill, who stayed just a short time, and a very cute, vivacious Philadelphia
girl who later developed into a topflight performer. This was "Pretty Kitty"
Kallen, who fell in love with young Garvin, then left with him when Jack
instigated his economic purge.

The revamped Teagarden outfit, which I heard late in 1940, was equally
good. The lesser-paid musicians worked hard, and by the latter part of 1940
Jack was again fronting a band of which he could be proud. Stylistically, it
reflected many of its leader's musical qualities: it sounded full-bodied, earthy
and masculine. It also introduced a boy singer, David Allen, who was to
become a musicians' favorite after the war. But for some inexplicable reason,
it did not feature enough of Teagarden's trombone.

Perhaps this criticism is a biased one, because, as I review the years during which I have been listening to jazz, I can think of very few musicians who have worn as wonderfully well as Jack Teagarden. "He was like an old shoe," Red Nichols told me some years ago, "warm and comfortable—always was and always will be." He was one of the few musicians who never seemed to be trying to impress anyone: he just naturally did so. Never was there the slightest strain; never was there a feeling that he was trying to sell something. He blew so easily, so effortlessly, as if there was always more where it came from, and by so doing he invariably left you wanting to hear more. His was true artistry.

Teagarden's obvious desire and ability to communicate so readily with people is pointed up by something he told me during the early sixties. We were discussing conditions under which jazz was being played and how it was being confined more and more to clubs to which people came mainly to listen. This depressed him. He said that he much preferred playing his music for dancers, "because I can see people enjoying themselves more. Dancing to dixieland jazz," he said, "is the easiest and happiest thing to do."

Jack loved people and people loved him. He also loved and understood mechanical gadgets, which occupied much of his spare time. But he felt little affinity for anything to do with business (for years his wife, Addie, handled all financial matters). In the early forties in California he assembled one more big band that featured two famous jazz trumpeters, his brother Charlie and Jimmy McPartland. But by the end of 1943 this group disbanded, and Jack began fronting outfits assembled especially for each occasion. Then, when the gigs became less and less frequent, he accepted an offer from Louis Armstrong, with whom he had recorded as far back as 1929, to play with his sextet, and for many years thereafter the two of them spread their music and good cheer throughout the world via some of the most beautiful jazz sounds of all time.

Eventually Jack went back to leading his own band—but only a six-piece dixieland group—and for several years he did well. There had been times when he had not taken proper care of his health, but when I saw him last in the early sixties, he was his same old warm, wonderful, relaxed self—happy, healthy and content. But then Jack started slipping, and by the mid-sixties the reports seeping into New York about him were not good. He had settled in Florida, but he would tour with his small group. In 1964, out of New Orleans, the city always associated with Jack's blues-tinged trombone and singing style, came the final report: Jack Teagarden had been found dead in a hotel room, apparently of a heart attack. Thus one of the greatest horns ever to play in a big band, a small band or even just all alone, was stilled. Once again Jack had left us wanting to hear more.

Claude Thornhill

FOR sheer musical beauty, for gorgeous musical moods, for imagination and wit and taste and originality and consistently fine musicianship, there was never a band that could match Claude Thornhill's. It was gentle yet virile, soft yet strong, subtle yet bright, witty yet profound. And in all of these characteristics it reflected much of the personality of Claude Thornhill himself, one of the warmest, one of the vaguest, one of the most talented and one of the most charming men I have known.

Claude's talents had been appreciated by other musicians long before he ever decided to form his own band. He arrived in New York in the early thirties, after having studied at the Cincinnati Conservatory and the Curtis Institute in Philadelphia, and was soon accepted in the inner circle of the town's top studio musicians, the Dorseys, the Goodmans, the Shaws, the

Berigans, etc., with whom he proceeded to record and broadcast. Intermixed were short periods with the bands of Freddy Martin, Hal Kemp, Russ Morgan, Benny Goodman and Ray Noble, followed by a longer stint as arranger and pianist for Andre Kostelanetz.

In the summer of 1939, after a long stay on the West Coast, where he had served as musical director of the Skinnay Ennis band on the Bob Hope Show (and where he had lost forty pounds and gained a temporary mustache), Claude announced that he was going to have a band of his own. But, in his charmingly vague way, he added that he didn't have the slightest idea what it would be like! He had already received some national recognition via his recording of "Gone with the Wind," which featured singer Maxine Sullivan and an even more successful side, "Loch Lomond," arranged by Claude, which skyrocketed Miss Sullivan to fame.

Some months later Claude announced that he had written forty new arrangements for his contemplated band but that he still hadn't started looking for musicians. Some indication of his band's future musical style was revealed when he stated, "It seems to me that touch and tone are pretty much overlooked by pianists who are leading bands nowadays. You can get so many more and better musical effects if you pay attention to those little, shall I say, niceties."

One of Claude's closest friends was Glenn Miller, and during the band's formative period it subbed several times for Glenn's band at the Pennsylvania as well as for Sammy Kaye's at New York's Commodore Hotel. Then early in 1940, it started out on its own, primed to set the rest of the country on its collective ear.

Its first engagement, a two-week stint, was scheduled for a swank spot in Virginia Beach. The night before the opening, the place burned down to the ground.

Panic followed panic as the booking office tried to find quick gigs. Eventually the band wound up on the West Coast, all primed for a big job at Balboa Beach. But the "big job" turned out to be a small one when the manager decided to open his club only a few nights a week.

Next, another swank spot, a San Francisco hotel that loved piano players. The one trouble was that Claude didn't sound at all like Henry King or Joe Reichman, the flashy society-type tinklers who were local favorites, and soon the Thornhill band was invited not to come back.

So back to the East Coast, this time for a club in Hartford, Connecticut. An important spot? Hardly, for when Claude asked a taxi driver to take him there, the cabbie replied that he'd never heard of the joint. This job lasted two nights. On the third night, the men arrived (someone had finally found the place) only to find the doors padlocked. The boss had vamoosed with all the money.

Claude, whose highly developed sense of humor included the ability to laugh at himself, once recalled that nightmare. "We came back from the place, and we were walking through the hotel lobby feeling about as low as any group could feel. Here we'd come all the way across the country for that job and look what happened. No job. No money. But then came the *real* blow. As we walked by the desk in the lobby, the room clerk called out, 'Say, aren't you Mr. Toenail? We have a message for you.' Imagine that. 'Mr. Toenail!' I've been called just about everything else, starting with Clyde Thornton, but that was the worst. Can you just imagine going through life as 'Claude Toenail and his Orchestra!' "

But like his friend Glenn Miller, who two years earlier had reached what he considered his all-time low, Claude Thornhill quickly revived when he was booked into Glen Island Casino, where, starting on March 20, 1941, his career really zoomed.

Claude had gathered such exceptionally good musicians as clarinetist Irving Fazola, trumpeters Conrad Gozzo and Rusty Diedrick, and trombonists Tasso Harris and Bob Jenney. The latter, brother of the more famous Jack Jenney, also sang, along with Betty Claire and Dick Harding.

"Truly, it's an amazing aggregation," I raved in the May, 1941, *Metronome*. "For not only has it struck upon a style that's musically unique and thrilling, but it also shows a flare for commercialism that's lacking even in most bands whose only claim to fame is cow-towing to the public's demands."

Of all its qualities of fine musicianship, the one that set the band several notches above almost all others was its magnificent use of dynamics. It would achieve a soft, mellow mood, either through Claude's extremely delicate, one-fingered piano solos or through six delicately blown unison clarinets; then suddenly it would burst forth into a gorgeous, rich, full ensemble sound, highlighted by the brilliance of Conrad Gozzo's lead trumpet.

Such exciting displays of contrasts in mood were especially effective in person. On the air, however, much of this impact was lost because the network engineers, invariably surprised by the sudden switches in sound, would cut the volume drastically whenever the band burst forth, or else raise the level too high whenever it tried to achieve its soft clarinet moods. The result was totally undynamic.

For two months the band continued to thrill those of us who traveled regularly to Glen Island to hear its gorgeous reed sounds, its brilliant brass and Claude's delicate, sometimes witty, sometimes romantic piano. Then, in May, its engagement completed, it set out on a road trip from which it hardly ever broadcast, and within a couple of months the band had dropped out of sight and sound.

Fortunately it had made some excellent recordings that helped sustain at least its memory—lovely ballads like "Where or When," "Sleepy Serenade" and the theme that Claude had written, "Snowfall," plus some brilliant arrangements of the classics, such as "Traumerei" and "Hungarian Dance No. 5," as well as one of the most fascinating instrumental originals ever recorded by any band, a Thornhill opus called "Portrait of a Guinea Farm,"

The Claude Thornhill band at Glen Island Casino (1942)
In front: *Claude, The Snowflakes (Buddy Stewart at left, Lillian Lane next to him, Martha Wayne at right);*
saxists George Paulsen, Conn Humphreys, Jack Ferrier, Ted Goddard
Second row: *French hornists Mike Glass, Vincent Jacobs; clarinetists Buddy Dean, Danny Polo; trombonists Tasso Harris, Bud Smith*
Back row: *bassist Marty Blitz; guitarist Barry Galbraith; drummer Irv Cottler; trumpeters Jakie Koven, Conrad Gozzo, Steve Steck*

which even today, a full generation later, still draws plaudits from musicians.

Until that period, Thornhill, aided by his friend Bill Borden, had written all the arrangements. Then, as suddenly as it had dropped out of sight, the band dropped into sight again, on the West Coast, where Claude became reunited with an arranger he had worked with in Skinnay Ennis' band. This was Gil Evans, the same Gil Evans who later became such an integral part of Miles Davis' career and who proceeded to augment Claude's and Bill's works with some tremendously imaginative manuscripts of his own.

Other changes were taking place in the band. Fazola had left to join Muggsy Spanier, so Claude brought in another fine clarinetist, Danny Polo, who had once been starred with Ambrose, the famous English leader. Randy Brooks joined and stayed for a short time (what a brilliant team he and Gozzo made!), to be replaced by a tasteful, Berigan-like trumpeter named Jackie Koven. Terry Allen became the new boy singer, and on several of the recording dates the rhythm section was bolstered by the addition of Thornhill's friend Davey Tough on drums.

Claude had done so well during his two months at Glen Island Casino early in 1941 that the management booked him for the full 1942 summer season.

By then the band had grown; it included, in addition to its seven clarinets, two French horns and a slew of vocalists, including Lillian Lane, Martha Wayne and Buddy Stewart.

The new band recorded some more impressive sides. One of these, "Somebody Else Is Taking My Place," offered a fine sampling of Claude's pixie-ish sense of humor. It started off with a honky-tonk piano, befitting the tune's corny construction, and then, when that mood had been firmly established, unexpectedly burst forth into some rich, romantic sounds that held on until the last half chorus, when back came Claude, cornier than ever, winding up the piece all by himself.

Some of the Evans scores also saw the light of wax, like his lovely arrangement of "There's a Small Hotel," and his brilliant swinger, "Buster's Last Stand," one of the first of many instrumentals that were to stamp Thornhill's as one of the greatest of the modern jazz bands.

Claude wasn't entirely satisfied with the way his musicians played some of the progressive jazz scores, though he could understand their difficulties. "It's hard," he explained, "to get guys to play strange harmonies with a beat." His reasoning was simply that playing jazz is always easier when the chords are familiar; when they are not, some of the freedom and spontaneity are more difficult to achieve.

However, getting the men to play jazz soon became one of the least of Claude's problems. His biggest one was simply getting men. The draft kept taking one musician after another—and it wasn't long before the most important one of them all, Claude himself, went into the service too.

According to Jack Egan, the well-known press agent who had been helping the Coast Guard to recruit musicians, Claude could have entered that branch of the service with a Chief Petty Officer's rating. But Thornhill had other ideas. "I'd just as soon stay away from music," he said, and so on October 26, 1942, he entered the Navy with the lowest possible rank, that of apprentice seaman.

He spent three years in the service, seldom away from music. Part of the time he played in a band led by his long-time friend Artie Shaw; more of the time he helped put together special shows and dance band units made up of Navy personnel and organized especially for service on newly captured posts in the Pacific. One of his drummers was Jackie Cooper; one of his singers, Dennis Day. Claude worked closely with two admirals, Nimitz and Halsey, who learned to depend upon his judgment in matters musical.

Unlike other bands that had started shortly before the war and whose leaders had been drafted, Claude's lost little of its popularity during the years it was disbanded. Its fine records were musical enough to warrant longevity. As for Claude himself, an indication of how much his former sidemen enjoyed working with him was the number who returned when he started anew in 1946. At his beckoning back came four of his five saxists, two of his three trumpeters (the third one returned later), one of his two French horn players and both his trombonists. Back too came both arrangers, Evans and Borden. Only in the rhythm section were there changes, and all three of these were for the better. It was quite a tribute to Thornhill.

In many ways the new band was even better than the old. The rhythm section, sparked by bassist Iggy Shevack and drummer Billy Exiner, helped propel a looser, more swinging jazz beat. Bob Walters, the only new addition to the reeds, supplied a wonderfully warm sound. And soon a girl singer named Fran Warren came along to bring even greater emotional depth to the band.

Fran, a very hip Bronxite, made one recording, "A Sunday Kind of Love," that really established her. But she sang numerous other songs, some with far subtler feeling, that showed even better what a good artist she really was. The male vocals came from singer Gene Williams, who later led a band of his own.

Gil Evans kept on writing more and more material for the band, often adapting some of the small group jazz compositions to a big band sound. Thus came such outstanding Thornhill sides as "Anthropology," "Donna Lee" and "Yardbird Suite," which featured several new modern jazz stars like Lee Konitz and Red Rodney. By this time the band was so filled with good jazz sounds that none other than Thelonious Monk went officially on record as citing Thornhill's as "the only really good big band I've heard in years!"

But by this time the big band boom had burst. Musicians loved the jazz that Claude's outfit had been playing, and some of the public was still attracted to the lush ballad sounds it brought to such recordings as "My Old Flame," "Lover Man," "For Heaven's Sake" and "Let's Call it a Day," which turned out to be a prophetic title. For shortly after the record was issued in 1948, Claude, who had held out stubbornly and longer than almost any of his compatriots, broke up his band.

Some months later he returned to the music scene, but his appearances became less frequent, though often quite exciting—thanks especially to Gerry Mulligan's arrangements from time to time and brilliant jazz solos by Tony Scott, Hal McKusick, Nick Travis, Gene Quill and Bob Brookmeyer.

By the mid-fifties, not only Claude Thornhill's orchestra but Claude himself had pretty much disappeared once again. Rumors drifted into New York that he was in poor physical shape and that he was eking out a living by fronting a small unit in various inconspicuous spots, either in Florida or in Texas. It was a depressing thought, this great man living out the rest of his days in that way, and I, like many of his good friends, had pretty much given up the thought of ever seeing him again, when all of a sudden, in the spring of 1965, he appeared in my office, looking healthier and happier than I had ever seen him look in all the thirty years I had known him.

The reason was simple. Following a collapse, brought on in part by problems begun during his hitch in the Navy, he had taken thorough stock of himself and had embarked on a health kick. He and his charming wife,

Ruth, had bought a home in New Jersey. There, when he wasn't going out on one-nighters with any one of three semi-permanent units he kept at his disposal in different parts of the country, he devoted himself to the new role of master of his home, to the relaxed, contented life of part-time gardener, part-time carpenter, part-time man-in-charge-of-everything-that-had-to-be-taken-care-of-around-the-house.

Never had I seen him in such wonderful spirits. Together he and I began talking about his future: about a Columbia reissue of his greatest sides and about new recording plans as well—all sandwiched between numerous gratuitous bits of advice from Claude on subjects like how to lose crabgrass and improve real grass and similar earthy topics. He was a mighty happy man, this witty, warm, whimsical cherub—up until those fateful moments on the night of July 1, when he was felled by two heart attacks.

Many people phoned Ruth Thornhill during the next few days, and one of the most moving calls came from another great man, who stated so well what so many of us felt about Claude. Said Duke Ellington: "I wonder if the world will ever know how much it had in this beautiful man . . . this beautiful man. He never wanted anything from anybody. If he called you, he just called to talk—or else he might want to give *you* something. You know, there aren't many of his kind left. . . . He was a beautiful man."

Claude: "He was a beautiful man."

Chick Webb

"I'LL never forget that night," Gene Krupa wrote several years ago, "the night when Benny's band battled Chick at the Savoy—he just cut me to ribbons—made me feel awfully small. . . . That man was dynamic; he could reach the most amazing heights. When he really let go, you had a feeling that the entire atmposhere in the place was being charged. When he felt like it, he could cut down any of us."

The battle of bands Gene referred to took place in Chick Webb's own bailiwick, Harlem's Savoy Ballroom. The date was May 11, 1937, and the Goodman band, just reaching its peak, had hoped to show the uptown people how great it' really was. It turned out to be quite a night! With cops lined around the stage, and police and fire reserves in readiness in case the crowd —four thousand inside, plus five thousand outside who had been turned away— rioted, the two bands battled each other. According to my report, Benny's band played first and made a great impression. Then "the Men of Webb came right back and blew the roof off the Savoy. The crowd screamed, yelled and whistled with delirium." From then on the Webb band led the way, and, according to most people there that night, truly topped the Goodman gang.

To those of us who used to migrate regularly to The Track, the "in" name for the Savoy, the result wasn't especially surprising. Little Chick had himself one helluva fine band in those days, one that's best known now for having uncovered Ella Fitzgerald, but which also produced some topflight instrumental jazz.

Its spark plug was little Chick, a hunchback who could barely reach the foot pedal of his bass drum. He wasn't a tremendous technician, as drummers go, partially because he didn't have the necessary physical power or stamina, but he could propel such a drive, simply by beating such great time and exploding at just the right moments, that he would, as Krupa put it, charge the atmosphere of any place in which he played.

Chick also knew how to take charge of his band. He was a very sharp, aware little man, kind and generous but surprisingly rough and tough with people who tried to cross him. For Chick Webb had been around a long time, and he knew the score.

Specifically, he'd been around the Savoy Ballroom, a second-floor walk-up

*Chick (lower left) swings, Ella (upper right) sings on the stand
in Harlem's Savoy Ballroom. Saxist at lower right is Louis Jordan.*

at least twice as wide as it was deep, with two bandstands in the center of one of the long walls, since 1928, when the management had seen his band cut down those of Fletcher Henderson and King Oliver and had offered him the house-band job.

By the time the Big Band Era had begun, Chick was heading a swinging thirteen-piece outfit that featured a couple of fine trumpeters, Bobby Stark and Taft Jordan, who did a whale of an imitation of Louis Armstrong, a strong bassist in John Kirby, an amusing vocalist in tenor saxist Louis Jordan, who later became a successful leader, and a brilliant saxist named Edgar Sampson, who not only arranged most of the music but also wrote instrumentals like "Don't Be That Way," "Blue Lou," "If Dreams Come True" and "Stompin' at the Savoy," all of which the Webb band was playing before the Goodman band made them famous.

The band also played some "head" arrangements that used to rock the joint. I remember one of its specialties was a long, twenty-minute version of "Stardust," played at a medium swinging tempo, with the whole band getting into the act with maracas, claves and other percussion instruments, building and building, and rocking and rocking until the whole ballroom floor was literally moving up and down from the dancers' reactions. It used to amaze me that it never caved in!

Another thing I remember was the enthusiastic new singer who came into the band in mid-1935. When she wasn't singing—and how she could sing!—she would usually stand at the side of the band, and as the various sections blew their ensemble phrases, she'd be up there singing along with all of them, often gesturing with her hands as though she were leading the band.

This, of course, was Ella Fitzgerald, whom Bardu Ali, a sleek-looking gent who would often front the band for Chick, discovered one night at an amateur contest held in the Harlem Opera House. Bob Bach, an inveterate jazz fan who later became one of the chief executives of the "What's My Line" TV series, was there that night, and according to his remembrances, printed in the November, 1947, *Metronome,* Ali, after hearing Ella sing a Hoagy Carmichael song called "Judy" (she entered as a dancer but, out of sheer stage fright, switched to singing), "insisted upon her being hired for Chick's band. The little drummer refused to listen to her, and Bardu had to smuggle Ella into the bandleader's dressing room, lock the door and practically hold Webb in his chair while she sang. Chick was sold but still not convinced. . . . 'We'll take her to Yale tomorrow night,' said Chick, 'and if she goes over with the college kids, she stays.'"

Well, the boys of old Eli loved Ella, and so she stayed. She started recording with Chick, and some of those first Decca records are really musical treasures —things like "I'll Chase the Blues Away," "Sing Me a Swing Song and Let Me Dance," "A Little Bit Later On" and "If You Can't Sing It, You'll have to Swing It." But her biggest all-time hit, one that continues these many years later to plague her (how many times can you sing a song without getting bored stiff?), was her recording of "A-Tisket, A-Tasket," as arranged for her and the band by Van Alexander (then Al Feldman) and for which Ella herself wrote some special lyrics.

This took place in the spring of 1938, after the band had begun an engagement at a Boston restaurant called Levaggi's, to which the college kids (the Harvards appreciated Ella and Chick just as much as the Yalies did!) used to flock.

Ella's value to the band was tremendous. The guys loved her, she loved the guys, and the whole spirit of the band perked up perceptibly. She was, as she continued to remain throughout her entire career, dedicated to her music, never fully willing to recognize her own greatness but forever encouraging and even revering the talents of others.

One of her earliest idols was Billie Holiday. "Once when we were playing at the Apollo," she told me, "Billie was working a block away at the Harlem Opera House. Some of us went over between shows to catch her, and afterwards we went backstage. I did something then, and I still don't know if it was the right thing to do." "What was that?" I said. "I asked her for her autograph. Do you think I should have done that?"

Ella, magnificent and admired and beloved as she is, has never seemed to recognize her greatness. Few singers suffer so before an appearance; none that I have ever seen becomes so completely immersed as she in an immediate performance. During her first days with Chick's band, when she appeared before perhaps two hundred people, she lived every single note that she sang. Today, before thousands upon thousands of fans who come solely to hear this great artist, she remains just as dedicated, just as devoted and just as anxious to please not merely her listeners but her musical conscience as well. Ella may have started as the idol of the Ivy League, but her fame was soon to pass far beyond those cloistered walls. (One indication of her greatness: among the hundreds of singers and musicians whom I have interviewed over a period of thirty years, I estimate that between eighty and ninety per cent of them have named Ella as their favorite singer.)

Ella and Louis Jordan on a Webb recording date

After Levaggi's, the late Moe Gale, Chick's manager, who also owned the Savoy, booked the band into other top spots, including the Paramount Theater for several engagements. Its most important New York hotel job was at the Park Central, which until then had never played a Negro band. Chick's did very well there, although I sometimes felt that it was bending over backward in an attempt to please the downtown patrons. Perhaps it had orders from the management—who knows? Certainly its great spirit was not always evident.

Chick himself was inconsistent. It became obvious that he wasn't feeling well, and soon we found out why: he had contracted tuberculosis of the spine, and month by month the pain was growing worse and worse. While his band was playing the Paramount for the second time early in 1939, Chick fainted after several of the shows. But he was determined to carry on. "I'm gonna be *so* well in another couple of months," he would tell his friends.

But his friends knew better, and inwardly Chick must have known, too. The beginning of the end came in June when he was playing on a riverboat outside Washington, D.C. He collapsed and was rushed to Johns Hopkins Hospital in Baltimore, where he was operated on. The prognosis was not good, and Chick didn't have to be told. After six days he told his valet, who had been staying at his side, to go home and get some sleep. "I know I'm going," he said. The next evening, with friends and relatives gathered around his bedside, he turned to his mother and asked her to raise him to a sitting position. Then, with that crooked little smile that used to play across his face, he called out, "I'm sorry, I gotta go!" And on that June 16, 1939, he was gone. He was only thirty years old.

The band stayed pretty much intact for several years thereafter. Ella fronted it, and two saxists, Ted McCrea and Eddie Barefield, acted as musical directors. But it was never the same without little Chick. His spirit and dynamism simply couldn't be replaced. By the middle of 1942 Ella was out on her own as a single and the Chick Webb band was nothing more than a wonderful memory.

Ted Weems

THE Ted Weems band was a singer's delight—or, to be completely accurate —a many singers' delight. It was a good though never great musical outfit that turned in a whale of a job entertaining in a modest, intimate sort of way, presenting a whole slew of singers, one after another, all of them different-sounding and all well above average in talent.

The most famous of them, Perry Como, says simply that "the band was really built around its singers. I can't recall that it ever played a straight instrumental."

Weems, a college man who had started on violin, switched to trombone and, realizing his own limitations, had settled for a baton, devoted most of his time to dates in the Midwest, especially in and around Chicago, where he was starred at several hotels and the Aragon and Trianon ballrooms. He interspersed his crisp, unsophisticated ensemble sounds with the crooning of Como; the sweet, ingenue-singing of little Mary Lee; the more sexy emoting of Marvell Maxwell (who later changed her name to Marilyn Maxwell and became a Hollywood star); the novelties of Red Ingle, whom Como calls "one of the most talented men I've ever met" and who later made a hit record

Ted Weems and vocalists Mary Lee and Perry Como

of "Timtayshun" with Jo Stafford; the straightforward rhythmic singing of Parker Gibbs, later a top NBC producer; the stylized, semi-hillbilly performances of "Country" Washburn, and the whistling of Elmo Tanner.

"Ted was a good businessman and a gentleman in every sense of the word— in his actions and in his dress and everything," recalls Como. "I don't think the man had a mean bone in his body, unless you could call what he did once in a while to Elmo Tanner 'mean.' "

Tanner's whistling was one of the band's features, and Weems depended on Elmo to deliver when called upon. But once in a while, for reasons best known to Tanner, himself, his precious lips would pucker up uncontrollably. Perhaps to impress upon Elmo the need for remaining in proper condition, Weems would, on those special occasions, call for the most virtuoso whistling bits in the book, such tunes as "Nola" and "Canadian Capers" and "Stardust," for Tanner to wrap his lips around. "I used to sit there on the bandstand and watch, and my heart would really bleed for the guy," says Como.

Weems was in a good mood in Warren, Ohio, the night in 1936 when he offered Como a job. As Perry tells it: "I was singing with Freddy Carlone's band in a gambling casino. Ted came in and played the 'double oh' in roulette and it came in. Then he came downstairs where we were working, and he heard me sing. Art Jarrett had just left him, so he offered me the job."

Weems recalled that evening too. "Como was introduced in the floor show," he wrote several years ago, "and had to do about six encores before the audience would let him go—a scene I was to see repeated many times in clubs and hotels throughout the country.

"I talked to Perry about joining my band, and he was interested. I believe Paul Whiteman's manager phoned from New York that same night and asked him to come to New York for an audition, which he didn't want to do."

Como joined Weems several weeks later. According to Ted, "We were on stage when he arrived, and during the show I saw him standing in the wings. I interrupted our regular program to tell the audience about hearing Perry in Warren and I would like them to hear his first song with us. He came on stage and sang one number to a wonderful hand."

However, reaction to Como during the first year was not always enthusiastic. When the band played the Palmer House in Chicago, radio station WGN threatened to discontinue Weems's broadcasts if, according to Ted, "the new singer didn't improve. I had recordings made of a number of Perry's songs taken from air shows, and one night I had Perry stay and listen to them. He commented, 'I can't understand what I'm saying.' I told him that he had been endowed with a fine voice and there was no need to embellish it with vocal tricks. Just open up and sing the words from the heart. From then on his enunciation improved and so did his professional stature."

Perry, as relaxed and as personable then as he is now, stayed with Weems for six years and grew to love the band. "It was a really happy group and a good entertaining one too. It did especially well when Ted could get us all close

Ted Weems and his singers (in the thirties and in the fifties)
Left to right: *Weems, Perry Como, Elmo Tanner, Parker Gibbs,*
Country Washburn, Red Ingle

to the people, like in hotel rooms. But when we went out on one-nighters and followed the big swing bands like the Dorseys and Goodman and Miller into those huge ballrooms, it was a different matter. After all, you've got to remember that we had only eleven musicians, just three brass instead of the six or seven or even eight that the others had, and four saxes and four rhythm. Sometimes I'd notice groups of kids hanging around the bandstand, sort of giving us the eye, and then after two or three sets of our novelties and singing, one of the hipper ones would slip up close and lean over and say something like 'Are you guys kidding?' "

Weems very wisely never tried to compete with the big swingers. He concentrated on making the most out of what he had, even if it was something as basic and simple as a whistler, a whistler who helped him create his band's biggest hit record.

Ted had probably forgotten all about that record of "Heartaches" when a North Carolina disc jockey began plugging it on the air in 1947. Weems had recorded it back in 1933, but for some inexplicable reason, the novelty version, with its washboard rhythm sound and Tanner's homespun whistling, suddenly caught on fourteen years later and within a few weeks Ted had a huge, full-sized hit record on his hands. And it was an arrangement that he had nearly tossed aside.

As Weems reported in 1947: "We were working in Chicago about fifteen years ago, and the publishers of 'Heartaches' had been begging us to put the tune on the air. So one night we introduced it. We played it just the way you hear it on the record, with that corny sort of half-rumba rhythm and with all those effects. After the broadcast, the writers and the publisher called me on the phone and they really let me have it. They claimed I was ruining their song, that we had given it the wrong interpretation and all that. We never heard from them after that. And do you know that I still haven't heard a word from them, even though they're raking in all the dough from the performances —not even a word to say that maybe I wasn't such a complete idiot after all."

The "Heartaches" rediscovery revived a Weems band career that had begun to fade like those of the other name bands. "Funny how surprised a lot of the kids are when they see me in person," he noted, perhaps a bit ruefully, at the time. "Lots of them are so young that they'd never heard of me until they heard 'Heartaches,' and so naturally they expect to see some young upstart."

Ted Weems, who died in May, 1963, at the age of sixty-one had already paid his dues by 1947. He had completed approximately a generation of successful bandleading (there had been a hitch in the Merchant Marines with almost all his musicians during World War II), when he was suddenly "discovered" by the kids. And so "Heartaches" turned out to be just a welcome dividend for one of the kindest men the band business has known.

Lawrence Welk

FRANKLY, I don't remember very much about Lawrence Welk during the days of the big bands, even though he had been leading a band since 1925 and was becoming a favorite among mickey-mouse and polka band fans in the early forties. I do recall that we used to receive an inordinate amount of publicity about Welk in the *Metronome* office, and every once in a while, generally around Christmas time, a bottle of champagne would be delivered, which Barry Ulanov would grab because, he claimed, he had been giving Welk better notices than I had.

Of course, all of us have seen since then what Welk has accomplished through television. His has easily been the most successful of the dance band shows, even though the music could hardly be termed adventurous or thrilling compared with that of the better bands a generation earlier.

But times and tastes changed. As Woody Herman noted some years ago when Welk's band held sway, "Let's face it. Welk has the most successful band in America. Maybe it's because the music is in keeping with the times. People don't have to think about it. No effort. It's automatic. They don't even have to

The young Mr. Welk

Welk: his years of one-nighters taught him what the people want.

listen to it. It can be great music for talking to, or great music for watching a ball game to."

Today, Welk's music has all the subtlety and polish of a used-car salesman's pitch. It has a job to do, and it does it well, and though the product may lack musical imagination, it does satisfy those who are looking for nice, clean, Rotarian entertainment.

During a recent golf game with TV executive Ted Bergmann, Welk, who has also golfed with General Dwight D. Eisenhower, admitted that his music was directed toward the middle of the country. He refuses, Bergmann reports, to take the counsel of what he refers to as "New York, Chicago and Hollywood entertainment types. My years of one-nighters in small towns throughout the country taught me what the people want," he emphasizes.

While learning what the people wanted, Welk obviously also picked up some additional musical savvy, for the band improved tremendously since I first heard it back in 1941 at the Rustic Cabin in New Jersey during the course of an evening that has long since been forgotten. Referring to my review, I note that the band dispensed mostly corn, "so much of it and done with so little exaggeration that you're not sure whether the men are doing it as a gag or whether they actually mean it. In fact, by the end of the evening, you find yourself wondering if the boys, themselves, are sure."

The trumpets were described as possessing "a vibrato that reminds you of the temperature graph of a pneumonia patient." The rhythm section "rushes and drags and crunches in a listless manner." As for Welk, himself, his personality and accordion playing were described as "pleasant." Far less pleasant, however, were his solos on a electrified instrument called a solo-vox, from which he projected "a grating, unmusical tone, not too far removed from the sound you get when you blow across a blade of grass." (No wonder Ulanov claimed the Christmas champagne!)

Yet, despite such obvious musical deficiencies, the band received a top commercial rating. "You may never be able to relax to it," the review concluded, "what with its tempos and continuous tricks and obvious attempts to make you notice what's happening on the bandstand. But, in any event, you've got to notice it, and you're going to remember it, and after all, those are two highly important factors within the field of commercial dancebandom, aren't they?"

Little did anyone realize how highly commercial Welks' gimmicks would turn out to be! Ten years after I had written that review, the band was starred on a Los Angeles TV show and drew so much attention that ABC signed it for its entire network. There it remained for sixteen years, featuring such steadies as the Lennon Sisters, Norma Zimmer, Myron Floren and even jazz players like Pete Fountain and Peanuts Hucko. After ABC dropped the series, Welk syndicated his show on over two hundred stations to prove that perhaps he knew more about the general public than did his critical network bigwigs.

Regarding criticism, Welk wrote to me in 1970: "Needless to say, our band has always been the subject of countless reviews during a career of [then] 45 years. They have been both flattering and derogatory, witty and dull, friendly and hostile. I guess it's just as well I developed a thick skin early in life. . . . I also discovered that the reviewers' opinions did not necessarily reflect those of the paying public, and I could always console myself with this thought when the notices were especially bad."

Welk has always believed strongly in his music, and, as it got better in later years, listening to it in itself could give him big thrills—perhaps even greater than those he could get from his enormous wealth that included his own music and real estate empire worth many millions of dollars. "Sometimes when we're home alone," he once confessed to a writer from *Crawdaddy* magazine, "I'll roll up my sleeves for my wife and let her see the goose-pimples I get just watching myself and my band perform on TV!"

Paul Whiteman

BY THE time the Big Band Era had begun, Paul Whiteman was approaching his twentieth anniversary as a famous bandleader. National recognition began coming to him as far back as 1918, and for almost a full generation he had been leading a colorful and distinguished career during which he had pioneered a symphonic approach to dance music and had gained the misnomer of The King of Jazz. For a true jazz band he never really had. And yet within his usually pompous arrangements he did sometimes feature some of the era's top jazz soloists, who, were it not for Paul (Pops) Whiteman, would never have had an opportunity to reach an audience as broad as his. Among those jazz stars and others who owed much of their success to the magnanimity of the show-wise gent who displayed their talents were Jimmy and Tommy Dorsey, Jack and Charlie Teagarden, Bix Beiderbecke, Frankie Trumbauer, Joe Venuti, Eddie Lang, Henry Busse, Mike Pingatore and Roy Bargy, plus singers Bing Crosby, Mildred Bailey, Johnny Mercer, Morton Downey, Red McKenzie, Ramona, Jack Fulton and Joan Edwards. It is quite a list!

Working with Whiteman was a rewarding adventure. He may not have been the world's greatest musician, he really couldn't conduct very well, and he tended to be overflamboyant at times. But he was all heart, and perhaps even more importantly, he was all for his men. He was proud of them and set an example for future leaders when he pointedly starred those musicians and singers whom he so obviously admired, leaving the spotlight entirely to them when they performed.

He was, of course, a great showman, and as a great showman he was well aware of the worth of his helpers. He was also a great salesman—especially at selling himself to hotel managers, to radio sponsors and to anyone else who could do him and his band some good. He spoke well and with enthusiasm and, I felt during the time I knew him, with great candor. Sometimes he'd exaggerate a bit in making a point or telling a story, but it was exaggeration born much more of enthusiasm than of any intent to deceive. Whiteman thought big, talked big and, most important of all, acted big. He was a rare man.

He was just as interested in encouraging writers as he was in giving musicians a chance to be heard. Thus in 1924 he premiered in concert a brand new composition that he had commissioned a young composer to write for his orchestra. This was George Gershwin; the piece was his famed "Rhapsody in Blue."

Whiteman had imagination and he had guts. He would try anything, even the unorthodox, just so long as he believed in it. His was the first dance band to popularize arrangements, the first to use full reed and brass sections, the first to play in vaudeville, the first to travel to Europe. His was the first to feature a girl singer, Mildred Bailey, and a vocal trio, the Rhythm Boys with Bing Crosby, Harry Barris and Al Rinker. Whereas other bands eventually played at New York's Paramount Theater for several weeks at a time and considered themselves fortunate to do so, Whiteman appeared there for two *years* at $12,500 a week! There was only one stipulation in his contract, he recently told me. "They thought Bing Crosby was such a bad singer that they insisted I not let him sing a solo. Two years later he came back there as a star!"

Whiteman's enthusiasm for music, and perhaps even his vanity, caused him to continue leading a band well into the mid-forties, long after his best outfit had broken up and at a time when it wasn't financially necessary for him to work so hard. During the mid-thirties he still had some good men—the Teagardens, Trumbauer, Roy Bargy, George Wettling. But his musical style was beginning to sound old-hat alongside that of Goodman and Shaw and the Dorseys. In 1938 he tried to revise that style by bringing in Joe Mooney and Tutti Camarata to write new arrangements and the Modernaires to sing, but the band was still stocked with too much dead wood that was unable to interpret the music properly. So Whiteman finally decided to chuck his outfit and start anew.

His first revised edition, which he started late in 1939, wasn't much of a success. It did show some promise, thanks to Mooney's arrangements, but before it ever had a chance to get off the ground, Whiteman accepted an offer to make a movie without his band, and in May, 1940, he disbanded again. Six months later he was on the scene once more.

The new band was more modern. It featured some exquisite arrangements by Camarata and young Buddy Weed, who also played a brilliant piano, and the virtuosity of Murray McEachern, who quintupled on trombone, sax, clarinet, trumpet and violin! There was also an extremely impressive young alto saxist, Alvy Weisfeld, who later became better known as Alvy West; an exceptionally strong bassist in Artie Shapiro; a colorful drummer, Willie Rodriguez, who contributed some fine Latin rhythmic effects; two good singers, Frank Howard and Dolly Mitchell, and in time some good, jazz-tinged arrangements by Jimmy Mundy.

When Capitol Records started, one of its three initial partners, Johnny Mercer, who was a former employee of Whiteman's, prevailed upon his old boss to cut some sides. "Pops" had been steadfastly refraining from recording because of his avowed opposition to the free use made of his discs by radio

stations. But this time he gave in, and out came two especially impressive sides, "Travelin' Light," featuring Billie Holiday (she used the pseudonym "Lady Day") and "I've Found a New Baby," spotting Weed on piano.

The new band was strong, but the draft was stronger, and soon Whiteman, like so many other leaders, found it difficult to staff his orchestra with good musicians. So he gave up his band, although in 1944 he did organize a group for theaters, which played the old arrangements and evoked more nostalgia than good music. After the war he settled down for a while at the ABC network, where, with the help of numerous good studio musicians, he conducted on a regular television series. In 1955 he appeared as host on a CBS summer replacement series, backed by Jackie Gleason, which featured more than fifty of the big bands (some of dubious distinction) that had managed to survive. Whiteman, himself, died in December of 1967.

The Whiteman band in the early 1930s with pianists Roy Bargy and Lenny Hayton.

Much of the love and respect and admiration accorded Whiteman by his alumni was reflected in an album recorded for Command in 1956. Titled "Paul Whiteman—50th Anniversary" (he had begun playing violin in 1906), it featured the Dorseys, Teagarden, Mercer, Venuti, Hoagy Carmichael, Weed, plus an air check of the Original Rhythm Boys.

Whiteman's warmth and refreshing philosophy are reflected in what he had to say about the project. "I'm touched and thrilled by all this," he stated. "And yet, if I want to talk about American music, I must confess that as much as I enjoyed the past and appreciate the present, it's the future that seems most important of all to me, because it's in the future that we ought to be able to create even greater music as we reap the benefits of our numerous mistakes and, I hope, of our even more numerous achievements. . . . Let us always remember that there is only one way to go—and that is forward!"

Pops ponders as Joe Mooney's Quartet
plays softly in the background.

Part Three:
Inside More of
the Big Bands

The Arranging Leaders

AS A group, the most musical of all bands were those led by arrangers. Some of these, like Glenn Miller's, Duke Ellington's, Les Brown's, Claude Thornhill's, Stan Kenton's and Larry Clinton's, gained great commercial acceptance. But there were others, not so well known, which, because they were led by the kind of men whose talents and training enabled them to draw the optimum from their music and their musicians, achieved much acclaim from musicians and the more musical-minded big band fans.

VAN ALEXANDER, the bright New Yorker who had arranged and co-composed "A-Tisket, a-Tasket" for Chick Webb and Ella Fitzgerald, organized his own band in 1938 after a productive stay with Webb. It was a good band, though never startlingly so, which made some Bluebird recordings and concentrated more upon ensemble sounds than it did on individual soloists— not too bad an idea since its arrangements were generally better than its musicians. However, Van did give starts to future stars like Butch Stone, Si Zentner, Ray Barr, a fine pianist who later carved himself a long career as Frankie Laine's accompanist, and two excellent drummers, Shelly Manne and Irv Cottler. In the forties Van, an easygoing though thoroughly alert man, gave up his band and concentrated strictly on writing, eventually establishing himself on the West Coast as one of the most highly successful and respected composers and arrangers in the television and movie fields.

ARCHIE BLEYER, best-known in the forties and fifties first as Arthur Godfrey's musical director and then as head of Cadence Records, had already established himself as one of the foremost writers of stock arrangements by the time the big bands came into vogue. A shy, retiring person, who looked more like a guy who

had built his own computer than a maestro, he was actually an excellent leader of men. He arranged and conducted expertly for shows and spent a good deal of time in the later thirties leading an orchestra at Earl Carroll's Club in Hollywood, just across the street from the spot where the Palladium was eventually erected.

SONNY BURKE inherited Sam Donahue's young Detroit band when Gene Krupa snatched the tenor saxist for his own outfit. A very personable and energetic graduate of Duke University, where he had led a college group, Sonny, with John Hammond's encouragement, brought his young Detroiters to New York, rehearsed them, helped support them and eventually landed an engagement at the Roseland in Brooklyn plus an Okeh recording contract. What Burke's men lacked in musical polish, they made up for in enthusiasm, so that at times they did quite well with Sonny's arrangements, good ones that crossbred the styles of Jimmie Lunceford and Count Basie. There were times, though, when the musicians' ears seemed to be bigger than their horns, though the band did produce an impressive pianist, Wayne Herdell; a good drummer, Harold Hahn; and an attractive singer, Lynne Sherman. In 1940, when Donahue left Krupa, he asked for his band back. Sonny left the

Arranger Sonny Burke in his post-band-leading days (when he switched to writing for singers like Mel Torme)

decision to the sidemen, who decided that since Sam had organized the group, had continued writing for it while with Gene, and could provide a great front with his dynamic sax playing (Burke merely dribbled over the vibes), he should get his band back. So Burke bowed out—which turned out to be the break of his life—and soon began a successful career as chief arranger for the bands of Jimmy Dorsey and Charlie Spivak, as well as one of the West Coast's leading arranger-conductors in the recording and television fields. He produced many of Sinatra's albums, including his ambitious 1980 "Trilogy: Past, Present and Future," served as musical director for Reprise and Warner Brother Records, and headed his own Daybreak Records, before he died in 1979.

TED FIO RITO, a prolific and successful songwriter (he wrote "I Never Knew," "Toot, Toot, Tootsie, Goodbye," "Laugh, Clown, Laugh" and other hits), started his band in the twenties in conjunction with Dan Russo. Known as the Oriole Terrace Orchestra, it was an early success, though by the time the big band boom had begun, Russo had left and Ted had the band all to himself. When I first heard it late in 1935, I found it to be one of the more enterprising sweet bands, employing trick rhythms, temple blocks, lots of musical triplets and a Hammond organ, played by Fio Rito. It also sported a funny bass player, Candy Candido, who did all sorts of tricks with his voice,

and a pleasant singer, Muzzy Marcellino, but not the pretty, blonde girl vocalist who had already left, Miss Betty Grable. As the years went by, Ted veered away from the tricks, modernized his band, and for a while featured a vocal group, Kay Swingle and Her Brothers, including one brother, Ward, who later formed the famous Swingle Singers.

RALPH FLANAGAN, an arranger in the forties for the bands of Charlie Barnet, Hal McIntyre, Tony Pastor, Gene Krupa, Boyd Raeburn, Blue Barron and Sammy Kaye, was an easy-going man, who always claimed he didn't want to lead a band. But he was catapulted onto the podium when a sharp record producer, Herb Hendler, induced him to arrange and record a salute to Glenn Miller album for a minor label called Rainbow Records. When Hendler left Rainbow for RCA Victor, he suggested that the company record Ralph as a sort of Miller-sequel band, and it has been reported that the Victor powers, thinking Ralph Flanagan was Bill Finegan, the man who had written so many of Miller's hit arrangements, went right along with the idea. The result was a series of successful records, and the start of a let's-make-the-most-of-Glenn-Miller's-music-now-that-he's-dead campaign that brought some juicy returns to Flanagan, who had never had any connection with Miller, and to such Miller alumni-turned-bandleaders as Tex Beneke, Jerry Gray and Ray Anthony.

JERRY GRAY was another reluctant arranger-turned-leader, and the direct cause of the switch was the post-Big-Band Era hoopla created by Ralph Flanagan's blatant Glenn Miller band impersonation. Jerry, a round-faced, round-tummied, alternately worried-and happy-looking Bostonian, began his career with Artie Shaw and, later, conducted the Miller AAF radio orchestra in Europe after Glenn had disappeared. Before then he had been a long-time arranger for Glenn's civilian band. He knew his Miller music and showed that he did when he headed the best of the bands that aped Miller's. He was helped by the lead clarinet of Willie Schwartz, who had played that role (and horn) in the Miller civilian band and whose distinctive sound was difficult to copy. Jerry stayed with the band as long as he felt he had to in order to make his point,

Arranger Ralph Flanagan and fans

then returned to conducting and arranging in the West Coast studios, where he served as musical director of the Bob Crosby show for many years. Eventually he settled in Dallas, Texas, where he served as musical director of the Fairmont Hotel, fronting a hotel-type band, until he died there on August 10, 1976, the victim of a heart attack.

JOE HAYMES led one of the most productive and most tragic lives among bandleaders. A handsome man (he looked like the typical collegiate hero in a 1927 movie) and a fine arranger, he organized, arranged for and conducted one of the best but least publicized bands of the early thirties, one that included such outstanding musicians as Bud Freeman, Peewee Erwin and Toots Mondello. After it broke up, Joe whipped into shape another unit that was so good that the astute Tommy Dorsey, looking for a group after his split with brother Jimmy, induced twelve out of fourteen of Joe's sidemen to let him become their new leader. Undaunted, Joe went ahead and organized still another outfit—another good one, too—which included two fine trumpeters—Chris Griffin, who later moved into the Goodman

brass section, and Zeke Zarchy, who went on to lead the Dorsey, Crosby and Miller brass sections—plus a fine young pianist, Bill Miller, who was to become Frank Sinatra's accompanist. But Haymes's bands never became successful commercially, perhaps because he never was able to discipline himself sufficiently to market the fine music he was creating.

LENNIE HAYTON is best remembered for his conducting and scoring of some of the best MGM musical spectaculars, as well as for his musical direction of, and marriage to, Lena Horne. But those of us who were in New York during the mid-thirties will also recall his very good, large dance orchestra, full of colorful arrangements that he, Deane Kincaide, Bill Challis and Fulton (Fidgey) McGrath had written for some of the best musicians around town. Lennie was a sensitive pianist and a vibrant leader. He was energetic and intense, yet he exuded great natural charm and controlled his music and his musicians wonderfully well, enjoying the same warm respect he received several years later in Hollywood, to which he continued to contribute his talents until his death in 1970.

CARL HOFF left his position as conductor of the Lucky Strike Hit Parade series in 1941 to start his own band and play leading hotels and ballrooms throughout the land. For a time he remained under the influence of the Hit Parade, setting tempos better suited for the sponsor's musical tastes than for the public's dancing feet. He did, however, introduce some interesting sounds through his voicing of trumpets and clarinets as one section in contrast with the lower-toned combination of trombones and tenor saxes. (Other bands continued to pit the saxes against the brass and let it go at that.) Hoff also featured a fine girl singer, Louanne Hogan, and introduced a promising boy singer, Bob Haymes, Dick's younger brother, who eventually became a top songwriter. By 1942 the Hoff band had loosened up a great deal, and Carl, one of the most likable guys in the world, had developed into a fine front man. His later edition featured two more good singers, Betty Norton and Al Nobel, a well-blended vocal group, the Murphy Sisters, one of whom, as Dottie Evans, was to become one of the country's top jingle singers, and a fine pianist, Ray Barr. The arrangements continued to be interesting, and with Hoff's humor and good cheer pervading the proceedings, hearing and watching the Hoff band was one of the more pleasurable ways to spend an evening.

QUINCY JONES, an alumnus of the bands of Lionel Hampton, Count Basie and Dizzy Gillespie, for whom he played trumpet and arranged, came into his own as a bandleader with a clean, beautifully rehearsed, infectiously swinging outfit. But this was long after the big band era. It was organized for a European jaunt in the late fifties; in the early sixties it played several engagements in the United States, impressing all by combining the rhythmic looseness of the best of the Big Band Era's swing bands with some of the more advanced harmonic sounds of a later generation. Highly respected for his talents as a leader-arranger and also for his bright, direct, I-never-take-myself-seriously approach, Quincy continued to write arrangements for others. He was picked by Frank Sinatra as conductor-arranger on numerous recordings. He eventually became one of Hollywood's most successful composers, creating scores for such major motion pictures as *In Cold Blood* and *The Centurions*, as well as for the highly-rated and much-acclaimed television series of *Roots*.

BILLY MAY never had a band until well after the Big Band Era had gone. But the happy-sounding, highly danceable and almost always swinging outfit, which this former Charlie Barnet and Glenn Miller arranger headed, became one of the few remaining joys for those of us who in the fifties were looking for good, new, big band sounds. May, a huge man with a dry wit that was reflected in much of what he wrote, featured slyly slurping saxes, voiced in

Arranger Billy May (right) with former bandleader and Meadowbrook owner Frank Dailey

thirds, which gave his music its distinctive style. Later he wrote mainly for others. (made some great sides with Sinatra), was musical director of many TV shows and of Time-Life's Swing Era recreation series.

SY OLIVER, whose arrangements played such an important role in the success of the Jimmie Lunceford and Tommy Dorsey bands, waited until the big band boom had burst before he formed his own outfit. It played not only some of his great arrangements but some by others that weren't so great, and featured several excellent sidemen. But the star was Sy himself, a round-faced, wide-eyed, handsome man, who led his band with great enthusiasm and supplied its brightest moments with his superb vocals. After arranging for Jackie Gleason, Sinatra and others, he formed a small dance band that supplied fine swinging sounds for dancers at New York's chic Rainbow Room.

DON REDMAN helped a flock of big band-leaders in the thirties and forties with his brilliant arrangements—Harry James, Jimmy Dorsey, Paul Whiteman, Charlie Barnet, Jimmie Lunceford, Bobby Byrne and others —both during the time he was leading his own band and after he disbanded it in the late thirties. A well-schooled, prolific and imaginative arranger, he had established himself during the twenties as a writer as well as a splendid alto-saxophone player in the Fletcher Henderson band, and then as arranger, musical director and vocalist (he had a captivating, semi-whispering style) of the famed McKinney's Cotton Pickers outfit. In the early thirties he started his own band, best remembered by the general public for its alluring theme song, "Chant of the Weed," written by Don, and for his romping arrangements of numerous pop tunes, including his famous version of "I Got Rhythm." It also featured one of the finest of all band vocalists, Harlan Lattimore, who sounded like a hip Bing Crosby. Don was a small, dynamic man, tremendously well liked and respected by all who worked with him, with a great talent for handling people and for drawing forth their greatest potential. (He was, incidentally, one of the few left-handed conductors in the business.) After the Big Band Era, Redman concentrated on writing for singers, radio and the legitimate theater. His ever-

Arranger Don Redman who led his own band and McKinney's Cotton Pickers.

broadening career ended when he died on November 30th, 1964.

JOHNNY RICHARDS, one of the most progressive of all arrangers, formed an interesting band in the forties. He had been writing in the Hollywood studios, and some of the complicated scores he contributed to his own band (he claimed to have penned 408 out of the band's library of 500) turned out to be pretty difficult for his less experienced musicians to play. But Johnny, a pleasant and patient chap, worked hard and finally whipped his band into shape. But it was never very successful, so Johnny returned to writing for others like Kenton, Gillespie and Sarah Vaughan and some modernists before his pen was stilled forever in 1968.

The SAUTER-FINEGAN band, one of the most colorful and musicianly of all groups, came along after the Big Band Era. Formed in 1952, it featured a whole slew of brilliant arrangements by its two highly respected but sometimes impractical leaders, Eddie Sauter and Bill Finegan, plus a group of talented and deeply devoted musicians who worked hard to produce a wide variety of intriguing sounds, ranging all the way from such up-tempoed, novel instrumentals as "Doodletown Fifers" to such moody, jazz-tinged ballads as "Nina Never Knew," which featured a great vocal by Joe Mooney. Both leaders were serious musicians; yet each had a keen sense of humor, often reflected in the band's scores. Neither would deviate from the idealistic attitudes they shared, refusing to compromise their music to satisfy the tastes of the public or the whims of producers, managers and other more commercially minded associates. Sauter and Finegan remained deeply dedicated to their music and musicians. But dedication wasn't enough, and when the money stopped coming in, each had to take his talents elsewhere. Eddie took his into the theater and the movies, in neither of which, because of commercial restrictions, he admitted he could ever feel quite comfortable or as truly creative as he wanted to be. Then on April 21, 1981, he succumbed in his West Nyack, New York home to a massive heart attack. As for Finegan, he tried his hand at teaching, and also wrote some excellent arrangements for the official Glenn Miller Orchestra and later for Mel Lewis.

BOBBY SHERWOOD had so many talents, he didn't know what to do. He arranged, composed, sang, played trumpet, guitar, trombone and piano and announced every number his band played. He also gave up a lucrative career as a Hollywood studio musician to start his band, which featured his arrangements, some very good and some that sounded as if they'd been written to meet a deadline, his Bobby Hackett-like trumpet, his full-chorded, musicianly guitar, his relaxed, drawling singing and a bright, teen-aged tenor saxist named Jack (Zoot) Sims. Bobby also had good looks, a warm, easy-going, Huckleberry Finn personality and a hit record, "The Elks' Parade," which he wrote and arranged. What he didn't have was a well-disciplined organization (his original band was one of the most slovenly looking crews I ever saw on any bandstand), an image—as either arranger, singer, trumpeter or guitarist—on which the public could focus, or very much commercial success. Too bad, too, because this was one of the real talents of the Big Band Era. Bobby died of cancer on January 23, 1981, while in semi-retirement in Auburn, Massachusetts.

The Horn-playing Leaders

LEADERS who blew trumpets and trombones had a big advantage over those who played other instruments. They could play louder, they could play more emotionally, and their very instruments made them look and sound like leaders.

Louis

Some of those leaders packed such an emotional wallop that they could rise above the unimpressive bands they led. Most important of these was one of the greatest jazz instrumentalists of all time, Louis (Satchmo) Armstrong. His trumpeting was glorious, his singing delightful; but his band seldom achieved even mediocrity.

During the Big Band Era, Louis performed primarily as a jazz soloist and an entertainer. He appeared in movie, in nightclubs and in theaters. He also recorded, but his most impressive recordings were made not with a big band but with all-star jazz groups, with small outfits that he fronted, or as a singer dueting with other top artists like Bing Crosby, Ella Fitzgerald, the Mills Brothers, Frances Langford and Jack Teagarden, with whom he was associated for years.

A wonderfully warm and gracious human being, Armstrong worked part of the time with a run-of-the-mill big band, led by Luis Russell and sporting, on occasion, such good musicians as drummer Sid Catlett, trombonist J. C. Higginbotham and trumpeter Henry (Red) Allen.

Yet it was seldom considered really to be Louis' own band, the way Goodman's or Miller's or Ellington's were their own. It seemed to be more of an "extra added attraction"—and, for those of us who loved Louis' playing and deplored the inferior musicianship supporting him, more of an "extra added distraction." For Armstrong was far apart from, and far above, the big band with which he worked, and it is to his everlasting credit that he not only survived, but that he also continued to blow his magnificent horn throughout those years with such feeling and warmth and vitality. Little wonder, then, that musicians throughout the world, when Louis was still among them and after his death on July 6, 1971, two days beyond his seventy-first birthday, continued to accord him the respect and admiration he so richly deserved.

As for the others:

RAY ANTHONY emerged as a well-known big band leader after the era had ended. He had broken in with Al Donahue's band in the early forties as a kid protégé, then was hired by Glenn Miller with Donahue's blessings. He and Glenn never hit it off especially well; Ray was not featured, merely playing fourth parts in the section. After six months, he returned to his hometown, Cleveland, where he formed a group with a unique instrumentation: one trumpet, one French horn, five saxes and three rhythm. Soon thereafter he went into the Navy, where he did yeoman work as leader of an entertainment group in the Pacific. While in the service, he met a bright sailor named Fred Benson, who, after the war, became Anthony's manager and guiding light. Together they built and promoted a good swinging band, featuring Ray's gutty, low-registering

horn. Then, when Ralph Flanagan started the parade of Glenn Miller mimics, Anthony fell in line and, like the other imitators, made good money. His band appeared in many of the country's top spots, recorded for Capitol and featured a good singer named Tommy Mercer. And Ray's glamour stock rose perceptibly when he married Mamie Van Doren. Eventually Ray's band melted away (so did his marriage), and he settled down with a small unit that played the lounges. In 1980, he formed an organization Big Bands 80s, to service radio stations, schools, and fans with all kinds of big bands sounds.

RANDY BROOKS built his band around his trumpet and some interesting arrangements by John Benson Brooks, a talented writer with a financial interest in the outfit. Started near the end of the Big Band Era, it

Ray Anthony

Henry (Hot Lips) Busse

Randy Brooks

tried mighty hard—sometimes too hard—to make an impression and enjoyed a modicum of success. Randy, built like a guard on a football team, was a very intense man. He had played lead horn in several name bands, impressing especially in Les Brown's, before he decided in 1945 to become a leader. Blessed with a fine technique, he could play both a brilliant, blasting, blaring horn or, when muted, one that was delicately discreet. His band was colorful, thanks to its leader's trumpet, the scores, the piano and excellent vibraphone of Shorty Allen, and an exceptional lead saxist, Eddie Kane, whose alto was also featured on numerous solos. And in 1946 the band introduced a promising young tenor man, his name: Stan Getz. Randy's intensity (he was a charming fellow with a refreshing State of Maine hominess) typified much of his band's music men. This was unfortunate because, when Randy's band took things easy, it produced some very persuasive musical sounds. Had it been able to relax more often, it might have developed into one of the major bands of its day. Randy eventually married another bandleader, Ina Ray Hutton, and they moved to the West Coast, where Brooks suffered a stroke that ended his career. In 1967 he was burned to death in a fire in his Maine home where he had been living with his mother.

HENRY BUSSE, usually identified with corn because of his "w-a-a-a-t d-o-o" style of trumpeting, led a surprisingly musical band during the late thirties. Its long, steady stay in Chicago's Chez Paree helped its musicians develop into a polished unit, so that when it finally appeared in New York in 1938 at the Hotel New Yorker, its musicianship, versatility, excellent arrangements and exceptional tone colorings were impressive. Featured, naturally, was Busse's soft, muted trumpet with its exaggerated vibrato, which didn't grate too much when cushioned by some rich, sonorous ensemble sounds. The band also sported its shuffle rhythm, a bright, six-eight–time sort of beat, which probably seemed more natural to Henry, a German, than did the more Americanized four-four swinging beat. Busse fronted in a charming bierstube style, willingly played his two big numbers, "When Day Is Done" and his theme, "Hot Lips," night after night and year after year, and remained fairly active as a leader until his death in 1955.

BILLY BUTTERFIELD possessed a great potential. He was a sensational trumpeter whose big, broad tone and emotional phrasing was widely acclaimed when he was featured with the Bob Crosby band and on Margaret Whiting's highly successful recording of "Moonlight in Vermont." Yet Billy never really made it as a leader. He formed his band near the close of the Big Band Era, in the spring of 1946, in conjunction with Bill Stegmeyer, who wrote most of the arrangements and who was featured on alto sax and clarinet almost as much as Billy was on trumpet. For me the band lacked both warmth and distinction. Butterfield's horn was improperly showcased. Billy, like two other great trumpeters with his initials, Bunny Berigan and Bix Beiderbecke, was not a great self-disciplinarian. He even allowed himself to sing—a sad mistake. What could have been an exciting musical venture thus never really came off, and so the Butterfield try, despite a strong buildup from Capitol Records, went down as one of the Big Band Era's more unfortunate misses.

LEE CASTLE, as featured trumpeter with the bands of Artie Shaw, Tommy Dorsey, Benny Goodman, Will Bradley, Bunny Berigan, Red Norvo and Joe Venuti, was an impressive sideman. As a leader of his own band he was less effective. Before his band-leading days, when he was known as Lee Castaldo, his full tone, good range and all-round musicianship, plus an ability to play good jazz in the Berigan-Armstrong style, kept him working regularly. But Lee yearned to have his own band so that he could play more solos. During the early forties he fronted two different editions, both of which appeared at the Pelham Heath Inn and featured not only Lee's jazz but also some sweet trumpeting à la Harry James. But neither band, even though each fielded some good musicians, ever matched Lee's own musicianship as a trumpeter. Lee, who always took himself and his work very seriously, remained extremely dedicated to the big bands even after their popularity had waned. It was not surprising, therefore, that years later he was selected to take over the late Jimmy Dorsey's band and that he turned in a first-rate job as its leader.

LES ELGART, who had played excellent lead trumpet but little or no jazz for Charlie Spivak, Bunny Berigan and Hal McIntyre,

Billy Butterfield

Erskine Hawkins

Lee Castle

formed his own band in 1945. A musical group it was, too, thanks to exceptionally fine arrangements by Bill Finegan and Nelson Riddle, a good, young jazz trumpeter, Nick Travis, and Les's brother, Larry, a colorful, enthusiastic saxist. Les, a handsome man, presented a rather lethargic front, but Larry imbued the band with so much spirit that eventually some of the men began looking toward him for leadership. Finally this conflict, together with other causes, produced a split between the two brothers, after which each lead his own outfit. But soon, having found that there wasn't that much business to go around, they patched up their differences. Their reorganized band of the fifties featured light, airy arrangements by Charlie Albertine, refreshingly fluid saxes led by Larry, and an overall, watered-down sound that made it one of the most underwhelming bands of the times. Yet it fared better commercially than the 1945 edition, chiefly because of its Columbia records and frequent appearances on the college circuit.

MAYNARD FERGUSON spent the big band days in his native Canada, not coming to the United States until 1948, and then first appearing with the bands of Boyd Raeburn, Jimmy Dorsey and Charlie Barnet. He made his biggest impact, though, when he joined Stan Kenton in 1950, with whom his sensational, if not consistently tasteful, high-note trumpet chilled the more impressionable cats. Eventually, ten years after the big bands had died down, Maynard, an articulate, bright, colorful man, formed his own outfit that featured his horn and some modern, swinging arrangements. In the sixties he formed another exciting band that occasionally migrated to the U.S. Then he resettled back in the States, leading a well-rehearsed group that of course featured his horn and whose torrid tempos and blasting bombast appealed more to youngsters than to big band or jazz purists.

ERSKINE HAWKINS brought his enthusiastic, swinging, though not always in-tune Alabama State Collegians out of the Deep South in 1936 and immediately began to attract musicians and the public through his Vocalion and Bluebird recordings. Hawkins, a pleasant man, though an awkward-looking leader, blew a stratospheric-styled trumpet that amazed some of his less-initiated listeners. But the really musical solos came from

the horns of the two Bascomb brothers, Wilbur on trumpet and Paul (and later Julian Dash) on tenor sax. It was Wilbur's delicate but swinging solo on "Tuxedo Junction," often credited to Hawkins (who was always quick to point out that it was Willie's), that helped make this the biggest of all record hits for the band. Its next most important recording, "After Hours," was a moody but swinging blues written and arranged by Avery Parrish, who also played good piano. Hawkins spotted numerous ballads, none of which the band played especially well but which were sparked from time to time by two good girl singers, Ida James and Dolores Brown. There was also 'a saxophonist, Jimmy Mitchelle, who sang frequently. Hawkins kept his big band working for a number of years after most of the others had folded, but eventually he settled for a small combo, which, following the Jonah Jones craze, worked in some of the swankier clubs that his big band had never been able to enter.

JACK JENNEY was an extraordinary trombonist and a mediocre bandleader. His style of playing was beautiful and imaginative; he

Jack

blew his instrument with great feeling, producing what for me is the warmest, most personal sound I've ever heard from any horn. He created lovely, melodic variations on themes, like his gorgeous chorus on Artie Shaw's hit record of "Stardust." His solos supplied the only musical attractions in recordings made by his own short-lived band, which suffered from uninteresting arrangements and lack of discipline. When his close friend Artie Shaw reorganized in 1940 and wanted him, Jack accepted, and stayed until he suffered a physical collapse late in 1941. Six months later he formed a trio with his pretty wife, Bonnie Lake, as vocalist, and Lester Ludke as pianist. In 1943 Jenney entered the Navy. After his discharge he settled in Hollywood. Apparently incapable of leading a well-disciplined life, he developed kidney trouble, and in December, 1945, following an appendicitis attack, he passed away. He was only thirty-five years old, and his loss was not only a great one to music but a deep, personal one to those who had known and admired this warm, too easygoing, talented gent.

HENRY JEROME led one of the most enthusiastic bands in the New York area during the early forties. Called "Henry Jerome and His Stepping Tones," it at first featured a style much like Hal Kemp's. The arrangements were generally good but Jerome's men didn't play them very well, so that the effect had little of the light charm of Kemp's group. Henry was featured on his very reserved trumpet, and the band also spotted a good singer named Kay Carlton and a strong guitarist, Billy Bauer, who later helped spark Woody Herman's First Herd. In 1944 Jerome dumped his "Stepping Tones" and surrounded himself instead with some of the city's young, eager, modern musicians. Johnny Mandel wrote the scores, and Al Cohn and Lenny Garment (he later became Richard Nixon's lawyer) played saxes, and Tiny Kahn played drums. "The band was great. We played bop scores, but we were too far ahead of the times. Hardly anybody ever came to hear us," recalls Jerome. Eventually he gave up this band also, headed for the studios, and with the help of many of New York's top musicians, created some very commercial recordings.

CLYDE McCOY will always be remembered for his version of "Sugar Blues," a corny novelty which, I've never openly admitted before, fascinated me the first time I'd heard it. It created an unusual sound, this talking-trumpet device that McCoy featured so effectively in the early thirties and continued to play incessantly and insistently for years to come until it became seemingly impossible for the corn to ripen any further. Actually, McCoy was a much better trumpeter than he was given credit for; through the years—as late as the mid-sixties—he had been heard blowing such a good brand of dixieland jazz that nobody really knew what kind of musical impression and reputation he might have made during the big band days if he hadn't boxed himself in with the "Sugar Blues" approach.

JOHNNY McGHEE led a very good hotel-room type of band in the early thirties, but it featured his own cornet in a rather disappointing way. Johnny, who looked a lot like the then Prince of Wales (the Duke of Windsor), could play lovely, melodic jazz, and some of us figured that he might turn out to be the next Bix Beiderbecke. But instead he latched onto a corny gimmick, changed the spelling of his name to McGee (a slang word for corny), and proceeded to blow forth some overly cute sounds. Eventually he gave up his affected style; then he produced some very impressive sounds in front of a well-rehearsed but poorly promoted band.

BUDDY MORROW was a brilliant trombonist who, as Moe Zudecoff, played for Tommy Dorsey and Artie Shaw, as Muni Morrow for Bob Crosby, and then took his strong, steady and well-toned horn into the studios. After the Big Band Era ended, Morrow was talked into leading a band, caused quite a furor for a while with his version of "Night Train," and impressed many with his group's discipline and good musicanship. He returned to the studios for awhile; then took over the Glenn Miller band; went back into the studios again, and then in the late 1970s led the Tommy Dorsey band, turning it into a first-rate organization, the best of the various so-called "ghost" bands.

PHIL NAPOLEON had already established himself as a top jazz musician through his Original Memphis Five and the many fine recordings they made, and as a studio musician, where he had been working for eight years before he decided in 1937 to form his own big band. Musically, it was a good outfit, with Phil's well-modulated and melodically pleasant trumpet featured along

Louis Prima

with Fulton McGrath's piano and Ford Leary's trombone. Phillie, as his friends called him, was a gentle person who wanted assurance that he was doing the right thing and that he wasn't offending anyone, especially the many admirers he had attracted. Though his band never achieved outstanding commercial success, despite some Herculean efforts by Napoleon's devoted manager, Walter Bloom, it did rank for a while as one of the more musical outfits on the scene. After the Big Band Era, Phil returned to fronting a small dixieland group, which performed regularly in the Miami area where he eventually settled down, leaving occasionally to appear on some nationwide TV shows.

LOUIS PRIMA, who started off as one of the better jazz trumpeters out of New Orleans, brought a lot of fun onto the dance band scene with his wild antics, while at the same time managing to retain a high level of musicianship. "Prima's success," I wrote in June, 1945, "is both a healthy and a happy phenomenon. For it proves once again that even if you're not the world's greatest musical genius, you still don't have to invent a lot of rickety tricks to make

folks like you and to make money for yourself. All Louis does is go out front and have himself a helluva good time, acting like a natural showman, kidding around, poking fun at folks out front, at guys in his band, and, most of all, at himself." Then, after noting that he was a much better trumpeter of the Armstrong school than most people gave him credit for being, and that he was a first-class musician insofar as directing a band was concerned, I added, "Louis has a fine ear, good musical sense and taste, a feeling for right tempos, a feeling for jazz." The bands he led, therefore, were generally fairly good ones, always colorful, with plenty of zany vocals from Prima, plus duets first with Lily Ann Carol and later with Keeley Smith. During his later years, he worked mostly with small lounge groups before being felled by a massive brain hemorrhage. He lingered in an unconscious state for a long time before his death in 1977 in his native New Orleans.

SHORTY (CLARENCE) SHEROCK was better known as a sideman than as a leader of a band he formed in 1945, which played Glen Island Casino but achieved little national recognition. Sherock, an attractive, round-faced, perennially juvenile type, was overshadowed when he first came to New York in 1936 with Ben Pollack's band. Why? Because the other trumpeter was Harry James. Shorty soon did all right for himself, however, starring in the bands of Jimmy Dorsey, Bob Crosby, Gene Krupa, Tommy Dorsey and Horace Heidt, the last of whom eventually groomed Sherock for his short leader's career by presenting him with a library totally unsuited to Shorty's musical style.

MUGGSY (FRANCIS) SPANIER led a superb fifteen-piece dixieland band in 1941 that rivaled the Bob Crosby band at its best

via "a broad, direct, hard-hitting type of jazz with a straightforward, unrelenting rhythmic attack," as I described it in a November, 1941, *Metronome* review that overshadowed the one I gave on the same page to Stan Kenton's band. And Barry Ulanov, a few months later, said about one of its broadcasts: "For a half hour the comparatively new Muggsy Spanier band stood up and blew music that all by itself should account for a place in the Hall of Fame for these musicians. Yes, the dominant quality of this broadcast was one of thrills." Deane Kin-

caide, who'd written many of the Crosby and Tommy Dorsey bands' arrangements, penned a fine library for Muggsy's too, one that was played wonderfully well by such stars as Irving Fazola, Vernon Brown, Ralph Muzzillo, Nick Caiazza, Dave Bowman and, of course, Spanier himself. He blew a soulful, pungent, but ever-driving cornet, never trying to produce more than he could, always delivering his music forcefully and straightforwardly. That's the sort of a guy he was, too—direct and honest and very vital. A short, slight man of intense spirit, he once had ambitions of becoming the first left-handed third baseman in major league baseball. He played his cornet with Ted Lewis' band for many years; recorded with many of the greats of jazz; made a miraculous recovery after a severe, long and almost fatal illness, and before and after his band fronted several outstanding dixieland combos, including one that recorded some memorable sides for Bluebird. His big band managed to make only seven sides for Decca before the recording ban began. The band spent its best days at the Arcadia Ballroom in New York; when it left there, many of its stars quit, unwilling to leave town for the salaries Spanier could afford to pay them. Muggsy tried hard to continue but couldn't make it. By the spring of 1944 he was back again with Lewis. He stayed for a while, then resumed leading smaller combos until his death in 1966.

COOTIE WILLIAMS, the great growl trumpeter who first achieved national recognition with Duke Ellington, for whom he played for many years, before he was featured with Benny Goodman, led one of the least known but most promising big swing bands in 1942. It was an exciting outfit, jumping at all tempos, with Cootie's prodigious trumpet starred in solos and as leader of a powerful brass septet that used to rock the rafters of the old Savoy Ballroom in Harlem where it appeared for long spells at a time. Unfortunately, first the recording ban and then the draft hampered the progress of the promising outfit. Eventually, Williams, described by Leonard Feather in his *Encyclopedia of Jazz* as "probably the best all-around trumpet player in jazz," was forced to settle for a smaller combo, one that featured mostly rhythm and blues, some unimpressive singing by Cootie and an uncom-

Cootie

fortably exaggerated commercial approach. Too talented and too honest a musician to settle for this sort of music, Williams soon organized a good little jazz group, made some exciting records on the Jazztone label, and finally found his way back into the Ellington band, which, thanks to Cootie's presence and spirit, began to sound more vital than it had in years. Cootie was a giant all right!

SI ZENTNER never had a big band in the thirties or the forties or the fifties. In the sixties, he fronted a very-post-Big Band Era outfit, a smartly rehearsed, especially clean, crisp unit that attracted a great deal of attention with its hit recording of "Up the Lazy River" and the highly pressurized campaign that the high-pressured Mr. Z. put on for himself and for the return of the big bands. (He had become a top Hollywood studio trombonist, but he couldn't fight the big band bug.) During the forties he was a much respected lead trombonist, best remembered for his work in Les Brown's band. He was also, he claims, a well-respected gent: "We had a new girl singer in the band when Les played at the World's Fair, and I was the one her mother trusted to take her to work and bring her back home every night." The singer? Doris Day.

The Reed-playing Leaders

PLAYING a reed instrument—a sax or clarinet—permitted a leader almost as much impact as playing a brass horn. The latter, of course, could sound louder and, especially with the trumpets, rise more easily above the rest of the band. But the saxes had their emotional wallop, too, and certainly, after Goodman had led the way, the clarinet achieved great acceptance. Some of the reed leaders weren't very good musicians, but by holding a horn they at least looked like leaders of a typical big band (more so than violinists, for example) and thus were able quite easily to establish rapport with their audiences.

GEORGIE AULD, a volatile, dark-haired, squat, intense Canadian first attracted attention with his hard-swinging tenor sax in Bunny Berigan's band, then with Artie Shaw's. When Shaw suddenly quit in 1939, Auld was selected to front the remnants. But without Artie, the band meant little; it disbanded after a few months, and Georgie wound up with Benny Goodman, recording some memorable sides with a sextet that included Goodman, Cootie Williams, the late Charlie Christian and Count Basie. After an Army stint, Auld finally organized his own big outfit, built along Basie lines. The band swung consistently but seemed to be less interested in pleasing the public than in providing musical kicks for itself and its too small coterie of admiring fans and musicians. Its music was often brilliant, thanks to some fine arrangements by Manny Albam, Al Cohn and Neal Hefti, singing by Sarah Vaughn, the piano (for a short period) of Erroll Garner and a batch of exciting trumpeters which, from time to time, included Dizzy Gillespie, Sonny Berman, Billy Butterfield, Freddy Webster and Al Porcino. Auld's tenor sax, brilliant, biting and forever rhythmic, pervaded much of the music of a band that was featured mainly in jazz clubs. In 1946, when a spot was discovered on his lung, Auld disbanded. In the late 1970s he played the role of a big bandleader in the movie *New York, New York*.

JOHNNY BOTHWELL had been featured on alto sax in the bands of Gene Krupa, Tommy Dorsey, Boyd Raeburn and others before he formed his own band in 1946. It centered around his flashy, flowery horn, one that he blew very well and on which he sounded most impressive when he wasn't overphrasing. Johnny was a likable guy. He had an attractive, boyish face, with an incongruous-looking mustache that made him look more like a salesman in a woman's shoe salon than like a bandleader. His band was inconsistent; sometimes, especially when Johnny was blowing easily, it showed great promise; at other times it seemed to flounder. He had a very good boy singer, Don Darcy, and a very attractive girl vocalist, Claire (Shanty) Hogan, with whom Johnny established close rapport. Under-recorded, and a late arrival on the big band scene, Bothwell's band really never had much of a chance for even instant fame.

SAM DONAHUE, talented, self-assured, virile and dynamic, was one of the most respected musicians ever to appear on the

475

Sam

big band scene. A forceful saxophonist and an inspiring leader, he started his first band in Detroit in the early forties, gave it up to Sonny Burke when Gene Krupa offered Sam a job, then reclaimed it after leaving Krupa and was fashioning it into one of the most impressive bands around when the draft called and he entered the Navy. There he took over Artie Shaw's band after the latter's discharge and developed it into one of the most magnificent bands of all time, recorded for posterity on V-Discs. After the war, Donahue assembled a civilian group, composed of many of his loyal former sidemen. But plagued by booking problems, it managed merely to subsist, and in a few years Sam disbanded. However, in the sixties, when the Tommy Dorsey estate was looking for someone to carry on with the band after Tommy's death, it selected Donahue, who had played sax in the band. Once again he turned in an expert job, drawing good music out of a batch of inexperienced youngsters which included Frank Sinatra, Jr. As a molder of musical, though seldom successful commercial bands, Sam Donahue, who died in 1974, had few equals. And few maestri can lay claim to so many enthusiastic alumni.

SAXIE DOWELL, a pleasant, heavy-set, mustachioed tenor saxist with Hal Kemp's band made some sort of ultra-minor musical history when he wrote "Three Little Fishes," a tune more suited to the repertoire of a nursery-school teacher than that of a professional musician. But Saxie survived; in fact, after Kemp's death late in 1940, he formed his own outfit. This particular unit never gained much musical fame, but his brave Navy band, assigned to the ill-fated U.S.S. *Franklin,* brought a new and even more thrilling recognition for musicians for its magnificent heroics when the ship was torpedoed.

TEDDY HILL led a compact, swinging band that appeared frequently in Harlem's Savoy Ballroom during the early and middle thirties. The outfit swung wonderfully well primarily because Teddy had a great knack of setting just the right tempos for each tune. Hill seldom spotted himself on sax, featuring instead the great tenor saxist Chu Berry, as well as several outstanding trumpeters: Roy Eldridge, Bill Coleman, Bill Dillard, Frankie Newton and, as early as 1937, before practically anybody had heard of him, Dizzy Gillespie. In 1940 Teddy retired as a bandleader and soon opened a Harlem nightclub, Minton's, where he encouraged musicians to play what they wanted to and which, because of Teddy's policy, eventually became the birthplace of bop.

LES HITE confined most of his bandleading activities to the West Coast, where, during the early thirties, he fronted a band that included such future stars as Lionel Hampton, Marshall Royal and Lawrence Brown. During the Big Band Era he occasionally migrated east, spotting such musical stalwarts as Dizzy Gillespie, Joe Wilder and T-Bone Walker. Though Hite's band didn't win major acclaim, it enjoyed a fine reputation among West Coast musicians and achieved national attention when on several occasions Hite lent his entire band to Louis Armstrong.

HARLAN LEONARD and His Rockets was one of the unheralded bands from Kansas City which played in the swinging Basie style but never received sufficient exposure either on the air, on records or in the better clubs. Leonard, a good saxist, though never a startling soloist, featured other musicians, including for a short time Charlie Parker. The band attracted musicians and the hipper audiences that frequented the lesser-known clubs and ballrooms that his band played throughout most of its career.

NYE MAYHEW threatened during 1937 to have one of the most successful sweet bands. Backed by Hal Kemp, with scores by Kemp's arranger, John Scott Trotter, who also played piano for Mayhew, Nye, a handsome tenor saxist, appeared first at 'the Hotel Pennsylvania and then at the important Glen Island Casino. His was the only band that didn't emerge a national success after a summer at the Casino. Why? Who knows? The band was good—it even had Hugo Winterhalter on sax!—but it lacked a unique sound and spark, and by the end of the thirties it had become a forgotten nonentity.

The McFARLAND TWINS, two handsome saxophonists who looked like football heroes, fronted a mickey-mouse band in the late thirties and early forties which offered nothing more musicianly than a good

The McFarland Twins

girls' trio, the Norton Sisters, and an effective glee club, in the style of Fred Waring, from whose band the Twins had been graduated. Then suddenly, in 1942, the boys pulled a musical about-face, and showed up with a thoroughly musical outfit that spotted a fine sax quintet, led by George, and played some delightfully modern arrangements. It also featured an exceptionally good pianist, Geoff Clarkson, who later became a Les Brown mainstay, and two singers, Betty Engels and Dick Merrick, who were obviously influenced by Helen O'Connel and Bob Eberly. The band worked regularly, attracting many a customer with its two-pronged charm. It's too bad the McFarland Twins didn't come along a generation later, though: imagine what a novelty it would have been recording them in stereo!

JOHNNY MESSNER, an especially personable Juilliard graduate, led the band in the Marine Grill of New York's McAlpin Hotel for many years, a ten-piece outfit that by the early forties had become so well knit that it managed to sound much bigger than it was. Its well-scored arrangements helped. So did the doubling of the musicians, who managed to field a trombone quartet, though there was just one regular trombonist in the band. Messner presided smartly over the proceedings, featuring himself and a very attractive lass, Jeanne D'Arcy, on vocals, as well as the toy piano of Paul Kuhlthau, whom Johnny dubbed "Professor Coleslaw." After his long stay, Johnny eventually moved up and out of the cold, marble-lined Grill and into the Army. But after the war, another grill beckoned him, and down he went again, this time into the Hotel Taft, as vocalist, saxist and assistant leader of the Vincent Lopez band.

GERRY MULLIGAN wrote some superb arrangements at the close of the Big Band Era for the bands of Gene Krupa, Claude Thornhill and Elliot Lawrence, but it wasn't until more than a decade later that he organized one of the really great bands of its day. Bright, articulate, dogmatic and for a time totally unpredictable and undisciplined, Gerry had also played his beautifully controlled, highly creative and ever-swinging baritone sax in several name bands, then had organized a magnificent jazz quartet,

Gerry

and in the sixties and again in the seventies created two of the outstanding big bands of all time. Staffed with fine, young musicians, attracted by Mulligan's charts and by his imposing, persuasive personality (he had matured beautifully by this time.), the thirteen-piece outfits featured a style that Gerry once described to me as "controlled violence. I learned the art of underblowing and still getting a full, rich sound, from working in Claude Thornhill's band—the most underrated, if not the finest, all-around big band of all time." Like Thornhill's, Mulligan's band sounded as if it were going to erupt at any given moment; yet it succeeded in suppressing any musical violence in favor of subtle, persuasive, swinging sounds. If ever there was classic proof that big band jazz needn't be loud or blatant to be effective, the Gerry Mulligan band has been it.

GEORGE PAXTON, an excellent arranger, pretty fair tenor saxist and bon vivant ran Ina Ray Hutton's band for her in the early forties. In 1944 he split and started his own outfit. It was always a musicianly crew, hampered for a while by a string quartet that got in the way, but aided by an outstanding lead trumpeter, Guy Key, a lovely toned, swinging tenor saxist, Boomie Rich-

man, and two very effective singers, young Alan Dale and Liza Morrow. By 1945 Paxton had dropped the strings and having replaced the weaker men with some of New York's best musicians, began playing the better spots. He soon disbanded and became one of the town's more successful music publishers and head of a less successful record company.

TOMMY REYNOLDS looked and played like a hungry Artie Shaw. Lean and intense, he blew his clarinet with great fervor, reaching for high notes as Shaw often did, screeching as Shaw seldom did. His band, which he formed in 1940, was one of the loudest of all time; its raw enthusiasm was as contagious and often as aggravating as a case of German measles. When it didn't sound like Shaw's, it sounded somewhat like Glenn Miller's, always with spirit but seldom with finesse. By 1942 Reynolds, a pleasant, dedicated man, had toned down his band and himself. New arrangements began to lend distinction to his music. So did a good tenor saxist, Serge Chaloff, described by critic Barry Ulanov as "a tenor man with a good tone and unremarkable ideas," who a couple of years later made musical history as baritone saxist with

Woody Herman's Herd. In later years, Reynolds received recognition of a different sort; he became one of the most respected producers of musical radio shows, first in the New York area and then in Los Angeles. And they weren't all loud ones, either.

DICK STABILE, a handsome, smiling, gentle sort of Lothario, was featured saxist with Ben Bernie's band before he organized his own in 1936. Built around its leader's horn, it was a joy to those who admired his amazing technique, an embarrassment to those who didn't like to tell this nice guy that he had no business trying to play jazz. The band supplied much musical color via a reed sextet ranging from clarinet to bass sax, highlighted, sometimes with overpowering effect, by its maestro's horn. By the early forties Dick had discarded some of his more blatant blowing, applying his prodigious technique to lovely shadings rather than racy runs. He had in the meantime taken himself a beautiful wife, Gracie Barrie, whose visual charm and vocal talents added musical and commercial appeal to a band that had developed into one of the most attractive outfits on the scene. After the end of the era, Stabile, a well-schooled musician, divided his time between conducting for Dean Martin and Jerry Lewis and leading his dance band at the Roosevelt Hotel in New Orleans, where he died in 1980 following a sudden heart attack.

CHARLIE VENTURA, whose booting tenor sax had been a spark plug in Gene Krupa's band, left the drummer and for a while in 1946 tried his hand at bandleading. It was a brave gesture that failed. Ventura, a serious, straight-forward gent, attracted some of the country's top young talent. Neal Hefti arranged and played trumpet. Tony Scott was on clarinet; Margie Hyams played vibes and wrote additional scores. Other contributors to a well-stocked library included George Williams and Justin Stone. The band was a colorful one, with Ventura featured on soprano and alto sax, in addition to his tenor. It recorded a few sides for National which revealed little of the band's attractions, played several dates, mostly in the East, but never really got off the ground. Charlie returned to Krupa for a while, then settled in Springfield, Massachusetts, where he led a swinging quartet.

JERRY WALD sounded like Artie Shaw, a comparison that Jerry often resented and about which Artie couldn't have cared less. Shaw had always been Wald's idol, and this showed clearly not merely in the sound of Jerry's clarinet, but in that of the whole band. It wasn't a bad sound by any means, but everywhere Wald went there'd be some-

Jerry Wald with saxist Bobby Dukoff, guitarist Art Ryerson, bassist Sid Weiss

one accusing him of copying Shaw. It annoyed Jerry, which may be why he glowered more than most leaders. But he just couldn't hide the obvious, either aurally or visually, in a band stocked with such illustrious Shaw graduates as lead saxist Les Robinson, jazz trumpeter Bernie Privin, bassist Sid Weiss, singer Anita Boyer and arrangers Ray Coniff and Jerry Gray. Wald's outfit also spotted some other fine musicians: saxists Larry Elgart and Bobby Dukoff, trombonist Ray Sims, guitarists Billy Bauer and later Artie Ryerson. With such talent, the band was bound to sound good and it often did. But distinctive, seldom.

The Piano-playing Leaders

THE WIDEST variety of bands stylistically were those led by pianists. Some featured jazz; others concentrated on society-type music. Some were fronted by great musicians; others by attractive personalities. Some concentrated on arrangements; others just played simple chorus after chorus of medleys of tunes. Few of the leaders could offer as much emotional impact as a horn player or singer who stood in front of his band and established direct contact with his audiences. Yet most of them, because they had studied piano rather than a simpler instrument, were well versed in music.

CHARLIE BAUM was a much sought-after studio pianist before he started his own band late in 1937. He himself was exceedingly impressive. "Baum's playing produces the kind of thrill that never wears off," I noted in my review, "because he's pulling such interesting stuff so quickly that you're still trying to find out what happened by the time the next bit of musical astonishment greets you." Otherwise, the band amounted to little, however, chiefly because it wasn't content with playing straight dance music but tried, instead, to play swing arrangements. "Once they try to play hot," the same review pointed out, "they're really awful."

NAT BRANDWYNNE, the "other" and more musically impressive pianist in the two-piano team that Leo Reisman had featured so successfully in the early thirties, never achieved the popular acclaim of his handsome, flashier former partner, Eddy Duchin. After Eddy left to start his band, Nat followed suit, fronting a pleasing outfit that featured his lovely, light and tasteful piano. An especially pleasant and articulate gent, with an eager face, brightened all the more by a receding hair line, Nat became very popular in the "smart set" circle in which he moved, while still retaining the respect and admiration of his fellow musicians. He died in 1978 of a heart attack.

LOU BRING was an attractive, facile pianist who had played with Vincent Lopez before he formed his own group in the mid-thirties. His was one of the better society type bands, primarily because of Lou's own playing and the singing of an attractive lass named Frances Hunt, who left the band for a short period to work with Benny Goodman, only to return to Bring and eventually to marry him.

CARMEN CAVALLARO was, so far as I was concerned, the best of all the flashy, society-music pianists. He had an extraordinary technique and touch, great dynamic control and, surprisingly, more than a slight feeling for jazz. I first heard him in 1935 with Al Kavelin's band (he was then simply billed as "Carmen") and gave him a rave review. After he left Kavelin, he led a small and unimpressive group for a while; then, as his fame and fortune grew, he blossomed out with an attractive fourteen-piece outfit that spotted a very good singer, Larry Douglas, who later became a successful musical-comedy and nightclub performer. In repose, Carmen had a face like a sad clown (without makeup, of course), but as soon as he started playing, his whole expression changed and he became the dynamic personality

Carmen

showman. Since the big band days, Cavallaro has enjoyed a very successful, semi-pop concert career.

JACK FINA, a handsome man, left Freddy Martin's band after he had starred on the "Tonight We Love" record hit, looking for success as a piano-playing leader. But at the beginning, success wasn't on his side, because Fina couldn't resolve a personal problem. Eventually, however, after an absence from the musical scene, Jack returned to lead a good, musicianly group that for a while featured an excellent singer named Harry Prime, and which played on the west coast until Fina's death in May of 1970.

JOHNNY GREEN, best known for his songs—"Body and Soul," "I Cover the Waterfront," "I'm Yours," "Out of Nowhere," "Coquette" and many other musical melodies, including his and my favorite, "Hello, My Lover, Goodbye"—led a good, hotel-room type band in the mid-thirties. Replete with interesting sounds from a reed section that included flutes, oboes and English horns, it featured both the expert piano and the enthusiastic charm of Green himself. But the band was short-lived.

Johnny soon went to Hollywood, pursuing a highly successful career first as a writer, then as a musical director and conductor (he appeared for several years on many of the Oscar telecasts). Most recently Green has evinced a preference for more serious music and, to emphasize the change, now makes it clear that professionally he prefers to be known not as *Johnny* but as *John* Green.

SKITCH (LYLE) HENDERSON may never have led his own dance orchestra if he hadn't been talking with his friend Bing Crosby one night in the Stork Club when Jimmy McCabe, head of the Pennsylvania Hotel, happened to pass their table. According to Skitch, "Bing said to Jimmy that he ought to put my band into the Café Rouge." McCabe liked the idea, so Skitch, who didn't have a set band, put one together, played three one-nighters, "in Mahoney City, Pennsylvania, some college date and Old Orchard Beach, Maine, and then we opened." The band, presided over by pixieish, talented Skitch at the piano, was a musical one, featuring two French horns, in addition to the usual sax, brass and rhythm section, and a superb singer named Nancy Read. It lasted about two years. "I didn't realize then that I was starting *after* the big band era had ended. By 1949 the business was pretty bad and, after a disastrous trip through blizzards in Michigan, I got a call one night in the Blue Flame Café in Lexington, Kentucky, from Frank Sinatra. He'd gotten wind that we weren't doing too well, and so he offered me my old job back as his musical director." That ended the Skitch Henderson band. "It also saved my musical life," he has noted. Later he achieved national fame as leader of the orchestra on the "Tonight" TV show, then went on to conduct various symphonies.

CLAUDE HOPKINS, a graduate of Howard University, had become well established by the time the big band boom began. His band played a very light, dainty, harnessed kind of swing, highlighted by the solos of Hopkins, a gentle, watery-eyed pianist, clarinetist Ed Hall, trumpeter Jabbo Smith and trombonist Vic Dickenson. The band also featured two popular vocalists, Orlando Robeson, who had a high, thin, yet attractive tenor voice, best known for his version of "Trees," and Ovie Alston, a trumpeter,

Claude

whose breathy, singing style huffed and puffed attractively through up-tempoed tunes, like Claude's theme song, "I Would Do Anything for You." In the seventies, Hopkins was still performing delightfully as a solo pianist.

HENRY KING, a thoroughly accomplished pianist, seldom played anywhere except in the poshest hotel rooms, which were well suited to his set style. During the mid-thirties his was considered among the best of the society bands, but it never seemed to appeal to other than those for whom the automated businessman's bounce was the answer to all dance music needs.

VINCENT LOPEZ had made a name for himself long before the Big Band Era ever got under way. Starting in the early twenties, he led an outfit that invariably focused on his piano, with a sharp pinspot on his fleet, facile, corny interpretation of "Nola." Lopez, who often seemed more interested in astrology and numerology than in music, did a reasonably good job of keeping up with the times, for the band he fronted in the late thirties and early forties produced fairly up-to-date if never distinguished or inventive music. He will perhaps be best remembered for "Nola," for having discovered Betty Hutton and for his seemingly thousands of broadcasts from the Grill

Room of the Hotel Taft, where he played year after year. Working for Lopez was always considered one of the most attractive jobs in New York, not because the music was so great, not because he was a particularly sympathetic or brilliant leader, but because of the 9 P.M. closing time (there were also afternoon sessions), which permitted the musicians to hear how the rest of the big band world lived. Thus Lopez was able to hire some of the town's best men. Had he featured better arrangements, he might have been more successful. Lopez died in September, 1975, after a stroke.

JAY McSHANN came out of Kansas City, a direct descendant in the big band lineage from Count Basie. Heralded by the public in the early forties for his commercial boogie-woogie solos, he soon proved himself to be something much more—a fine, updated, swinging pianist. His band, too, had a great deal to offer: a whole night's barrage of romping, riff-filled arrangements, blown with enthusiasm by the entire ensemble, and interspersed occasionally by the advanced solos of a young alto saxist who often confused some of us simply because we were not yet ready for Charlie Parker. In addition to Parker, the band introduced sev-

"Lopez speaking, Hutton mugging"

eral other embryonic jazz stars, bassist Gene Ramey, drummer Gus Johnson and tenor saxist Paul Quinichette, as well as the inspired blues-shouting of Walter Brown.

PANCHO led one of the very best of the half-Latin, half-society bands that played in the country's swankier hotel rooms. He made a volatile appearance as he attacked the piano with great gusto and managed, despite such showmanlike tactics, to produce on occasions better than average dance music.

JOE REICHMAN was one of the most exuberant of the piano-playing leaders. Always ready with a smile and quip, he portrayed the typical society-music piano player. He'd roam all over the keys, and when I reviewed the band in the mid-thirties, he even had a second pianist trying to outroam him. It was pretty awful. But Joe sold hard and he sold well, and though he never achieved much recognition for his musical efforts, he made a lot of hotel room managers and businessmen happy—not to mention the gals, who loved his thin mustache and handsome leer.

FREDDY SLACK had something big going for him when he left the Will Bradley band in 1941. He had been featured there on a batch of boogie-woogie big band arrangements, and the world seemed ready for him and his band. But Freddy, who was an excellent pianist in more than the limited b.w. vein (he had been featured with Jimmy Dorsey for several years), never seemed to take his career as a leader seriously enough. He did make a few sides with his vocalist, Ella Mae Morse, for Capitol, most successful of which was "Cow Cow Boogie," and he did lead a band, mostly on the West Coast, throughout the early forties. But Slack, a pleasant, vague man muddled along in a boogie-woogie rut almost until his death in August, 1965. A clue to his apparent lack of ' enthusiasm for a commercial career: "You might not believe it," he said in 1941, "but writing boogie woogie doesn't give me near the thrill that writing sweet stuff does." Apparently, Freddy, who made frequent attempts to reestablish himself, just kept barking up the wrong piano bench.

TED STRAETER was a warm, friendly, sensitive man who delighted New York's smarter supper set with his breezy, musical treatment of show tunes, always played at danceable tempos. He played piano with refreshing verve and he sang in a breathy style, sounding like a confident Skinnay Ennis. Today his theme song, "The Most Beautiful Girl in the World," is as closely associated with the late Ted Straeter as it is with its composers, Richard Rodgers and Lorenz Hart.

TEDDY WILSON led a fine band for a short time—much too short a time. A delicately swinging pianist, he organized his outfit shortly after he left Benny Goodman, who had called him "the greatest musician in dance music today, irrespective of instrument." The band featured some of the top musicians of the times: Ben Webster and Rudy Powell on saxes, Doc Cheatham and Hal Baker on trumpets, Al Casey on guitar, Al Hall on bass and J. C. Heard on bass, with vocals by Thelma Carpenter. Its style was very polite—like Teddy himself. But "polite" black bands were difficult to sell in those days: "Everybody kept saying we sounded too white," recalls bassist Hall. But for those of us who heard the band downtown at the Famous Door on Fifty-second Street or uptown at the Golden Gate Ballroom, it offered some delightful listening.

Teddy

especially when it featured Teddy's superb piano playing. During its one year of existence it recorded twenty sides, including a beautiful version of "The Man I Love" which featured a Webster tenor chorus that is still considered a classic, and a lovely theme, "Little Things That Mean So Much," composed by Wilson, who also wrote many of the band's arrangements. Perhaps the band remained too polite; perhaps it needed more flash to attract a public that associated excitement with black bands. In any event, Teddy gave up the band in 1940, formed a sextet and thereafter remained associated with small groups, all of them filled with the sort of musical good taste and distinction that typified Teddy Wilson himself. He also devoted himself to teaching and nurturing a son, Ted, a first-rate drummer, as well as appearing in clubs as a soloist and occasionally rejoining the Goodman Quartet.

BOB ZURKE, like Freddy Slack and Teddy Wilson, also gave up his job as a pianist in a name band to take on the role of a leader. His alma mater was Bob Crosby's outfit, to which he had contributed some intense yet high-swinging solos. By 1939 Zurke, a squat, mustachioed man in his late twenties, whose undisciplined way of living undoubtedly was one of the causes for his looking at least ten years older than he really was, had become so popular with big band fans that he decided to see what he could do on his own. The results were disappointing. His band—several of its members were discarded veterans from other outfits—had little to offer, and Bob's playing, often trying to make amends for an inferior rhythm section, suffered. Within a few years he let his men go and settled down on the West Coast, where he worked with a small unit until death overtook him at thirty-three.

The Violin-playing
Leaders

PLAYING a fiddle didn't create an especially exciting sight or sound for a leader during an era that heaped greater glories on brass and reed players. Nevertheless, some maestri managed to do quite well with their violins tucked either under their chin or under their arm.

MITCHELL AYRES and "His Fashions in Music," one of the more musical hotel-room-music bands, usually sounded larger than it actually was, thanks to good arrangements. Composed of refugees from Little Jack Little's orchestra, this was a cooperative unit, which elected Ayres, a pleasant, powerfully built violinist, as president. It was a homey-looking group—some looked like assistant zoology instructors, others like successful milliners, some like musicians—which evinced a good deal of team spirit among its principals: Ayres; "Goldy" Goldmark, his chief lieutenant, who began as a violinist and developed into a mediocre bass player; "Count" Ludwig Flato, a very good pianist; tenor saxist Phil Zolkind, who played good jazz, and the band's most distinguished and distinguishable musician, lead saxist Harry Terrill, whose lush lead alto was predominantly (often too much so) displayed. The band also featured two better-than-average singers, Maryann Mercer and Tommy Taylor, as well as Meredith Blake. It specialized in some fairly good swing versions of the classics, plus numerous other novelties, like glee club effects, that never quite came off. Throughout its career the group was plagued by weak rhythm sections, so that even though it tried to swing, it never really did. After the band disbanded in the mid-forties, Ayres, a very good conductor, took over as musical director of the Perry Como show and Columbia Records, the start of a highly successful

career, cut too short when he was killed by a car in Las Vegas, Nevada, in August, 1969.

EMERY DEUTSCH may have been putting everyone on. Nobody really ever knew. He played the saddest, most unctious fiddle in the world, every musical strain and facial grimace a reflection of his theme song, "When a Gypsy Makes His Violin Cry." The cry and the violin were there, all right, but Deutsch was much too hip and suave to qualify as anything even remotely resembling a gypsy. Obviously, he knew where the loot was, and when he gained a large following through his CBS broadcasts, he went out to dispense his weeping wails in person. "Sway and Loitch with Emery Deutsch," suggested one wag, and press agent and band commentator Gary Stevens wrote: "Emery used to soak his violin bow in chicken fat." But the fat and the tears attracted the customers, and Deutsch did very well for himself for several years.

AL DONAHUE began his career as a society band leader, landed a coveted and very successful engagement in the Rainbow Room, where he featured a young singer named Phil Brito, and then, in 1940, suddenly decided he'd rather lead a swing band. Two years earlier the U.S. Bureau of Standards had sunk a capsule, tested to last five thousand years, into the ground. Inside were memorabilia of the year 1938, including a photo of a swing band leader who up till then had never swung in his life: Al Donahue. Conceivably encouraged, embarrassed or perhaps conscious-stricken, Al, a mild-mannered, unassuming graduate of Boston University Law School, revamped his band. Soon it did swing. It featured some good jazz musicians plus a very pretty, talented young singer named Paula Kelly. "I'm getting the greatest kicks since I've been connected with the music business," announced Donahue, who had packed his fiddle into its case and joined the swing parade. It would be nice to be able to relate that his new band was a big hit, but it wasn't. Still, Al had tried hard to achieve the stature that a thoroughly unhip government agency had accorded him.

ENOCH LIGHT explained his musical philosophy twenty-five years ago when, in describing his new band, he noted that "there are no tricks, just straight dance music, arranged as tastefully as we know how but without a lot of unnecessary embellishments." An embryonic concert violinist, he had just reorganized his Light Brigade after a lengthy recuperation from a shattering automobile accident that had interrupted his already well-established career. A well-spoken, deep-thinking Johns Hopkins graduate, Enoch had played the European circuit before the Big Band Era had begun. Concentrating thereafter on New York and its environs, he fronted several different hotel-type bands, none of them ever especially scintillating but each well rehearsed and well routined. From time to time he featured such diverse attractions as Lazy Bill Huggins, a homey singer, Peggy Mann, a very musical one, Ted Nash, a good jazz

tenor saxist, and three girl fiddlers—all heard during his hundreds of broadcasts from the Grill Room of New York's Hotel Taft. Light did all right then. But many years later he did sensationally well—as head of the immensely successful Command and Project Three record labels before his death on July 31, 1978.

ENRIC MADRIGUERA, a well-schooled, effervescent musician, led a series of slick hotel-room orchestras that played good typical society music and sparkled on its well-orchestrated Latin melodies. It employed colorful reed doubles and over the years featured a variety of impressive vocalists: the exciting Helen Ward (before she joined Goodman), an attractive debutante, Adelaide Moffett, the Mullens Sisters, Tony Sacco, Manuel Fernandez, and a very pretty girl, Patricia Gilmore, who left NBC to sing with Madriguera's band and eventually to marry its leader.

JOE VENUTI was one of the truly great jazz violinists of all times—perhaps the greatest. He was also a phenomenal screwball whose wild antics have become legendary among musicians. But the leader of a great band he was not. Why? Possibly because Joe, an immensely lovable, volatile man, never disciplined himself or his musicians enough. His band sounded spirited but sloppy, playing a few good arrangements and many that were merely adequate. During the early forties it featured a vibrant, jazz-tinged young girl singer, Kay Starr, and a colorful speed demon of a drummer, Barrett Deems, who seldom laid down a solid beat. But most of all it featured Venuti himself, a magnificent musician, whose great talents had been more effectively displayed on a batch of great jazz sides he'd made in the early thirties with guitarist Eddie Lang. For many years after the end of the big band era, Venuti dissolved into semi-obscurity. But then in the 1970s, he emerged from the State of Washington, where he had been living, to be "discovered" by young jazz fans and welcomed back by those who had never forgotten his magnificent talent. He played in concerts and made a slew of recordings, including some with younger jazz violinists who also gasped in wonderment at his stupendous playing. He died back in Washington on August 14, 1978.

Venuti: lovable, volatile screwball

The Singing Leaders

SURPRISINGLY few singers led successful outfits during the Big Band Era. Why? Perhaps because the emphasis during those dozen years was upon instrumentalists and a singer didn't fit into the image that the general public had of a leader. Star vocalists like Sinatra and Como and Haymes and Bob Eberly must have realized this, for none, despite their popularity, even tried for a career as a maestro. Perhaps this was because, even though almost every big band needed a singer in order to be successful, no big singer really needed a band. Nevertheless, there were several singing leaders, including a few big band graduates, who did fairly well for themselves.

BOB ALLEN, who played second singer to Skinnay Ennis in Hal Kemp's band, had a deep, rich, romantic-sounding voice that he used in a lazy, scooping way. After Kemp died, Bob, a handsome lad, took over Vince Patti's Cleveland band. It featured some of Kemp's mellow clarinet sounds in addition to deeper voicings that used a bass sax, some excellent arrangements by Hal Mooney, Randy Brooks's brilliant lead trumpet and, naturally, Allen's voice. With Kemp he had seemed shy and reserved. In front of his own band he was much more dynamic, waving his baton enthusiastically and beaming at the dancers—many of them young girls overcome by Allen's good looks —and acting like the old personality kid. He succeeded in doing all this without sacrificing his basic talent: an excellent voice which he used intelligently and tastefully. His band, though, never became very successful, and so later Bob took up woodworking, settled down in Encino, California, and at last reports was turning out some excellent objects.

ZINN ARTHUR, leader of "the other band" that played opposite most of the big names in New York's Roseland, had an unusually warm, good baritone voice, a gorgeous theme song, "Darling," which he wrote and sang, and one of the biggest-sounding small bands in the country. It featured a raft of excellent arrangements, the lovely alto sax of Alvin Weisfeld (later known as Alvy West, leader of a good little recording band) and Arthur's singing. An extremely well organized gent with the mind of an accountant but the soul of an artist, he was just beginning to impress nationally when he was called up as one of the first Army draftees. He became an important part of Irving Berlin's "This Is the Army" show. After the war, he developed into a successful photographer, then took over as administrative assistant to producer Joshua Logan. A man of taste and intelligence, Arthur owned a prominent Long Island restaurant before settling down in Florida.

SEGER ELLIS, an attractive man with a ready smile and a musical style (he recorded many vocals with all-star instrumental groups in the early thirties) and a happy, swinging approach to piano playing which covered the full keyboard, led his Choir of Brass band during the mid-thirties. It used no saxes; just brass horns and rhythm, plus Seger's vocals and those of his wife, Irene Taylor, an equally impressive singer who had replaced Mildred Bailey in Paul Whiteman's orchestra. The interesting and unique Choir of Brass idea never caught on commercially, however, so Ellis eventually settled for a smaller but still musicianly group, which toured the country until Seger finally settled down in Texas.

SKINNAY ENNIS, who always sounded as if he didn't have enough breath in him to sustain his alarmingly slim body, let alone more than two successive notes, started his own band after he had left Hal Kemp's, in which he had made a national reputation.

Skinnay

Focusing on his singing, some fine arrangements by Claude Thornhill and Gil Evans, and using his version of "Got a Date with an Angel" for its theme song, the band settled on the West Coast, where it found a conspicuous resting place on Bob Hope's radio series, on which Ennis performed both as conductor and stooge. Skinnay was a quiet, slow-moving, gentle, thoroughly likable gent who in June, 1963 met a violent death —while dining in a Beverly Hills restaurant some food lodged in his throat and he choked to death.

EDDY HOWARD, a pleasant, relaxed, natural singer with the looks of a clerk in a country store, became so popular in Dick Jurgens' band that he decided to go out on his own. His vocal manner was soft and intimate and often more musical than he was given credit for. He made several Columbia recordings with jazz musicians,

Eddy, Teddy Wilson,
John Hammond (front)

including the great guitarist Charlie Christian, then started touring with a compact but rather good sweet band. His stock shot upward after he recorded "To Each His Own," which became a smash hit and helped him sustain through several successful years before he died in 1963. I liked his singing tremendously, for which I was labeled square by some colleagues.

ART JARRETT took over the Hal Kemp band in the spring of 1941, several months after Kemp had been killed in an auto crash. (The real, working leader of the band was Porky Dankers, who had played sax for Kemp for many years.) Jarrett, a likable dreamer with a tenor voice that really didn't fit the band's style, made a good front man, charming the customers. But the real excitement of the band, which continued to feature Kemp's unique style, was generated by the brilliant trumpeting of Randy Brooks and the good looks of Gale Robbins. The valiant attempt to carry on without Kemp was in vain, however, and after engagements in some of the country's better spots, the band faded from the scene.

LITTLE JACK LITTLE sang in a very personal now-I'm-singing, now-I'm-talking manner that had made him a radio favorite before the big band days. During the mid-thirties he led a pretty good band whose fiddle player, Mitchell Agress, became Mitch Ayres when he and several other men left Little to form their own co-op group. During the late thirties Little Jack formed another outfit, which featured bolero tempos but wasn't nearly as popular as Jack had been on radio as a full-time singer and part-time pianist.

FRANKIE MASTERS was one of the most amiable of the big band leaders. During the late thirties he began making some commercial sounds with his "Bell Tone Music," a trick device which consisted of staggered chords. He sang in a pleasant if somewhat thin voice, and he also spotted a good girl singer named Marion Francis. Later Frankie went in for straighter, more musicianly, thoroughly danceable but never especially identifiable music. He featured a new girl singer, a very pretty one named Phyllis Miles, whom he later married, a good tenor, Lou Hurst, and his own easygoing personality, which won him a host of friends if never very many overly zealous big band enthusiasts.

LEIGHTON NOBLE took over some of the remnants of Orville Knapp's band when some of its members grew dissatisfied with George Olsen who had assumed leadership of the band after Knapp's death. Noble, a very handsome man with a pleasant voice, and Chick Floyd, a talented arranger and pianist, formed a partnership, using many of the Knapp band's stylistic tricks, such as its exaggerated brass dynamics and the unison saxes. They also featured the same pretty vocalist, Edith Caldwell, and Floyd's playing of an electronic instrument called a novachord, which could sound pretty awful but which Floyd managed to play quite well. Essentially a sweet band, the Noble outfit appeared mostly in the smarter rooms, satisfying the customers with its danceable music and dignified presence.

WILL OSBORNE was one of the most delightful leaders I ever knew. Before the Big Band Era, he had waged numerous pitched battles with Rudy Vallee for top spot in what we used to call the Single Nostril School of Crooning. I doubt, though, that Will ever took these battles seriously: his sense of humor was too sharp, his attitude toward life too relaxed for that. He actually loved jazz and headed a good swing band in the early thirties. In 1935 he formed a stylized outfit that featured rich, deep-toned brass, emphasizing, of all things, slide trumpets plus glissing trombones blown through megaphones. Several years later he came up with a less formal outfit, one that featured a kooky singer named Dick (Stinky) Rogers. Several years after that Will fronted still another group, this one spotting a gorgeous girl vocalist named simply Marianne. Whenever I saw Osborne, he always seemed to be enjoying his work, often poking light fun at other bands and even at himself. His singing style changed little; it remained intimate and pleasant and to me warmer than Vallee's. But for reasons best known to Will he featured it sparingly, preferring to spotlight others, including some excellent musicians who filled the ranks of his various groups.

CARL RAVAZZA was best known for his theme song, a pretty ballad called "Vieni Su," which he sang with the same sort of tearoom charm that pervaded his orchestra. Much of Ravazza's success—he was a friendly, smiling fellow who looked just like the guy every girl's mother would want her daughter to marry (only the daughter would think he's just *too* nice)—came during engagements on the West Coast, where the band had originally been organized by Tom Coakley, a lawyer who returned to his practice and later became a prominent judge in California. The band did play in New York during a period when Carl had changed his last name to Ravell. Like several other West Coast sweet bands, it looked better than it sounded, producing relaxed, hotel-room music with much spirit and little finesse.

ORRIN TUCKER was a pleasant singer whose band was doing well enough until his girl vocalist, Bonnie Baker (nee Evelyn Nelson of Orange, Texas), happened to latch onto an old World War I tune called "Oh, Johnny, Oh." To it she added her own coy enunciations of such provocative words as "Oh!" and "Uh-uh!" and a few extra sighs,

*Orrin Tucker with Wee
Bonnie Baker cutting a
fifth anniversary cake
(1941)*

and all of a sudden Orrin had himself a hit record and one of the hottest bands in the land. This all happened late in 1939. For several years thereafter the Tucker band rode along on the crest of Bonnie and Johnny's waves. But unlike some other leaders who had been catapulted to prominence by a single record, Tucker, friendly and intelligent—he had studied to be a doctor—maintained his equilibrium. He knew he had a good, if not sensational orchestra that was at its best playing for middle-aged dancers, and that is just what he kept on doing. After Bonnie left, Orrin took on some even better vocalists: first Scottee Marsh and then, several years later, when he had his best band of all with seven brass, including a French horn, an especially musical singer named Helen Lee. Orrin knew his music, his public and his own limitations, and so, a generation after most of the big bands had faded away, he was still around, still playing his pleasant music in some of the country's smarter spots.

The Mickey-Mouse Bands

MICKEY-MOUSE bands had their place on the big band scene—most often in the Midwest, where for some reason that may be related to the section's inherent conservatism, bands that phrased in an old-fashioned way and blazed few new trails found ready acceptance. Most of these bands were led not by first-rate musicians (few could stomach those sounds!) but by businessmen, many of whom were top-flight executives who knew how to keep their mechanical men operating at maximum efficiency.

BLUE BARRON made out so well booking bands in and around Cleveland that he formed his own band (and changed his name from Harry Friedland). Having been associated primarily with numerous mickey-mouse bands that infested the Midwest, he had little difficulty assembling one that sounded like a mixture of Sammy Kaye, with whom he had worked closely, Kay Kyser, Guy Lombardo, Jan Garber and Horace Heidt, and soon posed a serious threat for the Master Mouse title. He had the style down pat, as I noted in a February, 1938, *Metronome* review of the band: "obnoxious over-phrasing, saxes with whining vibratos, trumpets that growl and rat-a-tat and slur into harsh, irritating mutes, a trombone that glisses all over creation, all sorts of over-slurring, an electric guitar, a rhythm section that puts most of its emphasis upon a tuba burping on the first and third beat, singing of song titles, attempted glee club effects, and all similar, musical tricks that associate corn with commercialism and commercialism with corn." Rough at first, the band gradually assumed a slick sheen. Russ Carlyle was its featured singer for years; later two even better singers, Clyde Burke and Jimmy Brown, a Sammy Kaye graduate, moved in. Barron, a short pudgy, effervescent man, had what some of the other mickey-mouse leaders didn't have: a sense of humor about himself and his music. He didn't take either too seriously, nor did he try doggedly to defend his music; in fact, if there weren't any fans within hearing distance, he'd kid about the sounds he was making. More than most leaders of such bands Blue Barron was at least a musical realist.

DEL COURTNEY, an affable gent, led a band that was part mickey and part society. Its style was complete unobtrusive, with the saxes subdued, the rhythm section almost nonexistent. It offended no one, except perhaps musicians. "After listening to it for a full evening," I noted in a 1939 review, "you may get a bit weak and commence yearning for something more substantial—like a ham sandwich." Such reviews notwithstanding, Courtney, who'd started his band in the Far West, continued for many years to play many of the top spots, especially around Chicago, and, in fact, outlasted many a more vital band.

CHUCK FOSTER, a tall, quiet, blond, country-type of fellow, made an impressive appearance as a bandleader, even though his band seldom played very good music. Its sound was indistinguishable from that of other bands of its ilk, but Foster, whose real name was Chuck Fody, found a following for his "Music in the Foster Fashion," first on the West Coast and later throughout the midwest area.

JAN GARBER, "The Idol of the Air Lanes," was the Dr. Jekyll and Mr. Hyde of bandleaders. In the early twenties his band swung as well as many others of the era and recorded some exciting sides for Columbia and RCA Victor. Then, in the late twenties, when the Lombardo boom exploded, Garber, a short, intense man with the flamboyancy of a, carnival conductor, took over another Canadian orchestra, Freddy Large's, which had already assimilated the Lombardo sound. Jan's new group succeeded handsomely, thanks in part to a fine baritone named Lee Bennett, but mostly to Jan's good timing and business sense. It played all over the country and appeared on the Burns and Allen radio series. Then, in 1942, Garber pulled a complete switch and reverted to his swinging ways. He junked the mice, engaged Gray Rains to write some fine arrangements, Liz Tilton, Martha's talented and pretty kid sister, to sing them, and a bunch of young musicians to play them. The results were musically rewarding, commercially indecisive. So, after the war, Jan returned to his more simpering style. When the band era had ended, he continued to appear, centering his activities for a time on the West Coast and in Las Vegas. He became a wealthy man, thanks in part to real estate holdings in Louisiana, and he remained semi-active there until some time before his death in Shreveport on October 5, 1977.

GRAY GORDON is best remembered for his "Tic-Toc Music," consisting of several Kaye-Lombardo-type slick tricks accentuated by a montonous beating of two temple blocks to reassure listeners that they weren't listening to Sammy, Guy or any of the other mice. The band wasn't consistently annoying; sometimes the men, many of them good legitimate musicians, even swung a bit. The total effect, according to my 1939 review, was like "a juicy steak over which you've just poured a quart of maple syrup." Gray, a sensible, sensitive man, admitted with obvious embarrassment that his tricks weren't musical. He had

known purer musical days: many years earlier he had played hot clarinet and sax and had fronted Elmo Mack's Purple Derby Band, which also featured jazz stars like pianist Joe Sullivan and drummer George Wettling. Apparently Gordon couldn't stomach his new sounds indefinitely. In 1943 he chucked his tic-toc tactics and formed a pretty good, swinging outfit, which didn't do much for his bank account but did revive his self-respect. Later Gray turned to personal management and was guiding the careers of Les Paul and Mary Ford in New York when he succumbed to cancer in July of 1976.

EVERETT HOAGLAND was once a jazz clarinetist who led a swinging band that featured arrangements by its pianist, Stan Kenton. Then Hoagland became head of RKO Pictures' arranging department and in the late thirties met George Mayes, one of the backbones of the recent Orville Knapp band. Together they worked on plans for a stylized group, receiving vigorous support from MCA, and began playing not the ballrooms that had once featured Hoagland's swinging sounds, but some of the plusher hotel rooms. In my review of the Hoagland band during its early 1940 engagement in the Empire Room of the Waldorf-Astoria I described it as "the most danceable and least boring of music's mickey mice." Its leader's knowledge and appreciation of good music apparently could not be completely suppressed, so that whatever the band did, it did well. Few other mickey-mice bands could make the same claim.

ART KASSEL, a friendly, hand-shaking maestro, built his "Kassels in the Air" around Chicago, and years before he adopted his mickey-mouse ways, had featured a young local clarinetist named Benny Goodman. Kassel's sweet band appeared at the Bismark Hotel for years. It also frequently played in Chicago's Aragon Ballroom, from which I caught a broadcast in the summer of 1942. I wrote: "Intonation must mean nothing to these boys. On the show it was a toss-up which were more out of tune, the trumpets, the trombones or the saxes. But then along came the clarinets. They won." Kassel's musicians may not have been as impressive as Goodman and some of Art's earlier sidemen, but he did have some above-average singers in Gloria

Art Kassel

The ambivalent Mr. Garber

Orville Knapp

Hart, Harvey Crawford and Jimmy Featherstone. And he also had a very loyal following.

ORVILLE KNAPP led a band for less than three years, but in that short time it made a tremendous impression. Knapp, the bright, handsome, boyish-looking brother of movie star Evelyn Knapp, formed his band in 1934 for a short engagement at the swank Beverly-Wilshire Hotel. It was a smash and stayed for two years, then migrated east. I heard it at the Waldorf-Astoria and found it to be an especially attractive-looking and colorful-sounding group. It used many mickey-mouse effects, including exaggerated vibratos, featured an electric guitar and an organ and jolted its listeners with sudden,

dramatic brass outbursts and subsequent sharp diminuendos. But it obviously did create the impression it was after, and it was getting a great deal of attention when on July 16, 1936, near Boston, Knapp was killed in the crash of an airplane he was piloting. Said Larry Barnett, the MCA executive who knew Knapp well, "He had great class. His would have been one of the big bands of the country." Veteran leader George Olsen took over the band after Knapp's death, but, added Barnett, "when Knapp died, his style died."

TOMMY TUCKER, a short, gentle man with a bright smile and a Phi Beta Kappa key, used to wave a long, thin baton with broad sweeping motions at an orchestra

Tommy Tucker with Amy Arnell

that produced most of the usual sweet staples plus several very good singers: Don Brown, a handsome lad with a great baritone voice and direct, musicianly phrasing seldom heard in a mickey-mouse band; Kerwin Sommerville, an enthusiastic, homey novelty singer; and an extremely pretty girl, Amy Arnell, who sang some songs better than others but projected a truly haunting quality with a vocal group that sang the band's lovely theme, "I Love You (Oh, How I Love You)." Tommy worked regularly and in good spots for many years, thanks in great part to an especially astute and dedicated manager, Joe Galkin. Then, in 1941, Tommy blazed when his record of "I Don't Want to Set the World on Fire"

became a smash hit. During most of the band's career it had suffered from emaciated-sounding arrangements, which invariably made the band seem smaller than it actually was. But in 1944, Tommy took on Van Alexander, Claude Hopkins and Fred Norman to write new arrangements, and suddenly what had been merely an adequate outfit blossomed into a highly impressive musical one. Unfortunately, Tucker had by this time become so identified with mickey-mouse music, that his fans didn't go along with the switch, and so he reverted to his rodent routine. Eventually he returned to academia as an assistant professor of fine arts at Monmouth College in New Jersey before settling permanently in Florida.

The Veterans

SOME of the pre-Big Band Era leaders had hung up their horns before the boom really got underway. Others hung around, and a few, because of their ability to keep up with the times and/or because of their commercial savvy, made out well for a number of years. Still others, unwilling or unable to adjust to the tastes of the newer generation, stuck tenaciously and unsuccessfully to their old styles and gradually faded from the scene. A few had left indelible marks, but more had made impressions that time and tastes could easily erase.

GUS ARNHEIM, a soft-spoken, deep-voiced gent, led the top West Coast band during the late twenties and early thirties. Ensconced in the Cocoanut Grove in Los Angeles, it was a hard-driving, well-rehearsed outfit that featured a raft of good singers, including Bing Crosby. In the mid-thirties, Arnheim's revamped and updated band scored a big hit at the Congress Casino in Chicago. Built along Goodman lines, it was sparked by a potent brass section and spotted some arrangements by its long, lean, lanky pianist, whom I complimented in a 1937 review for playing "not only good rhythmic piano, but interesting fill-in figurations as well." His name: Stanley Kenton.

BEN BERNIE, "The Ol' Maestro," fronted one of the top bands of the twenties and earlier thirties. His familiar "Yow-sah," his

"The Ol' Maestro"

warm, homey way of one-eighth singing and seven-eighths talking a lyric, and his two lovely theme songs, the opening "It's a Lonesome Old Town" and the closing "Au Revoir, Pleasant Dreams," highlighted his many broadcasts from the top spots in the country. His band, during its highly publicized stay in the Pabst Blue Ribbon Casino of the Chicago World's Fair, featured one of the best crooners of the times, Frank Prince, along with "Colonel" Manny Prager and Pat Kennedy and an outstanding saxophonist, Dick Stabile. Bernie was immensely well liked by everyone, including his musicians and Walter Winchell, with whom he carried on a synthetic but very rewarding radio "feud." During the late thirties he organized a more modern band with good arrangements by Gray Rains and some exciting trombone solos by his new discovery, Lou McGarity. Bernie's radio commercial featured another newcomer, a singer recently out of Nashville, Miss Dinah Shore. He tried very hard to keep her on the show, despite objections from a sponsor who claimed she didn't sing loud enough. "The Old Maestro" lost the battle. (Later Eddie Cantor hired Dinah for a series whose sponsor liked her, and thus it was he, rather than Bernie, who took credit for having discovered her.) Bernie, by then financially well off and extremely popular among the elite of the entertainment world, settled down in his Beverly Hills home, where he died in October of 1943.

DON BESTOR, best known as leader of the orchestra on Jack Benny's radio series —remember Benny's standard exit line, of "Play, Don, Play!"?—led one of the best bands of the twenties, the Benson Orchestra of Chicago. Its music was rhythmic, crisp and clean. During the Big Band Era he fronted a less impressive outfit. Its saxes at times sounded like Lombardo's; its rhythmic potency was nil. Occasionally it flashed some color via four flutes and an oboe, but too often its music sounded like Bestor looked—mild and pleasant and innocuous—more like an egghead chemistry teacher than a bandleader.

The COON-SANDERS ORCHESTRA, co-led by Carlton Coon and Joe Sanders, entertained not merely the dancers at the Muehlebach Hotel in Kansas but also radio listeners throughout the country who, during the late twenties and early thirties, could pull in the band's clean, straight-ahead, commercial music via a strong radio station, WDAF. The broadcasts created such a demand for the band that it soon went to the famous Blackhawk Restaurant in Chicago. There its numerous network air shots

"The Old Left-Hander"

attracted even more people. After Coon died, Sanders, billed as "The Old Left-Hander," took over the band. It became known simply as Joe Sanders and His Orchestra, continued to find some success, mainly in the Midwest, but didn't engender the excitement it had during the days when it sported a hyphen.

JEAN GOLDKETTE led a legendary, star-studded band that was long dead and gone by the time the Big Band Era began. But its music will never be forgotten by those who heard it during the mid-twenties, when it was recognized by musicans throughout the nation as one of the truly great bands of its day. Goldkette, originally a concert pianist who had been born in France, raised in Greece and educated in Russia, owned one of Detroit's top night spots, the Greystone Ballroom. Deciding that he'd like to have a band as good as Paul Whiteman's, which was then considered to be the best of them all, Goldkette, a studious-looking man with glasses, went right ahead and began organizing it. It turned out to be a

Top: *Don Murray, Howdy Quicksell, Frank Trumbauer*
Bottom: *Ray Lodwig, Irving Riskin, Spiegel Wilcox, Doc Ryker, Bill Rank,*
Chauncey Morehouse, Bix Beiderbecke, arranger Bill Challis,
Steve Brown, Fred Farrar—all Goldkette band members

magnificent outfit, full of spirit, musical kicks and such brilliant musicians as Bix Beiderbecke, Jimmy and Tommy Dorsey, Joe Venuti and Eddie Lang, Frankie Trumbauer, Pee Wee Russell, Russ Morgan, Don Murray and many others who migrated in and out of the band between 1924 and 1927. Its original base of operation was Detroit; later it appeared throughout the country, filling a memorable but farewell engagement in New York's Roseland in 1927, when the strain of high-priced and sometimes unmanageable prima-donna sidemen finally took its toll on Goldkette. When Whiteman offered some of the men jobs with his band and others took jobs in the New York studios, Goldkette gave up his magnificent group. He remained in the music business, however, leading units of varous sizes until as late as the mid-forties. But his days of real musical glory had ended on that last night at Roseland in 1927.

JIMMIE GRIER, who arranged for Gus Arnheim's band, followed his former leader in the early and mid-thirties as the steady attraction in the famed Cocoanut Grove of the Hotel Biltmore in Los Angeles. A good musician, who played clarinet and sax, Grier fronted a colorful and musical band that reflected his personality—relaxed, communicative but seldom very disciplined. It made a succession of good recordings that featured some excellent vocalists: Dick Webster, a very virile-sounding singer who later became a top Hollywood agent; Larry Cotton, a good tenor who went on to Horace Heidt's band; Donald Novis, who soon started a career of his own as one of the country's top pop tenors; Harry Barris, who had been one of the original Rhythm Boys

that included Bing Crosby, and Pinky Tomlin, who recorded his famous "The Object of My Affection" with Grier's band. Jimmy, a gregarious gent, liked music and people, liked to entertain, liked to live well, and seldom seemed to take either himself or his orchestra very seriously.

PHIL HARRIS was drummer and co-leader of the Lofner-Harris band on the West Coast, where it enjoyed great success during the late twenties and early thirties. Eventually Phil took over the band entirely, becoming a front man and dispensing his big grin as somebody else played drums. Harris, as gregarious in real life as he seemed to be when performing, obviously loved jazz. Proof: the swinging sounds he introduced into the Waldorf-Astoria in 1935 to patrons who weren't entirely appreciative. His singer at that time—a gorgeous girl named Leah Ray, who later married Sonny Werblin of New York Jets fame. Eventually, Phil settled on the West Coast radio studios, married movie actress Alice Faye, became conductor and chief foil for Jack Benny on his radio series and made numerous recordings, the most successful of which was "That's What I Like About the South."

TED LEWIS, "The High Hat Tragedian of Song," who died in 1971, was more famous as an entertainer than as a band leader. Still, his fame began when he fronted a band, one which at times had some good jazz musicians, like Muggsy Spanier and George Brunis, but had to withstand the impact of Lewis' hopelessly corny clarinet. His biggest success came from his glissful talking of lyrics, such as those of "When My

"Is Everybody Happy?"

Baby Smiles at Me" and "Me and My Shadow" and for the most persistent question ever sprung by any bandleader: "Is Everybody Happy?"

ABE LYMAN (né Simon) worked successfully in nightclubs, in hotel rooms and on records more than a decade before the big band boom began. He also appeared before and during the era on various radio series, the most successful of which was "Waltz Time," beamed at the older generation and conveniently sponsored by Philips' Milk of Magnesia. Lyman, a burly, loquacious extrovert who started out as a drummer, became especially good at selling himself and his band. Never an outstanding conductor (Jacques Renard and Victor Arden held the stick on his radio series), he was, however, excellent at organization and had a good sense of what the public wanted. As late as 1943 he put together a band of outstanding musicians—Si Zentner and Ray Heath on trombones, Billy Bauer on guitar, Marty Gold on violin, Wolffe Tannenbaum on sax, Bill Clifton on piano—which played adequate, if never startling, arrangements. Spotted also was Lyman's wife, Rose Blaine, who had been associated with him maritally and musically during many of the years in which Abe had established himself as a dominant, if never predominant, figure on the dance band scene.

McKINNEY'S COTTON PICKERS, one of the great swinging bands of the late twenties and early thirties, was originally a quartet out of Paducah, Kentucky, led by drummer William McKinney. It grew first into the "Sinco Septet," then into the ten-piece Cotton Pickers, and played at the Arcadia Ballroom in Detroit. Nearby, at the rival Greystone Ballroom, Fletcher Henderson's band was holding forth, with great arrangements by Don Redman. McKinney, a good businessman, wooed Redman for more than a year, won him and made him his band's musical director, and soon the Cotton Pickers, before then strictly a show band with all the funny-hat routines, were transformed into a splendidly disciplined, high-swinging crew. Redman drilled the men doggedly, until they had mastered his intricate yet always swinging scores, some of which, by the way, were copied from manuscript to score paper by two then-unknown local musicians, Glen Gray and Bob Zurke. The band featured several outstanding soloists—trumpeters Sidney DeParis and Joe Smith and saxists Prince Robinson, George Thomas and Redman. Thomas and Redman, along with Dave Wilborn, also sang, and sang well. The Cotton Pickers recorded for RCA Victor, coming up with two hits, "If I Could Be with You One Hour Tonight," inspired by Jimmy Rushing's singing of the tune at a party in Kansas City, and "Baby, Won't You Please Come Home?" both featuring great vocal solos by Thomas and arrangements by Redman. Don left the band in 1931, and though the Cotton Pickers lasted several more years, they never again achieved such musical heights.

BENNIE MOTEN led a hard-driving, swinging band that played mostly in Kansas City in the late twenties and from which were graduated several future jazz greats—William (Count) Basie, Jimmy Rushing, Ben Webster, "Hot Lips" Page and Walter Page. (The last replaced bassist Abe Bolar in 1927. Forty years later I rode in a New York taxi driven by the same Abe Bolar!) Moten's band may not have been heard by many big band fans, but certainly its influence (Basie's band was originally patterned after Moten's) was to be felt for many decades.

GEORGE OLSEN was an important bandleader in the twenties. His orchestra played in many of the country's major spots. It recorded regularly and successfully. It put on a great vaudeville show. And it featured the omni-present vocals of Fran Frey and one of the better girl singers, Ethel Shutta, who soon became Mrs. George Olsen. The band had spirit and color then but, unfortunately, didn't have them during the late thirties and forties. When Orville Knapp was

The Ben Pollack Band, 1929, with clarinetist Benny Goodman, trombonist Jack Teagarden and (between them) cornetist Jimmy McPartland

George Olsen and Ethel Shutta

killed, Olsen took over that orchestra but met with little success. In 1942 I reviewed one of his broadcasts and found his music hopelessly old-fashioned and poorly played. He definitely belonged in the pre-Big Band Era.

BEN POLLACK led one of the greatest big bands of its day, one that broke up just before one of the many brilliant musicians he had uncovered, Benny Goodman, started the whole big band craze, and several years before another graduate, Glenn Miller, took over as the Number One Leader. It had been a sensational orchestra—bursting with exciting, musicianly, great instrumentalists. It featured in addition to Goodman and Miller, who wrote many of the arrangements, Jack Teagarden and his brother Charlie, Charlie Spivak, Jimmy McPartland,

Bud Freeman, Fud Livingston, plus the nucleus of the future Bob Crosby band— Eddie Miller, Matty Matlock, Yank Lawson, Ray Bauduc, Nappy Lamare, Dean Kincaide, and Pollack's confidant and the future president of the Crosby band, Gil Rodin. By 1934 Pollack, a driving drummer and aggressive human being, and obviously a superb organizer, had grown weary of leading a band. He seemed more interested in furthering the career of his very attractive wife, Doris Robbins, who had been singing with him. And so he lost his big stars. But once the big band craze started, Ben couldn't stay away. In 1936 he organized a new unit, again packed with great undiscovered talent: trumpeters Harry James and Shorty Sherock, clarinetist Irving Fazola, saxist Dave Matthews and pianist Freddy Slack, all of whom migrated to other bands. Undaunted, Ben organized another outfit on the West Coast, where he had settled. Like all his bands, this one was also musically good, though it never greatly impressed the public. After 1938, Ben occasionally led a small dixieland group that featured his dynamic drumming. But he spent more of his time in business ventures, running his own club and short-lived record company and instituting an occasional law suit against some of the big bands. He grew increasingly bitter and more disappointed, and finally in 1971 came his tragic death— by hanging in his Palm Springs home.

LEO REISMAN started his band in Boston, where he impressed the blue bloods with his melodic, society-styled dance music. In the later twenties he came to New York and established an even greater following. His tea dansants and broadcasts from the Central Park Casino, near the East Seventy-second Street entrance, were some of the most "in" happenings of the era. Reisman, who looked and acted like Ben Casey, had a good ear for talent. He gave both Eddy Duchin and Nat Brandwynne their starts. His recordings of some highly musical tunes had a good sound; on some he featured such singers as Fred Astaire, Harold Arlen and Lee Wiley. After the more exciting bands came into prominence, Reisman's music seemed pale by comparison. His arrangements sounded like stocks, and though he worked in many of the smarter rooms for years, he no longer impressed the general public. In 1939 at the Strand Theater in New York he let an unknown girl singer take a quick chorus of "Hurry Home." Her name: Dinah Shore. But generally, his music projected little freshness, and by 1941 his band had deteriorated into such a dull nothing that all I could note as commendable in an August radio network review was "the fact that Mutual kindly cut the broadcast to fifteen minutes."

BEN SELVIN was the most prolific recording artist of all time. Starting in the early twenties, he led orchestras of all sizes and instrumentations, often employing top studio men like Benny Goodman, Glenn Miller and the Dorseys, during a career that spanned two generations. According to Joseph Murrell's *Book of Golden Discs,* published by the London *Daily Mail,* Selvin recorded over nine thousand different selections. His nearest competitor was Bing Crosby, with approximately twenty-seven hundred numbers. Selvin, who was also a leading conductor on radio, the guiding light in the electrical transcription field, the head of Majestic Records and a top man at RCA Victor, remained active for years as a consultant to large corporations interested

in music. A short, spry, enthusiastic gent, who invested his money well in real estate, his eyes would light up as he talked about the days when he recorded for nine different labels under nine different names. Obviously an extraordinarily efficient conductor, he managed to combine good musicianship with a commercial approach that brought him enduring respect. Still active at age 82, he died on July 15, 1980 in Florida.

NOBLE SISSLE led one of the first black orchestras to be featured in white nightclubs, one that specialized in playing for floor shows. Sissle was a well-schooled musician in the early twenties, who had written the score for a very successful show called *Shufflin' Along.* His band seldom projected much rhythmic excitement, though from

Noble

time to time it featured such diverse jazz soloists as Sidney Bechet and Charlie Parker and, in 1937, spotted a young singer named Lena Horne. What Sissle seemed to want to do more than anything else as a bandleader was to repudiate the stereotype of the black musician by showing he could play something other than jazz. In this he was eminently successful.

RUDY VALLEE will never go down in history as leader of a great band. Actually, his Connecticut Yankees sounded like a

Rudy

and a smart one, spotlighted his crooning pretty much to the exclusion of his musicians. Many of them resented what they called "his superior attitude" and had little respect for his musicianship. And he was inconsistent. He would pinch pennies almost viciously; yet if one of his musicians was in trouble, Vallee would support him for a long period, sometimes without letting anyone else know about it. By the time the Big Band Era had begun, Vallee was concentrating almost exclusively on his crooning and his activities on radio, especially on the Fleischmann Yeast program, on which he was starred for many years.

FRED WARING started as a professional bandleader in the early twenties, after leaving Penn State, with a polished dance orchestra that recorded for Victor and Columbia. Some of the sides were strictly instrumentals; others featured some good singing by Fred's brother, Tom. Later, Waring developed his famed glee club, and by the mid-thirties his major emphasis was on singing. He was self-admittedly a perfectionist who drove his men and women hard. Some hated him; many admired him; few ever really knew him. In my dealings with

pretty dreary group, but Vallee himself, of course, was a stellar attraction. Starting in 1928, he and his megaphone and his tantalizing tonsils captured feminine hearts throughout the country. Rudy, a Yale grad

A few of Waring's Pennsylvanians (brothers and sisters all)
Front row: saxists George and Arthur McFarland
Middle row: singer Priscilla Lane, maestro Fred Waring,
pianist-vocalist Tom Waring, singer Rosemary Lane
Back row: trumpeter George Culley, girls' choir director Kay Thompson (center)
flanked by singing sisters Blanche and Marian Thompson, violinist Fred Culley

him I found he could be utterly charming as well as frustratingly condescending and brutally dictatorial. But his strong will, plus his love and respect for good musicianship, paid off. His outfit invariably performed faithfully. It was the training ground for such future stars as choral directors Robert Shaw and Kay Thompson and movie stars Rosemary and Priscilla Lane. It enjoyed sensational success for many years on its radio broadcasts, not merely because of its precise musicianship but because Waring understood and exploited the tastes of the great American public. His was the common man's approach. "We don't sing music," he told *New York Times* reporter George Gent in August, 1966, "we sing songs." During that same year, Waring was accorded a fiftieth anniversary party, marking a career that included, in addition to the Waring Glee Club and Orchestra, publication of hundreds of band and choral arrangements, a

monthly magazine, *Music Journal,* a yearly music workshop, his tremendously successful Shawnee Inn on six hundred acres in Pennsylvania, and the invention of the world-famous Waring Blendor.

ANSON WEEKS led a pleasant-sounding though never exciting dance orchestra. During the early thirties it harbored some colorful sidemen and women—singers Tony Martin, Bob Crosby and Carl Ravazza and future leaders Xavier Cugat and Griff Williams. In the mid-thirties Dale Evans was his girl vocalist. Weeks, a very pleasant man, suffered serious injuries in a 1941 auto crash. After his recovery, he reorganized and for many years thereafter played in some of the West Coast's leading hotel rooms, including The Top of the Mark in San Francisco, from which he broadcast regularly and where he waxed his "Dancin' with Anson" record album.

Fred Waring and His Pennsylvanians at Des Ambassaseurs in Paris during a 1928 tour of Europe. Brother Tom is at the piano; Poley McClintock on drums.

And Still More Bands

IRVING AARONSON'S COMMANDERS, first in all alphabetical listings of bands, was primarily an entertaining, well-trained stage band that played in theaters, featured arrangements by Chummy MacGregor, Glenn Miller's future pianist, and nurtured such budding stars as Artie Shaw, Claude Thornhill, Gene Krupa and Tony Pastor, all of whom appreciated Aaronson's gentle, paternal guidance.

AMBROSE was an English bandleader, whose slickly rehearsed and at times semi-swinging group rivaled Ray Noble's in the early thirties and captivated American audiences with its recordings, especially one called "Hors d'Oeuvre."

PAUL ASH, bushy-haired, dramatic-looking, idol of female matinee audiences, conducted his large, semi-symphonic orchestra in big movie houses, mostly in New York and Chicago, during the late twenties and early thirties, giving employment to such future leaders as Benny Goodman, Glenn Miller and Red Norvo.

KEN BAKER assembled a group of young West Coast swingers during the mid-thirties, producing exciting sounds in the Goodman manner and introducing Liz Tilton, Martha's talented kid sister, and several musicians who later formed the nucleus of Stan Kenton's band.

SMITH BALLEW, an extremely handsome and musical singer, led a fine band during the early thirties, featuring Ray McKinley's drumming and Glenn Miller's trombone and arrangements until it broke up shortly after both sidemen migrated to the Dorsey Brothers, after which Smith made several good vocal records, then became a movie star before settling down for good in Texas.

ALEX BARTHA, mustacheod and trim, fronted the house band on Atlantic City's Steel Pier, often vying against name bands there with his crisp, clean attack and once in a while scaring them, especially when he unleashed his young trumpet find, Ziggy Elman.

LEON BELASCO, who tried very hard to please those who came to hotel rooms to dance to his music, varying tempos, introducing such goodies as the Andrews Sisters and "flitting around like a molested moth trying to find a place to alight" (a quote from a review), eventually wound up an actor in the movies, still trying hard to please, this time via roles as the perennial butler.

HENRY BIAGINI, who led the Casa Loma in its earliest days, continued during the thirties and early forties to front a ballroom-type orchestra that emphasized strident ensemble sounds, finding some success in the Midwest until his death in an auto accident in 1944.

JERRY BLAINE, pleasant, wide-eyed and moon-faced, led a fairly good band, in which he and a pretty girl, Phyllis Kenny, sang, and which spotted a good pianist in Jack Matthias in the late thirties, and played mostly around New York, where Blaine later established his Jubilee Records plus a successful distributing company.

BERT BLOCK, now a successful agent specializing in folk groups, led two very good bands, one a bright, swinging outfit that featured arrangers Alex Stordahl (then called Odd Stordahl) and singer Jack Leonard, before both joined Tommy Dorsey; the other a more stylized group, his "Bell Music Orchestra," which spotted numerous bell and celeste sounds, a good drummer, Terry Snyder, and an impressive vocalist, Bill Johnson.

CHARLIE BOULANGER put together a pleasantly subdued orchestra that eschewed the usual blatant brass and crunchy rhythms prevalent in the Broadway-type nightclubs it played, while still satisfying customers with its light, lilting, melodic sounds.

LOU BREESE was most successful as conductor of stage shows in Chicago's Chez Paree, though this serious-looking trumpeter with the thin mustache (he played stiffly and rather sharp) did have an interesting musical outfit in 1936 which featured an excellent woodwind quartet long before woodwinds became popular in dance bands.

FRANK and MILT BRITTON bashed instruments over various bandsmen's heads, put on a whale of a wacky show and still managed to play fairly good music during vaudeville presentations that often had their audiences in stitches and sometimes their musicians in bandages.

WILLIE BRYANT, a sleek, suave gent who was to become the "Unofficial Mayor of Harlem," led a swinging band at the Savoy, featuring some great, young musicians like Teddy Wilson and Cozy Cole, catchy riff tunes like "Viper's Moan," novelties like "Steak and Potatoes" and a moody, sentimental theme, "It's Over Because We're Through."

PUPI CAMPO led a Latin-type orchestra near the end of the Big Band Era, later benefiting from exposure on the Jack Paar TV show and the publicity surrounding his marriage to Betty Clooney, Rosemary's sister.

REGGIE CHILDS, a compact, energetic, serious-looking violinist, enjoyed a long and fairly successful career as leader of a band that never played exciting music but did emerge from the ordinary when it emphasized its clarinet quartet and the vocals of Paul Carley.

GAY CLARIDGE led a band mostly in the Chicago area, where it played a good deal for stage shows while also spotting its versatile leader as singer, saxophonist and trumpeter.

BUDDY CLARKE, not to be confused with the singer whose last name didn't have the final "e" ("His real name was Goldberg and mine was Kreisberg," Clarke explained.) was a genial man with a fairly good band that featured numerous doublings and played for many years at Montreal's Mount Royal Hotel and in leading East Coast rooms.

JOLLY COBURN, a clean-cut Columbia graduate with an uppish reserve, provided an excellent front for one of the better society bands, which reached its zenith when it preceded Ray Noble's orchestra in the Rainbow Room atop the RCA Building in Rockefeller Center.

EMIL COLEMAN, ultra-suave and urbane, a master at mesmerizing blue bloods who could be more impressed by the sight and name of a bandleader than by his music, was extremely successful with his better-than-average society orchestra, playing some of the country's top debutante and other balls, and for years at New York's Hotel Waldorf-Astoria.

RUSS COLUMBO, the handsome Valentino-like crooner who rivaled Bing Crosby in the early thirties (both had worked for Gus Arnheim, Columbo as a violinist), led a good band which at various times spotted Gene Krupa and several other jazz-oriented musicians—until Columbo, cleaning a hunting rifle in 1934, accidentally shot himself to death.

FRANCIS CRAIG had a home for himself and his band at The Hermitage in Nashville, Tennessee, where he played regularly, dispensing good, if never startling, music, gaining his greatest fame after the Big Band Era with his recording of "Near You."

BERNIE CUMMINS, handsome, intense, a former boxer, a close friend of leading sports celebrities and a master of all "genial maestro" mannerisms, kept working steadily in leading spots before the Big Band Era, faded as musical standards rose, invested his money well and led a happy, post-big band life in Boca Raton, Florida.

BEN CUTLER, a good-looking Yale graduate who once made headlines when he drove his car into New York's East River, led one of the more musical society bands that featured a good accordionist, fiddler and a pianist with the unlikely name of Seymour Fiddle, plus a talented and pretty vocalist-pianist with the likely name of Virginia Hayes.

FRANK DAILEY, owner of the famed Meadowbrook, led several bands, one an outstanding musical crew with arrangements by Joe Mooney, great trumpeting by Ralph Muzzillo and Corky Cornelius and excellent singing by Louise Wallace; another, a less-musical, trickier unit, called his "Stop-and-Go Orchestra," which didn't go very far.

DUKE DALY fronted one of the loudest East Coast bands that played—not too well —some good swinging arrangements by Horace Henderson, and featured an outstanding tenor saxist in Bobby Dukoff.

JOHNNY (SCAT) DAVIS was a comedian-trumpeter-singer who'd made a name for himself as one of Fred Waring's Pennsylvanians before embarking on a career as leader of a band that never achieved musical greatness but did showcase Davis well.

MEYER DAVIS supplied orchestras, some huge and some small, some good and some horrible, for hotel rooms, deb parties, Presidential and other balls, for which they usually played stock chorus after stock chorus, hour after hour, seldom varying their approach, seldom appearing on records or radio, yet managing to please the right people at the right time so many times and in so many places that Davis, who reportedly instructed his pick-up groups not to shake hands on the bandstand, made himself a fortune.

BOBBY DAY, one of the first electric guitarists to lead a band, played mostly in the New York area with an outfit that sometimes had mickey-mouse overtones and then later tried, without much success, to emulate Goodman's style.

PETER DEAN, one of the best of the scat-singing, dancing maestri of the early forties, led an enthusiastic swing band that spotted several promising musicians and an unknown girl singer named Dinah Shore, before Dean became a successful personal manager and then in the 1970s a recording personality via several delightful albums of his own.

JACK DENNY, who before the Big Band Era had been one of the more consistently employed of the big band leaders, especially at Montreal's Mount Royal Hotel, stuck doggedly to his old-fashioned style that featured an accordion and dull arrangements (he did spot a good singer, Frances Stevens, when he played New York's Pennsylvania Hotel) and faded slowly away.

BOBBY DUKOFF, whose warm, emotional tenor sax graced the bands of Jimmy Dorsey, Jerry Wald and others, headed groups of studio musicians and singers that produced some mood-filled RCA Victor sides that pioneered a style later made popular by Ray Coniff, then eventually settled in Miami with his wife, singer Anita Boyer, to pursue a successful, dual career as musician and audio engineer.

RAY EBERLE led a musical crew that impressed more with its arrangements by Billy Maxted than when it featured vocals by an ill-at-ease leader; later the ex-Miller singer relaxed more as a solo entertainer and in his Florida home before succumbing to a heart attack in August of 1979.

WILLIE FARMER, a very pleasant gent, was more successful as a society band leader playing New York's posh clubs than he was with his mickey-mouse band, which he organized in the late thirties.

HAPPY FELTON, who in the fifties led the Brooklyn Dodgers' Knot Hole Gang on TV, spread his girth and cheer in front of a good, entertaining band of the mid-thirties which featured a fine kid trumpeter, Shorty Solomson, and an outstanding jazz fiddler, Armand Camgros.

LARRY FUNK satisfied many requests in some of the country's top supper rooms with "His Band of a Thousand Melodies," which introduced Helen O'Connell to its dancers and eventually to Jimmy Dorsey before Funk hung up his baton to become a top booking agent.

DICK GASPARRE may not have known as many melodies as Funk, but he did remember the birthdays and anniversaries of the many patrons who danced to the music of his piano, tenor sax and fiddle orchestra in such swank spots as New York's Plaza Hotel and the Ambassador in Los Angeles.

TOM GERUN led one of the better bands of the early thirties, one which featured several good vocalists, including Al Morris, who later changed his name to Tony Martin, Virginia Simms, later to be known as Ginny Sims, and a clowning singer, hoofer, saxist, and clarinetist named Woodie (that's how he spelled it then) Herman.

BOBBY HACKETT, as gentle and warm as the sound of his horn, led a big band for a short time, also worked in the studios, concertized everywhere, but found most contentment in the 70s, leading his own group on Cape Cod until he died in June, 1976.

JOHNNY HAMP, a pudgy, nervous, aggressive little man, was more successful with his Kentucky Serenaders in the twenties than during the big band days when he fronted a band which introduced two fine singers, Johnny McAfee and Jayne Whitney.

EDGAR HAYES, a pianist, became best known after his commercial recording of "Stardust" appeared, a rendition not up to the swinging caliber of a band that was sparked by drummer Kenny Clarke and successfully toured Scandinavia in the thirties.

TED HEATH, a dignified, dedicated Englishman, organized his beautifully rehearsed and often high-swinging outfit near the close of the Big Band Era, creating a furor with its London Palladium concerts, its regular broadcasts and its succession of outstanding recordings, which resulted during the fifties in the first and successful American tour of an English jazz band.

NEAL HEFTI, acclaimed during the Big Band Era for his writing and trumpeting with Woody Herman's band, led his own outfit on and off during the fifties, then con-

Bobby Hackett with idol Louis Armstrong

centrated on composing and arranging for Count Basie (e.g. "L'il Darlin' " and "Cute") and for movies and television.

RAY HERBECK, an amiable saxist, first attracted attention with a mickey-mouse band; then, in the early forties, drew accolades, especially from musicians, with a more modern, swinging band.

ART HICKMAN, who started his band in 1915 in San Francisco, set the stage for many other bigger bands, gained considerable recognition when Florenz Ziegfeld brought him to New York in 1919, and even though he faded from the big band scene before the mid-thirties, deserves the appreciation of all for his pioneering efforts.

TINY HILL, 365 pounds of him, half-hid and half-led a band that parlayed a heap of corn and some pleasant dixieland jazz into an entertaining, successful dance band formula that managed to appeal greatly to hillbilly music fans without offending those with more sophisticated tastes.

RICHARD HIMBER, fidgety and often flamboyant, had been a successful leader on radio (in 1938, radio columnists voted his the top band in the field) before he entered the big band scene seriously with his tricky "Pyramid Music," which really wasn't as good as the music the band played when it performed some excellent, less-stylized arrangements of Bill Challis.

DEAN HUDSON, personable, handsome and ambitious, emerged from the University of Florida in 1941 with a good band, to which he soon added two impressive kid musicians, Tommy and Jimmy Farr, and a good singer, Ruthie Vale, and in 1944, after Dean, first of the leaders to enter the service, was discharged as an Army captain, fronted another good unit, which spotted his singing and that of Frances Colwell.

JACK HYLTON, a tremendously successful leader in England (his "Just a Gigolo" was considered a record classic), fronted an orchestra that emphasized pretentious though musical arrangements but, because of visa problems, never performed in America.

SPIKE JONES, once a top Hollywood studio drummer, developed a magnificently trained organization which, with split-second timing, exceptional instrumental technique and excellent mimicry, created marvelous takeoffs on other musical groups as well as wildly imaginative and original comedy routines of its own.

LOUIS JORDAN, a likable, humorous, unassuming saxist whose chief connection with the big bands had been his tenure in Chick Webb's and Ella Fitzgerald's bands, combined fun and some good jazz within his Tympany Five for musical pleasure and financial gains, especially through such record hits as "I'm Gonna Move to the

Louis Jordan (center) with Woody Herman (left)
and Al Jarvis of the West Coast's "Make Believe Ballroom"

The John Kirby Sextet—Kirby on bass, pianist Billy Kyle, Jr., trumpeter Charlie Shavers, clarinetist Buster Bailey, saxist Russell Procope, drummer O'Neil Spencer

Outskirts of Town" and "Choo Choo Ch' Boogie" and "Caldonia."

JIMMY JOY, who could play two clarinets simultaneously, led the band that many considered the greatest in the Southwest during the late twenties, recording some good jazz sides for Okeh, but, apparently looking for greater financial security, switched in the thirties to a sweet band style that captivated ballroom patrons in the Midwest, where he became a great favorite.

ROGER WOLFE KAHN, heir to a gigantic fortune, loved big bands so much that he organized his own excellent one, stocking it with such top musicians as Gene Krupa, Jack Teagarden, Red Nichols and Miff Mole for record dates and sporadic personal appearances.

GENE KARDOS, a man with a kooky sense of humor and a knack of pleasing dancers, led a good swing band during the early thirties, then formed a more sedate group that entertained at top spots in the Catskills and occasionally in New York City.

AL KATZ and His Kittens, originally out of Kentucky, were Chicago favorites in the twenties and early thirties, where and when their emphasis on novelties drew them their greatest popularity.

AL KAVELIN led one of the best sweet bands of all time during the mid-thirties, one that achieved a lovely ensemble sound while at the same time featuring its outstanding young pianist, then named simply "Carmen" but later better known as Carmen Cavallaro.

HERBIE KAYE, a handsome man who married Dorothy Lamour, fronted a sweet-tenor-sax-lead band that deviated from the dull norm by playing college songs in dance tempos for its favorite audiences in the Chicago area.

JOHN KIRBY, an outstanding big band bassist for Fletcher Henderson, Chick Webb and Lucky Millinder, organized his successful, gently swinging sextet in 1937 with four other Millinder alumni—trumpeter Charlie Shavers, clarinetist Buster Bailey, pianist Billy Kyle and drummer O'Neil Spencer— plus saxist Russell Procope and proved that swing could be polite, musical and commercial all at the same time, thereby gaining acceptance in such a plush spot as New York's Waldorf-Astoria and on a network radio series that also featured Maxine Sullivan, then Kirby's wife.

EDDIE LANE, a man seemingly dedicated to pleasing people (he later became a hotel executive), turned in an outstanding job of filling on-the-spot requests with his compact nine-piece outfit, which concentrated on the New York area and spotted an excellent though then unknown pianist named Cy Walter.

LESTER LANIN, a nervous, hard-working man, once less-known than his brothers Sam, who led the Ipana Troubadors, and Howard, who played top society dates, easily surpassed them in the fifties when, with the help of a series of recordings, he established himself as the most successful of the new society bandleaders.

BERT LOWN, who once admitted that he hadn't intended becoming a bandleader, struck pay dirt early in the thirties when he hastily formed a unit for a New York hotel engagement and recorded a hit version of "Bye Bye Blues," which featured a splendid trombone solo, not by Lown, as many thought, but by Al (Tex) Philburn.

CLYDE LUCAS fronted an extremely versatile though musically unexciting orchestra before and through the Big Band Era, specializing not only in a wide variety of dance tempos but also in much doubling of instruments, such as Clyde's parlay of a trombone and a marimba.

RICHARD MALTBY, serious, be-spectacled, talented, during the forties wrote arrangements for various leaders, including Goodman and Whiteman, and in the fifties organized a good, straight-ahead band which made some successful recordings, played good spots for a time, then settled for fewer dates as Maltby concentrated more on writing for recordings and television.

MATTY MALNECK, Paul Whiteman alumnus, top-notch fiddler, led a colorful, musical, West Coast octet that spotted Milton DeLugg's accordion and Mannie Klein's trumpet, performing, according to DeLugg, "with everybody—Bing, Bob Hope, Jack Benny, Jimmy Durante and you name 'em," on records, on radio and in dozens of movies before Malneck's death in March of 1981.

RALPH MARTERIE after the Big Band Era led a thoroughly musicianly, though seldom thrilling band that featured its leader's well-toned, straight-ahead trumpet, and which received a big build-up from Mercury Records.

BILLY MAXTED for a short time near the close of the Big Band Era led a band that sounded like he looked—solid, powerful, aggressive—featuring Billy's vital, two-handed piano and the same sort of potent arrangements he wrote at various times for the bands of Red Nichols, Will Bradley, Benny Goodman and Ray Eberle.

LANI McINTYRE led a band that featured mostly Hawaiian music, saturating the Hawaiian Grill of New York's Lexington Hotel with his specialty.

BENNY MEROFF fronted an entertaining band (Benny Goodman, as a kid imitator of Ted Lewis, performed with him in the early twenties), which was more effective in its shows than it was in trying to create anything outstanding musically, though it always managed to turn in an adequate job when playing for dancers.

LUCKY MILLINDER, a superb showman and expert organizer, first led the Mills Blue Rhythm band, then his own, often exciting group, made so during the big band days by such outstanding sidemen as trumpeters Henry (Red) Allen, Charlie Shavers, Harry Edison, Dizzy Gillespie and Freddy Webster (a brilliant musician who died much too young), pianists Billy Kyle, Ellis Larkins and Bill Doggett and the formidable and exciting Sister Rosetta Tharpe.

ART MOONEY, genial and toothsome, began with a corny band, then, in the mid-forties, switched for a time to a swinging one that featured Fran Warren, and finally, in the fifties, reached his commercial zenith with his rousing, corn-filled hit recording of "I'm Looking Over a Four-Leaf Clover."

SPUD MURPHY, arranger for many of the top swing bands, organized an avant-garde outfit during the forties which fascinated the musicians who heard it but failed to attract any appreciable segment of the paying public.

RUBY NEWMAN, charming, intelligent and intense, ruled the society-band roost in Boston for many years, brought a small group into New York's Rainbow Grill in 1936, scored some success, but eventually returned to Massachusetts to continue a rewarding career that eventually made him a very wealthy man.

HARRY OWENS and His Orchestra, among the top exponents of Hawaiian music, were featured for years in and around Honolulu and also made regular pilgrimages to the States to spread their own particular type of musical gospel.

LOUIS PANICO could play good jazz trumpet but found himself boxed in when his "wah-wah" version of "Wabash Blues" became a big hit, thereby relegating him and his band to the cornball class, where they really didn't belong.

RAY PEARL had a fairly musical band for a while, one that apparently didn't bring him much recognition, which, reportedly, is why he switched to a Lombardo-type outfit, which brought him greater financial rewards.

PAUL PENDARVIS, a handsome man with a rather good sweet band that played into cup mutes and featured clarinets, began his career in the Midwest and eventually settled on the West Coast without ever achieving his reported ambition: to play New York City.

PEREZ PRADO, "King of the Mambo," sparked a Latin-American rhythm movement during the mid-fifties with a well-disciplined, showmanly band that first scored a big success in Mexico, made a batch of commercial recordings for RCA Victor and appeared in top nightclubs and on important TV shows.

BARNEY RAPP formed his New Englanders in Connecticut, then attracted enough attention with their well-arranged, well-played music to create a demand for his music elsewhere, including Cleveland, where he unveiled his young singing find, Doris Day.

JOE RICARDEL, ebullient, outgoing and always ' anxious to please, played society music for New York's upper strata, bowed a good fiddle, sang pleasantly, and wrote songs, the most famous of which was "The Frim Fram Sauce" epic.

RILEY and FARLEY (Mike and Eddie), two big band graduates, had only a six-piece band, but they made a mammoth impression during the 1930s when they co-wrote (with Red Hodgson) and introduced "The Music Goes 'Round and 'Round."

RITA RIO, a very sexy-looking lass, led a band that had a radio commercial, played ballrooms and was staffed by a bunch of rather unattractive girls who looked as stiff in their imitation tuxedos as their music

Phil Spitalny and His Hour of Charm Orchestra (1939)

sounded, thereby setting off Miss Rio's undulating torso all the more dramatically.

BUDDY ROGERS, a pre-band-era movie idol, had a rather good outfit that featured not only top musicians like Gene Krupa but also Buddy himself playing trombone, trumpet and a whole slew of other instruments, none very well but all with enthusiasm and a good deal of natural charm.

DICK (STINKY) ROGERS inherited Will Osborne's band in the early forties, kept it in good musical shape, thanks to fine arrangements by Jerry Bittick, and added an extra spark with his mugging, singing and attractive personality.

LUIGI ROMANELLI and his King Edward Hotel Orchestra were Canada's oldest and most famous outfit, having started at the hotel as far back as 1915 and for more than a quarter of a century bringing to its supper room and other Canadian spots a wide variety of music that varied from salon to concert to out-and-out dance music.

SAL SALVADOR, former Stan Kenton guitarist, attempted with valor and dedication during the sixties to launch a big band, which spotted his expert playing, several good sidemen and a batch of modern, well-played arrangements, but which eventually proved such a financial drain upon Salvador's resources that he returned to fronting a small group and teaching young guitarists.

TERRY SHAND, a flashy, swinging pianist and persuasive vocalist, featured himself and a very fine ballad singer, Louanne Hogan, who had superb intonation and an emotional, low-pitched voice, in a band that played primarily in hotel rooms, supplying entertaining and thoroughly danceable music.

MILT SHAW and His Detroiters were the house band in New York's Roseland Ballroom, playing opposite Fletcher Henderson's and Chick Webb's bands during the early thirties and giving them good competition, thanks to some fine arrangements and such topflight young musicians as Ray McKinley, Will Bradley and Snub Pollard.

BEASLEY SMITH led a good all-around orchestra in Nashville, where, in addition to featuring some of the area's top musicians, it helped further the budding career of a Vanderbilt undergraduate, Dinah Shore.

PAUL SPECHT played mostly in theaters and ballrooms during the late twenties and early thirties, fronting a musicianly band that included, from time to time such superior instrumentalists as Artie Shaw, Charlie Spivak and Russ Morgan.

PHIL SPITALNY, once the leader of a very good dance and radio orchestra, lowered his musical and raised his visual appeal in the thirties when he surrounded himself with a bevy of girl musicians, including Evelyn and Her Magic Violin (Arlene Francis was the Mistress of Ceremonies on Phil's "Hour of Charm" radio series) who, as a group, didn't play very well—and didn't always look so great either.

HAROLD STERN led what would have been just another hotel-room-styled band, with the usual tenor saxes and fiddles, if it hadn't been for a wonderful singer, Bill Smith (he also played drums), a handsome man who emoted intimately and musically, with a rich vibrato and a resonance that made the band's theme, "Now That It's All Over," a highlight of each of its radio broadcasts.

EDDIE STONE, veteran vocalist with Isham Jones and Freddy Martin, formed his own band in the mid-forties, featuring, of course, his delightfully "impish" singing style as well as a sound notably large for nine men and three girl fiddlers.

JUSTIN STONE, a handsome, urbane-looking man and a talented arranger, put together a nineteen-piece band in 1943, played some ambitious and interesting scores, but couldn't find enough spots that could afford so many musicians.

LEW STONE led an excellent English orchestra, which was considered by many to have been the British Isles' finest dance band during the thirties and which spotted some of the country's outstanding instrumentalists as well as two fine vocalists, Al Bowlly and Jack Plant.

BOB STRONG, a good musician who played various single and double-reed instruments, led a studio band in Chicago before he organized a dance orchestra that featured various woodwinds plus a French horn, played a short engagement at Glen Island Casino, spotted a good singer in Jo Ann Tally but, because of inferior showmanship, failed to capitalize on its attractive and sometimes unique sounds.

The SUNSET ROYAL SERENADERS under "Doc" Wheeler, later a top gospel and rhythm and blues disc jockey in New York, was a spirited, entertaining, imaginative group that played both jazz and stage show music and created the version of "Marie" which Tommy Dorsey later recorded.

PAUL TREMAINE and his *Band From Lonely Acres* was a rich-sounding outfit of the early thirties which broadcast full if never terribly exciting ensemble sounds regularly from Yoeng's Chinese-American Restaurant on New York's Broadway, afternoons and evenings, occasionally featuring a jazz solo by young Sonny Dunham.

FRANKIE TRUMBAUER is better remembered as an outstanding saxist with Jean Goldkette and Paul Whiteman and as a close associate of Bix Beiderbecke than as the leader of a band that unlike Trumbauer, who became a flying instructor, really never got off the ground.

FATS WALLER, who gained most of his fame with his sextet, did front a rather impressive thirteen-piece band for a rather short spell during the early 1940s that appeared mostly in theaters and made a few records, invariably featuring its leader's superior piano-playing and his delightful, tongue-in-cheek singing.

ALVY WEST, talented alto saxist and arranger, serious-looking but often witty, fronted a six-piece group that made some very impressive sounds both in supper clubs and on numerous Columbia recordings.

RAN WILDE was a misnomer, inasmuch as his orchestra was quite subdued, ideally suited to hotel rooms, yet distinguished from other bands of its ilk through its selection of really good, unhackneyed tunes.

Fats Waller

GENE WILLIAMS, handsome, affable and dedicated, who had proved himself one of the better singers during his days with Claude Thornhill, tried valiantly after the Big Band Era to make a success of an always musical but not always commercial band, finally winding up as confidant, friend, and drink-dispenser at one of the New York jazz musicians' favorite hangouts.

GRIFF WILLIAMS led a very conservative-sounding band that was a favorite among dancers in midwest and West Coast ballrooms but whose old-fashioned music caused reviewer Barry Ulanov to note in 1942 that "it's like keeping a dead fish around for twenty-five years."

BOB WILLS began to bridge the gap between country and western music and big band swing during the forties by presenting the simpler C & W songs in more sophisticated, up-dated arrangements, a compromise that resulted in thousands of dedicated, West Coast fans, attracted by the sight of cow-boy attired musicians who sounded more like city-slickers.

GERALD WILSON, whose trumpet was once featured in Jimmie Lunceford's band, created some interesting arrangements for a band formed in 1944 that met just fair success, disbanded, and then in the sixties blossomed as one of that decade's most impressive big bands.

BARRY WOOD, younger brother of bandleader Barney Rapp, quit the Buddy Rogers band because Buddy wouldn't let him sing, then formed his own pleasant outfit in New York, caused such a sensation with his singing that he was signed for the "Lucky Strike Hit Parade" and eventually wound up a top TV producer, with many major credits, before his death in the late sixties.

AUSTIN WYLIE led a very musical band in Cleveland, which broadcast regularly, featuring Claude Thornhill's piano and Artie Shaw's clarinet and his arrangements in the late twenties and the clarinet of Clarence Hutchenrider in the early thirties.

AND there were still more big bands playing during that 1935 to 1946 period, as well as before and after those dozen years. Many have been forgotten completely, but not all. Here are some you may still remember:

Charlie Agnew, Barclay Allen, Mickey Alpert, Don Alvin, famed composer Leroy Anderson, Luis Arcaraz, Jerry Arlen (Harold's brother), Desi Arnez with his conga drum, Bob Astor, Buddy Baker, Jimmy Baker, Dick Ballou, Claude Bampton, Bill Bardo, Barnee, Hughie Barrett, Dick Barrie, "Bubbles" Becker, Denny Becker, Gene Beecher, Larry Bennett, Don Bigelow, Billy Bishop, Billy Bissett, Teddy Black, Neil Bonshu, Boots and his Buddies, Earl Bostic, Tiny Bradshaw, and Mario Braggiotti, who also played duo pianos with Jacques Frey.

Ace Brigode and his Fourteen Virginians, Earl Burtnett, Tony Cabot, The California Ramblers led by Ed Kirkeby, Blanche Calloway, Del Campo, Joe Candullo, Russ Carlyle, Ike Carpenter, Del Casino, Cato's Vagabonds featuring a wonderful singer named Nedra Gordonier, Tom Clines, Christopher Columbus, The Commanders, Zez Confrey, Irving Conn, Spade Cooley, Al Cooper and the Savoy Sultans, who made "The Home of Happy Feet" even happier, the very big Jack Crawford, and Chris Cross.

Eli Dantzig, Doc Daugherty, Hal Derwin, Frank Devol, Charlie Dornberger, who was on the back of many Paul Whiteman records, George Duffy, Mike Durso, Baron Elliott, Phil Emerton and his Blue and White Diamonds, Jim Europe, a very early trail-blazer, Felix Ferdinando, Dick Fidler, Herbie Fields, Scott Fisher, Charlie Fisk, Eddie Fitzpatrick, Basil Fomeen, Larry Fotine, Roy Fox, Jerry Freeman, and Snooks Friedman, who also used the name of Hale Hamilton.

Louis "King" Garcia and his potent trumpet, Dick Gardner, Glenn Garr, Emerson Gill, Ernie Golden, Cecil Golly and his "Music by Golly," Claude Gordon, who was a late starter, Lew Gray, Hal Grayson, King Guion, who introduced a double rhythm section, George Haefely, Cass Hagan, Sleepy Hall, Henry Halstead, Coleman Hawkins, the great tenor saxist who led a big band for a small time, Ralph Hawkins, Tal Henry, Ray Heatherton, whose daughter Joey, later became a big star, Ernie Heckscher, and Billy Hicks, who played like Bix, and his Sizzling Six.

Bert Hirsch, Bill Hogan, Herbie Holmes, Ernie Holst, Paul Howard and his Quality Serenaders, Lloyd Huntley, the Jeeter-Pillar Band, Nick Jerrett, Brooks Johns, Charlie Johnson, Johnny Johnson, Paul Kain, Whitey Kaufman, Leonard Keller, Sonny Kendis, who played at the Stork Club and who, according to one wag, may have borrowed Stan Kenton's and Sammy Kaye's old music stands, Larry Kent, Ted King, Ray Kinney, the well-named Korn Kobblers led by Freddie Schnickelfritz, Bennie Krueger, and Dick Kuhn.

Howard Lally, Frank LaMarr, Art Landry, who was a real old-timer, Allen Leafer, Eddie LeBaron, Ada Leonard and her All-Girl Orchestra, Phil Levant, David LeWinter, Dick Mansfield, Jack Marshard, Harry Marshard, Paul Martell, Paul Martin, Mel Marvin and his "Take It Easy Music," Bill McCune, Jimmy McHale, Hughie McPherson, Bobby Meeker, Stanley Melba, Rafael Mendez, Benny Meroff, Dick Messner, who was Johnny's older brother, and Harold Mickey, who led Argentina's Number One band before retiring to North Carolina.

Ray Miller, who in the twenties had a fine band filled with budding stars, Carlos Molina, Noro Morales, Carl "Deacon" Moore, Billy Murphy, Stan Myers, Freddy Nagel, Oliver Naylor, Paul Neighbors, who was a late mickey-mouser, Will Oakland, Husk O'Hare, Eddie Oliver, Don Orlando, Jimmy Palmer, Doc Peyton, Teddy Phillips, Graham Prince, who was a fine arranger, Roger Pryor, who was the son of famed military bandleader Arthur Pryor, Tito Puente, Gray Rains, who was another fine arranger, Arthur Ravell, Floyd Ray, Joe Rines, Sam Robbins, Don Rodney, and Adrian Rollini.

Bill Scotti, Boyd Senter and his Centipedes, Seymour "May I Come In?" Simons, Phil Sobel, Mike Speciale, Nick Stuart, Blue Steele, Ted Steele, George Sterney, Roy Stevens, Charley Straight, singer Joseph Sudy, Billy Swanson, Bob Sylvester featuring his wife, Olga Vernon, Dan Terry, who led one of the most interesting of the post-era bands, Henry Theiss, Lang Thompson, Tommy "Red" Tompkins, who featured an exceptional guttsy-sounding singer named Sally Ann Harris, George Towne, and Al Trace, who fronted one of the more entertaining novelty bands, Clyde Trask, and Vincent Travers.

Alphonse Trent, whose band spawned quite a few future black jazz stars, Anthony Trini, Evalyn Tyner, Herman Waldman, who was very big in the southwest, Garwood Van, Buddy Wagner, Jimmy Walsh, Sammy Watkins, Marek Weber, Ranny Weeks, Zach Whyte's Chocolate Beau Brummels, who uncovered Sy Oliver and others, Julie Wintz, Sam Wooding, Julian Woodworth, and Sterling Young, who, except for Si Zentner and Bob Zurke, ended just about every alphabetical listing of the big bands.

Part Four:
Big Bandleaders
Revisited

Big Bandleaders Revisited

Back in 1971, just a quarter of a century after the big band era had reached what many have felt was the end of those glorious times, I decided it would be interesting to interview and photograph some of its most illustrious bandleading alumni. And so with tape recorder and camera in hand, I went to visit some of them. They'd all changed on the outside, as you can readily see. But on the inside I found that they had changed remarkably little.

Count Basie impressed me as always before: warm and gracious, slow to express himself, but once he got going exciting and exuberant and very tolerant of everyone and everything.

Benny Goodman talked openly and frankly about his music, hemmed and hawed in his delightfully vague manner about a few other topics, then suddenly decided he'd had enough and started practicing his clarinet.

Woody Herman was as easy-going as ever, completely relaxed, perfectly willing to let everyone else do his own thing, forever the optimist about music and people.

Harry James, alert and lively, still seemed to be as boyishly enthusiastic about the importance of good swinging sounds and the St. Louis Cardinals baseball team as he was thirty and more years ago.

Stan Kenton was still tirelessly probing, still constantly analyzing, still as charming, still as dogmatic as more than a quarter of a century ago.

Guy Lombardo, forever the successful businessman, continued to delight in quoting record sales figures and other barometers of commercial success in such a disarmingly charming way as to make the listener wonder if he were putting someone on.

Artie Shaw, forever the searcher, for whom there just don't seem to be enough words in the English language, continued to propound all sorts of theories about his music (which he usually doesn't like to discuss anymore), and about why what happens when, where and how, and possibly even if.

Unfortunately, back in 1971, there was one major bandleader whom I could not arrange to revisit at that time. But in a phone conversation, I found

Duke Ellington was still running true to form, still sleeping almost all day every day, still parrying queries with remarks like "I don't like to look back because it destroys my perspective of writing music," and—while turning on that amazing Ellington charm—"I'm not sure I want to talk about those other things you mentioned because, you see, I am writing a book myself. But why don't you read *my* book, instead?" And then, he closed the conversation, probably going back to bed or back on the road again. His book, *Music Is My Mistress,* did appear a few years later, but unfortunately that great man was not around very long to appreciate its warm reception.

Count Basie Revisited

WE WERE SITTING in his living room between his band's engagements in East Orange, New Jersey, and Zurich, Switzerland. It was one of the few days in the year when Count Basie was able to relax in his St. Albans home with its outdoor swimming pool, a symbol of Bill Basie's commercial success. Then we went inside, and there stood or hung the dozens upon dozens of statuettes and plaques and certificates that the Basie band had been awarded for outstanding musical creativity. Who said you couldn't be both an artistic and a commercial success! And for thirty-five years yet!

Of course, there had been some scuffling times, like during the slow, early fifties, when Basie was forced to cut his group down to six men in order to get gigs. "That was a good experiment. I learned a lot." But business got better, and the band soon grew to normal size, and there were, as before, times when his band sounded absolutely great and times when Bill Basie knew it wasn't making it. Which of all his groups—the early one with Lester Young and Herschel Evans; the next one with Illinois Jacquet; the one that introduced "April in Paris"; the one that featured all those Neal Hefti and Quincy Jones arrangements; the one that Sinatra invited to tour with him; or the current one that was sounding so-o-o-o good—which of all those great outfits was his personal favorite?

"I could tell you," the Count replied, "but, no, maybe I couldn't, because a lot of times you think it's the right band because everything is working just right, but then gets stagnant. Then, after a while, the band seems to try and it gets good again. But then, if the band knows it's getting good, then automatically, it seems to me, it gets bad. You know, a band has to keep on trying and to keep that feeling that they just want to play and drive—that's when I think I've got a good band. You know, I think I'm happiest with my band when they're still not *sure* they're the greatest."

Certainly his band when it arrived in New York's Roseland Ballroom early in 1936 wasn't the greatest. I'd said so in my original review, and Bill hasn't forgotten, either. "It's going to be in MY book, what you said. I even mentioned it at the dinner they had for me a few years ago at the Waldorf. I remember: 'If you don't think the band is out of tune, just listen to the reed section. And if you don't think the reed section is out of tune, just listen to the brass section. And then, if you don't think *they're* out of tune, just listen to the *band!*' "

We laughed about it now. And for some crazy reason, I felt I should now try to excuse the band's performance. "You know, that was a terribly dead bandstand and you could hear everything that was wrong with a band." But Basie wouldn't let me off the hook. "You could hear everything that was good

in there, too, you know," he pointed out. "Woody was playing there at the same time, remember? And he had a good band in there. They were together —really."

I'd given Woody's band a much better review, and John Hammond, who had discovered Basie and helped bring him to New York, was furious. "That John," Bill murmured softly, "he's been so good to me through the years. If he hadn't come out to Kansas City, God knows what would have happened to me. I might still be out there, or back in New York doing something else, or just doin' nothin'! Or maybe I'd have gone out to the coast, because I had an offer to play organ in one of the theaters out there. But I couldn't see that, really. I was just having so much fun with this little band in Kansas City that it hadn't dawned on me yet to think seriously about the band at all."

And when did he start thinking seriously about it? The Count looked at me deadpan. "Oh, maybe about the year before last, or something like that."

The musicians in that early band were colorful and exciting and very much individuals. Count recalls them fondly—people like Lester Young and Herschel Evans, two of the greatest tenor saxists ever to sit in one band at the same time. "There used to be so much going on there. There was such a great

Count Basie in 1971

difference in their playing. It was such a big, wide space, but they were both so very good. And both so beautiful.

"And then there was Jimmy [Rushing] the gem of the ocean. He could always swing the blues. Jimmy meant an awful lot to us. Right now we look forward so much when we know we're going to work with him. The time can't go too fast, because we know we're going to have some fun. After he left, it was a long time before that gap could be filled in our band, and there was only one guy could really do it and that was J. W. [Joe Williams].

"And, of course, there was Billie—I mean Lady Day—she was just so wonderful. There was soul in those years, too. She was a stylist, like you would say now 's-o-m-e-t-h-i-n-g else!' How did she come with the band? Through John Hammond, of course. He took me by the arm up to Munro's one night and said there was a little girl there he'd like me to hear. After she joined our band, I used to be just as thrilled listening to her as the audience was. But she played only one location with us, the Savoy Ballroom. Otherwise, it was just the road. I remember she and Freddie Green and Lester were real buddies."

Obviously, Basie loves and respects the great jazz artists with whom he has been associated. But there's one musician whom he respects above all others—and envies, too. That's Duke Ellington. "I wish I could think like that, think that beautiful, be that imaginative, like Edward. I just don't have that type of a mind. Edward, he thinks beautiful. And he talks like that. He has that sort of a brain. That's what made it so wonderful when he first went into Carnegie Hall—actually, it was a *real* concert, not just another jazz thing, but a *real* concert."

And how does Bill Basie think? More in terms of foot-tapping audiences, perhaps? "Well, I tell you, they got to like jazz and swing. When they come to hear me, they got to expect just that, because that's the only way I can think and the only way that I could be."

How does he react to critics who sometimes wish Basie would be something else—more far out or less bluesy, for example? "Some of those writers, nothing you're gonna do is gonna please them, anyway. They write just how they feel. But I think there should be more to criticism than just how a person feels. Sometimes you wonder, do they really know, and sometimes, when you actually get to speak with them, you find they actually don't know. So I ask them, 'How could you write a column like this when you really don't know what it's all about?' Now, I don't think that's really fair. If you don't understand, you just don't understand.

"Like when people who interview me ask me about certain types of things in music, like little things that's going on—I can't comment on some of them, because *I* don't know what it's all about. Of course, when they ask me about rock, I tell them I think some of it is real great and I think a lot of the kids are composing some nice songs. We don't know how long they will last. I do think the Beatles have done some fine things. Everybody likes 'Something' and 'Yesterday' and 'Michelle.' And they have lasted."

How does one begin to understand types of music that at first hearing don't make too much sense, or at least strike some affirmative response? "Well, let me tell you what happened when we played on the same bill with a group in San Francisco a couple of years ago. I really didn't know what was going on the first night, so I went back very early the next night to listen. The kids were all sitting on the floor, listening. And I began to understand it a little better than I did the night before, and I began to see that there was something going on there that was a little interesting. And then, more and more I heard a little more and more and more of this thing, and finally I began to get a little closer to this movement."

What did "this movement" show Basie? Did it mean the kids were into something of substance? "It's got to be! It's got to be! Anytime you can catch a bunch of kids—and these kids weren't full of anything—they weren't juiced—they weren't drugged—all sitting on the floor, strictly obedient, listening—this has got to mean something. Now, if they could be that obedient to an artist or a group, something's got to be happenin' there. Later, when we played, they all stood up and some of them danced when we played some of our slower things. Then, when we played our faster things, they looked up and they tried to understand what we were doing. I don't know whether they respected our age, or whatever it was, but they were very nice to us and they were very receptive. And then, when we were done and *their* kids came on, they sat down again and listened. There's something there—really!

"Let me tell you something strange about this thing we call the generation gap. We've been like getting away and not even trying to meet them in any kind of way. But it's a little different with them. They have tried more to get close to us than we have tried to get close to them. They are always sittin' around and thinking, and listening, too. It's wonderful. Like they say, 'We want you to know, Mr. Basie, we really enjoyed your concert tonight, and I'm only fourteen, or I'm only seventeen, and we liked it very much.' They're *trying* to dig it. And sometimes, when we play universities, they ask us to play certain charts they play, because they say they want to see if they sound anything like them.

"All the kids are beginning to dig the big bands now. 'We like the sound,' they say. But, if there's going to be hope for the big bands, they're going to have to play a little different music. Maybe you can still play your style, but it's got to bend toward their way—meet them halfway, at least—give it a little of their flavor. We do a little of that—not too much—just a couple of little licks, or two or three, here and there, just enough to let them know that we know they're alive. That means so much. And the adults want to hear those new touches, too. Of course, there are still the die-hards who yell, 'Play "Shiny Stockings" ' or 'Play "Every Tub." ' But they're gettin' fewer and fewer now."

Then Bill turned to the great musical leveler, the blues. "Now, you *know there's* one thing that won't EVER die! In some way, there'll always be room for the blues—maybe some slight changes, like a little note here and a little note there, but it's still the blues and it still makes it and it always will. Today, it's got to be a little 'contemp' in there, but you can still hold on to your own identity. You just can't stay back there anymore. You got to step up a little bit. The kids are tryin' to step back a little bit toward you, so who are you not to step up a little bit toward them!"

Benny Goodman
Revisited

BENNY GOODMAN was in an expansive mood both times I interviewed him in his sumptuous home in Connecticut. We talked about many things—music mostly, of course—but also a good deal about something else that seemed to concern him very much: my right knee. I had torn a cartilage and was using a cane and Benny, who'd suffered for years from a bad back, kept emphasizing that the best therapy was swimming. "Why don't you drop by whenever you can and use our pool? It's the best thing you can do, believe me," he kept on insisting. So I did come and used the pool (Benny even tried to teach me to swim correctly). And he was right, because soon my knee got better, and I began to appreciate more thoroughly what old Goodman friends, like Glenn Miller and Gil Rodin, had said about how warm and kind the guy can be when he thinks about caring. Later, during the second interview, I asked him how come he had the reputation for being such a hard person to get along with, and he told me. But that's for later.

We talked about the band's early days, about the contributions of Fletcher Henderson: "A marvelous arranger, especially if he felt like arranging a certain tune. He didn't like to arrange pop tunes so much, but he managed to make just about every arrangement into a little gem."

And about Gene Krupa: "I always felt he was a very talented musician and a very hard worker—a real workhorse—and an inspiration to the band. And completely reliable."

And Lionel Hampton: "All the guys in that first band were hard workers and loved what they were doing, but particularly Lionel. John Hammond found him in a little club on Central Avenue in Los Angeles, you know, and he took me there and I played with his group and I offered him a job. So he drove all the way from California to New York and joined us at the Hotel Pennsylvania, and that was the beginning of the quartet. He was just as excited and exuberant about playing music then as he is now. He used to go around sitting in with bands because he only appeared with us about two or three times a night for only a half hour at a time and that wasn't enough for him. His *big* trouble simply was that he didn't get to play enough with us."

And Harry James: "He was a big kick in our band—sure. He played anything, lead or jazz, you name it. He was always a very flexible trumpet player, you know." Was he easy to get along with? "Yes. I didn't know Harry that well. I mean, we weren't buddies, but we certainly got along very well. When Harry started his own band, I think I helped him out, if I'm not mistaken." Financially? Enter the vague B.G. "I think so—yes. I loaned him some money, I think . . . I'm pretty sure I did."

Benny seemed to be a little surer about Ziggy Elman. "He was excellent, too. A terrific first trumpeter in those days." As for Ziggy personally: "Oh, he was sweet, worked like hell. He had a great sense of humor and was very understanding, and you had to like the guy."

It was Ziggy who was directly responsible for one of the band's biggest hits. "He had recorded 'And the Angels Sing" for Bluebird with a small group and he asked me to listen to it and I said, 'Gee, I thought it was great!' He had done it without a vocal, and I thought it would sound good to get lyrics to it and I asked Johnny Mercer to write some. It wound up being a star number for Ziggy."

How did another hit in a minor key, "Sing, Sing, Sing," come about? "Well, Jimmy Mundy had made the original arrangement, and we didn't particularly like the effect of the whole arrangement and the song. But we gave it a try. Helen Ward was singing with us then, but she couldn't stand singing the song and she said, 'Lookit, I'm out of this one,' or something like that. But we played it through anyway and joked about it, and then Gene continued to play with that tom-tom bit. He liked the idea of playing in a minor key, I guess. Then somebody took a solo still in that simple minor key, and somebody else played after him, and it sort of grew right after the first or second time we played it. We didn't use any music for that for years—never did— it was all a head arrangement."

Some of the greatest numbers the band played, Benny feels, sounded almost as if they hadn't been arranged, especially a batch of those early Henderson arrangements, whose very directness and simplicity created an especially free feeling. "I think when you get to know pieces and play them as if you're faking—really like a small band would—then they get to sound spontaneous, almost like an ad-lib performance. Naturally, we couldn't do that with some of the more complicated pieces that Eddie Sauter wrote for us later on."

When Sauter started writing for Goodman, his band took on a whole new sound. Benny agrees with many followers that the 1936 group with Harry, Ziggy and Gene, etc., and the early forties unit that featured Eddie's scores, were the two most outstanding of all Goodman bands. "Eddie was and still is a great arranger. I was really taken with his sort of style and the different kind of a sound that he gave to the band. I don't know just how the public took to it in those days. I don't think it was as good for dancing as a lot of Fletcher's arrangements were, but, in any event, they were great arrange-

Benny Goodman in 1971

ments. For example, when we played a piece like 'Clarinet a la King' for a dancing audience, they might walk off the floor. That was because the rhythm wasn't continuous; there were little breaks in the middle of it and ad-lib things."

Did Benny consider his a band primarily for dancing or for listening? "Well, we used to play for dancing most of the time. Even after Carnegie Hall, we still continued to play dances. I never thought that music should be continually in the concert hall, but, of course, that's about all anybody ever does nowadays. But playing for dancing has never distracted me the way it has some other musicians. I suppose there are musicians who couldn't stand having anybody dance to their music these days."

Which kind of music did Benny like to play better, the 1936 or the 1941 style? Specifically, what, in retrospect, have been his favorite recordings? The first side he mentioned was a Sauter original, "Benny Rides Again." But then he went on, "and, of course almost anything that Fletcher did: 'Sometimes I'm Happy,' 'King Porter Stomp' and 'Wrappin' It Up.'" He also recalls fondly the three sides Ella Fitzgerald made with his band, "Goodnight, My Love," "Take Another Guess" and "Did You Mean It," all of which were immediately recalled after their release "because Ella forgot to tell me one little fact, that she was under contract to Decca at that time and was not allowed to make records with anyone else. Well, that didn't make any real difference to me, because I had such a good time recording and listening to her sing that I sort of fulfilled whatever I wanted."

From time to time, Benny has, for some strange reasons, tried to fulfill

one other need: his need to sing. What was his favorite side of the perhaps too many sides on which he sang? "I'd have to say ' 'Taint No Use,' because that really characterized my singing. And later there came 'Gotta Be This or That.' And that was the end of my career."

Benny reacted just as candidly when I got around to his personal relations with his musicians, about which just about everybody, except Benny, has had very much to say. "I'm sure you've heard stories about Benny Goodman as a person," I started to say and Benny caught on immediately: "You mean difficult? Well, there's no doubt about it that I'm kind of a moody guy. You know, I think I am. I've got my moods, and sometimes it's hard to restrain a bad mood from an orchestra."

I asked him if he would take out his moods on his musicians. "I would think so. I'd take it out on them, I suppose." Did he become so preoccupied with what was on his mind that he didn't realize how he affected other people? "You mean hurting other people's feelings? Oh sure, I guess. When you're so preoccupied, you wouldn't have any idea about that. Why, I remember a lot of people coming to hear the band during a recording session, and I'd be so engrossed in what I was doing, I didn't even know they were there. And later on they'd say, 'Why didn't you talk to me?' And I'd say, 'Were you there? I didn't know you were there.' I suppose you'd have to call that devoted to what you're doing, you know. You've noticed this, George, I'm sure. Sometimes you came around and I didn't know you were there."

I remembered something like that having happened on occasions, and I told Benny that after it happened a couple of times I began to accept it, not taking it as a personal affront, but more as a Benny Goodman way of life. "You were probably engrossed in something else." "That's it, exactly. I probably was."

But how about his musicians, especially those who claimed he was giving them the evil ray? "Some of the time I guess I was probably just thinking of something else and maybe didn't even notice them. But most of the time I think it was projection on my part. You know, if you can't get what you want out of an orchestra, you get mad at somebody else, but you're really mad at yourself, and so maybe I did take it out on others. But, I'll tell you one thing. It's true. You know that when I play music that's all I think about. I'm really completely absorbed in what I'm doing. And I expect other people to be, too."

I asked Benny if he were more concerned with what people thought of him as a musician than as a person. "I think so," he replied slowly. "But nobody likes to be disliked, you know. There's an easy way. Gene used to say it. He'd say he only expected as much out of other people as he expected out of himself. Now that can be asking a little too much sometimes!"

Benny had admitted he was a moody guy. Finally, I asked him point-blank, "Benny, do you ever consider other people's moods as much as your own?" Whereupon Benny gazed at me with that three-quarter smile, one-quarter ray, and said quite simply, "No, I don't. But I do worry about some of your questions, I'll tell you that!"

Woody Herman
Revisited

THE REASON Woody Herman still leads a band is pretty simple: he wants to. He could have ended his career a long time ago, financially secure, and just coasted along amiably for the rest of his life. And for some people as amiable as Woody, that wouldn't have been difficult at all. But for Woody it would have been impossible. The urge to create, to develop and to communicate musically remains as strong within him today as it was when he first started hoofing as a kid vaudevillian a half-century ago.

From a dollar-and-cents point of view, his wisest move, he admits, would have been to have stayed retired after his two stupendously successful years, 1945 and 1946. "If I were a banker," he emphasized during our full evening interview in his handsome hilltop house with its breathtaking view of all of Hollywood, "I wouldn't have invested in a band after 1946. Only romantics would. But I was a romantic, so in 1947 and '48 and '49, I reinvested practically all my money in my bands."

A big financial mistake? Very possibly. Ever since then, Woody has been working steadily, partly from choice, but also partly from economic necessity. Business has never again been as good as it was in 1945 and 1946.

If he had it to do all over again, which role would he have played, the banker's or the romantic's? He claims he's not entirely sure. But he does say, "That's one of those games people play: counting their mistakes. And I'm very good at it. I've made many mistakes, including lots of musical ones." And Woody takes full credit for each of them—and for a laudable reason. "In the thirty-five years I've been recording, since the earliest days when we were a house band at Decca, I stood up for our rights. Anything that sounded very weird or very poor or was really rotten and showed my name, I did completely on my own. I feel there are too many people who for years have been hiding behind the excuse of 'Well, that wasn't my idea,' and blame somebody like the A&R man at their record company for making records that didn't sell. The decision still had to be mine, whether I gave in or stood up for what I believed in. After all, nobody was making me stand up there like an idiot and play it or sing it. Right? I could have taken a hard left and started walking anytime I wanted to."

This philosophy of complete responsibility for decisions has also permeated Woody's relationships with his musicians. "As long as you are the leader," he explains, "you are the boss, and as long as the fellow is in your band, he is an employee, and you can be the tightest of friends and the whole thing, but in the final analysis the musician knows—'You're still the boss, you dirty, rotten bastard, and I'm the one who has to take all the s - - t.'

"As a matter of fact, the best compliment I ever received during my entire career came from an old-type nightclub operator in Buffalo, New York. He came over on a cold, stormy night—he was a fan of the band for years—and he said, 'I wanna tell you one ting. I hope ya don't mind me, Woody,' he says. 'Ya know, Woody, you're de Vince Lombardi of de band business.' And that's how I really do feel about my players. If I'm given that respect, they'll get that respect."

Big band followers in the mid-forties wondered why Woody held on to a notorious group of hard drug users in his Second Herd. His explanation is purely pragmatic: he continued to respect their musicianship. Also, he says, "I don't think anyone ever proved anything by saying, 'You are involved with narcotics so get out of my band.' I had no personal knowledge of each man's personal needs. That was neither my concern nor my right. Their health was pitiful in some instances, but if they were well enough, they played extraordinarily well; if not, they might have played only adequately. One thing, though, dope never made them play better. I have never approved of narcotics of any kind, but I feel that if a person has ability, he must be given the chance to show that ability." And so Woody's understanding of addiction as a disease paid off with some of the best big band jazz ever blown by any band, the great sounds of the Four Brothers band. "And it still stands up well today in the state that it was put together."

Drug-users certainly weren't new to Woody. "Smoking grass," he recalls, "is something the kids were doing back in the twenties. I remember before my sophomore year in high school even, I was playing with a band in Tulsa, Oklahoma, for several hundred high school teen-agers. There were the little girls with their maxi-length country gowns, skin-tight, with nothing on underneath. They were known as pigs. And then there were the little boys, hung-up-looking cats with their sneakers and stale pants—this was way before zoot suits—and they were known as toads. At intermission, the pigs and the toads would run out to the oil fields and listen to the oil pumps and drills go make all those weird sounds, and they'd pass the stick of marijuana around and get high. This was back in 1929, and it was a universal thing among great groups of kids in parts of the midwest."

During the late twenties and early thirties, Woody, as a sideman, played with different types of bands. And after he became a leader he kept on fronting different types of bands, too. First the band that played the blues; then the

Woody Herman in 1971

band that played like Duke Ellington; then the roaring, romping First Herd; then the more subdued, super-talented Second Herd; then the bop-filled Third Herd, and then more and more Herds, constantly changing in style, constantly evolving into something new and different, invariably keeping up with the times like no other band has ever kept up with them, culminating in the early seventies in a completely modern, rock-tinged, kid-oriented, yet still-roaring Herd.

Why the constant changes? "If I thought there weren't any more challenges —just doing one thing over and over again, and maybe polishing it just a little more and taking another tune and making it sound like that—in other words, looking for *fresh* material so that I can make it sound like *old* material —I would have thrown in the towel for real!"

The amazing progress of popular music during the past ten years thrills him. Credit must go, he feels, to some of today's music education systems. "They're fantastic. What a kid can learn today in two or three semesters used to take us years to figure out. This is especially true if the kid happens to be in the right school, like Berklee, which is a fantastic place, or in the music departments of some of our universities. Yes, you're right, a lot of today's instructors are musicians out of the Big Band Era—or at least devotees of it. It's a whole different world we're living in. The stage band project alone covers thousands of high schools and thousands of colleges in all parts of the country. What is a stage band? It's nothing more than a big band. Many kids have become deeply involved in this sort of music. Some have gone on to rock groups, and that's why we have some rock groups that have gone way beyond the scope of the earlier rock groups.

"I think all this can very easily evolve into another Big Band Era, but it will be a whole different kind of band, not necessarily for dancing, because the whole attitude about dancing is now so completely different. Sometimes you'll walk into a place and see eight hundred kids all moving at the same time. But it's *their* world, *their* kind of dancing, and then on the next tune, they'll all be like sitting or lying on the floor."

The innovations in music thrill Woody even more. "So many of the barriers have been taken down. So many of the limitations have been wiped out. There are many changes of tempi, and odd amounts of bars, both unheard of during the big band days. Now you can do any damn thing you want, if you have the courage and the ability, and young composers and young writers and young arrangers are proving it every day. And as their music improves, the players have to improve, or else they can't play it. It's not easy; in fact it's damn difficult. But it's much more fun, because the challenge is there again. As long as there's a challenge, then it's fun. . . . But it was in 1902, too. Right? Then it was a challenge to get born!"

Unlike some other Big Band Era leaders, Woody digs many of the young composers. "Take the Beatles. As composers, as individuals and collectively, they have proven that they have a complete understanding of the music they dig and want, and they can produce it and produce it very well. And it has stood up extremely well, right from the beginning, songs like 'Michelle' and 'Yesterday' and 'Something'—the ones that the Boston Pops and all the legitimate people throughout the world picked up on. This proves that their melodies, their lyrics and their harmonic structure have lasting qualities. For me, 'Something' is one of the most unusual pieces of all times. Every one of their pieces has had something to say with a certain amount of freshness. Probably their only predictable thing is 'Let It Be,' which is like 'Sittin' in the Amen Corner' or 'Amen' or all the things that we did a hundred years ago. Of course, I'm not talking about the teeny-bopper things they wrote for a specific audience and sang and played for a specific audience, because that was just taking care of business."

Woody finds Burt Bacharach's work "very unusual and never trite, with very good musical taste." Jim Webb especially intrigues him. "He has proven he has some things that people never thought of before. He advocates no special form. If you feel like writing an extended thing, then extend it. And if you feel like writing a very short thing, it's quite all right. Or if you want to add a bar if for no other reason than the fact that you like the bar there, you do it. They used to criticize the country people because they used to throw in that extra bar now and then—but that was the bar that gave them that special feeling. And we find that all of us get that special feeling now when we get one of those rhythmic bounces or something that hits you in the back of your conetta."

The new jazz sounds Woody especially likes. "Things that Pat Williams and Gary Burton and Gary McFarland are doing all evolve out of these new tunes and new sounds and new ways to express yourself. And some of the pop groups have come up with some very strong things, particularly the ones with the horns, like Blood, Sweat and Tears and Chicago. And there's the group called Chase, led by Bill Chase [Herman's discovery and lead trumpeter during the sixties], that has four trumpets all miked up to an acid, heavy rhythm sound with an organ. It's a gas. You walk in and get pinned right against the wall with the sound."

How many other big band leaders will admit to such a reaction to an acid rock group? Hardly any. But then how many have kept up with today's sounds? Hardly any. Woody has. And obviously he relishes them. "Some of the things the guys in my band are writing and playing right now are positively phenomenal, and they're just beginning to scratch the surface. There's just no telling what will happen next."

And which, of all the many and completely different-sounding bands he has led is Woody's all-time favorite? "That's simple," says the man who refuses to grow old. "It's the band I'm going to have next year!"

Harry James Revisited

HARRY JAMES was in a wonderfully warm and receptive mood the night we talked between sets during his band's one-night stand in the Pan-American Hotel in Elmhurst, Long Island. His band sounded good, too, just as it had a generation and a half ago, only a few miles away on the Astor Roof. The Astor was long gone and the big band days were long gone, but Harry was still swinging and schmaltzing away, and the people loved him.

"Bet you didn't know," he told me, "that I almost went with Lawrence Welk's band. It must have been back around 1934 or 1935. I auditioned for him at the Baker Hotel in Dallas. It was just a seven-piece group, and he liked my trumpet all right. Then he asked me what else I could play and I told him drums. But that wasn't enough. He wanted guys who could play at least four or five instruments, so I didn't get the job."

He did get a job shortly after that, though, with Ben Pollack's band, and he reminisced about that too, about the write-up I'd given him, "the first write-up I ever had in my entire life. Remember? We were playing in Pittsburgh and we had a good, hard-rockin' band, and all of a sudden we pick up *Metronome* and we see this review of the band, and it was so favorable, and I said, 'Oh my goodness, this is so nice. We've got to find this man.' But we couldn't find him and it wasn't until this minute that I realized that you weren't in Pittsburgh at all but were hearing the band on the air!"

Benny Goodman soon heard about the great kid trumpeter playing in the band of his old boss Ben Pollack and sent for him. "As soon as I checked into the Pennsylvania Hotel, I called Benny's room to ask what time rehearsal was. Benny was in the bathroom, so his brother Harry took the call and Benny told him to tell me the rehearsal was the day after tomorrow. So I had to go down and just start playing.

"Well, Benny wasn't there for the first set. He and Gene and Teddy were somewhere with the trio playing a benefit and Lionel was playing drums and sort of leading the band. I remember we were playing a stock orchestration of 'A Fine Romance,' and after the first ensemble everybody would play choruses. I took one and then Lionel called out, 'Pops, play another!' And then he called out 'Play another!' again, and the next thing you know I'm playing six choruses in a row at the dinner session! Finally Benny came in, and after the set I was standing in back, but I could hear Lionel saying excitingly to Benny, 'Hey, hey, hey, pops, this guy can *play!*' "

Later there were times when Harry took over as leader, especially during the band's "Camel Caravan" radio series. "One thing Benny could never do was read lines and beat off tempos at the same time. It used to be terrible. He'd finish an introduction for a band number and then there'd be dead air while Benny just stood there getting set to beat off the tempo. So finally they had me beat off all the tunes."

Benny's problems with beating off tempos while trying to read lines were nothing compared with those that soon beset Harry and eventually led to his leaving the band. "I don't think I ever told anybody this, but I was going through a real mental thing and it was all built around 'Sing, Sing, Sing.' I'd been sick and they gave me some experimental pills—sulphur pills—only they weren't very refined yet. Well, they wigged me out, and it happened the first time just as I was supposed to get up and play my chorus on 'Sing, Sing, Sing.' I just couldn't make it. I fell back in my chair. Ziggy said to me, 'Get up!' but I couldn't, so when he saw what was happening, he got up and played my solo. I was completely out of my mind.

"It happened again another time, too, and so every time the band played 'Sing, Sing, Sing' I'd get bugged and scared it would start all over again. You know, that Stravinsky-type thing that the trombones and then the trumpets play just before the chorus? Well, that would really set me off. I tried to explain it to Benny, and I'd even ask him to play 'Sing, Sing, Sing' early in the evening, so I could relax the rest of the night. But, of course, that was his big number and I couldn't blame him for wanting to hold off. So finally I just left the band. I couldn't trust myself anymore. At least with my own band, I could play the tunes that *I* wanted to play.

"A funny thing happened years later when they asked me to play the trumpet part in the movie *Young Man With a Horn*. The director asked me if I could miss a note on purpose—you know, play like I was wigged out. I turned to him and I said, 'You may not know it, but I'm your man!' "

Even when he had his own band, that old fear would sometimes return, especially when Harry was called upon to play "You Made Me Love You" over and over and over again. "Funny thing about that record. It was the first one we made with strings. As you know, the band hadn't been doing too good and, oh, I guess about a month or so after we'd recorded the tune, we were booked into the Brooklyn Paramount. When we got there, people were lined up all around the block. I thought there had been an accident or something because we hadn't seen a crowd since we had the band. So I walked up and I asked, 'What's wrong? What's everybody doing?' And they said, 'We're waiting to hear Harry James.' I said, 'You're kidding. We're a hit?!' I didn't have any idea. But Martin Block had played our record of 'You Made Me Love You' so many times in New York, and all of a sudden it had caught on. But, you see, we'd been in Pittsburgh and we didn't know this.

And when Helen Forrest got there she went through the same thing. 'What's wrong?' she asked. 'Is something on fire or something?' "

Helen often has raved about Harry. The raves are reciprocal. "She was such a wonderful person! You know, anyone with talent is nice. You never have trouble with people with talent. And it's the same on the ball field. It's those .210 hitters who give you your problems in any league."

Harry expresses similar sentiments about another non-.210 hitter who sang with his band. "When Frank joined the band, he was always thinking of the lyrics. The melody was secondary. If it was a delicate or a pretty word, he would try to phrase it with a prettier, softer type of voice. He still does that. The feeling he has for the words is just beautiful. He could sing the wrong melody and it would still be pretty. Of course he matured a lot after he left our band. As a friend of mine said once in Las Vegas: 'It's amazing that they never give a trophy for experience.' How true!"

Experience and hard work both figure in the James success story. "Whatever success I may have had was due to my father sitting me down and really making me practice and practice and practice. I think that if the young musician of today would really work and study hard for three or four years to get his foundation, he'd be eligible to get into any field of music. Why should you be able to go only one way? If you're a real musician, you should be able to play whatever type of music you're asked to play."

One of the most difficult pieces of music Harry was ever called upon to play was "Trumpet Rhapsody," which wound up as a two-sided recording, and also as one of his two favorite James records. "But you know what? I've

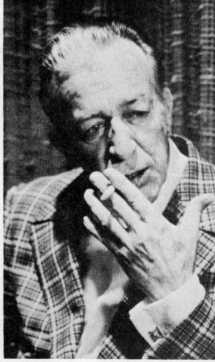

never played it at concerts or in theaters or anyplace in person. It's so difficult to play—just about impossible—so I'll let the record speak for itself."

Harry's other favorite James record is titled "Sentimental Rhapsody." "That was one of the very first records where a solo instrument played over an orchestra track. That came about because I wanted to conduct the strings and obviously I couldn't do that and play horn at the same time. It's such a beautiful theme. I really enjoy listening to it—still—and there are very few records of mine I enjoy because most of the time I listen to a record we have made and I say, 'Oh, gee! I could have done this better or that better,' and, being a perfectionist, I'm never quite satisfied with what's happening. But this particular record is so great for me to listen to. But it never sold, so evidently my opinion means nothing."

Harry's opinions about today's music reveal the same degree of tolerance and respect for true talent that has characterized his earlier opinions. Of rock, he says, "It has definitely matured. The singers are singing better, and the bigger orchestras have made it all more interesting. And some of those young musicians play very well. You know, I was one of the first Blood, Sweat and Tears fans. I got them into Las Vegas. I loved the fact that they were all such good musicians."

James has found in recent years a growing enthusiasm for big bands. "You can see it in the bigger bands the kids are using and listening to. But there's more to it than that. There are the adults, too. They're coming out more again. It seems like they're saying, 'To hell with the kids having all the fun. Let's us have some too!' And they are—thank goodness!"

Harry James in 1971

Stan Kenton in 1971

Stan Kenton Revisited

STAN KENTON has never given up. He's as dedicated as he ever was to creating new musical sounds. He remains the tallest bundle of nerves in the music field. He's still driven by some sort of compulsive enthusiasm that even he probably can't explain, as he keeps trying to prove one, two or even several points—all at the same time.

In recent years he has fronted a large neophonic orchestra, which played concerts with a fair amount of success. He has been running band clinics all over the country, uncovering, teaching, encouraging and developing young musicians. He has spearheaded a drive in Washington for federal legislation that would give copyright protection to arrangers and musicians. He has started his own record label, working out a deal with Capitol for his band's old masters, because he felt the company wasn't doing enough with them. At the same time, he continues to create and sell even more of his new material. And he still manages to go out on the road throughout each year, always with an enthusiastic, pro-Kenton group of musicians.

Stan has stayed as charming, as persuasive, as dogmatic as ever. He has grown more defensive, more reactionary (strange for one so dedicated to progressiveness in music), more bitter and somewhat disillusioned. And he has slowed up a bit—at least in his speech, for now, when he talks, he actually uses punctuation! When I mentioned this to him in his Hollywood office, where he presides over his Creative World, Inc., enterprises, he let loose one of those typical Kenton guffaws. "Jesus Christ!" he bellowed. "Maybe I'm growing up!"

Kenton has slowed in other ways, too, notably in his fervent, fearless campaign to sell, sell, sell himself and his progressive music. Now he admits that he "tried too hard to force things on people. But I've found that the fans can only go so fast; you can't lead them too fast. We made mistakes in years back when we decided to just forge ahead and confronted audiences with two hours—maybe even two and a half hours—of music they had never heard before—not one familiar thing. It used to be that years ago we had tension going all the time. That's where you were right in your original review of our band at Balboa. There was too much forcing.

"But now there's not so much of it, because now I am able to do things in a more sensitive, sensible manner. These things come to you as you get older. You begin to say, 'Am I playing music for children or am I playing music for adults? Am I playing for mature people, people who have perception, or for people who have no perception?' You have to learn how to assess your audiences.

"You know, I used to believe that if you would be patient, you could almost make a jazz fan out of anybody. That'll never happen. I am now fully convinced that in order to love jazz music, a person has to be gifted with a certain amount of perception, and if they don't have that, they're never going to get it. It gets back to what Fats [Waller] said years ago: 'If you don't know what it is, don't mess with it!' "

And what about today's audiences? Do the kids have the proper perception, or shouldn't they be messing with jazz? Stan isn't sure. "I have a feeling that many of the young people are getting more sophisticated in their desires. A lot of them are through with this kindergarten music. But I still think that the big problem is that today's tunes are so adolescent. The lyrics are so childish. The melodies are so simple. As far as the Beatles are concerned, I think most of their music is still children's music."

When Stan wants to make a point, he talks very slowly—for him. "If the Beatles can be credited with one thing," he almost drawled, "it is that they came along and they made fans out of six- and seven-year-old kids. They took it down that low. And the adults went for that stuff, because I think it's natural that an adult feels a kid is more perceptive and hip. And so they started looking at those things and started reading things into them. But there really wasn't anything there. It's just children's music. You compare the Beatles' lyrics with those of some great writers like Johnny Burke, Johnny Mercer, Jimmy Van Heusen or Sammy Cahn—are we kiddin' each other?

"Fifty percent of Americans are beneath twenty-five years old today. Does that mean the rest of us have to live like kindergarteners? But radio is programmed today to appeal to the young kids. TV is now geared to the eight- and ten-year-old mentality. Where the hell do people go that are hungry for something more sophisticated? Do they have to eat all that s - - t all the time? To me, you look at pop art and that's what you see on kindergarten walls. That's not mature. There's nothing there."

Kenton, as forceful, as hopeful, as conscientious as ever, would like to help fill that vacuum. "I'm in a position right now in my life to help a whole lot of people express themselves; help them find their identity; help clear up a whole lot of confusion in music education; help clear up some of the confusion today that's in the recording industry that is rank; help people discover what is the doughnut and not the hole. The important thing is to keep interested in people. What else counts? Birds and the sky and trees and all that crap? That doesn't really mean anything. The people are the most important thing."

Obviously, Stan Kenton has been doing a great deal of soul-searching.

Obviously, he has grown beyond the man who for years seemed to be obsessed with only his music. "Now I deal in human beings all the time, just like ministers deal in human beings and football coaches deal in human beings. Bosses and executives and everybody deals in human beings, and whether you make wheelbarrows, whether you play music, whether you're in religion, your whole human obligation is how do you bring people out of themselves and make people out of human beings. You bring a young musician along—you nurse him—and all of a sudden he tells you to f - - k yourself and he flies away. It's beautiful!"

And just how beautiful is life for this hyperactive almost-sixty-year-old who has no thoughts of retiring? "I'll tell you this: I'm happier right now than I've ever been. I've gotten over a lot of things. I've passed a lot of goals I thought would be barometers of success and found they were only passing milestones to where you're supposed to go. I've long since stopped worrying about whether I'm going to be a millionaire or not. I don't give a s - - t about that."

And what about his role in the future of progressive music? "I could drop dead this moment and I'm sure that everything is going to be straight. No, whatever I may be able to do in my future life, I'm sure will be done by someone else anyway. What needs to be done will be done. But if I can help, then I just make it easier for people. . . . That's all."

Guy Lombardo
Revisited

THE CHAPTER in this book about his band seemed to please Guy Lombardo, and he said so. It included, in addition to some direct quotes from him, a portion of my 1942 review of his band. Later, while preparing another book, I sent him a copy of the complete review, which had questioned his band's musical qualities, and asked him to comment on it. "It's absolutely ridiculous," he stated and he quoted total sales figures of 100 million Guy Lombardo recordings to substantiate his argument.

Now, I've always liked Guy. I've respected him as a gentleman, as a businessman and as an excellent salesman of a highly commercial product that has always appealed more to Middle America than to the great majority of musicians I've known, who have had neither the desire nor the stomach to assimilate his style.

Certainly, as a person, Lombardo is a stylish guy. He has class and he has guts. Despite criticism from many of us, he has never deviated. He has remained stubbornly and consistently dedicated to his commercial music and philosophy, and he'll defend them both against all comers.

"You and I have had a helluva lot of differences of opinion all of our lives. The trouble is, you have not studied the music business as you should," he began. "As a critic, you've just been picking on eighth notes." And what I'd hoped would be more of an interview started to turn into more of a lecture.

"Paul Whiteman in the twenties changed popular music entirely. Then, in 1929, we changed the whole music approach again. People liked Whiteman and us and later on Benny Goodman and Glenn Miller and the Dorseys. These have been the real contributors. But confusion has arisen between them and their imitators—in our case, between us and Sammy Kaye and Blue Barron and Jan Garber. They weren't creators; they were just bastardizing our music."

The phrase "popular music" draws different emphasis from different folk. Guy likes to dwell on the first word. "History has proven," he said, "that we have been important innovators and that we have created more styles and sold more records than any other band.

"But," he went on, "there are audiences for all styles. I think rock and dixieland and opera and symphony styles are all great, and there has always

Guy Lombardo in 1971

been enough for everyone's taste. Bing Crosby may not be in a class with Jan Peerce as a singer, but he has more showmanship. That doesn't mean they have to be compared. That bothers me, when you try to compare styles. Thank goodness there is enough around for everyone's taste."

When it comes to discussing the music business, Guy insists he likes to be "factual." "In the last twenty-five to thirty years, which band has sold the most records?" he asks almost rhetorically. His, of course. "So who likes who? What does the public say? Lawrence Welk going off TV has caused an uproar. Now that's being factual. But TV has been very foolish toward good music."

Asked to review some of the high points of his career, Guy admitted, "It's a very interesting life I've led. We rode in on Paul Whiteman's coattails. Luckily, our style embraced all types of music—even calypso. We had a number one record with it. Then we played country and western and did well there. And we had our twin pianos style that sold eleven million records in one year!"

Guy has always and very generously credited his late brother, Carmen, with having created the band's style. "He refused to have that reedy sound that other saxes had. He was a virtuoso on the flute, and he tried to use those talents on the sax."

Lombardo's generosity has also extended toward other bandleaders. "When we'd leave the Roosevelt Grill in the spring, we would make sure that they gave jobs to our friends. That's how Benny Goodman went in there. Later on we did the same thing for Lawrence Welk. We believed in taking care of the people we liked. That's why we got Eddy Duchin away from Leo Reisman's band and put him with MCA."

With forthright enthusiasm, and perhaps some extra imagination, Guy likes to take credit for having brought swing to 52nd Street in the mid-thirties. "In 1934 and 1935, if you didn't play like Lombardo, you couldn't get a job," he points out. While he was visiting New Orleans, Guy came across a musician who didn't play like Lombardo, but in whom he saw a great deal of promise, as a showman as well as a trumpeter. "I found Louis Prima in a little broken-down club," he recalls. "And I brought him to New York and tried to get him a job at Leon and Eddie's on Fifty-second Street. But they thought he was colored, and so they wouldn't take him. So I had him live with my folks and eventually I turned him over to Irving Miller to manage him. Well, as you know, Prima finally got to play at the Famous Door and he and his gang started swing on Fifty-second Street and I guess you could say I was responsible for it."

Has Guy discovered anything new in music these days that has excited him? Hardly. "I just don't think the way they do. Those guitars don't thrill me a goddamn bit. I've had too much musicianship in my background. But rock and roll certainly hasn't hurt us any," continued Guy, returning again to his commercial approach. "Our business is as good as, if not better than it's ever been.

"You know whose music I really used to love? Hal Kemp's. And today, I think the Tijuana Brass is just great." And again the shift to commercialism, "People who buy their records buy our records."

And then, finally, Guy offered what could be either his overall philosophy or his prescription for success in music—or both. "Anything that's popular," he said very simply, "I like."

Artie Shaw Revisited

INTERVIEWING Artie Shaw can be like driving a magnificent car. All you have to do is to turn on the ignition by saying "hello," step on the gas by feeding him some subject matter, and off he goes—smoothly, directly and amazingly well attuned. Then, once in a while, if you want a little turn in the conversation, all you do is given him a gentle steer, and he responds beautifully—as he did during our two conversations in his New York apartment-office.

Most bandleaders, when asked what they would have done differently if they had their lives to live over again, respond with vague answers. Not Artie.

"If I were now what I was then, I would have done exactly as I did. But if I knew then what I know now, I'd have done just about 180 degrees opposite.

"I'd have changed many things. I'd have been a bit less ebullient and a bit less convinced that everything was going to work out perfectly in this 'all-so-perfect' world, which I have since come to realize is one horrible mess of a world. I'd have been a bit more cautious and maybe a bit more conservative and invested my time and energies in different manners. I certainly wouldn't have gone off half-cocked in as many different directions as I did when I believed the bus was never going to stop.

"You know, you go back to when you're a kid—you've had no kind of training for the kind of success of adulation or money that's suddenly being showered on you from all sides. It's a head-turning experience, so, at a certain point, your head, in order to accommodate itself to that new set of circumstances, begins to accept it. Well, when you begin to accept the incredible, you're in kind of serious psychological trouble because at that point you expect the incredible to continue."

The mention of psychological trouble made it easy to turn the conversation directly to the famous Shaw flight from the Café Rouge of the Hotel Pennsylvania to Mexico at the very height of his first band's success. What happened?

"I just got up and walked away in the middle of the night—just got up literally and left, leaving all the debris behind and letting anybody who wanted to scrabble for what was left. Looking back at it now, I'd have made arrangements. What I really *should* have done would have been to present my agents and lawyers with a much more viable set of alternatives. As it was, I kept saying 'I need a vacation! I need a vacation!' But, like a little kid who argues with Daddy and gets frightened and hysterical and nervous, I overreacted. They were killing the goose with the golden egg kind of thing, getting their commissions and selling ninety-nine bands like tails to my kite. And I kept saying 'Fellows, I can't go on at this pace anymore.' Well, what I should have done was said, 'Look, fellows, goodbye. I'm going to take a vacation. Now, you make your *own* arrangements. Either that, or I'm going to walk out.' Instead of that, I just got up and walked out. Well, that was kind of a stupid thing to do without any thought of your future. But, you see, when you're twenty-eight and you're making umpteen thousand dollars a week anytime you want to work, it never occurs to you that the future is going to be any kind of a problem. It's like young kids. They don't believe they're ever going to grow old. The world is showering all sorts of goodies on them and they don't think it's ever going to stop. But, when it stops, it's a tremendous shock!"

Artie feels he was much more mature and far less stupid about his music. "I don't think I'd have done much different, because I think the music I played was the best I could contrive to play, given all circumstances, given what audiences would accept, given the length of the records you had to make. What I did try very hard to do at the time was to put our work into the context of concerts, because we were, in effect, playing concerts. Even though the locales were ballrooms, nobody danced. The people just stood in front of the bandstand. Maybe seven couples were out there dancing, out of maybe eight thousand.

"But I wasn't concerned with their dancing, anyway. We weren't playing dance music. Our music was for listening primarily. Within the so-called dance-music format, we were playing concerts. So I kept saying, 'Why don't we do this on a concert stage and let the people pay and sit down instead of letting them pay and come in to a dance hall and just stand there?' It was considered an outré proposal at that time. Well, as you know, not too long afterward, that's what it became. People finally got the idea that American jazz was a music *worth* listening to, that you didn't *have* to get up and dance, that you could dance to Meyer Davis if you just wanted to dance. If we had wanted to play just *dance* music, I could have saved myself an awful lot of money on some of the sidemen I paid."

Of all those sidemen, Artie likes to discuss the two who influenced his band greatly. One is Georgie Auld; the other Buddy Rich. "As you know, I'm kind of a perfectionist and I always insisted on a lot of control. Well, that can stifle some of your men and that was beginning to come true with my band. Then, at a certain point, I heard Georgie play. Now, Georgie used to do a lot of things that went against my grain, musically. They weren't what *I* felt music should sound like, and yet I was aware he knew precisely what he

was doing. So I hired him and he started the band sounding in a way that I could never have done myself.

"So I was very aware of that by the time I hired Buddy. He had enormous youth, enormous energy, enormous vitality in his playing and a beat that couldn't be topped. But he was a totally undisciplined musician. The hardest job was to keep him within the bounds of what I was trying to get the ensemble to do. But as soon as things started to jell, I must say he made the band into practically a new band overnight. I always let him know that, too. I was quite grateful to him."

Not all of Artie's personnel, let alone his personal changes, turned out that well. Take his matrimonial life. "I'd have done a lot of changes there, too. Come to think of it, I did anyway, didn't I! If variety is the spice of life, I guess I'd had a pretty spicy life, haven't I!

"It must be pretty obvious to anyone who knows me that I've been blessed, or cursed, with a large curiosity bump, and one of the things that has resulted is that I've spent most of my life probing and exploring into ways of life. This includes both people and interests. And I think it's one of the reasons I quit music.

"You see, music is such a horrendously all-consuming discipline. To play it up to the standards I had, I knew finally that I had to become such an overspecialized human being that there was nothing left for anything else. I just didn't want to become just a half-assed human being in order to become a whole-assed musician. So I gave it up."

Artie Shaw in 1971

Now, fifteen years after he has blown his last note, Artie Shaw still gets asked why he doesn't play anymore.

"How *could* I play? It would take me six months to produce a sound I could stand. Then they ask, 'Don't you play even for your amusement?' Well, then I say, 'What's amusement? What's amusing about the physical labor it takes just to get a note out of that thing?' It's like asking a prize fighter if he shadow-boxes or trains just for his own amusement. It's sheer, hard physical work, so I don't play anymore, and I have no intention of ever playing again. I miss it, sure. You miss anything that has so much of your life wrapped up in it."

Now that his music has become a part of the past only, how does Artie feel about the music of the present, like that of the Beatles or Blood, Sweat and Tears?

"I don't know. I'm really not terribly interested in singers. I never was. I mean, a singer to me is Billie Holiday. But I don't care very much about people getting up and telling me 'Hold my hand and I'll understand.' I don't care who it is. If that sounds terrible, I'm sorry. I mean, I have nothing against the Beatles. They created a way of living. They were also the product of a mass medium."

And what about what the Beatles have contributed musically? "Not very much. Basie has done more. Ellington has done more. I did more. Goodman did more. We *did* something musically. These people haven't done very much *musically*. Sure, they wrote some fairly nice songs, but then so did Cole

Porter, and so did Larry Hart and so did Rodgers. So did Hammerstein. As I said, the Beatles have written some fairly good things, but you're not going to ask me to take 'We All Live in a Yellow Submarine' very seriously, are you? I mean, hardly as a musical statement."

On the subject of songs in general, Artie insists that he, "like any good jazz musician, doesn't give a damn about the song itself. You care about what can be done with it. A song is merely a series of chords with a melody loosely attached, and then you say, 'What can we do with this one?' That's what it's all about."

Having disposed of melody and harmony, Shaw turned to today's rhythm. "Some of the beats have been exceedingly good. There is an energy and ferocity to them that's good. But then, take the energy and ferocity of what was going on in the late thirties and early forties. That's hard to beat. It's hard to top what a Basie does or an Ellington does at his peak. It's hard to top what I was doing at my peak, or what Benny was doing at his peak, or Tommy at his. You see, I didn't mention Glenn, because Glenn, too, was the recipient of an enormous amount of mass publicity—the fact that he died in the mysterious circumstances that he died in, and all that. But musically, his was essentially ground-out music—ground-out like so many sausages. On the other hand, take Jimmie Lunceford—that's not a name that comes up that often. But that was a great band, too.

"Now, I don't want to leave this subject on the basis that it sounds like some guy looking at the present and saying, 'Well, we were better in the old days.' I don't believe that. I think that the best of today ranks very favorably with the best of any day. But the best is *rare*. There is very little of that nowadays.

"And I don't think that because the Beatles were the *biggest* that they were necessarily the *best* musicians around. I read that little piece by Paul McCartney where he was talking about the Beatles corporation busting up, and they sounded like something out of Gulf and Western and a merger between that and McGraw-Hill."

The dimensions of the success of some of today's groups astound Shaw—and distress him as well. "They can't seem to have any kind of humility about them, these kids. Don't they know how lucky they are? Do they think they *really* deserve all that adulation? It's kind of dumb. Beethoven never got it at his peak. Mozart never got it, Bach never got it. It's kind of strange to say, 'I'm a Beatle. I'm getting all this money, and, man, I'm important!' They're an important piece of mass phenomenon—that's all—who caught on with a bunch of liberated kids who had enough money to buy records and dictate tastes, and could scream and yell. But the very fact that they screamed so loud that you couldn't hear the music told me a great deal about how much the music actually had to do with it.

"You know what? They weren't buying music. They were doing just what they did in my day—screaming too loud to hear what they were screaming for. And stopping anyone else who wanted to hear it."

And here he was once again: Artie Shaw, complaining as strenuously as ever about the very conditions that contributed to his sounding off more than a generation and a half ago with some highly publicized blasts at jitterbugs, the original freaks of the thirties and forties. Obviously, there are negative as well as positive ways of spanning that generation gap.

Part Five:
The Big Bands—
Now

*The Duke and the King
in the sixties*

The Big Bands—Now

Thirty-five years after the big bands began to fade from the scene, a few of the originals are still around along with quite a few later arrivals. Their popularity and their commercial success can't begin to match that which they enjoyed when the country was teeming with all those bands listed elsewhere in this book. But there's still a hard core residual of fans, along with many recent converts—including, by the way, many members of the younger generations—who make it possible for these bands to exist.

A few of those bands never stopped playing, and they're proud of it. Whenever some seemingly surprised fan asks Woody Herman, "Where have you been?" he quickly replies, "*We've* been around. But where have YOU been?"

Woody and Basie and Harry James and Les Brown and Lawrence Welk, as well as Duke Ellington and Stan Kenton and Guy Lombardo before they died, never gave up. Other top names of the big band era kept going on less regular schedules, sometimes organizing outfits just for occasional appearances, letting their fans know that Cab Calloway, Frankie Carle, Bob Crosby, Xavier Cugat, Dizzy Gillespie, Benny Goodman, Lionel Hampton, Dick Jurgens, Sammy

Harry James, Les Brown, Lawrence Welk and Freddy Martin in the sixties,
when there were just a few bandleaders left on the scene

The Count, who never gave up, with the Chairman of the Board,
himself forever a big band supporter

Kaye, Wayne King, Freddy Martin, Ray KcKinley, Charlie Spivak, Orrin Tucker and others who were willing to buck the musical tide were still very much around.

In the late 1940s, that tide began to change gradually but steadily. America was slowly becoming a nation whose economy centered around kowtowing to the whims and tastes of its younger generation. And if the Swing Era kids hadn't wanted to hold on to the likes of Victor Herbert or the Charleston or Rudy Vallee, who could blame the next generation for not embracing Benny Goodman or Glenn Miller or Duke Ellington or the Lindy Hop or Bob Eberly and Helen O'Connell?

The change in musical tastes reflected the new generation's attitude toward life—less naive, less romantic, more aggressive, more self-centered. The sentimentality reflected in the ballads of the big bands seemed silly to them, while the happy swinging and more sophisticated sounds of the big bands bore little emotional resemblance to the more overpowering, intense, often simplistic and even angry outpourings from at first twangy guitars, and then from high-powered, impersonalized, electrified instruments that more clearly reflected their own emotions and life styles.

But other factors also intruded to diminish the big bands' popularity. Television was an important one. Why go out and spend money when you could be entertained in your own home for free? And where would you go to dance to their music? With the demands for the bands' appearances reduced, many ballroom operators had renovated their places to cash in on the growth of bowling and of super markets.

Economic and social changes among the bands also contributed to their demise. Transportation costs had become almost prohibitive. And many of the musicians, tired of being away from home (especially those who had returned from the armed services), and no longer basking in the adoration of an entire country, simply decided it all wasn't worth it anymore and quit.

But the tide did change slowly. While many bands hung in, others even *came* in! Some were especially musical, like the great Sauter-Finegan orchestra, formed in 1952, and Billy May's inventive outfit, organized a year earlier. Ralph Marterie also debuted in 1951 and two years later Les and Larry Elgart came along with their highly personalized style. And in the mid-1950s, just about the time that it all came pretty much to a halt, Maynard Ferguson burst upon the scene with his exciting sounds, a harbinger of the much more intense music that was to follow.

No bandleader tried harder to stem the tide than did Tommy Dorsey, as pointed out in the chapter devoted to his band. When he died late in 1956, the big bands had lost their most dominating spirit. Sure, there was Stan Kenton, too, forever a beacon in a fading scene. But Stan, rather than reflecting the past, had always been setting his sights toward the future. And perhaps there is where he made his greatest contributions of all to the big bands.

It was Kenton who sent the big band movement into an entirely different direction—right into America's colleges and high schools. Forever one concerned with change and what was new, as well as with encouraging young, emerging musicians, he continued to believe in the youth of America. If *they* wouldn't come to hear big band music, why not take those sounds into *their* schools for them to hear *there*?

Stan believed what many of us did: that if young Americans could just hear—IN PERSON—the sounds of the big bands, they might immediately develop both an appreciation of and enthusiasm, for them. (I can recall when in the later 1950s I took my two young kids to Freedomland, a place in New York's Bronx, to hear Harry James and Benny Goodman and Woody Herman and how amazed and thrilled they were hearing those *live* sounds, especially the pure, pulsating brasses, for the first time, in person. The impact was just tremendous: "Gee, Dad, I never thought they sounded like that! They're much better than your records!")

Ironically, the economics of the band business helped Kenton in his move to get jazz and big band music taught in the schools. Instructors of previous generations had been content to follow established procedures, by pushing their musicians astride dull, old warhorses, like the "William Tell Overture," or some of Sousa's Marches, and encouraging them to play them just "as rote." But the newer instructors, many of whom had been forced to turn to teaching

Stan Kenton at North Texas State University with pioneering jazz educator Leon Breeden.

Woody Herman and arranger Alan Broadbent chat with students at Berklee College.

Clinician Clark Terry joins in with student bandsmen at the University of Utah.

because there were so few big bands job available, had different ideas. For them, playing had been fun. They had exulted in the freedom of jazz and in the opportunities of self-expression that the big bands had given them. "There's so much more to music than just the mechanics of playing notes," they told their students, as they began to share with them all that they had learned, and also enjoyed, during their working days and nights.

Not surprisingly, the students responded with enthusiasm, especially when idols, such as Kenton and his musicians, came directly into the schools to illustrate what the newer instructors had been teaching, and to actually play side by side with the youngsters. Stan wasn't alone in this movement, either. Other bands followed, and, as Charles Suber, publisher of *Down Beat* and a leader in musical education, has noted, the list of "name" clinicians appearing each year in schools has been growing steadily. With Kenton gone, Woody Herman's band took over the lead, closely followed by such leaders as Maynard Ferguson, Buddy Rich, Mel Lewis, Louie Bellson and Toshiko Akiyoshi and Lew Tabackin. Both "Doc" Severinsen and Tommy Newsom have taken time off from leading the "Tonight Show" band to appear in schools and colleges. And trumpeter Clark Terry, who toured with a band of youngsters early in 1981, trombonist Bill Watrous, arranger Ernie Wilkins, saxophonists Lee Konitz and Pepper Adams and many dozens more well-known musicians, most of them alumni of top big bands, have also served as enthusiastic, dedicated and often idolized clinicians.

According to Suber, there are now close to 20,000 big bands playing swing and more modern sounds in today's schools, some beginning as early as the fifth grade of grammar school, with, of course, the best working at the college level. These bands average twenty musicians apiece, some sporting as many as a dozen brass players. Simple multiplication reveals that, as of the winter of 1981, there were approximately 400,000 young musicians directly involved with playing big band music. So, as you can see, the sound had not exactly died.

Matt Beeton, a founder and the executive director of NAJE, the National Association of Jazz Educators, a strong organization formed in 1968 to bring together the various schools and instructors in the field, estimates an even larger number of big bands—20,000 to 25,000 of them, 60% in high schools, 30% in colleges and 10% in junior high schools. There are now two dozen colleges offering complete degrees in jazz, with 300 to 400 more offering varying degrees in the field. "And the best high school jazz players," he notes, "tend to gravitate toward those colleges with jazz programs, just as top athletes are attracted to the colleges with better sports programs."

Woody Herman, who, like Buddy Rich and others, has been stocking his bands with young graduates from such colleges for many years, has observed that "it has been a long, uphill battle. For a long time we had been fighting athletics for attention. But now jazz is getting some of that as well. It has," he adds a bit wryly, "finally become very respectable in school systems."

Clem DeRosa, a former director of NAJE and a leading educator, finds that

Leading jazz educator Clem DeRosa conducts
young students at Huntington (NY) Junior High School.

"youngsters who are totally immersed in jazz are more dedicated and more highly motivated than other students. Many of them found that rock music, with its limitations, just wasn't challenging enough for them. Now some of them *want* to expand into classical music as well."

What has impressed both educators and veteran bandleaders about the young graduates, in addition to their dedication and instrumental facility, has been their life style. "Because they are so secure in what they are doing," DeRosa has pointed out, "they have no need for getting 'high'." Emphasizing that his latest band is the "cleanest I've ever had," Woody Herman added, "It's a pleasure dealing with today's young musicians. They're so well-educated in every way, including music. It's not like dealing with some of the idiots we had when I was much younger."

Most of Herman's 1981 band graduated from the Eastman School of Music, long a bastion of classical music, but now right up there as a major source of superior musicians with Berklee College, which has always concentrated on jazz, and North Texas State University, which as far back as the late 1940s introduced the concept of college degrees in jazz.

Unfortunately, some of the very best students fail to find big bands jobs after graduation. The reason is pure economics: the supply exceeds the demand, a demand that could be increased significantly, Herman and others are convinced, if the record companies devoted a small portion of the money, time and energy they concentrate trying to hype overnight, non-lasting hits, to records that would sell over a longer period. "Unfortunately," Woody has pointed out, "record companies generally are run and guided not by people who care about music, but by accountants who are interested only in big numbers."

Willard Alexander, the man who helped start Benny Goodman, Count Basie and others, and whose booking agency has never failed to support big bands, agrees that they haven't received the support they deserve and which, he believes, in the long run could pay off well for the record companies and radio stations that have until now ignored them. For evidence he points to the increase in big band grosses from 1980 to 1981: Basie's as much as 50%, the Tommy Dorsey band from 30 to 40%, Herman, Harry James and the Glenn Miller band from 25 to 30%, and Larry Elgart and the Jimmy Dorsey band about 25%.

Meanwhile, the list of radio stations playing big band music has continued to expand as well. In almost every large city, at least one, and often more stations concentrate almost exclusively on big band sounds. New York's famed WNEW, the single most important station during the big band era, returned to that format in 1980. Immediately its rating zoomed upward. Washington's WEAM was completely revived after it went to all-big-band programming. A station in nearby Baltimore followed suit. Its ratings reportedly rose from something like 2.8 to 7.5 of the audience. And west coast Chuck Cecil's syndicated big band series, *The Swingin' Years,* gained a 25% increase between 1980 and 1981. Also, Ray Anthony, head of an organization called *Big Bands 80s,* which lists Les Brown, Les Elgart, Woody Herman, Harry James, and Sammy Kaye, Freddy Martin and Alvino Rey among its 40 bandleader members, reports that "close to one thousand radio stations are now (1981) playing big band music."

But don't get the idea that during this period only nostalgia pervaded the big band scene. Sure, there were the so-called "ghost" bands, with Buddy Morrow

A modern Buddy Rich

A modern Gerry Mulligan

leading the Tommy Dorsey band the most impressive. The Glenn Miller band, directed by Jimmy Henderson, continued to do big business, while Mercer Ellington kept his dad's name alive, first with a band that played some of the original Ellington music mixed with some more modern versions of his tunes, and later when he fronted the great band that appeared on stage during the Broadway musical, *Sophisticated Ladies*.

But the most interesting and certainly freshest sounds came from the newer big bands. In the latter 1970s, Gerry Mulligan created one of the finest bands of all time, a thirteen-piece outfit that played his colorful arrangements with delightful enthusiasm. Before him, Thad Jones and Mel Lewis had organized a group that played mostly Thad's charts with expertise but with a bit too much emphasis upon never-ending solos, a failure that Mel corrected after Thad settled in Europe and Lewis became sole leader. Some of the most exhilarating and progressive sounds came from the band co-led by Toshiko Akiyoshi, the brilliant Japanese pianist/arranger, and her husband, Lew Tabackin, a wonderful tenor sax and flute player, and from the high-swinging bands of two drummers, the forever dynamic and probing Buddy Rich, and the thoroughly musicianly and inventive Louie Bellson.

Up in Canada, Rob McConnell led the brilliant Boss Brass, composed of many of that country's top studio musicians, while out in California, Bob Florence and Bill Berry produced modern, swinging sounds with similar refugees while Bill Toll recreated some of yesteryears, as did Lynn Oliver's and Stan Rubin's bands in New York.

So, as the 1980s rolled on their way, it was obvious that the big bands were not dead. Sure, there were fewer of them. And there were many less places in which they could play, though colleges were beginning to notice them more and more and offered them additional employment. And several Big Band Societies, like those in Atlanta and Phoenix, for example, as well as in other cities and towns throughout the country, welcomed Harry James and Les Brown and Woody and the Count and the "ghost" bands with enthusiasm and a fair degree of regularity.

Still, changed tastes and attitudes, economic and social factors, plus obviously different life styles have pretty much precluded the resurrection of the big band era as it once was. But indications for a greater acceptance among members of the younger generation continue to grow, just as the kids themselves have. Three-chord guitarists and their musical immaturity don't appeal to them so much anymore. And the constant struggle to try to understand limited singers shouting their incomprehensible lyrics has become rather tiring.

Toshiko conducting; co-leader/husband
Lew Tabakin far left

The author of The Big Bands *with Count Basie in the spring of 1981*

Besides, for a decade or so, more and more reed and brass instruments have been used by rock performers—not only by such instrumental groups as Blood, Sweat and Tears and Chicago and others, but also in the backings for a number of the most famous singers. After all, if Stevie Wonder can use a full brass section, or if Billy Joel can feature a hot alto sax, maybe all those things that their parents had been telling them about what it was like during the big band days may not have been so stupid after all!

Certainly the signs of an instrumental revival of some sort are all there. Perhaps music may even be coming full circle. Who knows? Willard Alexander, who helped set off Benny Goodman's big band explosion in the summer of 1938, insists that another big band boom, almost a half a century later, is not out of the question. "After all," he points out, "it took just one big band then. So who's to say that if the right new band came along, it wouldn't happen all over again!"

Could be.

Part Six:
A Selective
Big Bands
Discography

A SELECTIVE
BIG BANDS
DISCOGRAPHY

The long-playing records and sets listed and described in this section include primarily big band music played and recorded during the big band era, and thus reflect the actual sounds of those times. Of course some bands, like those of Count Basie, Duke Ellington, Benny Goodman, Harry James, Stan Kenton, Buddy Rich and others who survived, have made many records since then. And so have those bands that came along later: Toshiko Akiyoshi and Lew Tabackin, Don Ellis, Maynard Ferguson, Thad Jones and Mel Lewis, Gerry Mulligan and many more.

However, what follows is intended primarily to *bring back* some of the best of the *original* sounds of the big band era to those of you who would like to hear them again, and to acquaint those of you who never heard them in the first place with what they were like.

By no means are all the records of each band listed. I have tried to pick out those that are either the best of the lot or else most indicative of a particular band's music. Nor are all the bands whose music you might want to hear listed. That's because some of the record companies, Columbia and RCA Victor especially, have been terribly remiss about reissuing some of their better material, or at least about retaining earlier reissues in their catalogue. Among their lost leaders are Will Bradley, Larry Clinton, Horace Heidt, Isham Jones, Kay Kyser, Ray McKinley, Ray Noble, Red Norvo, Tony Pastor, Jan Savitt, Charlie Spivak and Claude Thornhill!

Fortunately, Wally Heider's remarkable Hindsight series has filled in some holes. And so have some of the bootleg companies that have issued many unauthorized recordings, some of simply horrible quality, and none of which, because they are ripping off the artists, I can in good conscience recognize in print. They're there, but buyer beware!

At the conclusion of this discography I have listed a number of big band collections, many of which cover a side spectrum of the era's music. These are especially recommended to those unfamiliar with the various sounds, and of course will bring back copious memories, in abbreviated forms, to those who'd like to hear many of the bands again. There's also a listing of the various companies' addresses, including mail order houses, which must of course be contacted directly, since their product is not available in stores.

LOUIS ARMSTRONG: BACK IN NEW YORK—1935. Some of Satchmo's more popular works with a big band, including "I'm in the Mood For Love," "You Are My Lucky Star," "Shoe Shine Boy" and "I Hope Gabriel Likes My Music." (MCA-1304)
—THE BEST OF LOUIS ARMSTRONG. More jazz and standard fare with big band backing like "Dippermouth Blues," "Mahogany Hall Stomp," "Lazy River," "Georgia On My Mind," "Blueberry Hill," "When It's Sleepy Time Down South" and eighteen more. (MCA 2-4035)
—SWING THAT MUSIC. The title tune, plus "Skeleton in the Closet," "Dipper Mouth Blues," "Jubilee," "Struttin' with Some Barbecue" and "When the Saints Go Marching In" and more (MCA 1312)

GEORGIE AULD: GEORGIE AULD AND HIS ORCHESTRA. Some of the more exciting sides by a band that included Dizzy Gillespie, Erroll Garner, Al Cohn, Billy Butterfield, plus the leader's booting tenor sax. (Musicraft 501)

THE BEST OF CHARLIE BARNET. Two dozen swingers, including "Skyliner," "Smiles," "Things Ain't What They Used To Be," and "Share-Croppin' Blues," featuring Kay Starr, by Barnet's mid-forties crew. (MCA 2-4069). (Apparently RCA has withdrawn its album that contained original recordings of "Cherokee," "Red Skin Rumba" and other big Barnet hits.)

BLUE BARRON, 1938–39, 1941. Eighteen selections with vocals by Jimmy Brown, Russ Carlyle and Charlie Fisher taken from radio broadcasts to comprise the first 12-inch LP ever issued by this band. Fine notes by Brad McCuen. (Hindsight HSR 110) More of the same can be heard on Blue Barron, Vol. II. (Hindsight HSR 137)

COUNT BASIE: APRIL IN PARIS. A reissue, beautifully re-recorded in Japan, of one of the band's most important post-big band era collections, complete with the original "April in Paris," "Shiny Stockings," "Didn' You," "Midget," "Corner Pocket" and five more outstanding performances of the band during some of its most swinging times. (Verve/Polydor UMV-2641)

—THE BEST OF COUNT BASIE. The classic two-record set that includes the best of the 30's band that featured Lester Young, Herschel Evans, Jo Jones, Walter Page, Buck Clayton and Jimmy Rushing performing numbers like "One O'Clock Jump," "Swinging the Blues," "Blue and Sentimental," "Sent for You Yesterday," "Jumpin' at the Woodside" and more. (MCA 2-4050)
—THE COUNT MEETS THE DUKE. An exciting record combining the bands of Basie and Ellington blowing extended works of standards and originals. (Columbia CS 8515)
—ECHOES OF AN ERA. Late 1950s and early 1960s remakes of some of the band's biggest recordings like "One O'Clock Jump," "April in Paris," "Goin' to Chicago Blues" with Joe Williams, "Every Tub," "Lil' Darlin'," "Jumpin' at the Woodside," "Sent for You Yesterday" again with Joe Williams, and thirteen more. (Roulette RE-102)
—GOOD MORNING BLUES. 32 selections of real blues and blue-tinged performances that include "Dark Rapture," "The Fives" and "Thursday." (MCA 2-4108)
—SUPER CHIEF. An interesting two-record set that presents performances by several small groups plus many by the big band as well. (Columbia CG 31224)
(For more modern Basie, look for its recent Pablo albums.)

BUNNY BERIGAN: I CAN'T GET STARTED. The title song plus some of the better sides like "Davenport Blues," "I Cried For You" and "Peg O' My Heart" that the great trumpeter recorded during his all-too-short stay with RCA Victor and on earth. (Pickwick QJ 25081)
—TAKE IT BUNNY. Not exactly big band, though close to it, and still plenty of Berigan's potent horn. (Epic JLN 3109)

LES BROWN: THE BEAT OF THE BIG BANDS. Ten of the biggest hits in their original versions including "Leap Frog," "I've Got My Love To Keep Me Warm," "Bizet Has His Day" and Doris Day singing "Sentimental Journey." (Columbia 32015)
—THE BEST OF LES BROWN. Later versions of 24 of the band's more important numbers, like "Midnight Sun," "Mexican Hat Dance," "Montoona Clipper," plus other standbys, all expertly played and recorded. (MCA 2-4070)

—LES BROWN 1944–46. Sixteen of the band's instrumental and vocal works, some never before on records, with five Doris Day vocals, all resurrected with elegant sound from a series of transcriptions. (Hindsight HSR-103)

—LES BROWN 1949, Vols. II and III. Each contains sixteen more performances by a later, swinging group with good vocals by Lucy Ann Polk. (Hindsight HSR 132)

HENRY BUSSE 1935. Sixteen standards, including a full version of "Hot Lips" plus "When Day Is Done" and many other standards featuring Busse's puckish horn and his shuffle rhythm as they sounded on air-checks. (Hindsight HSR 122)

CAB CALLOWAY: HI-DE-HO MAN. Twenty selections on a two-record set that features the band from 1935 to 1947 on Calloway specialities like "Minnie the Moocher," "St. James Infirmary," "Nagasaki," "Jumpin' Jive" plus an "I'll Be Around" that shows how well the maestro sang ballads. Among the sidemen: Chu Berry, Cozy Cole, Dizzy Gillespie and Milt Hinton. (Columbia CG 32593)

THE BEST OF FRANKIE CARLE. One dozen clear, crisp, clean performances of numerous hit songs by the veteran pianist and his very straight-ahead orchestra. (RCA Victor ANL 1-1079)

BENNY CARTER: GIANTS OF JAZZ. Among the forty selections in this superb coverage of Carter's music are a dozen sides by his American big band plus more by groups he led overseas. Included are such gems as "Meloncholy Lullaby," "Sleep" and "More Than You Know" from Vocalion, "O.K. for Baby" from Decca, "Ill Wind" and "Sunday" from Victor, and "I Surrender, Dear" from Capitol. The well-documented and illustrated booklet by Monroe and Edward Berger is a big plus. (Time-Life STL-J10)

CARMEN CAVALLARO 1946. The only recordings by the "Poet of the Piano's" regular working band (others were studio assemblages) featuring 16 standard tunes played by a 17-piece orchestra with lots of musical frills from the talented maestro. (Hindsight HSR 112)

LARRY CLINTON 1937–38. A mixture of many ballads, mostly featuring Bea Wain, and light swingers by the band during its Glen Island Casino heyday—"Martha," "You Go To My Head" and an unusual "Dipsy Doodle" with a vocal by Wain. (Hindsight HSR 109) (A few of the original Clinton RCA recordings can be found in some of the anthologies listed later.)

THE BEST OF BOB CROSBY. By far the most inclusive of all the outstanding recordings of "The Best Dixieland Band in the Land," complete with Eddie Miller, Matty Matlock, Yank Lausen, Billy Butterfield, Bob Zurke, Bob Haggart, Ray Bauduc and others on "South Rampart Street Parade," "Big Noise from Winnetka," "What's New," "Honky Tonk Train Blues," "Boogie Woogie Maxixe," "March of the Bob Cats" and eighteen more. (MCA 2-4083)

XAVIER CUGAT: THE BEST OF XAVIER CUGAT. Two dozen selections, almost all with a Latin flavor, performed by a latter-day version of the famed maestro's series of bands. (MCA 2-4072)

THE BEST OF JIMMY DORSEY. All of the JD warhorses, including such Eberly-O'Connell cooperative ventures as "Tangerine," "Green Eyes" and "Amapola"; Eberly solos like "I Understand" and "Maria Elena," plus jumpers like "John Silver" and "Parade of the Milk Bottle Caps" and seventeen more. (MCA 2-4073)

—JIMMY DORSEY 1939–40. Sixteen performances, taken from transcriptions, of the band's renditions of ballads and instrumentals never-before released on records. Eberly sings such standards as "Imagination," "Fools Rush In," "The Nearness of You" and "Blueberry Hill," while O'Connell chimes in with "Just for a Thrill" and "I'm Stepping out with a Memory Tonight." (Hindsight HSR 101)

—JIMMY DORSEY, VOL. 2, 1942–44. Mostly up-tempoed material of standards and original instrumentals taken from broadcasts during the AFM recording ban and revealing a quality of this band heretofore seldom heard on records. There are also two O'Connell vocals. (Hindsight HSR 153)

THE BEST OF TOMMY DORSEY. A dozen of the band's most popular recordings including "Marie," "Song of India," "I'll Never Smile Again," "Boogie Woogie" and "Yes, Indeed." All the regulars are there: Bunny Berigan, Bud Freeman, Dave Tough, Jack Leonard, Frank Sinatra, Jo Stafford, Sy Oliver and on and on. (RCA Victor ANL1-1087)
—THE COMPLETE TOMMY DORSEY. Eventually to include everything the band ever recorded for RCA Victor—hundreds upon hundreds—but by mid-1981 covering only a small portion, including a lot of surprisingly dull sides of mediocre pop tunes. But when (and if ever) completed, this lengthy series will become the definitive T. Dorsey offering. (RCA Bluebird)
—THIS IS TOMMY DORSEY, VOL. I. An elongated, two-record version of "The Best of Tommy Dorsey" with such additions as "On the Sunny Side of the Street," "Opus One," "Hawaiian War Chant," "Street of Dreams" and "There Are Such Things." (RCA Victor VPM 6038)

A follow-up "Tommy Dorsey, Vol. II" offers some later recordings as well as some lesser-known earlier efforts. And if you'd like to hear what the band sounded like live, try to get a copy of a boxed set "That Sentimental Gentleman" (RCA Victor LPM 6003), which contains Sinatra's farewell broadcast and the only recorded example, "Daybreak," of Dick Haymes singing with the band.

EDDY DUCHIN: THE EDDY DUCHIN STORY. Thirteen standards, played with the usual Duchin piano flash, accompanied by a well-manicured orchestra that reflects the svelte society aura created by this handsome and somewhat talented gent. (Columbia CS 9420)

DUKE ELLINGTON: 1899–1974. An unusual, five-record collections of mostly Duke's own studio tapes, many never heard before, and samples of various broadcasts covering a huge breadth of the band's prodigious output, all the way from well-worn Ellington standards through his more obscure tunes to his extended works. (M.F. Productions MF 204/5)
—DUKE ELLINGTON '55. Extended versions of the hits of *other* bands (quite a change for the Duke), such as Basie's "One O'Clock Jump," Goodman's "Stompin' at the Savoy,"

Hampton's "Flying Home," Miller's "In the Mood" and Waller's "Ain't Misbehavin'." (Capitol M 11674)
—GIANTS OF JAZZ. Thirty years of Duke, from 1926 to 1956, are encompassed in this exquisite package of beautifully re-recorded works accompanied by expert notes by Stanley Dance and Dan Morgenstern and some truly wonderful photos. Most of the expected plus a few unexpected bits of Ellingtonia are included among the 40 selections. (Time-Life STL-J02)
—HI-FI ELLINGTON UPTOWN. Very extended versions of just five Ellington works: "Skin Deep," "The Mooche," "Perdido," "Controversial Suite" and "Take the 'A' Train" with Betty Roche's legendary vocal. A most unusual and interesting set, with some wonderful solos by Hodges et al. (Columbia Special Products JCL-830)
—THE MUSIC OF DUKE ELLINGTON. A dozen of the band's all-time hits, all the way from "The Mooche" and "Creole Love Call" through "Mood Indigo" and "Sophisticated Lady" and on to "Do Nothing Till You Hear From Me" and "Don't Get Around Much Anymore," (Columbia Special Products JCL-558)
—DUKE ELLINGTON: 1938, 1939, 1940. Three absolutely splendid packages, each with 32 wonderful sides that include several great, previously unissued takes as well as the well-known renditions that sparked these three glorious years of the band's history. The first two records come from Columbia's vaults; the last one from RCA Victor's. The exceptional notes make this a most revealing and rewarding set of recordings. (Smithsonian Collection P2-13367/14273 and DPM2-0351)
—THIS IS DUKE ELLINGTON. Twenty selections from RCA's vaults, about half from the 1930s, the rest covering the band at its height in the early and mid-1940s. Includes "Cottontail," "Take the 'A' Train," "I Got It Bad and That Ain't Good," etc. (RCA Victor VPM 6042)
—THE UNCOLLECTED DUKE, VOLS. 1–5. 64 performances all from transcriptions, none ever previously released commercially, with such prizes as a four-minute "Transblucency," Kay Davis singing "Come Rain or Come Shine," Duke's trio version of "Tip Toe Topic," Billy Strayhorn playing "A Flower Is a Lovesome Thing," a six minute and forty second rendition of "Happy-Go-Lucky," Ray Nance singing "St Louis Blues," and a rare "Park at 106th," complete with fine notes by Patricia Willard. (Hindsight HSR 125/6/7/8/9)

SHEP FIELDS' NEW MUSIC, 1942–44. What a delightful surprise! Sixteen tunes by this almost-forgotten but so very musical band that sported nine reed players (plus a rhythm section) utilizing 35 different instruments through some gorgeous arrangements. Rippling Rhythm was never like this, as Fields himself admits in the fascinating liner notes. (Hindsight HSR 160)

CHUCK FOSTER 1940. Sixteen selections taken from transcriptions by one of the mickiest of all mickey-mouse bands, every one with a vocal of some sort. (Hindsight HSR 115)

THE BEST OF JAN GARBER. Two dozen standards, like "You Are My Sunshine," "Girl of My Dreams," "I'll See You in My Dreams" and "When I Grow Too Old to Dream" by this dreamy band that imitated Lombardo so slavishly. (MCA 204028)
—1939–40. Live broadcasts and transcriptions are the sources of these sides that feature singers Lee Bennett and Fritz Heilbron. (Hindsight HSR 130)
—VOL. 2, 1946–47. An enlarged Garber band that sounds a bit fuller but still doesn't compare musically with the swing band Jan fronted for a few years with little commercial success. (Hindsight HSR 155)

BENNY GOODMAN: ALL-TIME GREATEST HITS. 20 of the King of Swing's most important Columbia sides such as "Benny Rides Again," "Clarinet a la King," and a 9½ minute version of "Sing, Sing Sing." Featured among others are Charlie Christian and Peggy Lee. (Columbia PG 31547)
—BENNY GOODMAN PRESENTS FLETCHER HENDERSON. Fletcher's great arrangements of "Honeysuckle Rose," "Somebody Stole My Gal," "Crazy Rhythm" and "Stealin' Apples," the last one of Goodman's special favorites, appear in this collection of a dozen of his charts, recorded in the period after Benny had re-formed his band in 1939 and including top sidemen like Charlie Christian, George Auld and Johnny Guarnieri plus an often-inspired Goodman. (Columbia Special Products JGL 524)
—BENNY GOODMAN PRESENTS EDDIE SAUTER. A dozen brilliant but seldom heard arrangements that turned the Goodman style completely around spark this collection that includes Cootie Williams on "Superman," Billy Butterfield on "La Rosita" and vocals by Peggy

Lee and Helen Forrest. (Columbia Special Products JGL 523)
—THE BENNY GOODMAN STORY. Well-recorded recreations of ten original hits, with Harry James, Mel Powell and Lou McGarity back as guests, Ruby Braff appearing for the first time, and Goodman sounding inspired. (Capitol SM-706)
—CARNEGIE HALL CONCERT. All the excitement of that great event of January 16, 1938, when Goodman introduced jazz to Carnegie Hall. Recorded with just one mike hung in the middle of the hall that captured the entire concert, including the breathtaking rendition of "Sing, Sing, Sing," climaxed by Jess Stacy's church-like solo. (Columbia OSL-160)
—THE COMPLETE BENNY GOODMAN—VOLUMES I through VIII. Eight two-record albums, with sixteen selections per record, comprising every recording the great mid-30s band made for RCA Victor, plus some extra takes. With loads of interesting sidelights in Mort Goode's copious notes. (RCA Bluebird AX2-5505/5515/5532/5537/5557/5566/5567/5568)
—THE COMPLETE 1937–38 JAZZ CONCERT NO. 2. Actually not a concert, but a whole series of takes from numerous Goodman broadcasts that projected even more excitement than most of the studio recordings, primarily because of the interaction between the band and dancers. A highlight: Goodman, Harry James and Gene Krupa on "Ridin' High." (Columbia OSL-180)
—GIANTS OF JAZZ: BENNY GOODMAN. A thorough review of Goodman's career from his first recordings as a sideman through all the various and varied stages of his band. Forty selections altogether plus an informative booklet dilineating both Goodman's career and the music on these three records. (Time-Life STL-J05)
—SOLID GOLD INSTRUMENTAL HITS. A great collection of the inventive, infectious jazz played by the Goodman band of the early 1940s with Cootie Williams, Lou McGarity, Vido Musso, Billy Butterfield and Mel Powell featured along with Benny through twenty brilliant arrangements, most of them by Powell and Eddie Sauter. (Columbia PG 31547)

GLEN GRAY AND THE CASA LOMA ORCHESTRA: THE BEST OF GLEN GRAY. Two dozen selections of the band at its musical best during the mid and latter 1930s, complete with such Casa Loma favorites as "Smoke

Rings," "It's the Talk of the Town," "No Name Jive," "Memories of You," "Under a Blanket of Blue" and "Casa Loma Stomp," with Kenny Sargent singing ballads, Billy Rauch and Peewee Hunt on trombones, Clarence Hutchenrider on clarinet, and Sonny Dunham and Grady Watts sharing the jazz trumpet solos. (MCA 2-4076)
—SOUNDS OF THE GREAT CASA LOMA BAND. Well-recorded versions of some of the original jazz instrumentals created by arranger Gene Gifford especially for the band during its early stages—"White Jazz," "Black Jazz," "Maniac's Ball" and "Dance of the Lame Duck," plus six other tunes associated with this slick outfit. (Capitol SM-1588)
—GLEN GRAY 1939–40. Sixteen familiar and unfamiliar Casa Loma numbers, taken from transcriptions, and featuring some especially fine trombone and alto sax playing by Murray MacEachren, plus the usual soloists and singers. (Hindsight HSR-104)
—GLEN GRAY, VOL. II, 1942–45. Trumpeters Red Nichols and Bobby Hackett solo on these transcription selections, along with Herb Ellis in one of his first recorded guitar solos and singers Eugenie Baird and Skip Nelson. (Hindsight HSR-120)
—THEMES OF THE GREAT BANDS. Excellently recorded and performed recreations of the themes of Barnet, Berigan, Brown, Tommy Dorsey, Goodman, Erskine Hawkins, Herman, James, Kenton, Miller, Savitt and Shaw. (Capitol SM-1812)

GEORGE HALL 1937. Part radio broadcasts and part transcriptions by this band heard almost daily at noon from New York's Hotel Taft, featuring of course Dolly Dawn. (Hindsight HSR 144)

THE BEST OF LIONEL HAMPTON. Two dozen swingers, most of them by Hamp's big band of the early and mid-1940s, including "Flying Home," "Hamp's Boogie Woogie," "Hey! Ba-Ba-Re-Bop," "How High the Moon," "Midnight Sun" and "Mingus Fingers," all reflecting the high spirit and totally swinging ways of its leader. (MCA 2-4075)
—SWEATIN' WITH HAMP 1945–50. More rocking performances by an even bigger outfit of nine brass, five saxes and rhythm and including such future jazz stars as trombonists Al Grey, Benny Powell and Jimmy Cleveland, trumpeter Kenny Dorham, guitarist Wes Mont-

gomery and bassist/composer Charles Mingus. (MCA 1331)

FLETCHER HENDERSON: SWING'S THE THING. Fourteen sides, mostly from the 1934 edition of the band, playing mostly Fletcher's arrangements, plus some by Benny Carter and featuring such soloists as Henry "Red" Allen, Buster Bailey, Coleman Hawkins Hilton Jefferson and Ben Webster on "Big John's Special," "Down South Camp Meeting," "Wrappin' It Up" and more. (MCA 1318)
For an even better appreciation of Henderson's gifts as arranger and leader, try to unearth a copy of "A Study in Fustration," the four-record set featuring Louis Armstrong, Carter, Hawkins, Rex Stewart and many more that Columbia has allowed to go out of print (Columbia C4L-19)

THE BEST OF WOODY HERMAN. Two dozen selections, most of them by "The Band That Plays the Blues" and containing such earlier Herman stalwarts as "Woodchoppers' Ball," "Golden Wedding," "Amen," "Blue Prelude" and its theme, "Blue Flame." (MCA 2-4077)
—EARLY AUTUMN. Ten numbers by the Second Herd and three more by the Third Herd make up this late 1940s compilation. The first group features Stan Getz, Zoot Sims and Al Cohn during the first four sides that include "Early Autumn" and "Lemon Drop"; then other fine soloists take over, Gene Ammons, Earl Swope and Terry Gibbs, along with holdovers Bill Harris and of course Herman. (Capitol M 11034)
—GREATEST HITS. Almost all are by the First Herd. Included are such major Herman gems as "Apple Honey," "Bijou," "The Good Earth," "Your Father's Mustache," "Northwest Passage," "Four Brothers," "Wild Root" and four more. (Columbia CS 9291)
—THE THREE HERDS. Pretty much the same as "Greatest Hits," except there are 12 instead of 11 selections. (Columbia Special Products JCL 592)
Both "Greatest Hits" and "The Three Herds" give an indication of the band's greatness during the mid-1940s, but are a far cry from the no-longer-available three-record set, "The Thundering Herds" (Columbia C3L 25), from which the tracks were taken. With its forty-five selections and illuminating comments

by Woody, this compilation is very much worth searching for.

—VOL. II, 1944. A compilation of some of the highlights of the First Herd's famed Old Gold radio series that displays the young band's amazing vitality, interpreting progressive arrangements by Ralph Burns and Neal Hefti, who appear along with Flip Phillips, Bill Harris, Pete Candoli, Chubby Jackson and Dave Tough and others in "Apple Honey," "Red Top," "It Must Be Jelly" and ten more tunes. (Hindsight HSR 134)

(For more modern sounds of Woody Herman, look for various albums on Century, Fantasy, Philips and RCA Records.)

TINY HILL 1944. Sixteen selections, by a seldom-recorded sweet band, all with the very personalized and for some quite tolerable vocals by the maestro applied to various pop tunes of the times. Primarily for mickey mousers. (Hindsight HSR 159)

EARL HINES: SOUTH SIDE SWING, 1934–35. This hard-swinging, high-spirited band is represented by some of its more outstanding sides, such as "Rosetta," "Angry," "Cavernism," "Blue" and "Julia" (Hines did not believe in wasting words with his titles!) that highlight the maestro's driving piano and other interesting solos by saxists Omer Simeon and Budd Johnson and vocalist Walter Fuller. Many of the arrangements are by Jimmy Mundy. (MCA 1311)

EDDY HOWARD: VOLUME I, 1946–51 VOLUME II, 1945–48. Lots of warm, sentimental Howard crooning with appropriate band backing on the first album, composed of good songs like "These Foolish Things," "Lazy River," "Our Love Is Here To Stay," "Don't Take Your Love from Me," plus Howard's standards, "Careless" and "To Each His Own." Volume II focusses a bit more on up-tempoed tunes but with plenty of Eddy's singing. (Hindsight HSR 119 and 156)

HARRY JAMES' GREATEST HITS. A good cross-section of the band at the height of its popularity, from 1939 to 1946, and featuring, in addition to Harry's horn, Frank Sinatra on "All or Nothing At All," Helen Forrest on "I Had the Craziest Dream" and "I've Heard That Song Before," Dick Haymes on "I'll Get By"

and Kitty Kallen on "It's Been a Long, Long Time." (Columbia CS 9430)

—HITS OF HARRY JAMES. Splendidly recorded recreations of ten of the band's big hits, with Harry in top form and Helen Forrest back to sing three of her hits. (Capitol M-1515)

—THE MAN WITH THE HORN. Lesser-known and thus in some ways a more interesting compilation that focusses more on the band's jazz talents than on its pop ventures, these dozen selections include several previously unissued masters and, in general, display a looser and more swinging band than is heard on most James sets. (Columbia P 14357)

—HARRY JAMES VOLUME I, 1943–46; VOLUME II, 1943–46; VOLUME III, 1948–49; VOLUME IV, 1943–46; VOLUME V, 1943–53; VOLUME VI, 1947–49. A revealing collection of almost 100 performances, all taken from live radio broadcasts, that provide a wonderful overview of the band during its most successful period. Volume I, composed of great standards, features Harry and Willie Smith and four Helen Forrest vocals; Helen Ward appears four times during Volume II; instrumental arrangements only by Neal Hefti, Johnny Richards and Jimmy Mundy fill Volume III with James, Willie Smith, Corky Corcoran, Juan Tizol and Don Lamond outstanding; more well-known standards with vocals by Helen Forrest, Buddy Moreno and Buddy DiVito fill much of Volume IV; Volume V is divided among early and later broadcasts, with Harry and Johnny Mercer featured on a hilarious take-off of "Sugar Blues," and Volume VI zooms in on a swinging band, that had just dispensed with its strings, romping through charts by Ray Conniff, Neal Hefti and Jimmy Mundy. (Hindsight 102/123/135/141/142/150)

LOUIS JORDAN AND HIS TYMPANY FIVE. Two dozen of this infectious, happy-sounding group's performances, including "Choo Choo Ch'Boogie," "Let the Good Times Roll," "Caldonia" and "What's the Use of Gettin' Sober." (MCA 2-4079)

DICK JURGENS 1939–39, VOLUMES I and II. A collection of thirty-two sides by one of the better sweet bands with many vocals by Eddy Howard and a few by Ronnie Kemper on a good selection of some of the era's more popular songs. (Hindsight HSR 111/138)

ART KASSEL 1944. The only long-playing record ever issued by one of the most syrupy sweet bands that enjoyed great popularity in the mid-west. (Hindsight HSR 162)

SWING AND SWAY WITH SAMMY KAYE. Twenty-four well-known standards, many of them excellently recorded after the big band era, and giving a well-rounded impression of this long-lived, very popular sweet band. (MCA 2-4027)
—SAMMY KAYE 1940–41. Sixteen tunes of the times, all with singing song titles and spoken introductions that lead into vocals by Tommy Ryan, Maury Cross, Alan Foster and the Three Kaydets, complete with good liner notes by Frank Driggs in which Kaye explains what made Sammy run. (Hindsight HSR 158)
—THIS IS SAMMY KAYE. A more complete picture of the band with the twenty musical examples stretching over a period of years and featuring a batch of vocalists like Nancy Norman, Tony Alamo, Don Cornell, Laura Leslie, Charlie Wilson, Clyde Burke, Jimmy Brown, Arthur Wright, Maury Cross, Tommy Ryan, Billy Williams and the Three Barons. Again Kaye provides illuminating remembrances of the singers and their songs, and of his own career. (RCA Victor 6070)

HAL KEMP 1934, VOLUMES I and II. The only available long-playing recordings by this very important band of the mid-1930s, they are culled from various radio broadcasts and feature the band's unique style and vocals by Skinnay Ennis, Deane Janis, Bob Allen and Saxie Dowell plus interesting notes based on recollections by Kemp's brother (Hindsight HSR 143/161). But what an outrage that both Columbia and RCA Victor have failed to reissue any of this band's many wonderful sides!

STAN KENTON: ARTISTRY IN RHYTHM. A batch of the band's most successful early sides including "Come Back To Sorrento" featuring Vido Musso and "Just a-Sittin and a-Rockin' " and "Willow Weep for Me" sung by June Christy. (Capitol SM-167 and Creative World ST-1043)
—ADVENTURES IN JAZZ. Later sides with more of a jazz flavor such as "Malaguena," "Misty," "Waltz of the Prophets" and "Body and Soul." (Capitol M-11027 and Creative World ST-1010)

—GREATEST HITS. Most of the band's early block-busters: "Artistry in Rhythm," "Tampico" with June Christy, "Eager Beaver," "Unison Riff," "And Her Tears Flowed Like Wine" with Anita O'Day and "Peanut Vendor." (Capitol SM-2327)
—STAN KENTON VOLUME I, 1941; VOLUME II, 1941; VOLUME III, 1943–44; VOLUME IV, 1944–45; VOLUME V, 1945–47. The first two volumes come from broadcasts direct from Balboa, where the band first caught enough attention to be recorded later on Decca and Capitol. The other volumes are taken from transcriptions and reflect the band's music of the particular years, divided between pop tunes and some of its outstanding instrumentals. Complete liner notes, including personnel, accompany each of the albums that in toto present 79 of the band's more easy-to-understand works. (Hindsight HSR 118/124/136/147/157)
—WEST SIDE STORY. One of the most famous and highly-regarded of the band's more pretentious works, full of typical Kenton passion and involved writing. (Capitol SM 12037 and Creative World ST 1007)
More albums by Kenton can be obtained through his record company, which purchased or leased many Capitol masters and created new albums of its own. For details, contact Creative World Records, P. O. Box 35216, Los Angeles, CA 90035.

THE BEST OF WAYNE KING VOLUMES I and II. A slew of top pop standards played with the light, lilting, suave semi-sophistication that the Waltz King imparted to just about everything he and his bandsmen blew. (MCA 2-4022/4023)

THE BEST OF ANDY KIRK. Two dozen well-played pop tunes and instrumentals by one of the most underrated of all the big bands. Mary Lou Williams is featured at the piano on such numbers as "The Lady Who Swings the Band" and "Little Joe From Chicago," while Henry Wells shines on the vocal of "I'll Get By" and Pha Terrell emotes his big hit, "Until the Real Thing Comes Along." (MCA 2-4105)
—INSTRUMENTALLY SPEAKING 1936–42. A dozen of the band's finest jazz performances, like "Walkin' and Swingin'," "Froggy Bottom," "Moten Swing" and "Mary's Idea," featuring at various times Mary Loy Williams' piano and Dick Wilson's tenor sax, plus Floyd

Smith on "Floyd's Guitar Blues" and Kenny Kersey on piano on "Boogie Woogie Cocktail." (MCA 1308)

GENE KRUPA AND HIS ORCHESTRA. A dozen of the band's biggest hits featuring mostly Anita O'Day, Roy Eldridge and of course Gene himself. Included are "After You've Gone," "Drum Boogie," "Disc Jockey Jump," "Let Me Off Uptown," "That's What You Think" and "Disc Jockey Jump." (Columbia Special Products JCL-753)
—GENE KRUPA'S SIDEKICKS. Twelve more sides, each featuring a different headliner like Roy and Anita, Benny Carter, Gerry Mulligan, Leo Watson, Charlie Ventura, Dave Lambert and Buddy Stewart and so on. (Columbia Special Products JCL 641.)
Amazingly, Columbia Records itself has no Gene Krupa in its catalogue. If you can find "Drummin' Man" (Columbia C2L 29), you'll have yourself the best non-available collection of all the Krupa big band sides.

THE BEST OF TED LEWIS. A smattering of good jazz but mostly pleasant, corn-ball fun pervade the two dozen sides, among them such Lewis war-horses as "When My Baby Smiles at Me," "St. Louis Blues," "Just Around the Corner" and "Down the Old Church Aisle." (MCA 2-4101)

THE BEST OF GUY LOMBARDO. The largest of the many Lombardo collections, this six-record set consists of 72 selections culled from Decca's extensive catalogue (now owned by MCA Records) and neatly segregated into various categories such as "Seems Like Old Times" (early songs), "Everywhere You Go" (geographical songs), "Every Night Is New Year's Eve" (happy songs) and even a record devoted to the band's twin pianos. (Reader's Digest RD4-161-1)
—THE BEST OF GUY LOMBARDO. Most of the band's more famous numbers appear in this two-record set: "Coquette," "Sweethearts on Parade," "You're Driving Me Crazy," "Boo Hoo," "Seems Like Old Times" and "St. Louis Blues," for example. The playing is precise and the recording very clean. (MCA 2-4041)
—THE BEST OF GUY LOMBARDO, VOL. II. Similar to the above, only most of the tunes

aren't quite as well known and come from a somewhat later period. (MCA 2-4082)
—GUY LOMBARDO AND HIS ROYAL CANADIANS. A two-record set with a dozen well-known fox-trots like "Arreverderci Roma" and "Around the World" plus twelve more waltzes, all very well recorded. (Capitol STBB-520)
—A LEGENDARY PERFORMER. Thirteen Lombardo favorites accompanied by a booklet with lots of photos and comments made by Guy just a few months before his death. (RCA Victor CPL1-2047)
—THIS IS GUY LOMBARDO. Twenty selections covering just about all of the band's big hits with the vast majority sung by Carmen. (RCA Victor VPM 6071)

JIMMIE LUNCEFORD: RHYTHM IS OUR BUSINESS—1934–35. Some of the early Decca sides, somewhat hotter but not quite as smooth as later efforts. Included are "Stomp It Off," "Dream of You," "Sleepy Time Gal," "Runnin' Wild," the title tune and nine more. (MCA 1302)
—HARLEM SHOUT—1935–36. The band had found its true groove here, as exemplified by "Four or Five Times," "Swanee River," "My Blue Heaven," "Organ Grinder's Swing" and "On the Beach at Bali Bali," with Sy Oliver's arrangements and vocals just about everywhere. (MCA 1305)
—FOR DANCERS ONLY—1936–37. And on they go, those wonderful men of Lunceford. Some of the standouts in the package are "The Merry-Go-Round Broke Down," "Annie Laurie," "Frisco Fog" and the album's great title song. (MCA 1307)
—BLUES IN THE NIGHT—1938–42. The pace never lets up. More than a dozen more including Trummy Young's great performance on "Margie," "Down By the Old Mill Stream," "By the River St. Marie," "Yard Dog Mazurka," and that splendid, two-sided version of "Blues In the Night." (MCA 1314)
—JIMMIE'S LEGACY—1934–37. There's just so much great Lunceford that MCA had to go back into those Decca vaults for more like "Sophisticated Lady," featuring Willie Smith's clarinet, Sy Oliver singing "The Melody Man" and, of all things, "Miss Otis Regrets," and supplying an arrangement of "Hell's Bells," Art Kassel's theme song, yet! (MCA 1320)
While MCA has done nobly by Lunceford,

Columbia, which has dozens upon dozens of gems in its files, currently makes nothing available. For shame! Try to locate an out-of-print "Lunceford Special" (Columbia CL 2713) that contains sixteen of the band's most outstanding 1940s performances.

THE BEST OF FREDDY MARTIN. Twenty-four of this sweet band's most famous numbers recorded after they had become hits on RCA Victor, which currently has no Freddy Martin in its catalogue. Included are "Tonight We Love," "Cumana," "Bumble Boogie," "Symphony" and "Warsaw Concerto." (MCA 2-4080)
—54 GREAT WALTZES. Precisely what the title implies: lush, legato playing with Freddy's full-toned tenor sax blowing above the string section. (MCA 2-4021)
FREDDY MARTIN 1940. Seventeen selections culled from transcriptions, including a version of Tchaikovsky's "Piano Concerto in B-Flat Minor," recorded well before the RCA Victor hit version. Clyde Rogers and Eddie Stone are featured in this collection of mostly ballads. (Hindsight HSR 151)

BILLY MAY: SORTA MAY. Nobody has had more fun arranging standard tunes than Billy May and this is the classic example of the novel way he uses slurping saxes, reed voicings and various percussion instruments, without ever sacrificing a swinging beat. (Creative World ST-1051)

CLYDE McCOY: SUGAR BLUES. Latter-day recordings of some of this controversial band's various offerings, including of course his famed title tune. (Capitol SM-311)

THE BEST OF GLENN MILLER. Some of the band's biggest hits interspersed with a few lesser ones in this 12-selection album that serves as an introduction to its music. (RCA Victor ANL1-3467)
—THE COMPLETE GLENN MILLER—VOLUMES I through IX. The set consists of 286 selections, all that the civilian band released on RCA Victor, packaged in nine albums that contain revealing as well as entertaining notes (plus photos) by Mort Goode. (RCA Bluebird AXM2-5512/5514/5534/5558/5565/5569/5570/5571/5574)

—REMEMBER GLENN. Healthy portions of the well-recorded sound tracks of the band's two movies, *Sun Valley Serenade* and *Orchestra Wives*, with interesting, expanded versions of "Chattanooga Choo Choo," "I've Got a Gal in Kalamazoo" and "Serenade in Blue." Unfortunately, this two-record set has dreadful notes with no singer or instrumental solo identifications. (20th Century-Fox T-904)
—A LEGENDARY PERFORMER, VOL. I. A dramatic musical history of the band's success, beginning with the opening announcement on opening night at the Glen Island Casino followed, between numbers, by pronouncements by Glenn, Martin Block and others, and a final emotional farewell from Miller at the conclusion of his final Chesterfield show. Interspersed are 23 previously unreleased air shots of many of the band's biggest hits with infectious crowd reactions that obviously spurred the men on to more emotional heights than they displayed on their more sedate studio sessions. The most complete aural history of the band ever assembled. (RCA Victor CPM2-0693)
—A MEMORIAL, 1944–1969. Thirty of the band's biggest hits, presented in chronological order from "Moonlight Serenade" to "St. Louis Blues March," plus seventeen photos and some very fond recollections and sincere admiration from Benny Goodman. (RCA Victor VPM-6019)
—THIS IS THE GLENN MILLER ARMY AIR FORCE BAND. Twenty selections by one of the greatest orchestras ever assembled, full of topnotch musicians from various civilian bands, sparked by drummer Ray McKinley, pianist Mel Powell, bassist Trigger Alpert and guitarist Carmen Mastren, playing charts written by Jerry Gray and other fine arrangers for a seventeen-piece dance band, sometimes augmented with a beautiful string section, plus vocals by Johnny Desmond and McKinley and the Crew Chiefs. Miller fans have argued among themselves about the relative merits of his civilian and Army Air Force band. Exposure to this album should help *you* make up *your* mind. (RCA Victor VPM-6080)
—THE UNFORGETTABLE GLENN MILLER. Seventy-six songs, most from RCA Victor's archives of studio and broadcast material, but six each from the sound tracks of *Sun Valley Serenade* and *Orchestra Wives*, elegantly boxed with very complete notes. (Readers Digest RD4-64)

Out-of-print but well worth looking for, if you are a Miller fan, are three five-record sets, "Glenn Miller Limited Edition, Volumes I and II," both composed of air checks, with the former the better of the two, and a simply marvelous "Glenn Miller and the Army Air Force Band" that shows both the depth and breadth of that organization. (RCA Victor LPT 6700/6701/6702)

THIS IS VAUGHN MONROE. Some of the best sides issued by this surprisingly good orchestra including of course "Racing With the Moon" and "There, I've Said It Again," with the too-often maligned Monroe, on second hearing, sounding a good deal better than most of today's singers. (RCA Victor VPM-6073)

THE BEST OF RUSS MORGAN—VOLUMES I and II. A couple of two-record sets, very typical of this band's stylized sounds, with its bigger hits, such as "Does Your Heart Beat for Me," "So Tired," "Somebody Else Is Taking My Place" and "You're Nobody Till Somebody Loves You" plus some of the bigger pop tunes in the first volume, and some lesser-known songs in the second. (MCA 2-4036/ 2-4029)

—RUSS MORGAN 1937–38. Eighteen renditions of very typical hotel-room music with Morgan, Mert Curtis and the Mullens Sisters singing material well re-recorded from a set of transcriptions. (Hindsight HSR 145)

OZZIE NELSON 1940–42. There's some pleasant singing by Ozzie and Harriet Hilliard as well as some surprisingly good jazz, arranged by Billy May with impressive solos by trumpeter Bo Ashford and pianist Paul Smith, and a pervading looseness too seldom found in bands of this sort. (Hindsight HSR 107)

RAY NOBLE/AL BOWLLY: VOLUMES I–VI. Each of these six albums contains sixteen examples of that wonderful English orchestra and its famed vocalist, Al Bowlly. Volume III contains more of the band's hits than do any of the others, such as "The Very Thought Of You," "By the Fireside," "Hold My Hand," "Love Locked Out," "Lying in the Hay" and "You Ought To See Sally on Sunday," while Volume I features two of

Noble's biggest songs, "Love Is the Sweetest Thing" and "Goodnight, Sweetheart." All are very worthwhile. (Monmouth-Evergreen MES 6816/7021/7027/7039/7040/7056)
—ENCORES. This consists entirely of instrumentals by a band that sounds somewhat dated but which still exudes a good deal of sophisticated musical charm. (Monmouth-Evergreen MES-707)
For examples of the Ray Noble American band that featured Glenn Miller, Claude Thornhill, Charlie Spivak, Will Bradley and Bud Freeman, try to find "Ray Noble and His Orchestra" (RCA-LPV-536) which Victor has permitted to go out-of-circulation.

RED NORVO: GIANTS OF JAZZ. Although this lush three-record set focusses primarily on Norvo, the jazz soloist, it does offer the only available reissues of his band's wonderful Brunswick recordings that feature Red's xylophone, Mildred Bailey's singing and Eddie Sauter's arrangements—"A Porter's Love Song to a Chambermaid," "Smoke Dreams," "Remember," "I Would Do Anything for You," "Russian Lullaby" and "Just You, Just Me." (Time-Life STL-J14)
—RED NORVO AND HIS ORCHESTRA, 1938. Taken from transcriptions, these sixteen selections are rather disappointing and seldom settle into the soft, subtle swing groove that made this such an outstanding band. Still, with Columbia hoarding its Brunswick stock, these are better than nothing. (Circle CLP-3)

LOUIS PRIMA: HITS OF LOUIS AND KEELY. Much good fun on most of these sides that project the uninhibited humor and often quite good musicianship that pervaded the music of this New Orleans trumpeter/singer and his then-wife, Keely Smith. (Capitol SM-1531)

BOYD RAEBURN: EXPERIMENTS IN BIG BAND JAZZ, 1945. Reissues of sides recorded for Guild by the era's most progressive band that included Dizzy Gillespie, Shelly Manne, Oscar Pettiford, Trummy Young, Johnny Bothwell, Serge Chaloff playing among others, Dizzy's "Night in Tunisia" and George Handy's "March of the Boyds." (Musicraft MU-505)
—BOYD RAEBURN'S JEWELS. A two-record set consisting of reissues of the eighteen

sometimes far-out sides the band recorded for Jewel, including Eddie Finckel's "Boyd Meets Stravinsky" and George Handy's "Dalvatore Sally" plus some beautifully arranged ballads with vocals by David Allyn and Ginny Powell and four additional sides by Allyn and strings. (Savoy SJL-2250)

CARL RAVAZZA 1941–44. Sixteen selections by one of the era's more pleasant bandleading crooners fronting a typical, smooth, more-or-less-nondescript hotel-type outfit that played primarily for dancing. (Hindsight HSR 117)

ALVINO REY 1946. Never recorded commercially, this amazing band is captured here on sixteen superb transcribed selections. Utilizing ten brass and five saxes, plus a strong rhythm section, it does full justice to fine charts by Billy May, Deane Kincaide and George Handy and features such outstanding jazz musicians as saxists Zoot Sims and Al Cohn, trumpeter Johnny Mandel and drummers Dave Tough and Don Lamond. Truly, quite a revelation! (HSR 121)

ARTIE SHAW: CLASSICS FROM 1945–46. These recordings by Shaw's post-war band reveal a looseness and sprightliness that his earlier bands didn't always project, as, for example, its rendition of the Basie-like "The Glider," and with Mel Torme and the Meltones "You Do Something To Me." There's also an updated "Begin the Beguine," complete with strings. (Musicraft M-503)
—THE COMPLETE ARTIE SHAW. Incomplete by mid-1981, but scheduled by the end of that year to run the full gamut of all the band's Bluebird and Victor recordings, this set will become the definitive display of the band at its height. Excellent notes by Burt Korall, with plenty of quotes from Shaw and his musicians, enhance the series, (RCA Bluebird)
—FEATURING ROY ELDRIDGE. A group of selections recorded by the rich-sounding mid-1940s edition that feature the great trumpeter as well as Shaw on tunes like "A Foggy Day," "Soon," "I'll Never Be the Same" and more. (Pickwick QJ-25191)
—ARTIE SHAW, VOLUME I, 1938; VOLUME II, 1938; VOLUME III, 1939; VOLUME IV, 1939. With RCA Victor having deleted the excellent "Artie Shaw in the Blue Room and

Cafe Rouge" from its catalogue, these four collections of broadcasts from those spots, plus one from Boston's Hotel Ritz-Carlton, help to fill the void. All contain fine examples of the band's crisp style, its leader's great clarinet, vocals by Helen Forrest and Tony Pastor, and in the latter sides Georgie Auld's booting tenor sax and Buddy Rich's driving drums. Interesting comments from Shaw about his band and its music appear in each of the liner notes. (HSR 139/140/148/149)
—THIS IS ARTIE SHAW, VOLUME I. Twenty of the band's big hits, including "Begin the Beguine," "Indian Love Call," "Any Old Time" with a Billie Holiday vocal, "Back Bay Shuffle," "Frenesi," "Star Dust," four numbers, including "Summit Ridge Drive," by the Gramercy Five, and Lena Horne singing "Don't Take Your Love From Me." (RCA Victor VPM 6039)
—THIS IS ARTIE SHAW, VOLUME II. Eighteen more of the original RCA Victor studio session opi, including the almost ten-minute "Concerto For Clarinet," the six-and-a-half-minute "St. James Infirmary" with a "Hot Lips" Page vocal plus fifteen strings, as well as many of the band's earlier hits, like "What Is This Thing Called Love," "Softly As In a Morning Sunrise" and "It Had To Be You." (RCA Victor VPM 6062)

CHARLIE SPIVAK 1943–46. With Columbia never having released an album by this fine band, these transferred transcriptions are most valuable and welcome, especially since the group comes across as a truly superior outfit, well-rehearsed, swinging through arrangements by Sonny Burke, Neal Hefti, Jimmy Mundy, Fred Norman and Nelson Riddle, and creating some truly romantic moods via its leader's gorgeous trumpet. Five of the selections have good vocals by Irene Daye. (Hindsight HSR 105)

JACK TEAGARDEN: KING OF THE BLUES TROMBONE. Only seven of the forty-eight selections in this three-record set contain the sounds of Teagarden's vastly underrated big band. All feature Jack's marvelous trombone, plus some good solos by his sidemen. Jack shines on his theme, "I Got a Right to Sing the Blues" and Dave Tough's drums propel the band through "Swingin' on the Teagarden Gate." (Columbia Special Products JSN-6044)

CLAUDE THORNHILL 1947. Can you imagine it! This is the only album by the band many consider to have been one of the truly greatest of the entire big band era. Fortunately, these transcriptions did capture the essence of Thornhill's gorgeous ballads, with their superb dynamics and lovely Fran Warren vocals, as well as their thoroughly modern renditions of such bop classics, brilliantly arranged by Gil Evans, as "Donna Lee" and "Anthropology." Most goose-pimple raiser: John Benson Brooks' "Happy Stranger." (Hindsight HSR 108)

For more Thornhill, look for "The Real Birth of the Cool," produced by Japanese Columbia, or for the slightly less effective "The Memorable Claude Thornhill" (Columbia KG 32906) recently deleted from the company's catalogue.

THE BEST OF CHICK WEBB. Twenty of the band's better sides, including the original, pre-Goodman versions of "Don't Be That Way" and "If Dreams Come True," plus Ella Fitzgerald on several songs, including "A-Tisket, A-Tasket," "Undecided" and "Rock It For Me," and little Chick's drums leading the band to rhythmic heights through "I Want to Be Happy" and "Liza." (MCA 2-4107)

—CHICK WEBB: A LEGEND. Some of the band's earliest recordings, including Edgar Sampson's "Blue Lou" and "Blue Minor" and "Don't Be That Way" and a rip-roaring, early vocal on "A Little Bit Later On" by Ella. (MCA 1303)

—ELLA SWINGS THE BAND. A self-explanatory album title, as a young Miss Fitzgerald sparkles through fourteen songs, including "Cryin' Mood," "Just a Simple Melody," "My Heart Belongs To Daddy" and "Little White Lies." (MCA 1327)

ANSON WEEKS 1932. Nineteen songs that were popular in 1932, and which have stood the test of time, played in typical hotel-band fashion by a group that has been a San Francisco favorite for generations. (Hindsight HSR 146). More recent albums by Weeks' latter groups are available on Fantasy Records.

THE BEST OF LAWRENCE WELK. Two dozen thoroughly popular songs, some from after the big band era, played with customary slickness. Included is the band's theme, "Bubbles in the Wine," ballads like "Twilight Time," "Blue Champagne" and "The Poor People of Paris," and Welk's foray into jazz with "Stompin'" at the Savoy" and "Lullaby of Birdland." (MCA 2-4044)

THE BEST OF LAWRENCE WELK, VOLUME II. If you like your Welk applied to mostly even older ballads, this two-selection set is the one for you. (MCA 2-4026)

THE BEST OF LAWRENCE WELK POLKAS. Resurrections of the kind of music Lawrence started playing back in the Dakotas; they're all here, "Beer Barrel Polka," "Friendly Tavern Polka," "Pennsylvania Polka" and on and on. (MCA 2-4104)

—CHAMPAGNE DANCE PARTY. More than one hundred songs make up this eight-record set which is categorized into long-playing sides such as "Themes from Stage and Screen," "Polka Party," "Country Classics," "Swinging the Classics," "Dancing Through the '30s," "New Hits" and so on. The original, well-recorded material comes from Welk's extensive Ranwood catalogue, and presents the band in its latter-day, sleeker manner, as opposed to its rougher, somewhat more personal ways that were once available from CBS Records. (Readers' Digest RD4-243-1)

THE BEST OF BOB WILLS. "San Antonio Rose," "Deep in the Heart of Texas," "Pan Handle Rag," "Across the Alley from the Alamo," plus sixteen less geographical songs make up this set of southwestern jazz performed with ebullience and excitement by the district's foremost exponent. (MCA 2-4092)

—LONE STAR RAG. Recorded between 1936 and 1941, considered "the hey-day of Bob Wills and the Texas Playboys," this collection presents a number of previously unissued performances plus some from the small Conqueror label to produce a very personalized feeling of what this specialized, but highly admired music (by both fans and professionals) really sounded like. (Columbia Special Products P-14390.)

Collections

BEST OF THE SWING YEARS. A recently-released eight-record set that includes many of the top names as well as the original studio recordings of those bands not available in their own collections: Bunny Berigan, Bob Chester, Larry Clinton, Erskine Hawkins, Hal Kemp, Johnny Long, Jan Savitt, Ted Weems and Bob Zurke. (Readers Digest RD4A-113)

BIG BANDS FOREVER: FOUR KINGS OF SWING. The second part of the title is a complete misnomer, since the four bands are Benny Goodman, Harry James *and* Sammy Kaye and Kay Kyser. Valuable primarily because of the Kyser sides, which are hard to come by, and the original Kayes, which are not available as a group. Only ten selections per band, however. (Columbia House 2V 8064/65)

BIG BANDS' GREATEST HITS, VOLUMES I and II. Twenty selections in each volume, many of them the anticipated "hits," but of special value to those looking for Claude Thornhill's original "Snowfall" and "A Sunday Kind of Love," Lawrence Welk's original "Beer Barrel Polka," complete with his accordion goofs, Orrin Tucker's "Oh Johnny, Oh Johnny, Oh," and "Billy," Charlie Spivak's "Autumn Nocturne" and Will Bradley's "Celery Stalks at Midnight" and "Beat Me Daddy Eight to the Bar." (Columbia CG 30009 and 31213)

BIG BAND MEMORIES. Ten big hits apiece from T. Dorsey, Goodman, Miller and Shaw; one each from Ellington, Gray, Kemp, Lunceford and Martin and five more hits of Helen O'Connell, more recently recorded by the dimpled one. (RCA Special Products DPL5-0015)

BIG BANDS REVISITED. Eighty-seven selections by thirty-nine different bands, some of them hits, some of them almost totally forgotten, thus giving you some of the high and low spots of the big band record era. (Columbia House P7S 5122)

BIG BANDS UPTOWN. Don Redman, Claude Hopkins and Benny Carter, reissued all too infrequently, share this 12-selection set that includes Redman's "Chant Of the Weed," "Shakin' the African" and "I Heard," Hopkins' "Chasing All the Blues Away," and Carter's own compositions, "Pom Pom," "Serenade to a Sarong," "Night Hop" and "O. K. for Baby." (MCA 1323)

THE FABULOUS BIG BANDS. An interesting melange of mostly semi-obscure to obscure selections from all sorts of bands, like Dean Hudson's "Ma, I Miss Your Apple Pie," Dick Jurgens' "Ragtime Cowboy Joe," Count Basie's "It Might as Well Be Spring," Red Norvo's wonderful "Remember," Duke Ellington's "Way Low," and Claude Thornhill's "We're the Couple in the Castle," plus quite a few expected standards. (Columbia Special Products P6 14007)

THE GREAT BAND ERA. The monster collection so far! One hundred and thirty selections in this ten-records-plus-bonus extravaganza that starts off with a dozen theme songs and then zooms in on many of the big hit songs of the era, all of them from the RCA vaults, many of them originally big hit records themselves and some of them obscure "cover" versions of others' original hits. In addition to the usual top bands, there are samples of such as Bob Chester, Hal McIntyre, Tony Pastor, Bunny Berigan, Shep Fields, Earl Hines, Rudy Vallee, Jan Savitt, Ozzie Nelson, Teddy Powell, Hal Kemp, and Xavier Cugat with Dinah Shore. (Readers' Digest RD4-25)

THE GREAT BIG BANDS. A budget-priced sampling of ten important bands including Goodman, Basie, James, Herman, etc. (Columbia Special Products CSS-1506)

THE GREAT BIG BAND VOCALISTS. More budget-priced fare offering 10 hits by Doris Day, Bing Crosby, Helen Forrest, Dick Haymes, Anita O'Day and others in a familiar setting. (Columbia Special Products CSS-1507)

GREAT VOCALISTS OF THE BIG BAND ERA. There are some recognized great ones in this six-record set, and also some more obscure, though often equally good band singers that makes this an unusual gathering—Carlotta Dale, Art Gentry, Taft Jordan, Liza Morrow, Durelle Alexander, Jane Harvey, Meredith

Blake, Harry Cool, Howard Dulany, Art Lund, Kathleen Lane, Cliff Weston, and Snooky Lanson among others. A good set to test your big band friends by. (Columbia Special Products P6-14538)

THE GREATEST RECORDINGS OF THE BIG BAND ERA.

A most ambitious undertaking: 100 records presenting 212 different big bands released at the rate of two records per month over a 50-month period. They're all mixed in together with most records including bands of vastly different styles. For example, set #1 has Glenn Miller, Will Bradley, Orrin Tucker and Don Redman; #3 has Vaughn Monroe, Gus Arnheim, Larry Clinton and Boyd Raeburn; #7 has Jimmy Dorsey, Erskine Hawkins, Ted Lewis and Les Elgart. And where else will you find Van Alexander, Mitchell Ayres, Will Osborne, Elliot Lawrence, Les Hite, Jay McShann, Buddy Rogers, Willie Bryant, Gray Gordon, Coon-Sanders, Orville Knapp, Al Donahue, Bobby Byrne, Bobby Sherwood, Johnny Messner, Seger Ellis, Ted FioRito, Henry Jerome, Hudson-DeLange and so many more that just may never have been heard again? (Franklin Mint Record Society)

GUY LOMBARDO AND HARRY JAMES FOR LISTENING AND DANCING.

Not the usual run-of-the-mill reissues; instead, fifty selections apiece, many previously unissued on records, by two of the era's big favorites. The James sides are 1969 recreations of many of the band's biggest hits, with Helen Forrest back as vocalist, while the Lombardo sides are a mixture of never-before-released radio broadcasts that Guy had collected plus some he cut for Capitol (Readers Digest)

60 OF THE GREATEST BIG BANDS.

A true bird's-ear sound of five dozen of the most important bands, each playing one of its most significant numbers. All the big regulars are there, ranging alphabetically from Louis Armstrong to Teddy Wilson and including such hard-to-get gems as Jimmy Grier's "The Object of My Affection," Hudson-DeLange's "The Moon Is Grinning at Me," Ina Ray Hutton's "Five O'Clock Whistle," Jack Jenney's "Star Dust," Johnny Long's "A Shanty in Old Shantytown," Tony Pastor's "Grievin' for You" with Rosemary Clooney; Charlie Spivak's "At Last," Jack Teagarden's "The Shiek of Araby" and Ted Weems' "That Old Gang of Mine" featuring a young Perry Como. (J. C. Penney/Columbia Special Products P6 13927)

SWEET BANDS OF 1932–34.

One of the more esoteric collections consisting of such hard-to-find items as Hal Kemp's "Heart of Stone" and "Living in Doubt;" Harold Arlen singing several numbers with Leo Reisman's band; Casa Loma's "Lazy Day;" a young Bob Crosby with Anson Weeks and His Orchestra, plus a slew of rather inconsequential but, in the aggregate, rather charming performances. (Nostalgia Book Club/Columbia Special Products P5 14843)

SWEET MUSIC FOR DANCING AND DREAMING.

Eighty selections divided among the bands of Sammy Kaye, Wayne King and Russ Morgan, and categorized into "Big Hits," "Sweet Bands at the Movies," "Among My Souvenirs' (oldies of course), "Broadway Show Hits," "Vienese Waltzes," "Go Hawaiian" and "Something Old, Something New"— all reassembled from Capitol's catalogue. (Readers' Digest RD4A-020-2)

THIS IS THE BIG BAND ERA.

A potpourri of RCA Victor's and Bluebird's big bands— twenty tunes by the usual T. Dorsey, Ellington, Goodman, Miller and Shaw, plus the less usual Barnet, Berigan, Clinton, Erskine Hawkins, Hines and Moten—all playing those great big hits. (RCA Victor VPM-6043)

THE RECORD COMPANIES' ADDRESSES

Most of the recordings listed in this Selective Discography, except those sold only through direct mail, whose companies are marked with an asterisk (*), should be available at or through your local record dealer. If he doesn't have what you're looking for, he may have to "special order" them for you. If you don't get the satisfaction you want, you might try contacting the record companies directly. As for those records sold only through direct mail, you must contact the companies yourself. Here are all their addresses:

Capitol Records, 1750 N. Vine Street, Hollywood, CA 90028
*Circle Records, c/o Collector's Record Club, 3008 Wadsworth Mill Place, Decatur, GA 30032
*Columbia House, 1211 Sixth Avenue, New York City 10036
Columbia Records, 51 West 52nd Street, New York City 10019
Columbia Special Products, 51 West 52nd Street, New York City 10019
*Creative World Records, P. O. Box 35216, Los Angeles, CA 90035
Epic Records, 51 West 52nd Street, New York City 10019
*Franklin Mint Record Society, Franklin Center, PA 19091
Hindsight Records, P. O. Box 7114, Burbank, CA 91510
MCA Records, 70 Universal City Plaza, Universal City, CA 91608
M. F. Productions, M. F. Distributors, 295 Madison Avenue, New York City 10017
Musicraft Records, 117 N. Las Palmas Avenue, Los Angeles, CA 90004
Monmouth-Evergreen Records, 1697 Broadway, New York City 10019
*Nostalgia Book Club, 333 Post Road, Westport, CT 06880
*J. C. Penney Company, 1301 Sixth Avenue, New York City 10019
Pickwick Records, 7500 Excelsior Boulevard, Minneapolis, MN 55426
*Readers' Digest Records, 750 Third Avenue, New York City 10017
RCA Bluebird Records, 1133 Sixth Avenue, New York City 10036
RCA Victor Records, 1133 Sixth Avenue, New York City 10036
Roulette Records, 1790 Broadway, New York City 10023
Savoy Records, 342 Westminster Avenue, Elizabeth, NJ 07208
*Smithsonian Records, Division of Performing Arts, Smithsonian Institution, Washington, DC
*Time-Life Records, c/o Time-Life Books, 777 Duke Street, Alexandria, VA 22314
20th Century-Fox Records, 8255 Sunset Boulevard, Los Angeles, CA 90069
Verve/Polydor Records, 137 West 55th Street, New York City 10019

*Records sold by direct mail only. All others available through regular retail channels.

Part Seven:
The Big Bands'
Theme Songs

The Big Bands' Theme Songs

What could be more evocative of the sounds of the big bands than hearing their identifying theme songs! At the beginning and end of dozens upon dozens of radio broadcasts, seven nights a week, you'd hear their special refrains, some composed just for the orchestra, others familiar songs that they had adopted as their own themes, each letting you know right off whom you were about to hear or whom you had just finished listening to.

Sometimes bands had more than just one theme. Some had one song for the opener and another for the closer, and for those bands appropriate identifications are included in the lists that follow. However, bands sometimes changed their theme songs, either because of some whim or, for awhile during the ASCAP music strike, because they weren't permitted to play them on the air. If any of those additional theme songs became important to a band, they too are listed here with appropriate explanations.

Irving Aaronson—*Commanderism*
Van Alexander—*Alexander's Swinging*
Barclay Allen—*Cumana*
Ray Anthony—*The Man with the Horn*
Louis Armstrong—*When It's Sleepy Time Down South*
Desi Arnaz—*Cuban Pete*
Gus Arnheim—*Sweet and Lovely*
Zinn Arthur—*Darling*
Georgie Auld—*I've Got a Right to Know*
Mitchell Ayres—*You Go to My Head*
Charlie Barnet—*Cherokee, Red Skin Rumba, I Lost Another Sweetheart*
    (early)
Blue Barron—*Sometimes I'm Happy*
Count Basie—*One O'Clock Jump*
Bunny Berigan—*I Can't Get Started*
Ben Bernie—*It's a Lonesome Old Town* (open), *Au Revoir, Pleasant Dreams*
    (close)
Archie Bleyer—*Business in "F"*
Bert Block—*Moonglow*
Johnny Bothwell—*Sleepy Alto*
Will Bradley—*Think of Me* (open) *Strange Cargo* (close)
Tiny Bradshaw—*Fascination*
Nat Brandwynne—*If Stars Could Talk*
Lou Breese—*Breezing Along with the Breeze*

SENTIMENTAL JOURNEY

By Bud Green, Les Brown and Ben Homer

Featured by LES BROWN and His Orchestra

LET'S DANCE

by FANNY MAY BALDRIDGE, GREGORY STONE and JOSEPH BONIME

Featured in

The *Benny Goodman Story*

Universal International presents

The *Benny Goodman Story*

Starring in TECHNICOLOR

CHEROKEE

(INDIAN LOVE SONG)

Words and Music by RAY NOBLE

RACING WITH THE MOON

WORDS BY
VAUGHN MONROE
PAULINE POPE

MUSIC BY
JOHNNY WATSON

Featured by VAUGHN MONROE

MOONLIGHT SERENADE

LYRIC BY
MITCHELL PARISH

MUSIC BY
GLENN MILLER

COMPOSED AND FEATURED BY
GLENN MILLER

JIMMY DORSEY
CONTRASTS

from the solo "Oodles of Noodles"
Decca Record No. 3198

Ace Brigode—*Carry Me Back to Ol' Virginny*
Randy Brooks—*Holiday Forever*
Les Brown—*Leap Frog* (open), *Sentimental Journey* (close), *Dance of the
  Blue Devils* (early)
Willie Bryant—*It's Over Because We're Through*
Sonny Burke—*Blue Sonata*
Henry Busse—*Hop Lips* (open), *When Day Is Done* (close)
Billy Butterfield—*What's New*
Bobby Byrne—*Danny Boy*

Cab Calloway—*Minnie the Moocher*
Frankie Carle—*Sunrise Serenade*
Benny Carter—*Melancholy Lullaby*
Carmen Cavallaro—*My Sentimental Heart*
Bob Chester—*Sunburst*
Larry Clinton—*The Dipsy Doodle*
Del Courtney—*Three Shades of Blue*
Bob Crosby—*Summertime*
Xavier Cugat—*My Shawl*
Bernie Cummins—*Dark Eyes*

Jack Denny—*Under the Stars*
Emery Deutsch—*When a Gypsy Makes His Violin Cry*
Frank Devol—*Dream Awhile*
Al Donahue—*Lowdown Rhythm in a Top Hat*
Sam Donahue—*I Never Knew*
Dorsey Brothers—*Sandman*
Jimmy Dorsey—*Contrasts*
Tommy Dorsey—*I'm Getting Sentimental Over You*
Saxie Dowell—*Three Little Fishies*
Eddy Duchin—*My Twilight Dream*
Sonny Dunham—*Memories of You*

Ray Eberle—*Serenade in Blue*
Les Elgart—*The Dancing Sound*
Duke Ellington—*Take the 'A' Train, East St. Louis Toodle-oo* (early)
Skinnay Ennis—*Got a Date with an Angel*

Willie Farmer—*Farmer in the Dell*
Happy Felton—*I Want to Be Happy*
Shep Fields—*Rippling Rhythm, Ritual Fire Dance* (all reed orchestra)
Jack Fina—*Dream Sonata*
Ted Fio Rito—*Rio Rita*
Ralph Flanagan—*Singing Winds*

Chuck Foster—*Oh, You Beautiful Doll*
Larry Funk—*Rose of Washington Square*

Jan Garber—*My Dear*
Glenn Garr—*I Love You Truly*
Benny Goodman—*Let's Dance* (open), *Goodbye* (close)
Gray Gordon—*One Minute To One*
Glen Gray—*Smoke Rings, Was I To Blame for Falling in Love with You*
    (early)
Jerry Gray—*Desert Serenade*
Johnny Green—*Hello, My Lover, Goodbye*
Jimmie Grier—*Music in the Moonlight*

Bobby Hackett—*Embraceable You*
George Hall—*Love Letters in the Sand*
Sleepy Hall—*Sleepy-Time Gal*
Mal Hallett—*Boston Tea Party*
Johnny Hamp—*My Old Kentucky Home*
Lionel Hampton—*Flying Home*
Phil Harris—*Rose Room*
Coleman Hawkins—*Body and Soul*
Erskine Hawkins—*Tuxedo Junction*
Edgar Hayes—*Star Dust*
Joe Haymes—*Midnight*
Ted Heath—*Listen To My Music*
Neal Hefti—*Coral Reef*
Horace Heidt—*I'll Love You in My Dreams*
Fletcher Henderson—*Christopher Columbus*
Skitch Henderson—*Anita*
Ray Herbeck—*Romance*
Woody Herman—*Blue Flame, Blue Prelude* (early)
Art Hickman—*Rose Room*
Teddy Hill—*Uptown Rhapsody*
Tiny Hill—*Angry*
Richard Himber—*It Isn't Fair*
Earl Hines—*Deep Forest*
Les Hite—*It Must Have Been a Dream*
Carl Hoff—*I Could Use a Dream*
Claude Hopkins—*I Would Do Anything for You*
Eddy Howard—*Careless* (open), *So Long for Now* (close)
Dean Hudson—*Moon Over Miami*
Hudson-DeLange—*Eight Bars in Search of a Melody*
Will Hudson—*Hobo on Park Avenue*
Ina Ray Hutton—*Gotta Have Your Love*
Jack Hylton—*She Shall Have Music*

Harry James—*Ciribiribin*
Art Jarrett—*Everything's Been Done Before*
Jack Jenney—*City Night*
Henry Jerome—*Night Is Gone, Nice People* (later)
Isham Jones—*You're Just a Dream Come True*
Jimmy Joy—*Shine On, Harvest Moon*
Dick Jurgens—*Day Dreams Come True At Night*

Art Kassel—*Hell's Bells, Doodle Doo Doo* (early)
Al Kavelin—*Love Has Gone*
Herbie Kaye—*Violets*
Sammy Kaye—*Kaye's Melody*
Hal Kemp—*Got a Date with an Angel* (open) (*How I'll Miss You*) *When the Summer Is Gone* (close)
Stan Kenton—*Artistry in Rhythm*
Henry King—*A Blues Serenade*
Wayne King—*The Waltz You Saved for Me*
Andy Kirk—*Until the Real Thing Comes Along Clouds* (early)
Orville Knapp—*Accent on Youth*
Gene Krupa—*Starburst, Apurksody* (early)
Kay Kyser—*Thinking of You*

Elliot Lawrence—*Heart to Heart*
Ted Lewis—*When My Baby Smiles at Me*
Enoch Light—*You're the Only Star*
Little Jack Little—*Little by Little*
Guy Lombardo—*Auld Lang Syne*
Johnny Long—*The White Star of Sigma Nu*
Vincent Lopez—*Nola*
Bert Lown—*Bye Bye Blues*
Jimmie Lunceford—*Uptown Blues, Jazznocracy* (early)
Abe Lyman—*California, Here I Come*

Wingy Manone—*Isle of Capri*
Ralph Marterie—*Trumpeter's Lullaby*
Freddy Martin—*Tonight We Love, Bye Lo Bye Lullaby* (early)
Frankie Masters—*Scatterbrain*
Billy May—*Lean Baby*
Clyde McCoy—*Sugar Blues*
Hal McIntyre—*Moon Mist*
Ray McKinley—*Howdy, Friends*
Johnny Messner—*Can't We Be Friends*
Eddie Miller—*Lazy Mood*
Glenn Miller—*Moonlight Serenade, Slumber Song* (during ASCAP ban)
Lucky Millinder—*Ride, Red, Ride*

Vaughn Monroe—*Racing with the Moon*
Art Mooney—*Sunset to Sunrise*
Russ Morgan—*Does Your Heart Beat for Me*
Buddy Morrow—*Night Train*
Benny Moten—*South*
Ozzie Nelson—*Loyal Sons of Rutgers*
Red Nichols—*Wail of the Winds*
Leighton Noble—*I'll See You in My Dreams*
Ray Noble—*The Very Thought of You* (open), *Goodnight, Sweetheart* (close)
Red Norvo—*Mr. and Mrs. Swing*

George Olsen—*Beyond the Blue Horizon*
Will Osborne—*The Gentleman Awaits*
Harry Owens—*Sweet Leilani*

Louis Panico—*Wabash Blues*
Tony Pastor—*Blossoms*
Ben Pollack—*Song of the Islands*
Teddy Powell—*Sans Culottes*
Louis Prima—*Way Down Yonder in New Orleans*

Boyd Raeburn—*Raeburn's Theme* (bits of *There Is No You* and *Dalvatore Sally*), *Moonlight on Melody Hill* (early)
Barney Rapp—*Skaters' Waltz*
Carl Ravazza—*Vieni Su*
Don Redman—*Chant of the Weed*
Joe Reichman—*Variations in "G"*
Leo Reisman—*What Is This Thing Called Love*
Alvino Rey—*Blue Rey* (open), *Nighty Night* (close)
Tommy Reynolds—*Pipe Dreams*
Buddy Rich—*Rain on the Roof*
Johnny Richards—*Young at Heart*
Buddy Rogers—*My Buddy*
Luis Russell—*New Call of the Freaks*

Joe Sanders—*I Found a Rose in the Snow* (open), *Nighty Night, Dear* (close)
Sauter-Finegan—*Doodletown Fifers*
Jan Savitt—*Quaker City Jazz*
Savoy Sultans—*Jumpin' at the Savoy*
Raymond Scott—*Pretty Little Petticoat*
Artie Shaw—*Nightmare*
Bobby Sherwood—*Elks' Parade*
Noble Sissle—*Hello, Sweetheart, Hello; I'm Just Wild About Harry*
Freddie Slack—*Strange Cargo*
Harry Sosnick—*Lazy Rhapsody*

MINNIE THE MOOCHER
(THE HO DE HO SONG)

Cherokee
(Indian Love Song)

I'm Gettin' Sentimental Over You

THE DIPSY DOODLE

GOT A DATE WITH AN ANGEL

When It's Sleepy Time Down South
Words and Music by LEON RENÉ, OTIS RENÉ and CLARENCE MUSE

ONE O'CLOCK JUMP
by Count Basie

The Song Favorite of the KING and QUEEN of England
GOOD NIGHT SWEETHEART

Muggsy Spanier—*Relaxin' at the Touro*
Phil Spitalny—*My Isle of Golden Dreams*
Charlie Spivak—*Stardreams*
Dike Stabile—*Blue Nocturne*
Harold Stern—*Now That It's All Over*
Ted Straeter—*The Most Beautiful Girl in the World*

Jack Teagarden—*I Gotta Right To Sing the Blues*
Claude Thornhill—*Snowfall*
Paul Tremaine—*Lonely Acres*
Frankie Trumbauer—*Singin' the Blues*
Orrin Tucker—*Drifting and Dreaming*
Tommy Tucker—*I Love You (Oh, How I Love You)*

Rudy Vallee—*My Time Is Your Time*
Joe Venuti—*Last Night*

Fred Waring—*Sleep*
Chick Webb—*Let's Get Together*
Anson Weeks—*I'm Writing You This Little Melody*
Ted Weems—*Out of the Night*
Lawrence Welk—*Bubbles in the Wine*
Paul Whiteman—*Rhapsody in Blue*
Griff Williams—*Dream Music*
Bob Wills—*San Antonio Rose*
Teddy Wilson—*Jumpin' on the Blacks and Whites*

Sterling Young—*Blue Is the Night*

Si Zentner—*Up the Lazy River*
Bob Zurke—*Hobson Street Blues*

PICTURE CREDITS

The photos listed in the section directly below are reproduced through the courtesy of *Metronome* magazine:

P. 6 (bottom right), NBC. P. 7, photo by Candid Illustrators. P. 9, P. 14, photo by Bill Mark. P. 18. P. 19 (top), photo by Ray King, Salt Lake *Tribune;* bottom, Official U.S. Navy photograph. Pp 21, 25, 26, 27. P. 32, photo by Barry Kramer. P. 34. P. 37 (first row, left; second row, left; second row, middle; third row, middle, photo by Maurice Seymour). P. 38 (first row, left, photo by Murray Korman; first row, right; second row, left, photo by Maurice Seymour; second row, right, photo by Lew Nichols; third row, middle; third row, right, photos by Bruno of Hollywood.) Pp. 39, 41, 43, 45, 47, 48, 50, 51, 53, 57, 60, 67, 69. P. 79, photo by "Popsie." P. 81, photo by M. Smith. Pp. 84, 86, RCA photo. P. 89. P. 92. P. 104, photo by Pell-Thomas. P. 108, photo by Ray Levitt. P. 110. P. 11, photo by Bill Mark. P. 116. P. 119, photo by Maurice. Pp. 121, 132, 134, 136, 141, 143, 147, 151, 154, 161, 164. P. 170, photo by Lew Nichols. P. 184. P. 189, photo by Zinn Arthur. Pp. 195, 201, 202. P. 205, photo by "Popsie." Pp. 210, 212. P. 223, photo by Ray Levitt. P. 241. P. 243, photo by Libsohn-Ehrenberg. P. 245. P. 246, photo by "Popsie." Pp. 250, 253, 254, 257, 259, 260. P. 263, photo by Bill Mark. Pp. 267, 270, 273, 280, 285. P. 289, photo by Drucker. P. 292. P. 295, photo by Zinn Arthur. Pp. 296, 297, 299, 308, 315 (top, right; bottom) 316, 319, 322, 323, 324. P. 326, photo by Ray Levitt. Pp. 328, 330, 331, 338, 340, 346, 347. P. 353, RCA Victor. Pp. 360, 366, 367, 369, 371. P. 379, photo by De Mirjian. Pp. 381, 384, 389, 395, 404, 405, 408. P. 411, photo by Zinn Arthur. Pp. 415, 425. 426. P. 428, photo by Barry. Pp. 433, 436. P. 460, photo by Gene Lester. Pp. 461, 462, 463. P. 467 (center, photo by Irvin Glaser); (bottom). Pp. 469 (bottom), 470, 472. P. 476, photo by Bill Spilka. P. 479, photos by Arsene Studios. P. 481. P. 482 (both). Pp. 483, 488, 490, 493 (all). P. 494, photo by Arsene Studios. P. 496. P. 497, courtesy of Irving Riskin. P. 498. Pp. 449 (left), 500. P. 501 (top), NBC photo; bottom. Pp. 507, 508, 510. P. 555, photo by Dave Pell.

Other Credits

P. 2, Walter Engel. P. 6 (top, left), RCA Victor. P. 10, Otto Hess. P. 15, Bill Gottlieb. P. 19 (bottom), courtesy of Guy Lombardo. P. 24, courtesy of Benny Goodman. P. 37 third row, right), Bill Gottlieb. P. 55, courtesy of Bonnie Lake. P. 72, Otto F. Hess. P. 74, Bill Gottlieb. P. 83, Bill Gottlieb. P. 89, Otto F. Hess. P. 96, Bill Gottlieb. P. 100, courtesy of Les Brown. P. 101, courtesy of Les Brown, photo by Arsene Studios. P. 106 (top), George T. Simon Collection; (bottom) courtesy of Les Brown. P. 114, courtesy of Frankie Carle. P. 123, CBS Records. Pp. 124, 125, courtesy of Dolores O'Neill. P. 128, courtesy of Larry Clinton. P. 130, George T. Simon Collection. Pp. 158, 169, 176, 177, RCA Victor. P. 180, Otto F. Hess. P. 181, Bill Gottlieb. P. 183, RCA Victor, photo by Drucker. P. 186, Bill Gottlieb. P. 189 (top and lower right) Bill Gottlieb. P. 192, Otto F. Hess. P. 199, Bill Gottlieb. P. 209, courtesy of Benny Goodman. P. 215, courtesy of Gene Krupa. P. 216, courtesy of Benny Goodman. P. 229, Otto F. Hess. P. 231, Fred Hess and Son, courtesy of Bonnie Lake P. 232, courtesy of Lionel Hampton. P. 234, Bill Gottlieb. Pp. 235 (top left), (top right), 238, 239, courtesy of Lionel Hampton, photos by Jean-Pierre Leloir. P. 251, George T. Simon. P. 265, courtesy of Harry James, photo by Central Studios. P. 272, courtesy of Harry James. P. 276, George T. Simon Collection. P. 278, CBS. P. 279, George T. Simon Collection. P. 283, courtesy of Sammy Kaye. P. 287, courtesy of John Scott Trotter. P. 291, CBS. Pp. 301, 303, *Down Beat*. P. 305, Otto F. Hess. P. 311, Charles Stewart. P. 312, CBS Records. P. 315 (top left) CBS Records. P. 327, Bill Gottlieb. P. 329, courtesy of Manny's Musical Instruments. P. 337, courtesy of Freddy Martin. P. 342, RCA Victor. P. 344, courtesy of Ray McKinley. P. 351, courtesy of Michael Badolato. Pp. 354, 363, 373, RCA Victor. P. 376, Decca Records. P. 377, CBS Records. Pp. 383, 393, Bill Gottlieb. P. 397, George T. Simon Collection. P. 398, Bill Gottlieb. P. 401, courtesy of Jack Egan, copyright 1941 RKO Radio Pictures. P. 414, *Down Beat*. P. 418, courtesy of Dave Dexter, Jr. P. 424, *Down Beat*. P. 431, Otto F. Hess. P. 439, George T. Simon. P. 441, courtesy of Dave Dexter, Jr. P. 445, courtesy of Paul Hutcoe. P. 446, Bill Gottlieb. P. 447, courtesy of Perry Como. P. 454, courtesy of Paul Whiteman. P. 465, Bill Gottlieb. P. 467 (top), Bill Gottlieb. P. 469 (top) photo by "Popsie." P. 473, Bill Gotlieb. P. 474, photo by "Popsie." P. 477, courtesy of Manny's Musical Instruments. P. 478, courtesy of Gerry Mulligan. P. 486, courtesy of *Down Beat*. P. 495, photo by "Popsie." P. 499, courtesy of Frank Driggs. P. 502, George T. Simon Collection. P. 506, George T. Simon. P. 512, RCA Victor. Pp. 520, 521, 526, 527, 531, 536, 537, 538, 543, 548, 549, George T. Simon. P. 554 (top) RCA Victor; (bottom) courtesy of Benny Goodman. P. 556, Phil Stern. P. 558 (top) North Texas State University News Service, (middle) Berklee College, (bottom) Irene Harris. P. 560, courtesy Clem DeRosa. P. 561 (Rich) RCA Victor, P. 562 (Mulligan) F. Rota, P. 563 (Toshiko) RCA Victor. P. 564, Chuck Pulin. Pp. 586, 591 Sheet music covers, courtesy of Bill Simon. Endpaper posters, courtesy of Robert Altshuler.

INDEX